MAINE
SEA
FISHERIES

*The Rise
and Fall of a
Native Industry, 1830–1890*

MAINE
SEA
FISHERIES

—

*The Rise
and Fall of a
Native Industry, 1830–1890*

Wayne M. O'Leary

Northeastern University Press

BOSTON

Northeastern University Press

Library of Congress Cataloging-in-Publication Data
O'Leary, Wayne M.
Maine sea fisheries : the rise and fall of a native
industry, 1830–1890 / Wayne M. O'Leary
p. cm.
Edited, updated, and rev. version of author's thesis.
Includes bibliographical references (p.   ) and index.
ISBN 1-55553-280-2 (cl : alk. paper).—ISBN 1-55553-281-0
(pa : alk. paper)
1. Fisheries—Maine—History—19th century. I. Title.
SH222.M2044   1996
338.3′727′00974109034—dc20   96-17724

Frontispiece: A pinky fishing schooner with
tanned canvas reducing sail under a threatening sky off
the New England coast. (Detail from a painting by an unknown
nineteenth-century artist. Courtesy Penobscot
Marine Museum, Searsport, Maine.)

Designed by David Ford

Composed in Galliard by G & S Typesetters, Austin, Texas. Printed and
bound by Edwards Brothers, Ann Arbor, Michigan. The paper is Glatfelter Offset,
an acid-free stock.

MANUFACTURED IN THE UNITED STATES OF AMERICA
00   99   98   97   96   5   4   3   2   1

For Elaine

Contents

———

Illustrations

———

Map of Maine customs districts, major fishing ports,
and coastal rail lines, 1860
2–3

Map of the major sea-fishing grounds
of the North Atlantic
78–79

Following page 111

Fishing pinky from the port of Friendship, Maine

Fishing vessels in Eastport, Maine

Grand Banks schooner at anchor

The *Sarah Franklin,* ca. 1880s

Maine fish gang unloading groundfish, ca. 1900

Fishermen dressing cod, ca. 1884

Groundfish drying on a wharf, 1892

Dried salt codfish being loaded onto the *Young America*

A herring smokehouse, ca. 1886

Advertisement for fishing salt

The *St. Leon,* 1835

The *George W. Pierce,* 1895

Preface

——

This book attempts to simultaneously fulfill two quite different but complementary objectives. First and most obviously, it sets out to tell the story of Maine's deep-sea fishing industry in the nineteenth century, a neglected saga untold in its full complexity and one that is significant in its own right. Second, the book tries, through that narrative, to examine the character of nineteenth-century capitalism in the United States and its relationship to social, economic, and technological change. In the process, the work seeks to use the experience of a particular maritime industry to address one of the recurring issues of American history, the role of government in the economy. To the extent that these dual objectives are realized, this history should shed light on both Maine's sea fisheries as an entity and the broader context in which they developed.

Methodologically, two approaches are used in the book. Keeping in mind Harold A. Innis's dictum that the fisheries are international in scope, Maine's native industry is presented here in part as a case study in the overall nature and operation of the North Atlantic sea fisheries during the age of sail. Also keeping in mind the importance of regional differences, the comparative approach is used as well, so that judgements can readily be made about Maine's historical experience in contrast to those of its North American neighbors and industry competitors, Massachusetts and Nova Scotia. It is both as part of a worldwide economy and as a unique component of that economy that Maine's nineteenth-century fishing industry must be viewed.

The Maine sea fisheries as a subject for serious study initially engaged my interest in the 1970s, during a brief tenure as curator of the Penobscot Marine Museum, located in the heart of coastal Maine's historical fishing region. The idea assumed tangible form when it became the subject of a research paper written for the late Dr. Robert G. Albion's graduate seminar in maritime history at the University of Maine. Professor Albion's suggestion that the paper be expanded led to its eventual transformation into a doctoral dissertation prepared under the direction of Dr. Arthur M. Johnson.

This book is essentially an edited, updated, and somewhat revised version of that dissertation.

For their critical advice and encouragement in seeing the study through to its completion at the dissertation stage, I would like to express my appreciation to Dr. Johnson and the other members of my doctoral committee, Professors David C. Smith, Jerome J. Nadelhaft, Kenneth P. Hayes, and the late Professor Edward O. Schriver. I would also like to acknowledge the research assistance of the staffs at the following institutions: the University of Maine's Raymond H. Fogler Library in Orono; the Penobscot Marine Museum in Searsport, Maine; the Nova Scotia Archives in Halifax; Harvard University's Baker Library in Cambridge, Massachusetts; and the National Archives in Washington, D.C. I am indebted as well to the University of Maine's Canadian-American Center for a research travel grant that permitted study in Nova Scotia, and to the John Anson Kittredge Educational Trust and the Henry P. Kendall Foundation for generous financial support that facilitated publication of the final manuscript. Lastly, I want to thank Richard D. Kelly, Jr., for drawing the first of the book's two maps, and my wife, Elaine T. O'Leary, for preparing the typescript.

MAINE
SEA
FISHERIES

The Rise

and Fall of a

Native Industry, 1830 – 1890

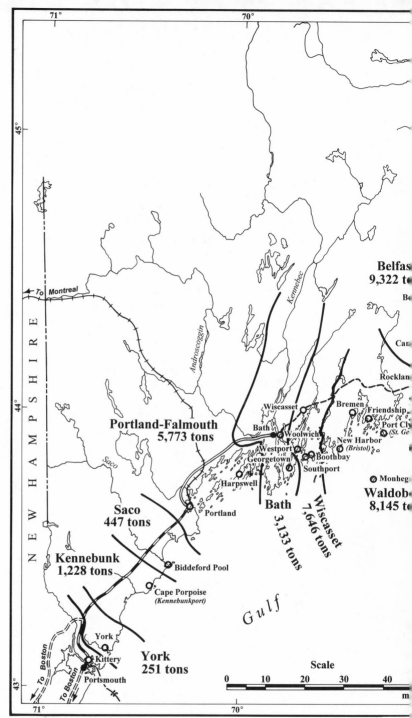

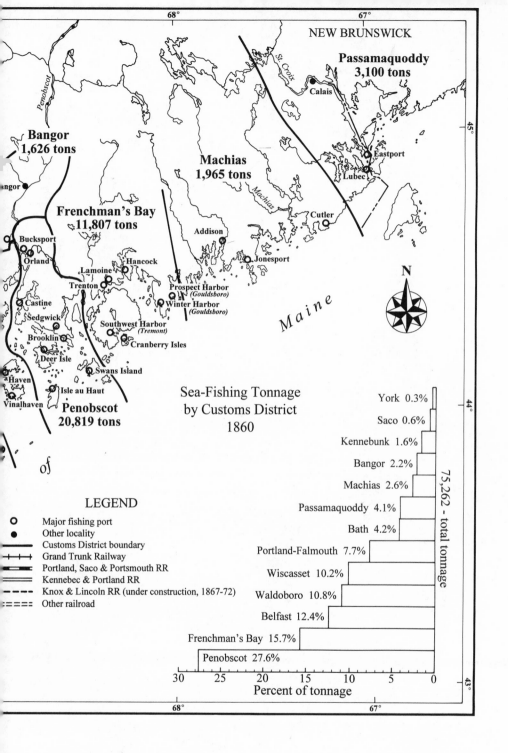

NEW BRUNSWICK

**Passamaquoddy
3,100 tons**

Calais

68°   67°

St. Croix

Eastport

**Bangor
1,626 tons**

angor

**Machias
1,965 tons**

Lubec

45°

Machias

**Frenchman's Bay
11,807 tons**

Cutler

Addison

Bucksport

Orland

Hancock

Jonesport

Lamoine

Trenton

Prospect Harbor
(Gouldsboro)

Castine

Winter Harbor
(Gouldsboro)

M a i n e

N

Sedgwick

Southwest Harbor
(Tremont)

Brooklin

Deer Isle

Cranberry Isles

Haven

Swans Island

Vinalhaven

Isle au Haut

**Penobscot
20,819 tons**

o f

Sea-Fishing Tonnage
by Customs District
1860

York 0.3%

Saco 0.6%

44°

Kennebunk 1.6%

Bangor 2.2%

Machias 2.6%

LEGEND

Passamaquoddy 4.1%

Bath 4.2%

○   Major fishing port

●   Other locality

Portland-Falmouth 7.7%

——   Customs District boundary

Wiscasset 10.2%

+|+|+   Grand Trunk Railway

Waldoboro 10.8%

Portland, Saco & Portsmouth RR

Kennebec & Portland RR

Belfast 12.4%

- - - -   Knox & Lincoln RR (under construction, 1867-72)

Frenchman's Bay 15.7%

=======   Other railroad

Penobscot 27.6%

75,262 - total tonnage

30   25   20   15   10   5   0
Percent of tonnage

43°

68°   67°

Map 1. Maine customs districts, major fishing ports, and coastal rail lines, 1860.
(Richard D. Kelly, Jr.)

CHAPTER 1

The Rise of the Maine Sea Fisheries

If the coast of Maine, is in some parts sterile, it stretches along nearly three hundred miles . . . and possesses as many harbors and inlets for vessels as all the rest of the coast of the United States. Nature herself seems to have pointed out the course of policy to be pursued.—*Report of the Joint Select Committee on the Fisheries*, Maine legislature, 1840[1]

The Impact of a Native Industry

On a summer day in 1852, the editor of the leading newspaper of Belfast, Maine, enthusiastic over the phenomenal growth and success of his city's fishing fleet, proclaimed that this small and heretofore undistinguished port on the western shore of Penobscot Bay was about to become the second Gloucester. It was, he insisted, almost an inevitability.[2] Sadly, the inevitable did not come to pass. Within a dozen years the fisheries of Belfast, like those of most other coastal Maine towns, were in decline, and all thoughts of challenging the fishing capital of North America had been forgotten. Still, the optimism of 1852 had not been without foundation, and the sudden change from exuberant vitality to economic decay is suggestive of a significant, if untold, story.

The Maine fisheries in general, and the deep-sea fisheries of the state in particular, have been neglected by history. They have been treated as a footnote to the immense fisheries of Massachusetts or not treated at all. In fact, they were of major importance in the maritime history of the United States during the nineteenth century and, more than that, a vital influence in the development of the state of Maine itself.

During the sixty years between 1830 and 1890, no fewer than seventy separate Maine communities sent men and vessels to the deep-sea fisheries of the North Atlantic.[3] In addition, virtually every coastal village was involved to some degree in the so-called shore fisheries, defined by fishermen as activity carried on within thirty miles of the coastline.[4] From the city of Portland eastward along the coast, fishing was an economic commonplace, if not a way of life.

At least one historian has largely credited the fishing industry with "the settlement and civilization" of Maine.[5] That, of course, is an exaggeration, but not as great a one as might be thought. The role of the fisheries in the original colonization of seventeenth-century Maine is well known. Places like Pemaquid and Monhegan began as stations for the English cod-fishing fleet. With the coming of settlement, however, the story of the Maine fisheries is generally relegated to vague references about the picturesque and noble character of the rustic Maine lobsterman, circa 1900. The years between have been unaccountably forgotten.

Yet in the decade of the 1820s a quarter of Deer Isle's population was to-tally dependent on the fisheries, and by 1860, when the island's industry reached its peak, that figure had increased to almost half.[6] Until 1850 cod fishing was practically the sole industry of Boothbay and nearby Southport, and ten years later the latter town employed virtually every able-bodied man and boy in the vicinity aboard its cod and mackerel schooners. By actual count, 410 of Southport's 708 inhabitants were directly supported by fish-ing at that time.[7] Of the effect of the mackerel fishery on Swan's Island dur-ing the 1870s and 1880s, the town's annalist recalled, "So alluring and profit-able was the occupation that almost every male inhabitant, except those enfeebled by old age or the younger boys, would be gone from the island."[8] At North Haven in Penobscot Bay, mackereling was the sole industry of the community in 1887, according to a contemporary observer.[9] During the 1850s, it was said that the smoked-herring business employed every male resident over the age of ten in the Washington County town of Lubec.[10] The wealth of Castine, the greatest per capita in the entire state in 1860, was directly traceable to the fisheries—the principal economic concern of that port.[11] And just before the Civil War, a visitor to Cranberry Isles, off Mount Desert, wrote, "The occupations of the inhabitants as well as the substantial arrangements of their tables, are furnished from the mute briny world."[12] The description could have been applied to dozens of small Maine coastal hamlets of the mid-nineteenth century, as well as numerous larger towns. In fact, the visitor who so succinctly characterized Cranberry Isles, Austin J. Coolidge, listed sea fishing as a primary occupation of no fewer than thirty-two Maine coast communities in his economic survey of New England, published in 1860.[13]

In purely monetary terms, the impact of the Maine fisheries upon the state was imposing. Measured by capital expenditures, fishing was the lead-ing industry of Knox County in 1860, absorbing over a third of that county's nonagricultural investment. In Lincoln, Hancock, and Washington counties, it was second only to lumbering. Based on product value, fishing was the second most important economic activity of at least three Maine coastal counties in 1860 and the leading maritime industry in four of them (Knox, Lincoln, Hancock, and Washington), ranking well ahead of shipbuilding. Statewide, the product value of the Maine fisheries on the eve of the Civil War exceeded $1 million.[14] As early as 1840, Maine's investment in the fisheries had been over $500,000.[15] By 1852 the port of Belfast alone had $100,000 invested in its fleet of cod bankers and mackerel hookers, including vessels and outfits.[16] Three years later, when the sea fisheries were approaching their zenith, Maine's Grand Banks cod-fishing operations were capitalized to the extent of $3 million, while the state's offshore mackerel fleet and attendant shore facilities occupied an additional $1 million in venture capital.[17] Even in 1880, well after the fisheries had passed their peak, Maine was still maintaining a total capital investment in excess of $3 million and producing an annual catch valued at $3.6 million.[18]

It is the human factor, however, that truly measures the impact of the Maine fishing industry. There were few great capitalists, merchant princes, or commanding personalities to dominate the scene, especially in the formative period. The archetypical Maine fisherman was relatively poor and unlettered. His business, if he was an entrepreneur, was in most cases small. There is little in the way of intimate, personal documentation to record the sociology of the Maine fisheries. Their importance lies simply in the number of people involved.

The fisheries ranked in the top ten among Maine occupations throughout the nineteenth century. In 1860, as published census reports indicate, Maine had more professional fishermen than in any other census year: the number was 4,607, the most for any state, and 21 percent of the national total. At the same time, fishing ranked only ninth among Maine occupations that year, and the 4,607 self-proclaimed professional fishermen constituted only 2.2 percent of the state's male work force.[19] The figures are not impressive unless other factors are taken into consideration.

First of all, for most Maine fishermen, fishing was only one of two or more occupations. Many were part-time farmers, woodcutters, or boatbuilders, at sea only part of the year. A seasonal voyage to the banks of Newfoundland or "the Bay" (Gulf of St. Lawrence), while occupying the better part of a spring or summer, did not necessarily constitute a vocation in their eyes and did not always show up as such in census statistics. Furthermore, many full-time fishermen were not properly classified by census takers, because of the nature of the industry in Maine, which involved minimal winter fishing. In general, the fishing season spanned the months of April through October. A typical pattern for fishermen devoted to life afloat

was to spend the balance of their year (November to March) aboard coasting vessels trading to southern United States ports or to the West Indies.
Thus over the years a considerable number of them were undoubtedly listed
as coastermen or common seamen.* It is known that this was the case in
1880, when census officials acknowledged that large numbers of fishermen
were reported as sailors, "while many who follow the avocation of 'fishermen' for only a portion of the year are reported under some other branch of
industry."[20] Perhaps the ultimate distortion in census data took place in
1850, when tabulators failed to find a single fisherman residing in the town
of Boothbay, a community totally devoted to the fisheries. Instead, Boothbay was credited with 382 "mariners" (a convenient catchall term for individuals with seafaring occupations) out of a total male work force of 698.[21]

The reality of the situation often differed considerably from the official
published statistics. In 1880, when the census showed 4,243 fishermen living
in Maine, George Brown Goode and Joseph W. Collins, of the U.S. Fish
Commission, estimated that at least 10,000 persons on the Maine coast had
engaged in mackerel-hooking during part of the season.[22] A generation earlier, in 1855, the *Maine Register* claimed that the state had 7,500 deep-sea
fishermen engaged in the cod and mackerel fisheries on a regular basis.[23]
The broad validity of such figures is supported by estimates offered by the
U.S. Department of Treasury for the year 1859. According to Treasury officials, who based their figures on government tonnage statistics, Maine was
home to 10,187 vessel fishermen, over twice as many as census takers recorded a year later. Of that total, 8,883 were thought to be engaged in the
state's primary industry pursuit, cod fishing.[24]

It is apparent that prior to the Civil War more Maine coastal inhabitants
went fishing than engaged in any other maritime occupation. Moreover, it
appears that more Maine workers fished than performed any other kind of
work at mid-century, with the exception of farm labor. The census of 1860
reported agriculture as the state's leading occupation, with nearly 81,000
farmers and farm laborers in residence; the occupation of "mariner" (11,375)
was next among the skilled trades.[25] But fishing employed at least 10,000
and probably more, and the enumerated mariners included sailors in the
two distinct activities of coasting and foreign trading, as well as numerous

---

*A related problem was the absence of fishermen from home when census takers collected
their data, which usually occurred around the first of June, at the height of the fishing season.
In 1870, the compiler of the industrial census for the town of Kennebunkport admitted that he
could not make a detailed report on the fishing industry there, "as the men are generally absent and therefore [I] cannot get accurate information." (Source: U.S. MS Census Ind., 1870:
York County, Maine, town of Kennebunkport.)

part-time fishermen. Keeping in mind the total male work force of 207,000 in 1860, it is likely that between 5 and 10 percent of Maine's workers engaged in fishing at the industry's height during the first months of the Civil War.

At certain places along the coast, the proportion of the work force involved in fishing was, of course, much greater. It was at the local level—in the individual townships of the rural areas—that the influence and impact of the fisheries was most dramatically measured. For the communities around Boothbay and those bordering Penobscot Bay, for instance, the fisheries were the focus of all activity. They dictated an entire life style and produced a distinct race of men. In 1860, exactly 50 percent of the combined male work force of the adjoining villages of Boothbay, Westport, and Southport was in fishing, with Southport reporting the astounding figure of 71 percent (141 fishermen out of 200 employed workers). Comparable figures for Penobscot Bay towns included 57 percent for Vinalhaven, 54 percent for North Haven, and 52 percent for Deer Isle, a community with over 500 resident fishermen.[26] And, as George Brown Goode observed in 1883, "For every man engaged in the fisheries there is at least one other man who is dependent to a considerable extent upon his labours for support."[27] Nor was it only the men who were involved. In addition to the 282 Vinalhaven fishermen working offshore in 1860, there were 68 female net and seine makers—mostly wives and daughters of the fishermen—employed on shore.[28] The fishing industry there was a true community enterprise.

Local and regional ramifications notwithstanding, consideration of the Maine sea fisheries would be a dubious scholarly activity if their impact had been felt only within the bounds of the state of Maine. In fact, through its sea fisheries Maine played a major role in feeding the nation up to the end of the Civil War. An analysis of the fishery tonnage statistics compiled on an annual basis over the years by the Treasury Department reveals both the extent of Maine's activity and its evolving pattern. The state's cod and mackerel (or sea) fisheries* were insignificant prior to the War of 1812, of marginal or moderate significance from the close of that conflict until about 1840, and of major importance from 1840 to 1865. The pinnacle was reached during the late 1850s and the years of the Civil War. Thereafter, the Maine sea fisheries slumped to their pre-1840 level, declining slowly until 1885 and rapidly after that date. By the 1890s they were no longer of national importance.[29]

---

*The term "sea fisheries" denotes those fisheries carried on mostly beyond the thirty-mile limit by vessels of twenty tons or more. It does not include such inshore activities as lobstering, scalloping, or (for the most part) herring fishing. It refers instead to the pursuit of mackerel and "groundfish"—the many varieties of bottom-feeders found on the offshore banks of the North Atlantic, the most prominent species of which was the cod.

Percentages present a more detailed picture. In 1805 Maine owned roughly 16 percent of the total cod- and mackerel-fishing tonnage of the United States, and just 12 percent of the tonnage in vessels over twenty tons. By 1820 these figures had risen to 23 and 19 percent, respectively, a plateau where they remained, with minor fluctuations, for the next twenty years. In the early 1840s an upsurge took place that gave the state ownership of more than a third of the American fishing fleet. For the balance of the decade, Maine's share, both in total tonnage and in large vessels alone, hovered around 35 percent. Another period of accelerated growth in the period 1850–1855 pushed the state's fisheries tonnage to 40 percent of the national total, and a final spurt after 1855 gave Maine owners control of nearly half of all the deep-sea fishing craft in American waters. Throughout the golden years of 1856–1865, Maine's share of the national tonnage ranged between 45 and 50 percent, actually exceeding 50 percent briefly in 1861 and 1865. Following the war, the figures dropped dramatically, leveling off to approximately 25 percent from 1867 to 1887. A further decline thereafter left Maine with just 16 percent of the total national tonnage by 1895 and only 12 percent of the tonnage in large vessels—the identical proportions the state had owned in 1805.[30]

The overall peak occurred in 1861. In June of that year, at the start of the Civil War, Maine had 98,694 tons in the cod and mackerel fisheries combined, or 51 percent of the national total. This was a figure exceeded only three times in the entire history of the fisheries, each time by Massachusetts. During the same year, Maine claimed 57 percent of the American cod-fishing tonnage, 44 percent of the mackerel-fishing tonnage, and 51 percent of all tonnage in vessels of twenty tons or more.[31] The year 1861 was one of three—the others being 1858 and 1865—during which Maine led all the other states in total deep-sea fishing tonnage. In every other year of the nineteenth century, it was second only to Massachusetts, and in the years 1852–1865 the difference between the two was negligible.[32]

The close competition between Maine and Massachusetts was particularly keen in terms of the celebrated cod, which was the principal food-fish of North America until the Civil War. Writing in 1911, fisheries historian Raymond McFarland asserted that "the deep-sea industries of Massachusetts since the Revolution have continuously outrivaled those of all other states to the present time."[33] As a generalization, McFarland's statement was accurate; in the specific case of the North Atlantic cod fishery, however, he was wrong. From 1849 to 1865 Maine dominated the United States cod fishery and in 1861 had 74,647 tons engaged in it, more than any other state before or since. During the five years 1858–1862, Maine consistently main-

tained over 60,000 tons of vessels and boats in the cod fishery. Massachusetts, as far as the record shows, never reached the 60,000-ton level during
the course of the nineteenth century. Even in cod-fishing vessels exceeding
twenty tons, a class in which the Massachusetts fleet specialized (Maine always dominated all New England small-boat or "shore" fisheries), Maine
led from the mid-1850s to the war's end. The latter's record of 68,680 tons
in the vessel cod fishery, achieved in 1861 and largely representing offshore
bankers, was never approached. Altogether, Maine was the national leader
in cod-fishing tonnage in thirteen of seventeen years between 1849 and
1865, and averaged 48 percent of the national total for each of those years.[34]

The foregoing tonnage statistics, while interesting in themselves, are most
important in terms of what they historically represent—namely, the means
by which a significant portion of America's food supply was obtained during
a crucial period in its national development. Actual catch totals for the early
and middle nineteenth century, unlike tonnage figures, are fragmentary.
Based on the size of its schooner fleet, however, it is apparent that Maine
supplied between 25 and 50 percent of the nation's food-fish during the
quarter-century preceding 1865. The year 1840, one of the few for which accurate information regarding fish production exists, bears this out. In that
year, Maine fishermen were responsible for 279,156 of the 773,947 quintals
of dried and smoked fish processed in the United States, as well as 54,071
of the 472,359 barrels of pickled fish produced.[35] A conversion of these
figures into weight indicates that out of 114.8 million pounds of prepared
fish processed for marketing, Maine's contribution was 42.1 million pounds,
or 37 percent.* It might be added that 1840 was a year in which the state's
presence in the American fisheries was only just beginning to be felt. For
twenty-five years thereafter, Maine fish was of increasing importance in the
national marketplace.

Clearly, the Maine sea fisheries were of more than passing interest during
the middle years of the last century. For a brief moment in time they were
all-encompassing in their influence, both within the state and on the national scene. Unforeseen circumstances and inherent weaknesses would ultimately combine to destroy this native "industry" and in the process alter
the character of a unique part of the American landscape, but before 1865
that was beyond the imagination or comprehension of thousands of coastal
inhabitants from Kittery to Eastport. To them, ocean fishing was, in every
sense, a way of life.

*A quintal of dried fish equaled 112 pounds, and a barrel of pickled fish equaled 200 pounds.
(Source: *U.S. FCB, 1898*, 398, 426–27. For this and subsequent condensed citations, see Reference Abbreviations, pages 293–97.)

The Environmental Imperative

The historian Walter Prescott Webb once drew an analogy between the "cotton kingdom" of the South and the "cattle kingdom" of the West based on their similar beginnings and relationships to the industrialized North. Both, he said, took root in the climatic and geological conditions of their respective environments, which were especially favorable to particular forms of development. Both were pioneering activities in their respective regions—representing the first uses to which the land was put. Both became subject to the whims of the nineteenth-century Industrial Revolution, because of a dependence on technology for their growth and expansion. And both produced for a time "a distinctive civilization, a thing apart in American life." [36]

Webb could have added a third realm, the "codfish kingdom." In a very real sense, the North Atlantic coast from Cape Cod to Nova Scotia was an environmental unit in which the natural surroundings dictated a particular form of economic development, one that resulted—after interaction with the requisite technological factors—in a distinct "civilization." Geological, climatic, and geographical imperatives turned this international region toward the sea and maritime enterprise, and the codfish became the common denominator of the resultant socioeconomic system. Coastal Maine was an integral part of the codfish kingdom. As such, its pursuit of the fisheries was natural and unavoidable. It was, in effect, dictated by the environment.

To begin with, there was really no viable alternative to a maritime economy. The Maine coast was harsh, rugged, and rather unproductive in terms of agriculture. As early as 1795, the state's first chronicler, James Sullivan, remarked, "The soil on the sea coast is hard, and reluctant to the plough." [37] One nineteenth-century observer went so far as to say that "the rocky character of the country forbids extensive agricultural interests, and the majority of those living along the coast are necessarily dependent upon the various industries connected with the sea." [38] The editor of Maine's official reference book for 1845 took note of the particularly sandy soil along the seacoast, which was rendered productive only by extensive tillage and enrichment with local kelp, mussels, seaweed, and rockweed. [39] To William Williamson, writing in 1832, the seaboard seemed a mixture of ledges, bluffs, and rocks, with "a half-starved shrubbery" as the chief vegetation. Only when the high ground above tidewater was reached did the rocky, sandy soil turn to relatively fertile loam. [40]

Numerous localities reflected the inhospitable nature of the Maine coast. Charles E. Ranlett, a master mariner who grew up in the mid-coast community of St. George, described the fishing and coasting town he remembered from boyhood: "In its natural aspect it is rough and rocky, affording much better crops to the stonecutter than to the farmer, though perhaps, upon the whole, at the time of which I write [circa 1830], its greatest revenues came in one way or another from the sea."[41] R. E. Earll characterized Vinalhaven Island in 1880 as "one huge mass of granite, with hardly a patch of soil large enough to warrant anyone engaging in agriculture."[42] Austin Coolidge, writing twenty years earlier, shared that assessment, estimating that only about one-third of Vinalhaven's land was arable. Its companion island, North Haven, he judged to be slightly more fertile, but farming there still consisted almost solely of hay harvesting.[43] Both islands, of course, were heavily involved in the fishing industry of Penobscot Bay.

Predominantly rocky and thin soil was not the only impediment to successful husbandry along the Maine coast. The cold and damp climate was another. It produced, among other things, a growing season shorter than that of southern New England by a full month. Wrote visitor Thomas Mooney of the mid-coast region in 1850, "The winters here are full seven months long, . . . vegetation is late and poor; consequently farming is a bad business."[44] William H. Bishop reported in 1880 that farmers on Deer Isle were handicapped by a five-month winter freeze that did not allow cultivation to begin until the ground thawed in early May. Even then, hay was the only important crop. Sufficient warm sunshine to yellow the corn was frequently lacking because of fog, and the island wheat, inferior to western varieties, would barely make white flour.[45] Like North Haven and Vinalhaven, Deer Isle looked to the sea for sustenance.

A correlation between poor agricultural resources and a substantial interest in the fisheries was characteristic of the Maine coast. Hancock County is a case in point. This eastern jurisdiction, encompassing the customs districts of Penobscot and Frenchman's Bay, was the single most important coastal county in the history of the Maine sea fisheries. Close to half of all the cod- and mackerel-fishing tonnage in the state was owned there during the pre–Civil War era.[46] Agriculturally, however, Hancock lagged far behind. It developed what Samuel Wasson metaphorically called "a 'stern-chase' agriculture."[47] In 1850, for example, Hancock was twelfth among Maine's thirteen counties in total farm acreage, eleventh in improved (cultivated) farm acreage, and tenth in the cash value of its farms. The contrast with more agrarian counties is striking. York County, the 1850 leader in farm assessment, had 223,000 acres—213,000 of them under the plow—valued at $8,350,000. Hancock County's 140,000 acres of farmland, only half of which were being worked, were valued at just $1,859,000.[48]

A decade later the situation had not changed. Farms in the coastal counties of Sagadahoc, Lincoln, Knox, Hancock, and Washington—all of them counties with considerable fishing interests—remained smaller and less productive than farms elsewhere in the state. And Maine farms as a whole were not very imposing or productive, considered within the national context.[49] Alexander Parris, U.S. senator from Maine, expressed the nature of his state's husbandry in lyrical fashion during a speech in 1828: "She is not blessed like regions of the West, with a mild climate and luxuriant soil. If therefore her seamen and her fishermen, whose farms have been upon the ocean, are driven from their accustomed employment, they can obtain but a scanty subsistence from farms on the land."[50] Another senator, James Simmons of Rhode Island, put it more succinctly thirty years later, during one of the congressional fishing-bounty debates: "You might as well live on a flat rock. They must fish or starve, and that is the reason they fish."[51] Senator Simmons had the fishermen of Marblehead in mind, but his observation was equally applicable in many parts of Maine.

The environment of coastal Maine was far from being a complete economic liability, however. Factors that hindered agriculture were positive influences with respect to the development of a deep-sea fishing industry. Maine was favored by a coastline that was not merely rocky but incredibly long and irregular. Including bays and inlets, the shoreline twisted its way for 3,750 convoluted miles from the mouth of the Piscataquis to Quoddy Head, a distance of only 230 miles measured linearly.[52] It possessed the attractions of innumerable deep and protected harbors and immense stands of evergreens, ready-made for shipbuilding, reaching nearly to the water's edge. Such features led the early publicist and proselytizer for the Maine interior, Moses Greenleaf, to conclude reluctantly in 1829 that the physical attributes of the coast had provided "strong temptations to the early inhabitants, in every part of the State, to engage in pursuits of commerce and the fisheries, rather than those of agriculture."[53] The U.S. Fish Commission survey of 1880 reached a similar conclusion: "With so extensive a coastline and such excellent harbors for vessels and boats in the near vicinity of the more important fishing grounds, Maine enjoys many advantages not possessed by other states for the prosecution of the fisheries."[54]

This last observation suggests a third environmental reason for Maine's rise in the fisheries, one that had less to do with soil quality and geological formations than with an accident of geography. Maine's location, an economic handicap in so many ways and eventually a factor in the decline of her fisheries, was initially a great advantage. When the state's sea fisheries achieved national prominence after 1840, they were centered east of Portland

and most especially around Penobscot Bay. This was no product of chance. Partly, of course, it was a function of geology, since it was east of Portland that the flat, marshy, sandy shoreline, more representative of southern New England, turned into the high, rocky, jagged shoreline that is typically associated with Maine.[55] It was from Casco Bay eastward, then, that the coast itself became progressively less conducive to other forms of economic development.

More important than this, however, was the simple matter of geography. Eastern Maine's very location relative to the major North Atlantic fishing grounds was a powerful incentive for its people to engage in deep-sea fishing. With the exceptions of George's and Brown's banks (seldom fished by Maine vessels), the chief North Atlantic banks and coastal grounds were north or northeast of New England. In general, eastern Maine ports were 100 to 150 miles closer to those grounds than were the ports of western Maine and Massachusetts. Eastern Maine was, to put it simply, a day's sail (or more) closer to the fish.[56]

The result was less time spent at sea by eastern Maine schooners, and less wear and tear on men and vessels. At the same time, eastern Maine fishermen were sooner able to begin drying or otherwise curing their fish for market. Where multiple trips in a season were commonplace, such as the Gulf of St. Lawrence mackerel fishery, the advantage was magnified. Even in the cod fishery, where multiple voyages were far less common, distance from the grounds was a factor. According to the report of a Maine legislative committee in 1840, the state's proximity to the major cod-fishing banks had resulted by that date in a significant transfer of vessel tonnage from Massachusetts to Maine registry.[57]

Until mid-century, when it gradually became more important to be near the market rather than near the fish, Maine's position was advantageous. Dried, smoked, or pickled fish, preserved indefinitely from spoilage and intended for export to the southern states or the West Indies, did not have to be rushed to its destination. Fast, costly vessels and expensive refrigeration were unnecessary; access to rail transportation was not essential. Market conditions and technology were such that until after the Civil War Maine fishermen could hold their own and, in fact, profit by their very location. Geography, then, encouraged Maine entrepreneurs who might otherwise have looked askance at the fisheries.

Patterns of Growth

Environmental factors, important as they were, do not by themselves explain the rise of the Maine sea fisheries during the decades leading up to the

Civil War. An additional explanation must be sought in the dynamics of demography, and it necessitates, first of all, an examination of the precise areas within the state where the industry was centered during its halcyon days. As suggested earlier, eastern Maine provided the impetus for the rise to prominence.

Until the War of 1812, the Maine sea-fishing ports were located chiefly in the coastal region west of the Kennebec River. York and Portland-Falmouth were the leading customs districts in fishing-tonnage ownership up to 1813, when hostilities virtually shut down all activity. The postwar revival, however, brought a change in the geographical distribution of the Maine fleet. Beginning in 1816, the "down-east" * district of Penobscot (see map 1) took over leadership of the state's vessel cod fishery, thereby staking its claim as the dominant customs district in the Maine fisheries.[58] Portland-Falmouth remained competitive throughout the 1820s and 1830s but by 1840 had ceased to be a major factor. From then until the Civil War years, Penobscot had no serious challenger. The emergence of Penobscot District was part of a gradual overall shift in vessel tonnage to eastern ports, a process that accelerated after 1830 as the western districts declined to insignificance. From 1840 to the mid-1870s the leading districts in almost all categories of the Maine fisheries were Penobscot, Frenchman's Bay, Belfast, Waldoboro, and Wiscasset—all east of the Kennebec River.[59] These central and eastern districts, especially those beyond Rockland, the traditional midpoint on the Maine coast, took over leadership of the Maine fisheries precisely when those fisheries began to assume national importance.

The singular dominance of Penobscot District was all-inclusive. It led in cod-fishing vessel tonnage statewide during most years from 1816 to 1841 and in all but two years from 1842 to 1867, when the tabulation of statistics on individual fisheries was discontinued. In the cod and mackerel vessel fisheries combined, the district was state leader every year from 1842 to 1861 and in all but a handful of years over the half-century between 1820 and 1870. Only in the boat or shore fisheries, which was Waldoboro District's forte, and in mackereling, the Portland specialty, were other areas of the state able to compete. In the major sea fisheries employing schooners over twenty tons, Penobscot was supreme, owning a quarter to a third of Maine's

*Down east is a relative geographic term meaning eastward of one's location within the limits of the northeast coastal region of North America. To reach Maine or points beyond, coastal mariners sailing from Boston usually ran downwind before the prevailing southwest winds of summer in a northeasterly direction—hence, "down east." To those in Massachusetts, Maine was down east; to New Englanders in general, Atlantic Canada was down east. In the context of this study, the term has been applied principally to Maine, but occasionally (for comparative purposes) to the eastern half of the state's coastline, which is down east from western Maine.

vessel fleet during the 1830–1870 period. On the national scene, Penobscot consistently ranked among the top three or four American districts in cod-fishing vessel tonnage from the 1830s through the 1860s and was second only to Gloucester or Barnstable (Cape Cod) during much of that time.[60]

The monopoly created by Penobscot and other eastern Maine districts after 1830 was such that in only five of the ensuing thirty-five years was a majority of the state's cod-fishing tonnage owned in districts west of Rockland—an almost exact reversal of the pattern for the thirty-five years prior to 1830.[61] The pinnacle was reached in 1861, when ports east of Rockland accounted for 61,000 of Maine's 93,000 tons of fishing vessels over twenty tons (66 percent); 51,000 of the state's 69,000 tons of *cod*-fishing vessels over twenty tons (74 percent); 53,000 of the record 75,000 tons of cod-fishing craft of all sizes and types (71 percent); and 63,000 of the 99,000 tons in Maine's overall cod and mackerel fisheries combined (64 percent). Most striking is the fact that on the eve of the Civil War eastern Maine fishing towns owned 40 percent of all American cod-fishing schooners exceeding twenty tons, a class that included the large and valuable offshore bankers.[62]

The quantitative growth of the Maine sea fisheries as a whole was directly tied to the growth of the industry in eastern Maine. The state's fisheries rose, therefore, in conjunction with the settlement of the eastern coast. Until the mid-eighteenth century, however, Maine east of the Kennebec River was a frontier. Initial pioneering in the area did not begin until after 1720, although much of southwestern Maine had been settled in the previous century. By 1760 the line of settlement along the coast had barely reached the western edge of Penobscot Bay, near what is now the city of Rockland.[63] Substantial settlement of the coastline east of Rockland—bringing with it a potential fishing population—took place only after the final removal of the French and Indian threat in 1763. Even at that, population growth was further hampered by the revolutionary war, which occupied much of the 1770s and the early 1780s and made the easterly reaches of Maine a no-man's-land and sometime battlefield. As late as 1772, there were only 5,563 occupants in the entire region beyond the Kennebec, coast as well as interior.[64]

The real influx began only around 1790, and much of the eastern coast remained a sparsely settled frontier well into the nineteenth century. Charles Eliot's charming biography of John Gilley, "Maine farmer and fisherman," chronicled pioneering activity on a small Hancock County island off Mount Desert in 1812, nearly thirty years after the end of the Revolution. Of that early settlement, Eliot wrote: "Even to get a footing on this wooded island—to land lumber, livestock, provisions, and the implements of labor, and to build the first shelter—was no easy task. A small rough beach of large stones was the only landing-place, and just above the bare rocks of the shore was the forest."[65] The experience of Eliot's pioneers, who did not establish a permanent foothold and produce a second generation of island seafarers and fishermen until the 1840s, typified the slow, painstaking development of the eastern coast. Their story, multiplied many times, goes far toward explaining the expanse of time over which the Maine sea fisheries grew to prominence.

Until 1830, or thereabouts, eastern Maine simply did not have sufficient population to take advantage of its resources and physical attributes. It has been said that forty years were normally necessary to turn New England wilderness settlements into mature, established communities.[66] Many eastern Maine coastal villages were just approaching that forty-year figure in 1830. Take for example the port of Belfast, the first incorporated town (1773) on the shores of Penobscot Bay. In 1779 this fledgling settlement, occupied for less than a decade, was broken up by a British expeditionary force. The inhabitants were forced to abandon their homes for the balance of the war and did not return to reestablish the township until 1784–1785. By 1790 the population was still only 245, and it was thirty years more before the modest total of two thousand persons was reached.[67] It was at this juncture, in the summer of 1822, that a visitor to Belfast made the following observations concerning its stage of development: "The place has grown entirely within this [past] twenty three or four years. . . . The town contains probably 250 houses tolerably compact and well built, one church, two public houses, three or four wharves, etc. . . . I conclude it will eventually be a place of considerable business."[68] The visitor, one Hezekiah Prince, Jr., a customs official with a keen eye for the possibilities of maritime enterprise, was describing a town not quite forty years old, dating from its postwar resettlement—a town in transition from frontier village to commercial center, a status not fully achieved until 1853, when it became a chartered city with a five thousand–plus population.[69] Coincidentally, it was only during this latter developmental stage, circa 1825–1850, that Belfast emerged as a major fishing port.[70]

The outports farther down east were even slower to develop than Belfast. Deer Isle, Gouldsboro, Trenton, Vinalhaven, Sedgwick, and Mount Desert, all important east-coast fishing villages, were not incorporated until 1789, despite the fact that they had been initially settled in the 1760s. Other incorporations followed at still later dates: Camden (1791), Bucksport (1792), Castine (1796), Eastport (1798), Orland (1800), Lubec (1811), Hancock (1828), Cranberry Isles (1830), Jonesport (1832), North Haven (1846), Tremont (1848), and Brooklin (1849), to name a few.[71]

The process of coastal development in the eastern sea-fisheries region can perhaps best be seen by examining the growth pattern of Hancock County, the core area of the industry in that part of the state. In 1790 Hancock's population was 5,763, an infinitesimal figure alongside such western coastal counties as York (27,560) and Cumberland (23,481). By the time Maine became a state, in 1820, the county's population had reached 17,856, still less than half that of the more populous counties to the westward but nevertheless an increase of over 200 percent. Much of the increase was directly traceable to immigration. Between 1790 and 1810 the population growth resulting from migration alone was 2,735, over a third of the total increase. During the same period, new settlements proliferated to the extent that in 1810 about one of every six county residents was living in a community that had not existed ten years earlier.[72]

The growth process did not terminate with the arrival of statehood, although it is probable that natural fertility progressively supplanted immigration. By 1830, about the time the initial generation of settlers was giving way to a second, Hancock County had a solid population base of 22,553 concentrated primarily along the shoreline, certainly enough to sustain a viable maritime economy. The period of greatest expansion was now at hand. Over the next thirty years the county's population grew by 67 percent, a 10 percent faster rate than that of the state as a whole.[73] The gain in actual numbers between 1830 and 1860 exceeded the previous thirty years' gain by a considerable margin. Significantly, population expansion occurred almost in tandem with the expansion of the fisheries, and both reached their maximal levels at approximately the same time, just before the Civil War. Hancock County's 1860 population of 37,757 marked its high point for the entire nineteenth century and climaxed seventy years of uninterrupted growth.[74]

A similar pattern manifested itself all along the eastern Maine coast. Every coastal county east of the Kennebec River experienced a population explosion during these years, and the impact on individual townships destined to play a role in the fisheries was dramatic. Bucksport, a small, sleepy village of 316 inhabitants in 1790, had become a major fishing port of 3,381 by 1850. Orland, Bucksport's twin sister in the Grand Banks cod fishery, grew from 240 people in 1790 to 1,579 sixty years later. Camden went from 331 people in 1790 to 4,005 in 1850, a twelvefold increase. Eastport, the heart of Washington County's fishing industry, saw its population soar from 244 to 4,125 during the same period. Deer Isle more than quadrupled in size from 1790 to 1850, and Gouldsboro, prime supplier of fishermen for the Frenchman's Bay District fleets, increased by a factor of five. Even Boothbay, a more westerly port with seventeenth-century origins, experienced a sixty-year population increment of 150 percent. Just as significant as this overall growth was its timing. Unlike Boothbay, which concentrated most of its growth between 1790 and 1820, the ports farther east blossomed particularly during the thirty years following 1820. Camden, Belfast, Bucksport, Orland, Deer Isle, Trenton, Gouldsboro, and Eastport all doubled their populations between 1820 and 1850.[75] In other words, the growth patterns of the individual fishing ports east of Rockland, like that of Hancock County, coincided exactly with the rise of the Maine sea-fishing industry. In effect, their development made it possible.

The potential of the eastern Maine coast for fishing could not be realized until the region acquired a substantial fishing population. Beyond that, the techniques and skills required of such a population had to be learned and instituted in succeeding generations until they became a hereditary birthright. John B. Brebner remarked that the German founders of Lunenburg, Nova Scotia, who emigrated from the farms and forests of the Rhineland around 1750, needed nearly forty years to evolve from European peasants into North Atlantic mariners.[76] A similar process of acculturation was taking place along the eastern shores of Maine after 1790. By the 1830s the process was completed, and the rise of the Maine sea fisheries was the result.

Economic Democracy

The question remains why the maritime development of the Maine coast in the first half of the nineteenth century, made inevitable by nature and possible by demographic patterns, had as its primary feature a fishing economy—and a cod-fishing economy at that. Given the environmental factors and the spread and size of the population, one might just as easily have expected a traditional mercantile society based purely on foreign trade and commerce. The answer lies in the economic nature of the state and, consequently, that of its fishing industry.

Maine was a poor state in relative terms,* and fishing was one form of business enterprise that required little capital investment. The average Maine entrepreneur, who could not afford to enter the foreign trade with a large square-rigger, could still purchase a small schooner for fishing and

---

*For example, in 1850—at the height of its influence upon the national economy—Maine ranked no better than tenth among the states in capital invested in manufactures and ninth in the product value of its manufactures. Even in New England, Maine was only the fourth state in capital investment and the third in product value. More specifically, the entire value of Maine's manufacturing production that year ($25 million) was just 2 percent of the national total, dwarfed by New York state's $238 million. In capital investment, Maine's $15 million was less than 3 percent of the national figure for 1850 and was barely one-sixth that of her mother commonwealth and chief competitor in the fisheries, Massachusetts. (Source: *U.S.Cen., 1860,* 3:729–30.)

coasting. The limited investor and the small vessel were typical of Maine's maritime industries during the pre–Civil War era of small-scale capitalism.

Take the case of the aforementioned John Gilley of Cranberry Isles, Hancock County. Gilley's first business venture took place in 1843, when, at the age of twenty-one, he borrowed $300 (part of it from his father) to purchase a one-third interest in a small, used coasting schooner. After several successful years carrying paving stones and dried fish to Boston in exchange for dry goods and other merchandise desired by Cranberry Islanders, Gilley branched out, investing the modest sum of $750 in a larger and somewhat better vessel, of which he became half-owner and master. Four years later, in 1854, he made the transition from coasting to fishing, dissolving his existing partnership and entering into a new one with his brother, Samuel. The two brothers bought a low-priced fishing schooner of thirty-five tons, a small vessel but large enough, with a crew of seven or eight men (including themselves), to work the cod and haddock grounds of Cape Sable and the Bay of Fundy. At the time he entered the fisheries, John Gilley had accumulated less than $1,000 in capital, and a considerable portion of that was expended as his share of the outlay for the new enterprise.[77]

The Gilleys were not great capitalists, and they were not atypical. Except at a few of the larger ports, the type of enterprise they represented—small, marginally financed, family-oriented—was characteristic of the early Maine sea fisheries. The nature of the craft employed was indicative. An estimated 80 percent of the hundred or so fishing vessels owned at Vinalhaven during the important 1845–1858 period registered less than fifty tons.[78] Similarly, 73 percent of the 160 vessels in the Penobscot District cod-fishing fleet of 1839 were under that size, the overall average being forty-four tons.[79] At Boothbay, in 1834, the entire fishing fleet was composed of small "pinkies," * most of them between thirty-five and forty tons.[80] Schooners of this type seldom exceeded fifty feet in registered length and carried no more than five or six crewmen.

Small size was matched by democratic ownership. The eighty-two vessels of the 1829 Penobscot District cod fleet had sixty-eight separate managing owners, a ratio of just 1.2 vessels per owner. Only nine of these sixty-eight

*The pinky was a small, beamy, double-ended (or sharp-sterned) schooner especially popular in the American and Canadian fisheries between 1820 and 1850 and, to some extent, beyond that time. It was characterized by exceptional seaworthiness and windward sailing ability, or "weatherliness." The pinky's signature feature, from which the name derived, was its "pink" stern, formed by an artificial extension of the bulwarks past the sternpost, ending in a peaked and narrow raking transom. In Maine the type was last in vogue among the fishermen of the Eastport-Lubec region. (Sources: Howard I. Chapelle, *The American Fishing Schooners, 1825–1935* [New York: W. W. Norton & Co., 1973], chap. 1; Howard I. Chapelle, *American Sailing Craft* [New York: Kennedy Brothers, 1936], chap. 9.)

owners had more than one schooner, and only one had controlling shares in more than three: David Thurlo of Deer Isle, the closest approximation of a fisheries monopolist in the district at that early date. Thurlo sent out four schooners in the spring of 1829, the largest being the *Lydia* of seventy-six tons, carrying a crew of seven. These four vessels were exceptions to the rule, however. Fully three-quarters of the schooners applying for bounty money in the district of Penobscot in 1829 had single-vessel owners. Furthermore, a solid majority (57 percent) were primarily owned by the very men who commanded them.[81]

This latter pattern persisted in the outports for years. A sizeable portion of the cod-fishing schooners operating out of Washington County's Machias District in 1853 were distinguished by a form of ownership in which the captain was majority shareholder. Typical of this group was the *Amaranth* of Cutler (sixty-one tons), whose skipper, John Grant, was three-fourths owner. Another example was the *Louisa* of Machiasport, a thirty-ton pinky in which the master, John Robinson, held half of the stock.[82]

It was also common practice for ordinary working crewmen to hold shares in vessels, and a kinship factor was part of the ownership pattern as well. When the schooner *Thistle* of Tremont outfitted at Castine in April of 1853 for a herring trip to the Magdalens, two of her four owners were aboard as members of the crew. One was the skipper and quarter shareholder, John S. Newman; the other was a twenty-two-year-old fisherman named John Stanley, who also owned 25 percent of the vessel. All four shareholders were from the same township (Tremont), two were related, and, according to the census returns for 1850, each was a working fisherman or seaman. The wealthiest among them was one Rufus King, whose stated occupation was "mariner." He owned $300 worth of real estate.[83] All in all, it was a tightly knit communal group, characterized by social intimacy and relatively low economic status.

The classic family form of enterprise was exemplified by the schooner *Banner,* also of Tremont. Her 1853 ownership consisted entirely of the members of one family, all brothers and all fishermen by trade. Two were members of the four-man crew: Lemuel Moore, age twenty-four, master and managing owner with a one-half interest; and John S. Moore, twenty-five, who owned a one-quarter interest. The remaining one-quarter share was held jointly by two younger brothers, William and Melvin, who remained at home or fished aboard other vessels. Their places on the schooner during the season of 1853 were occupied by two fellow townsmen. An interesting fact about the Moore brothers, in addition to their youthfulness (each being between the ages of nineteen and twenty-five), is that in 1850 they were all living with their father and had no discernible assets of their own. The elder Moore, who probably helped finance the cruise of the *Banner* three years later, was a farmer, with property valued in the 1850 census at only $280.[84]

Nor was kinship enterprise limited exclusively to small vessels. The *General Jackson* of Jonesport, which fished the Grand Banks of Newfoundland in 1852, was a 111-ton schooner with registered dimensions (length, beam, and depth) of 73' × 22' × 8'. Her four owners, including the captain, were all named Kelley and, from their ages, appear to have been either brothers or cousins. Of the three living in Jonesport in 1850, all were seamen, and only one owned any real estate.[85]

The extremely democratic ownership patterns prevalent in places like Tremont and Jonesport—control of vessels by fishermen and seamen, shareholding by crew members, extensive family involvement—were modified somewhat in the larger ports. There, ownership was more traditionally capitalistic, with merchants and other wealthy individuals playing a greater role. Merchants held majority shares in seventeen of Castine's twenty-three Grand Banks schooners in 1854, for example.[86] The vessels owned at the commercial centers also tended to be larger. In 1852 the city of Belfast's fleet averaged sixty-four tons, while that of Brooklin, a typically small, remote Penobscot Bay outport, averaged just forty-eight tons.[87] Nevertheless, the capitalism exhibited in the major ports was of a comparatively small-scale variety, and in the early years it had certain democratic aspects of its own.

If ordinary fishermen did not control the fishing schooners of Belfast, Bucksport, or Castine, it was still possible for small investors to own stock in them. Rarely did one merchant-shipowner claim exclusive title to a banker or mackerel hooker, although he might very well have a controlling interest. The Grand Banker *Mayflower* (104 tons) of Bucksport had no fewer than ten owners in 1859, including four farmers, two merchants, two sea captains, one shipbuilder, and one carpenter. That was exceptional, but an overwhelming majority of the banks schooners owned in Bucksport that year had between three and seven owners, among them several men of modest background and limited resources. All told, while Bucksport merchants held controlling shares in three-quarters of their town's banks-fishing fleet, they constituted just one-quarter of the total shareholders. In the case of four vessels, a plurality of the stock was actually held by farmers, master mariners, or artisans.[88]

An examination of the investment required to own such stock is enlightening. The 1859 taxable value of the schooner *Mayflower* (above) was placed by the local assessor at $1,440, which means that the share of the biggest stockholder (five-sixteenths) was worth $450 and those of the seven smallest (one-sixteenth) only $90 each. At the time, this vessel was just a half-dozen years old, scarcely an aged schooner in an era when some worked the banks for twenty years or more, and newer in fact than all but five of the eighteen identified banks schooners in the Bucksport tax list.[89] The *Mayflower* was not an isolated case. The cod banker *Accumulator* of Castine showed a similar pattern of small investments in 1850, when her taxable value, divided among seven shareholders, was assessed at $1,104. The biggest stockholders (three-sixteenths each) were two merchants, William Witherle and Benjamin D. Gay, partners in the firm of William Witherle & Company, whose combined investment was $414. They effectively controlled the disposition of the vessel with nearly half of the stock. The remainder, however, was held by five quite ordinary individuals—two farmers, two house joiners, and one fisherman—each of whom owned a one-eighth share worth $138.[90] Clearly, it took some money to buy into a fishing vessel during the prewar years, but not an exorbitant amount. At least through the 1850s, broad participation in the ownership of fishing schooners—if not large, seagoing carriers—was both a feasible proposition and a reality along the coast of Maine.

Of course, both of the vessels cited above had some years of service behind them, and participation in the ownership of a new vessel was a more expensive proposition. Even so, fishing schooners were relatively cheap compared to the large square-riggers used in the foreign and coastal carrying trades. A good-sized cod or mackerel schooner of the 1850s, built for offshore work, generally cost between $4,000 and $6,000 new, depending on tonnage, rig, materials, and the like. The 80-ton Boothbay clipper fisherman *C. G. Matthews,* for example, was delivered by a local builder in April 1851 at a cost of $4,000.[91] The cod banker *Olivia* (97 tons) was built at Belfast in 1852 for $4,500, and the mackerel schooner *Vesta* (100 tons) was launched there the same year for $5,000.[92] A somewhat larger schooner, the Castine Grand Banker *Martha Burgess* (118 tons), was built at a local yard for $5,500 in 1855, and the even bigger *Eothen* (130 tons), another Castine product, cost $6,000 new in 1860.[93] This represented the outer limits of cost for fishing vessels prior to the Civil War. The average was closer to $5,000, and smaller schooners could be produced for considerably less. The mackerelman *Castellane,* a 75-tonner, was reportedly built for $3,000 in 1850 at the Belfast yard of S. C. Nickerson.[94]

Compared to these figures, the outlay for a new square-rigger, especially of the three-masted variety, was enormous. It cost $46,787 to build the 876-ton ship *William Witherle* at Castine in 1851. The bark *Antioch* (646 tons), launched at Castine eight years later, was priced at $26,522. Even ordinary two-masted brigs, the common square-rigged carriers of the coastal and West Indies trades, could prove expensive. One, the *Susan Currier* of Castine (185 tons), was launched in 1847 at a cost of close to $9,000—or double that of most contemporary fishing schooners.[95] In the really large class of square-rigger—1,000 tons and up—the purchase price was higher still, especially at the prestige yards to the west. At Damariscotta, $62,000 was the going rate for a 1,200-ton ship in 1854, and $55,000 was the minimum for a 1,000-tonner at Yarmouth, Maine, during the late 1850s.[96]

Admittedly, the shares held by investors in large ships tended to be fractionally smaller than was the case in fishing-vessel ownership. Regardless of that fact, the very size of the overall expenditure necessary to buy a new vessel for the major carrying trades eliminated all but the most affluent investors. Shareholding patterns at Castine in 1854 are illustrative. A one-eighth share in the full-rigged ship *J. P. Whitney* was valued that year at $5,360, a one-sixteenth share at $2,680, and a one-forty-eighth share, the smallest available, at $895—roughly the cost of a good used fishing schooner. A one-thirty-second share in the fourteen-year-old ship *Adams* was worth as much as $435, and a twenty-fourth of the small bark *Sarah L. Bryant* was assessed at $415. It took $2,500 to own one-sixteenth of the full-rigger *William Witherle* and $2,335 to hold a one-twelfth share in the ship *William Jarvis*. The cheapest portion of stock owned in a Castine square-rigger in 1854 was a one-thirty-second part of the tiny and decrepit bark *Byron,* for which the holder was assessed $220.[97]

These half-dozen vessels were fairly representative, ranging from one to fourteen years in age and from about three hundred to a thousand tons in size.[98] They were neither new nor particularly large ships, and yet participation in their ownership was severely restricted. It is easy to see why. Just to own a piece of a major vessel required significant capital; to hold a substantial or controlling interest took immense resources. The primary owner of the Castine ship *Ostervald* (seven twenty-fourths) had a floating investment worth $13,000 in 1854.[99] Not many fishing entrepreneurs—and certainly no fishermen—could approach that level of finance.

This sort of capitalization was unnecessary in the fisheries. For one thing, purchase of a new vessel was not an absolute requirement, since used schooners were always on the market, often at very low cost. In 1850, three

Gloucester, Massachusetts,* fishermen of 1830s vintage were sold to Maine buyers at Deer Isle, Southport, and Cranberry Isles for prices ranging from $800 to $1,450, a fraction of their original cost.[100] Depreciation of such vessels tended to be based more on age than on actual condition, with the greatest loss of value taking place the first year or two and the decline continuing thereafter at a lesser but steady rate.[101] It was possible, therefore, to find schooners of considerable age and consequent low valuation, which had nevertheless been well built and carefully maintained and could give additional years of adequate service. Of course, the reverse could just as easily be true, and the use of old vessels in the fisheries was risky business. Still, with luck, it was one way for the small, marginal operator to enter the field.

The saga of the schooner *Meridian* indicates the extent to which the fishing business could be undertaken with minimum expense. The *Meridian* was a fifty-seven-tonner built at Gloucester in 1824. In 1850, when twenty-six years old, she was purchased and enrolled at Castine for the cod fishery. The four new owners paid just $500 for the aged schooner, with one stockholder putting up $250 and the rest sharing the balance of the investment equally. Two years later, in 1852, the *Meridian* was fishing the Gulf of St. Lawrence for mackerel. In 1854, when thirty years old, the vessel was still on the tax rolls and presumably still earning money for her Castine owners.[102]

Cod Fishers and Mackerel Catchers

While economic democracy was certainly the dominant theme during the years that Maine's sea fisheries rose to prominence, both in the small outports and the large centers of commerce, it would be misleading to imply that the merchant class and the mercantile firm did not play a primary role. They unquestionably did, despite the overall egalitarian tone of the industry's economic structure prior to 1860. What is significant, however, is the relatively small scale of mercantile enterprise at Maine's fishing ports and the precise form that enterprise took in terms of its objectives.

Maine, as suggested earlier, was a poor state, and its fish merchants were "poor" as well. This was clearly reflected in federal statistics on the U.S.

---

*Gloucester, the leading Massachusetts fishing center, provided an especially dependable market for cheap but serviceable used schooners, many of them built at nearby Essex, and it was resorted to regularly by the fishermen of rural Maine's outports from the 1840s onward. In the larger, more affluent Maine ports, however, relatively new, native-built schooners remained the rule until the Civil War. (Sources: Procter, *Fishermen's Own Book*, 211; *EA*, marine lists, 22 February 1855, 7 December 1860, and 2 January 1863; and see Wayne M. O'Leary, "The Antebellum Maine Fishing Schooner and the Factors Influencing Its Design and Construction," *The American Neptune* 44 [Spring 1984]:82–85.)

fishing industry just prior to the Civil War. According to the 1860 census, Maine had 350 business establishments engaged in the cod, mackerel, and herring fisheries, the largest number for any state. (Massachusetts was second with 169.) These 350 firms, however, were capitalized at only $687,000, compared to the $2,520,000* invested in the Bay State's 169 firms.[103] On an average basis, then, each Maine venture was capitalized at about $2,000, a trifling figure beside the $15,000 invested in each Massachusetts firm.

What were these smaller Maine establishments like, and what kind of fishing activity was occupying their energies and their capital? The Castine firm of Hatch & Mead provides a clue. This partnership was not typical of Castine. It was, in fact, the smallest of that town's eight fishing companies in 1854. Castine, however, was the wealthiest of all Maine fishing ports on a per capita basis, and its poorer entrepreneurs were a more accurate reflection of the industry statewide. Hatch & Mead had total capital assets of $5,000, of which $1,200 was in buildings and wharves and $400 in company trading stock. The remaining $3,400 was invested in the two schooners in which the firm held a partial or controlling interest. Both were Grand Banks cod-fishing vessels. The same pattern was evident in the investment practices of Castine's three other small firms, Stearns & Company, S. P. Hatch & Company, and C. K. Tilden, each with total assets of less than $14,000. Virtually all of their limited vessel capital was tied up in banks schooners.[104] In short, they were involved in cod fishing to the exclusion of almost everything else.

On a statewide basis, the Maine sea fisheries emulated the Castine pattern. During the nearly four decades that separate statistics were kept on the two primary American fisheries (1830–1867), 74 percent of Maine's vessel tonnage, on average, fished for cod, and only 26 percent for mackerel. The proportion in cod fishing was even higher during some years, notably 1859 and 1860, when it reached 87 percent, and 1841–1844, when it passed 90 percent. From 1830 to 1867 Maine never experienced a year in which its mackerel tonnage exceeded its cod-fishing tonnage. In Massachusetts, the situation was far different. Over the same period (1830–1867), the Bay State's mackerel tonnage exceeded its cod-fishing tonnage ten times, and on average less than 60 percent of its total tonnage was regularly employed in the cod fisheries.[105]

---

*Exactly what these dollar figures represent is not made clear by the census. In all probability, they measured the stock-in-trade and the investment in buildings and wharves. The comparatively low totals make it appear unlikely that vessel property was included, although in the case of Maine this may be explained by the fact that many vessels were owned by independent fishermen not connected with business firms. At any rate, since similar criteria were presumably used for all states, a valid comparison of Maine and Massachusetts can be made.

Actual numbers of fishing vessels (as opposed to tonnage figures) are sel-dom available for these years, but 1851 was an exception. An accurate tabu-lation for that year further delineates the contrast between the nation's two primary fishing states. The United States had 1,093 mackerel schooners afloat in 1851. Of these, 853 were owned in Massachusetts and only 200 in Maine.[106] A Newburyport, Massachusetts, fisherman best expressed the very real dis-tinction between the two states—albeit unknowingly—when he boasted to an international fisheries commission in 1877 that he was not a "cod-fisher" but a "mackerel-catcher."[107] Maine's fishermen, then as always, were pre-eminently "cod-fishers."

The cod fishery was more important to Maine than to any other Ameri-can state, Massachusetts included. Maine had a greater percentage of its coastal population dependent upon that fishery and remained committed to a way of life symbolized by the Sacred Cod long after the Bay State had diversified its fisheries and its entire economy. The reason was economic and can be traced to Maine's relative impoverishment.

Fishing for the elusive mackerel was, first of all, an economically risky oc-cupation, fraught with the possibility of financial disaster. Numerous con-temporary observers testified to the uncertainty of the mackerel fishery, a characteristic they blamed on the unpredictable nature of the species. In his 1853 report on the American fisheries, noted authority Lorenzo Sabine wrote, "The mackerel is a capricious and sportive fish, and continually changing its haunts and habits."[108] Success did not depend on skill and en-ergy alone, in Sabine's opinion. "The best masters make 'broken voyages,'" he pointed out, "for the obvious reason that the mackerel does not always appear in sufficient numbers in any of the seas or bays of New England or British America."[109] Zeno Scudder, political representative of the fishing districts of Cape Cod in the 1850s, echoed that sentiment. The mackerel fishery, he said, "is much more fluctuating and uncertain than the cod fish-ery. In one season it may yield a profit, and in another prove disastrous, . . . It seems in a great degree, to be a chance game or lottery."[110] A federal re-port discussed the problem more dispassionately in 1860:

> The true mackerel (*Scomber scombrus*) is a migratory fish of great fecundity and peculiar habits, which render the business of fishing for them a precarious one, involving considerable outlay and frequent loss. Though voracious, the mackerel is a capricious feeder, at one time taking the hook readily, at others refusing it altogether. Equal uncertainty exists as to the locality and numbers in which it may be found, whence it happens that mackerel fishers sometimes make quick and abundant fares, and at other times scarcely pay the cost of outfit.[111]

Despite the risk factor, fishermen from Massachusetts were more than willing to pursue the mackerel, especially fishermen from the Essex county port of Gloucester, who pioneered in the fishery as early as 1818.[112] Massachusetts always landed the bulk of the United States mackerel catch, and by the 1850s up to half of the Massachusetts catch was being brought in by Gloucester schooners. In 1847 mackerel was Gloucester's most important fish product in dollar value and was worth a third more than the town's codfish catch. By 1859 over half of the $1.3 million earned in the Gloucester sea fisheries came from mackerel, with cod a poor second and other species, like halibut, trailing far behind.[113] As of 1860, Gloucester owned ten thousand tons of mackerel vessels, over 50 percent of the Massachusetts total and more than the entire state of Maine put together.[114]

This emphasis on mackereling was no matter of mere chance. Fishermen from Gloucester and other Massachusetts ports went into the mackerel fishery because, regardless of the inherent uncertainty, money could be made in it.* Congressman Zeno Scudder developed statistics showing, among other things, that only the cod bounty allowed New England cod fishermen to earn more than mackerel fishermen in 1852. Otherwise, the mackerel catchers, who received no bounty, would have had a higher average seasonal income that year.[115] In 1880, when the bounty was no longer a factor, mackerel fishermen made much more, both per trip and per season, than fishermen in any other vessel fishery.[116]

The merchants and vessel owners also did well. Throughout the pre–Civil war era, wholesale mackerel prices rose at an accelerated rate, while cod prices remained almost static by comparison. In the 1830s, a barrel of pickled mackerel was worth roughly twice as much as a quintal of dried cod. In the 1840s it was worth three times as much, and by the 1850s, four times as much. From 1830 to 1860 the value of a quintal of cod (112 pounds) in the Portland wholesale market increased very slowly from $2.50 to $3.75, while the value of a barrel of mackerel (200 pounds) leaped from $4.75 to $16.00. On a per-pound basis, wholesale cod went from two cents to three cents, a 50 percent rise, but wholesale mackerel went from two cents to eight cents, a 300 percent increase.[117] Prices in the Gloucester market showed a similar pattern during the same period, although, significantly, the prewar high in mackerel prices at Gloucester ($19 per barrel in 1855) was a dollar greater than the prewar high at Portland.[118]

---

*The zeal of some fishermen in pursuing the valuable and elusive mackerel was exemplified in 1849 by an American schooner with a full fare (catch) of cod that was observed in the Gulf of St. Lawrence throwing her cod overboard to make room for a school of mackerel she had accidently struck. (Source: *Perley Reports*, 36.)

In addition to their general growth, mackerel prices tended to fluctuate wildly from year to year. Partly, this was a natural result of the marketplace responding to supply and demand, always a critical factor in this sensitive fishery. In both 1836 and 1853, unusual scarcity drove the price up at Gloucester.[119] There was another reason, however. Charles H. Pew, partner in the Gloucester fishing firm of John Pew & Sons during the 1870s, maintained that unlike other fish, mackerel was a speculative form of food, and he pointed to the common practice of holding it off the market until the price rose. Said Pew, "I think that the prices of mackerel are as much influenced by speculation as by the catch."[120] One instance of such speculative activity took place in 1857, when New York and Philadelphia agents sought to outbid one another for rights to the Massachusetts mackerel catch, in order to control the temporarily profitable export trade to California and Australia.[121]

In contrast to the fluidity of the mackerel market, cod prices varied hardly at all. From 1846 to 1860, codfish prices paid by Portland wholesalers stabilized at between three and four dollars per quintal, rising or falling only a few cents from year to year. Mackerel prices, on the other hand, fluctuated between nine and eighteen dollars per barrel during the same fifteen-year period, often varying as much as three or four dollars from one season to the next. The overall trend for mackerel was always upward, however, despite the bad years, and no matter how low wholesale mackerel prices fell, they never dipped below comparable codfish prices on a per-pound basis. During the 1840s and 1850s, mackerel was consistently worth at least twice as much as cod.[122]

What this all meant in the retail market was that by the end of the prewar period consumers were paying double the price for mackerel that they were for cod—eight cents per pound versus four cents per pound at Philadelphia in 1860.[123] What it meant to the fish merchants of Gloucester was prosperity. In 1877 Angus Grant, a Cape Breton (Nova Scotia) merchant and ex-fisherman who had once sailed out of Gloucester, assessed the importance of mackereling to that port's merchants in the following way: "When I first went to the United States Gloucester was a small place, but it is quite a place now. They own a great many vessels there; . . . They do some other business, but their principal occupation is mackerel fishing, in the greater part. They would not put one of these fine schooners years ago in the codfishing business; they were all engaged in the prosecution of the mackerel fishery in the Bay of Chaleurs."[124] To put it simply, the mackerel fishery offered a high return to the entrepreneur who could afford to risk the uncertainty of the catch and the vagaries of the marketplace. Massachusetts fish merchants, especially those of Gloucester, were in a position to do so. They were wealthy enough to survive the bad years and big enough to capitalize fully on the good years. Maine merchants were not.

The worst of the bad years were in the 1840s. From 1841 to 1844, Massachusetts newspapers were filled with stories of mackerel vessels returning with empty holds and fishermen receiving token wages.[125] Yet, the Massachusetts mackerel fleet survived and, by the last half of the decade, was more prosperous than ever. Not so in Maine. A customs official for the district of Portland-Falmouth reported in 1841 that the mackerel fishermen of Portland were giving up that fishery in discouragement, convinced that recent failures meant that the mackerel business was finished.[126]

Tonnage statistics tell the story. During the early mackerel boom of the 1830s, Maine, like Massachusetts, had committed a sizeable portion of its fishing fleet to mackereling—almost half of it for a few years. In 1836, when the catch was still good, both states had 46 percent of their respective fishing tonnages in the mackerel fishery. In 1840, after it had begun to tail off, 25 percent of Maine's tonnage was still in the mackerel business, compared to 34 percent for the Bay State. The next year the bottom fell out, and by 1843 less than 2 percent of Maine's fishing tonnage remained in the mackerel fishery, the rest turning to ground fishing. The lowest level for the Massachusetts mackerel fleet, however, was only 25 percent—also reached in 1843. Moreover, it quickly came back with the onset of improved fishing and marketing conditions and by 1849 again claimed over half of the Bay State's total tonnage. In other words, the Massachusetts mackerel fleet lost about half of its share of the state's fishing tonnage between the late 1830s and the early 1840s, and then rebounded, completely regaining its status by the late 1840s. The mackerel fishery in Maine never completely recovered, however, despite isolated successes here and there. Its initial decline was total—virtually 100 percent—and the recovery, when it came, recaptured only half of what had been lost in percentage terms. Until the last years of the Civil War, Maine's mackerel tonnage never constituted more than a quarter of the state's total sea-fishing tonnage in any one year.[127]

The actual tonnage figures are equally compelling. From 11,300 tons of mackerel schooners in 1838, Maine slid to just 232 tons in 1843—no more than five or six vessels. Not until 1850 did the state's mackerel fleet again exceed 10,000 tons. Massachusetts also suffered, but its low point (1841) was still a respectable 10,032 tons, and by 1850 the total was back up to nearly 43,000 tons. Maine fishermen did not give up fishing during the black days, however. They simply switched their attention to the less profitable but more predictable codfish. In 1843, during the nadir of the mackerel fishery,

Maine retained 15,000 tons of fishing vessels that hunted the unglamorous but dependable cod.[128]

A glance at the relative scale of operations at two fishing ports, one in Massachusetts and one in Maine, points up the problem of the Maine fishing industry vis-à-vis the mackerel fishery. The port of Gloucester, where the Massachusetts mackerel fishery came to be centered, had by conservative count 96 company-owned fishing vessels in 1832. These were controlled by seventeen mercantile firms. The average number for each firm was 6 vessels, and seven of the companies had more than that. The two largest owned 10 schooners each.[129] This was well before Gloucester reached its maximum development, yet considerable concentration was already noticeable. Another survey of Gloucester's internal industry structure a quarter-century later, in 1868, showed the number of fishing firms totalling fifty-two and the number of vessels approaching 400. By then, the top seven Gloucester firms owned 106 vessels between them, and each had more than a dozen. The leader was Joseph Friend, with no fewer than 18 schooners, and the average for all fifty-two companies was 8.[130]

The situation at Castine, Maine, center of the Penobscot Bay cod fishery, contrasted sharply. In 1854, when it was one of the leading fishing ports in the entire state, Castine had eight mercantile firms engaged in fisheries activity, fewer than half the number Gloucester had had twenty-two years earlier. Furthermore, these eight firms owned shares in only 48 schooners, and no more than two-thirds of those can be definitely identified as fishermen. In addition, several of the fishing schooners owned in part by Castine merchants actually sailed from other Maine ports. Altogether, about two dozen company-owned banks vessels operated out of Castine in 1854. If every schooner owned by Castine merchants, including those in the coasting trade, is taken into account, the eight firms averaged 6 vessels each. If only fishing schooners are considered, the average was closer to 4, and only one company, the firm of Samuel Adams, had more than 6.[131]

The capitalization of the fisheries at Gloucester and Castine further indicated their respective economic capabilities. Gloucester had a grand total of $989,250 invested in the industry in 1854.[132] The eight firms that dominated the Castine scene the same year were capitalized at $239,814, less than one-fourth as much. Actually, the true Castine figure was even smaller, since the total amount included well over $100,000 invested in square-rigged trading vessels. Eliminating them reduces it by nearly half.[133] The contrast in resources between the two ports was reflected in the money they spent on fishing vessels. In 1846 the Gloucester Georges Bank cod and halibut fleet was composed of twenty-nine schooners with an average individual value of

$2,800. The Castine Grand Banks fleet of 1854, which included twenty-three of the town's best cod bankers, had an average per-vessel valuation of $1,784.[134]

Because of their small size and limited capital, Maine's mercantile firms were forced to be somewhat conservative in their approach to the fishing industry. A merchant at Gloucester, Boston, or Newburyport, backed by substantial capital and owning numerous vessels, could accept short-term losses in exchange for long-term gains, which was the pattern of the mackerel business. The typical Maine merchant, on the other hand, having limited funds and only a handful of vessels, could be ruined by one or two bad years. If he could not reap windfall profits by fishing for the stolid cod, he knew that he could at least survive by doing so. And what was true for the small fish merchant of Camden, Bucksport, or Castine was doubly true for the independent fisherman in the outports, who lived from year to year and depended on the one small schooner he operated himself.

One additional factor needs to be taken into account in analyzing the character of the antebellum fishing industry in Maine. The dominant predilection of Maine fishermen toward cod fishing was directly influenced by needs and costs in the area of vessel ownership. As dictated by their economic situation, Maine entrepreneurs necessarily favored inexpensive fishing schooners. This meant purchasing practical, workmanlike vessels without lavish fittings when buying new, avoiding radical or experimental models that might prove costly, and getting good used schooners whenever possible. Most particularly, it meant obtaining all-round vessels with maximum utility rather than specialized craft.

The problem was that unlike cod fishing, mackerel catching was a highly specialized occupation. Any vessel, more or less, was suitable for the cod fishery. One sailed to the fishing grounds, anchored, fished off the bottom from the deck of the vessel, and returned home when the hold was full. The same general technique applied to the haddock, hake, pollock, and other ground fisheries. Mackereling was substantially different. A prime necessity was a fast schooner with the qualities of maneuverability that fishermen associated with a "handy" vessel.

Unlike cod and other bottom-feeding species, mackerel kept on the move, continually migrating in large schools near the surface of the water. Consequently, mackerel schooners had to be constantly under way, pursuing their quarry, fishing under sail, and often following the mackerel inshore, where the wind was light and the water shoal. Henry David Thoreau described a typical mackerel fleet operating off Cape Cod in 1849: "Though their sails were set they never sailed away, nor yet came to anchor, but stood

on various tacks, as close together as vessels in a haven, and we, in our ignorance, thought that they were contending patiently with adverse winds,
beating eastward; but we learned afterward that they were even then on
their fishing-ground, and that they caught mackerel without taking in their
mainsails or coming to anchor." [135] The ability to sail swiftly to windward—
a prized quality many ordinary vessels lacked—was a necessity in successful mackerel fishing. A Nova Scotian fisherman, explaining the success of
United States mackerel schooners in Canadian waters to a concerned government committee at Halifax in 1851, credited the American vessels with
superior sailing capabilities and better fittings. "It is of the first importance," he added, "to have a smart weatherly vessel—the current and drift
is usually off shore—the fish always make to windward." [136] The twin needs
of speed and weatherliness led to the development of a class of schooners for the mackerel fishery that contemporaries came to regard as the
finest and swiftest fishing vessels afloat.[137] "The American mackerel fleet,"
bragged a Wellfleet, Massachusetts, fish inspector in 1873, "is a fleet of
yachts calculated for fleetness and composed and constructed of the best
materials." [138]

Most of the design experiments carried out during the 1840s and 1850s in
search of fast-sailing fishing schooners had the mackerel fishery in mind.
Initially, the pinky had been favored by mackerelmen for its weatherly qualities.[139] Next came the "sharpshooter," a faster type, which became popular
with mackerel fishermen around 1848–1850.[140] By the mid-1850s the "clipper" model had evolved. Of its emergence Howard I. Chapelle observed,
"The class in which the clipper was the particular favorite was the mackerel
schooners. The mackerel fishery always attracted the fastest models of
schooners, including some of the most extreme designs." [141]

Hull speed was complemented by the practice of over-canvassing. American mackerel schooners working the Gulf of St. Lawrence in the 1860s were
distinguished by the huge sails they carried for fast sailing in light
breezes.[142] Joseph W. Collins, an astute observer, remarked that they carried "all the canvas which their rig will allow" and added that "the mackerel
schooners as a rule spread more sail, in comparison with their size, than any
other vessels in the world, except, perhaps, the extreme type of schooner-
rigged yacht." [143]

The need for speed, responsiveness, and windward ability meant that
mackerel fishermen had to put money into their vessels. The amount of
extra canvas for the sails alone meant a considerable outlay. Newness, too,
was important, since new wooden vessels tend to be sprightlier than older,
waterlogged vessels. And the demands of excellence under sail required an

attention to detail in all facets of construction and rigging that could only add to the cost.

All of this resulted in a contrast between cod and mackerel vessels that was exemplified by the fishing fleet of Belfast, Maine. Although most eastern Maine ports shunned mackereling, Belfast was an exception. One-third of her vessels were mackerel schooners in 1852. These twelve schooners were valued by local customs officials at $3,942 each, on the average, compared to $1,970 each for the city's twenty-three cod-fishing schooners. The mackerel fleet was both newer and larger in individual vessel size than its opposite number. Even among craft of similar age and size, those intended for the mackerel business were clearly superior. All three of the newly built mackerel schooners between 90 and 100 tons were worth $500 more than the one new cod schooner in that size category. Among one-year-old vessels, two mackerelmen in the 80-to-90-ton range were valued several hundred dollars higher than two cod schooners of similar tonnage. Based on the sample these eight vessels provide, a mackerel schooner of the prewar era was worth roughly 10 percent more than a cod schooner of comparable size and vintage. Overall, Belfast had fifteen cod-fishing schooners worth less than $2,000, while none of the city's mackerel schooners fell below that level.[144] The former were obviously the poor relations of the fleet.

Finally, added to the known expenses of buying and outfitting a mackerel schooner was the element of risk—the inherent uncertainty present in the search for speed. The serious mackerel merchant or fisherman was obliged to experiment with unknown quantities in the realm of naval architecture if he expected to outsail his competitors and outmaneuver his prey. A new departure in vessel design might cost no more to build than an old-fashioned type of schooner, but it could easily prove a total failure under sail. In the last analysis, this typified the kind of gamble that the Maine fishing community at large could not afford to take.

The Maine fisheries were dispersed, not concentrated. They were carried on by great numbers of small entrepreneurs, whose limited capital and relative poverty precluded more grandiose forms of enterprise. At the same time, those fisheries were narrow in their focus, concentrating on one species, cod, to the almost total exclusion of all others. The cod fishery did not require massive capital or particularly advanced technology. Like the one-crop cotton economy of the South, it stressed quantity, not quality or diversity, at a time when quantity production of one readily available commodity was in demand. In short, cod fishing was an activity perfectly suited to Maine's economy. This fact contributed in great measure to the rise of Maine's sea fisheries in the years between 1830 and 1860.

Slaves and Immigrants

There were other factors present in the antebellum era that tended to spur on the growth of Maine's fishing industry. Among these were developments outside the state. The Maine fisheries did not exist in a vacuum. They were part of a national—and in some ways international—economy. They were influenced by decisions made far from down-east fishing ports and by long-term trends taking shape far beyond the waters of the Piscataqua.

One decision, easily pinpointed, was the Crown Order in Council of November 5, 1830, which reopened the long-closed ports of the British West Indies to United States trade and thereby created new markets for New England fishermen. This action has been credited, at least in part, with the subsequent rise in importance of the Boothbay-area fisheries.[145] More important, although more difficult to measure with precision, were two evolutionary developments taking place simultaneously within the United States: the expansion of slavery and the rising tide of European immigration. Together, they resulted in the creation of a vast potential market for the products of New England fishermen—including those in Maine.

The growth of slavery, while the lesser of these two internal factors as measured by its impact on the fisheries, was nevertheless of considerable import to the industry. Most authorities have agreed that the basic staples of the American slave diet were salt pork and cornmeal, supplemented by such local produce as sweet potatoes, peas, or beans.[146] Recent investigators have concluded, however, that while corn and pork were the core of the plantation diet, fish was among the "less frequent, but not uncommon" commodities purchased by the southern slave owner for his labor force.[147]

The precise amounts of fish consumed by slaves cannot be determined. The cheapness of the article, though, must have made it attractive. At Philadelphia, in 1860, the per-pound retail price of dried cod was less than half that of salt pork and also much less than all other varieties of meat, fresh or preserved. Even a pound of pickled mackerel, the most expensive type of salt fish, could be bought a penny cheaper than a pound of salt pork. In interior agricultural regions, far from the seacoast but close to the hog raisers, salt pork was less expensive. All the same, it cost more than cod. Zanesville, Ohio, was probably typical. This southern Ohio town, situated near the Virginia border in the midst of cattle and hog country, retailed salt pork for six cents per pound in 1860. Dried cod, which had to be imported from afar, averaged five cents per pound the same year.[148] This price distinction cannot have been lost on southern planters, who purchased a substantial portion of the pork and hogs they needed, despite a presumed ability to raise their own stock on the plantation premises.[149]

However small the percentage of fish in the slave diet—and it certainly was a limited proportion—the total amount consumed necessarily grew during the prewar years, as the bonded labor force of the Old South increased in geometric fashion. The number of slaves in the United States doubled from 1800 to 1830 and doubled again between 1830 and 1860. In 1840, about the time Maine was emerging as a major factor in the American fisheries, the slave population was roughly 2.5 million. By 1860, when Maine's fisheries reached their maximum development, that population was up to 4 million.[150] In short, the slave system produced a large, expanding market for cheap food at just the right time for the rising Maine fishing industry.

Admittedly, the potential of the southern plantation as a market for New England fish products was never fully realized. For whatever reasons, it remained significant but tangential to the overall fishing economies of Maine and Massachusetts. The other major demographic phenomenon of the pre–Civil War era, however, the massive influx of European immigrants, was of crucial importance to the fishing industry. For one thing, the numbers were greater. Between 1815 and 1860, 5 million immigrants came to America. Most of them (3 million) arrived between 1845 and 1854 and constituted, in proportion to the total United States population at that time, the largest immigration wave in the nation's history. Not only did the immigrants come, they came in progressively accelerating fashion, increasing in each decade beginning with the 1820s and culminating in the 1850s, when various estimates place the number of arrivals at between 2.3 and 2.6 million.[151] Not coincidentally, this influx, especially that of the late 1840s and early 1850s, occurred simultaneously with the onset of Maine's boom period in the fishing industry.

More important than numbers alone was who the newcomers were and where they settled. Marcus Lee Hansen identified them as a fairly homogeneous group. "Three distinct stages of migration marked the nineteenth century," he noted. "The first . . . began in the 1830s and continued until 1860, reaching its crest in the years 1847–1854. To this exodus, the adjective 'Celtic' may be properly applied."[152] Hansen referred to the numerical dominance of migrants from Scotland, Wales, and (especially) Ireland. At least 2 of the 5 million immigrants entering the United States between 1815 and 1860—the largest single nationality group—were Irish. On the eve of the Civil War, the Irish-born in America, then totalling 1.6 million, constituted 40 percent of the country's entire non-native population.[153]

They had arrived, for the most part, during the preceding decade and had settled primarily in the cities of the eastern seaboard, the very urban centers that absorbed an increasing proportion of Maine's sea products in the late antebellum period (see chapter 4). Boston's forty-six thousand Irish, for example, made up three-quarters of that city's foreign element in 1855 and over one-quarter of its total population as well. Similarly, half of New York City's residents were foreign-born in 1855, and 54 percent of those were Irish.[154] Although the population centers of the Northeast received most of the impact, southern cities were not exempt. New Orleans, the South's largest metropolis, experienced an immigration flood of over a half-million persons during the four decades preceding the Civil War, a quarter-million of them in the early 1850s. Again, the bulk of these were of Irish origin. One out of every five citizens of New Orleans in 1850 was a native of Ireland.[155]

The exodus from Ireland was significant for the New England fisheries in two respects. First, it introduced Roman Catholicism to the United States on a massive scale. Second, it brought a particularly impoverished populace into urban America. Unlike any other sizeable immigrant group of the period, the Irish were almost uniformly Catholic.[156] They constituted, therefore, a ready-made fish-eating population bound by religious observance of meatless fast days. Furthermore, they came poor and remained in that condition for a considerable period of time, a fact of some importance in shaping their dietary habits.

As a class, the Irish entered American life with materially less than any other ethnic group. Most of those leaving the old country after 1835, when the great migration began, were dispossessed peasants living on the thin edge of starvation.[157] The economic straits in which they arrived meant that, once here, they were, to use Oscar Handlin's phrase, "completely immobilized."[158] The Irish landing at New York in the 1840s and 1850s, for example, could not afford to buy farmland or pay for transportation into the interior, as immigrants from rural Europe had traditionally done.[159] Of necessity they took the only avenue open to them, remaining in the cities and becoming unskilled laborers. Half of Boston's Irish-born workers were common laborers in 1850, and they constituted 82 percent of that city's entire unskilled work force. It was no different elsewhere. Most of the Irish who arrived in New Orleans between 1830 and 1860 were also relegated to "pick-and-shovel" work.[160] As a consequence, these newcomers, no matter where they arrived, evolved into a new urban proletariat, earning little money and adapting to living conditions no more ideal than the rural poverty left behind.[161] Other incoming nationality groups, notably the Germans, were a little better off, but not much. The result was that by 1860 most American cities, north and south, had heavy concentrations of foreigners—a third to a half of the population in most cases—the majority of them living on the lower end of the socioeconomic scale.[162]

Added to a potential rural slave market for Maine's fish, then, was a potential urban working-class market of considerable magnitude. As with the slave population, there is no way of knowing the exact extent to which the laboring immigrant masses of the cities actually consumed seafood. Nevertheless, the inferences are clear. The Catholicism of many new Americans— perhaps 2.3 million of the 4 million foreign-born living in the United States in 1860—demanded at least partial adherence to a fish diet on a regular weekly basis.[163] Beyond that, most of the newcomers were extremely poor, and until recent times, fish has always been the poor man's food.

Timothy Davis, a member of the U.S. House of Representatives from Massachusetts, made the following assessment of the place fish occupied in the American diet in 1857: "Dried and pickled codfish and mackerel enter largely into the list of articles of consumption mainly on account of their comparative cheapness. The laboring man can get along very well, if, for economy's sake, he can frequently get his dinner of dried or pickled fish."[164] Whether the working man got along "well" by buying fish, as Davis claimed, is debatable, but available statistics suggest that he could at least get along. On a list of eighteen meat and fish staples available to Philadelphia consumers in 1860, dried cod was the least expensive of all, and pickled mackerel also ranked near the bottom in price.[165] The new urban masses required a cheap, dependable source of protein, and fish, especially salt cod, provided it.

Essentially, Maine's deep-sea fishing industry grew from a regional curiosity into a cornerstone of the national economy because a number of various factors were in harmony. Between 1840 and 1865 a delicate balance was struck between national need, geography, environment, population, technology, and the nature of a state economy. Conditions were right for the creation of a Maine fishing industry. The alteration or loss of even one contributing factor, however, could upset the balance. After 1865, although the state's pace and character provided an illusion of permanence and continuity, Maine experienced not one but several disruptive changes.

The Role of Positive Government

On the whole, the historical view we have taken of these fisheries proves they are so poor in themselves as to come to nothing with distant nations who do not support them from their Treasury.—Thomas Jefferson, *Report on the Cod and Whale Fisheries*, 1791[1]

The Bounty: Economic Effects

One factor not previously discussed in relation to the rise of Maine's sea fisheries is the federal fishing-bounty law, a unique experiment in government subsidization that provided annual monetary payments to the codfishing industry for much of the nineteenth century. In a sense, the bounty law stands by itself and requires special treatment. Until the end of the Civil War, it was a constant presence in the consciousness of Maine fishermen, something that influenced their lives and colored their point of view. Yet its role has been misunderstood. That it shaped the character of Maine's antebellum fisheries is unquestionable; that it was the stimulus leading to their creation and development is highly debatable.

Some local historians have credited the bounty with being a primary force initiating the growth of the fishing industry in their regions of the state. Briefs to this effect have been filed on behalf of both Swan's Island and Boothbay.[2] Even so credible an authority as fisheries historian Raymond McFarland suggested that the development of the eastern Maine fisheries was spurred on by the bounty system established in the 1790s. McFarland did add a proviso, however, admitting that the fisheries would have achieved prosperity after 1845 anyway, regardless of the bounty.[3] In so doing he touched on the crux of the matter.

The element of time is the key to understanding the role of federal subsidies in the fishing industry. The first such subsidy, a per-quintal and per-barrel export bounty on dried and pickled fish sold abroad, was enacted in 1789 by the First Congress in lieu of a "drawback" or remittance of the onerous import duty on fishing salt. The pickled-fish export drawback remained on the books until 1846. In 1792, however, the dried-fish provision of the original act was replaced by the first truly comprehensive fishing-bounty

law, an annual allowance based on vessel tonnage, to be paid to all cod fishermen actively engaged for at least four months of the year. Under the system,
vessel owners received three-eighths of the allowance, and crew members
divided the rest according to their share of the fish caught. No stipulation as
to the disposition of the catch, whether sold at home or abroad, was attached to the law. It was a grant to fishermen for fishing, plain and simple.
This basic legislation provided the framework for governmental aid to the
fisheries for the next three-quarters of a century, subject only to minor periodic modifications. It was repealed in 1807 but, after a brief hiatus, was re-
enacted in 1813 and continued in force without interruption until 1866. The
last amendments to the act were made in 1819 and consisted chiefly of ad-
justments to the tonnage and rate structure.[4]

Initially, considered within the Maine context, the federal bounty law
was irrelevant, although it had a strong impact in later years. It was a product of the pre-statehood era and was in existence for a generation before
either Maine or its fisheries experienced any substantial growth. In its final
form, the bounty was already two decades old when the Maine sea fisheries
entered their major growth period (circa 1840) and rose to national prominence. Portland and Boothbay reflected the industry's comparatively late
start in Maine. Only one of the twenty fishing firms doing business at those
two ports during the mid-1870s had been in existence before 1830. Most of
them (two-thirds) were founded between 1830 and 1860, a majority in the
twenty-year period 1837–1857.[5]

Before 1820 the Maine fisheries were negligible, and what activity there
was appears to have received remarkably little impetus from the presence of
a government subsidy. Between 1796 and 1806, the ten years immediately
preceding the repeal of the first bounty law, Maine's cod-fishing tonnage
grew from 6,100 to 9,804 tons, hardly a dramatic increase. Within that ten-
year period, tonnage in the vessel class (twenty tons and over) actually fell
off for a time, from a high of 4,881 in 1798 to a low of 2,807 in 1803. With
repeal in 1807 there was a decline, but only in the larger vessels. In the
boat category (under twenty tons), the smallest class to receive bounty
money and presumably the most needy, its absence had no discernible
effect. Tonnage figures for boats under twenty tons remained generally
constant from 1805–1814 and actually showed a slight increase in 1808,
the first year in which no bounty was paid.[6] Moreover, the loss in large-
vessel tonnage was at least partly attributable to Jefferson's trade embargo,
which went into effect almost simultaneously with the bounty repeal and
shut off all export commerce, including the European and West Indian fish
trades.

Soon after the embargo ended, the United States was drawn into war with Great Britain. The War of 1812, with its privateering, naval blockades, and embargo resumption, further shackled the fisheries. The enactment of a new bounty law in 1813 had no immediate impact; Maine's cod-fishing tonnage was no greater in 1814 than the year before. There was a definite revival beginning in 1815, but that coincided with the end of the war, and the coming of peace had as much to do with the new fishing boom as did the bounty. Even at that, Maine's fishing tonnage as of December 31, 1817, after three years of peace and four years of bounty payments, was smaller than it had been ten years earlier.[7]

Of all the congressional actions taken in the area of fishing subsidies, the most important to Maine fishermen was undoubtedly the 1819 legislation amending the 1813 bounty law. Until 1819 the law's rate structure, while providing some aid to all cod fishermen, definitely favored the owners of large schooners. From 1797 to 1818 payment was made on the following basis: $1.60 per ton for vessels under twenty tons; $2.40 per ton for vessels twenty to thirty tons; and $4.00 per ton for vessels in excess of thirty tons (with a maximum payment of $272.00).[8] The amended version, which remained the rule for the next half-century, eliminated one of the three categories and lumped all vessels up to thirty tons together in one class. Furthermore, it increased the payment for that class to $3.50 per ton, while vessels over thirty tons remained at the $4.00-per-ton level. There was a sweetener for the owners of large schooners in that the maximum payment for the over-thirty-ton class was raised from $272.00 to $360.00—a bonus to vessels upwards of sixty-eight tons, which had formerly been limited to the sixty-eight-ton rate.[9] What the amended law essentially did, however, was provide additional encouragement to the owners of small craft.

Under the old system, a fifteen-ton cod-fishing boat received an annual bounty of $24.00. After 1819, the same boat received $52.50 for the season. Similarly, a small schooner of thirty tons got $72.00 under the old law and $105.00 under the new, amended version. Large schooners also gained under the 1819 act, but not by nearly as much, proportionately. A ninety-tonner, for example, earned $272.00 for a year's fishing prior to 1819 and $360.00 after that date, a 32 percent increase. By comparison, payments to the hypothetical fifteen- and thirty-ton vessels were increased by 119 and 46 percent, respectively.

Contemporary claims were made that one of the original purposes of the bounty law was to encourage the building of large banks vessels of the over-thirty-ton class.[10] The character of the rate structure up to 1819 makes it clear that such was indeed the case with the 1792 and 1813 acts. A man who could afford to build a large schooner of, say, thirty to seventy tons to go fishing received a reward from the government several times that of a poorer man who was limited to a small schooner or sloop. In effect, the original bounty was class legislation, favoring the most affluent among the fish merchants and shipowners—the "codfish aristocracy," as one critic labelled them.[11] Such individuals did not generally reside in Maine. Federalist Massachusetts was the beneficiary of the original tonnage bounties. From the enactment of the first bounty law until its democratization in 1819, Massachusetts proper claimed roughly 80 percent of all United States cod-fishing vessels over twenty tons. The District of Maine, then part of the Bay State, was a very poor second with about 10 percent. Upon the passage of the 1819 law, however, Maine's share immediately doubled to 20 percent of the national total.[12]

The inherent inequities in the bounty law were not totally erased in 1819; in fact, they were never completely eliminated. Still, they were modified by the essentially democratic thrust of the amendments, and the small operator, who was so characteristic of the industry down east, was given a new lease on life. For Maine, the key feature of the 1819 provisions was the added incentive given to owners of schooners in the twenty-to-thirty-ton class. These vessels were crucial to the development of the state's fisheries. They were small and inexpensive (about forty feet registered length) and carried only four or five crewmen. Nevertheless, they were large enough to visit some of the inner banks and engage in limited deep-sea fishing, an activity closed to smaller boats. Moreover, they provided a starting point for fledgling skippers seeking experience and were a convenient avenue for entrepreneurs lacking capital.

Numerically, these craft were the most important in the Maine sea fisheries, at least in the early period. In 1829, ten years after the amending of the bounty law, three-quarters of the vessels collecting government allowances in the district of Penobscot were under thirty tons, and exactly half were in the small-vessel (twenty-to-thirty-ton) category. The latter outnumbered large vessels of the over-thirty-ton variety by a two-to-one margin. By 1839 the movement toward larger fishing vessels was well under way, but half of Penobscot District's cod-fishing fleet remained under thirty tons, and twenty-to-thirty-ton schooners still constituted nearly a third of the total.[13] This contrasted sharply with the Massachusetts fishing districts. In 1829 a solid majority of Marblehead's cod-fishing tonnage was in Grand Bankers averaging sixty tons each.[14] Ten years later, only 3 of that district's 98 vessels were smaller than fifty tons, compared to 157 out of 200 in the district of Penobscot.[15] The lopsided emphasis on large schooners was nothing new in Massachusetts. It was a heritage of the first bounty law with its biased system of incentives. As early as 1807, Plymouth Bay had boasted a cod-fishing fleet of 62 vessels, the largest a 136-tonner and none of them under thirty-eight tons.[16]

Maine, however, did not have a codfish aristocracy, but rather a codfish democracy. The importance of the federal bounty after 1819 was that it nurtured the state's unique form of industry organization, allowing a system of small, democratic capitalism to survive and, for a time, even to flourish. Growth would take care of itself; Maine's fishing tonnage would expand because economic and environmental imperatives so dictated. The essential question in the antebellum era was not whether Maine would have a fishing industry of size and importance, but precisely what form it would take.

The existence of the bounty on cod fishing not only reinforced the natural tendency of poorer Maine fishermen to follow that fishery (thus contributing to Maine's development as a cod-fishing state), it also kept many of them in business as independent operators. This was its primary function at Portland in 1841, according to the port collector, who claimed that the city's cod fishermen relied heavily on the bounty to maintain their vessels and keep them operational.[17] On Swan's Island, the bounty was crucial in removing the necessity of local fishermen going into debt in advance for the expenses of outfitting their craft.[18] At Kittery the situation was similar, and fishermen there painted an ominous picture in an 1839 petition to Congress supporting the continuance of tonnage allowances. The petition, signed by eighty-eight owners and crewmen, warned that "the bounty now paid is the sole means which many have to procure their outfits for the voyage; and . . . , if it be taken away, all such persons will have to abandon the business, which will thereby fall into fewer hands, and will, in fact, be monopolized by capitalists." The ultimate result, the petitioners went on, would be a significant reduction in the number of fish taken and a corresponding increase in the price.[19] Senator John W. Davis of Massachusetts, a sympathetic spokesman for the bounty, concurred in that assessment. "Many now fit out vessels, who, when this encouragement is withdrawn, must withdraw also," he informed the Senate, "and these are persons either without capital or possessing limited means."[20] Elijah Kellogg, a Maine observer familiar with the fisheries of the Casco Bay region, summed up the meaning of the federal subsidy to fishermen in that part of the state: "It swelled their gains when the voyage was prosperous, and in the event of poor luck in fishing, the bounty saved them from loss, and it kept the vessels in repair."[21]

This last point, the indispensability of the bounty for vessel upkeep—for plant renewal, so to speak—was a common refrain of those who favored the law. The schooner was the essential component in the fish business: the better the vessel, the greater the potential profit. To countless Maine fisher-men, of course, the reality was not a better vessel, but any vessel at all. The government subsidy helped the large fish merchant to renew his fleet and bring new, efficient craft into play, an important contribution in its own right. In Massachusetts, it was not unusual for the annual allowance to serve as partial down payment on a new schooner or as the interest payment on a bank loan taken out for the same purpose.[22] Down east, a more crucial usage was in keeping old vessels afloat, "vessels which ought to have been dead," in the words of one old-time fisherman.[23] Aged and decrepit schooners otherwise destined for abandonment could, with a wise and judicious appli-cation of bounty money, be kept going for a few more years. In the process, marginal operators continued to function as independent entrepreneurs.

A variation on the theme was the phenomenon known as "bounty catch-ing," which was commonly practiced around Deer Isle. Ezra Turner, an Isle au Haut fisherman, described the procedure as he remembered it: "When the bounty was on, anybody who had an old vessel would let a man take her for nothing. If you had an old vessel you would say to me, 'I will give you her to use this season if you will give me the bounty.' The earning of the bounty would be no expense to you, and if I could make the vessel earn anything I would get it. That is the way bounty catching was carried on where I live."[24] Bounty catching—using the federal subsidy, in other words, as payment for a charter or lease—was also common at Portland in the 1840s.[25] This unintended benefit of the law had the salutary effect of per-mitting those not wealthy enough to own a vessel to function temporarily as entrepreneurs, accumulate capital, and eventually rise to a position of eco-nomic independence.

It was not only the owners or potential owners of fishing vessels who benefitted under the revised bounty law of 1819, but the men who worked aboard them as well. One political criticism of the bounty was that it was monopolized by the owners at the expense of ordinary fishermen.[26] The criticism was unjust. Of the $28,230 paid out by the collector of customs for the district of Penobscot during the first three months of 1840, $17,644 went by law to crew members and only $10,586 to vessel owners.[27]

Such annual infusions of money contributed in no small way to the sup-port of working fishermen and their families. In 1853 the highliner* aboard the Castine Grand Banker *Martha Burgess* made a grand total of $129.32

---

*The highliner on a fishing schooner was the crew member landing the greatest number of fish on a voyage and therefore making the most money under the traditional share system (see chapter 7). The term was also sometimes applied to the most successful vessel in a fishing fleet in terms of total seasonal catch.

for five months' work, of which $34.48 consisted of his bounty allotment. Among the individual owners of the same vessel, none realized more than $33.75 in bounty money. Of course, the other crewmen received less (the low sharesman made $64.16, including a bounty of $17.11), and the owners profited by a much larger share of the catch, but the fact remains that a substantial amount of the government subsidy found its way to those who needed it most. Not counting the captain, who was a part-owner, the sharesmen of the *Martha Burgess* depended on the government for no less than 27 percent of their seasonal income in 1853—33 percent after deducting outfitting debts. The owners, on the other hand, received an allotment that constituted 11 percent of their share of the proceeds from the voyage. Overall, the $360.00 paid out to the *Martha Burgess* that year made up 15 percent of the vessel's net stock, or profit after deduction of fishing expenses.[28] The crewmen of the *Martha Burgess* were not exceptional in their dependence upon government subsidies. A congressional investigator estimated in 1852 that 19 percent of the average seasonal income of all New England cod fishermen derived from bounty money.[29]

One of the vagaries of the 1819 bounty legislation was that while it encouraged small operators to own and outfit moderate-sized fishing schooners, it also encouraged potential crewmen to seek employment on larger vessels. In that sense, it was a mixed blessing. An examination of the disposition of the bounty funds distributed to Penobscot District fishermen for the 1839 season illustrates the point. The average payment to all 977 district cod fishermen that year was $18.06. However, those who worked in vessels of twenty tons or more averaged $19.26, compared to $9.34 for those employed in small boats under twenty tons. Moreover, there was a sliding scale of graduated compensation within those two categories that resulted in a direct correlation between vessel size and the bounty paid to individual crew members. The following are average payments for several typical crews, arranged in descending order by size of vessel: schooner *Charles Henry* (ninety-five tons, nine crewmen), $25.00; schooner *Pallas* (eighty-five tons, nine crewmen), $23.61; schooner *Economy* (sixty tons, seven crewmen), $21.43; schooner *Three Sisters* (fifty tons, six crewmen), $20.83; schooner *Fox* (forty tons, five crewmen), $20.00; schooner *Eight Brothers* (thirty tons, four crewmen), $16.25; schooner *Bonaparte* (twenty tons, four crewmen), $10.94; boat *Mary* (ten tons, three crewmen), $7.29.[30]

Generally speaking, fishermen who crewed aboard schooners larger than forty tons could count on $20 bounty money in addition to their share of the proceeds from the catch. Those who went in large bankers of seventy-five tons or more could expect up to $25. Crewmen in the small-vessel class (twenty to thirty tons), however, rarely averaged in excess of $15. The bounty, then, quietly encouraged the slow, inexorable drift away from independent entrepreneurship and small-scale capitalism. At the same time, the seeming economic foolhardiness of working aboard small vessels had a certain reverse logic to it, given the right circumstances. The smaller the vessel, the more likely she was to be owned by her skipper and some of her crew. This was particularly true in the case of family enterprises. In such instances, the owner's share of the bounty (three-eighths) reverted to the crew and allowed them to approximate the bounty receipts of fishermen serving aboard hundred-ton bankers owned by the merchant class.

The schooner *Grampus,* another Penobscot District vessel, fell into this category. The *Grampus* was a twenty-five tonner with crew of four, whose skipper was also managing owner. This vessel fished for cod for five months in 1839 and qualified for $87.50 in bounty, $54.69 of which belonged to the crew and $32.81 to the owners.[31] Assuming that the captain was a one-quarter shareholder and that his portion of the catch equalled those of the other three crew members, his total bounty payment came to slightly under $22.00, or about as much as a typical crewman on a large banks schooner. In the event that he owned a greater share, his percentage of the bounty increased accordingly. If one further assumes that some of his fellow crewmen were also part owners—a common occurrence in small vessels—it becomes clear that those who worked on small schooners could profit under the bounty system, provided they purchased shares in their vessels.

As suggested earlier, the bounty law of 1819 did not usher in an economic boom period. Its enactment was not the beginning of the "golden age" of the Maine fisheries, a claim made by at least one historian.[32] The golden age, such as it was, came after 1840. There is no doubt, however, that the bounty helped, and no question that countless fishermen came to depend upon it and to view it as a kind of birthright.

A sense of the importance of the fishing bounty can be gained by a brief look at the expenditure it represented over the years. From the passage of the first bounty law in 1792 until 1857, a little over $12 million was paid out by the federal treasury, most of it (about $11 million) to the fishermen of Maine and Massachusetts.[33] In the decade of the 1850s alone, $3.5 million was doled out, the peak being reached in 1857, when owners and crewmen shared $464,178 in governmental subsidies.[34]

Maine's portion of the bounty was substantial. Before 1820 almost all of the money went to Massachusetts fishermen, but that changed as the century progressed. In 1858, the Camden Custom House in the district of Belfast dispensed almost as much money as had all the custom houses in the state of Maine combined forty years earlier.[35] Over the period 1820–1857, Maine collected nearly $4 million, or close to 40 percent of all the bounty money paid out in the United States.[36] The bulk of it went down east to the great cod-fishing region of Penobscot Bay and beyond. The districts bordering Hancock County received 21 percent of the entire federal outlay in the 1840s. Penobscot District by itself was the recipient of $309,452, or 15 percent of the national total, during that decade.[37] And the town of Deer Isle, to cite one last statistic, was getting one-twelfth of all the bounty funds paid out annually by the federal government in the years just preceding the Civil War.[38]

A law expending so much public money was bound to become a political issue. From its inception to its final repeal, the fishing bounty was embroiled in controversy. The details of that controversy, which was so important to the fishermen of Maine, must next be considered.

The Bounty: Voting Patterns

The stormy career of the fishing-bounty law can best be traced through the activities of the United States Congress, where its fate was considered time and again over the years. There were three distinct periods in the political life of the bounty. The first, which might be called the era of establishment and solidification, ran from 1792 to 1819. During these years, the first battles were fought and won, the principle of the law was established, and the subsidy was built into the federal system. The second period, lasting from 1819 to 1839, was an era of quiet acceptance in which no serious political challenge to the bounty was initiated or apparently even contemplated. The third phase, beginning in 1839 and continuing until the law was permanently erased from the books, was one of retreat and rear-guard action. Throughout the 1840s, 1850s, and 1860s, supporters of federal aid to the fisheries were on the defensive, constantly fending off attacks of increasing intensity and bitterness.

Between the introduction of the first bounty bill and the final repeal of the law three-quarters of a century later, the question of allowances for fishermen came up in Congress seventeen different times—an average of about once every four and one-half years. To summarize briefly, congressional action began in 1792 with the passage of the first bounty. In 1797 Congress renewed the law and increased the subsidy. In 1806 the first repeal attempt was made, and it was carried through to success the following year. The second bounty law, essentially a copy of the 1797 version, was enacted in 1813 as a temporary measure; in 1816 it was re-enacted and made permanent. The following year, minor amendments were added, and in 1819 further amendments and a rate increase were passed. The next round of activity began in 1839 with a serious repeal effort, which made its way through the Senate and then stalled. Further efforts to repeal the law were made in 1840, 1846, and 1857; none of these got to the voting stage. In 1858 another repeal bill was introduced. It received Senate approval, but failed to reach the House of Representatives. Unsuccessful attempts were made again in 1859 and 1860. The Civil War then intervened, and the death blow was postponed until 1866, when the bounty law was finally voted out of existence.[39]

The fact that the bounty came up for a vote several times during its career, either in the enactment stage or in the repeal process, allows certain judgements to be made about the sources of its support and opposition. The first of these is that the measure was not a partisan issue in the traditional sense of the word. That is to say, the two dominant party and ideological strains present in the American political system up to 1866 showed no consistency either in favoring or rejecting the concept of a fishing bounty. Neither the Democratic party of Thomas Jefferson and Andrew Jackson, nor its Federalist-Whig-Republican opposition, were firm in their positions from one decade to the next.

It is true that the bounty began as a Federalist measure. Both houses of Congress were controlled by that party in 1792 and 1797, when the law was initially enacted and then upgraded. It is equally true that the Congress which repealed the fisheries subsidy in 1806–1807 was overwhelmingly Democratic-Republican. However, the same Jeffersonians who killed the bounty in 1807 revived it in 1813 and extended it in 1816. Furthermore, the Congress that increased and democratized the allowance system in 1819 was Democratic-Republican by a three-to-one margin in both houses. In 1839 and 1858, the two antebellum years in which the bounty came closest to extinction, Democrats controlled Congress and had three-to-two majorities in the upper chamber. Yet, when the law was finally repealed in 1866, it was repealed with Republican votes. As in 1819, there was no recorded division on the bounty question in 1866, but Republicans outnumbered Democrats by 149 to 42 in the House and by 42 to 10 in the Senate.[40]

The bounty votes in Congress are muddled somewhat by the fact that, beginning in 1797, the fishing allowance was tied to tariff legislation adjusting duties on imported salt. The law increasing tonnage rates in 1797 was entitled, "An Act laying an additional duty on salt imported into the United States, and for other purposes." The bounty increase was included in the "other purposes."[41] The theory, of course, was that if fishermen had to pay more for the salt used in preserving their catch, they deserved some kind of added compensation or rebate. Unhappily, the temporary expedient of making the bounty a rider on a revenue bill had the effect of confusing its status and complicating the meaning of votes cast on the subject for the next half-century. In 1839, for example, proposed repeal of the bounty was part of a bill to abolish the salt duty.[42] Congressmen voting on such measures were presenting their positions not only on fishing subsidies but also on tariff policy, and the emphasis naturally varied. Only in 1857, when Senator Clement C. Clay, Jr., of Alabama introduced a bill "repealing all laws, or parts of laws, allowing bounties to vessels employed in the bank and other cod-fisheries," was the bounty issue finally separated from the issue of salt duties.[43] During the interval—in 1806, 1807, 1813, 1816, and 1839—congressional votes on the bounty partly reflected tariff concerns. The 1813 vote, in addition, was influenced by the war policies of the Madison administration, which the Federalists, as a party, opposed. The major opposition speech that year was made by a Federalist representative, who viewed the bounty-and-salt-tariff bill as a tax measure to carry on an unjust war.[44] Despite these facts, the voting patterns are worth analyzing, if for no other reason than that the interests of the fisheries were at issue.

One might logically assume that, in the beginning at least, the commercially oriented Federalist party of Alexander Hamilton, rather than the more agrarian Democratic party of Jefferson, was the chief repository of pro-fisheries sentiment. This was initially the case, although not nearly to the extent that might be expected. On the vote for final passage of the first fishing-bounty law in 1792, Federalists in the House of Representatives voted 22 to 10 in favor of the measure, Democrats opposed it by an 8-to-7 margin, and those with unknown party affiliations supported it by a 9-to-3 count. The final tabulation was 38 to 21 for passage. The interesting feature of the vote is not that Federalists favored it and Democrats opposed it but that there was considerable sentiment on both sides of the issue in both parties. Almost half of the Democrats, including such luminaries as James Madison and Elbridge Gerry, voted favorably.[45] Similarly, when the bounty bill was passed to a final reading in the Senate, the vote again crossed party lines. Federalists voted for the measure by 11 to 2, but Democrats also favored it by a 7-to-2 margin. Five other senators with no identifiable party affiliation likewise voted for the bill. Prominent among the favorable votes was that of the Virginia Democrat and future president, James Monroe.[46]

To find the true significance of the 1792 vote, it is necessary to go beyond party labels. The first bounty law was not so much the product of a party struggle as it was the product of a regional conflict. The northeastern states favored it, and the southern states, generally speaking, were opposed. The breakdown in the House is indicative. Representatives from states north of the Mason-Dixon Line supported the bounty by a 30-to-1 count. The New England vote, which included the region's three Democrats, was 16 to 0. Southern representatives, on the other hand, opposed the measure by 20 to 8, better than a two-thirds majority.[47]

The 1792 vote—which, incidentally, was purely on the merits of a fishing subsidy, with no direct reference to a salt tax—set the pattern for all future confrontations involving the fishing bounty. By 1816, when the 1813 law came up for renewal, the party vote had reversed, but the regional trend remained relatively constant. The tabulation among members of the House of Representatives whose party affiliations are known showed Democrats favoring the bounty by 51 to 20 and Federalists opposing it 24 to 23. On a regional basis, the Northeast (New England and the Middle Atlantic states) cast a solidly affirmative 48-to-29 vote for final passage, while the South split evenly, with 23 members favoring the bill and 22 opposing it. The "New West" (Ohio, Kentucky, Tennessee, Louisiana), for reasons probably related to the tariff provisions, voted 18 to 0 for renewal.[48]

The emergence of a new interior region had important ramifications for the fishing bounty. On this, as on many other issues dividing the North and South, the rising West, with its own unique point of view, became the balance wheel. How that point of view evolved with regard to fisheries legislation is illustrated by two climactic votes in the United States Senate on proposals to repeal the bounty.

The first was in 1839. By that date, the movement of the frontier and the spread of slavery and southern "civilization" had brought Kentucky, Tennessee, Louisiana, and Arkansas within the sphere of what can broadly be called the South, while new states like Michigan, Illinois, and Missouri had been added to the western section. The party vote on final passage of the 1839 repeal bill was 19 to 9 in favor among Democrats and 10 to 1 in opposition among the Whigs, but a regional breakdown reveals flaws in what at first glance appears to be a straight party vote. A majority of the Democrats from the northeastern states, including Maine's two senators, voted to sustain the bounty. In fact, 6 of the 12 pro-bounty votes cast by northeastern senators were cast by Democrats. On a broad sectional basis, the vote showed the Northeast opposing repeal by 11 to 5, and the South and West favoring it by 8 to 7 and 7 to 0, respectively. Minus the border state of Kentucky, the South's vote was 8 to 5 for repeal, a clearer manifestation of that section's long-standing antagonism toward fishing subsidies.[49] The real significance of the vote, however, was that while the northeastern and southern parts of the country retained their traditional positions on the bounty, the West had moved from a favorable posture to one of opposition.

The North-South split appeared again in the Senate repeal bill of 1858. By party, Democrats voted 30 to 5 for final passage, and Republicans voted 17 to 0 to oppose the bill and maintain the bounty. The vote was a straight party-line affair and suggests an ideological split, except for the fact that by this date the two major parties had become hopelessly sectionalized. It was a case of the Republican North versus the Democratic South, with western members again wielding the balance of power. A sectional division indicates that senators from the Northeast voted 14 to 5 in favor of the bounty, while the South voted 18 to 2 for its abolition. Western senators, who split 8 to 8, indirectly gave the South its temporary victory: the measure passed 30 to 24. As they had in 1839, the states of the Deep South provided the bulk of the anti-bounty vote—they were unanimous for its repeal. The New England states, also voting in a bloc, were unanimous for its retention.[50]

What the scattered handful of recorded congressional votes on the bounty question really point out is that the fishing subsidy was increasingly dependent for its existence on support from outside the region it benefitted. As the nation grew, New England, in particular, became more and more a maritime region in a non-maritime country. The development of the great continental interior increasingly isolated the fishing states of Maine and Massachusetts. In 1792, the year of the original bounty law, the New England states claimed 31 percent of the membership of the United States Senate and 25 percent of the membership of the House of Representatives. By 1858, the year of the great repeal effort, those figures were down to 19 percent and 12 percent, respectively. The combined representation of Maine and Massachusetts in Congress fell from 13 percent to 7 percent of the total over the same period.[51]

The bounty was first enacted by northeastern votes, but it could not be kept on the books by northeastern votes alone. With the South unalterably opposed from the beginning, the new, developing western states became the key. In 1813 and 1816, the West was persuaded to hold firm for the bounty. After that time, the West was either uncommitted or negatively disposed. A growing southern-western alliance made the eventual repeal of the fishing bounty almost inevitable. It is ironic, then, that when repeal finally passed, in the Reconstruction year of 1866, the southern states—the center of anti-bounty feeling—were not even represented in Congress. The readmission of the southern states would have spelled the doom of the bounty system in any case, by the 1870s at the latest, but the fact that their votes were not needed suggests that other forces were at work. Regionalism was a major factor working against a federal subsidy for fishermen, but it was not the only one, and in the end, it was not even the critical one.

The Bounty: The Regional Debate

Although numerous arguments, some of them quite esoteric, were made for and against the fishing bounty over the years, the vast majority fall readily into a few categories. As the voting pattern in Congress suggests, proponents and opponents were motivated to a great degree by regional or sectional concerns. In the case of the opposition, this regionalism was translated into an ideological posture of sorts. It emerged as one of the two primary themes (along with accusations of illegality, fraud, and abuse in the operation of the allowance system) articulated by congressmen who found the law distasteful.

Regionalism emerged early in the debate over the fishing bounty. It was exemplified by the alignment of spokesmen addressing the first bounty bill in 1792. Prominent among members favoring the legislation in the House of Representatives were Benjamin Goodhue, Elbridge Gerry, and Shearjashub Bourne of Massachusetts, Samuel Livermore of New Hampshire, and, to a lesser extent, Madison of Virginia. Four of the five were New Englanders. Speaking in opposition were four Southerners, William Giles and John Page of Virginia, William Vans Murray of Maryland, and Hugh Williamson of North Carolina.[52] The pattern continued into the nineteenth century. In 1813 and 1816, three Massachusetts congressmen, William Reed, John Reed, and Timothy Pickering, carried the fight for the second bounty law. Their opponents were, with few exceptions, from the South, the most energetic representing the states of Maryland, Virginia, and North Carolina.[53] From 1839 to 1846, opposition to the bounty was monopolized by a Westerner, Senator Thomas Hart Benton of Missouri. A host unto himself, Benton singlehandedly battled pro-bounty senators from Massachusetts and Maine through three sessions of Congress.[54] During the 1850s Benton's standard was taken up by Senator Clement C. Clay, Jr., of Alabama. In the mammoth Senate debate of 1858, Clay, assisted by Senators Robert Toombs of Georgia, George Pugh of Ohio, and Trusten Polk of Missouri, waged a lengthy rhetorical struggle with northeastern bounty supporters, whose leading spokesmen were Hannibal Hamlin and William Pitt Fessenden of Maine and William H. Seward of New York.[55]

The Northeasterners who favored the bounty, especially those from New England, seldom raised the dangerous issue of section, except upon provocation. They were, after all, the sole recipients of the government's largesse in this instance. Their regionalism was understated, and their case was made with other arguments. To Southerners and Westerners, however, section was everything. They saw the bounty as a form of geographic favoritism. It was special legislation benefitting the maritime Northeast at the expense of the non-maritime interior sections.

Representative Giles of Virginia, the first member of Congress to address the issue, bluntly stated the premise of the sectional case in February of 1792. Said Giles, "Any man who takes a view of this country, must be convinced, that its real support rises from the land, and not from the sea."[56] His southern colleague, Williamson of North Carolina, carried the argument to the next logical step. The bounty, Williamson maintained, was a tax upon the agricultural South. "The certain operation of that measure," he said, "is the oppression of the Southern States by superior numbers in the Northern interest." Setting the agrarian South against the maritime Northeast, he told the House, "We shall not hear of a bounty for raising rice or preparing naval stores."[57] Another southern representative, Page of Virginia, went so far as to suggest the alternative of bounties for hunters in the western hinterland to promote the fur trade and serve as a barrier against the Indians. Fishermen, he added, would be more beneficial to the nation as farmers than as seamen.[58]

The sectional consciousness of the South and West was, if anything, accentuated in later years, when the bounty became closely intertwined with the tariff on imported salt. The tariff was uppermost in the mind of Benton of Missouri, as he began his crusade against the bounty law in the late 1830s. The salt levy and its allied bounty system, he told Congress, constituted "a tax on the people of the South and West, because it puts money in the pockets of the people of the Northeast."[59] In 1840 Benton, still adamant, called for the suppression of the salt tax "and the abolition of the fishing bounties and allowances founded upon that tax." Angry over the high price of salt in Missouri and neighboring states, he maintained that the tariff and bounty system were costing the rural, agricultural economy of the West millions of dollars annually.[60] Years later, long after the defeat of his numerous anti-bounty and anti-salt-tariff bills, Benton remained somewhat bitter and irrevocably sectional in his views on the subject. Writing in 1856, he noted, "In viewing the struggles about those bounties and allowances, I have often had occasion to admire the difference between the legislators of the North and those of the South and West—the former always intent upon the benefits of legislation—the latter upon the honors of the government."[61]

A year after those words were written, the South and the West tried again to restore "honor" to government. In January 1857, Senator Clay of Alabama introduced a bounty-repeal bill with the declaration, "Twenty-five States of this Union are made to pay tribute to the codfish aristocracy of but six states."[62] Clay's challenge brought on the harshest and most strident attacks ever aimed at the fishing bounty, but the culmination of the ensuing debate saw the sectional argument reach a new level of sophistication as well as vitriol. No longer was the question simply one of the equity of a tax on southern and western farmers to support northeastern fishermen, although Senator Pugh of Ohio did raise that venerable point on behalf of his agrarian constituency.[63] By the late 1850s the trans-Appalachian West had ceased being a simple frontier region peopled by the backwoods tillers of the soil whom Thomas Hart Benton had championed twenty years earlier. It was now a reasonably well developed area, with vested economic interests that transcended mere idyllic husbandry. If the South was the land of cotton, the West was the home of America's fledgling meat industry, which saw itself as a competitor with the fishing industry of the Northeast for the palate of the American consumer. Senator Polk of Missouri stated the case of the meat interests clearly during the 1858 debate: "I think myself the beef and pork in the western country are just as much entitled to drawback as pickled fish or cod fish, and I am not willing that either pickled fish or cod fish shall be left in a better position than beef."[64] In the House, an Ohio representative sarcastically called for a meat bounty on the sugar-cured hams of the West.[65] But it remained for the sponsor of repeal, a Southerner, to drive home the reality of a southern-western regional alliance against the fisheries based on economic interest. "Is it just," asked Clay of Alabama, "to require of the beef and pork packers of the West, and of the farmers of the entire Union, the payment of a duty on the salt which they consume, and to relieve the fishermen of the same burden in support of the Government?"[66] The answer of senators from the South and West was an emphatic "No!"

Political leaders from the Northeast, generally, and from New England, in particular, were quite conscious of their regional interests. At the same time, they were also conscious of their growing vulnerability in any sectional conflict and, as a rule, preferred to avoid sectional antagonisms. Periodically, however, they were caught up in the emotionalism of the fisheries issue. At such moments, it was the political representatives of Massachusetts who responded most vehemently to the gibes of the Southerners and Westerners. Elbridge Gerry, answering sectional attacks on the original bounty bill, inquired of the House of Representatives in 1792, "I wish to know on what principle gentlemen can expect, that the citizens of Massachusetts should contribute two hundred thousand dollars, or perhaps a greater sum, for the protection of the Western frontier against the Indians, when no contribution is made to support the commerce of Massachusetts."[67] In 1846,

Senator John Davis offered the following answer to Missouri's Senator Benton and other bounty opponents:

> I have often been moved by the eloquent descriptions of the hardships and sufferings of the pioneers of the West, which have fallen from the lips of gentlemen in this chamber; and I can assure Senators that, however great and affecting they may be, they fall far short of the courage, toil, suffering, and peril incident to these pioneers of the great ocean frontier; and I am sure that if Senators would witness the trials and hardships of a single voyage to and from the Grand Banks, I should be certain of their sympathies for the fishermen.[68]

A few years later, in 1852, Representative Zeno Scudder of Cape Cod made a more direct Bay State response to the sectionalism of the interior, accusing western agriculturalists of lacking a proper appreciation for New England's fishing industry and failing to take "a broad national view" of the subsidy question. Scudder, who, in a quixotic gesture, had introduced a bill extending the cod-fishing bounty to the mackerel fishery, suggested that western farmers needed the fishermen of the Northeast. Who else, he asked, would purchase the produce of the West? Fishing bounty money eventually found its way into the pockets of western agrarians by way of sectional trade. Without it, the eastern market for western food would dry up, and impoverished fishermen would be obliged to abandon the "sterile coasts" and move to the "rich West" themselves.[69] In a similar vein, Representative Timothy Davis of Gloucester asserted during the 1857 bounty debate that the agricultural interests of the country, unlike the fishing interests, did not need government aid. Agriculture was predictable, and western farmers required only up-to-date technical information and perhaps protection from marauding Indians. The eastern fisherman, however, uncertain of his catch, needed a bounty to survive.[70]

Aside from these and a handful of other outbursts, New England congressmen were remarkably silent in the face of continued regional attacks. This was especially true of Maine's senators and representatives, who almost never joined in the sectional fray. There is a probable reason for their behavior. Unlike Massachusetts, which was predominantly Federalist-Whig in its political orientation, Maine had Democratic leanings. It would hardly do for Maine Democrats to meet head-on the sectional offensives of southern and western members, who also tended to be Democrats. Thomas Hart Benton, for instance, the leading western antagonist of the bounty system, was virtually a Democratic institution. Instead of a direct approach, a more deflective and circuitous strategy seemed in order.

If Maine politicians were loath to raise sectional hackles, the Maine press was not. The *Eastern Argus* of Portland, a Democratic paper, laid the issue bare in an 1840 editorial: "The scheme of abolishing the Salt Tax and Fishing Bounties is a *Western Scheme*—originated by *western* men and likely to receive its strongest support among the *western* people. It is not a *party* measure—because while we find Democrats from the East opposing it, we find, also, Federalists in the west opposing it."[71] Opposition papers in Maine likewise made much of the regional conflict, although they naturally sought to turn Democratic sponsorship of anti-bounty bills to partisan advantage. The *Bangor Daily Whig and Courier* lashed out at southern Democrats in 1858 for opposing the fishing bounty on sectional grounds while supporting sugar duties that operated as a bounty to Louisiana and Texas sugar planters. Said the *Whig and Courier:* "The Senate has repealed the bounties. Southern democracy demanded the sacrifice, and there was not virtue or patriotism enough in the party at the North to stand by and defend this great interest. . . . Black Republican States only are engaged in the cod fisheries—and Black Republicanism must be punished."[72] Ironically, it was under "Black Republicanism" that the bounty was finally killed eight years later.

The Bounty: The Spectre of Fraud

Despite the prominence of the sectional favoritism theme, the opponents of the bounty did make consistent use of one other argument. Beginning with the passage of the second bounty law, accusations of abuse and fraud were continually levelled at the subsidy system. The attacks began in 1816, when the law, enacted as a temporary wartime measure three years earlier, came up for extension. During that session of Congress charges were made by two southern Democrats, Representatives John Randolph of Virginia and Richard Stanford of North Carolina, that since the 1813 act had gone into effect fishermen had been smuggling their salt—to avoid tariff payments— and collecting the bounty as well. Since the bounty was viewed (by opponents, at least) as merely a drawback to equalize the salt levy, fishermen were thus having their cake and eating it, too.[73]

The smuggling charge did not stand up, based as it was on ignorance of the situation and a lack of hard evidence. The thought of fishing schooners heading out to the grounds without salt on the chance of encountering incoming salt ships at sea struck several of the New England members as faintly ridiculous. "No man," said Cyrus King of the District of Maine, "would go to sea on the bare hope of meeting a vessel from Turks Island casually sailing with a cargo of salt."[74] Reed of Massachusetts added that salt was so bulky and of comparatively so small a value that the prospect of its being smuggled was inconceivable. Practicality, alone, would rule it out. If a customs duty could not be collected on salt, he wondered, on what *could* it be collected?[75]

The spectre of fraud next appeared in 1840, when Senator Benton made brief, sinister references to abuse of the law. Benton's primary concern was that, because of loopholes or ambiguities in the statute, foreign (especially Canadian) crews were improperly serving aboard United States cod-fishing vessels in numbers beyond the limit intended under the bounty. This, he contended, constituted a deliberate abuse of the system.[76] Benton's anti-bounty case, however, rested mainly on the inequities of high protectionism and monopoly as they applied to the domestic salt industry, and he did not stress illegalities in his argument.

The fraud issue re-emerged and reached full flower in the 1850s. By then, the supposed manifestations of corruption had taken different forms. Smuggling was no longer a concern. Instead, charges revolved around the specific points of the bounty law itself, which fishermen were presumably not observing.

The revival of the abuse litany began in the Treasury Department, which, as administrator of the law, had long been concerned with such things. Since the inception of the bounty, changes in the statute had periodically been made. Initially such changes or clarifications were handled by special acts of Congress, as in 1817, when legislation was passed requiring that the officers and three-fourths of the crews of vessels receiving allowance money be American citizens.[77] By mid-century, however, detailed regulations were being instituted by Treasury Department circulars of instruction, which were sent to customs collectors in the various seaboard districts.* In 1842, for example, a circular instructed that prior to each voyage a vessel owner be required to obtain a certificate testifying to his craft's seaworthiness and describing her fishing gear, and that the certificate be presented when collecting the bounty. In 1848 another circular demanded that sworn logbooks be shown before allowances were granted.[78] Finally, on February 20, 1852, the secretary of the Treasury issued a celebrated circular of some length and detail, which superseded all previous circulars and attempted to pull together and clarify the various regulations.[79]

As circulars and specific regulations multiplied, confusion and resistance increased. To Treasury officials, this smacked of fraud, pure and simple. De-

---

*Abridged versions of these circulars were also offered directly to fishermen by private publishers, usually in the form of addenda to blank logbooks intended for use on shipboard. (Source: *ES*, advertisement, 24 May 1854.)

partment reports in 1853 charged that bounty vessels were fishing for mackerel and still collecting the cod allowance, that the share system was not operating as required, that owners were not dividing the bounty properly with crewmen, that bogus logbooks were being made up after voyages, and that bounty recipients were marketing fresh fish instead of dried cod as the law specified.[80] Agent J. Ross Browne reported to Secretary James Guthrie that in New England "the community, to whom such practices are familiar, consider it fair and proper to take advantage of the government, and dishonorable to become informers."[81]

Such reports provided congressional opponents of bounties with considerable ammunition. Alabama's Senator Clay, who carried the brunt of the anti-bounty fight in 1857–1858, relied heavily on Treasury Department evidence, real or imagined, of fraudulent violations.[82] Clay outlined the essence of the fraud argument in early 1857, accusing owners and captains of monopolizing the bounty and reiterating earlier charges that proper logbooks were not kept, vessels were not inspected prior to voyages, and fishermen illegally pursued other fisheries without satisfying the four-month exclusive cod-fishing clause. The bounty, said Clay, was operating "in violation of almost every provision of the laws by which it was created." Furthermore, he added, the scope of the abuses was necessitating additional Treasury Department expenditures simply to enforce the law's regulations. The allowance was, in effect, "a premium to frauds and perjuries." The question, said the Alabama senator, was not merely one of political economy but of political morality.[83] A year later, Clay and his supporters were using the same arguments, adding only the old accusation—first made by Thomas Hart Benton in 1840—that American cod-fishing vessels were illegally using Canadian crews and still collecting the bounty.[84]

The real extent of fraud and abuse under the bounty law is speculative. It can never be known to a certainty. However, the reluctance of bounty supporters in Congress to be drawn into a thoroughgoing defense of the moral purity of the average New England fisherman suggests that some illegalities were perpetrated. Only two congressmen, Representative Timothy Davis of Massachusetts and Senator Fessenden of Maine, directly rejected the charges of fraud during the heated debates of the late 1850s.[85] Another finessed the subject and at the same time amusingly pointed out the unrealistic nature of certain government regulations. Said Senator John Hale of New Hampshire: "In the neighborhood of the cod are always found the halibut. There are friendly relations between the cod and halibut; and they frequent the same grounds with the pollock and haddock. The halibut not understanding that it is illegal for them to take hold of the bait, very frequently get hold of what is legally intended for a cod, and the fishermen haul them in. What should they do? Throw them overboard?"[86]

Senator Hale notwithstanding, there were undoubtedly some abuses. Charles E. Ranlett, a former fisherman from the midcoast Maine village of St. George, remembered that in his day (circa 1830) fishermen occasionally failed to observe the requirement that bounty recipients stay on the grounds for at least four months. "Now, the skippers, sometimes, did not too nicely distinguish in their own consciences between the fishing grounds and the beaches of their own farms," recalled Ranlett, "and so it was that 'a fisherman's oath' was held in light repute."[87] Another retired fisherman, Sylvanus Smith of Gloucester, related a rather accusatory description of "bounty catching" as practiced in Maine: "In many harbors and coves 'down east,' craft, which had long before outlived their usefulness for deep sea fishing, were to be seen lying at anchor, but collecting bounty."[88]

The official correspondence of several Maine customs collectors between 1823 and 1845 indicates that failure to spend the requisite minimum time on the cod-fishing grounds was, indeed, the principal violation of bounty rules. Transgressions appear to have been widely scattered, however. Even so avid a bounty opponent as Senator Benton was able to document fewer than a dozen legitimate cases of impropriety over the two decades preceding his 1839 investigation, and several of those arose from honest misunderstandings of the law.[89] At least one contemporary observer, John Anderson, the port collector for the district of Portland-Falmouth in 1841, insisted that cod fishermen in his area looked down on so-called bounty catchers and other violators, and volunteered information leading to their apprehension.[90] Similarly, Lorenzo Sabine, who was familiar with the situation at Eastport and vicinity in the early 1850s, debunked the charges of corruption, maintaining that instances of outright bounty fraud were highly exaggerated.[91] A recent student of the operation of the bounty law at Newburyport, Massachusetts, basing his conclusions on an examination of correspondence between the resident port collector and the secretary of the Treasury over the period 1829–1832, has determined that some violations took place but that intentional fraud was seldom involved. Instead, the irregularities were the result of ignorance of the law and lack of attention to detail on the part of both semiliterate fishermen and the port collectors themselves.[92]

It should also be remembered that several Treasury secretaries, under whose tenures the department was critical of the bounty, were Southerners or Westerners, with either a sectional axe to grind or a basic misunderstanding of the fishing industry. For example, Robert Walker (1845–1849) was a Mississippian, Thomas Corwin (1850–1853) was from Ohio, James Guthrie (1853–1857) was a Kentuckian, and Howell Cobb (1857–1860) a Georgian.[93] Cobb was prominent among those demanding abolition of the fisheries subsidy in the late 1850s, and he actively campaigned against the law while in office.[94] It was Guthrie who sent out the infamous J. Ross Browne, author of a scathing report on the operation of the allowance system in New England. Browne's report, which emphasized fraud and resulted in a call from Secretary Guthrie for repeal of the bounty, was greeted with scorn down east. Brown, it seemed, was an erstwhile compiler of Italian travel sketches and totally unschooled in the fisheries. The *Republican Journal* of Belfast commented, "Any one familiar with the practical business of fishing can not but smile at the naive simplicity of the author of the report."[95]

Guthrie, who fully endorsed Browne's findings, later claimed that the subsidy program was characterized by perjuries and false statements on the part of "hundreds" of fishermen seeking to illegally collect bounty money.[96] It was under Guthrie's predecessor and fellow Westerner, Thomas Corwin, that the 1852 circular was issued, which sought (among other things) to disallow the taking of other species in the process of catching cod for bounty purposes. Subsequent difficulties in enforcing this unrealistic stricture gradually led to a more liberal interpretation of the regulation by Treasury officials, in order to facilitate payment and soothe irate fishermen.[97]

Such compromises after the fact did not placate Representative Davis of Massachusetts, who angrily observed in 1857 that "out of all the heads of the Treasury that have filled the office since my remembrance, I do not believe there is one who ever saw a fisherman, or a codfish until the odor of antiquity was upon it."[98] Others felt the same way. A Gloucester observer, noting the maze of unwieldy licensing and reporting regulations that had grown up by the mid-1850s, sourly commented that if they had been administered by men who understood the fisheries, all would be well, "but when they are under the supervision of men from Missouri and Illinois, who have never seen a fishing vessel, and know nothing of the nature of the business and the difficulties attending it, what better can be expected?"[99]

There was strong justification for charges of ignorance. Not only were secretaries of the Treasury abysmally lacking in knowledge with regard to the fisheries, but so were congressmen from the interior sections of the country. One Senate committee, chaired by the ubiquitous Mr. Clay of Alabama, actually reported in 1860 that there was no difference between the mackerel and cod fisheries in terms of vessels used, techniques employed, waters fished, dangers faced, or seasons of the year pursued! On that basis, the committee contended that since mackerelmen did not get a bounty, cod fishermen should not get one either.[100] The ultimate commentary on the extent of congressional misunderstanding of, and lack of appreciation for, the fisheries came during a Senate exchange between Toombs of Georgia and Hamlin of Maine in 1858. Toombs volunteered that it was his impression that fishing schooners lasted for four or five years. When Hamlin corrected him and explained that fifteen years was closer to the mark, Toombs responded, "Well, I know very little about it; I am no sailor; I live away from the sea, and I have had very little to do with it, and I hope to have less, because I do not like it."[101]

The Bounty: The Naval Nursery

Faced with the double-barrelled assault of sectional accusations and corruption charges, supporters of the fishing bounty reverted primarily to one time-honored response. With remarkable consistency, they invoked the "school for seamen" or "naval nursery" argument. The proposition that the subsidized cod fisheries constituted the primary training ground for America's merchant seamen and naval personnel, particularly the latter, formed a basic part of the intellectual baggage of every elected politician from maritime New England from the founding of the federal government to the end of the Civil War.

The antecedents of the naval-nursery argument extend far back into the maritime history of the European nations. Clearly, it was not an American idea. The eighteenth century British economist Adam Smith cited it as one justification used by supporters of the herring- and whale-fishing bounties maintained by the English government in his time. These bounties, said Smith, did not necessarily add to the wealth of the nation, but it could be argued that they provided an inexpensive alternative to a large standing navy by encouraging the growth of a seafaring class adaptable to naval service in case of war.[102]

Actually, the concept of the fisheries as a training ground of seamen, irrespective of its use as a rationale for bounties, preceded even Adam Smith. As early as 1615, the French political economist Antoine de Montchrétien had argued that the cod and herring fisheries should be considered as a nursery for both the navy and the merchant marine of his nation, since they trained sailors in seafaring and long voyages. It was in the interest of the Crown to protect and encourage them, therefore, as a key to the growth of Gallic sea power.[103] The great French minister Jean Baptiste Colbert (1619–

1683) concurred in that judgement and made support of the fisheries as schools for seamen an integral part of his mercantilist program.[104] England, too, accepted the concept, and for a century prior to the American Revolution Parliament attempted on that basis to cultivate the fishing industry, eventually settling on a bounty system after various other experiments.[105]

The first apparent legislative application of the school-for-seamen argument in this country took place at the initial session of the First Congress, where it was employed by Federalist Representative Fisher Ames of Massachusetts as a rationale for the proposed export bounty on pickled fish. Said Ames, "The taking of fish on the banks is a very momentous concern, it forms a nursery for seamen, and this will be the source from which we are to derive maritime importance."[106] The idea was not a new one to Americans. Alexander Hamilton had made reference to the importance of the fisheries as a nursery of seamen in "The Federalist Number 11," written two years earlier, in 1787. They were, he had suggested, indispensable to the establishment of a national navy.[107] Hamilton's contemporary, Thomas Jefferson, was equally convinced of the crucial role of the fisheries at an early date, as evidenced by his 1791 *Report on the Cod and Whale Fisheries.* Although no friend of naval establishments and reluctant to suggest that the deep-sea industry might be used in providing military manpower, Jefferson did cite the fisheries as an important nursery for forming merchant seamen.[108]

More common was the approach used by Representative Goodhue of Massachusetts in the first major bounty debate in Congress in 1792. "My view," said Goodhue, "is only to appeal to the facts, to evince the importance of the fishery as a means of naval protection."[109] The fishing bounty, Goodhue maintained, was justifiable because it contributed to the prosperity of the fisheries, which, in turn, contributed to the national defense. The industry "furnishes a copious nursery of hardy seamen, and offers a neverfailing source of protection to the commerce of the United States."[110] This theme carried over into the 1797 debate on bounty renewal. The bounty, supporters argued, guaranteed the continuation of the fisheries as a nursery of seamen and, most importantly, as a naval militia for the United States.[111]

When the bounty was proposed anew in 1813, after a half-dozen years in limbo, proponents resuscitated the argument that had served so well in the 1790s. Noting the example of France, which had instituted fishing bounties as a means of raising seamen and achieving parity with England on the high seas, William Reed of Massachusetts advised the House of Representatives to emulate it. "The fisheries have been justly considered the nurseries of seamen; the best seamen in the world," he continued, adding that the poverty of the industry necessitated public patronage if it was to survive.[112] Three years later, bounty advocates, bolstered in their demands by the sweep of recent military events, were able to obtain an unlimited extension of the allowance system. The argument used by Bay State Representative John Reed typified the tone of the debate on the proponent side: "It seems now, by the consent and approbation of all, we are to have a navy. . . . It then behooves us to act wisely, and foster the fisheries, that should war unfortunately again happen, these fishermen . . . may enter on board our armed ships, and do as they have always done, bravely fight in defence of their country."[113]

By now the naval-nursery argument was virtually a doctrine. More and more, it became the central justification for continuing the bounty whenever the law was challenged. The experience of two naval conflicts within one generation—the French naval war of 1798–1800 and the War of 1812— had pointed up the uses of a navy and the apparent practicality of a training ground for seamen. For the next several decades, all bounty spokesmen in Congress had to do when under attack was hark back to 1812, or 1798, or even 1776, for the ultimate retort. Increasingly, it was Maine congressmen who led this effort. The emergence of Maine politicians as the primary defenders of the bounty system was one of the more interesting developments of the fisheries debate. In the early years, it was Massachusetts spokesmen who championed the pro-bounty forces. Later, however, Maine solons, spurred on no doubt by the fact that their state was becoming the leader in the American cod fishery, were in the forefront.

The first of these was Democratic Senator John Fairfield. On March 24, 1846, Fairfield wrote to his wife, "I made a little speech today upon the subject of the fishing bounties. . . . It was entirely off hand and without a minute for reflection."[114] As it happened, Fairfield's "off hand" remarks were elicited by the latest of Senator Benton's assaults on the bounty. Diplomatically, because Benton was his friend and political ally on most issues, Fairfield unveiled what amounted to a new, amended version of the naval-nursery doctrine. Since the passage of the second bounty act in 1813, he argued, the idea that "some encouragement should be extended to the cod fisheries as a school for seamen, and a nursery for the navy" had been the sole basis for the law. Earlier rationales relating to such things as the salt tariff and the drawback system had not been considered in the creation of the second bounty. "The law, therefore, though continued in form the same, assumed a different basis, and was continued for a new and different object." Continuing, Fairfield invoked memories of 1812 with the assertion that "all history shows that upon these men—those engaged in the fisheries—the country must rely, in case of war or other contingency, to man the navy." The history of the "last war," he added, was proof of the military value of fishermen. The subsidized fisheries were, in effect, serving as the naval equivalent of the army academy at West Point. "It is, then, decidedly for the interest of the country," the Maine senator concluded, "that this school should be continued."[115]

Fairfield's revival and refinement of the naval-nursery argument was followed in 1852 by a similar defense of fishing subsidies by Maine's Hannibal Hamlin—still, at this point in his career, a Democrat. Responding to a presidential message critical of the fisheries, Hamlin invoked the tried and true response: "We must have men for our Navy; we must have men for our commercial marine. Those men can only be had who have become proficient by a training in the sea service for a number of years. There is no nation that has ever existed which has not reposed with confidence on the fisheries as the great foundation of supply for its commerce and Navy."[116] Every great sea power, he continued, from Venice to Colbert's France, had relied on the fisheries for manpower. The decline of the French Navy after Colbert Hamlin traced to the concurrent decline of that nation's fisheries, which even now (1852) were being rebuilt by a system of bounties calculated to revive Gallic naval strength. The American government had traditionally given its fisheries such support, said Hamlin, and must continue to do so. "They are," he affirmed, "the school in which our seamen are trained to fight our battles on the oceans and on the lakes."[117] The thinly veiled reference to the naval battles on Lake Erie and Lake Champlain in 1813–1814 meant that the War of 1812 had still not lost its potency as a justification for maintaining a "school" for seamen, even after forty years.

In the course of his speech, Senator Hamlin exhibited an intriguing familiarity with the so-called Ancet Report produced by the French government in 1851. This document, which recommended that the National Assembly renew the expiring cod-fishing bounty law, argued strongly for the necessity of a school for naval seamen in the form of a heavily subsidized Grand Banks cod fishery.[118] The implied threat constituted by the naval power of a foreign nation like France, supported as it was by a fishing-bounty system, undoubtedly added to the congressional reluctance to abandon the American bounty system just yet. Moreover, the fact that foreigners were also using the naval-nursery argument—something Hamlin was careful to point out—reinforced the credibility of that rationale.

When the fishing-bounty debate came to a head in 1857–1858, supporters of the system were still clinging to the old argument. Maine Senators
Hamlin (now a Republican) and Fessenden, assisted by Seward of New York,
Hale of New Hampshire, and James Simmons of Rhode Island, outlined
the naval-defense case in the upper chamber. In the House, Representatives
Stephen C. Foster of Maine and Davis of Massachusetts led the fight. Without detailing the interminable and intricate unfolding of the naval-nursery
doctrine by these bounty defenders, it is worthwhile examining some of the
highlights of the debate in order to show the consistency and historical
continuity of their case. It could well be said that by the late 1850s the brief
on behalf of fishing bounties had figuratively hardened into plaster—firm
and able to hold a definable shape, but liable at any moment to crack and
shatter into a thousand pieces. Fortunately for fishermen, that did not happen in 1857–1858.

Senator Seward opened the defense on January 20, 1857, with a ringing
endorsement of the system that had originally been intended to establish
American commerce and promote American navigation interests but had
since been primarily maintained "for the purpose of increasing our mercantile marine, and supplying a nursery for seamen required by the United States
Navy."[119] In the House of Representatives a few days later, Davis of Massachusetts posed the ever-constant threat of naval war, despite the many years
of peace, and offered the bounty as a substitute for an increased naval budget. "If, by paying the sum of $350,000 yearly, we keep in readiness twenty
thousand American sailors, how," he asked, "can the Government make a
better investment?"[120]

The following January, when the debate was renewed, Senator Hale, a
Republican, proposed abolishing the military academies at Annapolis and
West Point on the grounds that if bounty patronage to the "school for seamen" was to be terminated, then patronage to the schools for officers should
also come to an end.[121] Senator Simmons of Rhode Island summoned the
ghosts of the Founding Fathers in defense of the naval-nursery case. Quot-
ing Fisher Ames, he claimed that the cod-fishing bounty was not a gratuity
but a means of promoting American commercial and naval power. It was,
he said, the "settled policy" of the country.[122] Fessenden of Maine added
that the 1813 bounty-resumption act was a direct result of the War of 1812,
which had clearly shown the need for naval seamen. Fessenden claimed, furthermore, that most of the sailors serving in that war had come from the
fisheries. The constitutional authority to impose a fishing bounty for military purposes originated, he said, in the war-powers provisions. The infor-

mal school for naval seamen, then, rested on the same constitutional basis as the formal school for naval officers at Annapolis.[123]

It was left to another Maine spokesman, Senator Hamlin, to make the classic presentation of the naval-nursery case. On May 6, 1858, he gave what one Maine newspaper called the most complete defense of the fishing-bounty system ever made.[124] Beginning with a characterization of the bounty as having a "national" purpose, despite the fact that the fishery itself was geographically localized, Hamlin went on to define that purpose as the training of seamen for the naval service. Having thus dismissed the charge of sectional favoritism, he reiterated earlier claims that the nature of the bounty law had changed during the War of 1812. The 1813 act and its finalized version of 1819 were specifically intended, the Maine senator said, to foster the fishing industry for the avowed purpose of "raising a corps of seamen who should always be found ready to participate in your commercial and your naval marine."[125] After citing once more the important military services rendered by fishermen in the wars against England ("Why, sir, in the War of 1812, you could hardly man a frigate without these very same fishermen"), Hamlin made a surprising offer: "If you can educate seamen in any other way, I am for abolishing the fishing bounties. . . . I am not advocating bounties to any class of citizens, . . . unless it be of national importance, for a national purpose, and be the most economical mode of effecting the object."[126]

This admission of tenuous legitimacy, by a leading advocate, indicated the single thread by which the bounty system now hung. The one and only reason for its continued existence, in effect, was that it was the basic means of obtaining needed naval manpower. If another source was found, or if the nature of naval requirements changed, the bounty would be doomed. Hamlin went on to make the assertion that since two-thirds of America's merchant seamen were actually foreigners, the native fisheries remained the only trustworthy naval nursery. "You cannot educate seamen as you can educate soldiers in the Army," he pleaded. "There must be time; and there is therefore a necessity for keeping up this school."[127] That school or nursery, Hamlin concluded, ought to be regarded by the Senate and by the country in the same light as the military academies.[128]

About three weeks after Hamlin spoke, Representative Foster, from eastern Maine, made what turned out to be the final speech ever delivered in defense of fishing bounties. Fittingly, it was an unalloyed version of the naval-nursery argument. Adapting an approach used by others, Foster compared the bounty's function to that of the service academies at Annapolis and West Point. Contrasting the $12.7 million Navy Department budget of 1857 with the average yearly bounty outlay of $300,000, he rhetorically asked, "Sir, can that be regarded as an expensive system of training seamen, which for the paltry sum of $300,000 gives the best kind of practical instruction to thirteen or fifteen thousand men yearly?" Foster added that with the aid of the subsidized cod fisheries the government was able to accomplish with a few thousand dollars what millions could not do without them.[129]

From a purely dollars-and-cents standpoint, the Maine congressman was right. If the cod bounties did, indeed, prepare men for the naval service—a supposition that remains debatable—the cost, at least, was modest and proportionately decreasing. Compared to the rest of the mushrooming national budget, the annual outlays for the bounty system remained relatively static. In 1838, the cod bounties represented 1 percent of all federal expenditures, but twenty years later that figure had fallen to 0.5 percent.[130] It is one of the many ironies surrounding the bounty conflict in Congress that while opposition to the subsidy was becoming increasingly more vociferous, the subsidy itself was becoming less and less of a factor in the federal budget. In that sense, by the late 1850s, the public investment was a comparative bargain.

Unwittingly, the last spokesman for the bounty continued the process of undermining the very system he supported, a process begun by other bounty advocates some years earlier. "I admit," said Congressman Foster, "that the system of bounties as a means of stimulating industrial enterprises is objectionable, and, indeed, indefensible." There was no justification for fishing bounties, he conceded, except the training of American seamen.[131] Presented with no other reasons to retain the system, Congress would soon find ample excuse to abolish it.

The obsession of bounty supporters with the nursery-of-seamen doctrine transcended the immediate scene of the debate in Washington. Throughout maritime New England, state politicians, newspaper editors, and the fishermen themselves trumpeted the idea. In Maine, state legislators twice advanced it as a primary justification for keeping the allowance system when they petitioned Congress against repeal in 1840 and 1858.[132] In 1854 a Democratic paper, the *Republican Journal* of Belfast, editorialized against repealing the bounty, a bounty, in its words, "for which, as we think can be clearly shown, the country and the government have been amply remunerated in the two contests this country has had with England."[133] Four years later, a Republican paper, the *Bangor Daily Whig and Courier,* used the same argument when it defended the bounty as crucial to the cod fisheries, which, in turn, were "not only important as a business interest to a large section of the country, but vitally important as a nursery of American seamen."[134] Various Maine writers joined in the chorus. Lorenzo Sabine, early chronicler of the fisheries and bounty enthusiast, dwelled at length on the naval exploits of those trained in the fishing "school" during the Revolution and the War of 1812.[135] Elijah Kellogg, the novelist, maintained that in addition to providing food, the fisheries "train up a class of rugged, resolute men, who are a most important aid in the event of war."[136] The idea never really died. Twenty years after the repeal of the subsidy law, some political figures persisted in referring to the New England fisheries as an indispensable training school for naval seamen.[137]

As a short-run expedient, the naval-nursery argument was effective. It even threw convinced opponents of the bounty system off stride. Representative William Giles, who led the congressional fight against the initial law in 1792, was forced to admit that the proposal might be considered in a favorable light if supporters could prove that it was essential to national defense.[138] And no less a bounty critic than Thomas Hart Benton noted the "great and lasting contribution of the northeastern cod fisheries as a nursery of seamen," although he steadfastly maintained that they had no exclusive monopoly in that regard.[139] Texas Senator Sam Houston, a Westerner who harbored deep reservations about fishing bounties, was, by his own admission, persuaded to vote for their retention solely on the basis of the need for a strong national navy.[140]

What gave the school-for-seamen doctrine its strength was the memory of the naval conflicts of the late eighteenth and early nineteenth centuries. The events of 1812–1815 had been particularly traumatic, with defeats on land and the ignominious burning of the Capitol offset only by the glorious successes at sea. Unfortunately for fishermen, the nature of naval warfare began to change in the years following the last war with Great Britain. As late as the 1830s, naval historians have noted, seamanship was still the chief qualification for a naval officer. By the 1840s, however, a revolutionary transition from sail to steam was under way.[141] The process was slow and painful until the Civil War brought it to dramatic and sudden fruition. The battle of Hampton Roads in 1862, involving the armored steam rams *Monitor* and *Virginia*, was particularly effective in altering attitudes.

In retrospect, the major lessons and consequences of the years 1861–1865, within the context of naval technology, were that steam had clearly triumphed over sail and that the ironclad and improved ordnance had rendered the wooden warship obsolete.[142] This left the fishing-bounty advocates, who had depended almost completely on the naval-nursery argument, without a proverbial leg to stand on. The kind of training provided by the fisheries "school" might have been helpful in preparing men for the old wooden sailing navy, where the premium was on seamanship. In the new age of steam, however, it was irrelevant. The ability to stoke furnaces, repair engines, or maneuver floating iron gunnery platforms was not learned on the Grand Banks. The Belfast, Maine, newspaper, *The Progressive Age,* hit upon the essence of the situation when it tried to explain the repeal of the bounty to its readership in August of 1866:

> It survived the early attacks through . . . the importance of the fisheries as a nursery for seamen to man our navy in case of war. But there has been such a revolution in our naval matters that this argument has lost much of its force, and this, together with the fact that our navy has been manned by men from the merchant and land service to a very large extent, has induced Congress to look upon the benefits actually resulting from this resource as of little importance.[143]

The Bounty: Mercantilism versus Laissez-Faire

Sadly, Maine's representatives in Washington, as well as other bounty supporters, seemed unable to get beyond the narrow, self-imposed military argument in defending the system of allowances. What was singularly lacking was a comprehensive, coherent economic rationale for what was essentially an economic policy. There were scattered attempts at an economic justification, of course, but they were never systematic and seldom a prominent part of any debate on the subject.

One tactic employed from time to time was to claim that the poverty of the fisheries—the marginal nature of the business—was such that government assistance was needed for its survival. This argument, occasionally buttressed by formidable collections of statistical data, was raised by Maine and Massachusetts congressmen at least a half-dozen times during the course of the fisheries debates. The essence of the case was stated by Representative Reed of Massachusetts, who first presented it in July 1813. "A view of the cod fishery," he said, paraphrasing Jefferson, "enables us to mark the fact that it is too poor a business to be left to itself, even with the nation most advantageously situated."[144] Representative Davis, another Bay Stater, put it a bit more strongly in 1857, warning his repeal-minded colleagues, "Take away the aid of the Government, and the death of the fishing business must be . . . as certain as the rising and setting of the sun."[145] However, the survival of the business was seldom advanced as an end in itself.

There was a higher motive, as Hamlin of Maine made clear a year later, when he said of bounties, "I am only in favor of them in this case because there is a necessity for them, from the nature of the business which requires aid to keep it alive; and to keep it alive is the only way in which you can get the force that is requisite and necessary."[146] The force in question was, of course, the U.S. Navy.

Direct economic arguments, unrelated to such things as national defense, were few and far between. A committee of the Maine legislature offered one in 1840, in the course of petitioning Congress to retain the bounty. Repeal of the law would adversely affect the entire economy of the state, the committee argued, because of the delicate interrelationship of various maritime activities. Not only the fisheries would be injured but also shipbuilding and commerce, and navigation generally. The welfare of the shipbuilding industry, in particular, was a special concern to the legislators, since the bounty had resulted in an increased demand for small vessels of the type used in the fisheries—a demand that might tail off with repeal.[147] An argument based on the special economic interests of one state, however, was not destined to have much impact. A more generalized approach was needed, but it was not forthcoming.

It is necessary to go back to the first debates on the fishing-bounty law in 1792 to find anything like a well-rounded economic argument. At that time, Benjamin Goodhue, a Massachusetts Federalist, defended the proposed subsidy in the House of Representatives on the grounds of national economic wealth and justice for fishermen, as well as national defense. In Goodhue's opinion, the fishing industry was deserving of support as an American resource. As he put it, "If nothing was in view, therefore, but to promote national wealth, it seems plain that this branch ought to be protected and preserved; because under all the discouragements it suffers, it increases, and every year more and more enriches the country, and promises to become an inexhaustable fund of wealth."[148] Furthermore, suggested Goodhue, the proposed bounty would help a deserving class of workers, important to the nation, whose just needs were not being met. The existing fisheries legislation, which gave a bounty on pickled-fish exports, was not aiding fishermen, but only export merchants.[149] This latter point was echoed by other New England members, who sought to bypass the middleman, in effect, and provide government support to the producing class—to those catching the fish. "By encouraging this class of men, your revenue will be increased," one of them argued, "for in return for the fish exported you will receive sugar, coffee, cocoa, indigo, molasses, pimento, cotton, dye-woods, rum, wine, salt, fruit, and other articles subject to duty and consumed in the country." [150]

Such spokesmen were proposing what amounted to an American form of mercantilism. Subsidies would be given to fishermen because they were a needy class of workers essential to the economic well-being of the nation. Along with the familiar naval-nursery argument, it seemed a plausible rationale in 1792. Only one representative, Giles of Virginia, rose to challenge it directly. The bill, he felt, contained a direct bounty on occupations and was, therefore, unconstitutional. As a strict constructionist, he opposed what appeared to be a use of the "ways and ends" or implied-powers clause of the document. He was, Giles said, opposed to bounties in any form as an unjust granting of exclusive rights and monopolies. If such use of federal power was allowed, he went on, the principle that the government or the State was supreme would be established, and tyranny would result. Finally, Giles assailed the bounty bill as an interrupting factor in the free operation of the economy: "All occupations that stand in need of bounties, instead of increasing the real wealth of a country, rather tend to lessen it; . . . and if an occupation is really productive, and augments the general wealth, bounties are unnecessary for its support; for when it reimburses the capital employed, and yields a profit besides, it may be said to support itself." [151]

Although the argument offered by the Virginia representative did not carry the day, lines had been drawn between two conflicting economic philosophies. The bounty, part of a quasi-mercantilist structure, would increasingly come under attack by the advocates of laissez-faire economics. The inability of mercantilist ideology to hold off the rising tide of laissez-faire in later years explains in large part the absence of a strong economic rationale for the bounty system after 1792.

Fundamentally, the bounty law that existed up to 1866 was a piece of eighteenth-century legislation. Its immediate ancestor was the tonnage bounty for vessels in the white-herring fishery of Scotland, which had been passed by the British Parliament in 1750. [152] This law, itself descended from a similar bounty given to English ships in the Greenland whale fishery in 1733, was vigorously attacked in the 1780s by economist Adam Smith, the very father of laissez-faire. [153] In a critique of fishing bounties covering several pages of his epoch-making *The Wealth of Nations*, Smith impugned such mercantilist legislation as economically inefficient, liable to frauds, and generally incompatible with the profitable operation of a free-market economy. [154] The herring bounty, based as it was on a per-ton allocation of payments unrelated to catch production, he found particularly offensive.

Under the existing British system, Smith declared, it had become "too common for vessels to fit out for the sole purpose of catching, not the fish, but the bounty."[155]

If Adam Smith had remained an obscure academic scholar, his opinion of fishing bounties would have made little difference. As it happened, he became the high priest of nineteenth-century economic thought, and his ideas—including those on government bounties—became dogma to most middle and late-nineteenth-century public men. In England, *The Wealth of Nations* was a major factor in ending a century of mercantilist policies; in America, it had a less immediate but just as pervasive impact.[156] As regards the fisheries, most of the arguments raised by Smith against English tonnage bounties were revived and used against the American system, which operated on the same basis. The language employed, in some instances, was virtually verbatim. Take, for example, the words of a southern senator who, in 1858, advised his colleagues that "these men go out, not so much to catch fish as to catch the bounty."[157] The senator had obviously read his Adam Smith.

What all this meant in terms of the bounty debate was that when the discussion turned to economics, bounty supporters were on the defensive. They were increasingly at odds with the prevailing climate of opinion. The best tactic, then, was to avoid the subject of political economy when possible and to use economic arguments only indirectly.

There were a few half-hearted attempts at economic justification in the years just preceding repeal. A number of bounty advocates had been politically nurtured within the Federalist-Whig tradition of American mercantilism. Memories of Hamilton's policies and Henry Clay's American System died hard, and in the 1850s scattered voices could still be heard in their behalf. Ironically, one such voice was that of the *Republican Journal* of Belfast, Maine, nominally a Democratic newspaper. Responding to claims that the cod-fishing bounty was an example of unwarranted government intervention in the economy, the *Journal* pointed to direct outlays for the transatlantic and California steamship companies, to federally subsidized river and harbor improvements in the West, to the pending homestead bill for farmers, and to high import duties protecting Louisiana sugar and Pennsylvania iron as evidence that government support of the private sector was a recognized national policy. In a classic disclosure of the gap between the theory and practice of laissez-faire, the *Journal* concluded: "When the 'powers that be' in Washington will reduce the government to a 'strict construction' system, and pay all the expenses of government by direct taxation, we will say nothing against the repeal of the bounties. . . . [A]t present we must decline to have Maine and Massachusetts experimented upon for the bringing in of such a simple and primitive form of government."[158]

Politicians were less straightforward and more reluctant to swim against the tide. In the entire history of the congressional bounty debates after the initial passage of the first law in 1792, only two men made any attempt at a direct economic defense of the system. Neither was from Maine. One was Timothy Davis of Massachusetts, who, in February 1857, rose to assure western critics of the bounty in the House that he favored a policy of government support for all needy sectors of the economy and not just the New England fishing industry. If it could be shown, said Representative Davis, that the production of any article of consumption would languish without public aid, he would vote to support it. "If the agricultural interest of the country was dependent upon governmental aid," he added, "it should have my vote in its support instantly, simply because there is no value to anything if productive industry fails."[159] Senator William Seward of New York also offered a quasi-mercantilist rationale. In 1857 he told colleagues that one reason for supporting continuance of the fishing bounty was that it encouraged "an adventurous and important branch of commerce, essential to the comforts of society."[160] A year later he defended the principle of bounties in general, pointing out to senators from the interior that the opening up of the public lands and their sale at nominal prices was, in effect, a bounty on agriculture.[161]

Against these voices in the wilderness were arrayed the children of Adam Smith, who came from all political parties and all parts of the country, and represented, beyond any doubt, the wave of the future. For a while they were found primarily in the party of Jefferson and Jackson, with its predilection against public largesse and special privilege, and its fear of government-business alliances.[162] By the 1850s, however, the Whig party of Henry Clay—last home of American neo-mercantilism—was dead, and even Republicans from the state of Maine were admitting that in principle the concept of direct bounties to any branch of industry could not be justified.[163] Others were more vehement. J. Ross Browne, author of the celebrated report calling for repeal of the bounty system, demanded that fishermen be forced to stand on their own feet. "The experience of every nation shows that the tendency of legislative protection is to depress individual exertion, and render unprofitable that which otherwise might be profitable," he said. Instead of appeals to Congress for aid, Browne suggested a greater application of industry and energy on the part of fishermen.[164] The last word belonged to Clement C. Clay, Jr., Democratic senator from Alabama and persistent critic of the fisheries. In the final debate of 1858, he levelled the following charge against the bounty:

> It encourages a sentiment already too pervading in the country, of dependence on the Government for support. . . . Such a sentiment is baneful to individual as well as national prosperity. It paralyzes the industry, enervates the mind, and enfeebles the will of man to look to Government as a natural or foster parent for support and aid in every enterprise. . . . Whenever Government undertakes to supply man's wants and relieves his labors, it violates a law of nature.[165]

To this, bounty supporters had no answer. They had no intellectual foundation from which to mount a philosophical counteroffensive. They could have pointed out, in the egalitarian spirit of Jacksonian Democracy, that the bounty law was a device which allowed poorer fishermen to compete with wealthy fish merchants. They could have truthfully presented it as a means of uplifting a deprived socioeconomic class rather than rewarding a prosperous special interest. They could have emphasized its real function, which was to democratize one segment of the American economy and protect it from monopoly capitalism. To say these things, however, the advocates of fishing bounties would have had to transcend at least a half-century of American history. The concept of an interventionist government operating not on behalf of the propertied and monied interests of society, nor on behalf of the nation-state itself, but for the benefit of the underprivileged elements of that society, was a theory of social engineering foreign to mercantilists and to nineteenth-century followers of Adam Smith, alike.

Even if the intellectual weapons necessary to make an incisive economic defense of the fishing bounty had been available, those using them would have had one more barrier to hurdle. Base economic interest is often more politically influential than economic philosophy, particularly if the interest to be served represents a powerful enough class or group of citizens. The fact is that by the mid-nineteenth century, the cod-fishing bounty had earned the enmity of one of the very groups it was created to serve—the large fishery capitalists, especially those of Massachusetts.

As Leonard D. White quite accurately pointed out, the federal bounty law of 1792 was an early American example of government involvement in employment contracts and industry regulation. It stipulated how the bounty money would be divided, dictated the labor system, outlined job responsibilities, guaranteed wages, and required specific written agreements between owner and crew.[166] With the passage of time other regulations were added, either by act of Congress or by Treasury Department decree. By 1852, when the secretary of the Treasury codified the various rules and regulations in the form of a circular of instructions to customs officials, a considerable body of bounty "law" had evolved.

A glance at the provisions, old and new, suggests why the system had become somewhat unpopular with certain owners of fishing vessels. First, the share system—division of profits according to the percentage of fish caught by each man—was mandatory, and the crew could not be paid in wages. Second, five-eighths of the bounty went to the men, while the owner got only three-eighths. Third, the master and three-quarters of the crew had to be United States citizens. Fourth, the vessel could fish only for cod while qualifying for the bounty, and fresh-market fishing during that four-month period was not permitted, bounty money being paid only when the catch was salted for dry-curing purposes. Fifth, the vessel had to be inspected and certified at the custom house before and after each voyage, and had to keep a formal logbook while at sea.[167] To the owner intent upon maximizing profits, these features were irritating obstacles. Inexpensive foreign labor— particularly Canadian labor from the Maritime Provinces—could not be used. Men could not be hired by the month and paid cheap wages. Profits had to be shared. The crew received a high percentage of the catch proceeds and the lion's share of the bounty. The owner could not instruct his skipper to go after fresh fish or mackerel (both of which were bringing increasingly high prices) while simultaneously qualifying for the dried-cod bounty. Finally, paperwork and red tape, that bane of all businessmen, was becoming burdensome. The keeping of a proper logbook required a reasonably literate captain, and the filling out of inspection certificates and licensing forms was time-consuming.

By the mid-1850s protests were being heard. The fishing community of Gloucester, Massachusetts, complained of petty annoyances and harassment on the part of the government.[168] Ultimately, in 1866 the large fishing firms of Gloucester, claiming that the bounty had become a "nuisance," petitioned their congressman for repeal of the measure.[169] In contrast, no such protests emanated from the Maine fishing ports. As late as 1861 Maine fishermen succeeded once more in persuading their legislature to instruct the state's congressional delegation to *oppose* repeal. The resolve emphasized the economic hardships that would result from ending the system.[170] Ordinary fishermen, however, had limited influence, and when the large fishing capitalists turned against the bounty, the last hope of retaining it disappeared. The hard reality for small entrepreneurs and working fishermen was that by 1866 the fish merchants of Boston, Gloucester, Newburyport, and even Portland had a vested interest in not opposing repeal. In the last analysis, that interest was the important one.

Map 2. The major sea-fishing grounds of the North Atlantic. The dark-shaded land areas indicate the coastal regions of Newfoundland and Labrador where American fishermen were permitted to fish inshore under the Treaty of 1818. The Quebec coastline adjacent to Labrador was considered an extension of the Labrador fishing grounds. (*Hague Arbitration Proceedings*, vol. 1, map. no. 1)

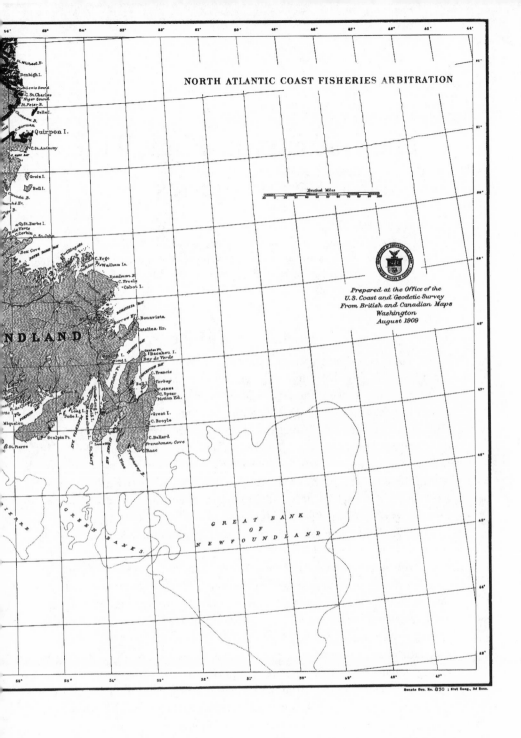

NORTH ATLANTIC COAST FISHERIES ARBITRATION

Nautical Miles

Prepared at the Office of the
U.S. Coast and Geodetic Survey
From British and Canadian Maps
Washington
August 1909

NDLAND

GREAT BANK
OF
NEWFOUNDLAND

BANKS

St.Michael B.
Dembigh I.
St.Lewis Sound
C. St.Charles
Niger Sound
St.Peter B.
Belle I.
C. Norman B.
Quirpon I.
C.St.Anthony
Groix I.
Bell I.
Canada B.
Orchard Hr.
B.
St.Barbe I.
Belle Verte
C.Corbin C. St.John
Bou Cove
NOTRE DAME B.
Tillingate
C. Fogo
Wadham Is.
Deadman B.
C. Freels
Cabot I.
BONAVISTA BAY
C. Bonavista
Catalina Hr.
TRINITY BAY
Grates Pt.
Bacaheu I.
Bay de Verde
C. Francis
Torbay
St.Johns
C. Spear
Motion Hd.
Great I.
C. Broyle
C. Ballard
Frenchman Cove
C. Race
Sculpin Pt.
Miquelon
St.Pierre

The Industry at High Tide: The Fisheries

[They fished] from the Grand Banks to Cape Cod, in
every place where they now carry it on. They had equally
as good vessels as anybody, and went all over the shores.
—Ezra Turner, Isle au Haut fisherman, on the fisheries of
eastern Maine, 1877[1]

General Characteristics

Maine engaged in most, although not all, of the important North Atlantic
sea fisheries during the nineteenth century. The favorite fisheries of Maine
vessels (see map 2) were the Grand Banks, Labrador, Gulf of St. Lawrence,
Bay of Fundy, Cape Sable, Western Bank, and Banquereau cod fisheries, the
Gulf of St. Lawrence and American shore mackerel fisheries, and the Magdalen Islands herring fishery.[2] The last named was not a deep-sea fishery in
the true sense and was a trade as well as a fishery. However, while carried on
within the sheltered waters of the Canadian coast, with native fishermen often landing the catch, it necessitated voyages from home of several weeks'
duration and is included for that reason.

In general, Maine's fisheries were basic, being confined to groundfish
and mackerel and limited to normal fishing seasons. Unlike Massachusetts,
Maine did not indulge in the more esoteric marine pursuits. The winter
haddock fishery, for instance, was carried on in Maine only by Portland vessels, and only after 1850. Maine did no swordfishing until around 1877, when,
again, Portland vessels became involved. Even then, the work was only a
part-time occupation for cod and mackerel schooners, and their catch in
succeeding years constituted a mere fraction of the U.S. total. Likewise, the
George's Bank halibut fishery, vastly important to Massachusetts, drew few
Maine schooners. Southport and Vinalhaven sent a handful of vessels during the period 1859–1862, but generally speaking, the George's Bank winter
fisheries, halibut or otherwise, were not for Maine.[3]

The fisheries important to Maine fishermen, however, were worked intensively. It is apparent that a minimum of thirty-one Maine communities
sent schooners to the Grand Banks of Newfoundland for cod. Twenty-four

were involved in the Gulf of St. Lawrence cod fishery, and seventeen pursued that species along the coast of Labrador. The Western (Sable Island) Bank cod fishery drew the vessels of twenty-four Maine ports, and Quereau Bank (Banquereau) attracted cod-fishing schooners from another twenty-three. No fewer than thirty-three towns had vessels fishing the Bay of Fundy for cod over the years, and at least seventeen were in the Cape Sable cod fishery. Another major Maine pursuit was mackerel catching in the Gulf of St. Lawrence and along the American coast. A total of forty coastal towns engaged in mackereling in Gulf waters, especially around Chaleur Bay on the Gaspé shore, and twenty-nine were active in the New England shore or "northern" mackerel fishery, carried on between Cape Cod and the Bay of Fundy. In addition to working the Gulf and more nearby offshore grounds, Maine mackerel schooners began to sail south in the spring during the 1860s to fish off Virginia and New Jersey. Probably a dozen towns participated in this "southern" mackerel fishery. Finally, at least twenty-one ports were involved in the Magdalen Islands herring fishery (or trade) during the nineteenth century.[4]

These fisheries, then, were the primary ones engaging the energies of Maine's deep-sea fishermen when the industry was at its height. To them must be added the less important but still significant local fisheries within the Gulf of Maine itself. It is likely that every coastal community possessing a harbor or waterfront of some kind periodically sent small vessels to the innumerable inshore banks for cod and haddock, or to the migratory haunts of the mackerel and herring when those species made their periodic visits to the immediate coast. Although so commonplace as to go virtually unrecorded, such activity added measurably to the state's annual fish landings. Nevertheless, it was the more distant fisheries, demanding large vessels and substantial investments of time, effort, and money, upon which the strength of the Maine industry was based.

The degree of participation in the sea fisheries varied from community to community. Some worked numerous fishing grounds and sought a variety of species. Others were more selective, visiting only a few locales or concentrating on certain types of fishing. In the diversity of their fisheries the individual ports of Boothbay and Deer Isle were unsurpassed; each participated in all of the major sea fisheries favored by Maine fishermen during the nineteenth century. Portland and Vinalhaven were close behind. If the Penobscot Bay mainland communities of Castine, Belfast, Camden, and Bucksport and the associated islands of Vinalhaven, North Haven, and Deer Isle are considered together, the extent and variety of their combined regional fisheries was historically unequaled anywhere on the Maine coast.[5]

The smaller Maine fishing ports, and the larger ones less totally devoted to fishing, tended to specialize. North Haven, for example, emphasized mackerel fishing and worked all of the major mackerel grounds. St. George also made mackerel a specialty, while Bucksport and Lamoine were particularly devoted to banks fishing for cod. Milbridge engaged in one, and only one, deep-sea pursuit, the Magdalen Islands herring fishery.[6] Aside from saying that Maine fishing ports primarily focused on cod, with secondary consideration for mackerel and herring, no other generalization about the sea fisheries statewide can be made. Fishing habits and priorities varied from locality to locality.

There were, however, some broad regional tendencies. That is, if the coast is divided into eastern and western sections with Rockland as the dividing point (see map 1), certain patterns emerge. Most of the towns participating in the Grand Banks cod fishery (twenty-four out of thirty-one) were east of Rockland. Eastern Maine similarly dominated the Bay of Fundy cod and Magdalen Islands herring fisheries, and to a lesser degree the Labrador, Quereau, and Western Bank cod fisheries as well. On the other hand, western Maine more than held its own in the Cape Sable and Gulf of St. Lawrence cod fisheries, and also in the various mackerel fisheries, which were eagerly pursued by both sections.[7]

Mackerel fishing, in general, was the one activity in which western Maine ports were able to compete successfully with those in the eastern part of the state. Western towns owned a majority of all the mackerel-fishing tonnage statewide in twenty-one of the thirty-five years prior to 1865. During most of that time it was customs districts well west of Rockland, usually Portland-Falmouth or Wiscasset, that led the state in supplying vessels for the various mackerel fisheries. In the all-important cod fisheries, however, the western region trailed badly. Between 1831 and 1865, eastern Maine owned a majority of the state's cod-fishing vessel tonnage in all but five years, and in the peak year of 1861 the region claimed three-quarters of the total. The leading cod-fishing district, almost invariably, was the eastern district of Penobscot.[8] In essence, eastern Maine was involved to a greater degree in those fisheries that the state made peculiarly its own.

The Cod Fisheries

Precisely when Maine vessels entered certain of the various fisheries is difficult to determine. This is especially true of the important Grand Banks cod fishery. Maine came late into Grand Banking, following the lead of Massachusetts. There are records of Bay State vessels visiting the Newfoundland banks as early as 1645, and several from the Gloucester region were there in 1724. Between 1770 and 1775, 70 to 80 Gloucester schooners were fishing the Grand Banks on a regular basis, and by the end of the Revolution nearby Marblehead claimed a fleet of 124 Grand Bankers.[9] It is doubtful, however, that any vessels from north of the Piscataqua sailed for the Newfoundland grounds prior to 1800. Portland and Castine sent schooners shortly after that date, and Bucksport and Orland were certainly involved by 1825. It is known that Monhegan was active on the Grand Banks for several years beginning in 1830, that Camden had vessels there in 1841, and that Bristol sent its first vessel in 1846. Beyond that, it is obvious that many towns participated up to 1865, and a few beyond that time. In general, Maine Grand Banking peaked during the 1850–1865 period. The towns of Swan's Island, Hancock, Lamoine (then East Trenton), and Tremont all sent schooners for the first time during those years, and numerous other communities, having started earlier, built their largest fleets during the 1850s and early 1860s.[10]

Although Grand Banks cod fishing does not appear to have been a major preoccupation of Maine fishermen prior to 1850, it took on much greater importance during the ensuing decade. There were several reasons for this development. As the nineteenth century progressed, the accumulation of capital from less distant fisheries allowed the building and outfitting of the large vessels necessary for extended trips to the waters off Newfoundland, and Grand Banking gradually became more of a practicality. A native of Grand Manan Island in the Bay of Fundy remembered a considerable fleet of small schooners from Hancock County, Maine, that annually visited his home region in search of cod prior to the mid-1850s. The Americans had since gone into Grand Banking. "They have built larger vessels, and consequently they have dropped our island fisheries."[11]

The Grand Banks of Newfoundland—composed of the Grand or "Great" Bank itself plus the adjoining Green, Whale, and St. Pierre Banks—had always been an attractive prospect. The Grand Bank proper, covering thirty-seven thousand square miles of the Atlantic southeast of Newfoundland (see map 2), was the haunt of the largest cod available to fishermen.[12] Hand-line vessels working there could expect to land fish that were roughly twice as large as those caught by hand-line in the Gulf of St. Lawrence and three times the size of those taken on the coast of Labrador.[13] Grand Bank cod also brought more per quintal in the wholesale market, as a rule, than other cod, although the highly prized Bay of Fundy variety occasionally challenged for top dollar. Prices in the Boston market for the week ending

September 5, 1850, were fairly typical: Grand Bank cod, $2.87–$3.00; Bay of Fundy cod, $2.62–$2.87; Bay Chaleur (Gulf of St. Lawrence) cod, $1.50–$2.37; New England shore cod, $2.00; and Labrador cod, $1.62–$1.87.[14]

Maine Grand Banking was further encouraged by the decision of Gloucester fishermen to forsake the Newfoundland grounds after 1820 in favor of the closer and equally rewarding George's Bank cod fishery, leaving something of a vacuum to be filled. Not until 1860 did Gloucester vessels resume Grand Banks fishing in any significant number.[15] In the interval, the Pine Tree State had a relatively free and uncontested hand there, with the fleets of Marblehead and Provincetown as the only real American competition. By 1855 the editor of the *Maine Register* could say, with ample justification, "Grand Bank fishing is here prosecuted to a much larger extent than in any other State in the Union."[16]

The heart of the Maine Grand Banks cod fishery was located in and around Penobscot Bay, bordering the counties of Waldo and Hancock. More specifically, it was the eastern shore of the bay, encompassing the district of Penobscot and the coastal towns of Bucksport, Orland, and Castine, that provided the leadership for the state's Newfoundland fishery. A careful perusal of Maine newspapers and logbooks for the decade of the 1850s reveals that while communities as far west as Kennebunkport and as far east as Jonesport were engaged in Grand Banking, the bulk of the Maine fleet sailed from Penobscot ports. Recorded returns for the months of July through November 1850–1860 indicate that during that time at least 126 different schooners from the Penobscot region made cod-fishing trips to the Grand Banks, the majority of them going several years in succession. Included in that total were vessels from such small fishing villages as Vinalhaven, Sedgwick, Brooksville, and Brooklin, but the greatest number came from the five large ports dotting the bay. Castine, Bucksport, and Orland on the eastern shore provided over 100 vessels, while Belfast and Camden to the westward accounted for most of the balance.[17]

Given the rather careless and incomplete newspaper reporting of the day and the paucity of surviving logbooks, these figures undoubtedly represent a conservative picture of eastern Maine's presence on the banks. Even so, they compare favorably to the more precise figures available for the Massachusetts fishery. Marblehead, center of the state's Grand Banks activity until its post-1840 decline, owned 54 bankers in 1832 and over 100 five years later. Marblehead's successor, the Cape Cod port of Provincetown, maintained 80 to 90 Grand Bankers throughout the 1850s.[18]

With the decline of Marblehead and the temporary absence of Gloucester, eastern Maine and Provincetown vessels exercised a shared monopoly on the banks from the late 1840s to the early 1860s. The port of Gloucester achieved parity with the combined Penobscot ports and then surpassed them upon its eventual re-entry into Grand Banks fishing. That, however, was not until the post–Civil War year of 1869—the greatest year in the town's celebrated fishing history in terms of active vessels and firms—when 120 of Gloucester's 435 commissioned schooners were on the Newfoundland banks.[19] Prior to that development, the Maine fleet had attained a definite, if brief and tenuous, supremacy.

Some sense of the proportions of that fleet can be seen through the eye-witness reports of vessel captains themselves. In the course of a five-month stay on the Grand Banks in 1853, Captain Joseph W. Sylvester of the Castine schooner *Martha Burgess* spoke nineteen other bankers, seventeen of which hailed from the Penobscot region of Maine.[20] These and other eastern schooners landed nearly three-quarters of a million banks cod at Penobscot Bay ports that year.[21] Further evidence of the down-east presence was provided by the Rockport, Massachusetts, schooner *Grampus,* which fell in with no fewer than twenty Maine vessels on the Grand Banks in the summer of 1859, all of them hailing from the three ports of Bucksport, Orland, and Castine.[22] So attractive had the prospect of a banks voyage become, in fact, that by the war years even so unlikely a fishing port as the inland city of Bangor, twenty miles upriver from the ocean, was sending vessels to the cod grounds off Newfoundland.[23]

Following the Civil War, things changed dramatically. By 1880 the formerly all-important Grand Banks fishery was engaging the energies of only a half-dozen Maine communities—Boothbay, Bucksport, Orland, Hancock, Lamoine, and Sedgwick—and some of those were employing only one vessel.[24] By 1888 just twenty-seven Maine schooners continued to fish the Grand Banks. A majority of the state's cod schooners were by this time concentrating on other fishing grounds, notably Western and Quereau banks off the coast of Nova Scotia.[25]

At its peak, the Maine Grand Banks fishery was supreme, but in terms of actual time other fisheries had an equal if not greater hold on the state's fishing population. A case in point was the Labrador cod fishery. Typically, Maine entered the Labrador fishery at a rather late date, at least in comparative terms. The first American schooner to fish Labrador went out from Newburyport, Massachusetts, near the end of the eighteenth century (probably in 1794), several years before the first down-east vessel was sent.[26] Nevertheless, when Maine did enter this fishery, it did so enthusiastically, and hand-lining for cod along the Labrador coast became the state's first, and in some ways its most representative, major sea-fishing enterprise.

The initial attraction of Labrador is not hard to understand. Fishing could be carried on cheaply there, which was always a consideration for Maine fishermen. A Boston merchant, describing the Labrador and Gulf of St. Lawrence fisheries in a letter to John Adams in 1815, noted that participating vessels not belonging to Massachusetts—including a number from the District of Maine—were mostly small sloops of little value.[27] These fisheries, as Samuel Eliot Morison observed, did not require large bankers, expensive outfits, or capitalist backing, and they could be easily prosecuted in small craft that fishermen built and owned on shares. As a result, most Massachusetts cod fishing prior to 1810 was carried on along the Labrador coast or in the Gulf rather than on the Grand Banks.[28] The same considerations of economy drew Maine fishermen to the northern grounds in great numbers up to the Civil War, long after wealthier Massachusetts had turned its fishing interests elsewhere. Eventually, they became specialties of the Maine fleet.

Eastern Maine pioneered on the Labrador grounds. During the early part of the nineteenth century, most of the fishing towns in the eastern half of the state were engaged there to a greater or lesser extent. Mount Desert Island first sent vessels north about the year 1800 or shortly thereafter. Vinalhaven followed suit in 1805, as did Cranberry Isles in 1810, with a 40-ton schooner. Eastport started in 1820, and Deer Isle sent its first two vessels in 1822. By the late 1820s the Passamaquoddy Bay ports were fishing the Labrador coast with increasing frequency, and by the end of the decade Eastport alone had a Labrador fleet of ten vessels.[29]

Most of these eastern vessels were small. The Labrador fleet belonging to the village of Southwest Harbor in the town of Mount Desert (later Tremont) in 1839 consisted of six schooners averaging 58 tons. The smallest of the group, the 35-ton *Four Sisters*, could not have exceeded fifty feet in length.[30] This is in striking contrast to the Grand Bankers sailing out of Penobscot Bay ports during the 1850s, which averaged over 100 tons and nearly seventy-five feet in registered length.[31]

It was the unique nature of the Labrador fishery that allowed participation by such small craft. Unlike the Grand Banks, where vessels anchored on the open ocean and men fished from the decks, the Labrador fishery permitted crews to moor their vessels in relatively safe harbors, unbend their sails, and carry on the actual fishing from small boats near the shore. This technique remained unchanged well into the 1860s.[32] It meant that vessels were seldom out of sight of land and always within reach of a safe refuge during storms. Beginning in June, a skipper merely ranged the coast—

usually the more southerly reaches*—until he found a likely looking inlet. There he remained through the quiescent summer season, until a full fare was taken or until an absence of fish in the immediate vicinity dictated a shift to a more promising but equally protected inlet nearby.[33] Lorenzo Sabine characterized the Labrador cod fishery in the following way in 1853: "It has been preferred to any other on account of its security, and a general certainty of affording a supply of fish."[34]

Western Maine entered the Labrador fishery somewhat later than the eastern part of the state, but with slightly larger vessels. The first known western schooner, the 115-ton *Ruby*, sailed from North Boothbay in 1817 under the command of Captain James Sennett, a Harpswell native. Two years later, this unusually large vessel was accompanied north by the *Union* (84 tons) and the *Dennis* (78 tons), both from the same town, and by an unidentified Westport schooner. About the same time, Wiscasset sent a schooner, but for several years these neighboring communities were the only regional participants. Even after 1825, when other towns like Harpswell became involved, the western Maine Labrador fishery continued to be dominated by the Wiscasset Customs District, encompassing Boothbay.[35]

Although pursued sporadically until the Civil War, the Maine Labrador cod fishery reached its peak in the 1840s. In 1844 greater Boothbay had a Labrador fleet of at least eight schooners, and Westport had four. Mount Desert Island had seven or eight Labrador schooners in 1840.[36] Other exact vessel figures are hard to find, but it is known that during this same general period "a great many went there from . . . the eastern shore about Castine."[37] By the decade of the 1850s, however, Maine's activity along the coast of Labrador had begun to wane. The main reason for this development appears to have been the Labrador fishery's inability to supply the large-sized cod increasingly demanded by the American domestic market, a demand satisfied after 1850 by the growing Grand Banks fishery.[38]

At any rate, there is no record of any vessels going to Labrador from Westport or Boothbay after 1852, and the *Osprey* of Southport, which made a trip in 1856, was practically the last western Maine vessel to fish Labrador

---

*American schooners normally worked the lower third of Labrador proper, from Cape Harrison southward to the Strait of Belle Isle. However, the cod grounds along the connecting eastern shoreline of Quebec, from Belle Isle to the vicinity of Anticosti Island, were considered an extension of the Labrador fishery, and the same inshore fishing methods were applied there. In the 1850s Maine "Labrador" schooners occasionally fished the Quebec inlets between Natashquam and Bradore Bay on their way northward. (Sources: *Goode Report*, sec. 5, 1:146; *Halifax Commission Proceedings*, 1416; *Perley Reports*, 8–9; *ES*, marine list, 21 July 1858.)

waters. Mount Desert Island and vicinity largely abandoned the fishery after 1845, although Cranberry Isles held on through the 1850s. By 1862 Cranberry Isles, too, had sent its last schooner. Lamoine (East Trenton), after dispatching two vessels north in 1850, gave up the Labrador fishery entirely the following year, while Eastport and Lubec both ceased operations in 1858. Among the Penobscot Bay ports, Vinalhaven ended its northern fishery shortly after 1840, and the last trip from Castine was made in 1851 by the schooner *Redwing,* a vessel that subsequently shifted her focus to the Grand Banks. The *Dolphin* of Camden, which returned home in the fall of 1850 with a fare of ninety-two thousand Labrador cod, made the last voyage of the decade from the western side of the bay. For all practical purposes, these vessels terminated the Penobscot region's involvement in the Labrador fishery, although newspaper reports do record a momentary revival in 1860, when two schooners outfitted at Camden for one final spring trip to the northern grounds.[39] By the end of the Civil War, not one Maine fishing port remained in the Labrador fishery, but throughout the thirty or so years preceding the rise of Grand Banking (circa 1850), it formed a cornerstone of the state's fishing industry.

Although less is known about them in detail, there were other cod fisheries besides those of Labrador and the Grand Banks that occupied Maine fishermen during the middle years of the nineteenth century. The ones carried on in the Gulf of St. Lawrence and the Bay of Fundy were among the most significant. Like the Labrador fishery, both began in the early years of the century, but unlike that northern enterprise, both lasted well beyond 1850 and in fact survived until the general post–Civil War collapse of the Maine fisheries.

The Gulf of St. Lawrence, or "the Bay," was most famous as a mackerel-fishing area, but during the 1840s and 1850s at least one hundred American cod-fishing schooners visited there each year.[40] The favorite fishing grounds for these vessels tended to be in the center of the Gulf on Bradelle ("Bradley") and Orphan banks north of Prince Edward Island, around the Magdalen Islands, along the coast of Cape Breton, and off the mouth of Chaleur Bay.[41] The last of these was especially favored by Maine vessels. The Bay of Chaleur, just south of the Gaspé Peninsula, was extensively fished by schooners from Castine, Belfast, Kennebunkport, Trenton, and Boothbay in the late 1850s and early 1860s, and most of the Gulf cod landed at Maine ports during the period came from that vicinity.[42]

In technique, the Gulf cod fishery (sometimes called the "North Bay" fishery to distinguish it from the activity in waters closer to Prince Edward Island) resembled that of the Grand Banks. Crewmen fished from the decks with hand-lines, although the vessels were sometimes allowed to drift rather than anchoring (as was the standard practice on the more exposed Newfoundland grounds).[43] In one respect, however, the Gulf fishery more closely approximated the one carried on off Labrador. Like their Labrador counterparts, the Gulf fishermen were able to utilize small vessels. During late August and early September of 1852, a provincial revenue schooner examining American fishing craft as they entered and left the Bay through the Strait of Canso boarded seven Maine vessels returning from Chaleur with cargoes of cod. The seven—two from Portland, two from Westport, and one each from the ports of Bremen, Waldoboro, and Boothbay—ranged from 36 to 62 tons and averaged 50 tons. Moreover, four of them were small double-enders of the pinky variety.[44]

The use of such small vessels was facilitated by the relatively protected waters traversed in common by Maine's Bay and Labrador fishermen (see map 2). The practice when outward bound was to cross the Gulf of Maine in the direction of Cape Sable, skirt the Nova Scotia shoreline as far as Cape Breton Island, and pass through the Strait of Canso into the Gulf of St. Lawrence, which was in some respects an inland sea. Fishermen bound for Chaleur then proceeded westward across the Gulf, while those heading for Labrador sailed north along the western coastlines of Cape Breton Island and Newfoundland toward the Strait of Belle Isle, bounded most of the time by land, the opposite shore being part of Quebec. That Labrador schooners took this "inland" route to and from their fishing grounds is borne out by the report of the revenue cutter H.M.S. *Daring,* which spoke four homeward-bound Maine Labradormen passing through the Strait of Canso in the late summer of 1852.[45] While not without its own unique hazards, the Gulf of St. Lawrence was not nearly as exposed to the buffeting of heavy seas as the Grand Banks. Neither was it as far from emergency repair and provisioning facilities. Its existence permitted the involvement in fishing of hundreds of small vessels owned by modestly capitalized Gulf and Labrador fishermen for whom Grand Banking on an individual basis was out of the question.

Fragmentary information suggests that Deer Isle was the first Maine fishing port to enter the Gulf cod fishery. It had vessels there as early as 1815. Beyond that, little is known about the origins of this fishery among Maine fishermen except that by the second quarter of the century it appears to have been well under way statewide. Castine was participating by 1825, Monhegan and Bristol sent vessels beginning in 1830, and the down-east village of Addison followed suit in 1835. Portland was involved by 1839, and Boothbay and Southport were both represented sometime prior to 1850.

The Gulf cod grounds were worked on a regular basis by these and other Maine ports until the late 1860s, when the fishery went into eclipse. Deer Isle, which had been the catalyst, ceased its involvement about the time of the Civil War, and by 1880 only the town of Bristol remained active.[46]

The cod fishery in the Bay of Fundy was among the first to engage Maine fishermen. Its proximity and the quality of its fish, which were superior to those found on the Labrador coast,[47] made it a favorite enterprise early on, and small craft from Matinicus Island and the Boothbay region were visiting the Fundy cod grounds shortly after the start of the nineteenth century.[48] The eastern towns, which came to dominate the fishery, entered it almost as soon as they had sufficient population to man vessels. Eastport, at the very mouth of the bay, was fishing there by at least 1820, if not sooner, and nearby places like Lubec, Dennysville, Harrington, Addison, and Jonesboro were all participants by the early 1820s. Among the more distant regional ports, Gouldsboro began sending vessels in 1830, Lamoine in 1835, Hancock in 1845, and Swan's Island sometime before 1850.[49] The likelihood is that schooners from every fishing village in eastern Maine went down to Fundy at one time or another before the Civil War. Penobscot Bay's numerous island communities were well represented by 1839, when Treasury Department estimates placed the total American Fundy cod fleet at between four and five hundred vessels.[50] Most of these, undoubtedly, were from ports in eastern Maine.

The type of craft utilized suggests the character of the Bay of Fundy fishery. Lorenzo Sabine wrote of this enterprise that "the vessels which are employed in it, though of greater variety, are neither so large nor so valuable as those which are required for the more hazardous and distant fishing grounds; and, unlike these, it allows of the use of sail-boats of the smallest size." * The larger Fundy vessels, he reported, worked on the outer grounds of the bay, while the numerous smaller boats, two hundred of which could occasionally be seen from Eastport in the early 1850s, fished close to the shoreline among the channels and ledges.[51]

Like the Gulf of St. Lawrence and Labrador cod fisheries, then, the Bay of Fundy fishery was one of those typical early Maine pursuits that could be

---

*Among the Maine fleet of vessels working Grand Manan Bank and other nearby Fundy grounds in 1824 were four schooners from the town of Addison, with an estimated average value of just over $600. The largest of these, the 41-ton *William*, carried a crew of only four, including the captain. The others were all under 30 tons. Fifteen years later, in 1839, Vinalhaven's Fundy fishery was being pursued in schooners of less than 40 tons with crews of no more than four or five fishermen. (Source: *Hague Arbitration Proceedings*, 2: 342, 347, 358, 360–61, 377, 419–20, 430–31.)

effectively followed in small vessels. It was simple geography that made this possible. All of the Maine ports east of the Penobscot were within one hundred miles of the Fundy cod grounds, and those in the Passamaquoddy region were close enough to engage in fishing on a daily or weekly basis. As a result, the cod season began earlier in the Bay of Fundy than elsewhere and was carried on until later in the year.[52] Being close to home and in relatively protected waters, even small-boat fishermen could stretch their season beyond the normal summer months. An early spring departure was less discomforting when the destination was Fundy Bay rather than more northerly seas. Similarly, the long, open-water passage home in stormy late-fall weather, an experience common to banks fishermen, was something with which Fundy fishermen did not have to contend.

Two problems of a less serious nature did concern cod fishermen in the Bay of Fundy, however, and gave the fishery there a distinctive flavor. One was the great depth of water and rise of tide, which necessitated much longer than average hand-lines. The other was the strength of the water currents when that tide rushed in and out. This feature forced the smaller inshore craft to fish at the "slack tide" period just before high and low water, when the sea was less turbulent.[53] Farther out in the bay, it meant that the large vessels of necessity fished while drifting, since the tidal current would not permit them to anchor. Drift fishing to preserve cables and anchors in turn required crew members to fish only on the windward side of the vessel, which effectively reduced the number of men working at any one time. To fish over both rails, as was the standard practice in the Gulf and on the Grand Banks, would cause one set of lines to run under the bottom of the moving schooner from the leeward side, causing possible entanglement and loss.[54]

These minor problems did not cancel out the obvious logistical advantages of the Bay of Fundy fishery, and it continued in volume until the end of the Civil War. Numerous eastern schooners went there during and immediately preceding the war years from such Hancock County towns as Trenton, Lamoine, Sullivan, and Eden (Bar Harbor).[55] The general postwar malaise, however, brought an end to this fishery, as it did to the cod fishery in the Gulf of St. Lawrence. By 1877 barely a dozen eastern Maine vessels, most of them from Lubec, were still fishing on Grand Manan Bank, the principal offshore Fundy cod ground.[56]

Less commonly frequented, but still important, was the cod-fishing region around the southwestern tip of Nova Scotia and its adjoining coastline. This area, which encompassed the popular Seal Island ground, constituted the Cape Sable and "Cape Shore" cod fishery. Strictly speaking, these were two separate fisheries, the Cape Shore referring more specifically to the south coast of Nova Scotia between Cape Sable itself and the old privateer port of Liverpool, about halfway to Halifax.[57] In practice, however, they overlapped and were indistinguishable one from the other.

Since this fishery was comparatively close at hand, it drew Maine's attention at an early date. A considerable fleet from the down-east coast was fishing the Seal Island ground in the first years of the nineteenth century.[58] Exact or approximate dates for the entry of individual Maine ports into the Cape fishery, as far as they are known, include Boothbay around 1800, Vinalhaven in 1817, Woolwich and Wiscasset in 1822, York in 1823, and Southport shortly before 1825. Portland vessels were also active in the area by the mid-1840s. The Cape fishery had a particular appeal for western towns, an attraction that transcended the Civil War in the case of Southport, which sent vessels there as late as 1880.[59] Generally, however, the Cape fishery was of secondary importance, especially after the larger cod grounds on neighboring Western and Quereau banks began to be worked intensively around mid-century.

Western (or Sable Island) Bank and Quereau Bank* (Banquereau to the French fishermen) were located east of Cape Sable, about one hundred miles off the southeastern shore of Nova Scotia and the island of Cape Breton (see map 2). They were side by side, close enough together nearly to constitute one large bank, Banquereau being the more easterly of the two.[60] Exposed and located a considerable distance from the New England coast, these banks, like those off Newfoundland, were late to be visited by Maine vessels. The earliest date at which Maine fishermen are supposed to have been active there was about 1825.[61] The first specific references that can be documented were in 1839 and 1844, when the *Eliza* of Portland and the *Tasco* of Boothbay made respective voyages to Western Bank, and in 1847, when two Castine schooners, the *Patapsco* and the *George Washington,* were reported fishing on Quereau.[62]

For the most part, though, the Western and Quereau banks cod fisheries were a post-1850 phenomenon. Hancock, Bristol, and Bremen entered the Western Bank fishery in 1852, 1854, and 1860, respectively.[63] The first recorded instance of Belfast and Vinalhaven vessels going there was in 1851,

---

*There is some confusion about nomenclature with regard to these banks. On occasion both were lumped together as the "Western Banks" to distinguish them from the more easterly Grand Banks. More often, Sable Island Bank (or Western Bank proper) and smaller nearby grounds, such as La Have Bank, were referred to collectively as the Western Banks. Most historical references, however, distinguished clearly between the two large adjoining banks off Nova Scotia and specifically labelled the more westerly one around Sable Island as *the* Western Bank.

while Westport, Southport, and Kennebunkport appear to have started in the middle 1850s. By the end of the decade, Bucksport and Castine were also active on the Sable Island ground.[64] The time frame for the Quereau Bank fishery was roughly the same. East Trenton (Lamoine), Belfast, and Vinalhaven all had schooners on Banquereau by 1851, but, so far as the record indicates, not before that time. The first known Boothbay vessel to fish Quereau Bank went there in 1852. The Penobscot District ports of Brooklin and Bucksport seem to have sent their first vessels in 1853 and 1854, followed in short order by Kennebunk (1855), Portland (1856), Camden (1858), and Tremont (1858).[65]

Unimportant at first, Western and Quereau banks together became, with the passage of time, one of Maine's major cod grounds, second only to the Grand Banks in overall significance. It was on Quereau, in 1886, that the Lamoine three-master *Henry S. Woodruff* landed the largest single fare of cod (4,500 quintals) taken by a Maine schooner in the course of the nineteenth century.[66] The *Woodruff* was a large vessel, over two hundred tons according to the register, and the two Western banks constituted, like the Grand Banks, an offshore, large-vessel fishery.[67] This accounts for their rather late exploitation by Maine fishing ports, a development that coincided roughly with that of the Newfoundland banks themselves.

The two fisheries were similar in many ways, differing really in only one respect, the quality of the catch. The Grand Bank cod were a superior stock, larger and fatter than those caught on Western Bank, which one fisherman described as thin and watery by comparison.[68] This perhaps explains the preference of Maine cod fishermen for Grand Banking—at least through the 1850s and 1860s. With the conspicuous exception of Belfast, the major fishing ports of eastern Maine were reluctant to work the Nova Scotia banks during the antebellum period. Castine, for instance, which sent numerous vessels to the Grand Banks each year during the 1850s—twenty-one in 1853—is only known to have had two schooners in the Western Bank fishery prior to 1860.[69]

The primary reason for this pattern was that the great distance to the Grand Banks made the fishery there an exclusive occupation, one that, unlike the fishery off Nova Scotia, could not be easily combined with other interests. The sailing time to and from the Grand Banks was one to two weeks, while Western and Quereau banks, only half as far, could be reached in less than a week's time. The *Mentora* of Castine, which was nine days making her fishing grounds on the western edge of Grand Bank in May 1852, passed over Western Bank on her fourth day out. If adverse winds or rough weather became factors, the transit could be even longer. The

Martha Burgess, also out of Castine, needed just eight days to reach the Newfoundland banks in 1853, but she was seventeen storm-racked days in returning.[70]

The average Grand Banks trip lasted three to five months, depending on the weather and the willingness of the cod to take the hook, and that did not include the considerable time needed for outfitting. Vessels ordinarily left in May and stayed on the grounds until September or October. Some of the voyages from Castine recorded in 1854 were typical. The schooner *Albion* left for the Grand Banks on May 17 of that year and returned on October 28, an odyssey of five months and eleven days. The *Mentora,* a schooner with a history of fast trips, left on May 30 and returned on September 7, just over three months later. The *Glendower, Fleet,* and *Redwing* all departed Castine during the third week of May and were back in port by mid-September, making similar voyages of four months each.[71]

These trips contrasted sharply in duration with those being made to Western Bank by Belfast fishermen around the same time. The schooners *Columbia, Cherub,* and *Nautilus,* for example, made two-month excursions to Western Bank in 1854, returning around the first of July in plenty of time to refit for other fisheries. The *Columbia* and the *Nautilus* did just that, proceeding north to the Gulf of St. Lawrence mackerel grounds for the balance of the summer-fall season.[72] Quicker trips than these were made to the Nova Scotia banks on occasion. The aforementioned *Columbia* got a fare of cod in three weeks on Western Bank in March 1853 and was able to complete two trips—one to Banquereau—within the space of three months in 1851.[73] The *Northern Chief* of Vinalhaven made a four-week journey to Western Bank in 1865, leaving in late March and returning in late April.[74] These were unusually fast voyages, but seldom did Western and Quereau bankers of the period stay out longer than eight weeks, and that meant landing a fare in about half the time taken by contemporary Grand Bankers.

The flexibility permitted by these fisheries was demonstrated by the activities of the *S. S. Lewis,* another Belfast schooner, in the season of 1853. The *Lewis* arrived home on June 15 of that year after a spring trip to Western Bank. She quickly disposed of her catch and headed back to the cod-fishing grounds, spending six weeks or so on Brown's Bank, one of the inner banks near Cape Sable. Returning in early August, the *Lewis* refitted for a one-month mackerel cruise that ended on September 7. She then spent the remainder of the fall shore-fishing close to home.[75]

Unlike Belfast, the preponderance of eastern ports—those concerned with Grand Banking—simply did not have the time to greatly diversify their fisheries, even had they wished to do so. Some of the smaller, less important vessels might be sent to various other fisheries, but the major vessels, once committed to the Grand Banks, could do little else during a given season. The result was that the early Western and Quereau banks cod fisheries functioned essentially as an added sideline for the minority of Maine ports— mostly in the western part of the state—interested primarily in mackerel fishing. The area around Boothbay, like Belfast, combined these two activities by fishing Nova Scotia waters for cod in the spring and sending its vessels north to the Gulf of St. Lawrence for mackerel in the summer.[76] The practice at Southport in the mid-1850s was to make one short banks trip in the spring, followed by two mackerel voyages to the Magdalen Islands region of the Gulf beginning sometime in early July.[77] For these and a few other Maine ports, the Nova Scotia banks provided an excellent opportunity to supplement their chief source of income and, at the same time, helped to qualify their vessels for bounty money—something mackerel fishing alone could not accomplish.

The Western and Quereau fisheries unquestionably took a back seat to the Grand Banks until the end of the Civil War, but during the last years of the deep-sea cod fishery they actually surpassed their Newfoundland counterpart in importance. The postwar decline of the eastern ports, which moved the center of the Maine industry westward, favored the less distant Nova Scotia banks. Then, too, Portland, Southport, and Boothbay, the towns that came to the fore after 1865, had always shown a marked predilection for the Western Bank fishery as opposed to Grand Banking. Of Boothbay's industry, one contemporary observer wrote, "The Grand Bank fisheries have never been extensively prosecuted."[78] Newspaper returns bear this out. There is no record of a Boothbay vessel visiting the Grand Banks until 1865, while as many as thirty-three schooners left there for Western Bank during one spring season in the late 1850s.[79] Neighboring Southport is not known to have ever sent vessels Grand Banking, but it did send vessels to Western Bank continuously after 1825.[80] Likewise, Portland had no schooners on the Newfoundland banks during the 1850s, but fishermen from that city were on Western Bank at least as early as 1857.[81]

By the 1880s, almost all the recorded trips being made to Western Bank were by schooners from Portland and the Boothbay region, while the two remaining eastern ports of significance, Bucksport and Lamoine, concentrated on the Grand Banks and, to a lesser degree, Banquereau.[82] In March of 1887, fourteen cod-fishing schooners started for Western Bank from Boothbay and Southport, a considerable number at that late date and something of an Indian summer revival.[83] The following year, the vessels of Maine's Western and Quereau banks fleet outnumbered the state's remaining Grand Bankers, and nearly all of them (twenty-nine out of thirty-three) were based in Portland or greater Boothbay. The active Grand Banks fleet had by that time been reduced numerically to a couple of dozen schooners operating out of Hancock County.[84] Ironically, as Maine's deep-sea cod fishery made its last stand during the twilight years of the nineteenth century, it was on the fertile grounds off Nova Scotia, not the historic banks of Newfoundland, that the quiet drama was largely played out.

The Mackerel Fisheries

Despite the overwhelming emphasis on cod in the fisheries of Maine, there were other species sought by the state's fishermen. Chief among them was mackerel. Although the mackerel fishery was more expensive and not as predictable as the cod fishery, it did have attractive features that consistently drew a modest percentage of the Maine offshore fleet. For one thing, it was less arduous than cod banking, nearly qualifying at times as a pleasant summer pastime and being exciting enough on occasion to appeal to the sporting instincts of certain fishermen. For another, it was (as recounted earlier) a highly remunerative vocation, assuming that one's luck held and the elusive mackerel could be found. An experienced observer of the Gloucester scene summed up the characteristics of this unique fishery quite succinctly in 1856. "It is much easier than cod fishing," he said, "though perhaps less certain in its results."[85] This very uncertainty shaped the way the fishery was carried on in Maine.

Because of its fitful nature, mackerel catching was rarely undertaken as a sole pursuit in the prewar bounty days, and it was only sometimes pursued exclusively during later years, even with the advantages of more sophisticated technology. Normally, it was sandwiched between cod-fishing trips. In the 1830s Portland vessels would fish for cod until the mackerel appeared on the coast in late spring or early summer. They would then go mackerel hooking during the height of the season and return to cod banking in the fall, in order to complete the requisite four months needed to qualify for the bounty allowance.[86] Not even the most avid mackerel port could resist the security of a guaranteed subsidy. A half-century later, although the absence of a cod bounty had begun to encourage season-long mackereling by a considerable number of vessels, much of the Maine fleet retained its traditional practice of ground fishing on Western Bank in the spring and turning to mackerel fishing in the summer months.[87] Specific data for the year 1880 indicates that at that time forty-two of Maine's ninety-five large mackerel vessels—nearly half—were still fishing for cod or other species during part of the year. For Portland, the figure was thirteen out of a fleet of thirty schooners.[88]

Altogether, there were three major mackerel fisheries of interest to Maine fishermen: the Gulf of St. Lawrence fishery and the so-called northern and southern fisheries. The first-named was by far the most important, especially in the years before 1865. The mackerel season in the Gulf began in late spring and ran until the middle of the fall. Most activity was concentrated in the months between June, when the migrating mackerel first appeared in the Bay, and October, when they departed. The fishery really began in earnest, however, during the first two weeks of July, which was the spawning period.[89]

The areas fished by Gulf mackerelmen were, more or less, the same as those worked by cod-fishing schooners. The popular grounds were the waters around Prince Edward Island (especially the northern shore of the island, known as "the bend"), the region in and around Chaleur Bay, Bradelle and Orphan banks, Cape Gaspé and vicinity, the northwest shore of Cape Breton Island, the New Brunswick coastline near Miramichi Bay, and the waters surrounding the Magdalen Islands.[90] Of these locales, Chaleur Bay was especially favored by Maine mackerel vessels. Scattered reports exist of a few Portland, Belfast, Deer Isle, and Georgetown schooners getting fares elsewhere in the 1850s and 1860s, notably on Bradelle and Orphan banks, and eastward from the Magdalens and the bend of Prince Edward Island to the Cape Breton shore. As newspaper returns verify, however, the emphasis was on the Chaleur fishery, particularly after the mid-1850s.[91]

Unsurprisingly, it was Massachusetts, the great mackerel-fishing state, that initiated the American Gulf fishery. The Gloucester schooner *Mariner* was the first to go mackereling there, in 1830.[92] Maine ports were not far behind, however. Portland and Freeport began to tap the rich spawning grounds of the Bay in 1832. Deer Isle followed in 1834, and Belfast shortly after 1835. Eastport schooners were also there by 1835, if not earlier, and in 1837, the pinky *Olinda* of Southport became the first vessel to go from the Boothbay region.[93]

Within a few years, great numbers of hook-and-line vessels from Maine and Massachusetts were visiting the Gulf for mackerel. A Quebec fisherman reportedly saw as many as 65 American vessels fishing at one time in Gaspé Bay during the early 1850s, and a resident of Tignish on the northwest tip of Prince Edward Island witnessed up to 200 American mackerel schooners working offshore nearby on several occasions in the 1860s.[94] The greatest number of New England mackerelmen ever reported in the Bay in any one season was the estimated 1,000 vessels said to have been there in 1851.[95] This was unverified by firsthand observation and may have been apocryphal. Various eyewitness accounts of fishermen who were actually on the scene placed the total figure during the 1850–1870 period at between 400 and 700 vessels annually. Whatever its exact size, the Gulf fleet was responsible for approximately 50 percent of all the mackerel taken by United States fishermen during the decade of the 1860s.[96]

Although Maine's contribution was considerable, there is no doubt that the majority of the mackerel vessels fishing in the Gulf of St. Lawrence were from Massachusetts. Maine mackerel schooners appear to have been in the Gulf fishery in approximately the same proportion as their numerical presence in the American mackerel fleet as a whole. Comprehensive figures are lacking, but a sample cross-section of the Gulf fleet, based on records of Canadian fisheries patrol vessels, is available for 1852. Between July 4 and November 30 of that year, provincial government vessels, enforcing legal restrictions on fishing in Canadian territorial waters, boarded and examined over 200 American schooners entering and leaving the Gulf in the vicinity of Port Hood, Nova Scotia. Out of 198 identified in the records by port of origin, 49 (25 percent) were from Maine and 138 (70 percent) from Massachusetts, the majority of the latter hailing from Gloucester. Fewer than half of the schooners in question were categorized as to fishing preference, but three-quarters of those (including two-thirds of the ones from Maine) were mackerel catchers.[97] A speculative estimate, therefore, is that roughly a quarter of the entire Gulf mackerel fleet of 1852 hailed from Maine. This approximates the state's share of the total United States mackerel fleet at that time—15,079 out of 72,546 tons, or about 21 percent.[98]

There were certain distinguishing characteristics, peculiarities perhaps, associated with the mackerel fishery in the Gulf of St. Lawrence. One was that the vessels engaged in it did not always fish exclusively for mackerel. Occasionally, like the schooners *Eagle* of East Machias in 1848 and *President* of Belfast in 1859, they combined mackerel hooking with cod fishing, taking whatever was immediately available and returning home with a mixed catch.[99] This may have been a way to deceive customs officials and collect the cod bounty for what was essentially a mackerel voyage, or it may simply have been an expedient forced upon fishermen anxious, in trying circumstances, to return home with a full hold. At any rate, it was a mode of operation well adapted to the Bay, where the cod and mackerel grounds were not only in close proximity but often identical.

More common than mixed fishing was the practice of pursuing both cod and mackerel in the Gulf, but on separate voyages. Rather than working the inner or Western Banks in the spring season, some vessels were in the habit of prefacing their summer-to-fall Gulf mackerel trip with a visit to the same waters for cod. Portland schooners were notable for their tendency to undertake successive cod and mackerel voyages to the Gulf. The *Maria* of that city spent three months in early 1857 hand-lining for cod around Cape Breton and the Magdalens and off the mouth of Chaleur Bay. After returning to Portland to unload and refit, she headed back to the Gulf to complete the season mackereling near the bend of Prince Edward Island. The Portland schooner *Ianthe* followed the same procedure in 1863.[100]

Multiple trips to the Gulf of St. Lawrence were confined for the most part to successive mackerel voyages, however. More than one mackerel trip a year was not at all unusual in the Gulf fishery, especially from ports where mackereling was a specialty. Deer Isle's large schooners almost always went north twice each season between June and November, as did the Southport fleet beginning in July.[101] Mackerel fishing was particularly adapted to this practice because of the short time in which a fare could ordinarily be obtained. The rapidity with which mackerel could be taken once they struck, together with the considerable distance fishermen travelled to reach the grounds, resulted in one of the oddities of the Gulf mackerel fishery, namely that vessels often spent more time in transit than they did fishing. The *Julia Franklin* of Georgetown, for example, got 360 barrels (a full fare) in ten days of fishing in 1856 but was fourteen days in reaching the Gulf and returning—a total round trip of twenty-four days.[102] The voyage was extraordinarily fast, but it was not an isolated case. In 1850 the clipper schooner *E. W. Merchant* of Gloucester made a successful fall mackerel trip to Chaleur Bay and back in twenty-seven days,[103] and in 1864 the *Archer* of Southport returned from a one-month summer trip there—the fastest ever made from Southport in the Gulf hand-line mackerel fishery—with a full load of 300 barrels, all taken within the space of ten days.[104] Even "slow" trips to the Gulf, such as the seven-week excursion of the Portland mackerelman *W. H. Rogers* in 1862,[105] were fast compared to most other fisheries.

The ability to get a catch in minimal time encouraged multiple voyages in the Gulf mackerel fishery, making it unique in that respect among the pre–Civil War salt fisheries. This, in turn, put an added premium on speed, already a key ingredient in mackereling because of the fishing techniques involved. Time, the dividend of fast sailing, was important for two reasons. First, a quick trip meant the opportunity to return to the grounds for a second or even third visit during the height of the season and thereby maximize the vessel's stock for the year. Goode and Collins, early chroniclers of the mackerel fishery, described the demands imposed by the multiple-voyage aspect of Gulf mackereling: "The fish being salted, the homeward passage was usually performed in a leisurely manner, unless indeed the return was made during the fishing season, and the skipper expected to make another trip, in which case the utmost expedition was used, and rapid passages were made."[106] Hard driving was no small part of a fishery characterized by fluctuating markets, stiff competition, and a limited season. Authorities agreed that two or three weeks was the usual time needed to sail home, pack out, refit, and return to the Gulf, but that it had been done in ten days on occasion.[107] The difference could be critical and no doubt separated the sail-carriers and superior vessels from the rest of the fleet.

The desire to travel to and from the grounds with maximum dispatch was reinforced by the need to preserve the catch. Salted mackerel required more care than salted cod and was subject to deterioration even in the pickled state. As a Canadian fish dealer of the time pointed out, "The fish . . . get worse by being kept in the hold of a vessel, as they have to be rehandled and repickled; they lose in weight, don't look so well, and they weigh less by being kept on board, and do not bring such good prices."[108]

The time element so crucial in the Gulf mackerel fishery eventually gave rise to the phenomenon of "transshipment," a practice unique to this branch of the industry. Transshipment was simply the process of landing the season's first mackerel catch at a convenient port on Prince Edward Island, or along the Strait of Canso, and sending it home by freighter or steamer. Thus unburdened, the mackerel schooner could refit at the same port and return immediately to the nearby grounds for another fare, thereby saving days or weeks normally spent in transit. Such a system had the added advantage of allowing vessel captains to watch the fluctuating mackerel market back home, particularly in later years when communications had improved, and to ship their catch accordingly. Observed one Prince Edward Island fish dealer, "They can send the fish in time to get good prices when the prices are up. They can get the fish in quicker by steam than if they took them on themselves."[109]

It was estimated during the 1870s that the right to transship cargoes was worth several hundred dollars yearly to American fishing vessels taking advantage of it.[110] In some instances, it enabled mackerelmen to get as many as three or four fares in a single season.[111] Maine schooners, as a rule, did not indulge in that kind of mass-production mackereling, generally being content with making one or two fares in a year. An exceptional case, however, does illustrate what could be accomplished with maximal use of transshipment. The *Abden Keene* of Bremen arrived in the Gulf on July 31, 1874, intent on catching mackerel. Despite the lateness of the season, this vessel got three fares totalling nearly five hundred barrels over the ensuing two and one-half months, of which two were landed at Port Mulgrave, Nova Scotia, for advance shipment. All but a hundred barrels of her catch had preceded the *Keene* by at least a month when she passed through the Strait of Canso homeward bound on October 19.[112]

Transshipment was not originally permitted by provincial authorities. It was, in fact, a product of the Reciprocity Treaty of 1854 between the United States and Canada, which provided (along with mutual free trade) American access to the inshore waters and coasts of the Maritimes for fishing purposes, with landing privileges included.[113] The Reciprocity Treaty terminated in 1866 but was succeeded by the 1871 Treaty of Washington (effective 1873–1885), which re-established reciprocal trade relations within the fisheries sphere and reinstituted the American rights of inshore fishing and landing for bait, supplies, and the transferring of cargoes.[114] During the interval between the treaties, as before Reciprocity, transshipment was not legally available as an option for American mackerelmen. However, from 1855 to 1865 and again from 1873 to 1885, it served as a ready alternative to multiple voyages.

Maine fishermen used the opportunity to transship from the very beginning. In 1855, the first year of Reciprocity, the schooner *Morning Star* of North Haven, having arrived too late in the season for two round trips, forwarded her initial fare of 250 barrels of Bay mackerel from Canso, Nova Scotia. The vessel—possibly the first from Maine to use this expedient—then refitted, returned to the Gulf, and eventually sailed home with another 310 barrels.[115] There are other recorded instances of Maine schooners transshipping during the 1850s. William A. Dickey, a Belfast fisherman, recalled that on his first mackerel trip to the Gulf aboard a vessel from that port, in 1858, the first of two fares taken was landed at Cascumpec, Prince Edward Island, and shipped to Belfast by way of a coastal freighter.[116]

In later years, rail transportation succeeded sailing vessels and steamships as the chief mode of transshipment. The building of a rail line connecting Shediac, New Brunswick (across the Northumberland Strait from Prince Edward Island) to the eastern Maine border and the New England rail network beyond was completed in 1869.[117] This convenient connection, with its railhead just a few miles from the principal transshipment ports of the Gulf, came into operation in time to serve as a major conduit for pickled mackerel under the second phase of fisheries reciprocity beginning in 1873. By the middle 1870s the transshipment of salt fish caught in the Gulf by American fishermen had become one of the road's primary uses.[118] Much of that catch was destined for western Maine. In August 1878 the *Eastern*

Argus, chief newspaper of the state's largest city and most important mackerel port, reported that "the Portland fishing fleet in Bay Chaleur are doing well, some of them having taken from 300 to 400 barrels of mackerel, which they are sending home via Shediac and the Intercolonial Railroad, so as to get another fare."[119]

The peak period for mackereling in the Gulf of St. Lawrence was between 1850 and 1870. By the late 1860s the fishery was already in decline.* In 1866, 454 American vessels visited the mackerel grounds of the Gulf, a substantial figure but well below previous highs. A year later, the number had dropped to 295, about one-quarter of that total from Maine.[120] Although the fishery persisted throughout the decade of the 1870s and into the 1880s, the number of vessels in the United States fleet never again exceeded 300 and, despite a brief resurgence in 1878, fell to less than 100 sail within a few years.[121]

Maine continued to send vessels during this period of gradual curtailment. The highliner of the 240-vessel Chaleur fleet of 1870 was the *Princess* of Bucksport, with five hundred barrels.[122] As late as 1878, 65 Maine schooners went north to the Bay for mackerel, a momentary reminder of the years when perhaps as many as 200 did so.[123] Nevertheless, except to a small minority of about a dozen Maine ports—Portland and Boothbay prominent among them—the Gulf mackerel fishery ceased to be important after 1865. In 1874, a typical year of the post–Civil War era, Maine's Gulf mackerel fleet consisted of just 39 schooners, half of them from Portland and Boothbay, and their combined catch of 11,849 barrels constituted slightly more than 18 percent of the American total for that year.[124] By 1880 only 10 Maine schooners remained in the Gulf of St. Lawrence fishery, and all but 2 spent a considerable part of the mackerel season fishing in American waters.[125]

The termination of the Gulf mackerel fishery did not mean the end of mackerel fishing by Maine vessels. Rather, it signified a reorientation, a shift to other fishing grounds closer to home. The ten schooners that went north in 1880 represented only a fraction of the nearly one hundred large mackerel catchers remaining in the Maine fleet. Two-thirds of that fleet fished exclusively in the Gulf of Maine in 1880, and most of the remainder worked the American shore south of Cape Cod.[126] The former group were part of the so-called northern fleet, named to distinguish it from the American mackerel fleet that congregated off the coasts of New Jersey and Delaware in the spring of the year.[127]

---

*The chief contemporary reason advanced for this decline was the development of seine fishing, which was well adapted to the American shore but could not be carried on successfully in the Gulf because of the shallow waters and rough bottom encountered there. (Source: *Halifax Commission Proceedings,* 3095–96, 3100–3101, 3185, 3188; see also chapter 6.)

The gradually changing focus of the Maine mackerel fleet from the Gulf of St. Lawrence to its own home waters following the Civil War was part of a broad trend not limited to Maine vessels alone. The massive Gloucester fleet formerly in the Bay was largely working the United States coast by the 1870s. Of Gloucester's 175 mackerelmen in 1875, 117 fished only along the American shore.[128] The northern fishery occupied most of them. It was estimated in the 1870s that 75 percent of the mackerel taken by American schooners was being taken along the coast of Maine,[129] and by the early 1880s authorities were calling the mackerel fishery there the most important in the world.[130]

The northern mackerel-fishing grounds extended the entire length of the Gulf of Maine, from Massachusetts Bay to the Bay of Fundy, and out to sixty miles seaward from the coast. Within these confines, the most favored areas were around Cashe's Ledge, the Isles of Shoals, Seguin and Boone islands, Cape Elizabeth, Monhegan, Matinicus Rock, and Mount Desert Rock. In addition, the Bay of Fundy north of Grand Manan was a prime region for some years, though less so as time progressed. The season along this portion of the coast ran from June to November, with the peak activity coming in the summer months of July and August.[131]

Although its prominence after 1870 suggests that the northern or "New England shore" mackerel fishery was a peculiarly post–Civil War phenomenon, this was not actually the case. The shrinkage of the Gulf of St. Lawrence fleet magnified the importance of the already-existing fisheries carried on along the American coast and created the illusion of sudden growth. There was some transference of vessels from one fishery to another, of course, but basically the northern fishery just received added attention after the war years. It had always been there, albeit overshadowed. In July of 1849, for instance, 200 mackerel schooners were reported working off the coast of Maine,[132] and on a September day in 1853 no fewer than 327 mackerelmen were sighted from the Portland Observatory, following the migrating schools northward.[133] Among the crewmen of the 1849 fleet was young Joseph W. Collins of Islesboro, who later rose to prominence in American fishing circles both as a noted vessel captain and as a crusading government official with the United States Fish Commission. Collins, then a ten-year-old novice, got his start that year aboard a Maine pinky jigging for mackerel off Mount Desert Rock.[134]

The antecedents of the northern mackerel fishery are obscure, and exactly when Maine fishermen entered it is uncertain. It is known that the first salt-mackerel voyage undertaken by an American vessel was a trip to Cashe's Ledge in the outer Gulf of Maine by a Gloucester schooner in 1818. It is further known that salt mackereling along the American shore was a substantial

business by 1820–1821 and that Gloucester had a fleet of ten pinkies engaged in it during the latter year.[135] Very probably, the random taking of
mackerel from inshore waters for immediate consumption in the fresh state
had gone on from time immemorial along the Maine coast. As an organized vessel fishery, however, mackereling in the region predated the Gulf
of St. Lawrence fishery by about a decade. Maine began to participate sometime in the 1820s, as nearly as can be determined. In 1830, two years before
any of its vessels ventured north to the Gulf, the state had a mackerel fleet
of ten thousand tons.[136] These vessels, it is clear, were among those working the shores of New England.

In technique and general mode of operation, the northern fishery differed little from that carried on in the Bay. Since the seasons of the two
fisheries coincided, it served as an alternative to fishing in the Gulf. The
reminiscences of a Belfast fisherman document, in the case of one vessel,
the practice of following the usual spring trip to Western or Quereau Bank
with one or more mackerel cruises along the Maine coast. The schooner
in question went in the northern fishery each summer from 1860 to 1865,
fishing exclusively between Mount Desert Rock and Cape Cod.[137] Other
Belfast mackerelmen went into Fundy Bay for fares. The schooners *S. M.
Libbey, Frederick,* and *A. M. Banks* of that port fished St. Mary's Bay, on the
Nova Scotia side of Fundy, in the fall of 1859.[138] By that date, St. Mary's was
rarely visited by Maine schooners, but between 1835 and 1850 it was a major
haunt of the northern fleet.[139]

In addition to providing an option for mackerel fishermen who chose
not to make the long trip to the Gulf of St. Lawrence at the end of the
spring cod-fishing season, the mackerel fishery of the New England shore
was useful in that it could substitute for a second trip to those more northern grounds, if necessary. This function was probably important to Maine
fishermen not blessed with especially fast vessels or, in the latter period, not
able to afford the privilege of transshipping their cargoes. Evidence of such
a recourse exists in the case of the schooner *Porpoise* of Isle au Haut, which
made a single summer trip to the Gulf in 1837 and spent the balance of the
season (until the first of November) mackerel hooking on the United States
coast.[140] It appears likely that the northern fishery functioned to some degree as an outlet for poorer fishermen from the more remote outports.
Otherwise, logic dictated that the Bay, whose mackerel were said to be
larger than those found on the American shore,[141] was the place to go for
the best catch.

The annual arrival of the first migrating schools of mackerel off Cape
Cod in mid-May, an occurrence that heralded the beginning of the north-

ern fishery, signaled the approaching season's end for the other of the two American shore mackerel fisheries, the southern or "southern spring" fishery. The southern fishery differed from that carried on in the Gulf of Maine essentially in geographical and chronological terms. The fish themselves were part of the same northward-moving schools that appeared off Cape Hatteras in early spring and worked their way up the American coast over the ensuing months.[142] Cape Cod served as the unofficial dividing line between the northern and southern fisheries, and the month of June as the seasonal demarcation.

Specifically, the fishing grounds of the southern fishery extended twenty to fifty miles offshore from the Virginia Capes to the Nantucket Shoals, except near New Jersey and Long Island, where the mackerel struck to within one or two miles of the coastline. The season stretched from late March to early June, and the fishery reached its height about the beginning of May.[143] The records of several Maine vessels of the 1870s indicate that at that time the first catches of the southern fleet were ordinarily made in mid-April in the vicinity of Cape May, New Jersey.[144]

The southern spring mackerel fishery began in 1817, when the schooner *Defiance* of Rockport, Massachusetts, went south as far as Cape May and returned with sixty barrels of mackerel. Between 1820 and 1824 numerous Gloucester vessels also became involved, operating off New York and marketing their first fares there.[145] The earliest mention of activity by Maine vessels concerned the successful trip of a Portland schooner in 1838.[146] This appears to have been an isolated incident, since no records exist of any other Maine mackerelmen going until the 1850s, when the fishermen of Georgetown sent some of their schooners. The first of these was the *Queen of the West,* which went south for several weeks in May of 1851. A number of other Georgetown schooners followed suit over the next two years.[147] Aside from this singular island port, however, there was little down-east interest expressed in the southern fishery during the antebellum period. A Deer Isle schooner, the *North Bend,* was reported at Newport, Rhode Island, in May 1857, bound for the mackerel grounds, and North Haven was sending a few vessels south by the spring of 1861.[148] For the most part, though, the southern mackerel fishery, unlike its northern counterpart, was a development of the post–Civil War era—at least as far as the state of Maine was concerned. The important mackerel ports of Boothbay and Southport did not send their first vessels until 1867–1868.[149]

Another difference between Maine's northern and southern fisheries was that while the former remained in large measure a salt fishery, the latter, in its postwar phase, evolved gradually into a fresh fishery. The primary catalyst

for this development was the presence of the vast, urban New York consumer market located within a few short miles of the best southern fishery
grounds. Throughout the 1850s and 1860s, New York's fresh-mackerel demands were adequately served by hook-and-line well-smacks* from Connecticut, and the few Maine and Massachusetts vessels in the southern fishery
salted their catch and carried it home. Beginning around 1870 this pattern
changed, and schooners from northern New England ports, equipped with
improved gear for faster fishing and ice to preserve the catch, began to run
their fares into the city. Initially, the practice was to market the first of the
season's catches as fresh fish and salt the rest, but during the mid-1870s some
vessels began fresh fishing for the New York market exclusively. By the 1880s
fresh fishing was virtually universal in the southern fleet.[150]

In addition to icing its catch—something the northern vessels also practiced, but to a considerably lesser degree—the southern mackerel fleet of
the post–Civil War era was unique in that it was composed exclusively
of full-time mackerel schooners. The southern fleet followed the mackerel
north after the spring season ended and became an integral part of the large
flotilla pursuing the species in the Gulf of Maine. The balance of the northern summer fleet consisted of a miscellany of craft that fished for cod and
haddock in spring and joined the mackerel fishery around the first of July.[151]
As a group, the vessels in the southern fishery were a superior class. Being
exclusively mackerel catchers, they tended to be more expensive and more
lavishly outfitted than the multipurpose vessels that made up the bulk of the
northern fleet. They also tended to be bigger. In 1880, for example, the
schooners in Maine's southern fishery were about a third larger in average
tonnage than the vessels that fished only the New England shore.[152]

Although many of Maine's best mackerel schooners belonged to the
southern fleet, it is easy to exaggerate the importance of the spring fishery.
Only a minority of the state's mackerelmen ever engaged in it, even during
the post–Civil War era. In 1880 slightly less than two dozen Maine vessels
engaged in the southern fishery, while sixty-six large schooners and eighty-
one smaller boats fished exclusively along the New England shore. Furthermore, almost all of the southern schooners hailed from just four ports—
Portland, Swan's Island, Boothbay, and North Haven.[153]

The southern fishery labored under the disadvantage that its season
conflicted with the major spring banks fisheries, an important economic
consideration in a cod-fishing state. In this respect, it differed from the New

---

*A well-smack was a specialized type of fishing craft equipped with a semi-enclosed hull
compartment, or "well," through which seawater could circulate and thereby keep captured
fish alive until marketed.

England shore and Gulf of St. Lawrence mackerel fisheries, both of which were summer-fall activities. Vessels going south in the spring could not make the usual early trip to Western or Quereau Bank, and they returned rather late to fit out for the Grand Banks. Then, too, the southern fishery created demands in the area of vessel performance that exceeded even those placed on the traditional salt-mackerel fisheries. The need for fast-sailing vessels— normal in any fresh fishery due to the sensitive nature of the cargo—was accentuated by the peculiar requirements of the New York mackerel market. By the 1880s, the practice of racing to Fulton's pier in the city with the season's early catches had become common. Supply and demand fluctuated enormously, and the first vessels in received the highest returns. Glutting of the market was not unusual, and the price for fresh mackerel, which sold by number and not by weight, could drop from ten cents each to fifty cents per thousand within the space of a few weeks.[154]

The upshot was that although it continued until the end of the century, the highly specialized southern fishery never involved more than 150 New England vessels, even at its peak in the mid-1880s, and not over a third of those were from Maine.[155] Most years, the spring fleet numbered between 50 and 100 schooners. By 1893 it was down to 60 sail, all but 11 from Massachusetts.[156] In general, Maine's mackerel fleet withdrew from the distant high-seas fisheries after 1865. The small southern fleet that continued to thrive for two more decades constituted the exception that proved the rule.

The Herring Fisheries

The last of Maine's major sea fisheries to be considered is the Magdalen Islands herring fishery. Herring, like mackerel, were found along the United States coast as well as in Canadian waters, and the fishery in the Gulf of St. Lawrence was only one of several. From about 1840 to 1870, a summer gill-net fishery existed off Jonesport that occupied as many as twenty-five vessels from surrounding ports.[157] In later years, from the 1860s through the 1880s, a fall fishery in the vicinity of Wood Island and Biddeford Pool, near the mouth of the Saco River, attracted numerous small vessels and boats from western Maine and Massachusetts.[158] Additionally, there were the important herring fisheries of the Passamaquoddy region. Between spring and fall of each year, herring appeared off Eastport, around Grand Manan Island, and along a considerable stretch of the Maine and New Brunswick coasts from the village of Cutler eastward for about thirty miles.[159] Fishermen from such Maine towns as Lubec, Perry, Pembroke, Eastport, and Machias worked this region extensively, particularly the Canadian side of Passamaquoddy Bay.[160] The herring fishery in this part of the Bay of Fundy was not a deep-sea fishery, however. It was primarily an inshore activity involving small boats, and the fish were taken in brush weirs that lined the shore. Furthermore, it did not become central to the Maine herring industry until the demise of the Magdalen fishery and the development of canneries after 1875.[161]

The herring fishery that concerned the deep-sea vessel fishermen of Maine during most of the nineteenth century was the aforementioned one carried on in the Bay. The principal herring ground in the Gulf of St. Lawrence was Pleasant Bay at the southeast end of Amherst Island, the southernmost of a chain of eight small islands located in the center of the Gulf and known collectively as the Magdalens (hence the name of the fishery). The spawning season at the Magdalen Islands lasted for three to five weeks, running from approximately the last week of April until June 1. It was during this period that the fish came near shore and could be easily captured in nets or seines.[162] The drag seines used at the height of the Magdalen fishery were in common use by 1852. These devices were simply long, finely meshed nets, with which the schools of herring were surrounded and hauled close to shore by work crews and small boats. Once in shallow water, the fish were taken by dip nets. This technique prevailed, along with the use of gill nets for supplemental offshore work, until 1865.[163]

In actuality, the Magdalen herring fishery was as much trade as fishery, consisting as it did of schooners either netting their own catch or buying from Nova Scotian fishermen already at the islands. Most American schooners, in fact, did the latter.[164] To some extent, vessel owners regarded the Magdalen trade as an alternative employment for schooners too small to join the general coasting trade during the off season. A British naval officer, observing the 146-vessel American fleet at the islands in May of 1839, noted that their average size was sixty to eighty tons, well below the banker class.[165]

In addition to being a small-vessel activity—and therefore very suitable to Maine's industry structure—the Magdalen fishery, or trade, possessed the added virtue of a short season. Vessels left early in the year and were seldom gone more than five or six weeks. In 1859, for example, the Lubec fleet departed in mid-April and returned in late May.[166] This left sufficient time for any number of other fishing pursuits. The Isle au Haut schooner *Porpoise* was able to follow a Magdalens herring trip in 1837 with several mackerel voyages, one of them to the Gulf of St. Lawrence.[167] Several vessels of the Belfast mackerel fleet went to the Magdalens for herring in April of 1859, and at least one of them, the schooner *Castellane*, found time for two successive trips to Chaleur Bay before the season ended.[168] The vessels of the Mount Desert Island Labrador fleet of the late 1830s, to cite another instance, all prefaced their usual June cod-fishing trips with quick spring jaunts to the Magdalens herring grounds.[169] In fact, prior to 1850 it was quite common to combine these two fisheries, and a large percentage of the early Magdalen schooners went to the Labrador coast for cod later in the year.[170] The northern herring trade, in short, was never an end in itself but rather an economic sideline, and one of its primary features was its compatibility with almost any other dominant fishing interest.

The special attraction of this fishery, however, was the size of the herring, which were larger than those taken on the American coast. When packaged after smoke curing, Magdalen herring would fit just 30 to a box, while other domestic varieties would fit from 40 to 150 per box. This, together with an inability to secure a sufficient abundance of the species at home to satisfy demand, drove American fishermen north to the Magdalens in great numbers before the Civil War.[171]

Although some Magdalens herring were pickled for shipment to market, most were lightly salted to retard spoilage during the voyage home and then smoked for preservation, a process requiring two to six weeks.[172] Smoked-herring production predated the Magdalen Islands fishery, even though that fishery provided its greatest impetus. The practice began on the Maine coast at Eastport in 1808 and at nearby Lubec in 1812.[173] By 1821 there were twenty smokehouses in Lubec producing fifty to sixty thousand boxes of fish annually, and the town quickly became the national leader in the smoked-herring business, a distinction it carried into the 1880s. Eastport maintained a position second only to Lubec throughout the period.[174]

The fishery upon which the smoked-herring trade of Lubec, Eastport, and other eastern Maine towns came to chiefly depend began in 1822, when a schooner from Isle au Haut, Maine, became the first American vessel to enter it. Characteristically, the Maine schooner responsible for initiating the Magdalens fishery had gone north for a "trip" of cod, had found them scarce, and had carried home herring instead. As always, everything was of secondary importance to the codfish. Following this rather accidental beginning, two or three Isle au Haut schooners sailed for the Magdalens the next year, and by 1825, Deer Isle, Vinalhaven, Mount Desert, Lubec, and Eastport were sending vessels. The closer eastern Maine ports anticipated western Maine and Massachusetts by a considerable extent in this particular fishery, and it was not until nearly 1830 that Bay State vessels entered the competition.[175] Westport, the first western Maine town to show interest, became involved about the same time, and Boothbay sent its first vessel in 1831. By that date the eastern port of Deer Isle already had a fleet of six schooners visiting the islands on a regular basis.[176]

The number of Maine vessels involved in the Magdalens herring fishery prior to the end of the Civil War is uncertain. The entire American fleet ranged between one hundred and three hundred sail during the late 1850s and early 1860s.[177] Many of those were Massachusetts vessels, however. Scattered information does indicate that sizeable contingents went each spring from several Maine fishing ports, most of them in the eastern part of the state. Westport and Vinalhaven had six and nine Magdalen vessels, respectively, in the 1840s, and Lubec about a dozen in 1860. The Hancock-Lamoine area fitted out as many as nine herring schooners for the island trade during the mid-1860s. Even so small and unimposing a fishing town as Cutler, a village on the eastern shore of Washington County, sent two or three vessels each year between 1860 and 1864.[178]

The fishery itself peaked in conjunction with the smoked-herring industry it served, both reaching their maximum developments just before and during the Civil War years. Numerically, the Magdalen fleet was largest through the 1855–1861 period, and that was reflected at Eastport, where in 1859 a record thirty thousand pounds of island herring valued at $90,000 were landed during the months of May and June.[179] Neighboring Lubec, the center of activity, packed out 300,000 boxes of smoked herring in 1854, a figure that rose to between 400,000 and 500,000 boxes annually within a decade.[180] A considerable amount of that total came from local waters, but it is clear that during the war years the demand for smoked fish made Magdalen herring the most important brand in the marketplace.[181]

Until about 1850, the major herring-smoking towns in Maine were Lubec, Eastport, Milbridge, Lamoine, Deer Isle, Boothbay, Southport, and Westport. Over the course of the next decade or so several of these communities gave up the business, and by 1860–1865, it came to be dominated by Eastport and Lubec. By 1880 the concentration of the industry down east was such that Lubec alone was putting up no less than half of all the smoked herring in the United States.[182]

The concentration of the Maine smoked-herring business after 1860 did not represent a major industrywide decline. There was some temporary slippage after the peak years of the Civil War, and production for the United States as a whole eventually dropped about 25 percent below the 500,000-box-per-year level maintained from 1845 to 1872. Beginning in 1885, however, the industry—still centered at Eastport and Lubec—returned to its former proportions.[183] What changed was the source of the herring used. No longer did the product come from the Magdalen Islands vessel fishery. Instead, the smokehouses of Lubec and Eastport turned to local sources, increasingly using the smaller herring found in Passamaquoddy Bay and supplied by small-boat fishermen. The advantage of an immediate supply of fish, an advantage the more westerly herring ports did not share, no doubt contributed to the down-east monopoly of the smoked-herring industry. The general post–Civil War fisheries decline, which resulted in the withdrawal from active use of many of the vessels formerly sent to the Magdalens in the spring, had less of an impact on the herring fisheries of Eastport and Lubec than it did elsewhere. For most Maine fishing ports, conversely, the end of the herring vessel fishery meant the end of the smoked-herring trade.

The decline of the Magdalen Islands herring fishery, as apart from the smoked-herring industry, can be dated from 1866. East of the Penobscot, it continued on for a few more years. Lamoine, near Mount Desert Island, retained a fleet of ten Magdalen schooners as late as 1870 and was still packing out 100,000 boxes of island herring annually near the end of the decade.[184] Aside from Lamoine, only Lubec and Eastport kept up the island trade throughout the 1870s, and their participation decreased with each passing year. In 1877 Eastport still had a number of Magdalen vessels, but they were used less and less frequently, and the town was gradually developing a fleet of small boats for the inshore frozen-herring fishery.[185] In the spring of 1883 only two schooners left Eastport for the Magdalens, and the same year witnessed the last recorded departure of a fleet from Lubec.[186] By the mid-1880s this unique fishery was a thing of the past.

A pinky fishing schooner from the Maine mid-coast port of Friendship laying to
an unidentified wharf, ca. 1880. Tubs, barrels, and other gear are in view on deck,
and the crew are drying their oilskins on the main gaff and boom. The "pink"
stern's function as boom crotch is in evidence. This type of double-ended craft
was commonly used by Maine fishermen prior to 1850, especially in the Gulf of
St. Lawrence and Bay of Fundy fisheries. (Courtesy Smithsonian Institution,
NMAH/Transportation)

The Eastport, Maine, waterfront in about 1885 showing several fishing craft. The vessel under partial sail (center) is a "clipper" schooner, typical of the type employed in the Maine sea fisheries from the 1850s through the 1880s, particularly in the mackerel fishery. (Courtesy Maine State Archives, Augusta, Davis Loring photo)

A Grand Banks schooner of the deck-fishing era at anchor on the Newfoundland grounds. The vessel is a "heeltapper" of about 1830, a craft characterized by bluff bows and a raised quarterdeck. The crew, clad in leather "barvels" (fishing aprons), are hand-lining for cod, with each man tending two lines. This was the standard means by which banks fishing was carried out until ca. 1860. (*Goode Report*, sec. 5, vol. 2, drawing by Henry W. Elliott and Joseph W. Collins)

Schooner *Sarah Franklin* (59 tons, n.m.; 56′ × 17′ × 7′) ashore during low tide at Bass Harbor, Tremont, Maine, ca. 1880s. This vessel was a small salt banker built at Essex, Massachusetts, in 1856 and purchased by Swan's Island fishermen in 1863 for use in the Penobscot District cod fisheries. She later fished out of Deer Isle, Maine. The *Franklin* was representative of the schooners employed in the eastern Maine outports for deck fishing around the time of the Civil War. She exhibits several characteristics of her type: burdensome hull, heavy ground tackle, and reduced rig with no fore topsail or jibboom. (Courtesy Smithsonian Institution, NMAH/Transportation)

A Maine fish gang unloading a fare of "round" or undressed groundfish from a schooner at a Mount Desert Island wharf, ca. 1900. The two men in oilskins (far left and center) are members of the vessel's crew. The fish are being handled with dual-pronged pitchforks called pews. They will be culled according to size and type, weighed (for payment) on the large scale in the center-right of the picture, and then prepared for salting and drying. Shore fishermen typically "weighed out" their catch unprocessed, as shown, while offshore banks fishermen dressed their catch at sea. (Courtesy Southwest Harbor, Maine, Public Library, G. A. Neal photo)

Fishermen dressing cod at Biddeford Pool, Maine, ca. 1884. The three-man dressing gang posing for the camera consists (left to right) of the "throater," who cuts the fish open transversely below the gills and lengthwise down the center; the "header," who breaks off the head, removes the viscera, and retrieves the liver; and the "splitter," who splits or lays apart the fish and extracts the backbone. In this condition, the catch is ready for washing, salting, and drying. The man on the far right displays the final product, two sun-dried cod. These are shore fishermen. On the outer banks similar dressing operations were carried out aboard ship. The two other prominent individuals in the picture (right foreground) are exhibiting a tub of trawl line and a stone anchor called a killick, items commonly used in the late nineteenth-century sea fisheries. (Courtesy Mystic Seaport Museum, Mystic, Conn.)

Groundfish drying on a wharf at Southwest Harbor, Tremont, Maine, on a hazy
day in 1892, while several fishing schooners maneuver offshore. The split fish, previously dressed and salted, have been sun dried on wooden stagings called "fish
flakes." They are now piled on the flakes for covering overnight or in the event of
wet weather. Dried salt groundfish, especially cod and haddock, was the principal
seafood in the American market until the mid-nineteenth century. (Courtesy
Southwest Harbor, Maine, Public Library, Henry L. Rand photo)

The small, Bath-built schooner *Young America* (6 tons, n.m.; 31′ × 11′ × 3′) of Portland, Maine, loading dried salt codfish in the 1880s at the C. & H. Trefethen establishment on House Island off Portland harbor, where much of the city's cod catch was professionally cured. The cargo, gathered in rough bundles, is being transferred from the nearby flake yard by wheelbarrow and stacked loosely on deck for delivery to a wholesale fish dealer. Upon arrival in Portland, it will be packed in large casks called "drums" for shipment to export markets. When ultimately consumed, the hardened and heavily salted fish will require soaking in fresh water before cooking. (Courtesy Smithsonian Institution, NMAH/Transportation)

A herring smokehouse at Eastport, Maine, ca. 1886. Fish hung for smoke curing can be seen through the windows, which are open for ventilation. They have previously been pickled in brine and then set out to drain and harden on wooden racks called "herring horses," such as the one being used in the center. A worker is in the process of transferring "sticks" of dried herring inside for smoking. To the right in the foreground are piles of spare drying racks, and to the left are the boxes in which the final product will be shipped to market. The majority of Maine's Magdalen Islands herring catch was processed in this manner. (Courtesy Maine Historical Society, Portland)

FISHING SALT.

JUST RECEIVED

PER BRIG RICHMOND,

TEN THOUSAND BUSHELS

Fine Ground Caicos Salt!

A SUPERIOR ARTICLE FOR

FISHING PURPOSES.

For Sale in Bond or Duty Paid by

W. H. WITHERLE.

An advertisement for fishing salt by William H. Witherle of Castine, Penobscot Bay's leading fish and supply merchant in the mid-nineteenth century. Spain and Great Britain were the chief sources of salt for Maine fishermen, but the Turks and Caicos islands of the British West Indies were an important supplementary source, especially after 1860. (Courtesy Penobscot Marine Museum, Searsport, Maine, Witherle Collection)

Ship *St. Leon* of Castine, Maine, entering Liverpool, England, to load fishing salt in 1835. The Liverpool run was the second leg of the triangular fish-cotton-salt trade crucial to eastern Maine's antebellum fishing industry. Maine cod and mackerel were shipped to New Orleans and exchanged for southern cotton, which was carried to Great Britain and exchanged, in turn, for rock salt destined for Maine fishing ports. The Civil War put an end to this important commerce. (Courtesy Penobscot Marine Museum, Searsport, Maine)

Clipper fishing schooner *George W. Pierce* (67 tons; n.m.; 73′ × 22′ × 8′) of
Southport, Maine, drying her headsails at a Portland wharf in 1895. A dory hand-
liner built at South Bristol, Maine, in 1867, this vessel was active in the Western
Bank cod fishery and typified the schooners used on the offshore grounds after
the Civil War. Dories, such as the ones shown on board and alongside the vessel,
enabled cod bankers like the *Pierce* to expand their range and surpass the catch
totals of the deck-fishing era. However, they added an element of danger to
the industry by separating crewmen from their vessel during fishing operations.
(Courtesy Maine Historical Society, Portland)

The Industry at High Tide: The Markets

We send to the West Indies the fish which we have caught with
our own hands, the lumber which we have cut in our own
forests, the agricultural products which we have raised on our
own soil. . . . All is from within ourselves.—Congressman
Peleg Sprague of Maine, 1828[1]

The Spanish Caribbean

The markets for Maine fish during the nineteenth century fell into two
broad categories, foreign and domestic, with the islands of the West Indies
accounting for most of the former. In this respect they closely paralleled the
markets for the state's other major commodity, lumber. Little specific data
exist concerning the disposition of Maine fish, but deducing from the national situation, it is apparent that foreign exports were initially very important. Until 1865 a significant percentage of American (and Maine) fish was
marketed abroad, although by that date, the peak years—1804 for dried fish
(567,828 quintals) and 1832 for pickled (102,770 barrels)—had long since
passed. In 1840 American fishermen produced 773,947 quintals of dried
or smoked fish, of which 211,425 quintals (27 percent), worth $500,000, was
exported. Ten years later, in 1850, 407,814 quintals of cod (the bulk of the
dried-fish catch) were processed. Dried- and smoked-fish exports that year
totalled 168,600 quintals,* or about 41 percent of cod production.[2]

Annual dried-cod exports hovered around 200,000–300,000 quintals
throughout the half-century preceding the end of the Civil War, except for
a few years in the 1850s, when they averaged closer to 150,000 quintals. Beginning in 1864, however, exports fell below 200,000 quintals per year on a
more or less permanent basis, only rarely thereafter exceeding that annual
figure.[3] The postwar low was reached in 1869, when just 88,415 quintals were
sent abroad. The following year, 111,672 quintals were exported, but that

---

*Dried and smoked fish were grouped together in government export statistics, but the
overwhelming preponderance of these shipments consisted of sun-dried products, principally
salt cod.

was less than 20 percent of the total national production in dried cod, hake, and haddock.[4] The percentage of American groundfish exported remained close to the 1870 level for the rest of the postwar era. From 1884 to 1894, for instance, no more than 20 percent of the cured cod landed by American fishermen was earmarked for foreign consumption.[5]

Pickled fish, consisting primarily of brine-salted mackerel and herring, was far less important in foreign markets than dried cod and smoked herring. The total value of dried- and smoked-fish exports in 1860 was $690,000, compared to only $192,000 for pickled products.[6] Furthermore, a smaller proportion of the nation's pickled fish was sent abroad. In 1850, when American fishermen produced 252,769 barrels of salt mackerel, 19,944 barrels (or roughly 8 percent) was exported.[7] The same small percentage was exported in 1870, despite the fact that the 30,935 barrels sent to foreign consumers represented an increased share of the total export market for mackerel vis-à-vis cod.[8]

Since dried cod, rather than pickled fish, was the major product of the Maine fisheries, it is fair to say that prior to 1865 probably a quarter to a third of Maine's fish catch was marketed outside of the United States. By far, the bulk of those foreign fish exports went to the West Indies. In the early years, though, the Iberian Peninsula provided a substantial market for Maine fish. Before the American Revolution, Boothbay vessels were carrying cod directly to Spain, as well as to the West Indies.[9] Maine fishermen also developed a profitable indirect fish trade with Spanish ports during the early 1800s. Between 1817 and 1840 the smaller cod caught by the Labrador fleet of Boothbay and vicinity were regularly salted, dried, and sold in Boston for exportation to Bilbao on the north coast of Spain. The small Labrador cod thereby came to be familiarly known to Boothbay fishermen as "Bilbao fish." Eastern Maine took part in the Spanish trade as well. In 1810, the first schooner from Cranberry Isles to engage in the Labrador cod fishery cured its catch at home and carried it to Spain.[10] In a variation of the indirect Iberian trade, Deer Isle schooners were accompanied to the Labrador grounds in 1822 by a Newburyport vessel, which purchased their catch on the spot and then sailed for Spanish ports.[11]

By the era of Maine's real importance in the sea fisheries, however, the European markets were negligible. Large-scale exports of salted cod to Europe came to an end after the War of 1812, and 90 percent of American cod exports were going south to the Caribbean by the 1830s.[12] The last important European markets were Gibraltar, Italy, and Malta, which together absorbed about 10 percent of the United States dried-fish shipments in 1821. A decade later Gibraltar remained the leading Old World market for American fish, but its share amounted to less than five thousand quintals dried (2 percent of the total exported) and almost none pickled.[13]

An examination of export statistics from 1840 to 1865, when Maine supplied nearly half of the nation's fish product, indicates that the two islands of Cuba and Haiti were by far the leading overseas markets and that the West Indies, in general, monopolized United States fish exports throughout the period. In the important dried-fish trade, Cuba was the leader until 1860, annually accounting for a third of all American exports. After that date it was replaced by Haiti, theretofore a secondary outlet occupying roughly one-fourth of the market. During the quarter-century ending in 1865, over half of all the United States fish shipped abroad—dried, smoked, and pickled—was sent to these two islands. Additional Caribbean markets included Puerto Rico, Santo Domingo, Dutch Guiana, French Guiana, the Dutch and Danish West Indies, and (to a lesser degree) the French and British West Indies.[14] A typical year was 1845, when Cuba and Haiti consumed 182,427 of the 288,380 quintals of dried and smoked fish and 23,796 of the 43,236 barrels of pickled fish exported from the United States. Out of $1,012,007 realized by American exporters that year, $655,629 came directly as a result of shipments to Cuba and Haiti. The Spanish islands other than Cuba, primarily Puerto Rico, followed with combined fish imports from the United States valued at $139,042.[15]

Perhaps more striking and significant than the figures for Cuba and Haiti were those for Cuba and the other Spanish islands taken together. Roughly half of all United States fish exports in 1845 went to Caribbean territories owned or originally colonized by Spain. Considering only dried and smoked items, the total swells to well over half.[16] For the entire period 1830–1860, an average of 46 percent of America's dried- and smoked-fish exports went to the Spanish ports of the Caribbean on an annual basis, and for a few years during the late 1840s, those markets accounted for close to 60 percent of the total.[17] The dominant role of the Spanish West Indies bespeaks the special economic relationship that existed between those colonies and New England's fish merchants. In a sense, the Hispanic appetite for dried cod—first on the European continent and then in the Americas—was the chief factor in the American foreign fish trade.

There were several reasons for this development. The first had to do with international trade policy. Beginning in 1818, Spain opened its Caribbean islands to free trade with all foreign nations, and from that date commerce between the Spanish West Indies and the United States steadily increased.[18] In contrast, the British West Indies, the other major markets of the Caribbean, were legally closed to American traffic after the thirteen colonies achieved independence in 1783, and they were not completely reopened to United States shipping until 1830.[19] American fish exports to British West Indian markets were further hampered by tariff preferences favoring Canadian exporters, which lasted until midcentury.[20] By that time, the cordial trade developed with the non-English islands of the region had reached a certain degree of maturity and permanence. Although a fair amount of American fish subsequently found its way to Jamaica and other British colonies, those markets never substantially altered the hold that the Spanish markets exerted through force of habit and familiarity.*

Another reason for the Hispanic flavor of the New England fish trade was related to religion. Spain was Catholic—possibly the most Catholic nation in Europe—and this preference of belief was transferred to her colonies in the New World. Like the immigrants to urban North America, the Spanish colonists and their descendants, as well as their culturally indoctrinated slaves, had spiritually imposed reasons for the periodic eating of fish.

More important was the economic factor of slavery. The Spanish islands of the Caribbean were among the final strongholds of the "peculiar institution." The transatlantic African slave trade flourished last in Puerto Rico and Cuba during the early 1860s, and Cuban authorities did not end the practice there until 1862.[21] Slavery itself, long since discontinued in most of Central and South America (1838 in the British colonies and 1848 in the French and Danish territories), lingered in the Spanish West Indies until the last decades of the nineteenth century. It survived until 1876 in Puerto Rico and was not completely abolished in Cuba until 1886, barely two years before Brazil became the final hemispheric nation to liberate its slaves.[22]

Altogether, over 600,000 bonded Africans were brought into Puerto Rico and Cuba between 1811 and 1870, about 90 percent of them to the larger island. This influx represented a historic shift in the focus of the Atlantic slave trade away from the French and British Caribbean, where it had centered in the previous century. Cuba, in particular, emerged in the nineteenth century as one of the three centers of demand for bonded labor, together with Brazil and the southern United States.[23] Of all the slaves brought to that island over the centuries, fully three-quarters arrived between 1800 and 1865, and one-quarter during the years 1832–1865.[24] This was a circumstance of great import to the fishing industry of New England.

---

*American dried-fish exports to the British West Indies did not commence until 1831, did not reach the thousand-quintal-per-annum level until the 1840s, and did not exceed four thousand quintals in any single year until the 1850s. (Source: *U.S.RFCN*, 1821–60, statements on domestic exports by country.)

The expanding slave systems of the Spanish islands required cheap but nourishing food for their laboring masses. Fish met that requirement.* In addition, it was necessary to acquire long-lasting foodstuffs that did not spoil in a tropical environment. Salted and sun-dried cod had this quality in abundance. Dried cod, if cured hard enough, would resist spoilage for at least nine months.[25] There were, of course, other fish suitable for salt drying. Because of their keeping qualities and relative cheapness, hake and haddock (or "scale fish") were sometimes preferred over the more expensive cod in Caribbean markets, where plantation owners, it was said, "desire to get provisions for their negroes as cheaply as possible."[26] Nevertheless, the greater accessibility of cod, as well as its more palatable taste and meatier texture in the dried form, made it the primary article of export. This was especially true as regards Cuba. The records of a typical Cuban sugar plantation of circa 1840 indicate that salt cod and jerked beef were the two protein staples of the slave diet at that time.[27] Over the ensuing decades, cod shipments to the island increased yearly, reaching sixteen million pounds in 1856, at which time close to 80 percent of all Cuba's fish imports were in the form of dried cod.[28]

There was another contributing factor to the historic relationship between the Spanish Caribbean and the fishing states of New England beyond the basic, uncomplicated desire for inexpensive and nonperishable foodstuffs. Gilberto Freyre, the eminent Brazilian social historian, summarized it in the words "latifundiary monoculture." In the case of colonial Brazil, he pointed out, the creation of an economic structure based almost solely on sugar production (hence monocultural), whose central organizational unit was the large, single-crop plantation (latifundium), led over time to the development of a native agriculture totally lacking in diversity. Massive crop specialization forced the preemption of land normally left for grazing animals or growing food. This meant—in the northeast coastal plain at least—that Brazilians, master and slave alike, were reduced to a severely restricted diet and a dependence on the outside world for food. Their diet, deficient in fresh beef, fowl, fruits, vegetables, and the like, was geared toward salted and otherwise preserved commodities. More specifically, the lack of good

---

*J. C. Burnham & Company, Havana provisions importers, informed their United States suppliers in late 1850 that fish would continue to do well in the Cuban market, despite a temporary abundance of salt beef, because "many Planters like to give Fish to their labourers." The same import house commented a few months later on the favorable competitive position of cod vis-à-vis Argentine beef because of its lower price. (Source: PMM, WP, Schooner *Commerce* Collection, file 5: price-current newsletters, J. C. Burnham & Company, 17 December 1850 and 20 June 1851.)

meat led to the evolution of an "ichthyophagous menu" in which that short-coming was compensated for by an overuse of fish—especially codfish.[29] Indeed, as late as 1825 Brazil imported a considerable amount of American dried fish—enough to qualify as this country's fourth-leading foreign market—although shipments fell off thereafter.[30]

Cuba, which became the chief American foreign fish market in the ensuing years, evolved a nineteenth-century economic structure remarkably similar to that of seventeenth- and eighteenth-century Brazil. Like Brazil, Cuba developed a sugar economy. By 1849 the island had already emerged as the world's leading sugar producer, far ahead of the British West Indies and Brazil. The smaller Spanish colony of Puerto Rico ranked ninth. In 1856 the two islands together accounted for 30 percent of the world's sugar, Cuba alone producing a quarter of the entire international output.[31] To achieve that position, Cuba embraced what can only be described as a monocultural economic system. Between 1840 and 1860, virtually all farms, capital, and labor formerly engaged in the production of coffee, the island's second-most-important crop, were turned to the cultivation of sugar, and by the end of that period the money invested in sugar plantations was five times greater than that invested in coffee and ten times that invested in tobacco, Cuba's only other significant cash crop.[32]

Cuban monoculture led to the same deficiencies of diet seen in Brazil a hundred years earlier, though perhaps to a somewhat lesser degree. Poor animal husbandry and a reluctance to fertilize land or vary crops were characteristic of the system.[33] Although the number of work animals on the island (horses, mules, and donkeys) increased during the 1840s and 1850s, the number of food animals, especially hogs and sheep, declined. The production of butter and cheese was nil, and shortages of dairy products were common.[34] Occasionally fresh foods were available, but salted commodities were the rule, and fruits and vegetables for slave consumption were largely limited to coffee farms. Urban areas were only slightly better off than the neighboring plantations. Mid-nineteenth-century Havana was a city in which the chief diet of the poor consisted of plantain (the starchy, cooked fruit of the banana plant), salt beef, and fish. While certain fruits were abundant, vegetables were scarce and native meat was poor.[35]

Cuba's monoculture never reached the extremes experienced elsewhere in the hemisphere. There was the saving grace of a small, independent yeomanry, and some minor agricultural diversity—notably cattle raising—did exist.[36] Nevertheless, the island was never self-supporting and, as a consequence of its status as a sugar factory, was dependent on outside forces for its livelihood and sustenance. The constant threat of malnutrition made the importation of food a necessity.* The lack of meat, in particular, made North American dried fish a welcome commodity. In 1852, for instance, the high price and scarcity of beef led to repeated calls by Havana provision importers for increased shipments of American fish, and local consumption of the article rose appreciably.[37] By the mid-nineteenth century, Cuban salt-cod imports were far in excess of bacon, ham, and pork imports combined and had achieved a position second only to salt beef in the island marketplace.[38]

Thus, the Spanish West Indies—Catholic, tropical, neo-feudal, monocultural, and always receptive to trade—were an ideal market for the products of the New England fisheries. As exemplified by Cuba, they were not only favorably disposed toward American cod as a food staple, they were utterly dependent on it. Until 1865 it was the catch of Maine fishermen that supplied a large portion of their needs.

It is likely that prior to the Civil War, a modest amount of Maine's West Indies fish trade was carried on in direct fashion by Maine vessels. It is known that most of the Magdalen Islands herring caught or purchased by Wiscasset District fishermen in 1830 was smoked and sent straight to the islands.[39] Southport, within that district, sent its fishermen on regular winter coasting voyages to the Caribbean in the antebellum period, and nearby Boothbay carried on an extensive trade there in the early 1800s, exchanging dried fish for "island products."[40] Among the eastern towns, Hancock carried its own smoked and pickled Magdalen herring to the Indies both during and after the Civil War,[41] and Lamoine's fishing fleet engaged in winter trade with the islands as late as 1890.[42] Eastport sent an occasional cargo to Cuba, as evidenced by the loss of the brig *Otis Norcross* of that port, bound for Havana with timber and fish, in 1848.[43] North Haven Island in Penobscot Bay did enough business with the Caribbean to maintain several "West India" goods stores in 1860, and it is apparent that the island dispatched some fish to Jamaica during the ensuing war years.[44] Comparatively little is known about the Indies commerce of the major fishing ports of the Penobscot region, although some of the Grand Banks cod landed at Castine and Bucksport obviously found its way to Cuban plantations aboard local coasters and foreign traders. The Castine bark *Sarah L. Bryant,* for instance, carried a cargo of cod, hake, herring, and mackerel to Havana in November 1847, as the first leg of a transatlantic triangular voyage that included a passage to London with Cuban sugar and a trip home with Spanish fishing salt from Cadiz.[45]

---

*At the end of 1850 Cuba was importing on a regular basis the following items: beef, cod, haddock, hake, ham, rice, lard, cheese, butter, flour, potatoes, onions, and cocoa. (Source: PMM, WP, Schooner *Commerce* Collection, file 5: price-current newsletter, J. C. Burnham & Company, Havana, 31 December 1850.)

Yet, certain as it is that Maine's fishing ports pursued some direct trade with the West Indies markets, it is equally certain that such trade was minimal at best. Moreover, the direct trade in fish products that did exist was extremely localized. In large measure it was restricted to the city of Portland. Unlike most Maine seaports, Portland was historically a foreign-trading port. Beginning in the eighteenth century, the merchants of the city had developed a barter trade with the West Indian islands in which cod was a prime component. In exchange for Caribbean sugar, molasses, and rum, cargoes of dried cod packed in drums went south accompanied by lumber, soap, and candles. The trade continued well into the nineteenth century and did not completely end until the post–Civil War era.[46] In its later stages, various foodstuffs were added to the cargoes, but the fleet of small square-riggers sailing from Portland concentrated mostly on mixed shipments of fish and "shooks"—prefabricated parts for the wooden boxes essential to the Caribbean export trade in sugar.[47] Cuba was the focus of this commerce, accounting for virtually all of the clearances of Portland vessels for West Indies ports by the middle 1850s. The Cuban trade, furthermore, was a Portland monopoly within the state of Maine. Of the 324 vessels clearing Maine ports for Cuba during the year ending June 30, 1856, 228 (70 percent) departed from the customs district encompassing the city. In contrast, just 5 cleared from the major fishing ports of Penobscot District to the eastward.[48]

Given its control of the state's trade with the Spanish Indies, Portland emerged quite early as Maine's dominant fish-export center. In 1826 the city sent out 18,790 quintals dried and 6,879 barrels pickled, far in excess of all other ports in the state combined.[49] Still, Portland's fish exports that year constituted no more than 8 percent of the total exported from the United States, a figure that did not appreciably alter over time.[50] In 1856 Portland was the fourth-leading United States port in terms of dried-fish shipments to foreign countries. Nevertheless, the city's 10,275 quintals, while over 90 percent of the total exported directly from Maine, constituted barely 6 percent of the national total—or about the same percentage as three decades earlier.[51] Even though Portland remained the leader within the state of Maine, the city's share of American fish exports declined rapidly thereafter until by 1861 it fell below 1 percent in both the dried- and pickled-fish categories.[52]

The extent to which Maine's control over its own fish exports had deteriorated by the eve of the Civil War is highlighted by statistics for 1860, a year in which the state's actual fishing tonnage was approaching its zenith. Of the nearly $1 million in American fish exports for this last prewar year, only $22,000 worth (less than 2.5 percent) was carried abroad in Maine vessels.[53] What had transpired was the flowering of a curious system of domestic neocolonialism in which the Pine Tree State had become in some ways as much an economic dependent of outside forces as the sugar island of Cuba. A truncated foreign fish trade was only one expression of this pervasive economic lifestyle, which eventually became endemic down east.

The roots of the system extended far back into the pre-statehood phase of Maine's development. Moses Greenleaf took note of it in 1816, pointing out that even then, the district's foreign commerce in fish, lumber, and agricultural produce—most of it bound for the West Indies—was largely an indirect commerce: "A very large proportion of the exports are shipped coastwise to Boston and other ports in Massachusetts, as well as to other parts of the United States, where they are partly sold for inland consumption, and partly reshipped for foreign markets, when they become absorbed in the general account of exports of the place, whence they are reshipped." Maine's foreign imports, Greenleaf added, arrived in much the same manner—indirectly, by way of Massachusetts or other states.[54] This status as a supplier of raw materials, perhaps an inevitable outgrowth of Maine's historical origin as the frontier hinterland of a mature mother-state, found its purest early expression in the operation of the Caribbean fish trade. Although it is possible that half of the American fish sent to the West Indies annually was caught by Maine fishermen, it is doubtful that much more than 10 percent of it was ever shipped directly to its ultimate destination.

It was Boston, and later New York, that marketed most of the Maine fish destined for foreign markets. The stranglehold of these two cities upon the American foreign fish trade increased throughout the century until by the 1860s their control was virtually monopolistic. As early as 1856 they already shared 72 percent of the exports in dried and smoked fish, a figure that rose to 85 percent within a decade and to 95 percent by 1875.[55] Boston was the clear leader until well into the 1870s, when it was gradually surpassed by New York City in both dried- and pickled-fish exports. Between 1870 and 1880 New York's share of the market went from about a third to over half, while Boston's decreased by the same proportion.[56] During the period when Maine's fisheries were most important, however, Boston was by far the dominant force. From 1855 to 1865, the Hub City marketed roughly half of all American dried- and smoked-fish exports, and New York about a quarter of the total. Boston also dominated pickled-fish exports during those years, although New York managed a greater share of that lesser trade.[57] Not coincidentally, Boston's exports peaked in 1861, the same year Maine's fishing fleet reached its maximum development. In the twelve months ending on June 30 of that year, the customs district of Boston-Charlestown shipped $508,000 worth of groundfish, mackerel, and herring abroad, or 58 percent of the total exported nationwide.[58]

In addition to dominating fish exports to the Southern Hemisphere,

Boston and New York also controlled the reciprocal West Indies import trade those exports helped to stimulate, and over time a steadily decreasing number of island cargoes came into Maine. As mentioned, the traffic with the Spanish Caribbean was to some degree a barter trade, based on acquiring sugar and its by-products in exchange for fish and lumber. Virtually all of the United States imports from Cuba in 1856, for example, were in the form of sugar and its chief derivative, molasses. Yet less than 2 percent of the Cuban brown sugar (the leading variety) entering the American market that year came in through Maine ports, while 75 percent of it arrived by way of New York and Massachusetts.[59] In 1827 Maine had imported about one-third of the molasses entering the country from the Caribbean, but by 1860 that share was down to roughly one-seventh, and, again, New York and Massachusetts dominated the trade.[60] Ironically, a significant portion of the Indies commerce in both fish and sugar products was transported in Maine bottoms. By the mid-1850s Maine schooners and square-riggers from ports like Wiscasset and Portland were taking cargoes of fish from Boston to Cuba and returning to Boston with loads of sugar and molasses.[61] Maine thus participated in, but did not control, an Indies trade based in considerable measure on its own ocean resource, a graphic illustration of the state's neocolonial mercantile status.

The Slave South

While the West Indies trade through Boston guaranteed a consistently dependable market for Maine's dried cod and added a touch of romance to the history of the fisheries, it was the domestic market that increasingly absorbed the bulk of the state's fish catch as the nineteenth century progressed. Between 1840 and 1860 Maine's fishing tonnage approximately tripled, while foreign fish exports remained roughly constant. There was even a slight decline in exports during the 1850s, when the Maine fleet experienced its greatest growth, and shipments abroad reached their pre–Civil War low during the early part of that decade.[62] These facts point indubitably to the rising influence of the home market.

Fish unquestionably played a major role in Maine's antebellum coastal trade. In the 1820s fish and lumber were the two principal domestic exports of Penobscot District, and those same two commodities, together with plaster, constituted most of the domestic trade of Passamaquoddy District as well. Over a quarter of Eastport's coastal trade was in fish products in 1826, most of it in dried cod and smoked herring.[63] Regrettably, a paucity of detailed information limits further quantitative judgements about Maine's coastwise fish trade. Nevertheless, the work of Robert G. Albion confirms that the ocean product was at least one of the four leading commodities—

lumber, lime, and granite being the other three—shipped out of the state on a regular basis to Atlantic Coast ports.[64] Lumber, of course, was always the Pine Tree State's leading export, but it is likely that salt fish was a strong second at times, particularly during the decade of the 1850s.

It has been established that a large part of the American coastal trade of the pre–Civil War period consisted of sending New England fish, lumber, and ice to the Middle Atlantic and southern states in exchange for coal, cotton, flour, and other bulk items.[65] To a considerable extent, Maine's domestic fish trade conformed to that pattern. Portland's extensive antebellum coastwise commerce, which was primarily with the population centers of the Atlantic seaboard, included occasional deliveries of salt mackerel to ports as far south as Savannah, where return cargoes of shipbuilding lumber from Georgia's pine forests were loaded and sent north.[66] A more common manifestation of Portland's domestic fish trade was the off-season trading pattern established by the city's larger cod schooners, which carried their cured catch to markets bordering Chesapeake Bay during the winter months and returned with flour and corn for local consumption.[67] The Virginia Tidewater river ports were the focus of much of this Chesapeake fish trade. During the two decades preceding the Civil War, shipments from such places in Maine as Eastport, Rockland, and Westport, as well as Portland, were sent by schooner to Richmond, on the James River, and Alexandria, on the Potomac. The cargoes were of an assorted nature, combining smoked or pickled herring and dried cod with potatoes, plaster, ice, and timber products.[68] The voyages of the *C. L. Allen* of Rockland typified this workaday commerce. In the mid-1850s the *Allen* went south to Richmond with fish and ice in the winter and sailed home with flour in the early spring.[69]

Not all the Maine fish destined for markets in the Upper South entered by way of the Virginia river ports. The city of Baltimore, farther up the Chesapeake, was perhaps the most favored entrepôt. Vessel losses provide melancholy but definitive evidence of the extensive trade with that commercial center during the prewar years. Coasting schooners from such timber ports as Bath on the Kennebec and Calais on the St. Croix were reported lost en route to Baltimore with combined cargoes of fish and lumber.[70] Vessels lost from the fishing ports themselves tended to be more exclusive in the composition of their southbound cargoes. A Deer Isle schooner, the *Blue Bell,* was run aground and wrecked in January 1856 while coasting to Baltimore with five hundred barrels of pickled mackerel, and another eastern schooner, the *Constitution* of Swan's Island, went down off Cape Cod in November 1860 while carrying a consignment of Chaleur mackerel and Magdalen herring to the southern metropolis.[71] As with Virginia, the Maryland fish trade revolved around obtaining return cargoes of agricultural staple products. Maine coastal communities from Portland to Eastport imported foodstuffs from Baltimore during the 1840s and 1850s. Corn and flour were the basic items, followed by occasional shipments of pork, beef, grain, and lard.[72]

One of the attractions of the commercial intercourse with Baltimore was the price Maine fish merchants could expect to get for their product. Foodstuffs demanded by the state's agriculturally deficient coastal towns could be obtained closer to home—at Boston and New York—but it paid to obtain them farther south since wholesale fish prices were higher in the southern market. In September of 1854, for example, cod could command a dollar more per quintal at Baltimore than at Portland or Boston, and mackerel was selling for up to two dollars more per barrel.[73] Those willing to undertake the longer and more hazardous ocean voyage around the Virginia Capes could count, therefore, on between 10 and 25 percent additional for their cargoes. Salt mackerel was especially valued in the Baltimore market, and by 1860 the city had become one the major domestic consumers of that product.[74] Following the Civil War, the Chesapeake Bay metropolis emerged as the overall distribution center for the southern mackerel market, reexporting large amounts to various places in the Deep South.[75]

Despite the importance and eventual prominence of Baltimore, it was the cotton city of New Orleans that formed the keystone of Maine's southern fish trade in the pre–Civil War years. Like the Chesapeake region, antebellum New Orleans was a prime importer of New England mackerel, especially the more expensive "number one" grade.[76] The Deep South's appetite for pickled fish was reflected in the wholesale prices it offered for that article in the 1850s, which substantially exceeded those prevailing in the northern states. According to market quotations for early November 1854, New Orleans merchants were paying as much as $10.50 per barrel for even the undersized and low-quality "number three" mackerel, which brought a maximum of $8.50 in the Boston market.[77] Dried cod was also highly prized in the Gulf Coast region, and while small cod were considered suitable for shipment to the West Indies, the larger, medium-sized variety were earmarked for that domestic market.[78]

Among Maine's fish-exporting centers, the Penobscot Bay port of Castine was most closely identified with the New Orleans trade. Cargoes of fish were sent to the Mississippi Delta aboard Castine ships as early as the 1820s. In November 1823 the ship *Canova* was dispatched to the Crescent City with fish, potatoes, and lumber, and instructions to her captain to "pay particular attention to the market at N. Orleans, . . . see what articles of the produce of this Country will do best, . . . [and] especially learn what can be done with Pickled Codfish."[79] From this tentative beginning the trade evolved into a local specialty, and it continued unabated until the outbreak of North-South hostilities, ending only with the wartime closing of the southern ports.[80]

The unique commercial relationship between Castine and New Orleans, which differed markedly in some respects from the more traditional coast-wise commerce alluded to earlier, warrants special attention. In the early period (pre-1840), lumber and agricultural products figured prominently as supplemental additions to the dominant trade in fish. Several recorded voyages of the Castine ship *Antioch* between 1830 and 1840 indicate that such items as pine boards, spars, hay, and potatoes were routinely added to the basic southbound cargoes of dried cod and haddock, pickled mackerel, smoked herring, and fish oil. Turnips, peas, and empty molasses barrels appeared on at least one shipping list.[81]

In later years, freight complements varied somewhat, but the Gulf Coast trade remained otherwise unchanged. An analysis of existing cargo manifests for the port of Castine from 1849 to 1858 indicates that outward-bound shipments during that ten-year period consisted mostly of cod and mackerel, with other types of fish, such as herring, haddock, shad, and halibut, making up the balance. Occasional supplementary loads of hay, ice, granite, or paving stones lent diversity to the cargoes, but fish products were the essence of the trade. Although an occasional schooner participated, the long run around the Florida peninsula was mainly the province of the modest fleet of square-riggers maintained by Castine's more prominent fish merchants. Shipments were typically joint enterprises, several merchants shipping cooperatively to a common agent in New Orleans in a vessel owned by one or several of them. As a rule, departures were made in November or December, well after the close of the fishing season, thus allowing a few weeks for curing* and otherwise readying the catch for market.[82]

A representative cargo was that of the ship *Adams,* which departed Castine for New Orleans on December 18, 1857. On board were 110 drums** of

---

*The months of October and November were the best time to dry salted cod on the New England coast. In summer, the sun was too hot and the air too moist for effective curing. The less direct sunlight and more favorable northwest and southeast winds of late fall provided optimal conditions—not too warm and not too humid. (Source: *U.S.FCB, 1898,* 394–95.)

**The drum, commonly used in the long-distance shipment of dried fish, was a large, round, wooden container of varying capacity weighing (when full) anywhere from 200 to 900 pounds. In 1850 Saint John, New Brunswick, exporters packed their cod in 440-pound drums. At Gloucester, in 1880, five sizes of two to eight quintals each were employed. Drums of 500 to 800 pounds were popular at Portland prior to 1850 for West Indies trade, and Castine merchants of the 1840s preferred a uniform size holding around 600 pounds of cod or approximately a half-dozen quintals. (Sources: *Perley Reports,* 170; *Goode Report,* 2: 83, 167; PMM, WP, Ship *Antioch* Collection, box 3, file 52: cargo invoices, Castine to New Orleans, 27 November 1840; PMM, WP, Bark *Sarah L. Bryant* Collection, file 3: cargo invoice, Castine to Havana, 12 November 1847.)

dried cod and 46 half-barrels or kegs of cod tongues and sounds* belonging to Witherle & Company, as well as 120 barrels and 174 kegs of mackerel owned by fish merchant Samuel Adams. The entire shipment was consigned to the Orleans firm of Robeson, Dennett & Company. Of the cargo's two owners, one, Samuel Adams, was also managing owner of the vessel.[83]

On occasion, a New Orleans-owned-and-registered vessel might make the trip, as when the ship *Picayune* of that port left Castine in November of 1857 with 200 drums of cod, 250 barrels of mackerel, and 120 tons of hay.[84] The *Picayune* was one of four square-riggers built at Castine during the 1850s for New Orleans interests. Significantly, Castine vessel owners maintained minority shares in all four and thereby ensured periodic visits to Penobscot Bay waters for cargoes of fish. In the case of at least two of the ships, the *J. P. Whitney* and the *Castine* (launched in 1853 and 1857, respectively), primary ownership was vested in the New Orleans firm of J. P. Whitney & Company, prominent in the importation of dried cod from Castine, while most of the remaining shares were held by one of the Castine fish merchants doing business with that firm.[85] Despite such arrangements, which testified to an exceptionally close interregional trade relationship, most of Castine's southern shipments were sent in vessels that were locally owned and managed.

The inner complexity sometimes attending this outwardly simple trade is revealed by the manifests of the full-rigged ships *William Witherle* and *Ostervald*. The *Witherle*, which cleared for New Orleans on December 17, 1851, carried cod, mackerel, granite, and hay on that year-end voyage. Ownership of the cargo was divided among six different Castine shipping firms or individuals; the cargo itself was consigned partly to two specific New Orleans agents and partly to the master for his own discretionary marketing. The fish portion of the consignment alone required an itemized list of fifteen different articles, packed variously in drums, half-drums, kegs, barrels, and half-barrels, each differing in size and weight. Similarly, the *Ostervald*, southbound with fish and paving stones in November 1852, had twenty-one separate entries on her manifest and a cargo owned by seven local merchants or traders, three of whom claimed partial ownership of the vessel.[86]

After their arrival in New Orleans, these and other Castine ships did not pursue the usual course of coasting home with bulk shipments of agricultural produce. Instead, they became participants in the celebrated triangular

---

*Cod "tongues" (actually the throat muscles of the fish) were considered a table delicacy by some consumers. Sounds, the air bladders located near the spine, were used in the production of isinglass, a gelatinous substance from which glues and jellies were manufactured. (Sources: Greene, 435–36; Reynolds, 99–100; Alan Davidson, *North Atlantic Seafood* [New York: Viking Press, 1979], 53, 308, 403.)

trade in cotton, which played so prominent a role in the development of the port of New York and the growth of American antebellum commerce.

As traditionally outlined, the "cotton triangle" consisted of New York ships sailing in ballast or with general merchandise to one of the southern ports (Charleston, Savannah, Mobile, or New Orleans), loading with cotton for Liverpool, England, or Le Havre, France, and eventually returning to New York laden with European immigrants or general freight.[87] The Castine version of this three-sided trade, in contrast, had as its first leg the shipment of fish to New Orleans. Castine vessels then carried cotton to a European port—usually Liverpool or Le Havre, but often some place in the Mediterranean. The nature of the third leg is somewhat obscure; documentation is scant on the cargoes carried by returning Castine fish-and-cotton freighters during the 1850s, and they did not always sail directly for their home port. Nevertheless, there is no question that in the early years of the trade the homeward-bound cargo was salt, most of it coming from the British mines near Liverpool, with smaller amounts from the solar salteries of Cadiz on the coast of Spain.[88]

Salt shipments were certainly the rule prior to 1850. The very first Castine vessel to carry fish to New Orleans, the ship *Canova,* completed the fish-cotton-salt triangle on her maiden voyage in 1823–1824.[89] This trip established a precedent that was followed by the entire Castine fleet during most of the next quarter-century. The voyage of the square-rigger *Antioch* in 1835 was typical. The *Antioch* left Castine in January of that year with cod, mackerel, and some lumber consigned by the owners of the ship, Messrs. Witherle & Jarvis and Thomas Adams, to the ship's master for discretionary sale in New Orleans. After selling the cargo at the best available price, the vessel sailed for Liverpool in May, when freight rates peaked, with fifteen hundred bales of Delta cotton shipped by two New Orleans merchants to eleven British owners. In Liverpool the cotton was exchanged for 470 tons of white salt, which was purchased from Alexander Gordon & Company for the *Antioch*'s owners and carried to Castine in late July.[90] Thus the Castine merchants disposed of their fish, obtained the salt necessary to sustain the next season's fishing, and made an extra profit as shippers on the intervening cotton run.

In its most classic expression, then, Castine's participation in the triangular trade took the form of sending fish to the South, carrying cotton to Europe, and bringing salt home for local consumption. However, that pattern began to change around midcentury. After 1850, only a minority of the fish ships sailed directly from Europe to Castine, and most of the port's salt was brought across the Atlantic by other vessels. The majority of those substitute carriers flew the British flag and participated in the transatlantic

timber trade between Canada and the United Kingdom.[91] Their availability
for regularized departures from Liverpool in March and April—the optimum time for salt shipments in order to facilitate spring outfitting in the
fisheries—freed locally owned vessels for other, more profitable pursuits.

Among the appealing alternatives to salt-carrying for Castine ships was
the emigrant trade out of Liverpool, which reached its peak during the 1850s.
It was common for ordinary transatlantic trading vessels engaged in the European cotton run to serve as emigrant carriers on their westward passages,
particularly those heading for New England ports.[92] The probability that
several of the Castine fish-and-cotton carriers dabbled in this commerce is
strengthened by the high incidence of outside ownership in the vessels. Although local merchants retained firm majority control in most instances,
virtually every square-rigger sailing out of Castine in the mid-1850s had
at least one non-resident shareholder.[93] Outside ownership (and influence)
tended to be focused in Boston, a center of immigration. The ship *William
Witherle,* for example, was one-eighth owned by a Bostonian. The *Witherle,*
moreover, was registered at that port in 1853, two years after her launching,
and sailed from there for the next several years, even though her managing
ownership remained at Castine.[94]

One round trip by a Castine freighter in 1850–1851 is perhaps typical of
how the town's triangular trade worked in the immediate prewar decade.
The ship *William Jarvis* left Castine in late October 1850 laden with cod,
halibut, and ice for New Orleans. After a three-week voyage and a six-week
stay in port, she cleared the Gulf Coast port on the last day of December,
bound for Liverpool with cotton. Four months later the *Jarvis* completed
the triangle, arriving in Boston on April 21, 1851, forty-one days out of
England. The vessel's incoming cargo went unrecorded, but since she was
quarantined for several days upon arrival, human freight was certainly a
large part of it.[95]

In common variation of the triangular trade, some fish vessels shunned
the usual New Orleans to Liverpool run in order to bring southern cotton
directly north for use in local textile mills or eventual re-export to Europe
from an East Coast port. Robert G. Albion found this two-sided route,
which had the virtue of providing an eastbound cargo for New York's
packet ships, to be as important as the normal triangular trade to the development of that city's prosperity.[96] Boston also participated in the domestic
cotton shuttle, and it was on the Boston axis of the two-sided cotton trade
that Castine ships figured prominently.

Until circa 1850 the Boston route was rarely traversed by Castine's fish
carriers, but after that time it served increasingly as a substitute for one of
the two consecutive round trips commonly made each year between New

Orleans and Europe along the south-to-east leg of the cotton triangle. Both the ship *Adams* and the bark *Ellen Noyes* sailed from Castine to New Orleans in November 1849—the former with over one hundred tons of cod, mackerel, and herring—in order to load cargoes for Boston, where they arrived in late February 1850. The subsequent voyages of the *Noyes* are unknown, but the *Adams* returned immediately to southern waters to ship cotton for Liverpool.[97] A third Castine vessel, the *St. Leon,* is also on record as having carried cotton on the Boston run. In February 1849 this ship interrupted her normal trafficking to bring eighteen hundred bales north from the secondary cotton port of Mobile, before resuming the New Orleans-Liverpool-Castine triangle.[98]

It is beyond the scope of this narrative to examine in detail whatever relationship may have existed between New England's "Lords of the Loom" and the fish merchants of Castine. Boston involvement in the ownership of Castine vessels, however, and the pattern of movement of those vessels, suggest a connection. Suffice it to say that the demands of the Massachusetts textile industry appear to have combined with the immigrant trade in significantly influencing the commerce of one eastern Maine fishing community in the years preceding the Civil War.

Whatever the subsequent disposition of Castine's fish ships following delivery of their primary cargoes, their transient wanderings do not detract from the importance of the town's New Orleans trade. On a purely local level, the southern fish shipments were indispensable to the operation of the dozen or so square-riggers sailing out of Castine in the 1850s, providing as they did a needed outbound cargo. They permitted, in effect, the participation of the town's merchants in the lucrative cotton trade and, in a broader sense, provided the national merchant marine with additional carriers for the international staple trade upon which the country's antebellum economy was considerably based. Most important, perhaps, from a regional perspective, the New Orleans connection presented a marketing outlet of sizeable proportions to the fishermen of the entire Penobscot region.

It was as a unique expression of economic independence, however, that Castine's southern fish trade was most significant. The irregular aspects and comparatively small scale of operations notwithstanding, it was one chapter in the commercial development of the state of Maine that did not smack of internal colonialism. Castine's triangular trade via New Orleans was generated, nurtured, and controlled by local merchants, not those in Boston or New York. In its purest form (pre-1850), it was totally self-contained: there was no transshipment, outside chartering, or middleman involvement; the exported commodity (fish) went straight to its ultimate market with no detours; needed imports, such as salt, came directly into Maine; the means of transportation were locally owned; and the profits were not shared by out-side economic interests. While it lasted, the New Orleans trade preserved a modicum of regional economic autonomy and did much to encourage the growth of an independent fishing industry in eastern Maine.

Most of the fish shipped to New Orleans was in the form of cod and mackerel, but those were not the only products in demand in the southern states. The slave markets of the region, in particular, absorbed large quanti-ties of the generally less popular species. Southern slaves were the principal consumers of the dried haddock procured in the Bay of Fundy by eastern Maine fishermen.[99] Herring, too, played a considerable role in the Ameri-can slave diet. If anything, the demand for herring on antebellum planta-tions was greater than that for any other seafood. According to one con-temporary authority, "Prior to the rebellion the bulk of the [American] pickled herring were consumed by the negroes of the Southern States."[100] This included Maine's Magdalen catch, which in the eastern part of the state was smoked and earmarked primarily for the slave South. As was the case with dried-cod shipments to the Caribbean, Maine's smoked-herring trade with the South was in large measure an indirect trade. When the Mag-dalen Islands fishery was at its peak, the Maine herring sold to plantation owners for their slaves went initially by schooner to Boston, where it was repacked and transshipped to its ultimate destination.[101] This indirect do-mestic trade provides added indication of Maine's economic dependency on outside forces—in this case the Massachusetts fish dealers, who served as middlemen for an important segment of the southern trade.

The South, significant as it was among the markets for New England fish, was eventually displaced by the vast and steadily growing interior section that bordered it. Within fifteen years after the close of the Civil War, much of the salt mackerel cured in Massachusetts was finding its way by rail to In-diana, Illinois, Minnesota, and Missouri, and most of the domestic herring catch was being marketed in western Pennsylvania and points beyond.[102] Ohio emerged about the same time as a significant wholesale market for fish landed at Portland, and the city of Cincinnati developed into a center of inland distribution for the catch of Maine fishermen.[103]

It was the West, in short, that eventually became the focus of a consider-able part of the American fish trade after 1865. This fact notwithstanding, the West was not a major factor in the years when Maine's fish products were most important in the national marketplace. This is not to say that no Maine fish reached the western states. A demand for seafood in the trans-Appalachian region certainly existed, as Massachusetts newspapers noted in 1838.[104] Some modest shipments of dried cod and smoked herring were reaching Cincinnati as early as 1846, by way of canal, river, and railroad, and they increased steadily, if slowly, throughout the 1850s.[105] Nevertheless, the West lacked the close connective ties with the Northeast that seaports provided the Gulf states, and the interior section awaited completion of the nation's railroad network for the implementation of a large-scale fish trade. Until that postwar development, most of the Maine fish reaching western tables did so indirectly via the river commerce of seaports like New Orleans.

Maine's only known direct contact with a western market in the early period—if, indeed, it can be called western rather than southern—was with the Gulf Coast state of Texas, which was able to accommodate seaborne trade through the port of Galveston. Texas imported small amounts of dried and pickled fish beginning in the 1830s, well before statehood.[106] Maine ships touched at Galveston on occasion in the 1850s. One of the itinerant Castine fish-and-cotton carriers, the *John H. Jarvis*, made an appearance there in 1858 to load Texas cotton for Liverpool.[107] For the most part, however, Maine's inter-regional fish trade was confined to southern ports east of the Mississippi, a fact of some considerable consequence to the state's fishing industry as it turned out.

The Urban North

Aside from the South, the major domestic markets for Maine fish, both before and after the Civil War, were the populous urban centers of the Northeast. There is no question that the northeastern coastal cities consumed by far the largest proportion of the Maine catch. Boston and New York emerged early as the leaders in that respect. Eastport was already shipping dried cod, smoked herring, and fish oil to both places in the middle 1820s, and Portland was sending most of its domestically marketed fish to the two metropolitan markets by 1840.[108]

Boston was the more important of the cities to Maine fishermen before the Civil War. The Mount Desert Island region sent large amounts of dried fish and cobblestones there in exchange for dry goods and important staples like flour and sugar.[109] Items of export to the Massachusetts capital from Cranberry Isles, Sedgwick, and Bristol included cod, herring, and fish oil, while Belfast and Boothbay shipped mackerel.[110] The Penobscot Bay island of Vinalhaven sold the bulk of its Magdalen herring in Boston, as well as its entire dried-fish production, forwarding $70,000 worth of cod to the city in 1855 alone. Island fishermen from Matinicus and Westport also carried their smoked herring there, the former supplying ten thousand boxes a year in the 1840s.[111] Among the mainland towns marketing almost exclusively in Boston during the antebellum period were the twin Grand Banks ports of Bucksport and Orland, which together provided Hub merchants with an average of twenty thousand quintals of dried cod annually throughout the

1850s.[112] The coastal towns around Passamaquoddy Bay were less closely tied to Boston but they did, nevertheless, look upon it as one of their primary outlets. Cargoes shipped from Eastport, Lubec, and Cutler over the period 1840–1860 included dried fish of all kinds and, of course, smoked herring, the "'Quoddy" specialty.[113]

Close economic ties between Boston and Maine were natural, given their geographic proximity. Boston was the nearest large, outside market for Maine's exportable raw materials, including fish, and the nearest source of supply for commodities not readily available down east. Even Castine, with its sizeable southern trade, relied heavily on the commerce it developed simultaneously with the Massachusetts capital. The marine lists of the 1850s are replete with entrances and clearances of vessels trading between the two ports. Traffic during the winter season, when fish cargoes were usually delivered, was uncommonly heavy. During the first two weeks of February 1854, for instance, three schooners from Castine were reported at Boston, either arriving to discharge freight or departing for home.[114]

Over time, the Castine merchants developed a regular trading relationship with a handful of Boston mercantile houses, a connection analogous in many respects to the special arrangements they cultivated and maintained with certain New Orleans firms. In both cases, longstanding business loyalties or force of habit had created by the 1850s what might almost be called an institutionalized commerce. Normally, several off-duty cod bankers would be sent "up" to Boston at the close of the fishing season with their own cured catch or, alternatively, with the fares of one or more other schooners belonging to the same owner. These trips were made between late fall and early spring, roughly in conjunction with the shipments sent south aboard the square-riggers of the foreign-trading fleet. They differed somewhat in that the cargoes were composed almost entirely of dried cod and rarely contained the mackerel, herring, and other, more exotic fish products customarily found aboard New Orleans–bound freighters. Settlements of the previous summer's banks voyages (crew payments, distribution of profits, etc.) awaited the completion of these coasting trips and were dependent on prevailing prices at Boston. There was, however, little or no discretionary marketing. According to the papers of several company-owned schooners, William Witherle & Company, the leading Castine firm, dealt with only three of Boston's two-dozen salt-fish wholesalers—D. Collins, B. Leavitt & Company, and Isaac Rich & Company—and, after 1855, exclusively with the last-named firm.[115]

The return cargoes of Castine vessels in the Boston fish trade consisted of assorted hardware, dry goods, and provisions, purchased for the most part from one particular establishment, the firm of Hall & Myrick. A detailed examination of the surviving manifests of several of these schooners reveals much about how the fishing economy of coastal Maine functioned in the 1850s. While the fish shipped from Castine to New Orleans provided the basis for a profit-making international trade—a monetary trade, in the case of cotton and immigrants—the cargoes sent to Boston during the same period provided the exchange medium for a barter system essential to the town's very existence. Freight items on the manifests of four typical Castine schooners arriving from Boston in the early 1850s fell for the most part into the category of foodstuffs. There were some manufactured products (clothing, crockery) and shipbuilding materials (oakum, hemp, anchor chain), but the cargoes were heavily weighted toward such basic staples as flour, corn, pork, sugar, molasses, coffee, tea, dried fruits, and rice.[116] These were all necessary articles to a seaport lacking an agricultural hinterland capable of supplying its own needs and those of the fishing vessels it serviced. The economic diversity permitted at Castine by the existence of dual fleets of coasting schooners and foreign-trading vessels allowed local merchants to take a substantial profit above and beyond mere subsistence. In the outports, however, the coastal trade with Boston—fish in exchange for agricultural foodstuffs and other necessities—allowed for survival and little more. It served, moreover, to keep most of coastal Maine securely within the Bay State's economic sphere of influence.

Maine's other chief northeastern market, New York City, played a subordinate role to Boston for much of the nineteenth century. Nevertheless, New York did compete with Boston for the Maine fisheries catch prior to the Civil War, notably for smoked herring from Boothbay and the Mount Desert region.[117] A portion of the banks cod landed at Boothbay and Southport also found its way to New York by way of Portland wholesalers, and a share of Portland's own catch was likewise earmarked for New York dealers.[118] In addition, there are isolated references to cod shipments leaving Deer Isle and the ports of Castine and Orland for the Manhattan market, suggesting that cargoes were sent there periodically from Penobscot Bay throughout the antebellum era.[119]

The real center of Maine's fish trade with New York, however, was located at the far eastern extremity of the state's coastline, in Passamaquoddy Bay. The fishing towns of Eastport and Lubec contrived somehow to remain outside the economic orbit of Boston, tying their maritime trade instead to New York City and (to a lesser degree) the city of Philadelphia. Between 1840 and 1860 a total of twenty-nine vessels from Eastport and Lubec were lost, run aground, or otherwise disabled while carrying fish to markets along the East Coast. Of this number, fourteen (or nearly half) were bound for New York, and five for Philadelphia. Only three were lost coasting to Boston during the same period.[120]

The reason for Passamaquoddy's ties to New York was related to the city's special interest in pickled and smoked fish, especially herring, which the Eastport and Lubec fisheries emphasized. Half of the fourteen coasters reported lost or damaged on the 'Quoddy–New York run were carrying smoked or pickled fish, meaning either herring or mackerel.[121] These cargoes were important to the city's re-export trade. During the last half-dozen pre–Civil War years, pickled fish (as opposed to dried) made up approximately one-third of the value of New York's foreign fish exports, compared to roughly one-fifth for Boston.[122]

Eastport and Lubec exported far more herring than any other part of Maine. It was the basis of their fish trade and one of the three commodities that formed the bedrock of their maritime commerce. The other two were ground plaster (from the plaster mills of Lubec) and wood laths, both key items in building construction. Cargoes composed of fish alone seldom left Passamaquoddy ports. The usual practice was to combine fish with laths or plaster, although at times all three were carried on a single voyage.[123] When herring or mackerel and laths constituted the cargo, the fish portion would be placed below deck in barrels or boxes,* and the lumber would be bundled and stowed topside in the open. On more than one stormy occasion, this meant the loss of an entire deckload of laths, an ever-present hazard on the dangerous fall-winter passage around Cape Cod and through Nantucket Sound.[124] A typical cargo was that of the schooner *Tilton*, which left Eastport in September 1860 with a load of fish and laths for Sturgess & Company of New York. The vessel carried 370 barrels and 63 half-barrels of pickled mackerel, 204 barrels of pickled herring, 500 boxes of smoked herring, and 283,000 laths, most of which was lost when she capsized in a gale in Long Island Sound, not far from New Haven.[125]

Like the Castine schooners that visited Boston, those transporting 'Quoddy fish to New York and Philadelphia brought back badly needed provisions to a maritime region almost totally lacking in agricultural resources.** Flour and corn were the commodities most in demand, and ma-

---

*Unlike pickled fish, which were packed in barrels, smoked herring were packed in small wooden boxes that measured (by law) 17″ × 11″ × 6″ before 1849 and 17″ × 8½″ × 6″ after that date. (Sources: *Me.PL, 1821*, chap. 150; *Me.PL, 1849*, chap. 91.)

**The barren nature of the Passamaquoddy coastline was such that in the 1840s Lubec was actually forced to supplement local hay production by bringing in shipments from the westward. (Source: *EA*, marine list, 18 February 1843.)

rine lists indicate that these articles, along with lesser amounts of other foodstuffs, were imported from New York for several decades beginning at least as early as the 1840s.[126] The flour-and-corn shuttle had some of the aspects of a scheduled packet trade. One Eastport mercantile house, C. B. & E. S. Paine, ran its own vessel, the *Z. A. Paine,* to and from New York on a twice-yearly basis during the late 1850s and early 1860s, often advertising anticipated shipments well in advance. The Paines imported flour, corn, pork, beef, rice, butter, cheese, molasses, coffee, lard, meal, and Puerto Rican sugar. Their business was both wholesale and retail, cash or barter. In the latter case, foodstuffs were exchanged for fish and lumber, which served as return cargoes for the company schooner.[127]

Despite New York's singular role in the development of the Passamaquoddy fish trade, it was not until after the Civil War, when Boston's foreign-export business declined, that the city became a truly important Maine market. Late in the 1870s, about the time Maine-coast herring replaced the Magdalen Islands variety in the smoked-herring industry, New York took over as the dominant market for that product.[128] Simultaneously, the city emerged as the focus of the southern spring mackerel fishery in which Maine vessels figured so prominently. Although some fresh spring mackerel were landed at Philadelphia and southern New England ports in the 1870s and 1880s, the famous Fulton Fish Market on the tip of Manhattan handled 70 to 90 percent of the annual output.[129] By 1880 New York was also the destination for half of the dried cod and two-thirds of the pickled mackerel landed at Portland, then Maine's leading fishing port.[130]

Throughout the golden era of Maine's fisheries, when the South and the urban centers of the East Coast were the prime domestic markets for the state's fish, there was also a constant local market, a market that grew with the passage of time. Southport's leading fishing firm during the 1860s, J. & J. Maddocks, prepared most of the cod taken by its Western Bank schooners for shipment to the West Indies. In addition, however, the Maddocks firm maintained a thousand accounts with retail merchants in surrounding towns.[131] The prominent Belfast retail establishment of Daniel McFarland carried on a flourishing barter trade with the surrounding countryside in 1860, exchanging fresh cod, hake, and haddock supplied by local fishermen for "good country produce," such as potatoes, apples, butter, and eggs.[132] Retail merchants at Portland, too, included native fish products as part of their stock. Dried cod ("Maj. McKown's best"), pickled mackerel, and pollock were among the items prominently displayed by city storekeepers in the 1840s and 1850s.[133] Maine fish fed the West Indies, the rural South, and the urban North during the nineteenth century, but it also fed Maine people as well.

The Civil War and Its Legacy

Not many years in the past, the fishing bounty was remorse-
lessly torn from our fishermen, and . . . tariff extortionate
was imposed upon them . . . until the industry lies fettered,
prostrate, helpless and lifeless under burdens too heavy to
be borne. . . . —letter to a Maine newspaper, 1888 [1]

In 1861 Maine was the most important sea-fishing state in the Union. Five
years later the Maine fisheries were in decline, and within twenty-five years
they were insignificant in national terms. The reasons for this abrupt turn of
events were many and complex. Some were interrelated and mutually reinforcing, creating a domino effect upon the industry structure. A few were
inherent weaknesses magnified in an era of crisis. Still others resulted from
outside forces working upon the socioeconomic fabric of the nation as well
as that of Maine. Their cumulative effect was to destroy a unique native industry and an entire way of life within one generation.

The Double-Edged Sword

The initial factor in the decline of the Maine sea fisheries was the Civil War.
The precise nature of the war's role in this process is less clear-cut than might
at first appear to be the case, and it has been generally misunderstood. In
several respects, the conflict was a doubled-edged sword: it cut both ways,
hurting but at the same time helping the fishing industry. On balance, however, its impact was negative.

It might be well, in assessing that impact, to first examine an aspect of
the war that did *not* contribute to the decline of the fisheries. A theory has
been advanced, from time to time, that military manpower needs undermined the industry by siphoning off potential crewmen. The primary nineteenth-century writer on the Maine fisheries attributed the disruption of activity at Vinalhaven and Gouldsboro to this factor, and it has also been used
to explain the demise of Marblehead, Massachusetts.[2] Other subscribers to
the labor-shortage theory have stressed the particular role of the Union navy.
George Brown Goode and Joseph W. Collins maintained that large numbers
of fishermen entered the naval service between 1861 and 1865.[3] Echoing that
claim, fisheries historian Raymond McFarland insisted that the fishermen of

New England had taken "an active part in the naval history of the Civil War."[4] A more recent writer, George W. Dalzell, has pointed to massive enlistment in the federal navy by fishermen, spurred on by recruiting bounties, as one of the chief causes of injury to the fisheries during the war.[5]

The picture painted by Dalzell of banks crewmen deserting their vessels at the wharves to become bluejackets does not square with reality, at least with reference to Maine. There is no evidence, first of all, that down-east fishermen were especially anxious to don uniforms and head south. If anything, the opposite was true. An 1862 newspaper report, under the headline "Great Fright at Winter Harbor," described the turmoil created in one Hancock County coastal town by rumors that local authorities were about to commence drafting men for military service. Wrote a correspondent on the scene: "The fright was general amongst the fishermen. Sunday night the people in the vicinity had their slumbers disturbed by the rattling of chains and other accompaniments to a fleet getting under weigh [*sic*], and in the morning every craft was found to have skedaddled. Even the old 'bounty catchers,' that had been rotting in the harbor for twenty years, left for the fishing grounds, much to the joy of the citizens."[6]

Lack of enthusiasm for the fray was not limited to Maine fishermen. Captain James W. Pattillo, retired skipper of a Gloucester mackerel schooner, recalled an extended trip to the Gulf of St. Lawrence in 1863 during which he transshipped two loads of fish home from Canso, Nova Scotia, rather than return to port with each catch. His crew, related Pattillo, were fearful of being drafted into the Union army and persuaded him to remain on the fishing grounds throughout the summer.[7]

There is little indication that fishermen cared any more for the navy, their supposed preference for that branch of service notwithstanding. Out of 160 Civil War servicemen from the western Maine fishing port of Boothbay, for example, only 20 went into the navy.[8] Muster records of several other Maine fishing towns show a similar disinclination to volunteer for sea duty. On average, no more than a quarter of the enlistees from the coastal villages appear to have chosen naval service.[9] Moreover, the total number of servicemen taken from the fishing ports, army and navy combined, was not sufficient in most instances to disrupt local economies. The case of Southport is particularly instructive. The 33 soldiers and sailors absent from that coastal hamlet during the war years represented less than 17 percent of the total 1860 male work force of 200 men and boys, which included 141 fishermen. Assuming all 33 enlistees were previously active in the fisheries, they were barely numerous enough to man three banks schooners, a minor loss to a town that maintained several dozen vessels.[10]

Enlistment figures aside, the very timing of the wartime decline of the Maine and Massachusetts fishing fleets strongly suggests that the loss of potential crewmen was not a crucial factor. The war, first of all, was under way a full four years before tonnage reductions became serious. It was not until 1865 that the number of enrolled fishing schooners dropped substantially.[11] Even the institution of a military draft in early 1863 appears to have had little effect. The conscription act itself was formulated in such a way that avoidance of service was a relatively simple matter for those having the means. Deferment upon payment of a lump sum to the government was permitted, as was exemption by use of substitutes.[12] There is evidence that both expedients were employed along the Maine coast. Between 1861 and 1865 the island community of Islesboro furnished the military with just twenty-five local recruits through draft or enlistment, but it provided an additional sixty-seven paid substitutes, who came from outside the town. Another ten residents bought their way out of the draft by paying commutation. Most of the substitutes were found not in neighboring fishing villages but in the Canadian Maritimes or among recent immigrants from Europe. In all, three-quarters of Islesboro's wartime obligation was satisfied by means other than direct service. A fifth of nearby Brooksville's quota was filled in the same way.[13] Admittedly, fishermen were less likely than more affluent members of society to avoid service by hiring substitutes. The opportunity was there, nevertheless, and some apparently took advantage of it.

The manpower impact of the Civil War on the fisheries was further reduced by the character of the war itself. The conflict was a young man's war, fought largely by soldiers under the age of twenty-five.[14] Since most Maine fishermen were mature men in their late twenties or early thirties, the disruptive influence on the industry was necessarily minimized. An examination of seven representative fishing ports for the year 1860 reveals the average ages of those in the fisheries to have ranged from a low of twenty-seven to a high of thirty-five, with an average of thirty-one years for the entire sample. The skippers or "master fishermen"—those most crucial to the operation of the vessels—were older still. At Vinalhaven Island they averaged thirty-six years of age, compared to twenty-eight for ordinary crew members. Overall, individuals between eighteen (the lower legal limit for military service) and twenty-four, the age cohort most likely to enlist, constituted barely a quarter of the fishing work force of the seven towns. Furthermore, a majority of the fishermen in the sample communities were married men with families.[15] Clearly, the great bulk of Maine fishermen fell into a social, as well as an age, group unlikely to go to war in large numbers.

A final observation may be made regarding the effect of the Civil War upon the work force of the Maine fishing industry. The war, irrespective of its impact in the short run, did minimal long-range damage to the numerical strength of the fishing population. There is no indication, for instance, that battle fatalities drained the Maine fisheries of their postwar manpower. Only one of the state's major fishing ports, Boothbay, suffered a rate of attrition that might be considered serious. This town lost 51 (or one-third) of the 160 men it sent to war, a figure that translates into 5.8 percent of the prewar male work force, of which about half were fishermen.[16] No other Maine fishing community suffered as great a proportion of war fatalities vis-à-vis enlisted personnel.[17] Deer Isle, which provided the antebellum fisheries with more fishermen than any other coastal village in the state (502 in 1860), lost 19 men through combat or disease, but that number represented just 2 percent of its prewar work force, all occupations included.[18] These loss percentages, though devastating in human terms, were certainly not large enough to constitute an economic disaster. In fact, as it turned out, there was no connection between the post-bellum economic health of Maine's fishing ports and their degree of wartime suffering. Boothbay, the hardest hit among Maine ports, prospered in the immediate postwar fisheries, while Deer Isle, which absorbed considerably fewer losses, underwent a severe industry decline.[19]

From the manpower perspective, the major impact of the Civil War on the fishing industry would seem to have been the periodic inconvenience involved in the necessary hiring of inexperienced crewmen to replace those fishermen who did leave for wartime service. Enlistments at Gloucester in 1863 forced owners of the port's three hundred mackerel schooners to take on a substantial number of "green hands" for that year's Gulf of St. Lawrence fishery.[20] Nevertheless, the vessels did sail, and while efficiency may have suffered, the Gloucester fleet continued to function; in fact, it increased in size over the ensuing year.[21]

In Maine the industry actually reached its highest quantitative development during the early stages of the Civil War. Not only did the state's overall fishing tonnage peak in the course of hostilities, its fishermen were also motivated to enter the mackerel fishery in large numbers for the first time.[22] Moreover, the war marked the heaviest participation in the industry for several individual customs districts within Maine. Waldoboro District owned more fishing tonnage in 1862 than in any other year, Passamaquoddy reached its all-time high in 1863, and 1864 was the peak year for the Wiscasset District fisheries. In addition, the initial war year of 1861 marked the pinnacle of fisheries development for the districts of Belfast, Penobscot, and Frenchman's Bay, the core region of the industry down east.[23]

The reason for this surge of activity was purely economic. It was an optimistic response to heightened demand and the higher prices accompanying that demand. The southern market for fish was, of course, lost as a result of the war, but other traditional markets remained firm and in some instances expanded. Exports to the West Indies, for example, increased during the first three years of hostilities. In 1861–1862, shipments to the island of Haiti alone were roughly double what they had been in 1859–1860.[24] This was despite the fact that militarily "the best prospect of all for the [Confederate] cruisers . . . was the great West Indian trade."[25]

In the domestic market, consumption was stimulated by the accelerating needs of the North's armed forces. The Union army, which used fish as a periodic substitute for its normal salt-pork or salt-beef ration,[26] was an especially good customer. According to one local fish merchant, Gloucester mackerel prices rose between 1861 and 1865 primarily because of the army's demands.[27] That was not a chance development. Gloucester merchant and sometime politician David M. Low had been in the forefront of a successful lobby effort during the early stages of the conflict to introduce fish into Union army rations. Resultant government purchases of cod and mackerel, he recalled, "made a better market for the fish and gave them higher prices. . . . It increased the demand."[28] By the last full year of the war (1864), the army's procurement of dried and pickled fish from all sources totalled 11.7 million pounds and cost the War Department slightly less than $900,000. That purchase approximately equalled the entire amount of fish exported to foreign markets during the same year from the port of New York.[29]

For a time, the needs of the military and the shortages they created in the home-front market had a positive impact on the New England fishing industry. High demand, coupled with the general wartime inflation, led in the short term to unparalleled high prices and some limited prosperity. "During the four years of the war," said Gloucester vessel owner Joseph Proctor, "I made money beyond what I ever did in my life at any other time."[30] On Cape Cod, mackerel from the Gulf of St. Lawrence sold in 1864 at prices higher than any within living memory.[31] The situation was similar in the Maine mackerel ports. At Boothbay, the fishing firm of Mc-Dougall & Race reached its peak of profitability during the "excitement" of the war.[32] A competitor, McKown & Reed, reported at the end of the 1864 season that one of its schooners had stocked $18,000 fishing for cod and mackerel during the year,* a munificent sum compared to the $3,000 to $4,000 typically realized by prewar cod bankers.[33]

---

*A vessel's "gross stock" was the amount of money obtained from the sale of her catch prior to any deduction of expenses related to the voyage. (Source: *Goode Report*, sec. 5, 1:292.)

Some eastern ports also shared in the economic euphoria of the moment. High wartime prices are said to have formed the basis for the postwar prosperity of Swan's Island by permitting several of the town's fishing captains to accumulate large amounts of capital and property.[34] Perhaps the ultimate commentary on the Civil War's stimulative effect on the Maine fisheries was the experience of Biddeford Pool's fishermen, who were actually able to make money catching dogfish for oil during the years of the conflict.[35] Such dramatic examples, combined with the undeniable increase in wholesale fish prices, apparently led one respected scholar to claim that "at the close of the Civil War the fisheries were prosperous in the State of Maine, probably beyond any other period to that date."[36]

Unfortunately, the wartime prosperity was mostly ephemeral. For one thing, it was limited primarily to mackerel-fishing ports, of which (Boothbay and Swan's Island notwithstanding) Maine had few. The prices Maine fishermen received for their products were, without doubt, extremely high. At Portland, bank-cod prices doubled during the war, reaching their highest point in history. Mackerel, too, brought the best price it had ever commanded up to that time.[37] The problem, from the viewpoint of the fishermen, was that these price increases were part of a generalized wartime inflation and that they were cancelled out by even higher costs.

The expenses associated with fishing began to rise early in the war, and the increases were cumulative. Everything fishermen used, directly or indirectly, rose in price. For about two years, the costs were manageable. A temporary decline in wholesale food prices—especially in basic staples like flour, pork, and molasses—kept the overall cost of outfitting for a banks voyage within reason.[38] Beginning in 1863, however, increased costs ceased being inconvenient and became clearly burdensome. Outfitting expenses on Cape Cod swelled during that year to double what they had been before the war, and profit margins suddenly became a cause for concern. For the first time, the price of gear and supplies began to produce attrition in the ranks of the region's mackerel-fishing fleet.[39]

The nadir, so far as Maine fishermen were concerned, was reached in 1864. Compared to May 1860, the Portland wholesale market of May 1864 showed an overall increase of 141 percent in the average price of twenty-five articles used in the fisheries. Salt, for example, which was indispensable in preserving the catch, had gone up 175 to 194 percent, depending on the variety used. Manila and Russian hemp cordage, employed in rigging and anchor cables, had risen 142 and 130 percent, respectively. Canvas duck for sails had increased nearly 300 percent. Tar, essential in treating hemp cordage against rot, had shot up over 900 percent. Oakum, the caulking agent, was up 100 percent, and iron for anchors, chains, and fastenings was as much as 200 percent higher. Vessels provisioning at Portland in the spring of 1864 also faced rising food prices. In comparison to the immediate prewar period, they were obliged to pay 231 percent more for their coffee, 150 percent more for rice, and at least 50 percent more for almost everything else needed to sustain their crews. Most distressing of all was the inflated cost of Cuban molasses,* the sea cook's traditional sweetener and multipurpose galley aid, which had suddenly jumped to a price 188 percent above what it had been in 1860.[40] Even the fisherman's everyday work clothes increased in cost during the war years. Flannel shirts, which were common apparel in the eastern Maine fleet before the war, doubled in price between 1860 and 1864.[41] Raw wool, of which so much seamen's clothing was made—including the "nippers" or mittens used by fishermen—nearly tripled over the same period.[42]

The inflation in fishing expenses would have scarcely mattered if the prices fishermen got for their catch had kept pace. They did not. Wholesale fish prices for September, when the banks vessels returned to port, moved steadily upward in Maine and Massachusetts markets during the war years, but their annual increases never equalled the cost increases faced each previous May at outfitting time. Large cod, for instance, were bringing $8.00 per quintal at Portland in the autumn of 1864, compared to $3.75 per quintal four years earlier, a 113 percent increase. Yet bankers benefitting from that inflated price had purchased Liverpool salt the previous May that wholesaled at $5.50 per hogshead, or 175 percent more than the prewar figure of $2.00 per hogshead.[43] When Portland prices reached their wartime peak in the desperate months of late 1864 and early 1865, items used in the fisheries were wholesaling on average at 222 percent above the prewar level, while fish and fish products were bringing only 172 percent more than before the war.[44]

The price structure maintained between 1861 and 1865, then, had a steadily eroding effect on the Maine fishing industry. Men left home with high hopes each spring, only to discover upon settlement of the voyage months later that their financial return was not what had been anticipated—that

---

*Eastern Maine schooners bound for the banks usually carried fifty to seventy-five gallons of this precious liquid for cooking, baking, and sweetening coffee. It was one of the small luxuries that made the fisherman's life bearable and could not be dispensed with, even at wartime prices. Coffee, however, became so expensive that it was not even carried aboard Maine schooners by 1864 and 1865. Tea, which had rarely appeared among the commodities stocked in the 1850s, was the substitute beverage of choice by the latter stages of the war. (Sources: PMM, WP, MS 125; BLH, WC, MS 176: Journal of Fishing Outfits, Witherle & Company, 1864–65.)

they were, in fact, falling further behind in their race with inflation. Some made money, of course, and a few got rich. As always, an inflationary economy held out the promise of profit for those shrewd enough to anticipate market fluctuations, powerful or clever enough to manipulate supply and demand, resourceful enough to reduce costs, or simply lucky enough to be at the right place at the right time.

In addition, the nature of the inflation plaguing the fishing industry was such that those enterprises operating with relatively new vessels and equipment at the start of the war—namely, the larger, better-capitalized mercantile firms—were able to temporarily avoid the worst effects of rising prices. Generally speaking, wartime inflation was greatest in the area of hardware and naval stores. With the outstanding exception of salt, items in those categories—anchors, sail duck, cordage, tar, etc.—accelerated in price at roughly twice the rate of other everyday commodities used in the fisheries, such as vessel provisions.[45] Salt and foodstuffs were, of necessity, purchased each fishing season. Other acquisitions could be delayed. A suit of sails and running rigging for a fishing schooner lasted two years, for example, while anchor cables were normally good for three years.[46] Owners of new vessels, therefore, had a built-in buffer against serious economic dislocation during the initial war years. Nevertheless, equipment does wear out, and by 1864–1865 all owners and fishermen were in the same dory, so to speak.* The unique character of the industry itself, as well as the distinctive peculiarities of the Civil War inflation, eventually interacted to depress all sectors of the Maine fisheries more or less equally.

The Burden of High Protection

To appreciate fully the economic impact of the Civil War upon the fishing industry, it is necessary to understand the nature of the inflation that accompanied it. The inflation of 1861–1865 was not just an ordinary market inflation related to wartime problems of supply and demand. To some extent, of course, price increases were a response to changed market conditions. Massive expansion of the military created chronic shortages and led to inevitable profiteering. In addition, the very absence of the South from the Union was

---

*Individuals or firms needing to replace their fishing craft or equipment faced one additional inflationary burden by the late stages of the war. The federal Internal Revenue Act of 1864, passed in June of that year, levied producer excise taxes ranging from 2 to 5 percent on all domestically manufactured vessel hulls, masts, spars, blocks, and sails. This war tax applied to fishing schooners and so contributed to higher industry costs for the duration of the conflict. (Source: *U.S.AppCG*, 38th Cong., 1st Sess. [1864], 222.)

a factor. The inflated cost of cotton goods (e.g., sail duck), for instance, could doubtless be traced to the secession of the southern agricultural states that normally provided the raw material. Nevertheless, the inflation visited upon the North's economy after the fall of the Fort Sumter was in large part a political inflation brought about by direct government action. The issuance of paper money, historians have agreed, was crucial.[47] But the inflation caused by the resort to paper currency affected all parts of the economy equally in terms of commodity prices. More critical to the fisheries in particular was the selective inflation intentionally created by the erection of high tariff barriers, a process facilitated by the withdrawal of the anti-protectionist southern delegation from Congress in 1861. The American policy of tariff reduction that had prevailed since the 1830s was completely reversed by the Morrill Act of 1861, which incorporated a radically new high-tariff system.[48]

The economic change of direction was both sudden and dramatic. Referring to the high-protection legislation enacted in 1861, tariff authority F. W. Taussig noted that "from that time till 1865 no session, indeed, hardly a month of any session passed in which some increase in duties on imports was not made."[49] After fifteen moderate years (1846–1860) during which import levies had consistently averaged between 20 and 30 percent overall, the war years saw them jump on a combined basis to nearly 50 percent.[50] These drastically higher duties compounded the effects of general inflation in the area of imported goods, making an already bad situation worse.

The New England fishing industry, more than most other sectors of the antebellum American economy, had a special vulnerability to the tariff inflation of 1861–1865. It was, quite simply, not self-sufficient in its means of production. It was an industry almost totally dependent on imports. Thomas Jefferson had discerned this weakness as early as 1791 in his *Report on the Cod and Whale Fisheries,* citing import duties on such items as salt, rum, molasses, tea, woolens, hooks, leads, lines, duck, cordage, cables, iron, hemp, and twine—all used in the fisheries—as being among the disadvantages under which the native industry labored.[51] A half-century later, in 1840, a joint select committee of the Maine legislature pointed out in support of the continuing need for fishing bounties that "those engaged in the fisheries are obliged to pay duties to government on the cordage, sail-cloth and iron used in building their vessels, as well as upon the salt with which they cure their fish."[52]

Over the next twenty years, the foreign dependence of fishermen lessened somewhat. Limited American production of fish nets and seines (formerly a British monopoly) began at Boston in the 1840s, and domestically manufactured cotton sail canvas was available in Maine fishing ports by the 1850s.[53] The fact remains, however, that on the eve of the Civil War the fisheries were still looking abroad for a major part of their operating necessities. Even the establishment of localized manufacturing of marine products failed to eliminate the ultimate dependence of overseas suppliers. After 1840, for example, fishing-vessel anchors could be purchased close at hand from a Bath, Maine, foundry specializing in that work, but the unfinished iron used by Bath's smiths continued to be imported.[54] During the year ending June 30, 1860, foreign imports entering Maine and Massachusetts customs districts included 76.1 million pounds of bar, hoop, and pig iron, 3.3 million pounds of iron anchors and anchor chains, 1.2 million pounds of Manila and Russian hemp cordage, 2.8 million pounds of raw hemp, 9.9 million gallons of molasses, 1.9 million pounds of coffee, and 2.5 million bushels of salt.[55] These were all products used extensively by fishermen, either in unprocessed or manufactured form.

Beyond any question, the most important single item employed in the prosecution of the fishing industry was salt. Salt purchases represented roughly one-third of the entire cost of outfitting schooners for the banks fisheries at Bucksport and Castine in the early 1850s, and some of the larger vessels carried upwards of 150 hogsheads* for a single season's work.[56] The salt used at sea to preserve fish caught and dressed during the voyage was only a portion of the total consumed, however. Upon arrival home, the catch was washed and resalted for sun drying or pickling, a curing or "making" process that consumed (in the case of dried cod) one-quarter to one-half bushel of saline preservative per quintal of fish.[57] According to one estimate, the entire sea-to-shore procedure required four-fifths of a bushel of salt (56 pounds) for each quintal of marketable dried fish (112 pounds) and one complete bushel (70 pounds) for each barrel of pickled fish (200 pounds).[58] Viewed another way, this meant that it took one pound of salt to transfer every two pounds of cured cod and every three pounds of preserved mackerel (or herring), respectively, from the processor to the wholesaler. By any measure, salt was the critical cost factor, on a day-to-day basis, in the operation of the antebellum fisheries. It was also a commodity that, as far as Maine was concerned, was totally subject to the vagaries of import policy.

Cape Cod fishermen made their own salt prior to the Civil War, by a solar-evaporation process that separated salt from seawater using a vast and complex system of windmill pumps and storage vats.[59] Maine, however, like

---

*A hogshead of salt was equivalent to eight bushels or 560 pounds. (Source: *Goode Report*, sec. 2, 210.)

the rest of Massachusetts, had no saltworks of its own* and was forced to turn exclusively to outside sources.[60] Merchants at Castine relied upon imports from Liverpool, England, and Cadiz on the Spanish south coast.[61] The state as a whole favored salt from the British Isles, and in the antebellum period a majority of its supply came from there. Northern Massachusetts, including the ports of Gloucester and Marblehead, looked primarily to Spain, Portugal, and the West Indies for its fishing salt.[62]

Although a commercial salt-manufacturing industry separate from Cape Cod's limited production-for-use did exist in antebellum America, there is no record of any Maine fishing schooner using anything but the imported variety prior to the Civil War. Penobscot District fishermen, for example, wetted only foreign salt in the 1850s.[63] The reason for this had largely to do with geography. The great interior salt deposits of western New York, southwestern Virginia, and what is now central West Virginia, the source of seven to eight million bushels annually around 1850, were too far away to be an important factor.[64] "It is . . . apparent," wrote Massachusetts senator John Davis in an 1840 congressional report, "that the larger portion of the value of salt consists in the expense of transportation; but it costs much less to bring it across the Atlantic, than to transport it into the Interior of the United States."[65] Shipping from the hinterland to the coast was equally expensive, and western salt moving east could not compete in price with imports from Europe or the West Indies, as Syracuse, New York, producers discovered to their frustration in the 1850s.[66] In 1850 Liverpool salt could be purchased in eastern-seaboard cities for one-third less than what western Virginia salt sold for in neighboring Ohio.[67] That sort of cost differential led fishermen and other classes of consumers on the East Coast to develop a decided preference for foreign salt during the middle third of the nineteenth century. Imports substantially exceeded domestic production from 1830 to 1860, increasing yearly,[68] and the transatlantic salt trade emerged as

*The reason for this lack of domestic production was environmental. Maine had few expansive open beaches of the sort found on Cape Cod and insufficient room, therefore, to accommodate the apparatus used in the solar-evaporation method. In addition, Maine's damp, rainy weather was inhospitable to the would-be saltmaker, who required sunny, dry conditions. Present-day climatology indicates that the state's coast annually experiences four hundred hours less sunshine and up to sixteen inches more rainfall than Cape Cod. Roughly speaking, Maine's marine weather is 10 to 15 percent colder, wetter, and cloudier than that of comparable areas in southern New England. Historical records also document these less-than-ideal conditions for solar saltmaking. In 1838, according to observations made at Portland harbor, well over a third of the days between the first of June and the middle of October—the optimum time of the year—were characterized by foggy, rainy, or overcast conditions. (Sources: Edward Powers and James Witt, *Traveling Weatherwise in the U.S.A.* [New York: Dodd, Mead & Co., 1972], 11–16; *Third Jackson Report,* 229–37.)

a little-publicized but important fixture in the maritime commerce of the United States. In some Maine customs districts, most notably Penobscot, salt eventually became the only direct foreign import of consequence.[69]

Until the Civil War, tariff duties on imported salt were relatively benign. They were so low, in fact, that toward the end of the antebellum period even Cape Cod fishermen were abandoning their historic reliance on local production and turning to cheaper imports.[70] These favorable salt duties, a by-product of the congressional dominance of the free-trade-oriented Jacksonian Democrats, reached their lowest level during the last two prewar decades. For a time during the early 1840s, foreign salt entered United States ports duty-free. A brief protectionist interlude under the Whig tariff of 1842 reimposed a charge of 8 cents per bushel, but the Democratic Walker Tariff of 1846 quickly reduced that again to a nominal 2 cents. In 1857, the salt tariff was reduced once more, to $1\frac{1}{2}$ cents per bushel (or 12 cents per hogshead), where it remained for the balance of the peacetime era.[71] Such token rates* were a major factor in the expansion of the salt-import trade that so disturbed competing producers. The onset of the war years and the coming to power of the protection-minded Republican party provided an opportunity for those discontented producers to recoup.

The Morrill Act of 1861, which increased tariff duties on imported iron and wool in order to attract Pennsylvania iron producers and midwestern wool growers into the Republican fold, also served to ingratiate domestic salt interests.[72] The duty on salt, set at $1\frac{1}{2}$ cents per bushel by the final Democratic tariff of 1857, was more than doubled in March 1861 to 4 cents. A few months later it went to $8\frac{2}{5}$ cents. In 1862 it was raised again, reaching a maximum of $12\frac{3}{5}$ cents per bushel,** the highest level in thirty years and eight times what it had been before the war.[73] This higher tariff effectively cancelled out the factor of overland transportation costs that had previously kept salt from the interior out of coastal markets, and it enabled producers in the Great Lakes states to offer their product to New England fishing outfitters at prices equal to or below those of imports.[74] By the immediate postwar period, salt from as far inland as Syracuse in western New York was finding its way via the Erie Canal and coastwise schooner to Portland, Maine, where it was being used in limited amounts by local fishermen.[75]

To some degree, burdensome tariff increases like those applied to salt could be explained away politically as emergency revenue-raising measures

---

*The duty imposed in 1857 amounted to no more than 6 percent of the wholesale price of an average bushel of imported Liverpool salt. (Source: Arthur Cole, 342.)

**The actual duty was 18 cents per hundredweight, which was $12\frac{3}{5}$ cents per seventy-pound bushel, or roughly one dollar per hogshead.

and as offsetting compensation for wartime taxes on domestic manufacturers. This, indeed, was the official rationale used to defend the new import policy.[76] It is true that federal assessments of 4 cents and 6 cents per hundredweight were levied on Northern salt producers in 1862 and 1864, respectively, but the fact remains that the import fees exacted on foreign salt during those same years were three to four times greater than the concurrent domestic taxes.[77] The essential purpose of the tariff increase on salt, as F. W. Taussig and others have suggested, was to put additional unearned money into the hands of producers in the salt-mining states, not to achieve economic fairness or help finance the war.[78] This act of political favoritism struck directly at the heart of the New England fishing industry. It was clear and ominous evidence of both the diminished influence of the maritime classes in national affairs and the basic industrial-manufacturing orientation of the newly dominant Republican party.

Salt, although the most important, was only one commodity used by fishermen to be affected adversely by the deliberately engineered tariff inflation of 1861–1865. The heavy-handed act of June 30, 1864, was particularly offensive. It was this tariff, coming as it did in conjunction with the peak in wartime prices, that did the greatest damage to the fisheries. In addition to retaining the severe duties enacted in 1862 on hemp sail duck* (30 percent ad valorem) and salt, it brought rates on a variety of other critical articles to unheard-of levels. Imported molasses, which had been subject to a levy of 5 to 6 cents per gallon during the first three years of hostilities (and only 2 cents prior to that time), was taxed 8 cents per gallon under the 1864 law, an increase of one-third. Pig iron, already paying six dollars per ton under the act of 1862 (twice the antebellum rate), absorbed an additional 50 percent increase that brought its impost to nine dollars. Iron anchors and anchor chains, both previously assessed at 2 cents per pound, had their rates raised by 12.5 and 25 percent, respectively, to $2\frac{1}{4}$ cents and $2\frac{1}{2}$ cents, approximately double that levied under the Morrill Tariff. Manila cordage reached an impost level of $2\frac{1}{2}$ cents per pound, the highest since the start of the war and twice the 1862 rate. The list was endless, and nothing was spared. Even so innocuous an item as hemp twine for cod-fishing lines, a cotton substitute, carried a 35 percent ad-valorem duty under the 1864 law.[79]

Worst of all for the fishing industry was the fact that the 1864 rate schedule, the highest in American history to that date, became the basis of the national tariff system for the next quarter of a century. No major revision

---

*Hemp canvas, or "Russian duck," was an essential substitute for scarce and expensive cotton sail canvas during the war years. It was used extensively on fishing schooners. (Source: *Halifax Commission Proceedings*, 2767.)

was undertaken until 1883, and even then the basic protectionist character of the war tariff was retained.[80] Minor reductions of interest to fishermen were made from time to time; in 1870 duties on pig iron, molasses, and coffee were slightly lowered, and in 1872 the duty on coffee was completely removed.[81] With these and one or two other exceptions, however, the tariff burden on the fisheries continued unabated throughout the postwar era and contributed greatly to the industry's gradual decline in Maine.

The tariff played a key role in perpetuating the wartime legacy of cost inflation, which in the fisheries meant continued high outfitting expenses. Prices paid by fishermen did moderate somewhat in the years after 1865, but they never returned to their pre–Civil War levels. Fishing industry necessities like salt, cordage, and naval stores were nearly double in 1870 what they had been ten years earlier, and even basic provisions cost substantially more than they had before the Civil War.[82]

Two specifics from the Grand Banks port of Castine will suffice to illustrate the lingering disadvantages under which the Maine fisheries, in particular, labored. Castine's resident cordage and twine manufacturer paid 40 cents per pound in 1870 for cotton used in the production of fishing lines, exactly double the 1860 price of 20 cents. During the same year, the town's leading sailmaker was forced to pay 40 cents per yard for sail duck and 25 cents per pound for his supply of bolt rope, considerably above the respective 1860 prices of 25 cents and $12\frac{1}{2}$ cents.[83] These increases, ranging from 60 to 100 percent, were naturally passed along to the ultimate consumers, the vessel owners and fishermen. One result was that by 1870 a typical banks cod-fishing schooner built in eastern Maine cost roughly twice as much to produce and equip as it had before the war.[84]

Where imports were concerned, a large part of the inflationary increase—both for building supplies and outfitting items—was added on at the custom house. For example, a large part of the increased expense involved in building a fishing schooner in 1870 could be traced to the rise in rigging costs during the preceding decade.[85] Higher rigging costs, in turn, were traceable in large measure to increased tariffs on the foreign hemp preferred by American shipbuilders. At Castine, the Russian hemp purchased as raw material by the local rope-walk wholesaled for $180 per ton in 1870, and close to one-quarter of that cost could be directly credited to the tariff duty.[86] The tariff had an even greater impact on certain outfitting commodities. Cuban clayed molasses, purchased wholesale in the Portland market, cost 16 cents more per gallon in the spring of 1870 than it had in the spring of 1860, and one-half of that price difference was due to the import fee. Similarly, imported Brazilian coffee wholesaled for $7\frac{1}{2}$ cents more per pound in 1870 than in 1860, and the impost accounted for two-thirds of the increase.[87]

Salt was a special case. The act repealing fishing bounties in 1866 contained a compensating proviso exempting fishermen from the duty on foreign salt.[88] This effectively reduced the wholesale price by about 25 percent beginning with the outfitting season of 1867. Within two years, buyers were paying three dollars per hogshead for Liverpool salt that had cost them two dollars before the war, an economic hardship but far better than the four dollars they would have paid without the exemption.[89] There was a joker in the law, however. Duty-free status was conferred only upon salt used aboard vessels as a temporary preservative and not on salt used ashore for final curing of the catch. It thus applied to slightly more than half of the salt actually consumed by the fishing industry.* In addition, the Treasury Department continued to exact a weighing fee based on hundredweights for each bulk cargo of salt brought through customs, which partially cancelled out the advantage of tariff removal.[90] The residual duty on curing salt, which had remained at its wartime rate for ten years, was eventually abolished under the exceedingly mild tariff reform act of June 6, 1872.[91] For the fisheries, however, that dispensation came after a decade of disastrously high salt prices had already taken its toll. The well-intentioned reform was too little, too late. In Maine, a state heavily dependent on salt fishing, the damage had long since been done.

The Price of Security

Civil War cost increases harmful to the fishing industry were not limited to the expenses associated with building vessels and outfitting them for the banks each spring. The crucial area of marine insurance was also greatly affected by the events of 1861–1865. Until the outbreak of hostilities, rates of coverage on fishing schooners and their outfits were relatively low and quite stable. For a voyage of up to six months, policyholders paid 2.5 to 3 percent on the value of their salt, gear, and provisions, and on whatever portion of the assessed value of their vessel—normally half to three-quarters—they chose to insure. These rates, which had been in force since at least the early 1850s, remained the rule through the first two years of the war.[92] Beginning in 1863, however, the charge for insuring a voyage more than doubled, to 7 percent. That sudden departure added substantially to the costs of fishing. The Castine Grand Banker *Redwing,* for example, paid $90.50 to insure her

---

*Approximately one-quarter of the salt used in the bank-cod fishery, virtually all of that used in the shore-cod fishery, and one-third of the amount used in the mackerel fishery was consumed during curing and packing operations on shore.

outfit at 7 percent in 1863, compared to $42.50 for the same coverage at 3 percent in 1860.[93]

The reason for this dramatic change was the perceived threat of seizure and destruction by Confederate commerce raiders, a threat magnified during the middle years of the war by the activities of such infamous cruisers as the *Tacony,* which burned several members of the Massachusetts fishing fleet in June of 1863.[94] Actually, the fear of seizure on the high seas was an inordinate one. Only six of the sixty-four Gloucester schooners lost between 1861 and 1865 were victims of hostile action. Five times that many sank in storms on dangerous George's Bank.[95] In 1863, at the height of raider activity, less than 2 percent of New England's entire fishing tonnage was taken by the Confederates.[96]

Although chances of encountering a Confederate cruiser were slim, the danger was very much on the minds of those involved in the fisheries. A crewman aboard the Boothbay schooner *Anna M. Nash,* bound for the Gulf of St. Lawrence in July 1864, wrote home with some relief that "we had a nice chance down to Canso [Nova Scotia] and escaped the Rebels."[97] If ordinary fishermen were concerned, money-conscious insurance underwriters were obsessed. Policies taken out with the Atlantic Mutual Fire & Marine Insurance Company of Provincetown, Massachusetts, in the spring of 1861 on behalf of two Castine Grand Banks schooners contained the following provision: "This company not liable for any loss resulting from the secession of one or more states from the Union."[98]

The unwillingness of companies like Atlantic Mutual to cover potential war losses forced Castine's fish merchants to terminate their long-standing relationship with Provincetown's conservative underwriters after the first year of the conflict and seek out companies less reluctant to take risks. One such firm was the Piscataqua Fire & Marine Insurance Company of South Berwick, Maine, which agreed to fully insure Castine fishermen at the traditional 2.5-to-3 percent premium rate in 1862 but altered its character under the impetus of the war from that of a mutual company (which it had been until 1861) to that of a standard capital-stock company.[99] This change relieved the insurers of the obligation to refund any surplus earnings resulting from high war-risk rates to policy-holding fish merchants and fishermen, the usual procedure followed by mutual companies during the war.[100] As a result, the fishing-vessel owners of Castine not only paid higher rates after 1861 but also lost the benefit of dealing with mutual-insurance firms, in which the insured were profit-sharing stockholders.

The burden of wartime insurance premiums—when, indeed, coverage was available—was magnified by the general inflationary spiral. During the war, for the first time, used fishing vessels could be sold at a profit. They were worth progressively more in paper money as they aged.[101] A good example of this phenomenon was the elderly Castine salt banker *Mentora,* which was appraised at $2,500 in 1862 and at $3,000 three years later as the war came to a close. For those selling schooners, such inflation was an economic bonanza. For those needing to insure them, it was something of a disaster. The owners of the aforementioned *Mentora* paid a premium in the spring of 1865 that was 17 percent higher than what they had paid for similar coverage in 1862, and that was after the news of Appomattox had reduced their premium rate by 0.5 percent. The difference was partly due to the inflated value of the vessel's outfit, but it was also due in large measure to the increased value of the vessel herself. The *Mentora* carried the same amount of coverage as previously (50 percent of assessed valuation) but was worth 20 percent more according to the underwriters.[102] In normal times, when fishing vessels depreciated at an annual rate of 10 to 15 percent,[103] this particular schooner would have decreased in value by at least a third.

Compounding the impact of vessel-property inflation on insurance premiums was the ever-rising wartime cost of fishing outfits, a factor of considerable import since outfits were typically insured at or near their full value. At Castine, outfitting coverage accounted in some cases for the biggest part of the premium increase faced by vessel owners.[104] In mid-1865, several months after the peak in wartime prices had passed, the insured value of fishing outfits was still half again greater than before the war. Despite vessel inflation, fish merchants were actually paying more by that time to cover operating gear and supplies than to insure their schooners, a complete reversal of the prewar pattern.[105]

One of the greatest ironies of the Civil War, from the perspective of the fisheries, was the extent of economic injury done to the industry by the very marine-insurance companies that were ostensibly helping to protect it from the effects of war-related disasters. Robert G. Albion wrote in regard to the war-risk rates on freight-carrying vessels that "they did more damage to the Northern merchant marine than did the actual burnings by Confederate raiders."[106] Some of these high rates may have been inspired by a genuine concern for solvency in the face of potentially crippling losses, but some were almost certainly due to profiteering. New York marine-insurance firms, in particular, made enormous profits during the course of hostilities.[107] Whatever the motives of those insuring Maine fishing vessels, the fact is that the percentage increase in rates of coverage on vessel outfits far outstripped the percentage increase in real outfitting costs. By the third year of the war, premiums were running 133 percent above the highest prewar rates.[108]

Measured against other cost factors, insurance was among the most inflationary necessities purchased by Maine's fishing community during the period 1861–1865.

Like the expenses of building and supplying schooners, the cost of buying insurance failed to return to its prewar level after 1865. Marine insurers, having accustomed themselves to the luxury of high wartime premiums, were reluctant to revert to the older, less profitable way of doing business. The standard antebellum premium rate of 2.5 to 3 percent for a six-month fishing voyage, which had risen to 7 percent at the height of hostilities, levelled off at 4.5 percent in the late 1860s and stayed there.[109] This meant that the Maine fisheries, already burdened by inflated domestic costs and ruinous import tariffs, entered the postwar era paying one-half to three-quarters more on a premium-rate basis for vessel insurance than before the war.

The impact on individual vessels and owners was dramatic. The schooner *Ella Rose* of Castine had been insured with her outfit for $2,500 in 1860 at a rate of 2.5 percent, resulting in a combined premium of $62.50. In 1870 the same vessel and her outfit were insured by the identical underwriter for $3,000 (the outfitting cost had doubled) at a rate of 4.5 percent, bringing the premium up to $135, or twice what it had been a decade earlier.[110] Like the retention of the war tariff, which lost its rationale with the coming of peace,* the continuance of high marine-insurance rates was arbitrary and without apparent justification. It was one more aspect of the Civil War's harmful economic legacy, a legacy that plagued the fishing industry for decades after the final shot had been fired.

In addition to swelling the basic costs of going fishing, high marine-insurance rates affected the Maine fisheries in one other way. They indirectly helped to destroy the New Orleans fish trade so important to the prewar marketing system of Castine and the greater Penobscot region. Prohibitive wartime premiums on American merchant vessels and cargoes encouraged Northern shipowners to transfer their tonnage to British or other overseas registry after mid-1863, in order to cut economic losses.[111] This so-called flight from the flag—an irreversible process due to postwar United States shipping laws—included many of the Castine square-riggers active in the triangular fish-cotton-salt trade of the 1850s. At least three such vessels were sold in Europe before the end of 1864.[112] They were never replaced. To these foreign sales and transfers must be added actual destruction by Confederate commerce raiders. The port of Castine lost no fishing schooners to marauding Southern cruisers, but one of her largest trading ships,

---

*Internal taxes on American manufacturers, the ostensible basis for protectionism, were repealed shortly after the close of the war. (Source: Taussig, 171–72.)

the *John H. Jarvis,* was seized below New Orleans in the early days of the war and condemned.[113] In all, the town lost an estimated $100,000 worth of shipping between 1861 and 1865, either through direct military action or through the sale of vessels abroad.[114]

Exacerbating the situation, of course, was the Union naval blockade, which closed all Southern ports (including New Orleans) to merchant shipping,* thereby ending the transatlantic cotton-export trade for the duration and giving New England vessel owners an additional incentive to dispose of their idle fleets. Historians have chronicled the disastrous effect this blockade had on the American carrying trade in cotton and, by extension, on the long-range health of the nation's merchant marine.[115] An equally severe, if more localized, by-product was the detrimental impact on the eastern Maine fishing industry. The New Orleans fish trade—the first leg of the cotton triangle for Castine's foreign-trading fleet—never recovered from the combined effects of the blockade and the transfer of domestic tonnage to foreign ownership. When the war ended and the port of New Orleans reopened, the ships that had sustained the trade were no longer under the American flag. Even had they been available, it is doubtful that the enterprise could have been resurrected in its original form. Too many factors had changed: old commercial ties had been severed by the war, Delta cotton growers were prostrate, and the important slave market for fish had ceased to exist. In short, the economic structure supporting Castine's interregional fish trade had been dismantled.

Despite the unquestionable difficulties caused by the disruption of the cotton trade and the loss of Southern markets, the major source of harm to the Maine fishing industry during the Civil War was cost inflation. Alternative markets could, after all, be cultivated; military demands for fish could, and did, offset the loss of the South in the short run. There was, however, no antidote for the inflationary virus. It was the combined impact of high domestic outfitting costs, huge tariff increases on essential imports, and surging insurance premiums—all reaching a peak in 1863–1864—that dealt the first crippling blow to the Maine fisheries. This three-pronged inflation undermined the favorable economic environment in which the antebellum fisheries had thrived. The stability produced by moderate costs, low tariffs, and cheap insurance disappeared with the war and never returned.

The influence of the inflation factor is evident in tonnage figures for the first half of the 1860s. Statewide, Maine's fishing-vessel tonnage remained at

---

*The following terse notice greeted shipowning readers of the leading newspaper of Portland, Maine, in early May 1862: "Vessels going South, excepting in Government employ, no matter what their cargo, will be confiscated." (Source: *EA*, marine list, 7 May 1862.)

a high level through 1862. The only significant decline took place in the eastern districts of Penobscot and Frenchman's Bay, both of which depended heavily on the marketing outlet created by Castine's New Orleans trade. In these two districts, vessel tonnage dropped by one-third within a year after the blockade of the South was imposed. Elsewhere it actually increased, so that on balance the state's fleet remained quantitatively about the same. A slow, but noticeable, overall decline began in 1863 and continued into 1864, as inflation began to take hold. Still, the amount of vessel tonnage engaged in the fisheries at the end of June 1864 was practically the same as it had been in 1860, and several districts showed increases over the preceding year. It was at this point that Maine's fishing industry went into the deep Civil War depression from which it never fully recovered. Vessel tonnage statewide was reduced by a third between June 20, 1864, and June 30, 1865, dropping from sixty-eight thousand to forty-six thousand tons. Reductions were across the board, and virtually every fishing community from Eastport to Kittery suffered losses. By the end of the war, Maine's total fishing tonnage amounted to a fraction of what it had been at the outbreak of hostilities.[116]

The timing of the decline, which began in 1863 and accelerated in 1864–1865, leaves little doubt as to its cause. It coincided exactly with the worst months of wartime economic dislocation. Hundreds of vessel owners, unable to stand the cumulative strain of rising operating costs, left the fishery, never to return. By the time inflation moderated in the late 1860s and fish prices began at last to catch up to outfitting expenses, other adverse economic developments were exerting an influence. Primary among these was the repeal of the federal fishing bounty.

The Political Economy of Neglect

The repeal of the fishing-bounty law in 1866 was one of the many wrenching economic changes arising out of the Civil War. This law, which provided for annual government payments to owners of cod-fishing vessels and their crews, had been in effect in one form or another since 1792. Its repeal, carried out by essentially the same forces responsible for the high war tariffs imposed on the industry,* ended three-quarters of a century of public support for the fisheries and ushered in a long, dark period of official neglect.

Writers who have examined the Maine fisheries have lent great weight to

---

*The Thirty-ninth Congress, which voted to end the bounty, was an extension of the war congresses of 1861–1865. Its membership was elected in 1864 and included no Southerners and few opposition Democrats. In terms of party composition, the Senate was 42 to 10 Republican, and the House of Representatives 149 to 42 Republican. (Source: *Historical Statistics, U.S.,* 691.)

bounty repeal as an explanation for the decline of the industry during the last third of the nineteenth century. Some have even viewed it as the sole cause of the decline.[117] This is at best an oversimplification. Like the war-time labor-shortage argument, the bounty-repeal explanation represents a facile answer to a complex historical problem. The Maine sea fisheries did not suddenly disintegrate and disappear at the end of the Civil War. Instead, they fell into a secondary position behind Massachusetts and levelled off, maintaining a constant (if reduced) presence in the national fishing industry for the next twenty years. It was only after 1885, and especially after 1890, that a total industry collapse in Maine took place.[118] To explain the decline of the state's fisheries solely or primarily in terms of the elimination of federal subsidies is to ignore its obvious two-stage process, as well as to neglect its character and chronology.

The precise date of repeal is instructive in assessing the actual effect that termination of the subsidy had on the fisheries. The measure ending the bounty, part of a broader bill entitled "An Act to protect the Revenue and for other purposes," was passed on July 28, 1866.[119] Therefore, it did not go into effect until more than a year after the decline, as measured by enrolled tonnage, had started. On the last day of June 1864, Maine had 52,054 vessel and boat tons (old measurement)* engaged in cod fishing. Exactly one year later—and thirteen months *before* repeal—the state had only 37,140 tons (o.m.) in the cod fishery, a 29 percent decrease. A year after that (and still one month before repeal), Maine's cod tonnage was down to 32,120 tons (o.m.). This amounted to a drop of nearly 20,000 tons (or close to 40 percent) over the last two years under the bounty law. In June 1867, one year *after* repeal, Maine's total cod-fishing tonnage fell to 19,770 tons (o.m.), a percentage decrease of 38 percent over the previous year, but just 12,000

---

*Much of the confusion about the role of the bounty repeal has arisen as the result of a change in the manner of measuring vessel tonnage that took place in 1865. After January 1 of that year, calculations were based on the so-called new measurement (n.m.) formula, which produced tonnage figures approximately one-third smaller than comparable figures derived under the "old-measurement" (o.m.) rules used from 1789 to 1864. Government statisticians continued to keep "old" tonnage figures for fishing vessels through 1865, but thereafter only "new" tonnage figures were recorded. Observers unacquainted with this nuance of difference have assumed a larger disparity between pre- and post-1866 tonnage figures than actually existed and have concluded that removal of fishing subsidies alone caused the dramatic decline in Maine's enrolled tonnage. Converting new to old tonnage by adding one-third (as below) allows the true picture to emerge. (Sources: *U.S.AppAC,* 1st Cong., 1st Sess. [1789], col. 2162; *U.S. AppCG,* 38th Cong., 1st Sess. [1864], 160–61; *Halifax Commission Proceedings,* 2298; *EA,* marine list, 26 April 1865; *U.S.RFCN, 1865,* 720–21, 728–29; *U.S.RFCN, 1866,* 438, 446–47; *U.S.RFCN, 1867,* 1:314–15.)

fewer actual tons. Two-thirds of the losses of the mid-to-late 1860s occurred, in other words, prior to the repeal of the government subsidy.

Among large vessels alone, the pattern was much the same. The state's cod tonnage in this category (20 tons-plus per schooner) dropped precipitously in 1864–1865 from 45,778 tons (o.m.) to 28,611 tons (o.m.), a loss of over one-third, and then fell on the eve of bounty repeal in 1866 to 23,801 tons (o.m.), half of what it had been two years earlier. The first year without government support saw an additional decline to 12,816 tons (o.m.), a substantial loss but, again, just a third of the total decline in tonnage Maine experienced between 1864 and 1867. Moreover, the state's vessel mackerel fishery, which was never subsidized, underwent nearly the same percentage decline in the year following bounty repeal (41 percent) as did the vessel cod fishery (46 percent), suggesting that other forces were at work.[120] The foregoing figures would seem to indicate that the loss of the bounty contributed significantly to weakening the overall health of the Maine fisheries, but that its impact was not critical. Obviously, it was not the initial catalyst for the post–Civil War decline. Nevertheless, it was a definite factor in that process, shaping the industry in a subtle but far-reaching manner.

The real effect of bounty repeal was twofold. First of all, it reinforced the negative impact of inflation, forestalling any recovery that might have taken place when operating costs moderated. The bounty was removed just as wartime inflation was beginning to abate slightly,[121] and the elimination of the subsidy discouraged the potential return of those entrepreneurs who had been forced out of the business by high operating costs during the last years of the war. Without the disheartening loss of the fishing bounty, vessel owners victimized by inflation might have undertaken to resume operations in the late 1860s. Conversely, without the ravages of inflation, the same operators might have survived the loss of their government subsidy. Together, the twin blows were too much to overcome.

A second effect of repeal was the structural reorientation of the Maine sea fisheries. The loss of the fishing bounty was most harmful to the small operator with limited capital, the same individual likely to be hit hardest by inflation. Penobscot and Wiscasset districts, home to innumerable independent owner-fishermen and economically marginal enterprises, bore the brunt of the dislocations caused in Maine by the loss of the bounty. Penobscot, the premier antebellum fishing district in the state, lost half of its cod fishery within a year after repeal, and Wiscasset lost the majority of its sizeable tonnage.[122] In the greater Boothbay region, small firms located in out-of-the-way places were the first to feel the effects of repeal, and many were driven out of the industry as a direct result.[123] The impact was similar in the outports around Penobscot Bay, where numerous older vessels owned by poor fishermen were removed from the active rolls when the tonnage allowance was withdrawn.[124] The drastic reduction of Deer Isle's fleet during the 1860s, for example, took place primarily in the last two or three years of the decade, after direct government aid had ceased. Two-thirds of the town's independent entrepreneurs went under during that period, most of them single-vessel owners of modest means.[125] The loss of the subsidy, therefore, eliminated many of the struggling operators who, with its aid, had somehow managed to cope with rising costs. Yet their absence did not result in a sudden curtailment of the fishing industry statewide.

Maine's overall fishing tonnage remained roughly constant during the twenty years that followed the initial downturn of 1864–1867. What happened was that the expansion of large, heavily capitalized merchant firms in a few select fishing ports, such as Portland and Boothbay, offset the loss of innumerable small, undercapitalized operators dependent on the fishing bounty. The industry did not grow appreciably smaller in the period immediately after 1867, but it was increasingly concentrated in fewer hands and at fewer places.[126] The shape of things to come was already apparent by June of 1867, when customs officials reported substantial post-bounty tonnage losses in most of the outlying cod-fishing districts in down-east Maine, but, significantly, a modest increase in the more centralized and merchant-dominated Portland-Falmouth District, as well as in the highly concentrated and heavily capitalized urban fishing districts* of Massachusetts.[127] This postwar trend toward industry monopoly and centralization, which came to characterize Maine's fisheries in the late nineteenth century, was a product of several forces. Nevertheless, its initial impetus was provided by the termination of government assistance to thousands of merchants and fishermen who required that aid to survive and remain economically independent.

For half a century, beginning with the rate-structure revision of 1819, the fishing bounty reinforced economic democracy by subsidizing small entrepreneurs and sheltering them from monopoly. It allowed a unique small-scale and broad-based industry arising from a peculiar mix of environmental,

---

*The fishing industry of Massachusetts experienced far less disruption from the repeal of the fishing-bounty law than did Maine's industry. The Bay State's overall cod-fishing tonnage, both in vessels and boats, remained virtually unchanged a year after the withdrawal of the allowance, and the major ports of Gloucester, Marblehead, and Beverly all recorded increases in vessel registration. Gloucester, where the commonwealth's fisheries were increasingly coming to be centered, saw its cod tonnage expand by one-fifth during the year following removal of the subsidy.

demographic, and economic factors to continue existing more or less in its original form. It encouraged individual vessel ownership, mandated profit-sharing between owners and working crewmen, prevented the rise of a debilitating wage system, and protected poorer fishermen from excessive credit dependency and extremes of indebtedness. In short, it safeguarded the fishing industry from the worst effects of nineteenth-century capitalism. As an entity, the Maine fisheries survived the removal of that safeguard in 1866. They remained viable, if diminished in stature, for another twenty years. However, their unique character was permanently altered, and they became increasingly vulnerable to a variety of insidious economic forces beyond the control of individual merchants and ordinary fishermen.

The New Technology

Harvey Cheyne: Why can't we always fish from the boat instead
of from the dories?
Dan Troop: Boat-fishin' ain't reckoned progressive. . . .
— Rudyard Kipling, *Captains Courageous*[1]

The Technological Revolution

Not all the forces threatening the traditional Maine sea fisheries in the new
era of laissez-faire were purely economic. One of the many benefits available
to the large fishing companies that emerged after 1866 was the financial
ability to capitalize fully on technological advances in the industry. An intimate relationship between money and technology developed in the fisheries
during the period immediately following the Civil War, when a series of revolutionary changes completely transformed the way in which fish were taken
and radically increased the expenses involved. This "Technological Revolution," coinciding as it did with the emergence of monopoly capitalism,
served to hasten the already rapid demise of economic democracy in Maine's
fishing industry.

Until the 1860s the New England sea fisheries were carried on in a relatively simple and inexpensive manner. Groundfish were caught by the time-
honored hand-line method, and mackerel were similarly "jigged" by hook
and line. Both forms of fishing were done from the deck of the vessel, and
neither required a major outlay of capital for purchase or upkeep of gear.
Beginning in the late 1850s and early 1860s, several innovations were introduced. In the cod fishery, dory hand-lining and trawling began to replace
vessel hand-lining. The trawl, a single multi-hooked line,* allowed each individual fisherman to multiply his catch. The use of dories, with or without
trawls, allowed a given vessel to fish a much wider area more intensively. In
mackereling, the purse seine, essentially a huge net with a drawstring, grad-

---

*Similar to today's "long line" and not to be confused with the modern trawl, which is a net
dragged along the sea bottom. The nineteenth-century trawl was a stationary line set and
tended by dory fishermen. Its numerous hooks were fastened to shorter lines (gangings) attached, in turn, to the main setline, which extended from the ocean floor to floats or buoys on
the surface of the water. (For a detailed description, see Pierce, 63, 66–69.)

ually supplanted old-fashioned hooking by hand.* It permitted fishermen to surround and capture entire schools of fish with minimal use of bait. Like the trawl and dory, the purse seine increased the catch potential as well as the efficiency of the vessel employing it, and it also speeded the fishing process. Dories and trawls were in common use among New England cod fishermen by 1860 and had completely superseded deck fishing twenty years later. Purse seining, widely adopted for the first time during the Civil War, was nearly universal in the mackerel fishery by 1870.[2]

These developments bore dire consequences for the traditional Maine sea-fisheries economy. The efficiency of the New Technology, however, was unquestionable. It meant more fish in less time. In 1853, when she was one of the highliners of the Penobscot Bay fleet, the schooner *Martha Burgess* of Castine caught 31,000 cod in five months of vessel hand-lining on the Grand Banks of Newfoundland.[3] Grand Bankers of the 1850s seldom took more fish than that, and ordinarily fares were much less. The deck fisherman *Black Hawk* of Bucksport, for instance, averaged 22,000 cod during five consecutive years (1848–1852) of fishing off Newfoundland and never landed more than 27,000 in any given May–September season.[4] Returns were similar in the other banks fisheries. The 33,000 cod taken on Quereau Bank off Nova Scotia in 1851 by the Vinalhaven schooner *Mirror* was the largest catch recorded on that ground by a Maine fishing vessel during the deck-fishing era.[5]

A quarter-century later the innovation of dory hand-lining had increased catch totals strikingly. Using the dory method, the Portland schooner *Gertie Lewis* caught 52,000 fish on one trip to Western Bank in 1879.[6] Another dory hand-liner, the *Lady Elgin* of Southport, took 64,000 cod within two months in 1886, also on Western Bank.[7] In eastern Maine, cod landings, which had rarely exceeded 30,000 (or a thousand quintals) per vessel in the 1850s, averaged close to 50,000 (or seventeen hundred quintals) in the 1880s, following the conversion to the dory system.[8] Even these increases paled, however, when compared to the results of trawl fishing. The first primitive Maine trawlers to fish the Gulf of St. Lawrence for cod around 1860 recorded catches that were double or triple those of contemporary hand-liners on the same grounds.[9] Technological refinements in ensuing

---

*Until the advent of the purse seine, mackerel were taken in two basic ways: "drailing," or troll fishing under sail with baited hooks attached to long poles, and "jigging," or drift fishing with baited hand-lines, using chopped bait thrown on the water to attract schools of fish. Drailing, the older form, was common until circa 1820–1830, while jigging predominated thereafter. (Sources: *Mackerel Fishery Materials*, 85–98, 117–18; *Goode Report*, sec. 5, 1:275–86, 298–300; *Halifax Commission Proceedings*, 2810.)

years were such that by the late 1880s, some Maine dory trawlers were averaging 5,000 fish in two days' time. Deck-fishing schooners of the pre–Civil
War era had considered that many fish a good two weeks' work.[10]

To some extent, of course, the increased efficiency of the latter-day dory
schooners was a function of size. Vessels—and, therefore, crews—were
larger in the 1870s and 1880s than they had been in the 1850s, but even so,
the rise in landed catch over the intervening years far outstripped the increase in tonnage. The six highliners of Hancock County's dory-fishing
fleet of 1883, for example, averaged 120 tons (o.m.) compared to 103 tons
(o.m.) for the six highliners belonging to the county's deck-fishing fleet of
1853—a 17 percent differential. At the same time, their average catch of
57,000 fish was 78 percent greater than the 32,000 averaged by the highliners of thirty years earlier.[11] Fishing technology, not vessel size, accounted
for most of the difference. The general rule, based on personal observations
by fishermen, was that hand-line vessels employing dories could land one-
third more fish in the same amount of time than comparable vessels using
the traditional deck-fishing method.[12]

When dories were equipped with trawls, still another element of efficiency was added. Trawling dramatically increased the individual size of the
fish caught, a distinct asset in light of the strong market demand for large
cod.[13] Increased fish size was a direct result of the gear and technique used.
Trawl lines were not individually manipulated by hand but were instead
baited, sunk to the ocean floor using weights, marked by buoys, and allowed to sit for a time before hauling by dorymen. As one fisherman explained it, "By trawling the bait lies on the bottom, and the big fish take it;
this is not the case in hand-lining."[14] In addition, trawls or "setlines" could
be used in deeper water than was practical with hand-lines, thereby maximizing chances for catching the largest of the ground-feeding species. Trawlers working the Gulf of St. Lawrence after 1860 consistently reported that
the cod they landed were at least triple the size of those formerly brought in
by hand-lining. Instead of seventy to eighty fish to the quintal (112 pounds),
their catches approximated twenty to twenty-five per quintal, and some trawl
cod ran as large as eighty pounds each.[15]

The increase in catch potential brought to the cod fishery by dories and
trawls was duplicated in the mackerel fishery by the adoption of the purse
seine. A writer for the *Republican Journal* of Belfast, Maine, described the
dramatic results of the transition in 1882:

> No branch of business in the past few years has undergone such a radical
> change as in the mode of capturing fish. This is particularly true with regard to

mackerel. Formerly mackerel were caught with hook and line. . . . It was not every day the fish would take the hook, but when they did the work was lively. . . . From 500 to 600 barrels of mackerel was considered a good season's work. Now everything is changed. . . . Hooks, lines and bait are no longer used and are seldom found on board. Every fishing vessel carries a seine with which the fish are caught. The fish are captured night or day, whenever they come to the surface. . . . In this manner hundreds of barrels are caught at one cast of the net.[16]

The impact of seining upon the mackerel fishery was, if anything, greater than that of dory trawling upon the ground fisheries. Seines allowed mackerelmen to quadruple their daily catch.[17] During the 1870s and 1880s it was not uncommon for schooners equipped with the new device to take 200 to 300 mackerel in one haul, about the same number that hook-and-line schooners of a generation earlier caught over the course of voyages lasting several weeks.[18] In the Gulf of Maine fishery, this added efficiency produced extraordinarily brief trips. The seiner *Dreadnaught,* for example, left her home port of Portland on an October day in 1881 and returned twenty-one hours later with a full fare of 205 barrels of mackerel.[19] By comparison, the fastest trip ever made from Southport in the Gulf of St. Lawrence hook-and-line fishery (in 1864) had resulted in 300 barrels being taken in ten days of fishing.[20]

The obvious superiority of purse seining was enhanced by periodic improvements in gear and continuing refinements in technique. One major technological advance was the invention and widespread adoption of the so-called mackerel pocket, or "spiller," around 1880. The spiller, a bag net that held fish alongside the vessel in a live and protected condition while awaiting dressing and salting, allowed more time for processing a large catch. Formerly, the seine's haul had to be brought aboard immediately, and whatever could not be accommodated was lost. Use of the new device led to an enormous increase in productivity.[21] Seasonal catches, which had already reached a range of 1,500 to 3,000 barrels per vessel in the 1870s, leaped to the 2,000-to-5,000 level the following decade.[22] By 1883 the most successful mackerel schooners were landing annual catches ten times larger than those of the hook-and-line era. Vessel stocks rose accordingly, climbing as high as $38,000 for some seiners.[23] The schooner *Alice* of Swan's Island, perennial highliner of the Maine fleet in the late 1870s and early 1880s, typified the revolution wrought by accelerated technology. In 1877, using an ordinary purse seine, this vessel took 1,500 barrels of fish worth the not-inconsiderable sum of $9,200. With the addition of a mackerel pocket, the *Alice* was able to pack out 4,900 barrels in the eight months between April and November 1881, and her proceeds totalled $28,000.[24]

Despite the effectiveness of dories, trawls, and purse seines in maximizing fish production, Maine fishermen were slow to accept the New Technology. Dory hand-lining in the major offshore cod fisheries originated with Marblehead's Grand Banks fleet around 1855–1856 and was for several years the sole province of Massachusetts vessels. It was not until the summer of 1858 that the first Maine schooner, the *American Eagle* of Southport, carried dories to the banks. The success of the *Eagle* and of other Southport schooners the following year encouraged Boothbay to try dory hand-lining in 1860 and Portland a short time later.[25] Other western Maine ports were slower to convert to the new system. Bristol vessels carried their first dories to Western Bank in 1868, and Westport did not begin to abandon deck fishing until 1872.[26] In eastern Maine, the first record of dory fishing was in 1860, when the Castine schooners *Redwing* and *Eothen* were equipped with a few boats for their annual voyages to the Grand Banks.[27] That was a full year after dories had become the rule among the Grand Bankers of Massachusetts.[28] By the early 1870s, dory fishing had become common at major fishing centers throughout Maine,[29] but the new method was never really accepted in some of the more isolated regional outports. At least as late as 1880, the seventeenth-century technique of fishing over the rail was reportedly still being used on the Grand Banks by "old-fashioned fishermen from the coast of Maine."[30]

The development of trawling in Maine followed a similar pattern of slow and only partial acceptance. The cod trawl, a European invention,* was introduced to America in 1851 or 1852 by immigrant fishermen from the west coast of Ireland, who used it to dominate the Boston fresh-market fishery during the 1850s. The success of their technique, carried on from dories or other small boats, inspired immediate imitation by native fishermen and led

---

*The trawl, also called the "bultow" or "Norman" line, is generally credited to the French, whose cod fishermen employed it extensively on the Grand Banks during the first half of the nineteenth century. In contrast to the dory trawls eventually used by North American schooners, the French bankers favored what may be described as vessel trawls—two to four lines strung out from the sides of ships with the aid of large lug-sail boats and retrieved by means of deck winches. Contemporary American fishermen, although aware of this technique, generally shunned it following an unsuccessful vessel-trawling experiment by a Provincetown banker in the 1840s. (Sources: Innis, 219, 329, 376; Sylvanus Smith, 88; Reynolds, 60–61; *Knight Report on Shore and Deep-Sea Fisheries*, 40; *Andrews Report*, 666; *Goode Report*, sec. 5, 1:158, 160–61; Louis Z. Joncas, "The Fisheries of Canada," *The International Fisheries Exhibition Literature*, vol. 5: *Conferences Held in Connection with the Great International Fisheries Exhibition of 1883*, pt. 2 [London: William Clowes & Sons, 1884], 12.)

to a rapid phasing-out of hand-lining in the Massachusetts Bay shore fisheries.[31] Within a few years, dory trawling spread to the offshore fishing grounds. Gloucester schooners started employing it in limited fashion on the "Cape Shore" and the Western Banks in 1854–1855, and introduced it in the Gulf of St. Lawrence cod fishery shortly thereafter.[32] Over the next two or three years, vessel fishermen from Provincetown, Newburyport, and other Massachusetts towns gradually converted to trawling, but it remained a novelty in Maine waters. In the spring of 1857, a Portland observer noted that despite the adoption of "scrawl [*sic*] fishing" elsewhere, hand-lining from the deck was still "the universal practice among our codfishermen."[33]

It was not until later the same year that trawling reached Maine. First to use it were the shore fishermen of Biddeford Pool, who worked the inner Gulf of Maine banks.[34] Another year passed before a Maine vessel (the pinky *Albatross* of Boothbay) experimented with the method offshore. In 1860 the *Albatross* was joined in the Gulf of St. Lawrence by a second Maine cod trawler, the *Island Queen* of Southport, and by 1862 the new mode of fishing had finally come into general use in the Boothbay region.[35] It was during this period (the early 1860s) that area vessels, which had originally trawled with pairs of eighteen-foot Hampton boats,* converted to the multiple dories traditionally associated with the American trawl fishery.[36]

Trawling eventually spread to other parts of Maine. It was adopted by Isles of Shoals fishermen in 1863 and by Matinicus fishermen in 1866. By the 1870s dory trawling was being employed as far down east as Eastport.[37] Nevertheless, Maine never became as enthusiastic about the New Technology as Massachusetts. Even after 1870 most of the American cod-trawling schooners continued to hail from Bay State ports, particularly Gloucester, which outfitted about two hundred of them annually. The majority of Maine's cod bankers persisted in equipping their dories with hand-lines rather than trawls.[38]

Purse seining, the third great change of the Technological Revolution, also came late to Maine. The purse seine, invented in Rhode Island for menhaden fishing around 1820, was first employed in the mackerel fishery at Harwich and Provincetown on Cape Cod in 1839. The device reached

---

*The Hampton boat was a double-ended, ketch-rigged sailing and rowing craft developed in the Hampton-Seabrook region of New Hampshire for inshore fishing during the early nineteenth century. Prior to 1860 it was commonly carried aboard New England schooners engaged in the Labrador cod fishery, which was a small-boat fishery pursued in protected waters close to shore. (For a detailed description, see Howard I. Chapelle, *American Small Sailing Craft: Their Design, Development, and Construction* [New York: W. W. Norton & Co., 1951], 137–40.)

Gloucester in the late 1840s and was in common use among vessel fishermen there by midcentury. In 1857 Wellfleet vessels, too, began to carry seines
for offshore mackereling.[39] Maine, however, did not become acquainted
with the new apparatus until 1859, when boat fishermen at Damariscove Island near Boothbay purchased one for inshore work. From there, use of the
purse seine spread to neighboring Southport in 1861 (where it was likewise
adapted to shore fishing) and to Monhegan Island in 1862.[40] Another year
passed before a Maine schooner, following the lead of Gloucester and other
Massachusetts ports, went into deep-water vessel seining. This was the
Dawning Day of Boothbay, which was joined in 1864 by the *Niagara,* also
of Boothbay. Schooners from other western Maine towns started shortly
after, beginning with Georgetown and Portland, which outfitted their first
seiners in 1865.[41]

For some time, mackerel seining in Maine was limited to a few fishing
communities in the general vicinity of Portland and Boothbay. Purse seines
did not reach eastern Maine at all until 1866, when they became popular
with the Magdalen Islands herring fishermen of Eastport, Lubec, and Lamoine, who had previously used more primitive gill nets for their inshore
work.[42] As a mackerel-fishing device, the purse seine was adopted in the
eastern part of the state only after 1870. The first towns to try it were Swan's
Island in 1872 and Deer Isle in 1873.[43]

On the whole, Maine's tepid response to the new method of catching
mackerel paralleled its reluctance to convert to dories and trawls in the cod
fishery. Even in the comparatively progressive Boothbay region, some fishing villages resisted the purse seine until well into the 1870s, and others never
fully adapted to it. The old-fashioned mackerel jig (hook, line, and lead
sinker) was still employed by some Maine mackerel schooners in the Gulf of
St. Lawrence as late as 1878, although purse seines had become nearly universal among Bay vessels from outside the state a decade earlier.[44] Statistics
for 1880 are useful in measuring the extent of Maine's technological lag in
the mackerel fisheries vis-à-vis Massachusetts, where the industry was much
more receptive to advanced ideas. That year, less than half (48 percent) of
Maine's fleet of 176 mackerel vessels was equipped with the modern purse
seine, while 86 percent of the Massachusetts fleet had gone over to the new
apparatus. Moreover, of the Bay State's 240 mackerel vessels, only 30 (13 percent) were still using the hook-and-line method. In Maine, 51 vessels (30 percent of the fleet) were still jigging in the old manner, and 40 others were
employing gill nets, an almost equally dated method.[45] Six years later, a
third of Maine's mackerel fleet had still not switched to purse seines.[46]

The Marriage of Capital and Technology

There is more than one reason for Maine's failure to adapt quickly and wholeheartedly to the dramatic mid-century advances in fisheries technology. A certain innate conservatism undoubtedly played a part, and so did geography. Up to a point, Maine's technical backwardness was a price paid for geographic isolation. Innovation in the New England fishing industry tended to move from west to east and from urban centers to rural areas. Starting from Greater Boston, where most of the technical changes and refinements originated (especially just north of the city in the coastal communities of Gloucester, Marblehead, and Essex), new ideas worked their way gradually northeastward up the coast, eventually reaching Maine. According to local sources, Swan's Island's fisheries expanded significantly around 1860 because "improved methods of fishing were learned from the crafts of the larger ports of Massachusetts, New Hampshire and [western] Maine."[47] That pattern of adaptation was common. For example, the bait mill—a device used by hook-and-line mackerel fishermen to grind bait*—was invented by a Massachusetts man in 1822 and introduced into Maine five years later by a Southport schooner captain, who purchased one in Gloucester.[48] The evolution of naval architecture in the Maine fisheries was similarly shaped by west-to-east influences. The "sharpshooter" and "clipper" schooner models, the principal innovations of the speed-conscious 1850s, both originated in Essex, Massachusetts, and were reproduced in Maine shipyards three to four years later, first in the western part of the state and later in the more easterly regions.[49]

Despite the importance of geography, which placed Maine at the end of the technological pipeline, the unusually slow process of conversion to dory fishing, trawling, and seining—almost two decades in all—suggests that something more fundamental was at work. What most set Maine apart from Massachusetts in its reaction to new technology was the basic economic structure of the state's fishing industry. In Massachusetts, economic concentration and the development of the large firm had come early. At the end of the Civil War, fully half of the Bay State's entire mackerel fishery was already centered at the one port of Gloucester, and a few large companies dominated the industry there, six of them controlling a quarter of the city's vessel fleet and most managing at least seven or eight schooners.[50] On a

---

*Ground bait, or "chum," was scattered on the surface of the water to attract schools of mackerel. This procedure, called "tolling," was an essential part of the jig fishery and was used to some extent in the seine fishery as well. (Source: *Mackerel Fishery Materials,* 58–59, 88–93.)

statewide basis, the typical Massachusetts fishing firm was worth $18,000 in 1870, compared to $4,000 for the average Maine operation.[51] This differ-ence meant that Bay State fish merchants had a considerable advantage in terms of the ability to finance new technology.

Where Maine's fishing industry was most similar to that of Massachu-setts—at Portland and Boothbay, for instance—the state was able to keep pace with accelerating technological change. Where it was not, the older methods continued to prevail. Boothbay, which possessed a highly concen-trated and well-financed fishery following the Civil War, was able to adapt rapidly to the latest innovations. Several of the area's most prominent fish merchants—all of them heavily capitalized operators with extensive fleets of vessels—reported in 1877 that they had completely given up hand-lining and jigging within the previous ten years and had fitted their schooners ex-clusively with trawls and seines.[52] Portland, the very center of big capital in Maine's postwar fisheries, was among the first New England ports to con-vert fully from deck hand-lining to dories in the cod fishery, and in the late 1870s its entire mackerel fleet was composed of purse seiners.[53] By 1886 Portland maintained forty-five purse-seine schooners, almost as many as the rest of Maine combined, and Boothbay was not far behind. Elsewhere in the state, however, hook-and-line schooners defied the march of progress. Among the dwindling ranks of mackerel fishermen in the outlying eastern districts, those fitting their vessels in the old style remained persistently in the majority.[54]

The resistance of these outport fishermen to change is not hard to un-derstand. The New Technology required an investment in equipment that was beyond the capacity of the traditional Maine operator. By 1873 it cost $2,000 to $3,000 (depending on vessel size and length of trip) to outfit a dory hand-liner for a cod-fishing voyage, compared to around $1,000 for an average deck hand-liner of the 1850s.[55] A large part of that increase was due to inflation, but changing fishing methods played an important role. As much as 14 percent of the expense of readying a cod banker for sea at Port-land in the early 1870s resulted simply from the addition of dories, which alone necessitated an outlay in excess of $300. The installation of trawling gear pushed costs even higher, adding another $700 to $1,000 to the over-head of banks vessels.[56] Outfits for mackerel schooners were only slightly less expensive than those of cod fishermen in the post–Civil War period, and contemporary estimates suggest that much of the increase in costs over the prewar period could be credited to the transition from jigging to sein-ing.[57] During the 1870s, the price of fitting out a mackerel seiner was judged to be two to three times greater than for a hook-and-line schooner, and equipping a vessel for the seine fishery added between $750 and $1,200 to her basic outfitting bill.[58]

There were several components that contributed to the overall cost of the New Technology. Common to all of the newly introduced fishing methods was the use of small boats. In the cod and haddock fisheries, this meant dories, which sold (circa 1875–1885) for about $25 each, oars included.[59] Hand-line schooners shipped one thirteen-footer for every member of the crew except the captain and cook, who normally stayed aboard the vessel. The total number varied between eight and twenty, with a dozen being about average in the 1880s. This was a far cry from the old vessel-fishing days, when schooners carried a single yawl boat at the stern for emergency purposes. Trawlers, because of the heavy gear they used, assigned two men to each dory, which cut the number of boats in half. A typical dory trawler of the 1870s stacked four to six dories.[60] That relative saving was more than compensated for, however, by the much greater cost of trawling equipment.

Compared to both deck and dory hand-lining, expenditures for hooks and lines in the trawl fishery were enormous. Hand-line vessels fished two lines to a man and two hooks per line, perhaps forty baited hooks for a typical banker with a ten-man crew. They worked in thirty to fifty fathoms of water, necessitating approximately one mile of fishing line altogether,* not counting replacement tackle.[61] This style of operation minimized costs. Deck fishermen outfitting at Castine in 1853 spent less than $50 per vessel for hooks and lines, and dory hand-liners of a generation later managed to keep their seasonal outlays for cod line well under $100.[62] Grand Banks trawlers, on the other hand, sometimes carried as much as fifteen miles of setline fitted with several thousand hooks, at an estimated cost (circa 1875) of over $600. A trawler of the mid-1870s might spend in excess of $100 for cod hooks alone (seventy-five hundred was an average supply), compared to $5 or $6 for a prewar hand-line schooner, which typically stocked two to three hundred hooks, far more than were actually used.[63]

Hooks and lines were not a concern in the mackerel seine fishery, but the purchase of expensive rowing craft was a prime necessity. In addition to two dories, at least one large "seine boat," double the size of a banks dory and costing up to $250 fully equipped, was needed to set and retrieve the seine. These specialized boats had an average life expectancy of half a dozen years, after which time a replacement was usually in order. On occasion, two might be carried, thus doubling the investment.[64]

*Replacement gear at least doubled the amount of line carried. In 1835 a typical Massachusetts schooner engaged in the Labrador hand-line fishery was supplied with $1\frac{2}{3}$ miles of tackle for an eight-man crew. Grand Bankers required more. (Source: *Goode Report*, sec. 2, 724.)

The cost of a new seine boat—equivalent, by itself, to the entire annual income of an average Maine fisherman in 1880[65]—was only a fraction of the capital expenditure required for seining. The bulk of that outlay was in the purse seine used to capture the catch. The first seines brought to Maine in the 1860s were so expensive that they were sometimes purchased in shares, each of four Southport owners putting up one-quarter of the $2,400 necessary to buy one in 1866.[66] In later years prices were lowered somewhat by a postwar reduction in materiel costs. Still, the price of a new purse seine remained imposing, ranging between $1,000 and $1,500 throughout the 1870s and 1880s.[67] Occasionally second-hand gear was available, but even that was of little help to the marginal operator. A "used" seine and seine boat sold for $750 at Gloucester in 1877.[68]

Technology was not static in the fishing industry, especially after the momentum for change began to gather force in the late 1860s. One result, and an additional problem for small entrepreneurs, was that the apparatus associated with dory trawling and purse seining grew steadily larger and more complex as time passed and became, consequently, ever more expensive. In the trawl fishery, for instance, the number of dories used and the length of the trawl lines themselves increased substantially. From four dories and 2,000 hooks per vessel in 1864, haddock trawlers expanded their gear to an average of six dories and 7,200 hooks in 1882, more than doubling the amount of line handled by each doryman.[69] In the Gulf of St. Lawrence cod fishery, the two miles of line and 2,000 hooks set by the first Maine schooners to trawl the Bay in 1860 had evolved by 1877 into twelve miles of line and 10,000 hooks per vessel.[70] Within another decade there were reports of some trawlers attaching as many as 5,000 hooks to the three miles of setline carried by each of their several dories.[71]

A comparable transformation took place in the mackerel-seine fishery. The boats used, for example, gradually increased in size to keep pace with a corresponding increase in the size of the seines they were designed to handle. From a length of twenty-one feet in 1857, when first developed by the Gloucester firm of Higgins & Gifford, seine boats grew to an average of thirty-four feet in 1877. By 1882 some were being built as long as forty feet overall.[72] This growth in size was naturally accompanied by a corresponding rise in price. At Gloucester in 1880, a thirty-one footer (minus oars, oarlocks, and pursing gear) could be had for $186, while a thirty-six footer cost $225.[73]

The purse seine itself was a marvel of sophisticated construction. It was made of three types of cotton twine and contained several thousand meshes. A typical net could incorporate up to 2,000 corks, 1,350 feet of hemp line, 40 iron rings, and 500 lead sinkers, and weigh as much as 750 pounds in all.[74]

Exact size varied according to the locale and depth of water fished, but in general it steadily increased as mackerelmen carried the device into deeper and deeper waters off the American coast. Prior to 1860, purse seines were about 100 fathoms long and 22 fathoms deep when hung, or roughly 79,000 square feet in area. By 1880 an average seine was 200 × 20 fathoms (or 144,000 square feet), and the largest type available measured 225 × 25 and encompassed over 200,000 square feet of mesh.[75] Toward the end of the nineteenth century, "modern" purse seines were said to contain four times as much twine as those commonly in use during the late 1860s.[76]

It was constant technical innovation that permitted such a rapid enlargement of the seining apparatus. An observer of the state of the art in 1881 wrote, "The purse-seines, like many other things, are being improved. Those we are making now are much lighter than we have been making them in former years, and can be handled with greater ease and rapidity."[77] Changes in weights, twine, etc., allowed manufacturers of the 1880s to produce seines that were double the size and capacity of those made twenty years earlier, even though they weighed roughly the same.[78] Yet improvements of this sort were a mixed blessing. The fitting, or "knitting," costs charged by seinemakers (exclusive of the price of materials) were calculated on a per-yard basis.[79] Accordingly, an inevitable consequence of the trend toward ever larger seines was an escalation in expenditures for fishermen choosing to keep pace with their most technologically advanced competitors. Nevertheless, failure to make the investment could prove equally expensive, because, as one industry authority noted, "it is in the deeper waters, where the immense purse seines can be freely used, that the large catches are made."[80]

The investment problem created by size was further aggravated when mackerelmen felt compelled to purchase more than one of the increasingly expensive nets, as many did beginning in the 1870s. At that time, owners of schooners operating along both the American and Canadian coasts resorted to equipping their vessels with two purse seines, one for the relatively deep waters off the east coast of the United States and one for the shallower depths of the Gulf of St. Lawrence.[81] This enabled them to be ready for any contingency, but it also added substantially to the cost of their outfit. Duplication of gear, like the increasing size of the apparatus itself, had the effect of creating a more and more capital-intensive seine fishery as time passed. In the process, it helped make purse seining an ever-more-exclusive occupation, as growing numbers of poorer mackerelmen found themselves simply priced out of participation.

The capital investment difficulties brought about by the new fishing technology did not end with the initial purchase of equipment. There were also periodic replacement and repair costs, which often assumed immense proportions. Short of losing the vessel herself, the most economically disastrous situation faced by hand-line fishermen of the old school was the loss of some inexpensive hooks and lines or the odd anchor. In contrast, the very nature of dory fishing, trawling, and seining led to outlays for lost or damaged gear that went far beyond anything experienced in the pre-technological era.

Most common were losses of small craft. In the cod fishery, reports of whole complements of dories being stove in or swept away by boarding seas were routine during the 1870s and 1880s. The Bucksport schooner *Annie G. Quiner*, for example, homeward bound from the Grand Banks in 1883, lost all twelve of her dories overboard in a September storm.[82] Everyday wear and tear could exact almost as great a toll. Banks vessels of the 1880s normally needed to replace five or six dories after each trip to the offshore grounds, even in the absence of storm damage.[83]

Seine boats were similarly vulnerable. While their more expensive and exacting construction precluded regular annual replacement, they were lost in large numbers because of the manner in which they were handled. Instead of being stacked on deck when not in use, like the smaller dories, seine boats were towed behind the mother ship in all kinds of weather while on the fishing grounds. As a result, they often foundered or capsized during gales.[84] A dozen mackerel schooners lost their seine boats in this manner during the stormy month of April 1884, while engaged in the southern spring fishery.[85]

Fishing apparatus was likewise subject to loss or partial destruction. Cod trawls could be easily damaged if set and left out during bad weather. Vessels on the Grand Banks commonly lost as much as half of their gear during storms in the late 1870s. Ordinarily, the damage occurred when the trawl was "hung up," or caught, on the bottom and torn, or was dragged along the sea bottom until chafing on the rocks caused breakage. Loss could also take place if lines were cut by sharks or if buoy lines were severed by the vessel's anchor cable.[86]

In mackerel seining, equipment damage was more apt to take the form of splitting or tearing the purse seine in the process of fishing, something that happened with distressing regularity.[87] Damaged seines could, of course, be repaired. A more serious occurrence was the complete loss of the apparatus, which often accompanied a vessel sinking. When the aged schooner *Lizzie Thompson* of Newburyport was run down and sunk by a steamboat in April of 1883, her new two-hundred-fathom mackerel seine, valued at $1,000, constituted one-fifth of the owner's entire investment.[88] In that instance—assuming the schooner was insured—the value of the lost seine was probably recovered. However, marine insurers of the time ordinarily refused to cover trawls, seines, dories, or seine boats except in cases where the fishing vessel herself was totally lost. Piecemeal replacement of individual items of equipment came directly out of the owner's pocket.[89] To remain solvent, therefore, the up-to-date fish merchant or owner-fisherman of the post-1870 period needed either extensive reserve capital or unusually good luck.

Elaborate and expensive fishing equipment was not the only aspect of the New Technology that drove costs steadily upward during the latter part of the nineteenth century. There were other expenses independent of the basic cost of the gear. In the cod fishery, it was considered necessary to provide trawling schooners with larger, more efficient rigs than comparably sized hand-line vessels. During the early 1870s, deep-sea trawlers began carrying flying jibs and fore-topsails, in order to facilitate periodic trips to bait stations on the coasts of Nova Scotia and Newfoundland, a hundred miles or so from the fishing grounds.[90] Trawlers normally spent several weeks "baiting up" in the course of a season on the banks, and any added speed that could turn some of those wasted days into fishing time was an economic asset.[91]

Baiting trips, a new phenomenon in the banks fishery, were brought about specifically by the development of trawling. The conversion from deck to dory hand-lining, however revolutionary in other ways, resulted in no appreciable change in the type or amount of bait used by cod fishermen. Throughout the nineteenth century, hand-line vessels depended almost exclusively on salt clams to lure their catch, and those working the offshore banks carried up to fifty barrels on each voyage. Around 1880 the price was $5 to $6 per barrel, so that a typical banker of the time spent between $250 and $300 in all. Since the original bait supply generally lasted the entire trip, this outlay was a one-time expense. Hand-liners rarely, if ever, visited a foreign port for bait.[92]

For a time, trawling schooners operated in similar fashion, staying at sea and using salt bait provided by their own outfitters. It was gradually discovered, however, that fresh bait was infinitely superior to the traditional salted variety in trawl fishing. Fishermen noticed that bank cod were reluctant to take the hook when salt clams were used and that fresh-baiters fishing alongside salt-baiters took many more fish on their setlines. In short order, it became axiomatic that only fresh bait would do for trawling.[93]

Since fresh bait brought from home would last only a limited amount of time—two or three weeks at the most—it was impractical to take much aboard at the outset, and usually none at all was carried. Instead, vessels tended to seek out ready supplies from the land nearest their fishing grounds and return periodically to re-stock as needs dictated.* American trawlers working Western Bank visited nearby Nova Scotia, while those operating on Grand Bank looked to Newfoundland (see map 2). These visits started in 1873, when Gloucester trawlers, responding to the resumption of baiting privileges afforded under the Treaty of Washington, pioneered in fresh-bait fishing on the banks. Within two or three years, nearly all of the Gloucestermen were stopping at Canadian ports for bait. Vessels from other ports followed suit, and by the end of the 1870s the practice was virtually universal among United States dory trawlers. Nova Scotian coastal towns from Shelburne to Arichat, as well as innumerable hamlets dotting the southern and eastern shores of Newfoundland, suddenly emerged as integral parts of the American bank fishery.[94]

The bait obtained at these places was not clam bait. Western Bank trawlers purchased fresh herring and occasionally mackerel, while Grand Bankers used fresh capelin (smelt) and squid, as well as herring, depending upon the time of the year. Beyond immediate availability, Canadian fresh bait had the advantage of being less expensive than the salted variety available at home. During the late 1870s fresh bait sold for only $1 to $3 per barrel in Nova Scotia—less than half the going rate for American salt clams—and it was even cheaper in Newfoundland.[95] Nevertheless, the vast number of hooks demanding daily preparation aboard trawlers meant that bait was consumed at a much faster rate than was the case in the hand-line fishery. Instead of fifty barrels for a season's work, trawlers required at least two hundred barrels and occasionally used three hundred or more. On average, Grand Banks trawlers put in at provincial ports about four times in the course of a voyage, purchasing approximately fifty barrels of bait on each visit, at a cost of close to $100. Some baited up more often, running in to port as many as a half-dozen times.[96] They thus used four to six times the amount of bait consumed by hand-liners and paid (assuming an average price of $2 per barrel) between $400 and $600 for their seasonal supply. At the very least, that was half again what hand-line bankers spent for bait in a season.

Bait was only one article sought by trawl fishermen in Canadian ports. Ice was the second essential ingredient in fresh-bait fishing. Unlike salt clams, which required no special attention, a supply of fresh herring, capelin, or squid had to be interspersed with layers of crushed ice for preservation.

---

*Some of the early trawlers operating in the confined Gulf of St. Lawrence carried drag nets and took their own fresh bait (herring and mackerel) in nearby harbors and coves. This was not practical on the major offshore Atlantic banks, however. (Source: *Goode Report*, sec. 5, 1:160.)

Ice lasted for about two to three weeks on the banks, after which time it melted, saturating the bait and causing decomposition.[97] It was therefore necessary to obtain a new supply with each baiting trip, and that need led to the growth of an entire new industry in the Maritimes. Observed a Port Hastings, Nova Scotia, fish merchant in 1877: "This supplying of Ice and fresh fish for bait to Codfishing vessels is becoming quite an extensive business. New Ice-houses are being erected every Year around the Coasts of the Provinces, and larger stocks of ice are stored, to be sold principally to the United States fishermen."[98] Trawlermen patronizing such establishments in Nova Scotia or Newfoundland purchased ice at a rate of $2.50 to $3.00 per ton in the 1870s. The ratio of ice to bait approximated one ton to every ten barrels, and vessels took four or five tons aboard on each visit, adding $10 to $15 to their individual baiting bills. In all, a trawler could expect to spend around $50 on ice each season.[99] This was one more annual expense not faced in the hand-line fishery.

Finally, in addition to paying for bait and ice, trawler fishermen frequenting the coasts of the Maritimes subjected themselves to various port charges, covering such items as harbor dues and water levies. These miscellaneous fees amounted to an estimated $18 per visit in 1877—or $72 for a projected year's fishing.[100] Added to the outlay for actual supplies, port charges pushed annual baiting costs for a typical banks trawler—one baiting up four times in a season—to more than $500, approximately double the comparable expenditure for an average hand-line schooner.[101]

The upshot of the high costs associated with the New Technology—whether direct in the form of capital expenditures for fishing gear or indirect in the form of increased outlays for bait and ice—was that only well-financed capitalists could engage successfully in trawling and seining operations. The independent operator characteristic of the early Maine fisheries could not compete. His choice was to stay with the less efficient methods of the pre–Civil War era or sell his vessel. As Joseph Collins pointed out in 1880 with reference to the mackerel fishery: "The expense of fitting out with seine, boat, etc., deterred many of the owners from sending their vessels seining, and the more conservative ones clung to the old method of jigging. . . . This, together with the fact that more or less risk is attached to seining— such, for instance, as losing the apparatus altogether, having the net torn, the boats stove, etc.—served to deter the timid. . . ."[102]

The inability of poorer fishermen to sustain periodic equipment losses not only prevented many from converting to trawls and seines in the first place, it also forced some who had tried the New Technology to abandon it. During the 1870s marginal vessel owners in the Southport area rebelled

against the high cost of gear loss in the modernized cod fishery and reverted to hand-lines rather than replace damaged or destroyed trawls. This
retrenchment, which began in 1873 as an attempt to compensate for declining fish prices, continued for the balance of the depression decade and significantly cut the number of active trawlers in the region.[103] The economic
pressure imposed by the New Technology was such that even at Portland,
where overhead was less of a problem, owners of cod bankers preferred dory
hand-lining to trawling because of the cost savings. Still, Portland schooners working closer to home in the Gulf of Maine haddock fishery (and able
to preserve their gear by running for port ahead of bad weather) continued
to be uniformly equipped with trawls, rewarding their merchant owners
with enormous profits as a result.[104]

Where it could be clearly shown that economic benefits outweighed
costs, merchant firms were more than willing to make the heavy initial investment necessary for trawls and seines. Moreover, once committed, they
tended to stay with the New Technology. For one thing, it permitted certain long-range savings. In the cod fishery, for instance, trawling reduced
labor expenses by reducing the number of experienced hands a vessel had to
hire. Trawling quite simply demanded less skill. In the words of one expert
observer, "It is merely a matter of putting on the bait and throwing it overboard, and it does not require the delicate manipulation and skill that the
hand-line fishery does, and therefore does not call into play to the same extent the functions of the practiced fisherman."[105] The only real qualification for a trawlerman was experience in handling a dory, and even that requirement was modified (vis-à-vis hand-liners) by the practice of fishing
two men to a dory, thereby halving the number of boats used and the number of seasoned boatmen needed.[106] Savings realized by slightly cheaper labor were available, of course, only to those having the wherewithal from
the start to equip their vessels with modern fishing gear. It was a savings
available, in other words, primarily to large industry units.

Reaction and Response

Unable to compete in the technology sweepstakes, ordinary Maine fishermen and small, independent operators became increasingly critical of the
advanced methods and equipment used by the larger owners. Opinions so-
licited by state government investigators in 1887 accused trawling and seining vessels of depleting the inshore grounds, killing and wasting fish through
careless operations, fouling the waters by dumping excess catches, and scar-
ing fish away by overfishing and breaking up schools.[107] Similar objections
had been voiced ten years earlier by both American and Canadian fishermen

during discussions relating to the Treaty of Washington.[108] To a certain extent, technology served as a visible scapegoat for those confronted by economic complexities that were affecting their lives but were beyond their comprehension. Yet there was some justification in the criticisms. Various international experts, including representatives of government and the scientific community, agreed that the new methods tended to deplete stocks, particularly by interrupting spawning cycles and taking "mother fish."[109]

Whatever the long-range ecological impact of trawls and seines, their short-term economic effect was to make life harder for the less affluent class of fishing operators, especially those involved in the shore fisheries. In Maine, cod fishermen owning small boats had to venture farther and farther from the coast to find fish,[110] and mackerelmen working with hooks and lines in the Gulf of St. Lawrence found that large seining operations in the area reduced their catches by about one-half.[111]

These distressing conditions led to demands for legislation against mass-production fishing methods. In 1878 a delegation of mackerel fishermen from Portland went to Washington to petition for a law prohibiting purse seines.[112] A decade later other Maine fishermen called for a total ban on both trawling and seining. Said one, summing up the attitude of his contemporaries:

> Seining has ruined the [mackerel-fishing] business, and until it is stopped and the old method of catching on the hook adopted there can be nothing better expected. . . . Now the same is true of trawling. When men went fishing with hand lines, fish were always plenty; they brought more money, and the men who caught them fared better than they do now. . . . Fishermen unite in saying that fish are growing scarce all the time, and agree that it is because of the trawling, and that it should be stopped.[113]

Some favored not complete prohibition but selective regulation, such as setting aside certain inshore grounds or restricting the use of mackerel seines at certain times of the year.[114] International agreements were also sought. In 1890 Ottawa's deputy minister of fisheries proposed joint regulations between the United States and Canada to curb seining operations in the coastal waters of both countries.[115]

Despite these initiatives, all efforts to impose limits on the New Technology ultimately failed. A protective sense of inevitability and inviolability surrounded it. To a generation schooled in laissez-faire and Social Darwinism, interference with technological "progress" was tantamount to tampering with nature itself. Moreover, there was a prevailing sense that any attempt at restriction would prove futile. In his 1867 report to the Canadian minister of marine and fisheries on industry conditions in Nova Scotia, Thomas F. Knight advised against a ban on trawling, "notwithstanding the remonstrances of individuals and committees," on the grounds that "this system has grown into such general use . . . that any legislative interference would be found unavailing."[116] American fisheries authority Spencer F. Baird of the Smithsonian Institution, queried ten years later on the same subject, responded that as one of the new modes of wholesale capture in the industry, trawling would be impossible to prohibit or regulate "because the tendency is to centralize, to accomplish the same work by less expenditure of money and human force."[117]

This state of mind, widespread among those in positions of authority and influence, was reinforced by the active opposition of elements of the fishing industry already committed to advanced technology. With respect to proposed international controls on mackerel gear under consideration in 1890, the annual report of the Canadian Department of Fisheries pointed out that "many of the masters of the United States fishing vessels admit that the unrestrained use of the purse seine has ruined the mackerel fishery, but some of them being part owners of vessels and gear are indisposed to support a measure, the passage of which would practically wipe out a portion of their capital for a time."[118] The overriding factor of economic interest was never far from the discussion about the relative merits of trawls and seines. In 1885 the Massachusetts fisheries alone had nearly $500,000 invested in trawling and seining gear, most of it the capital of Gloucester's merchant class.[119] To the large merchants, suggested government controls on mass-production fishing techniques were as much anathema as the federal fishing-bounty regulations they had earlier opposed. It was they who were most closely wedded to the new methods, and, as in 1866, theirs was the loudest voice.

Putting aside the long-range environmental problems created for the fishing industry as a whole by the triumph of advanced technology, its short-run effect in Maine was to enhance the growth of economic concentration. The Technological Revolution obviously allowed fishermen to catch more fish in less time, but it also made fishing more expensive. Poorer fishermen faced economic difficulties in converting to the new methods and equipment, but large, heavily capitalized merchant firms did not and were able to gain a decisive competitive advantage. Capital and technology were mutually reinforcing. An increase in one led to an increase in the other. The reverse was also true, so that while the rich got richer, the poor also got poorer. Thus the trend toward economic concentration, which began with the bounty repeal and wartime inflation, was accelerated. More independent operators went under, and more of the industry came to be centered at Portland, where the large postwar fishing companies were located.

Essentially, the period of Maine's dominance in the sea fisheries preceded the era of the Technological Revolution. Before 1860, numbers, not sophisticated equipment, were important; Maine possessed an abundance of fishermen and vessels. In the new era, when capital and equipment dominated and sustained one another, that portion of the Maine industry located outside the mercantile centers could not survive. Efficient technology did not destroy the Maine sea fisheries, but it did combine with big capital to help eliminate the distinctive form those fisheries took before the Civil War—independent entrepreneurship and small-scale capitalism.

A typical mackerel schooner bound for the fishing grounds under full sail, ca. 1880. She displays fore and main gaff topsails, a fisherman staysail, and a "jumbo" jib. The elaborate and lofty rig, calculated for maximum speed, was in marked contrast to the smaller and simpler sail plans characteristic of most cod-fishing banks schooners. (*Goode Report,* sec. 5, vol. 2, drawing by Henry W. Elliott and Joseph W. Collins)

Dory fishermen hauling and rebaiting (or "underrunning") a cod trawl on the offshore banks, ca. 1880. Their mother ship is visible on the horizon. The widespread adoption of trawls after 1860 produced dramatic increases in groundfish landings by permitting fishermen to tend hundreds of baited hooks simultaneously, but it also markedly increased outfitting costs and made fishing more strenuous and perilous. (W. H. Bishop, *Fish and Men in the Maine Islands* [New York: Harper and Brothers, 1885], drawing by Milton Burns; courtesy Maine Maritime Museum, Bath)

Mackerel seine fishermen dressing a haul of fish aboard a schooner off the Maine coast, ca. 1880. An awning has been set in the rigging for protection from the summer sun. After splitting and eviscerating, the mackerel will be washed, lightly salted, and placed in barrels like the ones shown on deck. Nearby, another schooner is servicing a seine boat that has just "pursed up," or closed, its net. Processing the catch became mass-production work in the frenetic seine fishery, which replaced hooking by hand-line in the 1860s. (W. H. Bishop, *Fish and Men in the Maine Islands* [New York: Harper and Brothers, 1885], drawing by Milton Burns; courtesy Maine Maritime Museum, Bath)

The Portland, Maine, fishing docks, ca. 1910. This quiescent scene could be from any time in the last quarter of the nineteenth century. Several of the city's market schooners are in from the grounds, among them the *Fanny Reed* (far left), a 22-ton (n.m.) vessel built at Kennebunk in 1872. A crewman is aloft repairing or adjusting rigging, and various small craft are at rest along the wharf. Foul-weather gear and other fishing paraphernalia are also in view. (Courtesy Library of Congress, Washington, D.C.)

Selecting, grading, and packing salted mackerel for shipment at Portland, Maine, ca. 1880. Each barrel held two hundred pounds of pickled fish. The large Portland mercantile firms dominated this aspect of the industry in Maine following the Civil War. (*Goode Report*, sec. 5, vol. 2, engraving from a photo by T. W. Smillie)

Life on the offshore banks, ca. 1880. The oilskin-clad crew of an anchored schooner cut bait and bait trawls prior to dory fishing for groundfish. The vessel's dories are nested between her masts, the normal position when not in use, and she has set a riding sail to aid in facing into the wind, which lessens rolling and increases comfort. The skipper, speaking trumpet in hand, is about to hail an approaching schooner. (*Goode Report,* sec. 5, vol. 2, drawing by Henry W. Elliott and Joseph W. Collins)

A typical Maine fishing crew. The men of the schooner *Emma* of Swan's Island
gathered near the mainmast for a group portrait at Bernard Harbor in the town
of Tremont, following a trip to the offshore grounds, ca. 1900. Judging from the
tubs of trawl along the port rail (center-right), they have been ground fishing.
The *Emma* was an 81-ton (n.m.) vessel built at Bath in 1883. Note the crew's
leather boots, standard fishing apparel throughout the nineteenth century.
(Courtesy Southwest Harbor, Maine, Public Library, G. A. Neal photo)

A rural Maine fishing station: the F. D. Hodgkins establishment on the Jordan
River at Lamoine, ca. 1880. Three large Grand Banks schooners are at the wharves,
one of them riding light after landing her salted cod, which will be stored in
one of the nearby fish houses until ready for sun drying in the adjacent flake
yard. Several unoccupied fish flakes are in view. The white, rectangular structures
atop them, called "flake boxes," were used to cover gathered stacks of drying
fish each evening to prevent damage from dampness or rain. Lamoine was
among the last Maine ports to engage in the traditional salt-cod banks fishery.
(Courtesy Lamoine, Maine, Historical Society)

Three small fresh-market schooners in port at Portland, Maine, sometime in the
1890s. Sails are furled and dories are neatly stacked or "nested." One man (center)
is overhauling a tub of trawl line. Fish warehouses form the backdrop. Portland
market schooners ground-fished on the nearest offshore banks of the Gulf of
Maine and made multiple trips in a season, returning at frequent intervals with
fresh catches that were iced on board, if necessary, to prevent spoilage. (Courtesy
Maine Historical Society, Portland)

The New Capitalism

The big fish eat the little ones.—Newfoundland proverb[1]

———

The Growth of Economic Concentration

Paradoxically, it is not possible to talk about the general decline of the Maine fisheries without discussing the concurrent rise of Portland's fisheries. The changes set in motion by wartime inflation, the repeal of the fishing bounty, and the development of new technology were not uniformly harmful to the Maine fishing industry. For those in a position to capitalize on the declining fortunes of others, the altered circumstances were actually beneficial. Such was the case with Portland, where most of Maine's fishery capitalists were based after 1865. This city became the focus of the industry following the Civil War and typified the movement toward economic concentration that government intervention under the bounty law had previously held in abeyance.

Portland was always a significant factor in Maine's fishing industry. Except for the war years, it dominated the state's mackerel fishery throughout the nineteenth century.[2] During the heyday of the cod fishery (1840–1865), however, Portland had been relegated to an overall position of secondary importance, and for a time it was something of a fisheries backwater compared to other parts of Maine. With the decline of the smaller outports and the eastern fisheries after 1865, that all changed. Portland's re-emergence began in the early 1870s, when it rose to challenge the districts of Castine (ex-Penobscot) and Wiscasset for leadership in the statewide vessel fisheries. By 1878 Portland-Falmouth* had become the leading Maine customs district,

———

*For all practical purposes, the district of Portland-Falmouth and the port of Portland were one and the same after 1865 in terms of fishing-vessel tonnage statistics. Although the district encompassed the entire coastline of Casco Bay from Harpswell to Cape Elizabeth, few large fishing vessels were owned outside of the city. Similarly, the fisheries of western Maine's other important postwar district, Wiscasset, were largely restricted to the port of Boothbay and its immediate environs. The fisheries of the eastern customs districts tended to be more dispersed, both before and after the Civil War. Castine (ex-Penobscot) District, for example, included the large fishing ports of Bucksport and Castine, as well as numerous smaller industry centers like Deer Isle and Swan's Island. For the boundaries of the Maine customs districts, see map 1. See also *Hough Report*, 104–6, and Richard Wynkoop, *Clearance and Entrance of Vessels in the United States of America* (N.Y.: D. Appleton & Co., 1882), 80–81.

as measured by tonnage owned in vessels over twenty tons. Within two years, it led in number of vessels as well and established a dominance that lasted for the remainder of the century.[3]

Portland's sudden prominence transcended the state of Maine. The city emerged in the 1880s as one of the three primary fishing ports in America, sharing that honor with Gloucester and Boston. As the decade began, it was second only to Gloucester in terms of vessel ownership, exceeding Boston and such other well-established New England ports as Newburyport, Provincetown, and Wellfleet.[4] Portland's mackerel fishery, always its forte, assumed national importance during the next few years and, for a time, made the city the second-ranking mackerel port in the United States. During the early 1880s the wharves lining Commercial Street accounted for nearly a quarter of all the salt mackerel landed in New England. Such activity enabled western Maine's "Natural Seaport" to seriously challenge Gloucester as the fishing capital of America by the middle of that decade.[5]

Portland retained its position of stature in the national fisheries for about fifteen years. Among customs districts, Portland-Falmouth was third in the nation in the ownership of fishing vessels over twenty tons from 1880 to 1894, behind Gloucester and Barnstable (Cape Cod). In total fishing tonnage, it maintained a place in the top four from 1879 to 1896.[6] Portland's peak year of the postwar era was 1883, when it claimed 113 large schooners and 38 smaller boats of the "smack" variety. Vessel tonnage that year was 6,522—or close to 8 percent of the national total. Servicing this impressive fleet were no fewer than thirty-one wholesale fish dealers, ranging the entire length of the city waterfront and specializing in all varieties of fish products.[7] A year later, the Portland fisheries were providing direct or indirect employment for three thousand workers, occupying a fleet of vessels worth an estimated $400,000, and accounting for an overall capital investment (including buildings and wharves) of $2 million, a figure equalled by the annual catch value.[8]

By the 1880s the city of Portland enjoyed a nearly monopolistic position in the Maine fisheries. Its share of the state's fishing tonnage in vessels over twenty tons, which had been 8 percent in 1870, increased to 26 percent in 1880, and was up to 36 percent by 1885. In terms of mackerel-fishing schooners alone, Portland owned roughly half of the entire Maine fleet after 1880.[9] Simultaneously, the city tightened its grip on the supply and marketing sectors of Maine's fishing industry. Its salt wholesalers, who had imported slightly more than half of the state's foreign salt at the close of the Civil War, increased that share to three-quarters of the total in 1880.[10] Within another five years, two-thirds of Maine's fish dealers and three-quarters of its outfitting firms were located in Portland, giving the city close to a monopoly over two aspects of the industry that had been relatively decentralized as late as the early 1870s.[11]

The rapid expansion of Portland's fisheries, though gratifying to local interests, was not really a healthy development considered within a broader Maine context. Unlike the comparable antebellum dominance of Penobscot District, Portland's monopoly of the postwar Maine fisheries was essentially negative. The city's position was not achieved by growing faster than other areas of the state within an industry that was expanding statewide. Rather, its growth was inversely proportional to the decline of the industry elsewhere. For fifteen years, beginning in 1870, Portland's fishing fleet grew steadily, approximately tripling in size, while Maine's overall fleet remained roughly the same in numbers and tonnage. The net result was a steady decline in areas outside of Portland, a decline that was in direct proportion to the city's growth. Between 1870 and 1885 the District of Portland-Falmouth gained five thousand tons of fishing vessels, very nearly the amount lost from all of Maine's other customs districts combined over the same period. Penobscot District, by contrast, had doubled its tonnage during the fifteen years from 1845 to 1860 but had managed only to retain its earlier share of Maine's total fishing fleet (29 percent), because other districts had increased their tonnage by the same ratio.[12] In short, Portland's rise was a product not of expansion in Maine's fisheries but of consolidation.

The clear implication is that Portland's growth during its brief golden era was accomplished in large part at the expense of other fishing ports in the state, and that was indeed the case. Large numbers of fishing vessels from Maine's smaller coastal towns were transferred to Portland after 1865.[13] It is possible, of course, to exaggerate the factor of vessel transfer in Portland's postwar expansion. Many new vessels also joined the city's fleet during that period. Portland was, in fact, the only important in-state market for Maine-built fishing schooners following the Civil War, and at least three dozen such vessels were launched for city merchants at Bath, Boothbay, and Kennebunkport, the state's principal postwar schooner-building centers, between 1866 and 1890.* Nevertheless, new construction cannot, by itself, explain

---

*Professional yards specializing in fishing-schooner construction for primarily outside interests were a prominent feature of Maine's coastal economy following the Civil War. The leading builders engaged in this work were Deering & Donnell and Hagan & Thurlow at Bath, George Christenson (or Christiansen) at Kennebunkport, and William Adams & Son, James McDougall & Son, and C. &. J. P. Hodgdon & Co. at East Boothbay. These and other Maine firms turned out 20 percent or more of the vessels in the Massachusetts fleet of the 1880s. (Source: *Mass.Cen., 1885*, 2:1422–23.)

the massive increase in Portland's fishing fleet, which expanded by eighty-two schooners between the years 1868 and 1883 alone.[14]

The phenomenon of vessel transfer began with the initial industry decline of the 1860s and especially affected the eastern seaports. Many of Penobscot District's larger schooners were sold "to the westward" during the last years of the Civil War, when its fishermen were forced by economic circumstances to seek employment on land or in the boat fisheries.[15] The process continued after the war ended and was typified by the sale of the Bucksport Grand Banker *Zenas Snow* to Portland interests in 1868. Most of Deer Isle's schooners were sold out of the district around the same time.[16] This east-to-west movement of vessels produced as its by-product a fundamental geographic reorientation of the Maine fishing fleet. Less than a decade after the close of the war, a majority of the state's tonnage was sailing out of western ports (principally Portland), totally reversing the pattern of vessel ownership that had existed for more than a quarter-century prior to 1865. The shift was massive. Between 1865 and 1880 that portion of Maine's cod and mackerel tonnage owned west of Rockland rose from one-third to two-thirds, while overall tonnage remained roughly static.[17]

The transfer of fishing tonnage to Portland did not affect eastern Maine alone. Smaller nearby towns sacrificed as well. Of Portland's continuing aggrandizement, contemporary observer R. E. Earll wrote in 1880, "This city now practically controls the fishing interests, not only of the district [of Portland-Falmouth] but also of the greater portion of western Maine."[18] Portland's hegemony in the western half of the state was reinforced by a considerable degree of regional absentee vessel-ownership. A number of city merchants began to dabble in that form of indirect control during the late 1860s, when they purchased shares in new Boothbay and Harpswell schooners. In the 1870s one of them, E. H. Chase, established branch facilities at Boothbay and began carrying on dual fishing operations, there and at Portland.[19] By 1880 city capital was extensively invested in several schooners of the Boothbay-area fleet, and arrangements had been made for those vessels to market their catch at Portland.[20]

Although the movement of tonnage to Portland was constant after 1865, the greatest number of transfers appear to have taken place at the end of the depressed decade of the 1870s. The following dozen members of the state-wide fishing fleet of 1879–1880, for example, were operating out of Portland less than four years later: *Lillian M. Warren* of Deer Isle; *S. L. Foster* of Cranberry Isles; *Fleetwood* of North Haven; *John Somes, Lucy J. Warren,* and *D. D. Geyer* of Swan's Island; *Venilia* of Brooklin; *Dreadnought* of Cape Elizabeth; *Young Sultan* and *A. H. Lennox* of Wiscasset; *Pearl of Orr's*

Island of Harpswell; and *Alice M. Gould* of Boothbay.[21] Characteristically, most of the transfers came from small eastern towns. The precise reason for their sales are unknown but may be inferred from the disposition of two other outport vessels around the same time.

In 1879 several fishermen from the small Hancock County town of Brooklin, near Deer Isle, decided to embark on an ambitious effort to enter the offshore mackerel fishery. They fitted out a large vessel with an expensive purse seine and pursued the major fisheries, working the southern waters during the spring, the Gulf of St. Lawrence in summer, and the New England coast during the fall. After a year of fishing, however, the enterprise proved economically untenable. Unable to refit for a second season, the owners sold their schooner to Portland interests in 1880.[22] A similar unfortunate case involved the schooner *George F. Keene* of Swan's Island, auctioned off at a United States marshal's bankruptcy sale held in Boston on August 18, 1888. The buyer was W. S. Jordan & Company of Portland, one of that city's larger outfitting firms, which purchased the vessel for fishing purposes.[23]

In both instances, economic failure precipitated the transfer to Portland ownership, and in each case the failure was that of a small, independent entrepreneurship, unable to succeed in the changed environment of the postwar fisheries. Low operating costs and the existence of the federal fishing bounty had minimized such mini-disasters in earlier times, but those ameliorating factors were no longer in play. High costs meant that for small operators success had to be immediate and substantial, and government aid was not available to carry enterprises over the rough spots.

The situation was especially bad during the decade of the 1870s. For the economy as a whole, the 1870s were years of severe retrenchment and dislocation. The famous financial panic of 1873 was followed in a matter of months by a general business downturn, which quickly evolved into the worst depression the United States had known up to that time. It lasted for six years, replete with bank closings, business failures, plummeting prices, and widespread unemployment.[24]

The fisheries were not immune to the hard times. To fishermen, the period 1873–1879 was one of drastically reduced returns on the catch they carried to market. Wholesale cod prices declined by a full one-third at Portland and Gloucester during the depression decade, dropping to a level not seen since before the Civil War.[25] Mackerel prices also fell, reaching such a discouragingly low level after 1873 that half of the Gulf of St. Lawrence fleet elected to remain in port rather than fish.[26] Costs incurred by fishermen, on the other hand, did not fall by nearly as much, even in a time of general price decline. There were exceptions, of course. The price of salt dropped at least as fast as the price of fish, if not faster, although that was a dubious benefit in an era when fresh fishing was increasingly in vogue.[27] Similarly, the cost of a suit of schooner sails was significantly reduced, falling by 25 percent between 1869 and 1877.[28] Such advantages were cancelled out, however, by other expenses. For example, the cost of many basic provisions carried on a fishing voyage—coffee, flour, rice, beans, bread, and potatoes, among others—remained steady or rose slightly between 1870 and 1877.[29] On balance, the expenses of going fishing remained fairly constant in the face of a declining fish market. Outfitting costs recorded at Castine in the depression year of 1874 showed price decreases over 1870 in only about half of the items purchased and actual price increases in several others. Banks schooners working out of Castine at the height of the depression were forced to insure their outfits for approximately the same value as in predepression years, even though cod prices were down substantially.[30]

More critical than the failure of outfitting expenses to keep pace with falling fish prices was the problem of vessel costs. The fisherman's schooner was his single biggest investment, and shipyards were slow to reflect the reality of a depressed economy. From 1873 to 1877, the average purchase price of a new fishing schooner built at Essex, Massachusetts, remained firm at around $8,000. That was approximately double the 1860 price and roughly equal to the cost prevailing in the inflation-ridden years of the immediate postwar era.[31] The continued price stability of the new vessel market—at Essex yards, prices even inched upward slightly in the middle 1870s[32]—was due almost entirely to the high cost of wood.

In Maine, timber costs had begun rising shortly before the Civil War. That process intensified during the 1860s, as gradually diminishing supplies close at hand necessitated an increased reliance on more expensive building materials shipped from out of state.[33] In the Trenton-Lamoine area of eastern Maine, the price of wood used in fishing vessels nearly tripled during the decade after 1860, and by 1870 lumber alone accounted for one-third of the total outlay for a banks schooner, compared to one-sixth ten years earlier.[34] Other construction costs began to decline at that point. Wages, which had risen somewhat during the 1860s, were reduced over the succeeding decade at Maine shipyards.[35] Timber, however, resisted the downward trend of wages and prices. In the Portland wholesale market, shipbuilding lumber was actually more expensive during the initial two years of the depression (1874–1875) than it had been before the 1873 crash, and, unlike most other commodities, it remained high throughout the 1870s.[36]

The results were predictable. As fishing profits shrank, fishermen and others in the industry were gradually priced out of the new-vessel market. By 1877 new fishing schooners built at Bath were sitting on the stocks for months at a time, unable to attract buyers.[37] Only at the tail end of the decade, after five years of general economic decline, did timber and, in turn, vessel prices begin to come down.[38] That was too late for many fishing entrepreneurs. The failure of shipyards to reduce their prices put a premium on used vessels and made them expensive as well. At the height of the depression, aging schooners that should have declined substantially in value were selling for the same amount of money their owners had paid for them several years earlier.[39] Such added overhead in the face of declining fish prices was a definite hardship on the operator in need of a replacement vessel to stay in the fishing business.

The depression of the 1870s, then, created an economic environment for the fishing industry that contributed to the already formidable problems of marginal operators. The disparity between costs and returns made the decade very similar to the inflation-ravaged years of the Civil War. The end result was more failed fishing firms in the smaller Maine outports and an increase in vessel transfers to Portland, where the large mercantile firms were better able to withstand the heavy economic weather of the times. Between 1870 and 1880, as Maine's fishing fleet outside the city was being reduced by a third, Portland's fleet was doubling in size.[40]

The Portland fish merchants were relatively immune to bad economic news. While other operators in Maine struggled to stay afloat during the depression decade, they remained insulated from serious economic difficulties by their very size and affluence. Most of the Portland companies were already comparative industry giants by the middle 1870s. In 1877 the city's eleven most prominent firms were capitalized at an average of $100,000,* and eight of them owned a dozen or more schooners, a concentration of vessel ownership matched by only four other operators in the state.[41] The Portland merchants could therefore afford the luxury of absorbing occasional losses or temporarily diminished profits. When smaller firms and independent fishermen went under, as happened with increasing frequency in the wake of the 1873 panic, they were there to pick up the pieces. The economic collapse of the 1870s thus reinforced the effects of postwar inflation

---

*Portland claimed five of the seven Maine fishing companies with capital investments of $100,000 or more at this time. The five were: E. H. Chase ($267,500), Jordan & Blake ($185,000), Thomes, Chase & Company ($130,000), Lewis, Whitten & Company ($110,000), and Charles A. Dyer ($100,000). These firms were engaged in all phases of the business and owned extensive shore property in addition to fleets of vessels.

and the bounty repeal in stimulating the growth of monopoly in the fishing industry.*

Although Portland was the chief beneficiary of increased economic concentration in the Maine fisheries after 1865, its expansion was not the only manifestation of basic structural change in the industry during the last half of the nineteenth century. The growth of concentration took place, albeit on a somewhat smaller scale, even where localized fishing operations survived independent of Portland's lengthening shadow. The greater Boothbay area was one example. In 1850 this region (including the fishing villages of Boothbay Harbor, Southport, and Westport) had a total of twenty-seven active fishing firms, which altogether operated 77 vessels. A quarter-century later, in 1877, greater Boothbay was home to well over 100 vessels, but the number of actual enterprises had been cut in half. Instead of two dozen small firms capitalized at less than $4,000 and operating an average of 3 vessels each, Boothbay's fisheries were now controlled by twelve large firms averaging $74,000 in capitalization and 11 vessels each.[42] Exactly when this process of consolidation gathered its greatest momentum is uncertain, given an absence of data for the Civil War period, but the depression of the 1870s appears to have had a major impact. One of the villages in the region, Southport, lost four of its six fishing establishments between 1870 and 1877, while its fleet of schooners and total capital investment remained roughly the same size. Two large companies thus inherited what six smaller firms had owned and managed prior to the economic slump.[43]

Similar developments took place everywhere in Maine, to a greater or lesser degree. At Deer Isle, in the eastern part of the state, the number of independent fishing enterprises declined by almost two-thirds between 1860 and 1870. Again, the money invested in vessels and shore facilities remained constant but was concentrated in fewer hands, as average individual capitalization rose from $2,000 to $5,000 in just a decade. Seven years later, Deer Isle's fisheries, once the industry's preeminent example of small-scale enterprise, were dominated by just three companies, one of them worth over $100,000.[44] On North Haven Island in Penobscot Bay the number of fishing firms decreased from eight to only two between 1860 and 1877, while the town's overall capital investment in the fisheries increased by several thousand dollars. The surviving operators, like their contemporaries on Deer Isle, enjoyed assets far greater than those of their predecessors in the busi-

*The impact of the depression of the 1870s on the fishing industry was not unlike its effect on other sectors of the American economy, such as oil and steel, whose consolidations were accelerated by the undermining and ultimate dissolution of numerous small companies following the financial crash of 1873. (Source: Thomas C. Cochran and John C. Miller, *The Age of Enterprise: A Social History of Industrial America* [New York: Macmillan Co., 1951], 143–45.)

ness.[45] Local consolidation of this sort was accompanied in eastern Maine by regional centralization. Fishing operations in the various customs districts tended more and more to be concentrated in one or two ports rather than in a multiplicity of towns and villages, as previously. Bucksport, for example, became the fisheries center for all of Castine District after 1880, gradually increasing its share of the district's formerly dispersed vessel fleet to well over half.[46]

The process of consolidation described above actually began early in the nineteenth century, even though it did not reach fruition until much later. A trend toward concentrated ownership of vessels was evident in the cod-fishing fleet of eastern Maine's Penobscot District soon after 1830. District statistics for the years 1829 to 1848 reveal an unmistakable, if slow, movement away from ownership by working fishermen and single-vessel owners and toward multiple-vessel ownership by wealthy individuals or mercantile firms.[47] By the 1850s merchant dominance was abundantly evident at such major regional entrepôts as Castine and Bucksport, and fishing companies in those places were beginning to extend their influence to smaller surrounding outports by purchasing controlling shares* in locally owned schooners.[48] The pattern was duplicated in western Maine. Portland's gradual absorption of the fishing interests of Portland-Falmouth District began as early as 1840, and the control of vessels owned in the city had already passed into the hands of large capitalists by 1850.[49]

Despite the inexorable spread of large-scale enterprise, economic democracy remained a reality in most fishing communities along the Maine

*This was especially the case with large Grand Banks schooners of one hundred tons or more, which by 1850 were already too expensive for the average outport operator to finance alone or through local partnership. A practice evolved whereby the majority owners of a new outport vessel would take a merchant from one of the large fishing ports as minority shareholder, accept his managing ownership, and permit their schooner to hail from the merchant's home port during the fishing season. The merchant thus guaranteed the vessel's outfitting and marketing trade for his own firm, while the majority owners gained capital assistance in building it. The Vinalhaven Grand Banker *Mary Brewer*—115 tons (o.m.) and registered dimensions of 77′ × 21′ × 8′, one of the Penobscot region's biggest cod-fishing vessels—exemplified this form of enterprise. In 1854, when two years old, she was valued at $4,000, having probably cost $5,000 new. Her four island owners, including the captain, were able to finance only ten-sixteenths of the schooner themselves. In exchange for the balance of the required outlay ($1,875), they accepted the managing ownership of a leading Castine merchant, Samuel Adams, who assumed a plurality share of six-sixteenths and supervised construction of the vessel at a Castine shipyard. The *Mary Brewer* thenceforth fished out of that port. (Sources: Colcord, 317; *Halifax Commission Proceedings*, 2250, 2610; *RJ*, marine list, 9 June 1854; *EA*, marine list, 2 October 1854; U.S. MS Census Pop., 1850: Hancock County, Maine, town of Castine, and Waldo County, Maine, towns of Vinalhaven and North Haven; Castine Tax Valuation Book for 1854: valuation of schooner *Mary Brewer*; NA, RBMIN [RG 41], VDR, Penobscot District Enrollments, vol. 40: certificate of enrollment, schooner *Mary Brewer*, 21 May 1852.)

coast for a considerable period of time. This was especially true down east. In 1848, close to half of the 267 cod-fishing vessels enrolled in the district of Penobscot still belonged to single-vessel owners, and despite the growth of merchant firms such small entrepreneurs continued to constitute the overwhelming majority of the district's vessel ownership bloc. Furthermore, these single-vessel operators, most of whom were working fishermen, actually increased in number during the decade of the 1840s. At midcentury, they remained the core of the industry in eastern Maine's premier fishing district.[50]

The broadly egalitarian tone of the eastern sea fisheries was sustained through the 1850s. Although merchants now ruled the larger fishing ports, they did not control the outports, and independent fishermen continued to flourish there. The contrast between the mercantile center of Castine and the outlying village of Deer Isle illustrates this point. Both fishing towns had similar amounts of capital invested in the industry in 1850, and both maintained numerically comparable fishing fleets. Beyond that, similarities ceased. Single-vessel ownership, rare at Castine, where the average firm owned four vessels, was the rule at Deer Isle, where there were nearly as many owners as vessels. A wide disparity in individual capitalization also existed between the two ports. While the handful of merchants controlling Castine's fleet had an average investment of close to $7,000, the typical Deer Isle operator claimed assets of less than $1,500.[51]

S. & H. Grove were representative of Deer Isle's class of small fishery capitalists. These two brothers owned and operated a single schooner with a crew of eight in 1849. The vessel and its equipment constituted their entire investment of $1,200, to which each of the partners had contributed $600. The Groves' total return from cod fishing at year's end amounted to $1,120, and from that sum they deducted $800 for payment of the crew. The remaining $320 and a bounty share of perhaps $100, minus whatever outfitting expenses had been incurred for salt, bait, etc., was their only reward for a full season's fishing.[52] This type of "democratic capitalism" continued to exist for another decade or so at Deer Isle and places like it. As late as 1860, half of the island's sixty-five fisheries entrepreneurs were single-vessel owners capitalized at less than $1,000, and some had entered the business with as little as $400 or $500. Such opportunity ended with the Civil War, however. Industrial census takers surveying the island in 1870 found only a fraction of the previous number of fishing operations, none of them capitalized at under $1,000 and few at less than twice that figure.[53]

Small-scale enterprise of the type found on Deer Isle in the 1850s was thoroughly undermined by the repeal of the fishing bounty and the inflation brought by the war. It lingered for a few more years, but by 1880 or thereabouts it was a thing of the past as far as the deep-sea fisheries were concerned. George Brown Goode, speaking to an international gathering of industry experts in 1883, delivered the eulogy on behalf of the United States Fish Commission: "The general fisheries are becoming concentrated in a few cities, and while formerly fifty small local fleets were recognized, the commercial fisheries [of the United States] are now carried on chiefly from Gloucester, Portland [and] Boston, though Provincetown, with Boothbay and some other minor ports of Maine, must still be recognized."[54]

The economic concentration and consolidation described by Goode—and evidenced in Maine by the rise of Portland—was the culmination of a long-term trend under way for decades, but one that had been blunted until 1866 by the intervening force of government subsidy and regulation. The removal of government from the scene allowed full play to an unfettered capitalism under which the natural tendency toward monopoly asserted itself fully for the first time throughout the fisheries. In the absence of offsetting subsidies to their lesser rivals, the merchant firms, with their "economies of scale," assumed an increasingly dominant role. The innumerable competitive advantages of large enterprises over small became obvious in the economically difficult years that followed the Civil War, when their superior capacity to withstand inflation, depression, and market fluctuations was proven time and again.

The End of the Independent Entrepreneur

The principal feature of the economic concentration characterizing Maine's fishing industry after the Civil War was merchant control. That in itself was nothing new, of course. Merchant firms had been economically dominant in the larger fishing ports well before 1865. What made the postwar mercantile influence unique was its pervasiveness. By the 1870s and 1880s the only remaining fishing ports of significance were the large ones, where the merchant class ruled supreme. As the fisheries became concentrated in a handful of commercial centers like Portland, therefore, they increasingly came under the aegis of a few large companies. In 1880 Portland's merchant firms directly managed three-quarters of that city's entire mackerel fleet and indirectly controlled (through minority shareholding) most of the rest of it.[55]

Merchant ownership of vessels at Portland differed in some respects from the pattern prevalent in the 1850s. The increased cost of schooners after 1865 led to an enlargement of the usual number of shareholders, as a means of spreading the burden of investment. Division of shares into thirty-seconds, rather than eighths or sixteenths, became common, and the typical number of shareholders per vessel approximately doubled.[56] This did not lead to more democratic shareholding by fishermen or other ordinary individuals, but it did produce changes in the nature of merchant ownership itself. Instead of exclusive control by fish dealers, as was the rule at leading Penobscot Bay ports a generation earlier, Portland's postwar vessel ownership included a wide range of maritime interests. In addition to traditional wholesale fish merchants, firms representing outfitters, provisioners, chandlers, coopers, shipbuilders, and sailmakers all purchased shares in the city's fishing fleet and thereby obtained control of its trade in their particular lines of business. Several outfitting companies went one step further and became actual managing owners of the vessels they serviced.[57]

If the economic environment of the post-1865 period broadened the range of mercantile involvement in the Maine fisheries, it did nothing for independent entrepreneurship. Compared, for instance, to pre–Civil War Belfast, whose fishing captains held managing shares in a third of their vessels and owned a fifth of them outright, shareholding in postwar Portland was restrictive indeed. Not one of the city's mackerel schooners was fully owned by its sailing master in 1880, and only a handful (18 percent) had a working captain as managing owner.[58] This pattern was in keeping with the broad trend in vessel ownership throughout the New England fisheries during the last quarter of the nineteenth century. In spite of extravagant contemporary claims that literally hundreds of fishing captains of the period managed, Horatio Alger–style, to attain ownership of their own vessels, the fact is that fewer and fewer were able to do so.[59] At Gloucester, where the largest single fleet was concentrated, less than one fishing schooner in six was independently owned by its master in 1882.[60]

In large measure, the demise of the independent operator can be credited to the repeal of the fishing bounty, the advent of sophisticated technology, and the impact of the disruptive cycles of inflation and depression that began in the 1860s. At the same time, there is little doubt that it was hastened by the market control established by the large fish companies. The independents—fishermen owning their own vessels and small operators selling to large wholesalers and distributors—were subjected to severe economic pressure by the integrated firms located at places like Portland, Gloucester, and Boston.

The adverse forces of the market operated at several levels. Partly, the problem facing independents was structural. Fishing was basically a two-tiered industry: there were those who fished—a description covering most of the independent operators—and those who purchased the catch, processed it, and distributed it to retailers. Often the two functions were combined. The majority of Portland's firms, for example, were integrated operations that engaged in both fishing and marketing.[61] They processed the catch of their own vessels and also served as fish buyers for fishermen not in the marketing business themselves. These wholesale packers and distributors—the infamous "middlemen" of the industry—had a tremendous economic advantage in their dealings with small fishing firms and unaffiliated fishermen, especially if they (the middlemen) owned their own vessels. Sylvanus Smith, a retired captain and fisheries chronicler, described the system as it functioned at Gloucester in the latter part of the nineteenth century:

> One great factor which has entered into the business, resulting in great injury, is the producers of fish becoming shippers of fish as well. This has a tendency to squeeze out the smaller firm, and the producer who was not also a shipper continually got the small price for his fish. The shipper, who was also a producer, would use his own fish when it was to his advantage to do so, but on a rising market, he would buy of a producer, saving his own supply for higher prices, and in this way, the producer was always getting the lower prices, while the shipper obtained the maximum.[62]

Numerous observers, viewing the scene from different vantage points, agreed that most of the money made in the fishing business after 1870 was made in the handling, not the catching, of fish. A critical fisherman offered the assessment that "as regards the profits of the business, the middle man makes the greatest, as is usual in most such cases."[63] An approving fish merchant concurred, describing the earnings derived from the catch as essentially "a mercantile profit."[64] Another merchant recalled that he actually lost money as a vessel owner at Gloucester in the 1860s but managed to recoup handsomely in the following decade as a wholesale distributor, buying from others. He credited his own, and Gloucester's, latter-day prosperity to a local post–Civil War integration of the producing and marketing functions, which eliminated the long-standing practice of selling exclusively to wholesale merchants in Boston. In the 1870s Gloucester's vessel owners emerged as middlemen in their own right, packing and shipping fish as well as producing the catch.[65]

There is no question that the middlemen of the industry benefitted substantially at the expense of the independent fishermen and vessel owners. During the late 1870s, Gloucester's wholesale merchants realized between seventy-five cents and one dollar on each quintal of salt cod they purchased from fishermen, a profit of 20 to 30 percent.[66] In the mackerel fishery, most profit taking was done at the packing stage, when the fish were transferred from sea barrels to shipping barrels and repickled for market. Profit margins for Gloucester's packing merchants ranged between 30 and 40 percent on each barrel processed.[67] Moreover, the packers appear to have gradually increased their margins during the postwar period, offsetting falling fish prices and applying a progressively greater squeeze on the independents in the process. Certainly, they sacrificed less in hard times than others in the industry. Despite several years of depression beginning in 1873, packing charges remained firm, not falling at all until 1876.[68] By the following year prices were twenty-five cents lower than their two-dollar-per-barrel peak, but most of that cut had been absorbed in reduced overhead. The packers' basic unit cost for barrels, salt, and labor fell by fifteen cents, while their per-barrel profit declined by only ten cents, resulting in a net drop in profits of just 3 percent, from 33 to 30 percent overall.[69]

Besides carrying the burden of working in an industry so structured that even when operating fairly (or at least honestly) it placed them at a distinct disadvantage, independent fishermen suffered from direct and calculated exploitation at the hands of those managing the postwar marketing system. In truth, abuses of one kind or another were as old as the fishing industry itself. Marblehead fishermen were complaining as early as 1834 about the unfair tactics of speculative merchants, claiming that such buyers, acting in combination, often obtained fish at one-third its true market value by employing trickery and deceit against unwary producers.[70] By the post–Civil War period such practices had become refined and almost institutionalized. Gloucester wholesale merchants routinely conspired in advance during the 1870s to set the price fishermen would get for their cod.[71] At the Fulton Fish Market in New York, which Maine's southern mackerel fleet frequented regularly during the Gilded Age, an alternative to ordinary price-fixing was the charging of a standard 12.5 percent commission on the gross sales of each vessel by dealers who doubled as wholesalers and retailers. That rate was agreed upon in advance by the three major wholesalers who controlled 80 percent of the market's transactions and was imposed on the rest.[72]

Maine itself was not free from such questionable business tactics. In the 1880s, Biddeford Pool fishermen, who marketed their catch at Portland, complained bitterly about price-fixing arrangements imposed there by marketmen and fish buyers.[73] Other Maine fishermen reported much the same thing. Said one independent operator, interviewed by state officials in 1887: "The fish business is monopolized to the injury of the fisherman, as the buyers are about all members of fish bureaus that control prices and sales. At best there is but a bare living and a life of hardship for those who catch the fish."[74]

There was considerable validity to criticisms of the role of fish bureaus, or "exchanges," as they were often called. In November 1882 one such organization, representing Boston's leading wholesale dealers, sought to gain control of that city's entire fresh-fish market, in order to force down prices paid to fishermen. The attempt was described in the following way by the *Eastern Argus* of Portland, whose readers in the fishing community followed its progress with keen interest: "The distinctive feature of the scheme is the purchase of fish only through an exchange, which fixes every morning the price which is to be paid during the day. It was claimed by the wholesale dealers that the new arrangement would benefit the fishermen as well as themselves, by giving a uniform price for their whole cargoes. The fishermen are unanimous in taking an altogether different view of the matter."[75] The would-be monopoly, known as the Boston Fish Exchange, ultimately failed, owing to a producer boycott. By refusing to sell at the low dictated price and carrying their fish to other ports instead, the vessel operators compelled the thirty-six member firms constituting the Boston "ring" to dissolve their association.[76]

Such cooperative efforts to ensure free competition at the marketing level were not always successful, however. The power of the exchanges and other combines was sufficient to overcome resistance in many, if not most, instances. The so-called halibut pool, another Boston-based monopoly, serves to illustrate. The New England Halibut Company, founded in 1866, had so cornered the market in that species by 1882 that under-compensated halibut fishermen proposed to break it by selling exclusively to several smaller wholesale dealers in the city and elsewhere.[77] Despite their resolve, the company not only retained its position and authority but expanded it, forming ironclad price-fixing agreements with its smaller competitors—the very source fishermen had looked to for relief. The pool of associated wholesale halibut dealers had spread by 1888 to include those in Gloucester as well as Boston, and the Fulton market in New York was also said to be "thoroughly permeated" with its influence.[78]

Luckily for Maine's fishermen, fresh halibut was not one of the state's staple fish products, and Maine's wholesale merchants were somewhat less heavy-handed in their excursions into market manipulation. This does not mean that there were no attempts to emulate the fish combines of southern New England. On April 4, 1884, thirty of Portland's "principal dealers in fresh, salt and pickled fish" met to organize the Portland Fish Exchange. The motives behind the initiative were not publicly revealed, except for an indication that the arrivals of fishing schooners and their fares would be carefully monitored and the suggestion that the new organization, with its committee on arbitration, was expected to "result in much benefit to the fish trade of Portland."[79] There is no direct evidence that the Portland Fish Exchange functioned like its short-lived predecessor in Boston, which enforced market discipline among its members and dispensed profit dividends in the manner of a corporation.[80] Still, the potential for abuse was clearly present in the pooling of information and the close confidentiality of the dealers.

The capacity of Portland's capitalists to exert market control was reinforced by the vagaries of Maine's curious fish-inspection law. The state was one of several in New England to regulate the pickling and shipping of mackerel during the nineteenth century. Among the very first pieces of legislation enacted by Maine's fledgling government in 1821 was "An Act to provide for the packing and inspection of Pickled and Smoked fish," which empowered the governor and his council to appoint local fish inspectors and established uniform grading standards for all pickled and smoked sea products approved for sale. Barrels of mackerel, in particular, were to be branded numerically, according to their size and quality.[81] By the post–Civil War period this system of inspection had produced glaring conflicts of interest. Portland, for instance, had nine fish inspectors in 1880, all of whom were also wholesale fish dealers. Seven of the nine, furthermore, were active mackerel packers.[82] Fish inspection was similarly implemented elsewhere, with the result that most packing houses in New England had an inspector who was a member of the firm as well.[83]

In effect, the packers were accorded the privilege of policing themselves, and there is reason to believe that they were less than totally scrupulous. A Gloucester dealer indicted the Massachusetts inspection law in 1877, saying, "I think there has been a great deal of fraud practiced by our own packers, and the quality of the fish packed has hence deteriorated."[84] Four years later, representatives of the United States Fish Commission agreed that dishonesty was widespread in all of the mackerel-packing states because of the incestuous relationship between dealers and inspectors, and they pointed to improper grading as the most common offense.[85] That particular charge was directed toward deception of retailers and (ultimately) consumers, but there was also ample opportunity for the mackerel packers, who controlled the inspection process, to take advantage of their independent suppliers. State inspectors were permitted considerable discretion in evaluating fish. They took into account not only size but relative quality as well. The final revision of Maine's inspection law in 1875 allowed for five separate classifications of pickled mackerel, based only in part on objective criteria. A fish exceeding thirteen inches in length might be variably judged a "number one," "number two," "number three large," or "number three" product.[86] As an indication of what the inspector/packer's potentially biased decision could mean to fishermen, the maximum per-barrel wholesale prices of mackerel at Portland on August 27, 1878, were: $16.50 for number one, $11.50 for number two, $9.50 for number three large, and $6.00 for number three.[87]

There was one brief attempt to reform Maine's flawed system of inspection. In 1832 the state legislature acted to make it illegal for any appointed inspector to officially brand any barrel of fish in which he had a direct or indirect economic interest. However, that amending statute was repealed four years later without explanation.[88] It was never re-enacted, and victimized fishermen were left only the recourse of improperly tampering with their fish before delivery to improve its appearance and quality rating. The usual process, called "plowing," consisted of splitting or cutting the fish during dressing operations in such a way as to make it appear thicker and fatter, thus creating the illusion of a higher-grade product. Unfortunately, wholesalers and inspectors were acutely aware of the technique employed and, by the 1880s, were in the habit of automatically downgrading the mackerel they received to compensate.[89]

The operation of the fish-inspection law was symbolic of the problems facing independent vessel owners in Maine after 1865. In contests between producer and wholesaler, the merchant or middleman had the overwhelming advantage. The economic struggle was essentially an unequal one, and the fisherman was the inevitable loser. Henry Demarest Lloyd, surveying the economic landscape of America in 1894, summarized the fate of independent entrepreneurship in words that accurately fit the situation in Maine's fishing industry. "We have been . . . leaving competition to regulate itself," he wrote. "But the flames of a new economic evolution run around us, and we turn to find that competition has killed competition."[90]

From Shares to Wages

In addition to small-scale enterprise, another casualty of the post–Civil War era in the fisheries was the traditional share system. This, too, was related to the emergence of the merchant firms, but other factors also weighed heavily, foremost among them the repeal of the fishing-bounty law. Until repeal in 1866, profit sharing—as opposed to a wage system—was mandated by law in the cod fishery. The original legislation establishing federal bounties in 1792 stipulated that to collect the subsidy a vessel had to provide a prior written agreement between captain and crew to the effect that "the fish, or the proceeds of such fishing voyage or voyages, which may appertain to the fishermen, shall be divided among them, in proportion to the quantities or number of said fish they may respectively have caught; which agreement shall be endorsed or countersigned by the owner of such fishing vessel or his agent."[91] This contract provision remained basically unchanged through subsequent revisions and administrative interpretations of the law for the next three-quarters of a century. It appeared virtually verbatim in the circular instructions on bounty payment distributed to customs officials by the Treasury Department in 1852 and, lest any misunderstanding exist, was made more explicit by the following addendum: "No fishing vessel of which the fishermen, or any one of them, are compensated for their services on board by wages, or in any other manner than by the division of the fish, or the proceeds of the same, as required by law, is entitled to bounty."[92]

While firmly establishing the principle that the profits from a cod-fishing voyage had to be divided between owner and crew, the bounty law left undefined the precise nature of that division. The share system thus evolved differently from place to place, taking a variety of forms in the years before the Civil War. Initially, the various economic arrangements developed in the New England fisheries were quite democratic. In the 1830s, the Massachusetts ports of Marblehead, Plymouth, and Beverly favored a division based on fractions of eight. The owner and crew together supplied the major outfitting items for the voyage (salt, bait, barrels, fuel, and lighting), known collectively as the "great general," and the crew provided its own provisions and fishing gear, commonly referred to as the "small general." Upon the vessel's return, five-eighths of the net stock (proceeds remaining after deduction of the cost of the great general from the gross) was proportionately divided among the crew, while three-eighths was delegated to the owner. The crew then paid the cost of the small general prior to apportioning its share.[93] In effect, the crew was responsible for five-eighths of the basic outfit, in addition to its individual tools of trade and subsistence requirements, and received five-eighths of the final profit from the sale of fish. On Cape Cod, a similar system evolved, except that fishing was more typically done "at the quarters." That is, the owner took just one-quarter of the net stock, leaving a more generous three-quarter portion for the crew.[94]

Maine's fisheries, too, functioned very democratically in the early years of the industry. A share, or "lay," system based on quarters or fifths—the owner in the latter case paying for one-fifth of the outfit and receiving one-fifth of the profits—flourished in the more isolated coastal regions of the state, including the island communities of Penobscot and Casco bays, prior to midcentury.[95] It is apparent, however, that the less egalitarian mode of fishing "at the halves" gradually became the most common form used down east.

Under the half system, owner and crew divided the net profits of the voyage evenly, each taking one-half of what remained following payment of the great general charge. For obvious reasons, the owners favored this method of division, and it was instituted early on by merchants at most of the larger New England fishing ports, to the comparative detriment of ordinary crewmen.* The half-lay was in common use at Gloucester, Massachusetts, well before 1850, and it replaced more democratic forms of apportionment at Beverly and Provincetown sometime after midcentury.[96] In Maine, the half-lay had become the customary arrangement at Portland and Boothbay by the 1840s and was used exclusively at Castine from the 1830s through the 1850s.[97] The system was also widespread in Maine's smaller regional outports by the middle of the nineteenth century, indicating a fairly broad range of acceptance. It was employed, for instance, at such places as Deer Isle, Sedgwick, and Swan's Island during the decade-and-a-half that preceded the Civil War,[98] suggesting that other, more equitable forms had largely disappeared by the late antebellum period.** Whether the lay was at the fifths, quarters, or halves, however, the fact remains that until 1866 some form of share system existed wherever American vessels carried on the cod fishery. The fishing industry thus stood at odds with the prevailing trend elsewhere in the increasingly wage-oriented national economy.

The end of government involvement in the fishing industry after the Civil War changed all that, by relieving vessel owners of the onerous necessity of sharing profits with their employees, the fishermen, and treating them as co-investors in a cooperative venture. The quasi-socialist concept of the worker as sharesman began to be replaced by the more common capitalist notion of the worker as wage earner. The erosion of the democratic tendencies inherent in the share system was, nevertheless, gradual. Tradition dies hard, and the fisheries were a tradition-bound industry.

The share format survived longest in those places most closely identified with the mackerel fishery and the emerging fresh fisheries. The reason for this is not entirely clear but was probably related to the higher profit margins

---

*The gross stock of a vessel was normally several times the cost of the outfit, so that the modest savings the men realized by paying for only half of the great general was more than offset by their lost percentage of the net profit. Occasionally they benefitted from the paternalistic custom at some ports whereby the merchant-owner incorporated the small-general charge in the great general or deducted it from his half-share. However, this gain too was often offset by the owner's taking the crew's share of the bounty allowance as compensation. (Sources: *Anderson Report*, 1; Kellogg, 61; *U.S.AppCG*, 34th Cong., 3rd Sess. [1857], 219; NA, RBC [RG 36], CDR, Penobscot District Fishing Articles of Agreement: articles for schooner *Olive* of Castine, 2 May 1854, and schooners *Anne* and *Andover* of Deer Isle, 21 April 1846 and 22 April 1848.)

phasing out of more fractional forms of share fishing appears to have been related to the concurrent decline of broad-based ownership. In Massachusetts, communities fitting out their vessels at the quarters or fifths tended to be those in which working crewmen were part owners. Cape Cod's outports fell into this category. Conversely, fishing ports devoted to the half system were more typically those where crew members had a limited economic involvement in the vessels on which they sailed, such as Gloucester. (Source: Morison, *Maritime History of Massachusetts*, 309–10.)

in those branches of the industry. Vessels engaged in the mackerel, halibut, and haddock fisheries at Gloucester, for example, normally produced higher net stocks than those working the cod banks, resulting in relatively higher incomes for both owners and crews.[99] Therefore, there was less pressure on merchants engaged in these fisheries to alter the prevailing way of doing business so as to increase their own portion of the returns, something attainable only through a conversion to wage payments.

At any rate, mackerel catchers and fresh-market fishermen continued on the share system until at least the 1880s. In the New England mackerel fleet, fishing at the halves was the general rule, and it was followed at Gloucester and Wellfleet, Massachusetts, as well as Portland, Boothbay, Swan's Island, and North Haven in the state of Maine. The half-lay was also used in the fresh-halibut fishery, a Gloucester specialty.[100] Perhaps the most stubborn survival of the share system was in the winter fresh-haddock fishery, pursued in the 1880s by several New England ports, among them Boston, Gloucester, and Portland. Haddock fishermen not only fished at the quarters or fifths in the ancient manner but (with the exception of Boston crews) provided their own dories, a rarity in the age of trawling.[101]

In the various salt-cod fisheries, remnants of the profit-sharing system also lingered well into the last decades of the nineteenth century. For years Gloucester retained a variant of the half-lay in which crewmen shared one-half of the net proceeds but often divided it equally among themselves, rather than proportionally according to each man's catch, as required by law in earlier times.[102] A number of Maine cod-fishing ports also clung to the half system. It remained in vogue at Castine in 1870, though in modified form, and survived at Southport as late as 1886. In addition, the minority of cod bankers belonging to the mackerel-fishing ports of Boothbay and Portland continued to work on half-shares throughout the 1870s.[103]

The above exceptions notwithstanding, share fishing rapidly became a thing of the past after 1866. This was particularly true for the bank-cod fishery, which remained for some time the primary occupation among both Maine and Massachusetts vessels despite the increased attraction of alternative employments.* Within a few years after the repeal of the federal bounty regulations governing work contracts, fundamental changes in the

---

*While the share system largely disappeared from the cod-fishing ports of New England during the late nineteenth century, it survived more or less intact in the Maritime Provinces of Canada. Fishing at the halves—called "on the half-line" by Canadians—remained standard practice in Nova Scotia from the 1840s to the 1930s. (Sources: *Perley Reports*, 248; *N.S.App JPHA, 1853*, 373; *U.S.FCB, 1884*, 10; *U.S.FCB, 1893*, 344; *Can.ODHC*, 4th Parl., 4th Sess., 1882, 1516; Mather B. DesBrisay, *History of the County of Lunenburg* [3rd ed.; Bridgewater, N.S.: Bridgewater Bulletin, 1967], 469; H. P. Jenkins, *Nova Scotia at Work* [Toronto: Ryerson Press, 1938], 135.)

traditional method of compensation had become readily apparent to long-time observers of the industry.[104] To some, this was a decidedly adverse development. Nicolas Gilman, a leading advocate of profit sharing, detected a growing reduction in upward mobility among fishermen, particularly as expressed through vessel ownership. Looking back in 1896, he observed, "Where the wage system has been introduced into the fisheries, as it has been to a considerable extent within the last thirty years, its effects have been distinctly unfavorable."[105] Nevertheless, its adoption in the postwar era was both swift and widespread.

In Massachusetts, Newburyport was among the first to go over to the wage system, and the new format was well established there by the middle 1870s.[106] Toward the end of that decade, Provincetown, Plymouth, and Beverly owners were likewise hiring their crews by the trip or by the month, and even at Gloucester, which was notable for maintaining profit-sharing arrangements, a significant portion of the crewmen engaged in the Grand Banks cod and Greenland salt-halibut fisheries were being paid monthly wages in the 1870s.[107] Maine converted to the wage system with less unanimity but with equal dispatch. Soon after the removal of federal restrictions, the cod fishermen of Bucksport, Orland, and Lamoine, the centers of the eastern postwar banks fishery, were uniformly working for seasonal wages, and by 1880 a majority of the state's Grand Banks vessels, like those of Massachusetts, were no longer fishing on shares.[108] The wage system also appeared in the smaller fishing fleets of southern New England. Nearly half of the crewmen employed in Connecticut's cod fishery, for example, were paid by the month in 1877.[109]

There were essentially two reasons for the changeover to a wage system in the cod fisheries, one related to technological developments in the industry and the other to simple acquisitiveness on the part of the merchant-owners, who constituted the preponderant vessel-ownership bloc in the post–Civil War era. To begin with, the triumph of trawling and the adoption of dories were antithetical to the practice of traditional share fishing. In its purest form, the share system imposed certain responsibilities on the fishermen that wage earning did not. The sharesman was expected, for instance, to provide his own fishing gear as part of the arrangement, fishing "on his own hook," as the phrase went.[110] Technological change introduced cost factors that made this difficult, if not impossible, in many cases. Individual fishermen could theoretically provide their own dories and tubs of trawl, and occasionally they did, but the expense was prohibitive for most potential crew members, who possessed little or no ready capital. Old-fashioned share fishing, therefore, became increasingly impractical as more and more owners converted to the New Technology.

The upshot was that at most places the vessel owner gradually assumed the responsibility of supplying the necessary fishing equipment, absorbing all or most of the cost of the so-called small general himself or transferring portions of it to the vessel's common overhead expenses. When dories were introduced at Castine, for example, their cost was factored into the great general, while at Boston and Portland they were directly provided by the owner.[111] At Gloucester, where trawling was the rule, all of a cod-fishing schooner's working necessities were paid for by the merchant.[112] The concept of the sharesman as co-investor in the fishing enterprise was thus undermined, and this blurring of formerly distinct lines of responsibility had broad ramifications. Once the men had been relieved of the traditional burden of providing their own tools of trade, the vessel owners naturally felt less duty-bound to honor their part of the fishing compact, namely the maintenance of a profit-sharing mode of payment. It was they, after all, who were increasingly the sole providers of investment capital, and the transition to wages could be seen, from their viewpoint, as totally justifiable. It lacked only legal authorization, which came in due course. The awkward fact that the owners themselves had initially upset the ancient joint-stock system by instituting the expensive New Technology in the first place was easily forgotten or rationalized.

Technological change thus provided a convenient and plausible justification for the abandonment of profit sharing, but the primary motivation was far more fundamental. Under a wage system, the owners quite simply had the potential to greatly increase their percentage of the profits from any given voyage. The crew's share was set, while the owner's remained on a sliding scale, increasing with the success of the enterprise. There was some security for the men in fishing for wages, of course. They were guaranteed at least something from the trip, regardless of the catch. Gone were the days when (as happened to the crew of one Marblehead banker in 1861) a schooner could return home with almost no fish, leaving the sharesmen with only their small bounty allowance as a reward for several months of hard but fruitless labor.[113]

The existence of an economic safety net in the form of a guaranteed wage was indeed comforting, especially after the elimination of subsidies, but, ironically, it proved less and less necessary. So-called broken voyages were the rare exception, not the rule, after the Civil War. Improvements in vessels and equipment, refined fishing techniques, and expanded knowledge of the cod grounds reduced the likelihood of total failure. Trawling and dory fishing, in particular, increased the catch and made it more predictable. Trawls, for example, permitted the taking of spawning mother fish that spurned moving hand-lines but were attracted by stationary setlines.

Thus, the reproductive cycle no longer worked to frustrate fishermen.[114] In the early cod fishery, it was not unusual for luckless banks fishermen to sail home with half-fares, or less. A more frequent occurrence in later years was for dorymen to participate in record catches, the value of which they could not share in because of their status as hired hands.[115] When the wage system went into effect, then, the fisherman involuntarily surrendered the possibility, or even probability, of an increased income for the certainty of a minimum wage.

There is no doubt where the owners stood on the question of compensation. In the mackerel fishery, which did not fall under the labor restrictions of the bounty law, random payment of monthly wages appeared as early as the 1830s.[116] By the 1850s it was the chief modus operandi at some mackerel ports, despite the overall predominance of the share system. "In those years," recalled a schooner captain familiar with Newburyport's Gulf of St. Lawrence fleet, "generally in fitting out vessels, four men were hired to take a risk with the owners, and the balance of the crew were hired by the month. If they had fourteen men, they shipped eight."[117]

The antebellum cod fishery, too, witnessed the periodic use of wage payments by owners who were willing to circumvent the loosely enforced bounty rules. A Canadian reporting on the Gulf of St. Lawrence fishery in 1851 noted that although wages were expressly forbidden under the American subsidy, "this regulation is constantly set at nought or evaded, monthly wages being paid by a large proportion of the vessels."[118] The illicit practice appeared occasionally in the offshore banks fisheries as well. Years after the bounty law had been erased from the books, Nathaniel Atwood, a retired Provincetown fish merchant, admitted having paid the entire crew of his Grand Banker monthly wages for one voyage in 1836. Atwood and his brother, co-owners, outfitted at their own expense and cleared $920 in net profit, roughly double what they would have realized share fishing at the quarters. Their crew of five hired hands received no more than $50 each for the three-month cruise, about half what they could have made as sharesmen. Three years later, the Atwoods went to the banks again, shipping one sharesman and what was described as "a cheap crew."[119] The desire to minimize crew expenses and maximize profits was permitted fuller, less surreptitious expression once the bounty no longer applied. Aboard Gloucester and Provincetown dory trawlers fishing for cod on the Grand Banks around 1880, it was said to be standard practice to employ numbers of "young men trained up in the shore fisheries of the British Provinces and Maine, who have not yet learned the routine of the vessel, and who can be hired at a low price."[120]

In contrast to the owners, the crewmen by and large preferred to go fishing on shares whenever they had the opportunity. "I have heard the

[American] fishermen say that they would sooner go on shares than on wages . . . because they could make more," a Canadian fisherman told members of the Halifax Commission in 1877.[121] There was good reason for such an attitude. Four mackerel fishermen working on shares aboard the schooner *Ellen* of Newburyport in 1854 averaged $140 for a fourteen-week trip to the Gulf of St. Lawrence, while several hired hands paid in monthly wages—Newburyport vessels carried mixed crews of sharesmen and wage earners—earned an average of only $88 for the voyage.[122] Similar disparities appeared elsewhere. Maximum seasonal wages paid to Grand Banks cod fishermen in the post–Civil War period ranged from $150 at Bucksport to $190 at Provincetown—not much more than Labrador cod fishermen from Boothbay had earned a half-century earlier working at the halves.[123] By way of comparison, sharesmen aboard the highliners of Gloucester's Grand Banks fleet were able to average from $250 to $325 for a season's labor during some postwar years, or close to double what their wage-earning contemporaries were paid.[124]

The obvious superiority of the wage system from the owner's economic standpoint raises the question of why it was not imposed universally in the fisheries. Evidence on this subject is scanty, but several factors appear to have come into play. One, the profitability of most of the fisheries in which profit sharing was retained, has already been mentioned. Another was almost certainly the increased prevalence of winter fishing during the latter half of the nineteenth century at such places as Gloucester, Boston, and (to a lesser degree) Portland.[125] The winter fisheries, which came to be concentrated at ports where share systems remained intact, involved greater-than-normal hardship and danger, and may therefore have necessitated the added attraction of shares as an inducement to fishermen. A third, and conceivably the most important, reason for the survival of profit sharing was probably the general attitude of the fishermen themselves. It was in their interest to resist the wage system, and they undoubtedly did so where feasible.

Ordinary working crewmen had few cards to play against the owners, but they possessed one trump, the threat of unionization. Labor unions, or "societies," for fishermen were proposed and discussed as early as the 1830s.[126] They were rarely formed but were always a possibility, especially in the volatile atmosphere of worker unrest that permeated the post–Civil War years. It is perhaps no accident that Gloucester, one of the few Massachusetts ports to retain vestiges of share fishing, had an active local chapter of the Knights of Labor during the 1880s.[127] The presence of this "Deep Sea Assembly" may well have motivated Gloucester's merchants to maintain some semblance of a share system, in order to discourage organizing activity aboard their schooners.

Whatever the roadblocks raised before the wage system, there was no way to fully halt its inexorable progress. From the perspective of the owners, capitalist logic demanded its adoption. Furthermore, if native American fishermen refused to work for wages, there were others who were more than willing to do so. In most cases, this meant Canadians from the Maritime Provinces, who became a major presence in the New England fisheries in part because of their willingness to work for low pay.

Canadian fishermen gained employment aboard American schooners in basically three ways. The most obvious means, and one chosen by many, was to emigrate to the United States, settle in one of the fishing ports, and become naturalized citizens. More common were the twin options of migrating temporarily to Maine or Massachusetts for the duration of a fishing season, or of signing on New England vessels that visited Canadian ports for the express purpose of hiring crews. For decades, these two avenues had been partially closed by fishing treaties limiting American access to provincial ports (1819–1854 and 1866–1872),[128] as well as by an amendment to the federal bounty law, enacted in 1817, which stipulated that the master and three-fourths of the crew of any cod-fishing vessel collecting a subsidy had to be United States citizens.[129] However, bounty restrictions on foreign fishermen were eliminated (along with wage regulations) when the subsidy law was repealed in 1866, and diplomatic barriers were lifted in 1873 by the Treaty of Washington, which gave the Yankee fleet full visitation rights in Maritime ports for the purpose of (among other things) shipping crews. The British-American fisheries agreement of 1888 further guaranteed those rights for the balance of the nineteenth century.[130]

These political and diplomatic initiatives opened the door to unlimited Canadian participation in the American fishing industry and made a greatly expanded pool of cheap labor available to New England's fish merchants, most of it transient in nature. Of the Prince Edward Island component it was said, "A great many come home for the winter and go back to the States in the spring."[131] Such nonresident Canadians were especially valued because, unlike the "whitewashed Yankees" who took up permanent citizenship, they did not become part of the share-oriented and potentially troublesome native work force. Nova Scotians and other Maritimers who shipped aboard American cod-fishing schooners on a temporary basis worked exclusively for wages.[132] Moreover, the wide differential between Canadian and American wage scales meant that they expected, and were satisfied with, less money than their Yankee counterparts. "The Americans ship a good many men down at our place now," reported a Port Hawkesbury, Nova Scotia, merchant in 1877. "Of course, the latter can be obtained at lower rates than is the case with men in the States, and these men take [their own] outfittings to an extent." [133] During the 1870s and 1880s, crewmen in the Maritimes normally earned less than half what American crewmen were paid for a fishing trip, a circumstance that led Portland's *Eastern Argus* to protest the shipping of crews in Nova Scotia as being "not in the interest of fishermen, but of the owners of fishing vessels." [134] In 1877 sixteen to twenty dollars was an average monthly wage for fishermen in Canada's Gaspé region, while New England vessel fishermen made twenty-five to fifty dollars per month, depending on their experience. [135] By the late 1870s the obvious economic advantage of hiring Canadians had become abundantly clear to the vessel owners of Maine and Massachusetts, and the new ease with which their services could be obtained had increased their presence in the American fleet to an unprecedented extent. One observer placed the number of provincial citizens serving aboard New England schooners each year at over two thousand. Others variously estimated the non-native component at between one-third and two-thirds of the region's total fishing work force. [136]

Besides stopping at Maritime ports on the way to the fishing grounds or signing on random migrants who turned up each spring at New England fishing ports, there was one other way to obtain an inexpensive crew. The relative cheapness of Canadian labor led for a time to the much-criticized practice by American fish merchants of hiring whole crews in the Maritimes on an advance-contract basis. The mass importation of alien wage earners for periods of up to twelve months, under what was essentially a form of indentured servitude, was made possible by the Contract Labor Law of 1864, which remained in effect until 1885. [137] It is not known how many contract fishermen were brought into New England during the intervening years, or precisely where they were all employed. It is known, however, that significant numbers were transported to the port of Gloucester in the 1880s, including some who arrived after the practice was outlawed. It was not until 1888, three years after the legal prohibition of foreign contract labor, that the ban was actually enforced for the first time in the fishing industry by customs officials at Gloucester. Commenting on that enforcement, *The Republic*, a local publication, offered the following appraisal of the motives behind the contract system:

> The action of the customs house authorities in this city in preventing the landing at this port of some Nova Scotian fishermen who came here under contracts, stipulating, of course, that they should work for lower wages than American fishermen demand for services, similar to those they were to perform, is highly commendable and in keeping with the law which forbids the importation of alien contract labor into this country. . . . The return of these Nova Scotia fishermen also illustrates how little sincerity there is in the regard which

capitalists profess to have for American labor. . . . The fish monopolists of Cape Ann have been caught in the act of bringing cheap . . . labor here to the injury of American fishermen, for whose welfare, however, they never weary of professing the greatest solicitude.[138]

The rapid influx of Canadian fishermen after 1870, by whatever means, had two major effects on the New England fishing industry. First, it reinforced the wage system in the cod fisheries—and kept wages low—by providing an alternative labor force willing to work on that basis. Second, it forced native fishermen unwilling to submit to wages to abandon cod fishing for more lucrative opportunities elsewhere. Most migrant Canadian fishermen of the post–Civil War period, it is clear, took employment on cod bankers, replacing recalcitrant or reluctant American fishermen. According to a Bangor, Maine, newspaper, the large numbers of Nova Scotians and Prince Edward Islanders who passed through that city in the spring of 1885 bound for the coastal fishing ports shipped principally on Grand Banks vessels.[139] Statistics tend to bear out that subjective observation. In 1889 a majority of the Canadians serving in the Massachusetts vessel fisheries, and nearly two-thirds of those in Maine's vessel fleet, were aboard cod-fishing schooners working the major offshore banks east of Cape Sable. Less than one-quarter of the combined Canadian work force of both states was in the mackerel fishery, and an even smaller proportion was engaged in the various fresh-market fisheries.[140]

The opposite side of the coin was that the share-oriented mackerel fishery, which had absorbed most transient Canadians before the Civil War (a reflection of the labor-restrictive cod-bounty law then in force), employed more native American crewmen than any other fishery by 1880. Most of Maine's own mackerel schooners were entirely crewed by native-born fishermen at that time.[141] This contrasted sharply with one of the state's contemporary Grand Banks cod-fishing ports, Bucksport, where wages prevailed and where several skippers and a large portion of the crews were "Provincials."[142]

The Making of a Maritime Proletariat

Although there is no doubt that share fishermen for the most part earned higher incomes than those paid in wages, their economic life was by no means easy. Despite changes in the industry that made fishing more predictable, working on shares remained at bottom a game of chance. This was especially true of the mackerel fishery, where vessels could still experience "broken" voyages, even in the technologically advanced post–Civil War period. In good years, of course, mackereling was the fisherman's most remunerative occupation. It paid better than any other fishery on a per-trip or seasonal basis in 1880.[143] Still, the spectre of failure was always present. "That there are very many families in this town who have no money wherewith to support life [during] the coming winter, on account of the poor returns of the mackerel season, is . . . a fact that stares us in the face in these dull and cheerless days of November," reported Gloucester's *Cape Ann Advertiser* in 1867.[144] The same sort of tragedy struck the mackerel fleet of Portland in 1886, the city's worst fishing year in half a century. In the words of one out-of-town newspaper:

> The season has been one of the most discouraging ever known. The total amount of mackerel packed at Portland this year was only 12,000 bbls. against 80,000 bbls. in 1885 and 155,000 in 1884. . . . Out of some fifty vessels which fitted out there this season only about half a dozen have realized a profit. . . . Very few of the fishermen have made any money, and this . . . will make it particularly hard for this class of the community the coming winter.[145]

Such years were experienced just often enough to keep Portland's share fishermen teetering on the thin edge of economic survival, if not perpetually in debt. In 1876 the cook aboard the mackerel schooner *Alice M. Gould,* the only crew member to earn monthly wages, made $200 from two unproductive voyages to the Gulf of St. Lawrence. His shipmates, who were sharesmen, made no money at all and came home in arrears from four months' fishing.[146] Unless they had reserve savings to fall back on, these men became instantly susceptible to the chronic malaise of indebtedness.

Indebtedness appeared everywhere in the industry, and it oppressed wage earners and sharesmen alike. Even a reasonably successful season was no guarantee against it. In the late 1870s, the average total income for fishermen employed ten months out of the year at Gloucester was no more than $300, about half the annual wage of local dock workers.[147] Experienced and skilled hands, working year-round at Gloucester and following the winter as well as summer fisheries, could increase that to $500 during exceptional years, but those in the Maine ports, where winter fishing was rare, were lucky to clear half as much.[148] From 1873 to 1876 vessel crewmen at Portland averaged just $239 a year for seven months' work. That came to $34 per month during the fishing season, or barely a third of the typical monthly wage earned at that time by the city's skilled manual laborers, who enjoyed the added advantage of full-time employment.[149] "The earnings of the fishermen are very small for a family to live on in Gloucester, as everywhere else," acknowledged one of that city's fish merchants in 1877.[150] "They make just about enough to live through the winter and start even next spring," a Noank, Connecticut, fisherman said the same year, referring to his contemporaries.[151]

The inability to put aside savings was a particular problem. An Eastport, Maine, fish buyer of the postwar period testified before the Halifax Commission that he had never known a fisherman able to save money.[152] That assessment was upheld by a working crewman, who told Maine state investigators in 1887, "I don't know of any one who did not own part or whole of [a] vessel, to lay up any amount of money."[153] Joseph Proctor, a leading Gloucester merchant, admitted that upward mobility through savings and investment was achieved by only about one fisherman out of a hundred, and even then advancement was limited to captains, who received a skipper's bonus from the owner and thus became "double sharesmen." Those not chosen as vessel masters, he pointed out, seldom rose above their class.[154]

Fishermen, of course, had always been poor. In 1850, those working in Maine ranked near the bottom of the socioeconomic scale according to such measures as real-estate ownership and property valuation, and their level of poverty was equalled or exceeded only by merchant seamen, stonecutters, and common laborers.[155] Had even that unenviable status been maintained, life would have been sufficiently hard. If anything, however, the economic situation of fishermen deteriorated further in the years following the Civil War. Between 1860 and 1870 the percentage of full-time fishermen reporting no real or personal assets whatever actually increased at eleven of twelve representative seaports. By the latter year a clear majority of the industry workers in these towns were without measurable assets, up considerably from a decade earlier.[156]

Such individuals eked out an existence that was quite literally from hand to mouth. Those fortunate enough to own homes were often forced to mortgage them, and it was quite common for the families of two married Maine fishermen to pool their meagre resources by living together in a single, small house.[157] At Portland, around 1880, most local fishermen made their homes not in the city itself but on the desolate harbor islands, where the lower cost of living was within their limited means.[158] Perhaps the most graphic commentary on the condition of Maine's postwar fishing population was R. E. Earll's vivid description of Portland's handcart fish peddlers, most of whom were retired vessel crewmen fallen on hard times. "This class," he wrote in 1880, "is made up largely of aged fishermen who have worn themselves out in their open boats, and are now satisfied with the small amount of money that can be made in that way."[159]

The increasing impoverishment of fishermen resulted from several factors. The growth of the wage system and the importation of cheap Canadian labor both tended to depress income levels. Equally damaging was the elimination of the fishing bounty. The bounty repeal hurt independent vessel owners, but it devastated ordinary crewmen. In terms of basic compensation, fishermen employed on shares had kept pace with the general upward trend of wages during the 1860s and 1870s, increasing their earnings by roughly the same percentage as had the working population of the United States as a whole. Annual wages for all American workers rose by an average of approximately 60 percent between the immediate prewar period (circa 1850–1860) and the decade of the 1870s.[160] Similarly, the $239 average wage earned by Portland's vessel fishermen in the 1870s was just about 60 percent higher than the $150 average annual wage prevailing throughout the New England fisheries during the 1850s.[161] The comparison is deceptive, however, because it does not take into account the loss of the federal subsidy. The bounty allowance, which averaged close to $20 per year, swelled the typical antebellum fisherman's income from $150 to $170.[162] In real income, then, the average yearly wage earned by Portland's fishermen in the mid-1870s represented an increase of not 60 percent but 40 percent. The difference was crucial, since it wiped out the margin that had protected the previous generation of fishermen from total dependence on the industry's notorious credit system.

Some idea of what the bounty meant in terms of individual solvency can be seen in the experience of Castine's prewar fishermen. In 1853, seven of the nine sharesmen belonging to the Grand Banker *Martha Burgess* of that port returned from their voyage owing money to the local outfitter, but the bounty allowance was sufficient by itself to retire the debts of four of them. In that particular case, the crew's average individual debt amounted to $17.31, while their average individual bounty payment was $24.95, just enough to save the men from the financial exactions of the "company store."[163]

The removal of these protective subsidies in 1866 exposed fishermen to the full brunt of the destructive credit system and thereby contributed greatly to their declining economic fortunes in the post–Civil War period. The credit system, which was based on the habitual practice of borrowing against the returns of a voyage, was the social curse of the fishing industry. It was not a new institution, having evolved over decades, and it was not limited to the Maine or even the American fisheries. Variations appeared wherever and whenever fishing was pursued. Nova Scotia and Massachusetts both maintained oppressive credit systems in the 1830s, and others flourished fifty years later in Newfoundland, Great Britain, and the Gaspé region of Quebec.[164]

The very nature of the fishing industry demanded some form of credit financing. Like the farmer, who required capital for tools and seed money in advance of his cash crop, the fisherman had to obtain gear and provisions in the spring in order to bring in a sea "crop" that was not fully harvested until the fall. Unlike the farmer, who worked at home, the fisherman left his family behind and thus added to his economic vulnerability. Moreover, the low wages and seasonal aspects of the occupation precluded his saving much money during the winter months in preparation for the following year. Someone had to provide him with the means to go fishing each spring, and someone also had to provide for his family in his absence. That need was filled by the outfitting merchant, who often doubled as fish dealer. He supplied the crewman with clothing, bedding, foul-weather gear, extra provisions, and whatever other amenities were needed for the voyage.* At the same time, he arranged a line of credit for the crewman's family so that their day-to-day necessities would be guaranteed over the course of the fishing season. A Massachusetts congressman described how the operation functioned in his district in 1857:

> After . . . [the skipper] has secured his crew, he arranges with a packer or a dryer to furnish all supplies to the vessel that may be needed during the fishing season. This inspector, packer or dryer, keeps a store containing a stock of ship chandlery and stores usually needed in the fitting of a vessel. He also, upon the order of that portion of the crew who have families, supplies to them a limited quantity of provisions in the absence of the vessel; and when she returns he takes the fish, if any are caught, sells them, and makes up the voyage, crediting the account of each man with the amount due, charging and deducting what may be, by agreement, his for services in packing, drying, and inspecting, and for outfits and family stores delivered.[165]

Given the realities of the industry, the merchant's role as "banker" was absolutely essential. As one veteran of the Maine fisheries remarked, "It was nothing but unlimited credit that ever kept the fishermen up."[166] Unfortunately, the system had a dark side. The men invariably returned from the fishing grounds in the merchant's debt for either their outfit or their families' living expenses, and they paid dearly for the privilege of deferred payment. At Harpswell, in the 1850s, fishermen obtaining their outfits on credit— the vast majority—were charged considerably more than the fortunate few who were able to pay in cash.[167] Interest was also applied to hooks and lines

---

*Among the items charged by individual crewmen belonging to Castine's Grand Banks fleet in May 1853 were the following: Boots, shoes, overalls, shirts, pants, underwear, jackets, woolen jerseys, slippers, stockings, mittens, nippers (wool fishing gloves), hats, suits of oil clothes, sou'westers (storm hats), barvels (fishing aprons), mattresses, blankets, towels, sewing needles and thread, calico and flannel cloth, buttons, belts, scissors, knives and spoons, books, pencils, cigars, pipes and tobacco, soap, hand mirrors, combs, hair oil, sea chests, "pain killer," raisins, currants, apples, sugar, pickles, eggs, cheese, butter, and lemon syrup. (Source: PMM, GC, MS 125.)

and basic provisions, which were purchased collectively by the entire crew. A character in Elijah Kellogg's semi-fictional account of Maine's antebellum fisheries attempted to explain this harsh fact of life to his novice fisherman-son: "You see, boy, this ere skipper and crew they'll go right ter Bickford's store, and they'll take up their provisions, lump it all together, have it charged, to pay out of the fare of the fish when they come back, and they'll have to give a high price, if he is a goin' to trust 'em four months; he'll want pay for trustin 'em, and for the risk, and the trouble of making out his account. Don't you see, boy?"[168]

The exact interest charged by merchant-creditors is open to question, but by the post–Civil War years it was considerable. A profit of 10 percent* was said to be standard for goods sold to fishermen on a cash basis in the 1870s.[169] However, purchases made on credit were marked up at least another 10 to 15 percent, and one Maine captain claimed that outfitters charged an additional 20 percent above the cash price for fishing essentials and added 25 percent on supplies credited to the men's families.[170] There were also occasional reports of outright cheating by unscrupulous storekeepers, or "longshore sharks," who dealt primarily with uneducated fishermen possessing a limited understanding of figures or bookkeeping methods.[171]

In addition to suffering high interest and overcharges, crewmen were victimized by the manner in which fishing trips were traditionally settled. Payment was rarely made at the end of the voyage. In the salt fisheries, vessel owners or merchants waited until the catch was processed and marketed before paying off the men. This could take months. The schooner *Glendower* of Castine returned from a season on the Grand Banks in late August 1858, but her crew received no compensation until the catch was sold in Boston the following March.[172] By then, the crew had remained debtors for the better part of a year, settling their accounts just in time to ship out again for the fishing grounds, once more in debt for the voyage. Each spring the cycle was repeated, and the fishermen were, in effect, carried on the company's books (at interest) more or less indefinitely.** Their dependence on the merchants who extended credit placed them, as Fish Commission in-

---

*On at least some items the regular markup was appreciably higher. In 1883 pairs of fishermen's wool mittens wholesaled for four dollars per dozen and retailed for six dollars per dozen, resulting in a healthy 50 percent profit. (Source: *MIJ*, news item, 5 January 1883.)

**This process of perpetual economic bondage bore a remarkable resemblance to the operation of the infamous agricultural lien system of the late nineteenth century, whose impact on southern tenant farmers was described in memorable fashion by C. Vann Woodward: "The lien system converted the Southern economy into a vast pawn shop. Its evil effects did not end when the farmer signed away his future crop, for that act merely started a vicious circle of compounded evils. It meant that until he paid the last dollar of his debt, and his crop was often found inadequate for that, he was dependent for his every purchase, clothing, food, imple-

vestigators delicately put it in 1880, "somewhat at the mercy of these men if they chose to be exacting."[173] Some fishermen, of course, never got out from under, and their eventual share of the previous year's trip, once settled upon, merely served as the annual payment on their permanent, ongoing debt.[174] In the era of government subsidies, a few never even saw their bounty money, which passed through the mercantile establishment and was credited toward their bills or was used as an advance on their annual spring outfits.[175]

Delayed crew payments, called "end-of-season" settlements, were standard procedure at most New England fishing ports, both before and after the Civil War.[176] The outstanding exception was Gloucester, where beginning around 1850 cash settlements with the crew were made immediately upon the vessel's arrival, as soon as the fish were weighed out. These "end-of-trip" payments, which eventually drew large numbers of fishermen to Gloucester from other ports,* allowed crew members to short-circuit the credit system somewhat by freeing themselves from interest charges for at least part of the year.[177] Unfortunately for most fishermen, the Gloucester scheme was not widely adopted elsewhere.

In Maine, the tradition of late payments carried over into the postwar period largely unchanged. (It was still adhered to at Castine in 1870, some twenty years after immediate settlements were first introduced at Gloucester.)[178] This became the source of considerable tension between the state's merchants and fishermen, especially when the timely annual distribution of bounty money—normally made around the first of January[179]—ceased in 1867. A contributing factor to the decline of the industry at Deer Isle after 1868, for instance, was said to have been an economic relationship between fitters and crews "whereby a settlement with the fisherman was often delayed for nearly a year, during which time they were subjected to all the disadvantages of the credit system in its worst forms."[180] Deer Isle fishermen registered their protest by increasingly deserting their home fleet in favor of employment on vessels from other ports. By 1880 seventy-five of them were regularly shipping out on Portland and Gloucester schooners.[181]

Sadly, those migrating to Portland merely exchanged one form of exploitation for another. Portland's merchants did, indeed, evolve a form of

---

ments, fertilizer, everything, upon his creditor merchant, who charged him from twenty to fifty per cent more than the cash price and dictated the amount and quality of the purchase." (Source: C. Vann Woodward, *Tom Watson: Agrarian Rebel* [New York: Macmillan Co., 1938], 129–30.)

*Gloucester also offered the attraction of debt assumption by vessel owners in cases of broken voyages. If a fishing trip showed no profit, leaving the fisherman without cash to pay an outfitting debt incurred at another merchant's store, the vessel owner assumed responsibility for the account and paid it. (Source: *Halifax Commission Proceedings*, 2589.)

the end-of-trip settlement by the 1870s, but unlike Gloucester's format it was optional and unrelated to wholesale fish prices.* Rather, it consisted of the men exercising the dubious choice of waiting, as usual, for the completion of processing or selling their share in the catch to the fitter or owner for immediate cash at what was termed by one observer as "a considerable sacrifice."[182] In effect, those who waited for the catch to be cured and sold ultimately realized a greater return, but the added income was eaten up by the interest they compiled in the meantime by living off the company store. On the other hand, those selling off their share of the catch avoided credit charges but earned far less money. It was a Hobson's choice that typified the economic trap Maine fishermen found themselves in as the nineteenth century entered its last decades.

The unregulated and socially debilitating credit structure produced as a by-product of the New England fisheries had disastrous long-range effects on the industry. In its final form after the Civil War, it combined with the breakdown of the share system and the elimination of government support subsidies to create a new, dependent class of fishermen—a maritime proletariat of sorts. By 1880 or thereabouts, a definite class division, not totally apparent a generation earlier, had emerged between those who fished and those who owned and serviced the vessels. To some, this was inevitable and desirable. According to one evaluation of the industry's New Capitalism, "The more extensive and more profitable the fishery, the more necessary and natural is the division of the persons engaged in carrying them on into two classes—the capitalists and the fishermen."[183] From the standpoint of pure economic efficiency and short-run profit, the absorption of independent entrepreneurs by large industry units and the conversion of semi-independent sharesmen into low-paid and impoverished wage earners may, indeed, have been praiseworthy. Nevertheless, it left a residue of economic dissatisfaction and social antagonism that was bound to undermine the internal vitality of the fisheries. In the end, it led to a wholesale desertion of the industry in Maine, as fishermen sought first to ply their trade elsewhere and, ultimately, to abandon that trade altogether.

---

*The universal end-of-trip payment system developed at Gloucester was facilitated by the city's status as a direct marketing center, whose wholesale merchants did not deal with other middlemen. This resulted in immediate price setting and prompt transactions at all levels. Portland's merchants, on the other hand, were primarily indirect marketers, who dealt with large wholesalers in Boston and New York. They were less able to predict ultimate prices and consequently discouraged immediate payment by means of arbitrarily low cash settlements designed to guarantee their own profits. (Source: *Goode Report*, sec. 2, 89–92, 147–49.)

The Hard and Dangerous Life

What a wretched life the fisherman has—with his berth a home,
the sea his labor and fish his wandering prey!—Moschos of
Syracuse, poet, 150 B.C.[1]

Perils and Hazards

The primary role of market economics and technological change in the re-
organization and ultimate decline of Maine's sea fisheries tends to obscure
another important element in that process. Not the least of the factors
slowly undermining the state's native industry was the hazardous way of life
it entailed. The sea in all its unpredictable moods was the fisherman's constant companion, and he was always in danger of losing his vessel or his life.
The United States Fish Commission did not exaggerate when it reported in
1886 that "probably no other industry carried on in this country shows
yearly such a large loss in life and property as the New England fisheries."[2]
In 1884, a rather typical year, the region as a whole sacrificed twenty-one
schooners and 134 lives in order to bring in the catch.[3]

Maine suffered its share of fishing-related disasters. In October 1841, for
example, six schooners belonging to the single town of Vinalhaven were
lost in the harbor of Matinicus Island, where they had unsuccessfully attempted to ride out a northeast storm.[4] Vinalhaven's loss was dramatic because it resulted from one sudden visitation of nature, but other Maine
ports paid an even greater cumulative price for their involvement in the industry. The Penobscot Bay town of Castine lost fourteen vessels and fifty-
one men in the fisheries during the twenty-nine years between 1839 and
1867, and nearby Belfast experienced eleven vessel losses and thirty fatalities
over roughly the same period. Altogether, during the half-century ending
in 1889 at least fifty-nine schooners and ninety-seven fishermen—approximately one vessel and two men each year—were lost from the various
fishing towns bordering Penobscot Bay.[5] Farther to the westward, the port
of Boothbay gave up fifteen schooners and fifty-four men in the forty years
between 1833 and 1873, a loss in lives exceeding the town's Civil War battle
fatalities, which were themselves proportionately greater than those of any
other fishing village in Maine.[6] Portland's losses were even more severe. In
terms of a concentrated multiplicity of disasters, few places matched the

experience of western Maine's largest fishing port, which surrendered fourteen of its vessels and forty-six of its crewmen to the sea in the four-year period 1873–1876.[7]

Portland, a large city and a port that drew many of its fishermen from other places, could adapt to such losses after a fashion. To smaller communities, however, they could be devastating, especially in human terms. When the schooner *Ocean Wave* of Penobscot disappeared en route to the Grand Banks in 1858, all nine of the crewmen aboard were natives of that one small eastern Maine town.[8] On occasion, the missing were not only from the same community but the same family. This was the case with four of the six crew members who went down with the Castine schooner *Active* in 1846.[9] Worst of all, perhaps, was the fact that lost fishermen typically represented the strength and future vitality of their coastal villages. The *C. G. Matthews* of Boothbay foundered in the Gulf of St. Lawrence in 1851 with a home-grown crew of thirteen, all but one of whom (the captain, age thirty-three) were under thirty years of age. Three of the missing hands were teenagers, and the average age of the entire complement was twenty-three years.[10] Seldom was a participant in the Maine offshore fisheries much over the age of forty, and the youngest were in their late teens.[11] Sea casualties, therefore, were concentrated primarily among those individuals in the active, early prime of life. The impact was much the same as that of battlefield casualties in wartime. Particularly in small communities, the best of a whole generation could be decimated in an instant, through an error in seamanship or a whim of nature.

The causes contributing to lost vessels and lives were several, and they varied according to the geographic locale of the particular fishery being pursued. In the Gulf of St. Lawrence, storms were the primary danger. The Gulf, or "the Bay," as it was familiarly known, was the single most dangerous fishing ground for Maine fishermen. Half of the schooners and about two-thirds of the men lost in the fisheries from the Penobscot region were lost there.[12] Part of the problem was the general weather pattern. The Gulf tended to be much windier after about the first of August than most other places. "It is a very blowy country," was the understated evaluation of one Canadian schooner captain.[13] An officer in Nova Scotia's revenue service concurred, saying, "It is generally a very boisterous place in the months of October and November, . . . and I am surprised that more fatal results have not been the consequence."[14] Added to the frequency and force of gale winds, which were particularly strong during the fall season, was the proximity of land. Fishermen working the Gulf, especially those following the mackerel inshore, were usually close to some coastline, whether it was Prince

Edward Island, the western shore of Cape Breton, the Gaspé Peninsula, or the Magdalen chain. The Gulf itself was essentially an inland sea, and many of the best fishing grounds within it were smaller bays, such as Chaleur and Mirimichi (see chapter 3 and map 2). Moreover, Prince Edward Island, which dominated the lower Gulf, formed an exceedingly treacherous land mass, its long, crescent-shaped northern shore presenting an exposed pocket with few good harbors and with sand bars at both ends. In short, fishing vessels in the Bay were constantly in jeopardy of being caught on a lee shore, especially the dreaded "bend" of Prince Edward Island, during a storm.[15]

The possibility of having to claw to windward off the land into the teeth of a gale was the mariner's special nightmare, and it was the primary risk of fishing in the Gulf of St. Lawrence. Most of the losses suffered in the Bay were not sinkings per se but strandings, vessels being driven ashore and wrecked, their hulls stove in or "bilged" and their crews drowned in the surf. The story of the Maine schooner *E. Atwood,* as related in a news column of October 1858, was typical: "The schooner E. Atwood (of Westport), Stinson Jewett, master, came on shore Saturday night near the North Cape [of P.E.I.]: all hands lost. One man was found locked in the rigging, and three others have since drifted on shore. The four bodies have been buried on the island. The crew consisted of ten. . . . The vessel is a total wreck, and but little will be saved from her."[16] This fate befell scores of fishing vessels and their crews in the waters of the Gulf over the years. In October 1852 twenty-one schooners were driven ashore and wrecked at Souris, Prince Edward Island, when gale-force winds shifted and trapped them in that exposed harbor.[17] Again, in late August 1873, forty-eight vessels out of a fleet of eighty-three American mackerelmen were run aground and stranded at Pleasant Bay and Amherst Harbor in the Magdalen Islands. Only nine of the vessels were able to make the comparative safety of open water, while the remaining survivors managed to ride out the storm at anchor near the land.[18]

The worst of all the Gulf disasters was the infamous "Yankee Gale" of October 3–5, 1851, so named because of the particular havoc it wreaked on the New England mackerel fleet. This memorable storm was a northerly gale that struck the coast of Prince Edward Island without warning on the night of October 3, driving the unsuspecting vessels onshore in the usual fashion, destroying dozens of them and exacting a frightful toll in lives. According to the best estimates of the time, approximately one hundred schooners and three hundred fishermen were lost altogether, the bodies of the latter drifting onto the beaches for days afterward.[19] "The whole shore is strewed with the wrecks of vessels, and the bodies of their crews," lamented Portland's *Eastern Argus* after hearing reports from the scene.[20]

The fortunate crewmen who survived were landed by ropes extended to their wrecked schooners by rescuers on shore. Those who did not were buried in mass graves on the island, one such tomb containing the bodies of sixty drowned American fishermen.[21]

In all, Maine sustained about a quarter of the losses suffered in the Yankee Gale. Fourteen ports from Kennebunk to Lubec were affected, and at least thirty vessels and seventy-seven men from those ports were among the victims.[22] Of the *Mary Moulton* of Castine, a fifty-ton schooner with a crew of twelve, it was said that nothing had survived but a box containing the ship's register case.[23] Other Maine schooners came ashore with various amounts of damage. A boat from the *Hickory* of Portland was later sold at auction for five dollars, while the remains of the vessel herself were thrown into the bargain for nothing.[24] Such was the great gale of 1851. Although it was never equaled, nearly a dozen similar storms struck the Gulf of St. Lawrence between 1839 and 1886,* resulting in tragic losses to Maine fishermen each time and lending credence to the Bay's contemporary reputation for perverse unpredictability.[25]

The problems faced by fishermen on the offshore banks of Newfoundland and Nova Scotia were somewhat different from those encountered in the more confined waters of the Gulf. Vessels fishing on the Grand and Western banks were also imperiled by periodic storms, and some foundered, but at least the North Atlantic bankers had "sea room" in which to maneuver (see map 2). The best fishing grounds off Newfoundland were on the southern two-thirds of the Grand Banks between 43 and 46 degrees north latitude, or one hundred to three hundred miles from the nearest part of Newfoundland's ragged coast.[26] Maine schooners favored the southeastern corner of the "Great Bank" in the vicinity of 44 degrees latitude and 50 degrees longitude, which placed them approximately two hundred miles away from any threatening shoreline.[27] Western and Quereau bankers likewise worked far from land. The inner edges of the Nova Scotian banks were from fifty to seventy-five miles offshore, and the banks themselves were up to fifty miles wide. Unless vessels approached Sable Island, located on the extreme eastern side of Western Bank, the danger of grounding on a lee shore was virtually nonexistent.[28] In its place, however, were sufficient risks to earn the banks fisheries a fearsome notoriety.

First of all, the exposed location of the major cod banks, those off Newfoundland in particular, meant that they took the full brunt of the normally heavy North Atlantic swells. Added to the difficulty of high seas was the fact

---

*Documented Gulf storms especially destructive to the fishing industry took place in 1839, 1848, 1851, 1852, 1853, 1858, 1860, 1867, 1872, 1873, and 1886.

that the banks were essentially large shoals in the midst of the open ocean, and the combination of rising swells and comparatively shallow water made them a remarkably uncomfortable place to spend one's time. If strong winds were part of the equation, the banks became a genuine triple threat to the seaman, producing storms that combined gale-force breezes with high seas and turbulent water. Even when the banks were relatively placid, there were dangers inherent in fishing there. On the Newfoundland grounds, strong and irregular sea currents were a continual hazard, and vessels had to allow for considerable drifting when under sail.[29] More dangerous yet was the fog. This unpleasant phenomenon occurred regularly along the coasts and on the contiguous banks of Newfoundland and Nova Scotia from May to July of each year. It was at its very worst on the Grand Banks, as G. W. Blunt made abundantly clear in the 1850 edition of his *American Coast Pilot:* "These banks are frequently enveloped in most horrid fogs, which . . . have been known to last 8 to 10 days successively. At such times they are often so thick that you will not be able to see any object at ten fathoms [i.e., twenty yards] distance."[30]

The unusual environmental conditions prevailing on the cod banks gave a definite character to the types of disasters or near-disasters befalling fishermen who spent any great amount of time there. Common mishaps experienced by vessels at anchor on the grounds included shipping seas and having the decks swept, being knocked over by high winds while under riding sails, and having rudders torn loose (with resultant leakage and weakening of stern timbers).[31] Numerous Maine schooners were severely damaged, and many crewmen were lost, in these sorts of accidents. In 1873, for example, the Orland banker *W. T. Emerson* was thrown on her beam-ends* during a late August storm on the Grand Banks. The vessel survived, but one crewman was lost overboard. In August 1881 the Grand Banker *Harvest Home* of Lamoine was forced to terminate fishing operations prematurely and return home after her anchor cable was snapped in a gale and two men were swept away by boarding seas. A year later the Portland banker *Elizabeth W. Smith* was knocked down on the Cape Shore grounds by heavy seas; her ballast shifted, and she barely recovered, losing several dories, tearing her riding sail, and suffering extensive damage to her bulwarks. Three fishermen were washed overboard but were miraculously saved.[32]

While such incidents exacted a heavy toll on individual crewmen, immediate vessel losses were rare. Nevertheless, the incessant pounding the bankers endured, year in and year out, often weakened them beyond their capacity

---

*A dangerous ninety-degree rollover in which masts and sails are brought level, or nearly level, with the water.

to absorb punishment, ultimately resulting in a surrender to the elements. The *William Tell* of Bucksport was a case in point. This schooner suffered a knock-down during a gale on the Grand Banks in 1873, losing all of her dories and nearly being swamped. In 1886 the same vessel lost her main-mast while riding out a storm at anchor on Quereau Bank and had to be towed home for repairs. Finally, in 1889, after a half-century of laboring on the banks, the *William Tell* simply opened her seams and sank on the fish-ing grounds, her captain and crew managing to survive and reach the safety of St. John's, Newfoundland.[33]

Schooners suddenly developing fatal leaks and foundering was a com-monplace occurrence in the offshore fisheries. During the 1850s one or more Grand Bankers from the Penobscot region succumbed in this manner on an almost yearly basis.[34] The causes were generally old age, or the after-math of storm damage, or a combination of the two. Several of the Maine bankers lost to leakage in the course of fishing were ancient craft, like the aforementioned *William Tell*. Others were vessels sustaining prior injury in storms—a sprung mast or cracked hull timbers—that indirectly led to their demise.[35] Schooners starting their planks on the offshore grounds seldom survived. The same distance from land that permitted them to run before storms without the fear of being wrecked on a lee shore worked as a disad-vantage when gradual flooding was the problem. Fishing captains operating on the Grand Banks had neither the option of making for a nearby port for repairs nor that of beaching the vessel in a protected cove before she sank, as those working closer to home sometimes did.[36] With land a hundred or more miles away, the only solution (once the battle at the pumps was lost) was to allow the schooner to expire and take to the boats. Fishermen leaving sinking vessels could normally expect assistance on the relatively crowded banks.* Most were taken aboard other schooners or passing merchant ships.[37] A prompt rescue was by no means guaranteed, however. The nine crew members of the abandoned Bucksport banker *Astoria* spent ten days in an open boat in July 1885 before being picked up with their water supply nearly gone.[38]

Rough weather, storm damage, and leaks were naturally worrisome to the fisherman, but they were problems that were amenable in some degree to advance preparation and good seamanship. The same could not be said for fog. Of all the natural hazards present on the cod banks of the North

---

*Captains Warren Hibbert and Joseph Sylvester of the Castine schooners *Mentora* and *Martha Burgess* reported fishing within sight of other vessels on numerous occasions during two trips to the Grand Banks in the early 1850s. (Sources: PMM, GC, MSS 6, 354.)

Atlantic, none was more frightening than fog, both for the helpless feeling it induced and the very real danger it posed. For one thing, it increased the likelihood of collision between vessels, which often fished in close proximity to one another. Schooners at work changed position periodically, moving from place to place in search of promising locations to anchor and fish, and in foggy conditions this entailed considerable risk. Torn sails, broken spars, and stove topsides were among the more minor forms of damage sustained by bankers coming in contact with one another at such times.[39]

For the most part, of course, the schooners were not under way at all. Their normal routine kept them anchored in one spot, sails furled, for days on end. Such immobility made them vulnerable to another, more serious, risk, that of being run down by a merchant ship. By a quirk of geography, the Grand Banks south of Newfoundland—and to a lesser extent the Western Banks off Nova Scotia—extended across one of the world's busiest sea lanes, the major transatlantic route between Europe and North America. This meant that schooners anchored on the fishing grounds were directly in the path of the innumerable packets and other large merchantmen shuttling between British and American ports like Liverpool and New York.[40] Intermittent fog conspired with the semi-sedentary activity of the bankers to create a deadly situation. Schooners were regularly run into on the banks throughout the nineteenth century, usually with fatal consequences. Three vessels from the Bucksport fleet alone were lost this way in the dozen years prior to 1860.[41]

Most of the accidents took place at night when darkness made the bankers even less conspicuous to oncoming ships. On occasion the fishermen sealed their own doom by lying-to without lights, an unaccountable invitation to disaster.[42] The low-slung design of fishing vessels only compounded the problem. Their minimal freeboard, an advantage in hand-lining fish, meant that they were not easily seen in the best of circumstances, especially if no sails were up. In 1848 a Gloucester fisherman was struck in broad daylight and in clear weather, despite all efforts to alert the approaching ship.[43] From the standpoint of lost lives, the worst recorded collision involving a Maine schooner took place at 2 A.M. on August 23, 1874, when the *Fleetwing* of Lamoine was hit and sunk on the Grand Banks by the French bark *Marseilles,* bound from Quebec City to Greenock, Scotland. The schooner sank within minutes, carrying nine of the twelve men aboard to their deaths. A shipping news description of one survivor's escape offers some idea of the traumatic suddenness with which such incidents took place: "The captain, Isiah Bowden, of Penobscot, was at the time in his berth, but awakened by the crash rushed on deck, and seeing that the vessel must sink, sprang for the main-chains of the barque, which he was fortunate enough to seize and was saved."[44]

As great as the threat of collision and run-downs were on the cod banks, they eventually became secondary fears among fog-bound fishermen. A more immediate danger after 1860 was the increased chance of being lost in a dory. This new hazard was a direct outgrowth of the Technological Revolution in ground fishing, which introduced dory hand-lining and, later, dory trawling to the offshore banks. Technological advancement is quite often uncritically portrayed as an unalloyed boon to mankind, a step forward in human progress leading to a better life for all. This was decidedly not the case with respect to the nineteenth-century fishing industry. The dory system, which separated fishermen from the comparative safety of their mother ship, added a new negative dimension to their working lives even as it was increasing the profits of the owners who hired them. George Procter, writing in 1873, described its adverse features:

> Since the introduction of trawl fishing, some twelve years since, another peril has been added to the fisheries, viz: that of being lost from dories while visiting trawls, or estrayed during the fog which oftentimes shuts in on the fishing grounds, enveloping them like a pall. Then the dorymen find it extremely difficult to discover their vessel. A fresh breeze springing up renders the situation still more dangerous, and notwithstanding the efforts made on board, by the firing of guns, blowing of horns, ringing of bells, and the continued cruising about in search of the missing men, the fact of not being enabled to find them, and being obliged to give up the search and return home is too often the case.[45]

The onset of trawling, as Procter noted, was an important factor in raising the danger level. Hand-lining from dories was bad enough. The men were on their own—most hand-liners fished from "single dories"—but they generally stayed within sight of the vessel. Trawl fishermen, on the other hand, worked two hands to a dory but strayed much farther afield. They often rowed two miles from the vessel to set and tend their trawls, thereby increasing their chances of not returning.[46]

There were basically two ways in which dory fishermen were lost. One was by drowning when dories capsized in rough weather; the other was by dehydration, starvation, or exposure when boats went astray and were not retrieved.[47] The former was perhaps the more merciful of the two, since the end came quicker. A surprisingly large number of accidents on the banks involved capsized dories. Despite the legendary seaworthiness of these famous small boats, they were still susceptible to overturning in rough seas, especially if empty of fish. Once overboard, most dorymen were lost. Many could not swim, and in any case they were weighed down by heavy boots and clothing. The newspaper marine lists of the late nineteenth century contain numerous melancholy accounts of schooners returning from the fishing grounds minus crew members who drowned when their dories upset in a seaway.[48]

In contrast, dorymen separated from their vessels by fog or sudden squalls sometimes survived, and their stories have become part of the lore and legend of the fisheries. Among the incidents involving Maine vessels, the saga of an unnamed fisherman belonging to the *George W. Pierce* of Southport was especially memorable. It took place in June 1876, when the doryman in question lost touch with his schooner on Western Bank in a thick fog. Missing for three days and four nights without food or water, he eventually drifted, weak but alive, past the bow of his own vessel, which had given him up for lost and shifted her anchorage forty-five miles away from the original location.[49] Happy endings resulting from good fortune were matched by those arising out of sheer human fortitude. Two fishermen lost from the Eastport dory trawler *Ida A. Thurlow* in May 1878, for example, rowed 120 miles from Western Bank to the Nova Scotia shore and landed through dangerous breakers 45 miles east of Halifax. That exceptional odyssey took nearly four days and was accomplished without food, water, or the benefit of a compass.[50] More often, survivors drifted until they were picked up by other vessels in the vicinity. Four dorymen from the schooner *A. M. Deering* of Portland, astray on the Grand Banks for thirty-six hours in August 1888, were among the fortunate few rescued in this manner.[51]

Those fishermen were the lucky ones. During the eight years from 1874 to 1881, 133 crew members were lost in dories from the single port of Gloucester, about two-thirds of them through drowning and the rest by going adrift in fog or storms. These victims of the New Technology represented fully 16 percent of that city's fishing fatalities during the period, and their number did not include the many who were rescued but suffered permanent disabilities as a result of their experience.[52] Such sobering statistics made a considerable impact on the more concerned observers of the fishing industry. Calls for reform, aimed primarily at the failure of vessels to equip their dories with emergency rations of food and drinking water, began to be heard in the early 1870s and continued into the next decade.[53] However, the vessel owners, who by then were fully responsible for outfitting at most places, steadfastly refused to make any added provision for occupational safety. One critic hinted that the expense, estimated at three dollars per dory, was a consideration, although general inconvenience and the reluctance of the men themselves to voice public objections to the prevailing system also played a part.[54] Whether the delaying factor was economic cost, callous insensitivity, or simple ignorance, the fact is that demands for safer conditions were still being ignored in the mid-1880s, a quarter-century after the introduction of dory fishing. In 1885 Maine's *Industrial Journal* suggested that fishermen take matters into their own hands:

> While the fish dealers and owners of fishing vessels are combining for protection against unjust legislation it is to be hoped that the fishermen themselves—they who man the vessels and do the work, will stand up for their rights also, and demand that measures be taken for the protection of their lives when away from their vessels in dories. The dories should be furnished with sufficient food and water to sustain life for a few days, so that when lost in the fog the men would stand at least an even chance of rescue.[55]

Ultimately, the problem was carried to Washington. A proposal for federal legislation, accompanied by a lengthy report, was submitted to the House Committee on Merchant Marine and Fisheries in early January of 1888 by W. H. Robertson, a Commerce Department official shocked by what he had learned of the effects of dory fishing as an agent in Yarmouth, Nova Scotia. The Robertson draft called for the mandatory equipping of banks dories with accurate and securely fastened compasses, as well as sufficient food and drink to sustain two men for up to ten days. Monetary penalties to ensure compliance were also suggested.[56] A bill incorporating these features was introduced the following month, but it never advanced beyond the committee stage.[57] At that point the futile reform effort died, and the fishermen were, once again, on their own.*

If they managed to survive their encounters on the fishing grounds with impenetrable fog, sudden squalls, and heedless merchant ships, banks fishermen had one more danger to overcome, the voyage home. It was at this point that their qualities as seamen, or lack thereof, came fully to the fore. In the Grand Banks cod fishery, the outward-bound spring trip was relatively easy and usually uneventful. Sailing to the banks from the coast of New England, fishermen had the benefit of prevailing westerly winds about two-thirds of the time. They enjoyed, in effect, following breezes. However, the same prevalent North Atlantic westerlies, or "southwest passage winds," became headwinds on the return trip, to the discomfiture of the west-bound sailor.[58] As a result, bankers waited and hoped for rare easterly

---

*Protective legislation on behalf of dory fishermen fared better in the more enlightened Canadian Parliament, where a bill incorporating the essential features of the Robertson proposal was enacted into law in 1898. (Source: *Can.AP,* 61 Vict., 1898, chap. 44.)

winds to make their fall departures. Most of the time, unfortunately, they had to face the full brunt of the westerlies, which could reach gale force late in the year during the hurricane season.[59] The Castine banker *Martha Burgess,* beating home in October 1853, was forced to heave-to several times and often made only a few miles a day with continual tacking under reefed sails. "This had been a hard wind to pass Cape Sable," was the captain's succinct but expressive evaluation of the last wearying homeward leg.[60]

It was in such conditions that many banks schooners foundered, proving unable to withstand the rigors of windward sailing in bad weather. Some homeward-bound vessels simply disappeared with their entire crews, leaving no trace. "Overdue and feared lost" was an epitaph that appeared frequently in marine lists late in the year, in reference to missing banks schooners.[61] It was not unusual for men to be lost overboard in the process of handling sail at this stage of the fishing voyage, and damage to the top-hampers of the vessels themselves was also quite common.[62]

Fishermen who visited the Gulf of St. Lawrence or the coast of Labrador had a somewhat less difficult time in transit to and from their fishing grounds. Here, too, however, there were inherent dangers. Trips to the Bay and beyond were essentially long coasting voyages during which schooners skirted the rugged and occasionally unfamiliar Maritime shoreline for days or weeks at a time (see chapter 3). This allowed them to duck into protected harbors to avoid inclement weather, but it also made them vulnerable to whatever unmarked shoals or hidden rocks the inshore waters contained. In the 1850s numerous Maine schooners were lost by running aground on the coast of Nova Scotia en route to, or returning from, the northern Canadian fisheries.[63]

The dangers associated with the northern enterprise were accentuated by the remarkably casual manner in which Bay fishermen, in particular, regarded ocean navigation. Offshore bankers were routinely equipped with up-to-date sighting devices, such as marine quadrants, for measuring latitude and longitude.[64] Schooners bound coastwise for the Gulf of St. Lawrence, on the other hand, rarely took observations and had little use for precise instruments. A table fork with a missing prong occasionally substituted for a pair of dividers in plotting a rough course on the chart.[65] Charts were not even used in the early years and were not adopted until nearly 1840 by some Maine fishing ports. The rudimentary taking of soundings to determine location remained a common way of negotiating the inshore waters around Prince Edward Island well into the 1860s.[66] Most of the Maine fishermen venturing northward in the nineteenth century were what Charles Eliot described as "coasting sailors," technically untrained navigators who found their way to the fishing grounds by "practice, keen observation, and good memory for objects once seen and courses once safely steered."[67] That admirable combination was usually sufficient, but not always, as vessel losses testified.

Hardships and Privations

As dangerous as the offshore fisheries were—and they were obviously very dangerous—most vessels did not sink, and most fishermen were not lost at sea. Gloucester, the most adventurous of American fishing ports, sacrificed an average of 13 schooners a year between 1868 and 1881 out of a total fleet that averaged 367 vessels.[68] The proportion lost annually was 3.5 percent. In other words, a fisherman had approximately a one in thirty chance of shipping aboard an ill-fated vessel. Those odds were certainly worth pondering, but they were only one aspect of the demanding life the fisheries entailed.

Fishing was, in the words of the chantey, "hardest in th' first hundred years."[69] It was, indeed, a hard life. Physically, the men worked long hours in harsh conditions. During the 1840s the crews of Boothbay schooners in the Labrador cod fleet often fished twenty-one hours a day at the height of the season, taking advantage of the extended daylight offered by the northern latitudes. A workday of 2 A.M. to 11 P.M. for periods of two to three weeks was not unheard of in that fishery.[70] Ordinarily, the fisherman's day ran from dawn to dusk and averaged fourteen to sixteen hours. Mornings and afternoons were given over to fishing, and evenings to dressing the catch. This regimen, which permitted time out only for meals, remained in force long after the ten-hour day had become the prevailing standard for employment on shore.[71]

In addition to long hours, the work environment was far from ideal, especially on the cod grounds. Joseph Reynolds's 1855 description of the typically unpleasant conditions endured by fishermen on the foggy Grand Banks could have been written at any time during the nineteenth century: "Every thing in the vessel was saturated with moisture. Their pea jackets and baize shirts were doubled in weight by the moisture which they had imbibed. The water hung in drops from the ceiling of the cuddy; even the bed and blankets in their berths, when they turned out in the morning, steamed like so many uncovered wash boilers. They had scarcely been dry for the last fifteen days, and their skins were completely parboiled."[72] That characterization, while colorful, was scarcely exaggerated. Aboard the Castine banks schooner *Martha Burgess* in 1853, crewmen hand-lined by the hour in pouring rain for days on end and endured a climate that ranged from cool and wet to warm and humid. Stormy spells were frequent as well, and they were equally hard on the men and the vessel. "This week has been one continual blow and a strong current," read the entry in the schooner's log for September 10th. "Rain most of the time, and upon the whole very rough and disagreeable."[73]

The physical effect on the fishermen was predictable. Constant exposure to cold, damp conditions gave rise to chronic rheumatism and neuralgia, both of which were common ailments among deep-sea fishermen throughout the nineteenth century. Professional crewmen also tended to age before their time, most of them worn out and finished by age forty-five unless they managed to become skippers.[74] Perhaps they were privileged to "breathe only the pure blasts of the mountain wave," as a Maine politician once euphorically put it,[75] but they could be identified in New England seaports by their rounded shoulders and stooped posture, the legacy of vessel handlining.[76]

Fishermen often suffered from one other physical ailment, namely dyspepsia, or what today would be called indigestion.[77] This can be traced no doubt to their diet, which was high in salted meats and heavy carbohydrates and low in fresh fruits and vegetables. Prior to 1860 the basic staples aboard fishing schooners were salt beef, salt pork, fish (until 1850), potatoes, flour, cornmeal, rice, beans, and coffee. Most of the cooking was done with lard, vinegar, and molasses. The only green vegetables carried were dried peas or cabbages, and dried apples and raisins constituted the fruit ration. Occasionally vessels took on a few fresh dairy products, such as butter and eggs, but these had to be consumed quickly before spoiling and so were not available after the first few days of the voyage. The majority of meals prepared by the ship's cook were of the meat-and-potatoes variety, interspersed with soups, chowders, and hashes, and supplemented by a conglomeration of puddings and shortcakes similarly made from flour, cornmeal, pork fat and scraps, and molasses.[78] Not only was the fisherman's daily diet nutritionally marginal and rather monotonous, it also deteriorated as the trip progressed. The Grand Banker *Martha Burgess* of Castine began to run out of essentials early in the fourth month of a five-month voyage in 1853, first exhausting her supply of potatoes and then, successively, her flour, beef, and peas.[79]

Gradually, food aboard New England fishing schooners did improve somewhat. By the 1870s canned goods were available, and such items as condensed milk, sugar, oatmeal, and baking powder were being stocked, as well as assorted fruits and vegetables not previously available. After 1880, furthermore, market schooners—those carrying ice for fresh fishing—began to provide fresh meat for their crews.[80] However, that practice was limited to places like Gloucester, Boston, and Portland. Most down-east vessels continued to go salt fishing in the 1880s and carried no ice with which to keep meats and other perishables fresh. Salted beef and pork remained the protein staples at Southport, for instance, although smoked ham and bacon were eventually added to the menu.[81] This was a slight improvement over the standard fare of the 1850s, but it was nevertheless not as good as what was available in the larger Massachusetts ports or, for that matter, on shore.

Chronic ailments produced by working in a wet, chilly environment and eating an unbalanced diet laced with salt were debilitating but not fatal. There was, however, a larger price to be paid for going to sea. Any serious illness suffered aboard a fishing schooner went basically untended until the vessel returned home or was able to reach a convenient port near the fishing grounds. A bottle of "pain killer" or castor oil, some liniment, and a jug of rum was all the medicine a schooner was liable to have on board to treat emergencies.[82] The problem was especially acute on the Grand Banks, which were far from any shore facilities. Schooners in the Gulf of St. Lawrence had access to any number of Maritime ports, while Western Bankers were able to run into Nova Scotia settlements like Port Mulgrave, a few hours' sail away, to land sick fishermen. Conversely, bankers on the Newfoundland grounds, especially in the early days, were forced to deal with situations on the spot as best they could, using home remedies and occasionally soliciting medical supplies from passing ships.[83]

Among the known maladies afflicting the crews of Maine fishing schooners over the years were measles, smallpox, and pneumonia.[84] There were doubtless others that went unrecorded or were not even diagnosed. When the sickness was a lingering one, fishermen often reached home in time for treatment.[85] On the other hand, sudden seizures or swiftly progressing illnesses requiring immediate attention were usually fatal. One such case, poignantly reported by a Portland newspaper in April 1855, was typical: "Sch Australia of Southport, put into Beaver Harbor [N.S.] from the Banks on Tuesday, 17th inst, to bury a hand named Webster, who on the day of his death had caught a qtl of fish."[86] Fatalities of this sort were not everyday occurrences, but they were frequent enough that small cemeteries scattered throughout the Maritime Provinces contain the grave sites of fishermen who sailed from Maine ports and never returned.[87]

Physical illness was not the only affliction experienced by men in the deep-sea fisheries. Mental and emotional problems, arising from the nature of the work, were common, although (given the prejudices of the time) they were seldom publicized. In 1880 Goode and Collins reported numerous cases of "nervous exhaustion" in the New England fishing fleet, especially among skippers at the larger ports where competition was intense.[88]

The special strain of withstanding seemingly endless bouts of bad weather at sea was a contributing factor. Ole Rölvaag, the Norwegian-American author who spent much of his European youth fishing on the Lofoten Banks of the North Atlantic, described the feeling with remembered trepidation: "Did you ever see the sea in all its madness? Then you have not known absolute insignificance. . . . The unearthly madness I am speaking of might last for days and for weeks, with no let-up, no breathing spell." [89]

On the Grand Banks, the terror of which Rölvaag wrote was abundantly present. To the men working there, however, storms could almost be blessings at times, since the danger relieved the awful boredom of their daily existence. Depression, more than fear, preyed on the minds of the banks fishermen. For one thing, they were absent from the land for interminable periods. An entry in the log of the homeward-bound banker *Martha Burgess* for October 12, 1853, noted that the vessel's sighting of the Nova Scotia coast was the first land seen for 143 days.[90] At work, the bankers often remained in one place for weeks at a time without even the diversion of shifting their anchorage to break the tedium. Moreover, entire days were sometimes spent without catching any fish, which was, after all, the primary purpose.[91] Confinement was another problem, especially in the pre-dory-fishing era. The restricted quarters and limited deck space aboard the average banks schooner gave rise to the nautical expression "a fisherman's walk," which, it was said, was three steps and overboard.[92] The Grand Banks themselves added to the oppressive mood. Their vastness combined with the ever-present fog to create a uniquely depressing workplace. Joseph Reynolds, writing in the 1850s, captured its essence perfectly:

> If there is any situation in the wide world where men feel solitary and alone, it is on the Banks of Newfoundland, with no object in sight to break the monotony of the scene. Neither sun, moon nor stars are seen for many days. They are enveloped in a dense fog, which shuts them up from all the world. In the long, damp, chilly nights, they are enclosed as with a solid wall of darkness. . . . There you lie, rocking to and fro, and rising and falling with the swelling surges, day after day and night after night; your deck slimy and slippery, the water trickling in streams down the windward face of your mast. . . . When fish are plenty, and the crew take from twenty to thirty quintals a day, the feeling of success enables one to bear the solitude. But when you are doing nothing, or only catching now and then a dog-fish, the feeling of dreariness is sometimes very oppressive.[93]

Some banks fishermen were simply unable to tolerate their situation. In July 1841 the schooner *Olinthus* of Castine put into St. John's, Newfoundland, for the purpose of replacing an anchor and ninety fathoms of cable, which a homesick crewman had cut in hopes of forcing the vessel to return to port. The *Olinthus* had at that juncture been on the banks only "a few weeks."[94] Older and more mature hands were better able to withstand the mental stress, but even experienced captains were susceptible to it. A reading of the 1853 log of the *Martha Burgess,* a typical banker of the pre–Civil War period, reveals a skipper progressively obsessed with the dreary weather, the poor quality of his vessel's food, the inferiority of his bait, and a general run of bad luck apparently ordained by Providence. Self-doubt and paranoia combined to produce a depression that lifted only when the schooner hove up for home after four long months on the fishing grounds.[95]

One means of alleviating the psychological side-effects of life at sea was the not-universally-approved use of alcoholic beverages. This recourse was especially prevalent in the years before the New England temperance movement reached full flower. Rum was a standard item in the provisioning stores of Gloucester schooners throughout the early part of the nineteenth century, and Provincetown vessels often stocked up to two barrels of the dark liquid for Grand Banks voyages as late as 1830, a practice that was said to have shortened many fishing careers.[96] Down-east fishermen were no less inclined to seek solace in "ardent spirits." In the 1820s, schooners from eastern Maine ports occasionally carried barrels of beer aboard to help relieve the tedium of cod fishing in the Bay of Fundy, and some were in the habit of putting in at Grand Manan Island to exchange fish for rum provided by the obliging inhabitants. Boothbay-area schooners, too, took significant quantities of rum aboard for trips to the cod-fishing grounds in the decades prior to 1850.[97] The use of hard liquor produced periodic reports of alcoholism in the Maine fleets during the first half of the nineteenth century, especially in the inshore fisheries, where proximity to land guaranteed steady access to drink for those so inclined.[98] The passage of Maine's prohibition law in 1851, however, largely closed that avenue, and the lengthy isolation of the offshore banks fishery imposed a sobriety of its own.[99]

With the passage of time, some aspects of the fisherman's life (notably his food ration, as mentioned) did improve. Unfortunately, the introduction of technological changes in the manner of fishing did much to cancel out any new benefits. In fact, the average crewman's daily work was made not only more dangerous by such innovations as dory fishing and trawling, but also much more difficult. Until circa 1860, life on the cod-fishing banks, while hard, did offer some minor amenities. Sunday fishing, for instance, was rare, the day being given over to rest and relaxation on most vessels.[100] However, this and similar customs were considered dispensable in the new age of accelerated technology.

Dory trawling radically changed the daily routine aboard bankers. Boredom became less of a problem, but only because the level of work intensified. Trawlers did not rest on Sundays, as had hand-liners. They also moved about the banks more often, rarely unbending their mainsails, and seldom stayed long in one berth. As a result, the men were constantly working the vessel. Furthermore, trawlers were sailed harder than hand-liners, making more trips in the course of a season and periodically racing into Canadian ports for fresh bait and ice.[101] On the fishing grounds, work went on around the clock in order to exhaust each new perishable supply of bait before it spoiled. The larger daily catches produced by trawling added to the task, necessitating a much greater amount of time to dress and salt the fish. In the process, crews were pushed to the limit, laboring longer and harder than in the past. Eventually it became standard practice to set and haul each trawl twice a day, which placed a considerable added burden on the men. Then, too, the trawls became progressively longer and had to be set farther and farther from the vessel, increasing the distance dorymen had to row to reach the gear as well as the time and effort needed to service it.[102] Finally, the act of tending a trawl was, in itself, physically taxing. It required far more strength and exertion than hauling a hand-line, and it often left scars. "I have got the marks to show about my trawls right on my hands," one veteran trawlerman joked when asked about his work.[103]

Rigorous exertion also became the hallmark of the offshore mackerel fishery once seining was introduced on a wide scale in the 1860s. Prior to the adoption of the purse seine, it was common for young and old alike to participate in mackereling. Hook-and-line schooners often carried several youngsters between the ages of ten and seventeen, who fished off the stern of the vessel in the summer months and learned the trade. Older men, past the prime of life, could also be usefully employed in this fishery, which required neither great strength nor exceptional endurance. Technology changed all that, converting mackerel catching from a sportive vocation into a grim task. Introduction of the massive, cumbersome seining apparatus quickly forced elderly fishermen to retire to the shore or to the boat fisheries, and it simultaneously pushed back to late adolescence the age at which boys could apprentice themselves.[104] The new breed of mackerel fisherman was chosen for his mature muscularity and willingness to work exceptionally hard at times, expending his energy in periodic bursts of strenuous activity necessitated by the critical pursing-up operation. He was

also expected to accommodate himself to a longer and less predictable
workday. Leisure hours and regular rest became vestiges of the past. As in
the cod trawl fishery, exclusive daylight fishing gave way to frequent periods
of nocturnal labor, during which time seiners often went several days without sleep in order to exhaust a school of fish.[105]

The sea fisheries, in short, meant an increasingly hard life, even if one did
not "go missing." Prior to the Civil War, it was the only choice for many inhabitants of coastal Maine. Hard labor and death at sea were accepted sto-
ically and philosophically. In time, however, the postwar world and the new
awareness and opportunities it brought would change that perspective.

The Economics of Risk

The dangerous and difficult aspects of the fishing way of life represented
more than a potential agenda for social reformers or a diversionary curiosity
for the land-locked public at large. Taken together, the innumerable small
tragedies experienced in the day-to-day operation of the deep-sea fisheries
constituted a socioeconomic problem of considerable proportion for the industry itself. In Maine, lost vessels, lost lives, and constant hardship contributed directly to the industry's decline by creating disincentives for both
the state's vessel owners and its fishermen.

As far as the owners were concerned, the negative factors were primarily
economic and focused on the perils of the trade, not its hardships. The
owners, after all—unless they belonged to the vanishing breed of owner-
fishermen—did not put themselves personally at risk. They did, however,
risk their vessels, and it was in the realm of property loss that they confronted the harsh nature of the fisheries.

One unpleasant economic reality of the business was the regularity with
which fishing schooners were damaged in the course of their work. Vessels
routinely suffered injuries to their spars, sails, and rigging, both in transit to
and from the fishing grounds and on the grounds themselves. Two incidents involving Castine schooners typified the sort of damage most commonly sustained. In September 1846 the *Lion*, homeward bound from the
Grand Banks, encountered a heavy gale east of Sable Island and lost her
foremast, jib-boom, and bowsprit, plus several sails. Similarly, the *Redwing*,
returning from the coast of Labrador in August 1851, was struck by severe
winds off Cape Canso and had both her bowsprit and headsails carried
away, as well as a large portion of her rigging. Both schooners survived.[106]
Episodes of this sort seldom resulted in the loss of a vessel. Jury rigs normally allowed dismasted fishermen to limp home or reach some other safe
haven for repairs, and torn sails were so commonplace as to warrant only

passing mention in marine disaster reports.[107] The economic cost to the owners was substantial, however. In 1881 the banker *W. T. Emerson* of Bucksport lost her mainmast when a stay parted during a storm on the Newfoundland grounds. The replacement bill came to $337. Two years later, the *Annie G. Quiner* of the same port had several spars and sails carried away in a hurricane, while en route to the Grand Banks. The cost to her owner was $500.[108]

The frequency of damage to masts, sails, and rigging, which together amounted to one-quarter to one-third of the cost of a new schooner,[109] increased in the years following the Civil War when changes took place in the manner of fishing. The onset of trawling meant that cod bankers began to carry additional spars and more sail, in order to commute quickly back and forth between the fishing grounds and the bait and ice depôts of the Canadian coast.[110] Fresh fishing brought similar alterations in the traditional practices of mackerel, haddock, and halibut fishermen. Widely fluctuating fresh-fish prices encouraged market schooners literally to race for port with their fares, carrying increased sail in all conditions and taking extraordinary chances.[111] Those wishing to compete in these fisheries had to accept additional risks and be willing to pay the higher "top-bills" that resulted.

While damage to the top-hampers of vessels was an economic burden to all fishermen at one time or another, those who worked on the cod banks had to allow for an added expense unique to their trade, the periodic loss of anchors and cables. Cod bankers almost always fished at anchor, and the constant strain of "holding on" in all kinds of weather often caused anchor stocks to break or mooring lines to part. As one Gloucester merchant put it, "Vessels which do not lose more than an anchor a year would be considered very fortunate."[112] Marine damage reports for Maine bankers tend to confirm that observation. In the 1850s scarcely a season passed without numerous incidents involving lost anchors and cables, and the French bases of St. Pierre and Miquelon off the south coast of Newfoundland became a favorite source of emergency replacements.[113]

Lost mooring gear constituted a steady economic drain on schooner owners throughout the nineteenth century. Moreover, since anchors and chain sold by the pound and manila cables were purchased by the foot, replacement costs increased with the passage of time. There were two reasons. First of all, banks schooners steadily grew larger in size (see chapter 6), and the weight of an anchor was directly proportional to the tonnage of the vessel using it. Secondly, trawling schooners, which began to proliferate after 1860, tended to fish in deeper waters than hand-line vessels, increasing the amount of cable used and (therefore) potentially lost.[114] From a monetary standpoint, the loss of a cable or anchor rope was worse than the loss of the anchor itself. Anchors ranged in size from 250 to 600 pounds and cost from $20 to $90, depending on the rate per pound and the actual poundage. Iron prices remained relatively stable from decade to decade, and during most years fishing anchors could be had for less than $50. The cost of the two-hundred-fathom manila cables attached to them, on the other hand, rose markedly between the prewar and postwar periods, increasing from about $100 in 1860 to well over $400 in 1877.[115]

What made lost gear and other damage to fishing schooners most serious was not just the ever-growing expense but the fact that marine insurance did not, for the most part, cover it. Anchors, cables, and outfits could not be insured at all, except as part of the overall loss in cases where the vessel was sunk or wrecked.* Explicit clauses freeing underwriters from any responsibility for mooring gear lost on the cod banks were written into every fishing policy. Insurers were more willing to pay for losses to spars, sails, and rigging, but only under certain conditions. The deductible principle was applied, and incidental damage was covered only if it exceeded a certain percentage of the total value of the vessel. That percentage was based on a sliding scale tied to vessel valuation—the less valuable the vessel, the higher the deductible—and it ranged from 10 to 35 percent in the postwar period.[116] In the mid-1870s, for instance, damage to the top-hamper of a Gloucester cod banker worth $6,700 would not be covered by the local insurer unless the loss exceeded 14 percent of the vessel's full valuation, or $938. Since the spars for such a schooner collectively cost $400, its standing and running rigging $550, and its sails $575, it is obvious that all but the most extensive damage was the responsibility of the owner. Only wholesale destruction above deck—say, the loss of all masts and sails—would entitle the insured party to compensation.[117]

In effect, those who chose to remain in the fishing business were forced to assume significant annual overhead costs in the form of piecemeal damage to their vessels and equipment. Only at times of more or less total disaster were marine underwriters obligated to come to their aid. Moreover, if owners elected to pursue the more dangerous offshore fisheries, employ the latest technology, and compete for the highest market price, they could expect an increased economic burden as time passed. This reality was sufficient reason after 1865 for many to simply leave the industry.

*This led to extremely imprudent behavior on the part of some economically hard-pressed fishermen. On George's Bank, schooner captains were loath to cut uninsured cables under any circumstances, often holding fast to their mooring lines and risking collisions with oncoming ships or drifting schooners whose own cables had accidentally parted. (Sources: *Goode Report*, sec. 4, 105; *EA*, marine list, 30 June 1848.)

The necessity of writing off a good portion of each year's investment in equipment was an economic problem faced by all owners of fishing vessels. It was undoubtedly more burdensome to the marginal operators found in many parts of Maine, but it was, nevertheless, universal in nature. There was another major difficulty created by the dangers of the fishing industry, however, one that affected the Maine fisheries in particular and contributed directly to their decline. This was the inability of many Maine entrepreneurs to finance the vessel insurance they needed to remain in business.

The great age of marine insurance in the fisheries began around 1850 and roughly coincided with the passage of vessel control into the hands of large merchants—those best able to afford coverage—at the major New England ports.[118] Prior to that time it was not unusual for owners of fishing schooners to operate without any security on their vessels and outfits. In the 1830s 33 percent of the schooners lost from the port of Gloucester carried no insurance, and that figure declined only slightly in the 1840s, to 24 percent. During the decade of the 1850s, however, the number of uninsured Gloucester vessels among those lost dropped dramatically, to 5 percent of the total. Thereafter, it never rose above 4 percent for any ten-year period.[119]

In marked contrast to their Massachusetts counterparts, many Maine owners continued to risk their vessels without proper coverage long after insurance had become the industry norm. This was particularly true of the lesser entrepreneurs, especially the owner-fishermen. The merchant-owners of Castine, Bucksport, Boothbay, and Portland did generally insure their schooners.[120] The independent operators, however, viewed vessel security in much the same way that they saw the New Technology—as a luxury they could not afford. Well into the 1870s, independent fishermen from the outports of eastern Maine continued to ply their trade in uninsured vessels.[121] Among them were the lingering minority of old-fashioned Yankee mackerel-catchers still fishing with hook and line in the Gulf of St. Lawrence, of whom a Canadian fisherman remarked, "Many do not insure at all."[122]

The results of such risk-taking were predictably disastrous for innumerable small operators whose capital was entirely tied up in their schooners. In 1851 the brand-new Boothbay clipper *C. G. Matthews,* built at a cost of four thousand dollars, went down in the Gulf of St. Lawrence on her maiden voyage. The two owners, one of whom was the captain, had no insurance whatever and were wiped out.[123] The loss of the *Jenny Lind* of Belfast while pollock fishing in 1865 was a comparable tragedy. According to Portland's *Eastern Argus,* which related this particular hard-luck story, "Capt. Clark who was the principal owner of the vessel had no insurance; and the probability is that by the fire at Belfast he has been stripped of the remainder of his property."[124] Another case of this sort was the sinking of the *Active,* one of a handful of Castine schooners not owned by that port's merchants. This vessel went missing in an October storm in 1846, while mackerel fishing along the Maine coast. The owners were among the lost crew members, but even had they survived the enterprise would have been terminated. Nothing but a few barrels and part of a cable were salvaged from the schooner, and, as usual, there was no insurance.[125]

Although uninsured vessels typically belonged to independent owner-fishermen, some of the smaller merchant houses in Maine also occasionally risked their property without coverage and suffered the consequences. Ezekiel Tarbox, a marginal outport operator who maintained a small fleet of vessels at Westport in the 1850s, chose to chance that investment on the vagaries of the Gulf fishery rather than purchase protection. It proved a poor gamble. His new schooner, the *E. Atwood*, wrecked at Prince Edward Island just months after launching in 1858, carried no insurance and became a total financial loss.[126] Three similar incidents of the post–Civil War period, involving Boothbay, Eastport, and Portland firms, produced unredeemable losses amounting to fourteen thousand dollars.[127]

In addition to a total lack of coverage among large numbers of entrepreneurs, the pattern of insurance usage in Maine's fisheries differed from that evidenced at Massachusetts ports like Gloucester in one other respect, namely in the small amount of coverage down-east owners purchased when they did take out insurance policies on their vessels. After 1850 most Gloucester schooners were insured at, or close to, the maximum allowed by local underwriters. The average coverage on all insured Gloucester vessels lost during the period 1850–1869 was 73 percent of assessed valuation.[128] By comparison, the coverage carried by Maine schooners, including merchant-owned vessels, was rather paltry. A sample of two dozen fishing policies purchased by Witherle & Company of Castine between the years 1850 and 1870 reveals that bankers operated by that firm were insured on average for only 55 percent of their full value.[129]

Castine's owners rarely insured to the allowable maximum, even when new schooners were involved. The policies of two one-year-old cod bankers, similar in size, illustrates how their approach to vessel insurance differed from that of Gloucester's fish merchants. In 1854 the Gloucesterman *Flight*, assessed at $4,000, was insured by E. & E. W. Merchant & Company for $3,500, or 87.5 percent of valuation.[130] In 1867 the *D. T. Patchin* of Castine, worth $7,000 in the inflated post-bellum market, was insured by Witherle & Company for $3,000, barely 43 percent of valuation.[131] Such token coverage was far from unusual in the Maine fisheries. The schooner *Medora* of Bristol went fishing in the fall of 1877 with a policy that guaranteed her owner no more than 20 percent of his investment in case of disaster.[132]

The failure of so many Maine fishermen and merchants to insure their vessels adequately was attributable to a number of factors. The relative poverty of the state's fishing entrepreneurs, the same marginal status that caused them to favor cod fishing over mackerel catching (see chapter 1), was one. Another (after 1866) was the absence of the fishing bounty, which many operators had depended upon for payment of their annual premiums.[133] There was one more important element, and that was the slow and stunted growth of mutual fishing-insurance companies in the down-east region.

Under the mutual principle, the insured became members of the company insuring them, serving as stockholders for the duration of their policies and sharing in both the profits and losses according to the size of their premiums. Mutual companies, or "societies," specializing in fishing insurance offered the advantage of low premiums, since their rates were calculated not to maximize profits but simply to cover anticipated losses. Their incorporators and officers tended to be fish merchants and vessel owners rather than professional insurance executives or general business investors. In short, they were engaged in what George Brown Goode, referring to the Gloucester model, called a system of "co-operative insurance."[134]

Ironically enough, the first American mutual societies devoted to covering fishing risks appear to have been organized in Maine. These were the Vinalhaven Mutual Marine Insurance Company and the Fisherman's Mutual Insurance Company of Eastport, founded in 1833 and 1837, respectively.[135] Little is known of these companies, however, and they seem not to have survived for any great length of time. The first permanent implementation of cooperative insurance in the fisheries was at Gloucester, where a mutual company was started in 1841 by five local merchants. Their motivation was to provide cheaper coverage for Gloucester vessels than was available from regular insurance companies, whose rates on fishing risks were deemed at the time to be prohibitive. This small society lasted until 1847, when it was succeeded by the larger Gloucester Mutual Fishing Insurance Company, which continued the practice of providing local merchants and fishermen with lower rates than those offered by outside firms.[136]

Under the auspices of Gloucester Mutual, cooperative fishing insurance reached a fuller development at Cape Ann than it did anywhere in the industry, and by the post–Civil War period Gloucester's numerous schooner owners, many of whom had formerly insured with expensive commercial offices in Boston, were universally covered by their own cooperative underwriters.[137] In 1877 Richard Henry Dana, Jr., the celebrated author, described the Gloucester experiment in mutual protection as a key ingredient in the port's economic success. It enabled local vessel owners, he said, to "insure themselves cheaper than any people in the world ever did insure themselves against marine risks; so much so, that merchants of Gloucester have told us that if they had to pay the rates that are paid in stock companies, the fishing business could not be carried on by merchants who own their ships; the difference would be enough to turn the scale." [138]

In addition to lowering premium rates, Gloucester's mutual society provided another critically essential service. It ensured that fishermen would actually be able to get the insurance they required. During the 1830s the availability of coverage, at whatever price, was by no means guaranteed. Gloucester's first marine-insurance company, a traditional firm, was not favorably disposed toward fishing risks or, for that matter, fishermen.* As Sylvanus Smith remembered it, "The Old [sic] Marine Insurance Company was controlled and managed by the retired captains of the square-rigged fleet, and these men carried their quarter-deck manners into business." [139] Smith, himself a Gloucester fish merchant, participated in the establishment of a second local mutual society, the Cape Ann Mutual Marine Insurance Company, founded on principles similar to those of the popular Gloucester Mutual Company and intended to guarantee the coverage denied by commercial underwriters. [140] This direct involvement of fishing interests in mutual companies was, as mentioned, a standard feature of the cooperative system. The presidents of the dominant Gloucester Mutual firm were invariably chosen from the ranks of active fish merchants, [141] and their presence assured that no bona fide application for fishing insurance would be turned down. Indeed, that precept was formally written into the by-laws adopted by Gloucester Mutual's stockholders. [142]

Given Gloucester's statistical dominance in the Massachusetts fisheries, it is probable that close to half of that state's fishing tonnage was already insured under the mutual concept by the end of the 1850s. [143] The same could not be said elsewhere in New England. Maine's fishing industry came late to the idea of cooperative insurance. Except for the Vinalhaven and Eastport ventures, only one mutual society was started down east prior to the Civil War. That was the Southport Mutual Fishing Insurance Company, founded in 1858. Two years later, it was still the only one of Maine's eleven marine-insurance firms offering mutual coverage to fishermen. [144]

Cod-fishing schooners sailing out of Castine during the antebellum period were forced to turn to Cape Cod underwriters, purchasing coverage from the Union Insurance Company of Provincetown, a standard stock

---

*A similar condescending attitude toward the fishing industry permeated Gloucester's banking community prior to the incorporation of the Cape Ann Bank, controlled by fishing interests, in 1855. Until that time fish merchants were extremely hard pressed to obtain loans for any purpose connected with their businesses. (Source: Sylvanus Smith, 119–20.)

company, through the early 1850s. In the middle of that decade, Castine's merchants availed themselves of the services of the Atlantic Mutual Fire & Marine Insurance Company, a general mutual company founded at Provincetown in 1854. Through this firm, which wrote most Castine policies up to and immediately after the Civil War, eastern Maine fishing interests did have recourse to a mutual insurer.[145] However, although a mutual company, Atlantic Mutual was neither controlled by fishermen nor concerned exclusively with fishing risks. Moreover, it strictly limited the type of coverage it offered, refusing to insure fishing vessels venturing east of Cape Canso between October 1st and May 1st, increasing rates for schooners fishing anywhere after October 1st, and writing no policies at all for those engaged in the dangerous George's Bank fisheries. By contrast, Gloucester's leading mutual society covered all fishing risks without exception, although it did add a surcharge on vessels operating in the winter months.[146]

It was not until the post–Civil War period that Maine fishermen obtained ready access to specialized insurance suited—or purportedly suited—to their needs. In 1868 the Boothbay Mutual Fishing Insurance Company was incorporated "for the purpose of making insurance against maritime losses on fishing vessels employed in the cod or mackerel fishery, or both."[147] Six years later, a similar charter was granted in the name of the Portland Mutual Fishing Insurance Company to seven of that city's fish merchants, who, unlike the stockholders of most locally oriented fishing mutuals (including Gloucester's), took upon themselves the responsibility of offering coverage to any and all cod and mackerel schooners statewide.[148] By the late 1870s vessel owners from as far away as Bristol, Cranberry Isles, and Swan's Island were insuring with Portland's fishing underwriters.[149]

Despite the establishment of mutual-insurance companies at Maine's two premier postwar fishing ports, the state's vessel owners remained at an economic disadvantage compared to their Massachusetts counterparts. The creation of a mutual company did not, in and of itself, guarantee low rates and blanket coverage, and indications are that Maine's fishing mutuals lacked a number of the features of Gloucester's cooperative societies. For one thing, the insurance provided at Gloucester was clearly superior with respect to its extent of coverage in case of total loss. Most fishing underwriters, including Maine's mutual companies, insured vessels only up to 75 percent of full valuation, leaving the owner responsible for the other 25 percent. In contrast, Gloucester's cooperative indemnified its members for up to a maximum 87.5 percent of valuation.[150] That difference could mean as much as $1,000 to a victimized owner in the inflationary years after 1865, when new-vessel prices ranged from $7,000 to $10,000.[151] One way around this problem, and the high cost of insurance in general, was to buy used schooners of limited value, thereby reducing premiums and minimizing potential economic losses. This approach, risky from the standpoint of safety, was taken of necessity by many Maine entrepreneurs in the 1870s and 1880s. At a time when the average vessel in Gloucester's cod-fishing fleet was worth $6,000, operators at a number of Maine ports were investing in second-hand schooners valued at $1,000 to $3,000 and reducing their insurance costs accordingly.[152]

There is evidence to suggest that in addition to their low percentage levels of coverage Maine's mutual fishing-insurance firms were deficient in other ways as well. For instance, although the precise rate structures of Maine's mutuals are unknown, it is clear that some down-east policyholders were paying at least 1 percent more for annual coverage than was charged at Gloucester.[153] Furthermore, there appears to have been an unwillingness on the part of Maine underwriters to emulate the Gloucester practice of insuring all fishing risks at reasonable cost, regardless of potential dangers and losses. This led to some confusion about the nature of the companies serving Maine's industry. In 1880, six years after the founding of Portland's mutual firm, the United States Fish Commission examined the reluctance of Maine ports to participate in winter fishing and offered the following explanation: "The reason why Maine fishermen do not engage in the offshore winter fisheries can probably be found in the fact that they have not the system of mutual insurance which prevails in Gloucester. The probability of vessels being lost on winter trips is so great that few individuals or firms care to incur the risk without insurance; and the cost of insuring in stock companies is too high to leave any profits."[154] The commission was mistaken in labelling Maine's fishing mutuals as stock companies but was correct in perceiving that they resembled stock companies in some respects. Like Provincetown's underwriters, those in Maine either did not offer coverage for the more distant winter fisheries or charged so much for it that there were few takers.

At any rate, schooners from the Boothbay region, served by two mutual firms, seldom went winter fishing on the offshore grounds. Likewise, Portland's merchant-owned vessels, insured by their own local mutual company, rarely ventured beyond the confines of the Gulf of Maine during the winter months, being content to fish for haddock on the inner banks within thirty or forty miles of the coast.[155] Gloucester's fleet, on the other hand, assiduously followed the offshore haddock and halibut fisheries between November and April, and visited the George's Bank cod grounds in large numbers after January 1st of each year.[156] Gloucester was able to afford its fishermen the cheaper and more generous insurance coverage that permitted winter fishing in part because of its sheer size as a fishing port. The great number of vessels participating in the insurance system there provided the cooperative underwriters with sufficient capital stock to offset the immense losses suffered annually in the winter fisheries without unduly raising premiums. In 1877, for example, the Gloucester Mutual Company wrote policies on $1.6 million worth of schooners, many of them George's Bankers.[157] The Portland Mutual Company, the likely insurer of any Georgesmen sailing from Maine, did not even open its books for business until mid-March, practically the end of the winter season.[158]

Combined with their other shortcomings, the unwillingness or inability of Maine's marine insurers to provide the coverage needed for the safe pursuit of the remunerative winter fisheries was a powerful incentive for the state's merchants to move their enterprises to Gloucester after the middle of the nineteenth century. One choosing to do so was Benjamin Maddocks, owner of a substantial fleet of schooners at Southport in the 1850s, who moved his business south following the Civil War. Formerly engaged only in the spring and summer fisheries, Maddocks converted to year-round fishing under the security provided by Gloucester's comprehensive mutual-insurance scheme, employing several vessels in the hazardous but profitable George's fishery.[159] His was not an isolated case. By 1880 several other fish dealers from Maine had set up operations in Gloucester.[160] They symbolized the dilemma facing Maine's postwar fishing companies because of the state's inadequate insurance system. Those firms wishing to participate fully in the increasingly important winter fisheries had little choice but to move out of state. The alternative was to continue operating in the traditional manner, depending on seasonal fishing and gradually falling behind competitors in places like Gloucester. For Maine's native industry, either path led toward economic decline.

The Coastal Exodus

If fish merchants from Maine were drawn to Massachusetts, so were ordinary fishermen. The attractions, however, were somewhat different. For merchants, the lure was purely economic, consisting of the desire to participate in the profitable winter fisheries and share in the full benefits of cooperative insurance. For fishermen, the motivations were mixed. In part, they, too, were attracted by economic opportunities. The chance to fish year-round and earn the top money available to sharesmen in the winter fresh fisheries was an obvious incentive to the more ambitious and adventurous among them. Also appealing were the Gloucester traditions of end-of-trip payments and cancellation of outfitting debts in case of broken voyages. Yet there was another factor, social in nature and growing out of the dangers and hardships of the industry, which was of equal importance. This was the elaborate system of social security—primarily survivor benefits of various kinds—maintained for fishermen and their families at Gloucester and most other Massachusetts ports.

More than half of all Maine fishermen were married, and in some places the figure was close to two-thirds.[161] The welfare of dependents, therefore, was a prime consideration to a sizeable proportion of the men employed in the industry. That concern was magnified by the dangers of the occupation and by the realization that one could easily be lost at sea, leaving a family behind to fend for itself. The events of December 29, 1876, illustrate in minia-ture what one brief storm could produce in terms of social dislocation. On that day a violent gale struck the Portland haddock fleet, winter fishing on Jeffrey's Bank in the Gulf of Maine. No vessels were lost, but two fishermen were drowned, one disappearing from a capsized dory and another being washed overboard while at the wheel of his schooner. Both men had fami-lies; they left behind two wives and seven children, a total of nine depen-dents suddenly bereft of a breadwinner.[162] That tragedy was duplicated manifold during the truly bad years. In 1846, for instance, the loss of eleven vessels and sixty-five men from the Massachusetts port of Marblehead cre-ated forty-three widows and 150 fatherless children.[163] An estimate made at Gloucester in 1873 was that fishing losses there over the previous forty years had produced 422 single-parent households containing 844 children, or an average of thirty new unsupported dependents each year.[164]

Until the mid-nineteenth century, fatherless families in New England fishing ports survived largely on their own, with the occasional aid of pri-vate charity. Widows depended on relatives and neighbors in times of great stress and earned pocket money tending flake yards, digging clams, or do-ing needlework in the home. Children were sent off to work as soon as they were able, and sympathetic storekeepers sometimes helped with a line of credit.[165] Nevertheless, it gradually became obvious that in times of con-centrated disaster, private charity was no adequate substitute for a depend-able system of public assistance. There was ample precedent for such aid. As early as 1771 the colonial government of Massachusetts had earmarked pub-lic funds for distribution to families left destitute by the results of a storm on the Grand Banks. In the nineteenth century it was the towns and cities that assumed responsibility for this form of welfare. By the eve of the Civil War, for example, both Wellfleet and Newburyport were providing support for deceased fishermen's families through their local marine benevolent societies.[166]

Not surprisingly, it was left to Gloucester, the Bay State's preeminent fishing port, to evolve the most generous and comprehensive program of social security. Beginning in 1862 with the establishment of the so-called Widows and Orphans Fund Society (renamed the Gloucester Fishermen's and Seamen's Widows and Orphans Aid Society in 1865), the city embarked on a full-scale effort to provide survivors' benefits for its fishing population. Money was initially raised by public subscription and by the sale of membership certificates to fishermen. Neither approach proved satisfactory as a long-term solution. Ultimately, the society settled on a funding scheme whereby fishermen agreed to donate a certain portion of their earnings—no more than 0.5 percent—upon the settlement of each voyage. This voluntary "tax," deducted from all crew shares by the fishing companies and transferred to the society at year's end, became the permanent financial basis of the system.[167] Refinements were made from time to time. By the 1870s, employer contributions were also being collected, the normal procedure being to assess each returning schooner 0.25 percent of its gross stock prior to the deduction of expenses and division of profits. For most vessels, this meant a levy of between five and ten dollars.[168] Since Gloucester schooners typically fished at the halves, the gross-stock levy meant, in effect, that both owners and crews (employers and workers) contributed equally, a funding concept adopted more than half a century later by the framers of the Social Security Act of 1935.[169]

During its first two decades of operation, the Gloucester Widows and Orphans Aid Society collected more than $115,000 through the mechanism of direct industry taxes and distributed over $95,000 of it to needy recipients in the form of food, fuel, clothing, and cash allotments. As many as two hundred families at a time were carried on the society's rolls. By 1880 standard guidelines had been established for assistance. A widow with three or four children was entitled to $50 per year, while smaller families received $30. In addition, each family could expect annual donations of clothing valued at between $75 and $125.[170]

Besides the industry-supported aid society, Gloucester's needy had recourse to a variety of other charitable organizations. After 1871, the Tenement Association for Widows and Orphans provided a primitive form of low-cost public housing by maintaining a building with apartments available to fishing widows and their children at token rents. In 1877 the Gloucester Relief Association, funded by voluntary contributions, was organized to engage in poor relief specifically related to fishing disasters and served to supplement the work of the Widows and Orphans Society in particularly bad years. Finally, there was the Gloucester Female Charitable Association, which distributed food and clothing to dozens of single-parent families in the community, mostly widows of fishermen and their children.[171]

Although hardly munificent by modern standards, the aid provided by Gloucester's social-welfare organizations went far beyond anything available in Maine. At Portland, the state's largest and most important fishing port after 1865, there was no organized help at all for the dependents of men lost in the fisheries, and destitute families had to depend exclusively on the city's poor laws.[172] Portland did support a flourishing marine society, which used a portion of its abundant resources to care for widows of merchant sea captains residing in the general vicinity. However, none of that relief found its way to the wives and children of either common seamen or fishermen.[173] At Boothbay and a few other Maine ports, masonic lodges offered some assistance to the families of deceased members who had been fishermen, but in most smaller communities private charity and church aid were all that could be relied upon.[174]

Together with various economic incentives, the total lack of survivor benefits in Maine ports drew hundreds of native fishermen to Gloucester in the post–Civil War period. A certain number of Maine fishermen, motivated perhaps by adventure or wanderlust, had always been attracted to Gloucester and other Massachusetts ports. Their names appeared on the crew lists of Bay State vessels throughout the 1850s and, occasionally, before that time.[175] Nevertheless, it was only after fundamental socioeconomic reasons arose for leaving the Maine fisheries—dissatisfaction with the continuance of the prewar credit and payment system or the desire to guarantee a modicum of financial security for dependents—that the trickle turned into a flood. By the 1870s and 1880s the migration from Maine fishing ports had become a virtual coastal exodus.

Examining the Gloucester fisheries on behalf of the United States Fish Commission in 1880, G. B. Goode and J. W. Collins observed that a large percentage of the port's manpower hailed from the down-east region.[176] Actual census figures for that year indicate that 348 of Gloucester's resident fishermen (roughly 8 percent of the city's crew members) were natives of Maine.[177] That did not include many who did not live in Gloucester but went there each spring to ship out on banks vessels, returning home for the winter in much the same manner as migrant Canadians from the Maritimes. Brooksville and Deer Isle, for instance, were among the eastern Maine coastal communities whose fishermen spent part of the year working out of

Gloucester.[178] The number of crewmen belonging to this transient work force was quite substantial. In early April 1885, a Maine newspaper reported that "nearly one hundred men have left South Deer Isle for Gloucester and other places, on their way to the fishing grounds."[179] There is evidence, moreover, to suggest that it was the best of Maine's deep-water men who annually left home to ship aboard Gloucester vessels. "In the sharp competition which exists among the fishermen of this port," wrote Goode and Collins, "those from Maine hold a prominent place and are second to none in bravery, hardihood and seamanship."[180]

Those men who left home permanently were, of course, the greatest loss to Maine's native industry. This group included many highly qualified "master fishermen," or skippers, a critical component of the fishing work force. In 1880 no fewer than forty of Gloucester's captains were from Maine, and they were said to be among the port's "most enterprising" skippers.[181] Their ranks included experienced vessel handlers from such widely scattered down-east fishing towns as Boothbay, Westport, Kittery, Islesboro, and North Haven.[182] These particular individuals had special reasons for migrating to Gloucester. As a class, they tended to be family men with a more-than-casual interest in survivors' benefits. Four out of five skippers residing at Vinalhaven in 1860, for example, were married, compared to only half of the vessel crewmen.[183] Furthermore, most Gloucester merchant firms offered a unique economic inducement to obtain and keep expert skippers. That lure was the chance for partial vessel ownership, an opportunity unavailable to master fishermen at most places after 1865. In the interest of the company, loyal and energetic captains were encouraged to buy one-quarter shares of the schooners they commanded,* with the merchants arranging financing if necessary.[184] Such an avenue for advancement made vessel captaincy in Gloucester an irresistible prospect for many of Maine's best professional skippers, and their consequent departure deprived the state of one of the key ingredients necessary to the maintenance of a strong and stable industry. They were, in a word, irreplaceable.

The manpower shortage plaguing the Maine fishing industry in the post–Civil War period was not simply due to the magnetic attraction of Gloucester and other Massachusetts ports. It was also rooted in a general abandonment of the fisheries as a way of life. For many, deep-sea fishing

---

*Only a small percentage of Portland's postwar schooner captains held shares in company-owned vessels, and those who did rarely owned more than a one-eighth or one-sixteenth interest. (Sources: *Mackerel Fishery Materials*, 420–29 passim; NA, RBMIN [RG 41], VDR, Portland-Falmouth District Registers and Enrollments, 1877–83, certificates for various schooners.)

was an occupation to be followed only if there was no alternative. As Maine's Senator Hannibal Hamlin remarked in an 1858 speech on the problems and hazards of the industry, "It is not that kind of business that invites individuals to its prosecution under an ordinary state of things."[185] By the postwar period, lost lives, chronic hardships, and minimal rewards had produced a cumulative inhibiting effect on the fishing population, encouraging a large portion of the younger generation to look elsewhere for its livelihood.

A great many looked out of state, not merely to the fishing ports of eastern Massachusetts but beyond. During the twenty years between 1860 and 1880 over half of all Maine's towns lost population, and among the coastal fishing villages that figure was closer to two-thirds.[186] To an even greater degree than the rest of the state, Maine's seaports participated in the huge out-migration affecting all of northern New England in the wake of the Civil War. That phenomenon was stimulated fundamentally by three factors: the upheaval caused by the war itself, the opening of the West, and the growth of the American city.[187]

The West had long been a subject of fascination to New England's fishermen, as to most Easterners. A Prince Edward Island fisherman who served aboard Yankee schooners in the 1840s noticed the intense interest engendered among his fellow crewmen by the news of the California gold strike: "In 1848 there was a great California fever among the fishermen of the United States, and California was a great deal talked about. Many thought there was no place like California, and it was talked about on board the vessels and in the boarding-houses."[188] Nevertheless, it was not until the post–Civil War years that actual migration to the West became a practical option for large numbers of New Englanders. After 1865, the various homestead acts, the building of the transcontinental railroads, the removal of the Indian menace, and the development of the cattle and sheep ranches of the Great Plains combined to create the stimulus needed for a mass movement.[189]

There seems little doubt that a significant number of Maine fishermen, or at least potential fishermen, took part in the westward population shift. Certainly, it is known that other classes of maritime workers did so. In October 1869, J. B. Coyle, president of the Portland Steam Packet Company, complained to a congressional committee investigating the decline of American shipbuilding that "our best men are drifting to the West," and added that "a great many of them are leaving our seaports, particularly our mechanics, who are the bone and muscle of the country."[190] Others agreed, citing a dramatic migration of both ship carpenters and merchant seamen out of Maine.[191]

Until around 1880, the West continued to draw the bulk of those dissatisfied with life in Maine and the rest of northern New England. At that point increased opportunities in the growing cities of the eastern seaboard, particularly the manufacturing centers of southern New England, began to attract the bulk of the rural workers who no longer cared for the drudgery of farm labor or the dangers and hardships of seafaring. Of particular impact were the changed hiring practices of the factories, which after 1875 began to employ fewer women and more young men.[192] One Maine fishing port affected by the drift to the urban centers was Southport. For generations, this midcoast village had manned its schooners for the most part with native crews, but after 1880 the town's skippers were forced to hire Canadians to replace the local boys who had forsaken the life of the fisherman and gone to the cities of Massachusetts in search of safer and higher-paying jobs.[193]

To one degree or another, Southport's experience became the experience of all Maine fishing ports—and in fact all New England fishing ports—in the post–Civil War period. The industry simply could not survive without periodic infusions of imported labor to replace native workers who had left the fisheries for what they perceived as better futures elsewhere. For the most part, the substitute labor force consisted of Canadians from the Maritime Provinces, who, unlike their American counterparts, were still willing to go to sea in the late nineteenth century. Writing in 1875, the collector of customs for Gloucester District pointed out what their presence meant to his city's economy: "These [Canadian] immigrants make up to a large degree the crews of our fishing vessels, and the loss of life falls primarily upon them. If the loss of life were confined to the native population of the town, Gloucester could not long maintain the fishing business."[194] There were solid economic reasons for the employment of Canadian workers. Their willingness to work for low wages made them a particularly valuable commodity to New England fish merchants anxious to phase out the share system and reduce labor costs (see chapter 7). Nevertheless, the overwhelming number of provincial fishermen in the American fleet after 1865 was due at least in part to the increased reluctance of native New Englanders to undergo the risks and hardships associated with deep-sea fishing.

The Canadians themselves came for a variety of reasons. Some of these were the same motivations that drew Maine fishermen to Gloucester, namely prompt cash settlements after voyages, the opportunity to rise quickly to the command and partial ownership of a vessel, and the desire to escape economic oppression by fishery capitalists at home. Other lures included the superior sea-keeping qualities of American schooners, the better food supplied by Yankee outfitters, and a general lack of employment opportunities in the provinces aggravated by the inability of Maritimers to finance their own vessels.[195] Food appears to have been a prime consideration. This is not surprising, since the fishing schooner became a home away from home, where men lived for weeks on end. Fish and potatoes remained the standard fare on board most Canadian vessels well into the 1870s, long after New England schooners had expanded their menus to include a variety of meats and vegetables.[196] At Lunenburg, Nova Scotia's most advanced port, bankers were stocking essentially the same provisions in 1876 that Castine bankers had carried in 1853, the only difference being a preference for sauerkraut over dried peas among the predominantly German Lunenburgers.[197] Still, despite the comparative attractions of life aboard Yankee schooners, the chance simply to work was likely the chief factor drawing Canadians to American ports. In the words of one Nova Scotian fish merchant, "the employment of so many men on board American fishing vessels is considered a great advantage to our people in a pecuniary point of view."[198]

Whatever their individual motivations, there were an estimated four thousand Canadians serving in the New England fishing fleet by 1880, most of them Nova Scotians, with a heavy sprinkling from Prince Edward Island and Newfoundland. Close to eight hundred of these migrant seamen were scattered throughout the various Maine ports, transforming the labor force in many places.[199] For Maine's fisheries, the presence of so many foreign workers was a relatively new phenomenon. Although Canadians had been coming to Gloucester in significant numbers since about 1830, relatively few had arrived at Maine fishing ports. Half of the crewmen in the New England fleet shortly before the Civil War are thought to have been of Canadian origin, but aside from Eastport and Lubec, nestled close to the New Brunswick border, no Maine port had more than a 10 percent provincial component in its resident fishing work force at that time.[200] The reason was simple. In contrast to Massachusetts (the destination of most migrant Canadians), Maine was essentially a cod-fishing state (see chapter 1), and prior to the repeal of the fishing-bounty law in 1866 no cod-fishing vessel could collect a subsidy without first establishing that its master and three-fourths of its crew were United States citizens.[201] That restriction effectively limited the number of Canadians in the Maine fleet until the last third of the nineteenth century.

This is not to say that no Canadians other than the few living in Maine seaports found their way aboard down-east schooners before 1866. On the contrary, beginning in the late 1830s, vessels (mostly mackerel schooners) from such Maine ports as Castine, Isle au Haut, Vinalhaven, Lubec, East

Machias, Southport, Belfast, and Portland regularly carried small numbers of provincial crewmen, often picking them up in their home ports on the way to the fishing grounds.[202] In these early years, before the labor-shortage problem became acute, Canadian crew members were valued principally for their knowledge of Maritime waters, especially the tricky Gulf of St. Lawrence. The Castine schooner *Minerva*, for example, signed on a Port Daniel, Quebec, fisherman in 1853 specifically for his familiarity with the region around Gaspé and Bonaventure Island, where the vessel intended to fish.[203] In later years the use of Canadian crewmen became less a luxury and more a necessity, as native Mainers departed for Gloucester or deserted the fishing industry altogether. After 1865 Maine schooners that stopped at Maritime ports were in need of whole crews rather than temporary guides. In April 1880 the undermanned *Astoria* of Southport, bound for Western Bank, was obliged to take on six men at Clark's Harbor, Nova Scotia, in order to fill out her normal complement of twelve. Sailing shorthanded and supplementing crews en route in this fashion became standard practice for the Southport cod fleet during the 1880s.[204]

The number of Canadians in Maine's fishing labor force increased dramatically in the post–Civil War period. Between 1860 and 1870 the proportion of foreigners among Portland's resident fishermen rose from 18 to 27 percent, and virtually all of that increase was due to an influx from the Maritime Provinces. This provincial contingent constituted 20 percent of the city's vessel crewmen by 1870, up from 10 percent a decade earlier.[205] Similar increases were evidenced elsewhere in the state. The Canadian component in Eastport's fisheries jumped from 42 percent in 1860 to 60 percent in 1870, and by 1877 the local fishing population was said to be composed almost entirely of "whitewashed Yankees."[206] Toward the end of the 1870s, Bucksport, eastern Maine's premier Grand Banks port, was likewise manning its schooners largely with provincial captains and crews.[207]

The Canadian presence in the Maine fisheries reached its peak around 1880, when close to one-fifth of all the state's vessel fishermen were from the Maritime Provinces.[208] Actions taken thereafter by the Dominion government in Ottawa to subsidize Canada's eastern fisheries began to gradually stem the tide of emigration (see chapter 9). Nevertheless, large numbers of Canadians continued to come, and they tended to be concentrated in those fisheries that native Americans were increasingly reluctant to pursue for reasons of danger and hardship. Many Nova Scotians and other provincials were imported to serve in the mackerel seine fishery, for example, which was characterized by strenuous work and harsh conditions.[209] In 1887 only half of North Haven's deep-sea mackerel fishermen were natives of that town, and several local seining vessels had entire crews composed of Nova Scotians.[210] Similarly, Canadians remained a crucial element in the hard and tedious offshore cod fishery, representing one-quarter of all the crewmen aboard Maine schooners working the Grand and Western Banks in 1889.[211]

Although the steady stream of migrant Canadian fishermen provided sufficient manpower to keep Maine's native industry alive in the 1870s and 1880s, it created a labor situation that was not altogether healthy. The New England fisheries in general had become dependent to a large extent on an outside labor force susceptible to any number of external influences. Gloucester fish merchant Joseph O. Proctor unwittingly highlighted the problem when in 1877 he described Nova Scotia and Newfoundland as the new nurseries for America's fishing industry. Said Proctor, "These countries now raise up our fishermen, and they do not come among us until they are of age."[212]

National origin was of no consequence in cases where alien fishermen became naturalized American citizens. Such individuals could be expected to remain permanently as dependable additions to the work force. However, only a portion of the Maritimers active in the New England fisheries ever took up permanent domicile. Reported the United States Fish Commission in 1880, "A great many fishermen are every year shipped by American vessels in the Provincial seaports, and a considerable proportion of these men, though yearly making up a part of the crews of our fishing fleet, never became residents of the United States."[213]

It is impossible to ascertain with any degree of certainty how many of Maine's Canadian-born fishermen of the post–Civil War period fell into the nonresident category, but for the New England fishing fleet as a whole it was somewhere between one-third and two-thirds of all the provincials serving aboard United States schooners. Most Canadian fishermen themselves reckoned the figure to be at the higher end of that spectrum.[214] On the other hand, the overseer of fisheries at Amherst Harbor in the Magdalen Islands speculated in 1877 that among provincial citizens shipping aboard Yankee vessels in the Gulf of St. Lawrence during the previous twenty-five years, only one-third chose *not* to settle permanently in New England.[215] Perhaps the best estimate can be obtained by examining the Massachusetts state census for 1885, which tabulated both resident and nonresident fishermen by nationality group. This source indicates that 824 of the commonwealth's 1,610 Canadian fishermen (or 51 percent) were nonresidents at that time.[216] It can be logically assumed that the percentage for Maine was similar.

For Massachusetts, the transient nature of the native Canadian work force was troublesome but not critical. Cosmopolitan Gloucester, for instance, could call upon a large pool of other foreign fishermen—Swedes, Portuguese, Irish, French, and the like—who could scarcely commute to their ancestral homes on an annual basis. More than half of Gloucester's foreign-born fishermen were non-Canadians by 1885, and all but a handful of them were permanent residents. The same was true of Provincetown.[217] In contrast, Portland's non-native fishermen were three-fourths Canadian in 1880.[218] Comprehensive industry statistics for both states in 1889 indicate little change. The foreign element in Maine's fisheries was still overwhelmingly (92 percent) Canadian, while Massachusetts' alien fishermen remained a broadly mixed group of predominantly (59 percent) non-Canadian heritage.[219]

The Maine ports did not draw the large numbers of European fishermen who made Gloucester a cultural kaleidoscope as well as a fishing community. Portland, Boothbay, and towns further eastward depended almost entirely on the Maritime Provinces to meet their labor shortfalls after 1865. This was a fatal weakness. Local fishermen could be, and were, replaced in the short run. As the native wellspring of trained manpower backed by generations of experience dried up, Maine's fish merchants were temporarily able to tap a convenient source of foreign labor that was equally skilled in all respects. Nevertheless, the ultimate allegiance of that work force was elsewhere. Many—perhaps most—transient Canadians would remain at home given the opportunity. When that happened, the decline of Maine's fisheries would accelerate. To remain viable, the native industry required either a dependable native work force or a continuing supply of permanent immigrant laborers. By the late nineteenth century it had neither.

Changing Markets in a Changing World

Within the past ten years, consumers have been using fresh instead of salt fish. The salt fish business on this continent is virtually at an end.—James W. Bigelow, fish merchant, 1877[1]

During the twenty years following the Civil War, the Maine sea fisheries were undermined by a multiplicity of adverse developments. The repeal of the fishing bounty, the persistence of high operating costs and periodic low fish prices, the growth of the New Technology and the New Capitalism, as well as the dangers and hardships that attended the enterprise, all coalesced after 1865 to depress the state's native industry, driving most small, marginal operators from the scene. Yet despite these negative factors, Maine's sea fisheries survived into the 1880s, albeit in a reduced and more concentrated form. It was only after 1885 that the down-east fleet experienced total eclipse, shrinking to insignificance in terms of vessels and tonnage.[2] This last stage of decline was produced by fundamental changes in markets and marketing for which a Maine industry that had withstood two decades of smaller disruptions to its economic base had no answer. Foremost among those changes were the arrival of new competitors in the domestic and international marketplace and a revolutionary alteration in the nature of food products and food-consumption patterns.

New Competitors at Home

Not all of the causes contributing to the decline of Maine's deep-sea fisheries were unique to the Pine Tree State. Insofar as Maine's industry was part of a regional economy, it suffered from some of the same problems faced by the New England fisheries as a whole. Among these difficulties was the rapid growth of competing fishing industries elsewhere in the United States after 1865, and especially after 1880.

Rival fisheries developed in essentially three sections of the country: the South, the Great Lakes region, and the Pacific Northwest. The first of these delivered a fatal blow to one of Maine's historically important markets, the states of the former Confederacy. The Civil War had already seriously disrupted the southern fish trade, and the South's creation of a native inshore fishery during the immediate postwar period effectively finished it, eliminating further need for large-scale imports of New England fish products.

In 1865 the coastal fisheries of the Middle Atlantic states were underdeveloped and insignificant, while those of the Gulf states had yet to come into existence.[3] By the late 1870s there was a healthy southern fishery in operation that exploited as many as fifty species of edible food-fish, among them mullet, menhaden, striped bass, bluefish, and snapper. The last-named was a groundfish caught in the Gulf of Mexico and along the Florida coast and marketed extensively not only in the Deep South but also in Cuba, formerly the great market for New England dried fish, where it sold at a "very high price."[4] The snapper (or, more properly, "red snapper") fishery became so economically attractive in the 1880s that it drew a number of New England schooners, including a few from Portland, south for winter fishing out of Pensacola, Florida.[5] Eventually, Pensacola emerged as a major independent fishing port in its own right, with a permanent fleet larger than any in Maine.[6]

The Florida snapper fishery was exceptional in its use of vessels. By far the majority of southern catches were taken with drag nets or seines by men working on shore or in small boats. It was, in fact, the absence of efficient seines that had been primarily responsible for the lack of a viable southern shore fishery prior to 1865.[7] By the 1870s proper apparatus was no longer a problem, and the southern coastal fisheries began to produce catches sufficiently large that native fish were challenging the market position of New England salted products throughout the South and Southwest, undercutting mackerel sales in particular.[8] The strongest competition came from the mullet, a species caught with shore seines along the southern coast from Chesapeake Bay to the tip of Florida and marketed either salted or fresh. The commercial mullet fishery began around 1870 and grew geometrically over the next several years. By 1877 mullet had become the dominant food-fish in Georgia and the Carolinas, displacing imported mackerel and herring. Ease of capture, freshness, taste, and low cost were said to be the key ingredients in its successful takeover of the southern market.[9]

While New England's fish trade in the South was being threatened by the development of the southern coastal fisheries, its exports to the western states were facing serious competition from the rapidly expanding Great Lakes fisheries. The fishing industry on the lakes predated the Civil War by several decades, becoming initially significant during the 1830s in conjunction with the settlement of the Upper Midwest.[10] By 1864 regional demand had resulted in an average annual production of close to 100,000 barrels of pickled products valued at around $500,000, and a report to the secretary of the Treasury claimed that "the lake fisheries are only second to the cod fisheries of the Atlantic coast."[11] Nevertheless, it was not until the 1870s that the great upsurge in lakes fishing began. Between 1872 and 1877 Great Lakes fish production increased over fourfold, from 36 million to 156 million pounds, most of it in whitefish, lake herring, and lake trout. The major outlets were Buffalo, Cleveland, and Chicago, and by the late 1870s the Chicago market alone was absorbing as much fish as the entire lake fishery had produced a decade earlier.[12] Accelerated growth continued until about 1890, when the commercial fisheries of the region, then centered on Lakes Erie and Michigan, reached their peak.[13]

Of special concern to New England's fish merchants was the fact that approximately one-third of the lakes catch was marketed as salt fish and therefore competed directly with their westward shipments of pickled mackerel to Ohio, Indiana, Illinois, Minnesota, and Missouri.[14] A Gloucester packer, queried in 1877 about the slump in sales of salt mackerel during recent years, replied that it was due "in a very large measure to the increase in the catch of our western-lake fisheries."[15] The particular villain was the lake herring, which was said to be pushing mackerel out of the western markets. Lake herring also competed with New England mackerel in the South, where it was shipped in large amounts by midwestern dealers after 1870.[16] The formerly secure southern markets of Maine and Massachusetts were thus subjected to a double-barreled assault during the postwar decades, besieged both by the native fish products of the South itself and by the overflow from the expanding Great Lakes fisheries.

The third fish-producing region competing with New England after 1865 was the Pacific Northwest. There were several Pacific species pursued from ports in northern California, Oregon, Washington, and Alaska beginning in the late 1860s. These included cod, halibut, and salmon, all of which were abundant in the waters north of Puget Sound. The first two were of little significance in the fortunes of New England's deep-sea industry during the nineteenth century. Neither the cod nor the halibut fishery became economically important until about 1890, and both remained quite localized in terms of marketing until after 1900.[17] Their growth was sufficiently slow, in fact, that New England groundfish was actually able to penetrate West Coast markets for a few years following the building of the transcontinental railroads.[18]

The real threat to the New England fisheries from the Far West was that posed by the Pacific salmon fishery, which began to assume importance shortly after 1870. Its development was spurred by the canning process, initiated in northern California during the Civil War.[19] In the late 1870s canneries were opened on Puget Sound in Washington Territory and in Alaska. By 1889 three dozen plants were in operation along the Alaskan coast, and the salmon "pack" there, which had amounted to just 8,000 cases a decade earlier, had reached 500,000 cases.[20]

Pacific salmon quickly gained a foothold in eastern markets. Shipments were being sent from California to Boston by rail as early as the mid-1870s.[21] In 1884 the first through car direct from the West Coast to Maine arrived in Portland with a consignment of canned salmon for J. & H. Dennis, commission merchants of that city.[22] Carload lots of fresh whole salmon began to come east the same year, and within a decade six million pounds of Pacific salmon was being delivered each year to Atlantic Coast markets like New York.[23] By the last quarter of the nineteenth century, then, New England's fish dealers were faced not only with local rivals within their formerly secure southern and midwestern preserves but also with an aggressive transcontinental rival challenging them at their very doorstep.

For the first ten or fifteen years of the post–Civil War period, the new regional fisheries of the South, the Great Lakes, and the Pacific Coast were more annoying obstacles than genuine economic threats to the traditional fish producers of the Northeast. During the decade of the 1880s, however, they began to seriously undermine New England's position as the premier fishing region of the country. Between 1880 and 1890 the New England fisheries ceased growing and experienced the beginnings of a definite, if slow, decline in terms of capital investment, product value, and size of work force. Meanwhile, their regional competitors increased significantly in all those categories. The southern, Great Lakes, and Pacific Coast states nearly doubled their combined product value during the 1880s and (most ominously) quadrupled their combined capital investment, achieving approximate parity with New England. In the process, New England's market share was cut from one-third to one-quarter of national fish production and sales, and its portion of American capital invested in the industry was reduced from more than one-half to slightly over one-third.[24] By the 1890s, the coastal states of New England, once overwhelmingly dominant in the fisheries, were only one of several regional sources of seafood and a declining source at that. Maine, which had once been second only to Massachusetts in the value of its fish products, was now eighth, outpaced by such unlikely producers as Virginia, Maryland, California, and Alaska.[25]

Domestic competition for Maine's traditional sea fisheries arose after 1865 not only outside the state but inside its borders as well. In its annual bulletin for 1890, the United States Fish Commission made the following

observation: "The vessel fisheries of Maine, while of considerable importance, are much less extensive than the shore fisheries, so far as the results of
the industry are concerned. Their specially prominent feature is the large
number of vessels of small size fishing on the shore grounds."[26] That statement accurately defines the evolving character of the Maine fisheries by the
last years of the nineteenth century, but, more than that, it suggests a contributing cause of the decline of the deep-sea branch of the state's native industry. The offshore fisheries were quite simply being abandoned in favor of
inshore fishing closer to home. Industry personnel figures clearly reflected
the transition. From 1880 to 1900 the total number of Maine fishermen remained stable at roughly 8,500. However, the number of shore or boat
fishermen steadily rose during that period, while the manpower in the offshore or vessel fisheries just as steadily dwindled. In 1880 Maine had 3,630
vessel and 4,480 boat fishermen. In 1889, the respective figures were 2,515
and 6,205. By 1898 vessel crewmen totalled only 1,734, while the ranks of
boat fishermen had swelled to 6,770.[27]

The growth of the shore fisheries at the expense of the deep-sea fisheries
may be traced to a number of factors. Shore fishing was less dangerous, less
arduous, and less expensive than deep-water ocean fishing. That was part of
its appeal for those rejecting the sterner virtues or simply lacking capital. In
addition, small-boat fishing permitted the maintenance of a relatively normal home life. Asked why he had switched to shore fishing in the 1870s, a
former Portland vessel crewman replied, "Because I could be home every
night to see my family."[28] Such motivations notwithstanding, the upsurge
in shore fishing could not have been as dramatic as it was had not the en-
deavor also been highly profitable. It was the money-making potential of the
inshore fisheries that was largely responsible for diverting much of Maine's
fishing capital away from traditional pursuits like cod banking and mackerel
hooking after 1865.

The first of the post–Civil War shore fisheries to exert an influence on
the Maine scene was the menhaden or "porgy" fishery. Formerly valuable
only as cod or mackerel bait, the lowly menhaden suddenly became important in its own right as a source of leather-tanning oil and fertilizer. This migratory fish, a non-carnivorous surface feeder that schooled close to shore,
was taken in seines by vessels operating within a mile or two of the coastline. By the mid-1870s its pursuit was considered to be among the most
profitable of all American fisheries.[29]

Although originating in the antebellum period, the porgy fishery reached
its peak during the years 1864–1878, the initial stimulus for its expansion
coming from the wartime demand for fish oil. That demand continued into

the postwar period and was augmented by the discovery that menhaden refuse was an admirable replacement for Peruvian guano as a fertilizer.[30] Between 1866 and 1876, eighteen oil and guano factories were built in Maine, nine of them at Bristol and six around greater Boothbay. By the latter year a total of seventy-two Maine vessels, forty-three of them large steamers,* were in the porgy fishery, and establishments in the mid-coast region were pressing over two million gallons of oil and turning out more than twenty thousand tons of guano. Statewide, the industry occupied 1,129 fishermen and factory hands, and its capital investment approached $1 million in buildings and fishing gear.[31]

The impact of the menhaden craze on the deep-sea fisheries was considerable in certain parts of Maine. Boothbay, which was second only to Bristol as a menhaden center, had much of its capital diverted away from banks fishing after 1865 by the porgy boom.[32] On Swan's Island the temporary upsurge in menhaden prices led to a similar neglect of traditional fisheries, and some island residents who had invested everything in menhaden equipment were nearly bankrupted when the bubble burst in the late 1870s.[33] At Deer Isle the porgy fishery drew sizeable numbers of fishermen away from the cod and mackerel fleet, until overfishing by seining steamers depleted menhaden stocks and terminated the business.[34]

It was this latter effect of the menhaden industry, its drain on available manpower, that most harmed the deep-sea fisheries. Porgy seining had become a favorite occupation of fishermen in the Boothbay region by the late 1870s. According to Luther Maddocks, a spokesman for Maine's organized oil and guano manufacturers, area fishermen were attracted to the steamer fleet by the short trips normally made (one to three days' duration), the suspension of seining in bad weather, and the prompt payoffs resulting from immediate sales of fish to plant operators on shore. These features weighed heavily against the competing cod and mackerel fisheries, where "the hands are obliged to wait until the end of the season for settlements, [and] the service is dangerous and comparatively full of hardships."[35] In 1870, well before porgy seining reached its peak in Maine, one out of every eight Boothbay fishermen was already a member of a menhaden "gang," as the steamer crews were called.[36] To those merchants with no special interest in the deep-sea fisheries, this was a positive development. Said menhaden processor Luther Maddocks of his industry's benefits, "It has secured to young men employment and kept them at home, instead of being driven to other States for occupation, or to sea at poor pay."[37]

*The menhaden fishery was an anomaly among shore fisheries with respect to its use of large vessels. Most inshore activity was carried on in boats of less than twenty tons.

Another shore fishery that kept Maine's fishermen at home in increasing numbers after 1865 was lobstering. The rise of the lobster industry was one of the most far-reaching developments affecting the state's coastal economy in the late nineteenth century. Among the new postwar shore fisheries, lobster catching was easily the most important, occupying more men and producing a larger, more valuable catch than any other.[38] Moreover, it was essentially a product of the last two decades of the century and, as such, impinged directly on Maine's deep-sea fisheries during the final phase of their decline, which began in the mid-1880s.

Lobstering was largely irrelevant in Maine prior to 1880, and its heralded position as a symbol of the state's fisheries is based entirely on its development after that time. Only a half-dozen towns (Harpswell, North Haven, Swan's Island, Deer Isle, Isle au Haut, and Eastport) are known to have had significant lobster fisheries prior to the Civil War, and in 1876 fewer than 200 men were engaged in full-time lobstering statewide.[39] As late as 1880, lobster ranked only sixth in pounds landed and fourth in product value among Maine species, trailing behind cod, herring, mackerel, hake, and haddock in quantity and all but the latter two in dollar value.[40] That quickly changed. Beginning in the early 1880s, the expansion of the lobster fishery was little short of phenomenal. The number of Maine lobster fishermen, which had begun to increase in the late 1870s, grew from 1,843 in 1880 to 2,628 in 1892. By 1898 there were 3,304 hands employed in landing and transporting the catch. The 20 vessels involved in the fishery in 1880—most of them small schooners or sloops of less than ten tons—increased to 130 before the turn of the century. The catch itself, which amounted to fourteen million pounds in 1880, reached twenty-five million in 1889. Its value doubled during that nine-year period from $269,000 to $574,000 and doubled again the following decade, to approximately $1 million.[41] Before the end of the 1880s lobstering was firmly established as Maine's most valuable fishery, surpassing even the historic ground fisheries.[42]

The meteoric rise of lobstering after 1880 was produced by at least three factors. One was the low cost to fishermen engaging in it. The basic equipment (lobster traps) could be made at home, and the fishing craft needed were very small. In 1898 the typical Maine lobster vessel averaged eight tons, carried two or three men, and was worth $475. Some lobstermen, working alone, were able to make do with small two-ton sloops (the famous "Friendship sloops"), and others tended their inshore traps in dories.[43] That sort of minimal capital investment was considerably less than what the offshore cod fisheries required.

A second factor that spurred the growth of lobstering was the development of tourism in Maine. Bar Harbor's first summer colony was founded in 1844, and by the middle of the nineteenth century the former shipbuilding town was already a major tourist center.[44] After the Civil War, numerous other coastal villages turned to summer visitation as an economic sideline. In 1868, for example, Islesboro built its first tourist home, a facility that was enlarged in the 1880s to meet increased demand.[45] With tourism came changing tastes in seafood. The unusual and the exotic—particularly shellfish—replaced the food-fish staples of an earlier era, and in this milieu the lobster fishery thrived. By the turn of the century, hotels and restaurants were absorbing the lion's share of the catch taken by lobstermen at places like Boothbay.[46]

A third reason for the upsurge in lobster fishing after 1880 was the increasingly high price the product commanded. Between 1880 and 1898 the wholesale value of the catch more than quadrupled on a per-pound basis. This drew ever more fishermen into lobstering, despite the fact that actual landings declined somewhat in the 1890s.[47] The price surge was produced by accelerated demand not only in resort centers but in the large urban markets of the eastern seaboard, which became major outlets for Maine lobster when canneries and live pounds made native shellfish available in convenient and appetizing form to vast numbers of out-of-state consumers. Numerous canneries were built along the Maine coast following the Civil War, chiefly by Portland interests. In 1880 there were twenty-three in operation, absorbing two-thirds of the lobster catch and shipping it in processed form to Boston, New York, and other cities.[48] After 1885 lobster pounds gradually replaced canneries, and fresh shipments became the rule, although the markets remained the same.[49]

The losers in the great expansion of lobstering were the traditional sea fisheries. Lobster catching supplanted the cod, mackerel, and herring fisheries at Matinicus, and at Deer Isle it combined with the menhaden and granite industries to siphon off numerous potential deep-water men. By 1880 most Harpswell fishermen were likewise pursuing the lobster fishery, and so were many of Vinalhaven's former vessel crewmen, who found it "more profitable than any other branch of the fisheries of the region."[50] In 1887 the Maine Bureau of Industrial and Labor Statistics interviewed a former deep-sea captain and vessel owner who had recently turned to lobstering. A cod and mackerel fisherman since the 1850s, he had reluctantly concluded after thirty-five years in that business—the last fifteen unrewarding—that lobster catching represented the hope of the future for men like himself.[51] After 1880 that attitude was not unique, and it explains much about what became of Maine's blue-water fishermen in the last years of the nineteenth century.

Although lobstering was the most important of the shore fisheries blossoming in the 1880s, it was not the only one. Of almost equal importance was Maine's eastern herring fishery. Herring catching was nothing new, of course. The pursuit of this species for smoking and pickling purposes, both along the immediate coast and in the Gulf of St. Lawrence, dated back to the first half of the nineteenth century. The last quarter of the century, however, produced a new and distinct herring fishery that owed its creation to the sudden rise of sardine canning in the eastern part of Maine. Largely untapped prior to 1875, this was the Passamaquoddy Bay fishery around Eastport.

The new 'Quoddy pursuit was essentially a weir fishery. That is, fish were captured in brush weirs lining the shores of the bay and transported to area canneries by small sloops called "carryaway boats."[52] The special virtue of the 'Quoddy herring was their small size.* Considered inferior to the larger Maine coast or Magdalen Island varieties for pickling or smoking, they were found to be ideal for canning as sardines. By 1880 these once commercially worthless fish constituted the largest herring catch taken anywhere along the Maine coast.[53]

The Passamaquoddy Bay herring fishery was similar to lobstering in that it could be undertaken with a limited amount of capital. Brush weirs cost only a few hundred dollars in the 1880s and could be serviced by one or two rowing boats using small seines. In 1886, it was possible to get into the business with an outlay of $300 for equipment and a hired crew of two or three men. Large weirs and boats cost more, but rarely was more than $1,000 in capital needed for a fisherman to become the owner and operator of a weir. It was similarly easy to enter the herring-carrying trade. The 'Quoddy sloops that ran fish from the weirs to the canneries were small (usually eighteen to twenty-five feet overall), and they cost on average no more than $300. Some single-handers were built for as little as $125.[54]

The returns to both weir owners and boat operators were attractive compared to earnings in the offshore cod and mackerel fisheries. Weir owners did particularly well in the mid-1880s, when the numerous canneries in the Eastport area competed vigorously for their fish supplies. Gross annual earn-

---

*Although Passamaquoddy Bay was the center of the sardine industry, small herring were also found in lesser amounts as far west as the Penobscot River. In the mid-1880s a handful of canneries were built in Hancock County, mostly around Deer Isle. (Source: U.S.FCB, 1887, 163–64.)

ings in excess of $10,000 were not unheard of at that time.[55] Boat owners, or "smackmen," were also comparatively well paid. By hiring out to the canneries, they could make up to $60 per month for their services and the use of their boats, about twice what a wage-earning banks fisherman could command. Weir fishermen—those hired to tend the weirs and load the carrying boats—earned less, but their average wage of $30 per month plus board was at least equal to the going rate for vessel fishermen.[56] Such positive prospects attracted a considerable number of coastal workers and small entrepreneurs in the 1880s. By 1886 there were 1,110 weir fishermen and 187 boatmen serving Maine's sardine canneries, about half of them Americans from the Eastport-Lubec area and the rest Canadians from the New Brunswick side of Passamaquoddy Bay.[57]

The canneries themselves were another source of alternative employment for eastern Maine's erstwhile sea fishermen. The first sardine cannery was built at Eastport in 1875, and the industry's growth thereafter was rapid. By 1880 there were eighteen canneries in Maine—virtually all of them in the Eastport area—employing 1,896 factory workers and boatmen and capitalized at approximately $400,000.[58] Within less than a decade, the canning industry more than doubled in size. In 1886 there were forty-five plants in operation, over half of them in the Eastport-Lubec region but many in surrounding locales. These employed 4,128 plant workers (a third of them women) and occupied a capital investment of over $1 million.[59] Toward the end of the decade, in 1889, eighteen million pounds of herring were being processed and canned, a threefold increase over 1880. Canned herring accounted for 14 percent of Maine's entire fish production by that time, second only to lobster and far ahead of dried cod and pickled mackerel.[60]

Unlike the menhaden and lobster industries, little of the capital invested in sardine canning was directly diverted from Maine's sea fisheries. The majority of packers were not native businessmen, and most of their capital originated in New York.[61] Nevertheless, the employment opportunities they provided for weir tenders, boatmen, and factory hands drew substantial manpower away from the traditional fisheries. Young men from Eastport, Lubec, and other eastern towns, whose fathers had braved the sea fisheries of Labrador or the Gulf of St. Lawrence, could now stay safely at home and make equal or superior wages working fewer hours in the sardine industry. The canneries thus placed one additional obstacle in the way of the successful prosecution of an offshore industry after 1880. Together with the lobster and menhaden shore fisheries, they undercut Maine's deep-sea activity at home, even as other forces were threatening it from the outside.

The Evolution of American Taste

Among the many reasons for the final decline of Maine's sea fisheries, few were of greater import than the revolution in eating habits that took place in the United States during the course of the nineteenth century. This radical alteration in consumer preferences, which reached its culmination in the period after 1880, drastically changed the nature of the fishing industry and simultaneously shrank its domestic markets.

Until about 1840, codfish and corn were the staples of the New England diet, particularly in rural areas, and cod also enjoyed a prominent place on the menus of the leading public houses in America.[62] Other fish products were popular as well. At midcentury Lorenzo Sabine could write in reference to one of the lesser Atlantic species, "The 'Quoddy pollock is a great favorite everywhere in the interior, and is to be found in almost every farm house of the North."[63]

Most of the fish consumed was salt fish. Dried salted cod, for instance, was standard fare in the lumber camps of eastern interior Maine until at least 1850.[64] It also appeared on the tables of the best homes in New England. Initially, the largest and most select cod were kept for domestic usage as "dun-fish,"* and only the less desirable were exported.[65] Maine fishermen prospered under the aegis of such dietary preferences. In 1852 the state's Bay of Fundy fishery was said to produce "a considerable part of the table or dun-fish which are consumed in the New England states."[66] Although most common in the homes and labor camps of the Yankee Northeast, salt fish could likewise be found in other parts of the country. Touring the United States in 1830, Frances Trollope, celebrated British chronicler of American domestic life, observed the consumption of salt fish in such widely disparate settings as the fashionable town house of a Philadelphia lawyer, the ramshackle dwelling of a poor Maryland farmer, and the public dining room of a Buffalo, New York, hotel. Salt fish with onions, she noted, was a particular culinary favorite.[67]

For a time, then, the national appetite was conveniently in tune with Maine's fishery resources, but the American infatuation with salt fish did not last. A dual change in national eating habits took place toward the middle of the nineteenth century. First, a preference grew for fresh foods at the expense of salted fish and meats. Second, fish itself was challenged as a protein staple by beef and poultry. After 1830 a diet formerly dominated by

---

*Dun-fish was lightly salted cod carefully dried for several extra weeks until reddish-brown in color. It was highly esteemed as a table delicacy, but large, firm fish, able to withstand the evaporative effects of extended curing, were required. (Source: *U.S.FCB, 1898,* 396.)

breads and salted fish and meats began to gradually give way to one emphasizing fresh fish and meats, milk, fruits, and vegetables. This improved regimen slowly gained support during the three decades preceding the Civil War, assisted by diet reformers, the influence of French cuisine, and the growth of cities with consumers who preferred and could afford the change.[68] As early as 1831, the effects were felt even in Maine, where expanding factory towns were demanding vegetables, fresh meat, and other perishables.[69] By the post–Civil War period the trend had become obvious to New England's fish merchants. One, bemoaning the decline of the formerly lucrative salt-mackerel trade, speculated as to its cause: "We cannot sell one-half what we could twenty-five years ago [i.e., 1850]; we cannot find a ready market. I cannot tell the reason for this fact, except that the people . . . are supplied with fresh fish, which they prefer to salt fish, and I don't blame them for it."[70] Another dealer summed up the situation more simply, saying, "People will not eat salt fish when they can get fresh."[71]

While fresh fish was replacing salt fish as a desired commodity, meat was simultaneously replacing fish. The process was slow, however. Up to the Civil War, good meat was a dietary rarity in America, and the meat most commonly eaten was salt pork, an unappetizing dish at best.[72] During the war itself complaints about the Union army's salted meats, particularly its pickled beef, or "salt horse," were rife. The saltiness necessitated soaking the product in water overnight before cooking, and preservation was generally poor.[73] Even in the immediate postwar period, the grade of beef marketed by American producers was less than excellent, according to authorities in the packing business.[74] Against such competition, fish fared well for a time in the marketplace. Nevertheless, the desire for meat, however poor its quality, was such that consumption grew steadily after the 1830s, especially in urban America. In 1833, for example, the average city family devoted 13 percent of its food budget to meat. By 1851 that proportion had increased to 33 percent. Overall, there was a general rise in meat consumption among the nation's working classes from 1840 to 1880.[75] That trend continued into the twentieth century. The use of meat among the American population as a whole increased by 25 percent between 1890 and 1905.[76]

The United States was, in effect, becoming a nation of meat eaters rather than fish eaters. In 1865 it ranked sixteenth out of twenty-two selected countries in per-capita outlays for seafood products,* spending (on aver-

---

*The average annual American expenditure was 25 cents, compared to 88 cents for Canada and 38 cents for all of Europe. The leading individual European fish consumers were Holland (83 cents), Sweden (76 cents), Norway (60 cents), Portugal (43 cents), Denmark (38 cents), Spain (35 cents), Great Britain (32 cents), Greece (30 cents), Belgium (27 cents), and France (26 cents).

age) half what was spent elsewhere in the developed world.[77] Not even the increased availability of fresh fish after the Civil War was able to reverse the predominant dietary inclination. A Boston fish dealer, asked about sales of his products in 1877, affirmed that fresh fish had outstripped the salted variety in the American market but added the significant postscript that "there are seasons in the year, as in winter, when people can get poultry of all kinds and fresh meats, when they do not care much about these [fresh] fish."[78] By the 1930s the decline of fish eating among Americans had reached the point that a Canadian analyst remarked on its unusually low level compared to other nations, including her own. Statistics at that time revealed Norway's annual per capita consumption to be seventy pounds, that of the United Kingdom forty pounds, and that of Canada twenty-one pounds. The United States trailed Canada.[79]

Nowhere was this dietary revolution more dramatically evident than in the very fishing fleets that suffered from it. Initially, most fishermen consumed little, if any, meat. Around 1830, the crews of Provincetown, Massachusetts, schooners had fish at least twice a day. A typical menu included fish chowder for breakfast and fried fish for supper. Gloucester schooners of the time often carried no meat at all, and fish served as the exclusive protein staple. Contemporary Marblehead vessels working the Grand Banks likewise leaned toward a fish diet, relying on halibut prepared various ways for their chief sustenance.[80] The situation was similar in Maine's Boothbay-area fleet, where fish and potatoes three times a day was standard fare aboard ship throughout the 1830s and 1840s.[81] The reliance on fish continued until the Civil War at some Maine ports. When in June 1863 the Southport cod schooner *Archer* was taken by the Confederate raider *Tacony* in the Bay of Fundy, her crew were about to sit down to a dinner of fish chowder and cod tongues. The Confederates, appreciative gourmets, joined the feast.[82]

By the postwar era, the food on most American fishing schooners had undergone a change. The change actually began during the 1850s, when salt pork and beef first found their way aboard in large amounts. Contrasting the provisions stocked by Gloucester's cod bankers in 1855 with those carried earlier in the nineteenth century, Joseph Reynolds commented, "Fishermen in those days ate much more fish on their trips than they do at the present time."[83] By the late 1870s Gloucester schooners always carried meat, either salted or fresh, and market vessels consumed more fresh meat than anything else. Gloucestermen ate little seafood at that time unless other provisions ran low. As a rule, fish was served only once a week, on Fridays, in deference to Catholic crew members. Fried fresh beefsteak was a popular item on board during the first few days out, and when exhausted it was typically replaced with boiled salt beef.[84] Southport bankers of the 1880s favored salt beef and pork, smoked ham, and even salt spareribs.[85] With unintended irony, a Souris, Prince Edward Island, merchant described the eating habits that prevailed after 1870 among American fishermen working in the Gulf of St. Lawrence: "The owners of these vessels have to furnish the men with the best possible kind of provisions; if the men are put on what they call salt provisions, they pretty soon rebel against it. The consequence is that the captains have to look [on Prince Edward Island] for fresh meats and vegetables and all that kind of thing for them."[86] The irony was that those crewmen—typically American in their dietary preferences—shared in the national consumer biases that were reducing the markets for traditional seafood and undermining the very industry in which they made their living.

There were several reasons for the turning away of consumers from fish. In the case of salt fish, the elemental factor of taste was no doubt important. The exposure to fresh foods diminished the public's liking for extremely salty products as time passed, and where domestic salt-fish markets did survive, there was a general trend toward lighter salting and softer drying.[87] The process was gradual, of course, especially in isolated rural areas, which were slow to alter time-honored habits of consumption. Some of the most stubbornly loyal salt-fish devotees were in the fishing districts themselves. A strong regional market for salt cod, pollock, hake, and herring existed in eastern coastal Maine throughout the 1870s, for instance, and was satisfied by local vessels fishing the Bay of Fundy.[88] In 1880 a visitor to Deer Isle noted that "it was the sun-cured salt-fish that was the favorite article of diet in the islanders' households, while very little account was made of the fresh."[89] Outside of coastal Maine, however, the demand was increasingly for fresh fish in the post–Civil War period. In large urban markets, such as Boston and Philadelphia, it was items like fresh haddock, well adapted to boiling or making chowders, that were chiefly sought after 1870.[90] The desire for fresh, rather than preserved, seafood in the cities of the Atlantic seaboard accelerated in the 1880s and 1890s and drastically undercut remaining domestic salt-fish sales.[91] By the twentieth century the market for dried and salted fish had been essentially reduced to the underdeveloped countries of the Southern Hemisphere, where a lack of ice limited the introduction of fresh fish and where a liking for the tangy and potently flavored traditional products persisted.[92]

In addition to changing taste standards, fish was plagued in the national marketplace by evolving social mores. As the nineteenth century wore on, dried and pickled seafood, which had always been the cornerstone of the fishing industry, developed negative connotations. Fish, especially salt fish, was stigmatized as being the poor man's food. It became something to be eaten if necessary and avoided when possible. This attitude was an inevitable outgrowth of one of the economic assets of the product, its relative cheapness. To conspicuous consumers, the more expensive the food, the greater its attraction. Cod, which formerly graced the best tables in America, began to be replaced by alternative main dishes, principally beef and other fresh meats.

The change was already evident by the late antebellum period. When the richest citizen of Providence, Rhode Island, died in 1859, the revelation that he had actually dined on salt cod was considered ample evidence of his eccentricity and proof that, despite his millions, he had "lived poorer than most men."[93] Senator William Seward of New York, discussing the market for dried cod during one of the interminable fishing-bounty debates of the 1850s, characterized its appeal in the following words: "I think it is hardly the aristocracy of society that are concerned in the cheapness of this article. It enters, like tea and coffee, and sugar and salt, into the consumption chiefly of the poor, rather than of the rich."[94] As if to confirm that observation, the bill of fare for an exclusive ball held at Maine's capitol in February 1854, attended by the state's most influential civic leaders, featured virtually no fish. The main courses on that occasion consisted of beef, pork, turkey, chicken, and ham. Aside from a few appetizers and side dishes, the products of Maine's own native industry were nowhere to be found.[95]

The socially restricted consumption of fish products became more pronounced in the post–Civil War period. By the late 1870s the best markets for Maine's Magdalen Islands pickled herring were the poverty-stricken mining districts of Pennsylvania and the immigrant enclaves of the urban Midwest.[96] The same was true by that time for most other traditional food-fishes. From the middle of the nineteenth century onward, the New England fishing industry depended primarily on the urban immigrants, the native-born white working class, and the black masses of the southern United States and the West Indies to consume its products. In an upward-striving, increasingly middle-class nation, which tended to emulate its monied aristocracy in matters of taste and life style, the identification of fish consumption with poverty was sufficient incentive for many to abandon the practice.

The dietary revolution in America was not due entirely to consumer whim, of course. Technology played a major role. The transition to fresh food was considerably eased by the development of the refrigerator, or "ice box," which permitted a more extensive use of perishables. Invented in 1803, the home refrigerator did not attain common usage until the middle 1830s because of the initial high cost of ice, but by 1840 the device was a standard household item.[97] Its introduction led to an upsurge in the use of ice for preserving food in northern American cities beginning in the 1840s. Boston, which had consumed 6,000 tons in 1843, used 85,000 tons in 1860. In New York, ice consumption climbed from 12,000 to 100,000 tons between 1843 and 1856.[98]

Fortunately for the short-term interest of Maine's salt-fishing industry, the transition to home refrigeration was gradual. Early ice boxes were primitive, and technological improvements came slowly until the late 1850s. Many city dwellers continued to depend on pantries or cellars for food preservation throughout the antebellum period and clung to the traditional American diet of salted, smoked, and spiced foods.[99] Nevertheless, the future pattern was clear by the eve of the Civil War. The postwar decades saw rapid advances in the development of the refrigerator. Improved models were introduced in 1868 and 1881. By the 1880s refrigerators were in use in all but the poorest urban homes, and sales of ice to private families rose to an all-time high, accompanied by a corresponding increase in the consumption of fresh meats, poultry, and dairy products.[100]

The importance of taste standards, social conventions, and home refrigeration notwithstanding, the major reason for the decline of fish eating among American consumers was simply the increased availability of fresh, inexpensive meat products, particularly beef, brought about by the rise of the western meat-packing industry. Until the Civil War, the consumption of fresh meats in the cities of the eastern seaboard was strictly limited. The leading cattle-raising areas were in the interior of the country, far from the centers of population. Droving, an expensive and time-consuming process, was the principal means of getting animals to the distant slaughterhouses, located (because of a lack of refrigerated transport) close to retail markets. Inadequate cooling facilities also confined most meat-packing operations to the winter months and severely reduced the distribution of dressed carcasses during the rest of the year. The meat industry was further held back by its decentralized and unorganized nature. Slaughtering and packing were separate operations, stockyards functioned independently of one another, and market communications were inadequate—all of which led to periodic gluts and shortages.[101] This chaotic state of affairs greatly favored the competing New England fishing industry. Unfortunately for the fish dealers, it did not last.

Beginning soon after the close of the war, a series of far-reaching changes revolutionized the American meat industry and corrected its earlier weaknesses. First, the numerous independent stockyards in Chicago were consolidated into one operation in late 1865. Buyers and sellers were thenceforth more easily able to determine supply and demand conditions, and a certain degree of order and efficiency was created in the Chicago market, which quickly made the city the livestock center of the Midwest. The success of this first central "terminal" market led to similar consolidations throughout the region over the next two decades.[102] Simultaneously, the building of the transcontinental railroads connected the reorganized stockyards with the great cattle ranches of the Southwest, and for the first time cattlemen in that part of the country had a dependable outlet for their product. Starting in 1867, Texas beef producers were able to drive their herds to convenient railheads in Kansas and load them aboard Union Pacific cattle cars bound for Chicago and its packing plants. Between 1867 and 1880 over four million head of Texas steers were sent east in this fashion.[103]

Another key postwar development was the invention of the railroad refrigerator car. Before 1860 the refrigerated transport of foodstuffs was largely limited to fish and dairy products, both of which could be easily packed in crushed ice.[104] The movement of fresh meat required a more technically sophisticated approach. The answer was provided by J. B. Southerland of Detroit, who patented the first properly insulated and adequately ventilated refrigerator car in 1867. Four years later, an improved model was used by a Detroit packer to carry the first shipment of western dressed beef east to New York.[105] However, it was left to Gustavus F. Swift of Chicago to fully exploit the new technology. In the late 1870s Swift began building his own refrigerator cars, using the principle of circulated cold air, and undertook the first commercially successful, large-scale shipments of dressed beef to eastern cities. Other packers followed suit, and rail shipments of processed beef grew steadily in volume after 1880, becoming a regular feature of the meat industry.[106] By 1889 there were nearly twenty thousand railroad refrigerator cars in operation in the United States, a quarter of them privately owned by dressed-beef shippers, and firms like Armour & Company of Chicago were marketing $15 million worth of cattle by rail each year.[107]

Hand in hand with the development of refrigerated rail transportation in the fresh-meat industry went the creation of a comprehensive distribution system. Railroads could carry the meat east, but they could not serve as storage facilities or wholesale outlets. To that end, regional distributing agencies or "branch houses" were established. These branch houses, directly owned and operated by the Chicago packers, were essentially refrigerator warehouses that maintained reserves of fresh products on hand to respond immediately to the demands of local retailers.[108] The first such outlet was opened in New York in 1884 by Armour. It was quickly emulated by other dressed-meat distributors, including Swift, and by the end of the decade, the major packers had in place a nationwide network of over five hundred regional facilities.[109]

Through the innovations outlined above, the domestic fresh-meat industry grew dramatically in size, scope, and influence between 1880 and 1900. The number of cattle passing through the four principal Midwest markets (Chicago, Kansas City, Omaha, and St. Louis) rose by 500 percent during those years, while the population of the United States was increasing by only 50 percent. Meanwhile, the fresh processors' share of that expanding production went from less than half to nearly two-thirds.[110] By the turn of the century, the packers, led by Swift and Armour, had annual aggregate sales totalling $700 million.[111] Most importantly, their operations were truly national. Two authorities on the meat industry have described its disparate, yet interconnected, parts as functioning with machine-like efficiency from one end of the continent to the other: "The gears were meshed and synchronized to a system of country livestock dealers and rails; terminals and rails; meat packers and terminals; packers and branch houses; and rail shipments to thousands of retail outlets."[112] The New England fishing industry, which had to compete in the marketplace against that organizational juggernaut, had nothing to compare with its nationwide delivery system and efficient marketing structure.

The fish merchants had only two things in their favor in the economic competition against the fresh-meat packers. One was a certain degree of consumer resistance to western range beef, based on a reluctance to eat meat that had been slaughtered hundreds of miles away and long before reaching retail markets. This bias, encouraged by eastern meat interests, led in the 1880s to hostile legislation in several states limiting the distribution of imported dressed beef, pork, and mutton.[113] Concern among consumers was quickly dissipated, however, by the technique of mass advertising, another innovation of Gustavus Swift, and by 1890 the fear of contaminated meat was no longer a major factor in the marketplace.[114]

Decreased opposition to refrigerated meats left the fish producers with just one competitive edge, the traditional cheapness of their product and its appeal to poorer consumers. It had long been recognized in perceptive fishing-industry circles that low cost was what made dried and pickled fish most attractive to the average worker and his family, and that he would cease buying it "if he can get a pound of fresh beef or mutton for the same price that it cost to furnish his table with salt fish."[115] After 1875 the vast improvements in meat packing and shipping came close to producing that dreaded situation of price parity. Fresh-meat prices never fell quite to the low level of fish prices, but they were reduced significantly through economies effected by the western packers, who were able to use their integrated operations to substantially undercut the prices charged by local slaughterhouses in the East.[116] Simultaneously, changes in preparing and packaging dried fish—primarily the movement toward "boneless cod"*—raised the cost of that most humble of seafoods.[117] Toward the end of the 1880s, the narrowing price gap between meat and fish** combined with aggressive marketing to give western beef a prominent place on the dinner tables of even the laboring classes. There was no question in the mind of Philip D. Armour about who deserved the credit:

> The cattle men of the United States are indebted to the dressed-beef industry . . . for the successful efforts of its promoters in opening up new markets in communities which were not formerly beef consuming. They have established themselves among the artisans and laborers of the East and North, and are today actively engaged in opening new markets throughout the South for the introduction and sale of Western beef. They are making beef more palatable, attractive, and wholesome, by a proper and advanced system of refrigeration . . . and they are distributing this beef throughout the country at the lowest possible charge for the service rendered.[118]

In the face of such aggressive, sophisticated, and highly organized competition, the New England fishing industry could not hope to retain its once preeminent position as protein supplier to the nation. Simple economic survival called for greater operating efficiency, better marketing, and (most important of all) an improved, more saleable product. For sea fishermen, long accustomed to salt banking, that unassailable truth pointed to the absolute necessity of a massive conversion to fresh fishing. Only by marketing their catch in the fresh state could they hope to slow the inroads of the dressed-meat interests and hold on to a portion of the American food market.

The Emergence of the Fresh Fisheries

Among the many reasons for the final decline of Maine's sea fisheries, the rise of fresh fishing in the last third of the nineteenth century stands out

---

*Boneless cod was simply dried salt fish with the bones and skin removed to improve handling and marketing. The final product was ordinarily cut into small pieces and packed in boxes for shipment. The boning process originated between 1868 and 1870, and was refined and perfected over the next two decades. It generally added two dollars per one hundred pounds to the cost of preparation. (Source: *U.S.FCB, 1898*, 400–405.)

**Between 1879 and 1889, the wholesale price of dressed beef in Maine's Portland market fell by more than one-third, while the price of dried cod increased slightly. By the latter year, beef, which had been three to four times more expensive than cod on a per-pound basis, was less than twice as expensive. (Source: *EA,* wholesale prices current, 10 September and 22 October 1879, and 30 August and 16 October 1889.)

above all the rest. It struck at the very core of the state's deep-sea industry. To keep a meaningful share of the domestic fish trade after 1865, Maine's merchants, who had historically keyed their operations to salt fishing, had to adjust to changing dietary preferences and begin marketing fresh products. Their failure to do so in sufficient numbers was largely responsible for the ultimate ruin of the state's sea-fishing economy.

Maine was slow to respond to the demand for fresh fish from the very beginning, and Massachusetts took an early lead in this new branch of the sea fisheries. Bay State interests pioneered in the practical development of the enterprise by introducing the technique of using layered, crushed ice to preserve the dressed catch. In 1838 a Gloucester halibut schooner became the first vessel to carry ice on a voyage.[119] By 1845 icing the catch had become standard practice aboard Gloucester halibut bankers, replacing the older methods of preservation* and converting fresh-halibut fishing from a limited wintertime occupation into a year-round pursuit.[120] Fresh fishing for cod and other species began shortly thereafter, and by 1850, specialized "market schooners" were being designed and built in Massachusetts shipyards specifically to carry ice in the various offshore fisheries.[121] Boston quickly emerged as the center of the fresh-fish trade, marketing the iced catch far beyond the confines of Massachusetts Bay by the middle of the nineteenth century.[122]

The growth of Maine's fresh fishery was agonizingly slow by comparison. The state's first fresh-fish wholesaler, supplied by local shore fishermen, began operations at Portland in 1838.[123] There is no record, however, of fresh fishing of any kind by Maine's large vessels until the mid-1840s. At that juncture, two or three schooners from the Boothbay area began to visit the George's ground for halibut, which they marketed in Portland. These vessels carried no ice and delivered their catch every few days to minimize spoilage, a procedure Gloucester halibuters had initiated fifteen years earlier.[124] Except for isolated ventures of this sort and some small-boat activity, there was little significant fresh fishing carried on from down-east ports prior to the Civil War, and no apparent effort to supply any but the most local markets. As late as 1860 the city of Boston had more fresh-fish dealers than the entire state of Maine. At that time, only one out of eight Maine dealers—nearly half of them located in Portland—were handling fresh products.[125] In 1880 Portland, the center of market fishing in the down-east

---

*Prior to that time, a limited amount of fresh fishing was done by halibut well-smacks, which carried their catch live to market, and by vessels making quick trips during the naturally cold winter months. Winter fishermen depended on low temperatures to retard spoilage of the catch and rarely stayed on the grounds more than a few days.

region, still had only seven fresh-fish establishments, about the same number as twenty years earlier. Boston, which had opened its first wholesale fresh-fish outlet in 1835, had three dozen such firms by then.[126]

The differing character of fisheries development in Maine and Massachusetts can best be seen in catch statistics for the post–Civil War period, when fresh fishing made its greatest strides and assumed a position of major importance in the industry. In 1880, for example, the amount of dried fish produced by Massachusetts fishermen exceeded their fresh-fish production by only a slight margin (163 million pounds to 124 million pounds). Maine's dried-fish production, on the other hand, exceeded its fresh catch nearly threefold (93 million pounds to 37 million pounds). In addition, Maine pickled more fish than it landed fresh, while Massachusetts' fresh catch was more than double the amount pickled. Figures for specific species of fish are equally graphic. Out of 22 million pounds of mackerel caught by American fishermen for the fresh-food market in 1880, Bay State vessels landed 18 million pounds, and down-east vessels only 3 million pounds. Massachusetts landings also far exceeded those of Maine in the fresh-cod fishery (24 million to 4 million pounds) and in the fresh-haddock fishery (21 million to 5 million pounds). In the salt-hake and salt-haddock fisheries, however, Maine outstripped Massachusetts, producing 24 million pounds of cured hake and 10 million pounds of cured haddock to 7 million and 3 million pounds, respectively, for its competitor.[127] Massachusetts was, in short, rapidly evolving into a fresh-fishing state by 1880, while Maine's salt-fish economy remained much as it had been before the Civil War.

Figures for 1889 revealed a continuation of the trend. By then, Massachusetts was a full-fledged fresh-fishing state. Whereas dried or pickled fish had been the leading catch in half of the commonwealth's ten customs districts in 1880, fresh fish was the leading product in seven of those ten districts nine years later. Statewide, Massachusetts fishermen landed substantially more fresh fish than salted in 1889, reversing the situation of a decade earlier.[128] Maine, however, remained essentially a salt-fishing state in 1889. Dried or pickled fish had been the leading catch in all but one of Maine's twelve customs districts in 1880, and nine years later salt fish was still the leading vessel catch in seven of the twelve, including all but one of the districts east of Portland. Statewide, fresh- and salt-fish landings were virtually equal, a parity resulting only from Portland's large fresh catch, which was nearly half the Maine total. Outside of Portland, salted fish were far and away the bulk of the catch, and salt cod remained the dominant product of Maine's vessel fisheries.[129]

The contrasting emphases of the Maine and Massachusetts deep-sea industries were most clearly evident in the specialized employment of their
vessels. By the end of the 1880s, close to 20 percent of the entire Bay State
fleet consisted of large vessels engaged exclusively in fresh-market fishing
for groundfish on the inner Atlantic banks. No more than 3 percent of the
down-east fleet was permanently employed in this work, which typically involved brief trips to George's or Brown's banks on a biweekly basis for iced
cod, haddock, halibut, pollock, and hake. In raw numbers, Massachusetts
had 201 market schooners in 1889—more than the number salt banking on
the Grand and Western banks—while Maine had only 18, a ratio of eleven
to one. Maine merchants still persisted in outfitting three-quarters of their
bankers with salt at that late date.[130]

Not only did Maine's fishing interests continue to process and sell cured
varieties of fish in the fresh-marketing era, they actively lobbied to perpetu-
ate the salt fisheries as well. The most visible effort of this sort took place in
the 1880s, when fresh mackerel began to seriously contest the dominance of
pickled mackerel in the marketplace for the first time.* The catalyst for the
rise of the fresh-mackerel trade was the southern spring fishery, which had
emerged as a leading source of fresh fish for the important New York market during the previous decade.[131]

Innocuous at first, the southern fishery was suddenly perceived as a major threat by salt-fish packers in 1885, when an unusually large catch glutted
the market and forced down prices for all kinds of mackerel, pickled and
fresh alike. The upshot was a campaign, instigated by Maine's fearful salt-
mackerel dealers and fishermen, to obtain a federal ban on springtime
mackerel seining south of New England. In the forefront of the prohibition
movement were Portland's packing merchants, acting through their fishing
exchange, whose initiatives included a formal petition to Congress in December 1885. Maine's salt mackerelmen were joined in their protest by opponents of seining and by fresh fishermen hurt by the supply glut, but the
key argument was a straightforward appeal for protection of the established
trade in pickled mackerel, which contained the bald assertion that the flood
of fresh southern mackerel was unfairly prejudicing consumers against salt
fish by exposing them to a more tasteful product. The mackerel packers won
their case in 1887 and obtained a five-year moratorium on fresh-mackerel
fishing in the spring months, beginning March 1, 1888.[132] It was a Pyrrhic

---

*The fresh-mackerel fishery developed more slowly than the other fresh fisheries. Until 1880,
80 percent or more of the mackerel taken by American fishermen was pickled rather than sold
fresh.

victory, however. Salt-mackerel production continued to decline despite the moratorium, and by the end of the 1890s the pickled catch was a mere fraction of what it had been two decades earlier, accounting for less than half of total mackerel landings.[133]

While Maine fish merchants fought losing battles, those in Massachusetts captured the modern fresh-fishing industry. In 1880 between two-thirds and three-quarters of all the fresh food-fish landed in New England was landed at Bay State ports, most of it at Boston and Gloucester. Boston alone accounted for close to $2 million worth of fresh products, more than half of the New England total.[134] The city's fresh-fish trade grew enormously during the quarter-century following the Civil War. Between 1869 and 1889 its number of dealers specializing in fresh fish nearly tripled, and in the 1880s the amount of fresh fish passing through its wholesale market approximately doubled. By the end of that decade there were three times as many Boston merchants engaged in fresh marketing as in the traditional salt-fish business.[135] This phenomenal expansion was greatly enhanced in 1884 by the opening of the celebrated "T" Wharf, a $5 million facility containing a three-story commercial block that could accommodate most of the city's fresh-fish dealers and service literally hundreds of vessels in one centralized location. It gave lease-holding merchants a tremendous advantage over their competitors and converted Boston's regional leadership of the fresh-seafood industry into a virtual monopoly.[136]

Among the Maine fishing ports, only Portland developed a fresh fishery viable enough (for a time) to contest Boston and Gloucester. Slightly over eight million pounds of fresh products were landed at Portland in 1880, about a fifth of the total fish processed in the city. Of that fresh catch, almost all was marketed directly as food-fish rather than being diverted for canning or industrial uses, as was the case with much of Maine's fresh production. Moreover, Portland's fresh landings consisted primarily of cod, haddock, and other popular groundfish, thus placing the city in direct competition with the fresh-fish dealers of Massachusetts. That competition extended to markets as well as products. Fully one-half of Portland's fresh fish was sold in the cities of the Northeast, including Boston, while the remainder went north to consumers in central Canada.[137]

Portland became Maine's fresh-fishing center for essentially two reasons. One was geography. As the state's southernmost major fishing port, it was closer than any other to the northeastern urban centers that accounted for the lion's share of fresh-fish consumption in the post–Civil War period. Within an in-state context, furthermore, the city was admirably located to tap the growing urban-immigrant market of Maine itself. That local market more than doubled in size between 1855 and 1889, because of an influx of Irish and French-Canadian immigrants.[138] Of special importance to Portland's fishing industry was the fact that most of those newcomers were drawn to the southwestern corner of the state, within easy reach of the city's fresh-fish distributors. The Irish settled in Portland itself, making it Maine's largest Catholic enclave by 1875.[139] Five years later, the combined first- and second-generation Irish-American population of Portland was over nine thousand and amounted to 27 percent of the city's entire populace.[140] The Gaelic influence in Maine's largest metropolitan area was more than equalled in nearby textile centers like Lewiston, Saco, and Biddeford by French-Canadian arrivals, who, together with their American-born children, numbered close to forty thousand in 1890 and constituted the single largest ethnic minority in the state.[141]

Portland's strategic location relative to Maine's Catholic immigrant population benefitted the city's market fishery in the short run, but geographic proximity to the best markets for unsalted fish, both in-state and out, was only one reason for its relative success at fresh fishing compared to other down-east ports. A far more important factor was its access to rail service (see map 1). Portland was initially established as a railroad terminus in 1842, through the building of Maine's first major line, the Portland, Saco & Portsmouth Railroad. The long-range effect of that pioneering transportation development upon the city was made clear in a report of the Maine Railroad Commission some thirty years later: "The road was opened for travel in 1842, and since that time has been distinguished as being the only line of rail communication from Maine to Boston, securing upon its single track, not only the local business incident to its location but the accumulated traffic of all the railroads running north and east of Portland, and centering at that city."[142] Within a decade of its construction, the P.S.& P. line was joined by the Atlantic & St. Lawrence (or "Grand Trunk") Railroad, which connected Portland to Montreal in 1853 and gave Maine's port city access to points as far west as Detroit. In the interim, local feeder routes were constructed, and by the eve of the Civil War five different state rail systems were coming together at Portland, making it Maine's sole rail center.[143] It was this rail network, expanded in the 1870s to include connector lines to southern New Hampshire and upper New York State,[144] that stimulated the growth of Portland's fresh fishery and established the city as the leading down-east distributor of unsalted seafoods.

The crucial importance of railroads for the swift distribution of perishable fresh fish to inland markets lacking water transportation was recognized as early as 1852.[145] In Portland's case, it was the "Grand Trunk" Railroad to

Montreal that facilitated the city's first tentative shipments of iced fish to an outside market, sometime prior to the Civil War.[146] By the 1880s the greatly expanded American rail network was being acknowledged as the very foundation of the fresh-market fishery. Commenting in 1884, the *Mining and Industrial Journal* observed:

> The fresh-fish business in its present magnitude is of comparatively recent date, and is the outgrowth of the modern railway and express system. . . . With the extension of the railroad system, and the use of ice in transportation, fish caught not only in Massachusetts Bay, but on the shores of the Gulf of St. Lawrence and as far away as the coast of Greenland . . . are sold fresh on the other side of the Mississippi.[147]

Fish merchants agreed that it was the expansion of rail service combined with refrigeration that made possible the dramatic shift away from domestic salt-fish consumption following the Civil War.[148]

The close interconnection between the growth of railroads and the development of a fresh-fishing industry was exemplified by Massachusetts. Boston, which became the center of the Bay State's market fishery, was also the hub of its railroad system. The first shipments of fresh fish beyond the Massachusetts tidewater were sent out by rail in 1837, no more than three years after the commonwealth's first lines were extended into the interior. In 1842 Bostonians obtained a trans-sectional rail connection as far west as Albany, and within a year or two they were delivering iced fish to customers in upstate New York.[149] A decade later, in 1852, Boston merchants became the first New Englanders to ship fresh fish to the Midwest, sending consignments of iced cod and haddock by rail to Chicago. Again, the venture followed directly on the heels of Boston's successful completion of its railroads* to the West in 1851.[150]

By the end of the antebellum period, Boston was the uncontested rail center for New England, just as Portland was for the state of Maine. Ten rail lines, twice as many as gathered anywhere else in the region, radiated out in all directions from the Massachusetts capital.[151] The existence of that network became a significant advantage in the late 1870s, when the introduction of refrigerator cars began to permit the unlimited shipment of fresh fish to far-flung interior markets without the restraints previously imposed by melting crushed ice.[152] Toward the middle of the following decade, Boston was supplying retailers throughout the Mississippi Valley and be-

---

*Fresh fishing at other Massachusetts ports was likewise tied to railroads. Gloucester's entry into fresh-fish marketing, for instance, coincided almost exactly with the arrival of the town's first railroad in 1846. (Source: Morison, *Maritime History of Massachusetts*, 309.)

yond, and had solidified its hold on most of the principal markets within a six hundred–mile radius of its fish wharves, including the cities of New York, Philadelphia, and Baltimore.[153] Rail facilities enabled Boston's wholesale distributors to market a regional catch whose value was five times that of the catch landed by their own local fishermen, and in 1889 they were able to dispose of $3.2 million worth of fresh products to customers all over the United States, realizing an enviable profit of 20 percent—considerably above the contemporary return on salt fish.[154]

Fish merchants at other places were less fortunate. Among Maine's fishing ports, only the city of Portland developed efficient rail connections with the rest of the nation. More common was the transportation network of Castine, antebellum center of the sea fisheries in the eastern part of the state. Castine had no railroad at all, and to say that it lacked adequate land communications with the outside world would be a gross understatement. George L. Wasson described the town's inaccessibility in words given a hard edge by personal experience: "In winter the roads were often blocked by heavy snow; the clay soil of the region produced deep, sticky mud until late in the season, and on long, steep hills, seldom to be equalled, protruding ledges of granite that must be climbed at intervals. No wonder that the Castine road was known as the worst among the many poor ones in the vicinity, and that steamboats took the bulk of travel in all directions when ice did not prevent."[155]

Water-borne commerce was, indeed, the only answer for places like Castine and remained so for most of the nineteenth century. Before the Civil War, the major transportation to and from coastal towns east of Portland was by steamboats that connected with the Portland, Saco & Portsmouth Railroad.[156] By 1860 much of the Maine coast was linked to Boston or Portland by steamboat lines, but these lines were an inadequate transportation basis for the successful prosecution of an eastern fresh-fishing industry. Early steamboat enterprise (circa 1840–1860) was characterized by numerous grand openings followed by ignominious closings. When steamer lines did survive, they tended to run to and from the major river ports on the Kennebec and Penobscot, not to relatively obscure fishing ports. Timetables and sailings were capricious, and regular daily departures could not be relied upon.[157] As late as 1880 a triweekly ferry service remained the only link between the Mount Desert Island area and Maine's easternmost railhead at Rockland.[158] Added to these difficulties were the obvious problems related to refrigeration and the transfer of delicate cargoes from coastal steamers to rail cars for shipment into the interior. Faced with such an uncertain means of marketing fresh products, Maine fishermen lacking direct access to a railroad really had only one practical option. That was to remain in the salt-fishing business, which placed no premium on speed and permitted leisurely deliveries under sail.

The decision to ignore the fresh fisheries was made, for the most part, out of sheer necessity. Rail development in Maine was painfully slow. Until the late 1840s, the Portland-to-Boston line was the state's only railroad. By the eve of the Civil War only 472 miles of track had been laid statewide, giving Maine fewer than any state in New England except tiny Rhode Island and no more than 13 percent of the total for the entire region. Construction accelerated somewhat in the postwar period, but Maine remained far behind Massachusetts in the extent of its rail system, acquiring only half as much mileage as the Bay State through the 1880s.[159]

Of particular import to the fishing industry was the location of those few miles of railway. Writing with overly abundant enthusiasm about the extent of Maine's rail network in 1860, Austin J. Coolidge proclaimed that "there are upwards of four hundred miles of track in operation, at a cost of from $15,000,000 to $20,000,000, penetrating all parts of the state west of the Penobscot."[160] Left unsaid was the fact that the overwhelming bulk of Maine's fishing tonnage was *east* of the Penobscot at that time.[161] The first rail line to reach beyond the Penobscot River was the European & North American Railroad from Bangor to Saint John, New Brunswick, completed in 1871, and it did not approach the coastal region.[162] Track spanned the continental United States before it pushed into some parts of eastern Maine.

Penetration of the Maine coast by railroads proceeded even more slowly than rail development in the state as a whole. The Kennebec & Portland Railroad was extended from Yarmouth to Bath in 1849, giving rail service to most ports west of the Kennebec River, but the laying of track beyond that point was delayed until after the Civil War.* The Knox & Lincoln Railroad from Bath to Rockland was not chartered until 1864, and its last spikes were not driven before 1872. Farther east, coastal Hancock County had to wait until 1884 and the opening of the Shore Line route from Bangor to Mount Desert Island for a rail outlet. Washington County obtained no coastal railroad until 1899, and parts of the lower Penobscot Bay region have never seen rail service to this day.[163]

Compounding the late arrival of the coastal railroads was their distress-

---

*In 1857 the Maine coastal villages east of the Kennebec River, including the vast majority of the state's sea-fishing ports, still had no rail facilities. In contrast, all of the major fishing centers of northeastern Massachusetts—Boston, Gloucester, Marblehead, Beverly, and Newburyport—were situated directly on rail lines at that time. (Source: Geer, 2–68, 136, 137, 155, 164, 169.)

ing tendency to bypass major fishing towns (see map 1). The coastal lines from Portland to Rockland, for instance, did not touch any of the important fishing ports of western Maine in the postwar period, including those in the Boothbay area, which were located several miles from the nearest rail station. Virtually all of the fishing ports west of Rockland suffered by virtue of being located on peninsulas. Seeking the straightest possible route, rail engineers avoided the jutting headlands of the mid-coast region entirely.[164]

The problem for ports east of Rockland was even more severe. Their closest postwar rail connections were at Rockland, the terminus of the Knox & Lincoln Railroad, and at Belfast and Bucksport, where branch lines were built inland in the 1870s to join trunk roads running through the center of Maine.[165] Important Penobscot Bay fishing towns like Camden, Vinalhaven, Castine, and Deer Isle were anywhere from ten to twenty miles by land or water to any of these three potential shipping points.[166] For those eastern ports situated beyond Penobscot Bay, the outer limit of Maine's coastal rail development in the age of the sea fisheries, the use of railroads was not even a remote possibility.

The stunted rail development of the down-east coast can largely be explained in one word: geography. Natural barriers created by Maine's rocky, indented shoreline slowed or halted railroad construction everywhere along the seaboard east of the Kennebec River. At least one proposed coastal route—from Bangor to Calais by way of the eastern shore—was abandoned in the 1850s as being too precipitous. Others were built, but with great difficulty. When the Knox & Lincoln Railroad was finally completed in 1872, it had just one straight stretch as much as a mile long.[167] A contemporary writer described its circuitous route as a veritable obstacle course: "The route of the Knox and Lincoln Railroad is very nearly at right angles to the line of the numerous water-courses over which it passes, and the cost of the road was necessarily heavy. At one point there is for several miles an almost unbroken succession, one after the other, of rock cuts, trestle-works, drawbridges, and high embankments."[168] There were problems even after the road was in operation. The Maine Railroad Commissioners' report of 1872 noted the inconvenience caused by snow blocking the tracks and holding up trains the previous winter. The report of the following year mentioned the difficulty of keeping the new road's many bridges in repair.[169] Given the nature of the terrain, the prospect of extending tracks beyond Rockland proved so discouraging that the Knox & Lincoln became the last significant segment of Maine's coastal rail system to be built for a quarter of a century.

There seems little doubt that lack of railroads, combined with distance from the major markets, was the outstanding reason for the absence of fresh fishing in Maine east of Portland. Catch statistics for 1880 indicate an exact correlation between the availability of rail connections and the extent of fresh-market fishing in each Maine customs district. In the four western-most districts of Portland-Falmouth, Saco, Kennebunk, and York, all of which had direct access to a coastal railway, the bulk of fresh fish landed was marketed for food. In seven of the eight more easterly districts, all of them having limited or nonexistent rail service, only a very small percentage of the fresh catch was sold for food; instead, it was purchased for bait by banks fishermen or used for industrial purposes. The sole exception to this pattern was Passamaquoddy District, which processed its fresh catch (herring) in regional canneries.[170] It was no accident that in 1889 the leading Maine county for fresh cod (3 million of the state's 3.7 million–pound vessel catch) was Cumberland, home of the state's rail center at Portland, while the leading county for salt cod (5 million of the 10 million pounds landed) was Hancock, almost totally lacking in rail facilities. Fresh food-fish constituted roughly half of the total vessel catch that year in the three western costal counties possessing full rail connections, one-quarter to one-third of the catch in the two mid-coast counties enjoying partial rail service, and almost none of the catch in coastal Maine's three rail-starved eastern counties.[171]

Among all of Maine's fishing ports, only the city of Portland truly prospered in the post–Civil War fresh-fisheries economy. Nevertheless, even Portland was in decline by the late 1880s and 1890s.[172] There were several reasons. As discussed previously (in chapter 8), Portland was a reluctant participant in the fresh winter fisheries. While rival ports like Gloucester were busy throughout the year, Maine's fresh-fishing center observed a spring-fall season for the most part, neglecting the offshore banks between November and March and falling behind as a year-round marketer.

More debilitating than its lack of a strong winter fishery was Portland's decentralized industry-support system. The most successful of the North American fishing ports, such as Gloucester and Lunenburg, Nova Scotia, were those in which all aspects of the fishing business were concentrated in one location. Economically and logistically, it was helpful to have outfitting supplies and equipment produced locally and to have vessel building and repairing done in the immediate vicinity. Costs tended to be lower, and related industries reinforced one another. Of Maine's fishing ports, only Boothbay approached the efficiency ideal of a one-industry town, but Boothbay had other problems—notably, the lack of a railroad—that prevented the realization of its potential.

Portland, which did have rail connections, lacked local supporting industries; it was not self-contained. In 1880 the city's fish merchants obtained their lines and trawls from Castine, their cordage and nets from Plymouth and Boston, their seine boats from Gloucester, and their dories from Newburyport, Salisbury, Gloucester, and Harpswell.[173] The same year, Portland's fish barrels (a critical item for a mackerel port) came from suppliers in such diverse regional locales as Bangor, Winterport, Camden, Bucksport, Milbridge, and Plymouth.[174] Portland was also lacking in specialized construction facilities for its vessels. While Gloucester, Lunenburg, and even Boothbay built and repaired their own fishing schooners—Essex, the schooner-building center of Massachusetts, was virtually a Gloucester suburb—Portland relied on shipyards at Bath, Kennebunkport, and East Boothbay, roughly thirty to forty miles away by water. Builders in those three places turned out virtually all of the large, new schooners constructed for Portland owners in the 1880s.[175]

In addition to its dependence on outside sources of supply, Portland had inherent weaknesses as a fish-distribution center. Unlike Boston and Gloucester, both of which marketed their fish direct to retail markets, Portland was primarily an indirect marketer. All of the city's dried cod, for instance, was sold to large dealers in Boston and New York for export to the West Indies or resale to buyers in the southern and western United States. Similarly, all of Portland's dried hake and most of its pickled mackerel and herring were also marketed through Boston and New York, and a large part of the city's fresh catch was delivered to Boston wholesalers as well.[176] This absence of independent marketing led investigators of the New England fishing industry to conclude in 1890 that, Portland notwithstanding, "Maine has . . . no very important trade center for fishing products."[177]

Portland did acquire some direct markets of its own in the post–Civil War period, but those outlets were insufficient to build and sustain a strong, independent marketing structure for its fresh fishery. Rail systems dictated the nature of fresh-fish markets, and Portland's railroads simply went to the wrong places. While tracks fanned out in westerly and southerly directions from Boston and Gloucester toward the population centers of the United States, Portland's rails ran mostly north and east, away from the large markets. Aside from the city's southern feeder line to Boston, which only reinforced its satellite status, Portland's out-of-state railroads were the Grand Trunk via rural Quebec to Montreal, the Portland & Ogdensburg to upstate New York by way of northern New Hampshire and Vermont, and the Portland & Rochester through southern New Hampshire to central Massachusetts. Except for the Montreal connection, these routes limited Portland's merchants to a handful of relatively small northern markets: Sherbrooke, Quebec; St. Johnsbury, Vermont; Ogdensburg, New York; and Rochester and Nashua, New Hampshire.[178] As a result, during the postwar period more than half of the city's fresh fish was sold to buyers in Quebec Province or in interior sections of New York State and northern New England.[179]

Unfortunately, these were not markets of sufficient growth potential to enable Portland's fresh-fish merchants to expand their fishery on anything like the scale market fishing was expanding at ports in Massachusetts. The city's northward-trending rail lines, initially visualized as indirect routes to the West, had difficulty establishing through connections and never lived up to their promise.[180] Effectively confined to a small corner of the northeast marketing sector by its stymied and ill-conceived rail system, Portland stagnated as a seafood distribution center. Maine's premier fresh-fishing port was barely able to hold its own through the 1880s, processing approximately the same amount of fresh cod and haddock in 1889 as in 1880, for instance, while Gloucester was increasing its production in those same species by almost 50 percent.[181]

Developments in Massachusetts reinforced Portland's decline. Gloucester and Boston gradually achieved an efficient division of labor in the fresh fisheries. Gloucester, though a direct distributor, was primarily a fresh-fishing port; Boston, though maintaining a fishing fleet, was essentially a distribution center, supplied in large part by Gloucester's market schooners. Each complemented the other, and both were superior to Portland in financing, transportation facilities, and location vis-à-vis domestic markets and major fresh-fishing grounds. Portland, attempting to combine both fishing and distribution, was less strategically situated and comparatively lacking in transportation outlets and capital. She was simply squeezed out by her rivals. After 1890 New England did not really need three major fresh-fishing ports. In the long run, the weakest of the three was eliminated from serious contention, and with its downfall, the fresh fisheries of Maine ceased to be important.

Rising Star in the North

While Maine's limited fresh sea fisheries were being undermined by the combination of an inferior rail system and competition from Massachusetts ports to the south, the state's traditional salt fisheries were being pressured from the north. Canadian influence upon the American sea fisheries has always been acknowledged, but has generally been considered from the point of view of international politics and diplomacy. Economic factors and internal Canadian developments have been relatively neglected.

Undoubtedly, various treaties with British North America figured in the general overall health of the sea fisheries of the United States and, by extension, those of Maine. Anti–free traders of the nineteenth century considered the Washington Treaty of 1871 to be the Devil's own work in this regard. Its admission of duty-free Canadian fish to the American market was suggested by some as the sole reason for the decline of the New England fisheries,[182] and when the treaty came up for renewal in 1885, Portland's fish dealers were among those who actively campaigned against it as a source of unfair competition for the domestic industry.[183]

Canadian competition did, indeed, have a bearing on the decline of the Maine sea fisheries, but not as a result of international treaties establishing free trade. The initial post–Civil War decline of the state's deep-sea fisheries took place before the Treaty of Washington was implemented in 1873, and the second stage of that decline process began after the treaty was revoked in 1885.[184] Imported Canadian fish did not hurt the Maine industry in the years following 1865. In that respect, the fears of the state's fish dealers were unfounded. However, Maine's merchants and fishermen *were* faced after 1865—1867 to be precise—with the challenge of a rising new nation to the north, whose Atlantic fishermen were interested in the same products and many of the same external markets as they, themselves. The result was a naturally competitive situation that did not depend on diplomatic reciprocity for its lifeblood. It was a competition in which Maine fared badly.

The Maine ports east of the fresh-fishing center of Portland were the ones most adversely affected by the rise of the Canadian fisheries, particularly the flowering of the deep-sea industry of Nova Scotia. Like Maine, the Maritime Provinces were slow to build railroads. At the time of Confederation (1867), Nova Scotia had just 145 miles of track and no lines at all leading out of the province.[185] Most Nova Scotian ports were not integrated into a rail network until the 1890s, and as a result commercial fresh fishing was unimportant to their economies until the early twentieth century.[186] Instead, Nova Scotia's fishermen emulated their eastern Maine neighbors by cultivating the salt fisheries, with special attention to cod fishing.

Writing in 1893, an authority on the Canadian industry proclaimed that "of all the deep-sea fisheries of Canada, the most important is the cod fishery, which furnishes employment to thousands of men and contributes most largely to our exportation trade."[187] That had always been the case. In 1883 the value of the Canadian cod catch was $6.6 million, compared to just $2.1 million and $1.3 million, respectively, for the Dominion's herring and mackerel catches. Furthermore, most of that cod (two-thirds) was landed in the one province of Nova Scotia.[188] Nova Scotians were as fully devoted to salt-cod fishing in the latter third of the nineteenth century as Mainers had been in earlier years. More than half of their fishing revenue was said to have come from that fishery in 1867, and the proportion fell only slightly during ensuing decades. In 1885 over 40 percent of the province's catch value was still derived from salted cod.[189]

Nova Scotia's singleminded concentration on cod banking, initially a minor concern to Maine, became a major threat to the state's deep-sea industry after 1865 because of the sudden and phenomenal expansion of the Canadian fisheries. In 1883 George Brown Goode of the United States Fish Commission expressed amazement at the "immense" growth of the Canadian fishing industry over the preceding decade.[190] He had reason to be impressed. The market value of eastern Canada's fish products, a modest $6.6 million in 1870, increased to $18.7 million in 1886. In 1869, two years after Confederation, the region's cod catch was just 154 million pounds. Annual increases thereafter brought the total to 328 million pounds by 1880.[191] Nova Scotia, the salt-cod specialist, was in the forefront of that expansion. The value of the province's fisheries doubled between 1870 and 1885, and its dried-cod production increased yearly from 1869 to 1888, reaching a peak just as Maine's fisheries were entering the final phase of their decline.[192] By the 1870s Nova Scotia's presence on the cod banks of the North Atlantic was already drawing the concerned attention of New England's fish merchants. Testifying before the Halifax Commission in 1877, Gloucester vessel owner Charles H. Pew told his provincial hosts, "We go to the Grand Banks, and you now fit out vessels to go there; and to all the places where our fishermen go, yours also go."[193]

The impact of Canadian competition was most keenly felt by eastern Maine, whose cod fishermen had exercised a near American monopoly on the Grand Banks prior to the Civil War. In 1848, well before it attained its antebellum peak, the single eastern Maine district of Penobscot claimed a cod-fishing fleet of 235 vessels. That was far more than any individual district in Nova Scotia had three years later (186) and nearly one-third the number (812) in the province's entire fishing fleet. Overall, Nova Scotia's fisheries recorded just 43,333 vessel tons in 1851 compared to Maine's 51,092 tons, most of which was owned in Penobscot and other eastern districts.[194] A decade later, on the eve of the Civil War, Maine still retained numerical superiority, employing half again as many schooners in cod banking as Nova Scotia, an overwhelming majority of them hailing from ports in the eastern part of the state.[195]

Within a generation, however, a complete transformation had taken place. By 1880 Nova Scotia fishermen were operating over twice as many vessels as their Maine counterparts and landing nearly four times as much salt cod, while the single provincial county of Lunenburg was outfitting as many bankers as all of eastern Maine combined.[196] Lunenburg's fleet, which first ventured to the Grand Banks in 1873, was there in force a decade later. In the mid-1880s it numbered approximately eighty large schooners and produced an annual banks catch of roughly 130,000 quintals dried. Meanwhile, the once-proud banks fleet of Hancock County, which encompassed Penobscot District and remained the core of Maine's dwindling salt-cod fishery, had been reduced to just thirty-six schooners with an estimated annual catch of 60,000 quintals.[197] Ten years later, Maine's entire Grand and Western banks contingent amounted to fewer than a dozen vessels, and the state was no longer even a minor factor on the offshore cod grounds.[198]

Nova Scotia displaced Maine on the Grand and other Atlantic banks for several reasons. One was its ability to capture the major West Indies markets for dried cod. Commerce with the Indies, whether direct or by way of Boston and New York, had always been an important outlet for Maine's dried-fish catch. It was potentially more so after the Civil War, as inroads by the fresh fisheries reduced the domestic salt-cod market to relative insignificance. By that time, however, the gradual Canadian takeover of the West Indies fish trade, which had begun to attract notice around the middle of the nineteenth century,[199] was a virtual fait accompli. At the close of the war, Nova Scotia's dried-fish exports to the Caribbean already far surpassed American exports to the region, exceeding them by threefold in the late 1860s.[200] The disparity grew in succeeding years. By the late 1870s and early 1880s, the port of Halifax by itself was exporting more than twice as much dried fish to the West Indies as the entire United States.[201]

Canadian cod benefitted from being much harder and more thoroughly sun-dried than its American counterpart, a significant advantage in tropical markets. This characteristic was in part a function of deliberately longer drying by Maritime fishermen, but it also resulted from eastern Canada's proximity to the cod banks, which permitted drying to begin sooner, before the debilitating effects of prolonged salting on board vessels* took place.[202] The end result was a vastly superior product for the Caribbean market. In addition to its keeping qualities, Canadian cod also tended to be cheaper than other varieties. By the immediate post–Civil War era, Nova Scotian dried fish averaged approximately a dollar less per quintal in world markets than its New England counterpart. Lingering wartime inflation in the United States, which had priced American fish almost twice as high as

---

*Heavily salted New England cod, which lay in the holds of vessels so long that it would not later dry thoroughly, was called "salt-burned" cod. It contained twice as much moisture as Canadian cod, an advantage in domestic markets, but it was not well adapted to the peculiar needs of West Indies buyers, who required a product with extra keeping qualities.

the competing product in the last year of the conflict, was certainly a contributing factor. Provincial salt cod, more expensive than American salt cod
in Cuban markets during the 1850s, sold there at substantially lower prices
over the following two decades.[203] The combination of better quality and
reduced price* was unbeatable in the long run, and toward the end of the
1890s American observers of the cod-fishing industry were forced to con-
cede that "the West India trade is almost monopolized by shipments from
Canada."[204]

From the point of view of Maine's cod fishery, the worst aspect of increased Canadian competition in the Caribbean export market was that it
was not limited, as might be expected, to the islands of the British West
Indies. Instead, it increasingly focused directly on those markets Mainers
and other New Englanders had long assumed to be their own. The Canadian provinces were British colonies, to be sure, and as such had easier access to the Crown's Caribbean sugar islands than did New England, whose
nineteenth-century Indies trade revolved around the Spanish islands (see
chapter 4). For a considerable time, therefore, the gravitational pull on
Canada's fish trade was in the direction of Jamaica, Barbados, and Trinidad.
In 1851, for example, 96 percent of all dried-fish exports from the port of
Halifax went to the West Indies, and three-quarters of those shipments
were sent to British possessions in the region.[205]

Nevertheless, some Canadian fish had always found its way to Spanish
and other "foreign" Caribbean markets. Havana was already an occasional
entrepôt for salt-cod shipments from Nova Scotia in the 1830s, and within
two decades the province's dried-fish exporters had achieved a rough quantitative parity with their American competitors in the Spanish West Indies.[206] Together with Norway and Newfoundland, Nova Scotia began to
challenge American dominance in the Cuban market, in particular, around
midcentury. Cargoes from United States ports, which had accounted for almost all of the dried cod entering Cuba in 1846, provided less than half of
the total ten years later.[207] In the 1860s Nova Scotia's dried-fish exports to
Cuba, Puerto Rico, and Santo Domingo rose to 100,000 quintals per an-
num—four to five times American shipments to those islands—and in the
1870s the figure doubled to 200,000 quintals—or about 40 percent of the

---

*These cheaper exports were made possible, at least in part, by the substantially lower re-
turns Canadian fishermen received for their catch, which wholesaled for about a dollar per
quintal (or roughly 25 percent) less than American cod during the late 1870s and early 1880s.
(Sources: *LP*, news items, 2 September 1879, 4 October 1881, and 3 October 1883; *EA*, wholesale prices current, 10 September 1879, 27 September 1881, and 25 September 1883; Procter,
Fishermen's Own Book, 19.)

province's total annual exports to the Caribbean.[208] Toward the end of the latter decade the Spanish islands, formerly the preserve of fish exporters in Portland, Boston, and New York, became the primary destinations for cargoes of dried fish outward bound from the city of Halifax, Nova Scotia's premier marketing center. As the 1880s began, over half of all Halifax cod shipments—upwards of 200,000 quintals a year from this one port alone— were being consigned to Cuban and Puerto Rican importers.[209] Not long after, in 1882–1883, the "foreign" West Indies statistically displaced the British Caribbean as the chief focus of Nova Scotia's overall dried-cod trade.[210] At that point Maine's last outside market for its own salt cod ceased, for all practical purposes, to exist.

There were, of course, other reasons for the Canadian takeover of the North Atlantic salt-cod fishery besides its product and price advantages in the West Indies export market. One was a growing population. As Harold A. Innis pointed out, the increase of settlements along the coasts of Newfoundland, Nova Scotia, and Prince Edward Island led, in turn, to an expansion of native fisheries in those regions, to the ultimate detriment of American fishermen.[211] A comparison of Maine and Nova Scotia is particularly graphic in this regard. Between 1860 and 1880, while Maine's population stagnated, Nova Scotia's expanded rapidly, growing by 110,000 over the period. Maine had twice as many people as Nova Scotia in 1860; twenty years later it had only one-third more.[212] That provincial growth was an obvious stimulus to economic activity.

Another advantage the provinces enjoyed was their close proximity to the major fishing grounds of the North Atlantic. While New Englanders had to sail several hundred miles to the Grand and Western banks or to the Gulf of St. Lawrence, Canadians had the fish, in the words of one fisherman, "at their very doors."[213] Being close to the fishing grounds produced several benefits. For one thing, money was saved on supplies and provisions. "They are nearer home, and do not require so extensive an outfit," said a Portland vessel owner of his northern competitors.[214] There was also the positive factor of time saving. The farthest of the major banks were no more than a few days from the fishing ports of the Maritimes, while New England ports were up to two weeks away.[215] Instead of one or (at most) two seasonal voyages to the banks made by Maine vessels, Nova Scotian salt bankers made several. Lunenburg schooners of the 1870s normally took three fishing trips in the course of a year, visiting the Western Banks in the spring and going to the Grand Banks twice between summer and fall.[216] Geographic proximity to the primary salt-fishing grounds thus increased potential production in the province's cod fishery and added to its overall success.

Production was also enhanced by Maritime Canada's receptivity to the New Technology. Compared to Maine (see chapter 6), Nova Scotia was quick to adapt trawling to its ground-fishing industry, starting as early as 1867 at some places.[217] The transition to trawling was most successfully carried out at Lunenburg, which used the technique to establish domination of the province's cod fishery around 1880.[218] Lunenburg had begun experimenting with trawls in 1873, about the time its vessels first visited the Grand Banks. By the mid-1880s close to half of the port's bankers were equipped with set-lines, and so were numerous schooners from surrounding localities.[219]

Nova Scotia's cod bankers were able to convert to trawling, an innovation many Maine operators could not afford, because they saved money in other areas of their business. Provincial fish merchants enjoyed a number of basic cost savings not available to Maine or even Massachusetts merchants. One of these was inexpensive vessels. "They can build vessels for much less than we can," a Boothbay fishing captain reported in 1873; other Maine fishermen and vessel owners concurred, estimating that Canadian builders could turn out a schooner for about half what New England yards charged.[220] Gloucester merchants of the 1870s, who had many of their vessels built in Maine, judged the cost of a new Yankee schooner to be close to $100 per ton compared to between $30 and $60 per ton for a provincial schooner.[221] The biggest difference was in the wood used. Maine and Massachusetts builders were primarily employing imported hardwoods and other non-native timbers by that time, especially white oak and yellow pine from the South, which were of superior quality but expensive. Canadian builders, on the other hand, were exploiting their own vast stands of native spruce to turn out shorter-lived but much cheaper softwood schooners.[222]

In addition to the advantage gained through the use of their famous softwood vessels, fishing entrepreneurs in the Maritimes benefitted from low outfitting expenses. Dories, for instance, which cost eighteen to twenty-five dollars new at Salisbury, Massachusetts, around 1880, were available for just fourteen dollars at Lunenburg, Nova Scotia.[223] A whole host of other items—salt, cordage, fishing lines, hooks, barrels, cables, anchors, chains, and provisions—were also less costly for Canadians than for their American rivals.[224] Some Yankee merchants maintained that fishing outfits were only half as expensive in the Maritimes as in New England. That was probably an exaggeration, but even the most conservative estimates of the 1870s placed the cost differential at 25 percent.[225]

On balance, New England operators agreed that if vessel prices and outfitting expenses were considered together, their Dominion counterparts could enter the fisheries with about one-third less overhead* than Americans faced.[226] Low timber and food costs—factors arising out of the natural workings of the Canadian economy—accounted for a large part of the difference, but these were greatly reinforced by beneficial British import policies, a reward for Canada's Empire membership. While American fishermen staggered under the burden of high tariffs on the foreign articles they required, Canadian fishermen paid low tariffs or none at all. "Many of the duties that the American pays are unknown to the Colonist," a retired Massachusetts fisherman noted in 1873.[227] Indeed, such critical items as salt, anchors, and chains were imported duty-free (or nearly so) to the provinces at that time, and imposts on such items as tea, coffee, sugar, molasses, woolens, cordage, and cotton duck were well below American levels.[228] From Gloucester to Castine, New England fishery interests were keenly aware of the tariff advantage enjoyed north of the border and gave it much of the credit for their difficult competitive position in the industry.[229] Unfortunately, they had no hope of obtaining a similarly enlightened import policy from their own federal government, whose officials looked after 1865 not to the sea but to the land.

Blessed with innumerable natural and economic advantages for the pursuit of their occupation, the fishermen of Nova Scotia and the other Maritime Provinces lacked only one ingredient to establish their superiority in the North American salt fisheries. That ingredient was a strong central government dedicated to the creation and maintenance of a national fishing industry. Confederation, which established Canada as a nation in its own right in 1867, added that missing factor of an activist State.

Canada's new Dominion government was dedicated to nation-building in all its aspects, and support of the fisheries was one such aspect. A year after Confederation Ottawa passed the Fisheries Act of 1868, which regulated inshore fishing and led to increased spawning in Canadian waters. Two years later a fisheries-protection fleet was inaugurated to enforce new legal restrictions against American schooners fishing within three miles of the Dominion coastline.[230] These actions, combined with the earlier system (in

---

*New England fishermen did get more for their product, but not enough to offset their greater overhead costs. In the fall of 1879, for example, large banks cod wholesaled for only 20 to 25 percent less at Lunenburg, Nova Scotia, than at Portland, Maine. By way of comparison, fishing salt could be purchased for 40 percent less at Lunenburg than at Castine, Maine, in the early 1870s, and most provisions were as much as 30 to 40 percent cheaper. (Sources: *LP,* news items, 2 September 1879 and 28 October 1879; *EA,* wholesale prices current, 10 September 1879 and 22 October 1879; PANS, ZC, MS 174: Ships' Account Book, Zwicker & Company, 1871–76; BLH, WC, MS 181.)

force from 1866 to 1869) of charging tonnage-based license fees for inshore fishing, had a particularly dampening effect on American activities in the Gulf of St. Lawrence.[231] It was another government initiative, however, that had the most far-reaching impact on Nova Scotia's (and, indirectly, Maine's) offshore banks fishery.

On May 17, 1882, the Canadian Parliament passed "An Act to authorize an annual grant for the development of the Sea Fisheries and the encouraging of the building of Fishing Vessels," which provided for an annual expenditure of up to $150,000 in government fishing bounties.[232] This law was strikingly similar to the United States bounty law revoked in 1866, calling as it did for tonnage payments divided between vessel owners and crews, but it was an improvement on its American predecessor in that it subsidized all sea fisheries and not just the salt-cod industry. Under the Canadian enactment, vessels over ten tons that were engaged in sea fishing for a minimum of three months each year were entitled to compensation at a rate of two dollars per ton (up to eighty tons), half of which was paid to the owners and half to their crews. Small boats were compensated separately on a per-man basis.[233] The new bounty remained in effect for the balance of the nineteenth century and into the twentieth, and its administration became the most important responsibility of Canada's newly created (1884) Department of Fisheries, accounting for half of that bureau's entire budget by 1889–1890.[234] The Ottawa government's continuing solicitous attitude toward its fisheries, which contrasted so sharply with the laissez-faire attitude prevailing in Washington, was summarized by a Canadian spokesman in 1893: "A large sum of money is distributed every year among our fishermen as premiums, and our public men are willing to continue to help the advancement of an industry which for the future of the Dominion is so necessary and important."[235] Maine fishermen were thus faced after 1880 not only with a new rival in the industry but with a heavily subsidized rival, able to count on the firm support and encouragement of its government.

The creators of the Canadian fishing bounty had two objectives in mind, and the legislation passed in 1882 achieved both of them. One was to encourage the construction of a larger and better class of vessels in the Maritimes, a goal explicitly stated at the outset by both the Ministry of Marine and Fisheries and its supporters in Parliament.[236] Until the onset of subsidization there was no question that New England schooners were superior craft in every way. During the early 1850s it was said that Yankee mackerel vessels were able to reach the fishing grounds and procure cargoes while their Nova Scotian counterparts were still under sail en route.[237] In 1853 a captain in the provincial revenue service sent the following dispatch to his superiors in Halifax: "The American fishermen deserve a great deal of praise. Their vessels are of the very best description, beautifully rigged, and sail remarkably fast. . . . The difference between the American and English [i.e., Canadian] vessels is very great, for [of] all the English vessels in the Gulf of St. Lawrence the past fall, there were only four or five could in any way compete with the American."[238] Twenty years later, knowledgeable observers still judged the Canadian fleet to be far below the American in vessel quality.[239]

That perception altered rapidly in the years after 1882. Under the encouragement provided by the bounty, a substantial building program got under way in the Maritime Provinces. In 1883–1884 alone, eighty new fishing schooners were added to the Canadian fleet.[240] The change was not just quantitative. Models of Nova Scotian bankers drew appreciative comments at London's International Fisheries Exhibition in 1883, and American representatives at that conference agreed that provincial fishing vessels were showing remarkable improvement in size, speed, and seaworthiness.[241] By the mid-1880s Canadian spokesmen were claiming that schooner builders in the Maritimes had achieved technical parity with their opposite numbers in New England. Addressing a meeting of the British Association for the Advancement of Science in Montreal in August of 1884, Louis Z. Joncas, of Canada's Department of Fisheries, gave the Dominion's bounty law full credit for that achievement: "Owing to the encouragement given by our public men during the last years, the building of Canadian fishing craft has progressed rapidly. The swift schooners of Nova Scotia, New Brunswick, and of the other maritime provinces, can already by their sailing qualities compete fairly with the American fishing vessels, reported to be the best of their class in the world."[242] Looking back a decade later, Joncas observed that a revolution in naval architecture had taken place in the Maritimes under the auspices of the bounty, and he credited improvements in fishing-schooner design with playing a large role in producing the increased annual catches realized since 1882.[243]

In addition to enlarging and improving the Maritime fishing fleets— and, in part, through that process—sponsors of Canada's bounty law also sought the more fundamental objective of persuading provincial fishermen to remain in their own home fisheries instead of emigrating to New England. A bounty, said one supporter of the idea, would have "a most salutory effect . . . in inducing our people to fit out a much larger fleet of fishing vessels and thereby afford remunerative employment to our young men, instead of them seeking employment abroad in the United States."[244] Keeping Canadian fishermen employed at home "was one object we had in view," acknowledged M.P. Leonard Tilley, floor manager of the bounty bill in Parliament.[245] The law admirably fulfilled that purpose in large measure. Eastern Canada's resident fishing work force increased by thirty-five hundred within a year of the bounty's passage, and by 1889 the provinces had eighty-four hundred more fishermen than in 1882.[246] Most of that increase represented new workers drawn to the industry by the offer of a subsidy, but a large part of it reflected the fact that veteran fishermen who had formerly worked out of New England ports were exercising their new options of either signing on local vessels or building their own schooners. Either way, the result was a drastic reduction in the potential manpower available to serve aboard Maine banks vessels, which had come to depend so heavily on Canadian crews (see chapter 8). Between 1880 and 1889 the number of Canadians serving in the New England fishing industry fell by over 60 percent, and in Maine the figure was closer to 70 percent, most of the decline coming during the first five years of the bounty's operation.[247] It was this aspect of Canada's new neo-mercantilist policy of fisheries support that more than any other had a negative impact on Maine's overall industry.

Besides its critical role in cutting off Maine's primary source of imported manpower, the Canadian bounty law produced one other lasting effect that directly undermined the salt fisheries in the eastern part of the state. As the Dominion Department of Fisheries pointed out in 1884, the bounty was especially effective in stimulating the cod fisheries of Nova Scotia, eastern Maine's new rival on the Grand Banks. Two-thirds of Ottawa's entire subsidy outlay went to Nova Scotian vessel owners and crewmen that year, and Lunenburg County's $23,000 share was the largest for any county in the Maritimes.[248] The province as a whole increased its vessel fleet by seven thousand tons (or 31 percent) between 1882 and 1884, the first three subsidy years, and added over $1.6 million to the value of its fisheries.[249] The massive infusion of public capital those figures represented was far more competition than eastern Maine's unsubsidized entrepreneurs could meet.

The rise of Canada's fishing industry after 1865, and especially after 1880, placed Maine's native industry in a figurative vice. The state was caught between two powerful and resourceful competitors, each of which possessed natural advantages grounded in geography and economics. Cold facts dictated that while Maine's fishermen could not compete with Massachusetts in the burgeoning fresh fisheries, they also had no free hand in the traditional dried and salt fisheries. As Portland struggled against Boston and Gloucester, eastern Maine was forced to contend with Lunenburg and other Nova Scotia ports. It was an impossible situation. The rise of the Maritime Provinces, and Nova Scotia in particular, guaranteed that Maine would not survive as a sea-fishing entity. Only if the Canadian salt fisheries had failed to develop could Maine have withstood the loss of her domestic market to the fresh fishermen of southern New England. Such historical cooperation was not forthcoming.

Reference Abbreviations

———

Government Documents (series)

Can.AppRFB	Canada, Ministry of Marine and Fisheries, *Appendix to the Annual Report of the Department of Marine and Fisheries, Fisheries Branch.*
Can.Cen.	Canada, Ministry of Agriculture, *Census of Canada* (decennial).
Can.ODHC	Canada, *Official Debates of the House of Commons.*
Can.RFB	Canada, Ministry of Marine and Fisheries, *Annual Report of the Department of Marine and Fisheries, Fisheries Branch.*
Can.S	Canada, *Statutes of Canada.*
Mass.Cen.	Massachusetts, Bureau of Statistics of Labor, *Census of Massachusetts* (decennial).
Me.LR	Maine, *Legislative Resolves.*
Me.PL	Maine, *Public Laws.*
Me.PSL	Maine, *Private and Special Laws.*
Me.RBILS	Maine, Bureau of Industrial and Labor Statistics, *Annual Report.*
Me.RRC	Maine, Railroad Commissioners, *Annual Report.*
N.S.AppJPHA	Nova Scotia, *Appendix to the Journal and Proceedings of the House of Assembly.*
U.S.AC	U.S., *Annals of Congress.*
U.S.AppAC	U.S., *Appendix to the Annals of Congress.*
U.S.AppCG	U.S., *Appendix to the Congressional Globe.*
U.S.Cen.	U.S., Superintendent of the Census, *Census of the United States* (decennial).
U.S.CG	U.S., *Congressional Globe.*
U.S.CR	U.S., *Congressional Record.*
U.S.FCB	U.S., Commission of Fish and Fisheries, *Annual Bulletin.*
U.S.MV	U.S., Bureau of Statistics, *Merchant Vessels of the United States* (annual).
U.S.RCFF	U.S., Commission of Fish and Fisheries, *Annual Report of the Commissioner.*
U.S.RCN	U.S., Department of the Treasury, *Annual Report of the Commissioner of Navigation.*

U.S.RDC	U.S., *Register of Debates in Congress.*
U.S.RFCN	U.S., Department of the Treasury, *Annual Report on the Foreign Commerce and Navigation of the United States.*

Government Documents (reports)

Anderson Report	U.S., Congress, Senate, Committee on Finance, *Document in Relation to the Bounties Allowed to Vessels in the Fisheries,* by John Anderson, 26th Cong., 2nd Sess., 1841, Sen. Doc. 148.
Andrews Report	U.S., Department of the Treasury, *Report on the Trade and Commerce of the British North American Colonies and of the Great Lakes and Rivers,* by Israel D. Andrews, 32nd Cong., 1st Sess., 1852, Sen. Exec. Doc. 112.
Benton Report	U.S., Congress, Senate, Select Committee on the Origin and Character of Fishing Bounties and Allowances, *Majority Report,* 26th Cong., 1st Sess., 1840, Sen. Doc. 368.
Browne Report	U.S., Department of the Treasury, *Report on the Bounty Allowances to Fishing Vessels,* by J. Ross Browne, 33rd Cong., 1st Sess., 1853, House Exec. Doc. 3.
Cutts Report	U.S., Department of State, *Report on the Commerce in the Products of the Sea,* by Richard D. Cutts, 42nd Cong., 2nd Sess., 1869, Sen. Exec. Doc. 34.
Davis Report	U.S., Congress, Senate, Select Committee on the Origin and Character of Fishing Bounties and Allowances, *Minority Report,* 26th Cong., 1st Sess., 1840, Sen. Doc. 368.
First Clay Report	U.S., Congress, Senate, Committee on Commerce, *Report on Fishing Bounties,* 35th Cong., 1st Sess., 1858, Sen. Rept. 10.
First Jackson Report	Maine, Office of the Governor, *First Report on the Geology of the State of Maine,* by Charles T. Jackson (Augusta: Smith & Robinson, 1837).
Goode Report	U.S., Commission of Fish and Fisheries, *The Fisheries and Fishery Industries of the United States,* ed. George Brown Goode (5 secs., 7 vols.; Washington: Government Printing Office, 1884–1887).
Hall Report	U.S., Superintendent of the Census, *Report on the Ship-Building Industry of the United States,* by Henry Hall (Washington: Government Printing Office, 1882).
Hough Report	U.S., Department of Agriculture, *Report Upon Forestry* (vol. 2), by Franklin B. Hough, 46th Cong., 2nd Sess., 1880, House Exec. Doc. 37.

Knight Report on N.S. Fisheries	Canada, Ministry of Marine and Fisheries, *Report on the Fisheries of Nova Scotia,* by Thomas F. Knight (Halifax: A. Grant, 1867).
Knight Report on Shore and Deep-Sea Fisheries	Nova Scotia, Office of the Provincial Secretary, *Shore and Deep Sea Fisheries of Nova Scotia,* by Thomas F. Knight (Halifax: A. Grant, 1867).
Lynch Report	U.S. Congress, House, Select Committee, *Report on the Causes of the Reduction of American Tonnage and the Decline of Navigation,* 41st Cong., 2nd Sess., 1870, House Rept. 28.
Perley Reports	New Brunswick, Office of Lieutenant Governor, *Reports on the Sea and River Fisheries of New Brunswick,* by M. H. Perley (Fredericton, N.B.: J. Simpson, 1852).
Robertson Report	U.S., Congress, House, Committee on Merchant Marine and Fisheries, *The Present Defective Method of Dory Fishing, its Unfortunate Features, and Proposed Remedies,* by W. Henry Robertson, 50th Cong., 1st Sess., 1888, House Misc. Doc. 206.
Sabine Report	U.S., Department of the Treasury, *Report on the Principal Fisheries of the American Seas,* by Lorenzo Sabine, 32nd Cong., 2nd Sess., 1853, Sen. Exec. Doc. 22.
Second Clay Report	U.S., Congress, Senate, Committee on Commerce, *Report on Fishing Bounties,* 36th Cong., 1st Sess., 1860, Sen. Rept. 41.
Third Jackson Report	Maine, Office of the Governor, *Third Annual Report on the Geology of the State of Maine,* by Charles T. Jackson (Augusta: Smith & Robinson, 1839).
Wasson Report	Maine, Board of Agriculture, *A Survey of Hancock County, Maine,* by Samuel Wasson (Augusta: Sprague, Owen & Nash, 1878).
Wells Report	U.S., Department of the Treasury, *Report of the Special Commissioner of the Revenue for the Year 1868,* 40th Cong., 3rd Sess., 1869, House Exec. Doc. 16.
Wright Report	Massachusetts, Bureau of Statistics of Labor, *Profit Sharing,* by Carroll D. Wright (2nd ed.; Boston: Wright & Potter, 1886).

Government Documents (miscellaneous items)

ASP, CN	U.S., Congress, *American State Papers, Commerce and Navigation* (2 vols.; Washington: Gales & Seaton, 1832–34).
BDAC	U.S., Congress, *Biographical Directory of the American Congress, 1774–1971* (Washington: Government Printing Office, 1971).

Fisheries of the U.S., 1908	U.S., Bureau of the Census, *Fisheries of the United States, 1908* (Washington: Government Printing Office, 1911).
Hague Arbitration Proceedings	U.S., Department of State, *Proceedings in the North Atlantic Coast Fisheries Arbitration Before the Permanent Court of Arbitration at the Hague,* 12 vols., 61st Cong., 3rd Sess., 1911, Sen. Exec. Doc. 870.
Halifax Commission Proceedings	U.S., Department of State, *Documents and Proceedings of the Halifax Commission, 1877, Under the Treaty of Washington of May 8, 1871,* 45th Cong., 2nd Sess., 1878, House Exec. Doc. 89.
Historical Statistics, U.S.	U.S., Bureau of the Census, *Historical Statistics of the United States, Colonial Times to 1957* (Washington: Government Printing Office, 1960).
Machias Registers and Enrollments	U.S., Works Projects Administration, National Archives Project, *Ship Registers and Enrollments of Machias, Maine, 1780–1930* (Rockland, Me.: The National Archives Project, 1942).
Mackerel Fishery Materials	U.S., Commission of Fish and Fisheries, *Materials for a History of the Mackerel Fishery,* by George Brown Goode et al. (Washington: Government Printing Office, 1883).
Meat Products Hearings	U.S., Congress, Senate, Select Committee, *Hearings, The Transportation and Sale of Meat Products,* 51st Cong., 1st Sess., 1890.
New Orleans Registers and Enrollments	U.S., Works Projects Administration, Survey of Federal Archives in Louisiana, *Ship Registers and Enrollments of New Orleans* (6 vols.; University, La.: Louisiana State University, 1941–42).
Salt Documents	U.S., Congress, Senate, Committee on Finance, *Documents Relating to the Trade in, and Manufacture and Uses of Salt,* 26th Cong., 1st Sess., 1840, Sen. Doc. 196.
Statistics of Commerce	U.S., Department of the Treasury, *Statistics of the Foreign and Domestic Commerce of the United States* (Washington: Government Printing Office, 1864).
U.S. MS Census Pop.	U.S., Superintendent of the Census, Manuscript Schedules for Population.
U.S. MS Census Ind.	U.S., Superintendent of the Census, Manuscript Schedules for Industry.

Manuscript Collections

BLH, WC	Baker Library of Harvard University, The Witherle Collection.
NA, RBC (RG 36), CDR	National Archives, Records of the Bureau of Customs (Record Group 36), Collection District Records.

NA, RBMIN (RG 41), VDR — National Archives, Records of the Bureau of Marine Inspection and Navigation (Record Group 41), Vessel Documentation Records.

NA, RDT (RG 56), GR — National Archives, Records of the Department of the Treasury (Record Group 56), General Records.

PANS, ZC — Public Archives of Nova Scotia, The Zwicker Collection.

PMM, GC — Penobscot Marine Museum, General Collection.

PMM, WP — Penobscot Marine Museum, The Witherle Papers.

Newspapers

EA — *Eastern Argus* (Portland, Maine)

EAm — *Ellsworth* (Maine) *American*

EH — *Ellsworth* (Maine) *Herald*

ES — *Eastport* (Maine) *Sentinel*

LP — *Lunenburg* (Nova Scotia) *Progress*

MIJ — *The Mining and Industrial Journal* (Bangor, Maine); name shortened to *The Industrial Journal* in 1885.

MN — *The Morning News* (Saint John, New Brunswick)

MU — *Machias* (Maine) *Union*

N.O.PC — *New Orleans Price Current, Commercial Intelligencer and Merchants' Transcript*

PA — *The Progressive Age* (Belfast, Maine)

RJ — *Republican Journal* (Belfast, Maine)

WC — *Bangor* (Maine) *Daily Whig and Courier*

Registers and Directories (series)

ALR — *American Lloyd's Registry of American and Foreign Shipping* (New York: various publishers and years).

MBD — *The Maine Business Directory* (Boston: Briggs & Co., various years).

PDRB — *The Portland Directory and Reference Book* (Portland, Me.: B. Thurston & Co., various years).

RAFS — *Record of American and Foreign Shipping* (New York: American Shipmasters' Association, various years).

Notes

Chapter 1

1. *Me.LR, 1840,* chap. 77.

2. *RJ,* news item, 6 August 1852.

3. Compiled from: *Goode Report,* secs. 2, 5; *Halifax Commission Proceedings,* vols. 1–3; *Hague Arbitration Proceedings,* vol. 2; *Mackerel Fishery Materials;* Emory R. Johnson et al., *History of Domestic and Foreign Commerce of the United States,* 2 vols. (Washington: Carnegie Institution, 1915), vol. 2; Wesley G. Pierce, *Goin' Fishin': The Story of the Deep-Sea Fishermen of New England* (Salem, Mass.: Marine Research Society, 1934); George H. Procter, comp., *The Fishermen's Own Book* (Gloucester, Mass.: Procter Brothers, 1882); *N.S.AppJPHA, 1853; Can.AppRFB, 1870;* PMM, GC, MS 6: Log of the schooner *Martha Burgess,* 1853; PMM, GC, MS 125: Journal of Fishing Outfits, William Witherle & Company, 1853; PMM, GC, MS 354: Log of the schooner *Mentora,* 1852; *EA, RJ, EH, EAm,* and *ES,* marine lists, 1840–90.

4. Joseph W. Smith, *Gleanings from the Sea* (Andover, Mass.: private printing, 1887), viii.

5. Raymond McFarland, *A History of the New England Fisheries* (New York: D. Appleton & Co., 1911), 144.

6. *Goode Report,* sec. 2, 40; U.S. MS Census Pop., 1860: Hancock County, Maine, town of Deer Isle.

7. Francis B. Greene, *History of Boothbay, Southport and Boothbay Harbor, Maine* (Portland, Me.: Loring, Short & Harmon, 1906), 367; U.S. MS Census Pop., 1860: Lincoln County, Maine, town of Southport.

8. H. W. Small, *A History of Swan's Island, Maine* (Ellsworth, Me.: Hancock County Publishing Co., 1898), 187.

9. *Me.RBILS, 1887,* 113.

10. George Adams, ed., *The Maine Register for the Year 1855* (Portland, Me.: Blake & Carter, 1855), 256.

11. A. J. Coolidge and J. B. Mansfield, *A History and Description of New England: Maine* (Boston: Austin J. Coolidge, 1860), 90.

12. Ibid., 97.

13. Ibid., passim.

14. *U.S.Cen., 1860,* 3:208–17.

15. *Sabine Report,* 175.

16. *RJ,* news item, 30 July 1852.

17. Adams, 256.

18. *Goode Report,* sec. 2:9–10.

19. *U.S.Cen., 1860,* 1:208–9, 663.

20. *U.S.Cen., 1880,* 1:780.

21. U.S. MS Census Pop., 1850: Lincoln County, Maine, town of Boothbay.

22. *U.S.Cen., 1880,* 1:826; *Goode Report* sec. 5, 1:305.

23. Adams, 256.

24. *Second Clay Report,* 16.

25. *U.S.Cen., 1860,* 1:208–9.

26. U.S. MS Census Pop., 1860: Lincoln County, Maine, towns of Boothbay, Southport and Westport; Knox County, Maine, towns of Vinalhaven and North Haven; Hancock County, Maine, town of Deer Isle.

27. George Brown Goode, "A Review of the Fishery Industries of the United States and the Work of the United States Fish Commission," *The International Fisheries Exhibition Literature,* vol. 5: *Conferences Held in Connection with the Great International Fisheries Exhibition of 1883,* pt. 2 (London: William Clowes & Sons, 1884), 22.

28. U.S. MS Census Pop., 1860: Knox County, Maine, town of Vinalhaven.

29. *ASP,CN,* vols. 1, 2, *U.S.RFCN,* 1825–92, and *U.S.RCN,* 1893–1900: statements on fishing tonnage by customs district.

30. Ibid.

31. *U.S.RFCN, 1861*, pt. 3, 508.

32. *ASP,CN*, vols, 1, 2, *U.S.RFCN*, 1825–92, and *U.S.RCN, 1893–1900*: statements on fishing tonnage by customs district.

33. McFarland, 169.

34. *U.S.RFCN, 1830–65*, statements on fishing tonnage by customs district.

35. *Sabine Report*, 175.

36. Walter Prescott Webb, *The Great Plains* (New York: Ginn & Co., 1931), 271.

37. James Sullivan, *The History of the District of Maine* (Boston: Thomas & Andrews, 1795), 6.

38. *Goode Report*, sec. 2, 8.

39. *Reference Book of the State of Maine for the Year 1845* (Boston: White, Lewis & Potter, 1844), 7.

40. William D. Williamson, *The History of the State of Maine*, 2 vols. (Hallowell, Me.: Glazier, Masters & Co., 1832), 1:97.

41. L. Felix Ranlett and Lincoln Colcord, eds., *Master Mariner of Maine: Being the Reminiscences of Charles E. Ranlett, 1816–1917* (Portland, Me.: Southworth-Anthoensen Press, 1942), 11.

42. *Goode Report*, sec. 2, 50.

43. Coolidge and Mansfield, 334, 336.

44. Thomas Mooney, *Nine Years in America* (Dublin: James McGlashan, 1850), 128–29; see also Charles E. Clark, *The Eastern Frontier: The Settlement of Northern New England, 1610–1763* (New York: Alfred A. Knopf, 1970), 9.

45. W. H. Bishop, "Fish and Men in the Maine Islands," *Harper's New Monthly Magazine*, 61 (August 1880): 352.

46. *U.S.RFCN, 1835–60*, statements on fishing tonnage by customs district.

47. *Wasson Report*, 37.

48. *U.S.Cen., 1850*, 12.

49. Clarence A. Day, *Farming in Maine, 1860–1940* (Orono: University of Maine Press, 1963), 3; see also Percy W. Bidwell and John I. Falconer, *History of Agriculture in the Northern United States, 1620–1860* (Washington: Carnegie Institution, 1925), 321–453 passim.

50. *U.S.RDC*, 20th Cong., 1st Sess. (1828), col. 744.

51. *U.S.CG*, 35th Cong., 1st Sess. (1858), 2027.

52. John Hay and Peter Farb, *The Atlantic Shore: Human and Natural History from Long Island to Labrador* (New York: Harper & Row, 1966), 35.

53. Moses Greenleaf, *A Survey of the State of Maine* (Portland, Me.: Shirley & Hyde, 1829), 217.

54. *Goode Report*, sec. 2, 8.

55. Hay and Farb, 37–38.

56. National Geographic Society, *Map of the Atlantic Ocean* (Washington: National Geographic Magazine, 1955); National Geographic Society, *Map of North America* (Washington: National Geographic Magazine, 1952); National Geographic Society, *Map of Canada* (Washington: National Geographic Magazine, 1961).

57. *Me.LR, 1840*, chap. 77.

58. *ASP, CN*, vols. 1, 2, statements on fishing tonnage by customs district.

59. *ASP, CN*, vols, 1, 2, and *U.S.RFCN, 1825–75*: statements on fishing tonnage by customs district.

60. Ibid.

61. Ibid.

62. *U.S.RFCN, 1861*, pt. 3, 496–99.

63. Douglas E. Leach, *The Northern Colonial Frontier, 1607–1763* (New York: Holt, Rinehart & Winston, 1966), 34, 131; Clark, 335–39.

64. Moses Greenleaf, *A Statistical View of the District of Maine* (Boston: Cummings & Hilliard, 1816), 50.

65. Charles W. Eliot, *John Gilley: Maine Farmer and Fisherman* (Boston: American Unitarian Assoc., 1904), 10–11.

66. Samuel Eliot Morison, *The Oxford History of the American People* (New York: Oxford University Press, 1965), 178.

67. William Williamson, 2:398, 517; Greenleaf, *Survey*, 217.

68. Hezekiah Prince, Jr., *Journals of Hezekiah Prince, Jr., 1822–28*, ed. Albert Spear (New York: Crown Publishers, 1965), 17.

69. *Maine Register, State Year-Book and Legislative Manual, 1974–75* (Portland, Me.: Tower Publishing Co., 1974), 850.

70. *Goode Report*, sec. 2, 45, 48.

71. *Maine Register, 1974–75*, passim.

72. Greenleaf, *Survey*, 140, 143, 149.

73. *Maine Register, 1974-75*, 509; *Historical Statistics, U.S.*, 651.

74. *Maine Register, 1974-75*, 509; Greenleaf, *Survey*, 140.

75. Greenleaf, *Survey*, 146-49; *Maine Register, 1974-75*, passim.

76. John B. Brebner, *Canada: A Modern History* (Ann Arbor: University of Michigan Press, 1960), 160.

77. Eliot, 31-39.

78. *Goode Report*, sec. 2, 51.

79. PMM, GC, MS 229: Penobscot District Customs Collector's Abstracts of Bounty Allowances Paid to Vessels Employed in the Bank and Other Cod Fisheries, 1st Quarter 1830 to 1st Quarter 1840.

80. Greene, 368.

81. PMM, GC, MS 229.

82. *MU*, news item, 9 August 1853; *Machias Registers and Enrollments*, 75, 530.

83. PMM, GC, MS 125; U.S. MS Census Pop., 1850: Hancock County, Maine, town of Tremont.

84. Ibid.

85. *Machias Registers and Enrollments*, 326; U.S., MS Census Pop., 1850: Washington County, Maine, town of Jonesport; PMM, GC, MS 354: 1 June 1852.

86. Castine (Maine) Town Office, MS: Tax Valuation Book for 1854; U.S. MS Census Pop. and Ind., 1850: Hancock County, Maine, town of Castine; Adams, 346; *EA*, marine lists, 1853-60; *RJ*, marine lists, 1850-54, 1859.

87. *RJ*, news item, 7 June 1852; PMM, GC, MS 231: Penobscot District Customs Collector's Record of Licenses Granted to Fishing Vessels at the Port of Sedgwick, 1852.

88. Fogler Library of the University of Maine, Special Collections, MS: "Vessel Property Owned in Bucksport, 1859"; U.S. MS Census Pop., 1850 and 1860: Hancock County, Maine, town of Bucksport; *EA*, marine lists, 1853-64; *RJ*, marine lists, 1850-54, 1859.

89. Fogler Library, MS: "Vessel Property Owned in Bucksport, 1859."

90. *RJ*, marine list, 14 October 1853; Castine (Maine) Town Office, MS: Tax Valuation Book for 1850; U.S. MS Census Pop., 1850: Hancock County, Maine, town

of Castine; George A. Wheeler, *History of Castine, Penobscot and Brooksville, Maine* (Bangor, Me.: Burr & Robinson, 1875), 237.

91. Greene, 292.

92. *RJ*, news item, 6 August 1852; George S. Wasson and Lincoln Colcord, *Sailing Days on the Penobscot . . . with a Record of Vessels Built There* (Salem, Mass.: Marine Research Society, 1932), 268.

93. *EH*, marine list, 29 April 1853; *EA*, marine list, 27 April 1860; BLH, WC, case 19: marine-insurance policies, schooners *Martha Burgess*, 14 November 1853, and *Eothen*, 14 May 1860.

94. *RJ*, marine list, 7 June 1850.

95. Wasson and Colcord, 317.

96. *Lynch Report*, 143, 197.

97. Castine (Maine) Town office, MS: Tax Valuation Book for 1854.

98. Wasson and Colcord, 315-17.

99. Castine Tax Valuation Book for 1854.

100. *EA*, marine list, 13 December 1850.

101. *Halifax Commission Proceedings*, 2610.

102. *N.S.AppJPHA, 1853*, 123, 158; Castine Tax Valuation Books for 1850 and 1854.

103. *U.S.Cen., 1860*, 3:218, 253.

104. Castine Tax Valuation Book for 1854; U.S. MS Census Pop. and Ind., 1850; Hancock County, Maine, town of Castine; Adams, 346; *EA*, marine lists, 1853-60; *RJ*, marine lists, 1850-54, 1859.

105. *U.S.RFCN*, 1830-67, statements on fishing tonnage by customs district.

106. *Mackerel Fishery Materials*, 250.

107. *Halifax Commission Proceedings*, 1923.

108. *Sabine Report*, 184.

109. Ibid., 186.

110. *AppCG*, 32nd Cong., 1st Sess. (1852), 920.

111. *U.S.Cen., 1860*, 4:535.

112. George H. Procter, comp., *The Fishermen's Memorial and Record Book* (Gloucester, Mass.: Procter Brothers, 1873), 62.

113. Procter, *Fishermen's Own Book*, 45, 108. See also *Sabine Report*, 175, 316; *Goode*

Report, sec. 2, 11, 108–9, 120–21, 285, 314; *Mackerel Fishery Materials*, 209; *U.S.Cen., 1860*, 4:536; *U.S. Cen., 1870*, 3:793; and *Mass.Cen., 1895*, 6:116.

114. *U.S.RFCN, 1860*, 621.

115. *U.S.AppCG*, 32nd Cong., 1st Sess. (1852), 920.

116. *Goode Report*, sec. 4, 95.

117. *EA*, wholesale prices current on or near 1 September 1830–60.

118. Procter, *Fishermen's Own Book*, 19.

119. *Mackerel Fishery Materials*, 229, 255.

120. *Halifax Commission Proceedings*, 2886.

121. *Mackerel Fishery Materials*, 262.

122. *EA*, wholesale prices current on or near 1 September 1846–60.

123. Wesley C. Mitchell, *A History of the Greenbacks* (Chicago: University of Chicago Press, 1903), 455, 462.

124. *Halifax Commission Proceedings*, 614.

125. *Mackerel Fishery Materials*, 235–38.

126. *Anderson Report*, 2.

127. *U.S.RFCN, 1830–65*, statements on fishing tonnage by customs district.

128. *U.S.RFCN, 1843*, 400.

129. Procter, *Fishermen's Own Book*, 208–11.

130. Sylvanus Smith, *Fisheries of Cape Ann* (Gloucester, Mass.: Gloucester Times Co., 1915), 66–67.

131. Castine Tax Valuation Book for 1854; U.S. MS Census Pop. and Ind., 1850: Hancock County, Maine, town of Castine; Adams, 346; *EA*, marine lists, 1853–60; *RJ*, marine lists, 1850–54, 1859.

132. *Goode Report*, sec. 2, 692.

133. Castine Tax Valuation Book for 1854; U.S. MS Census Pop. and Ind., 1850: Hancock County, Maine, town of Castine; Adams, 346; *EA*, marine lists, 1853–60; *RJ*, marine lists, 1850–54, 1859.

134. Procter, *Fishermen's Memorial and Record Book*, 69; Castine Tax Valuation Book for 1854; *EA*, marine lists, 1853–60; *RJ*, marine lists, 1850–54.

135. Henry David Thoreau, *Cape Cod* (Boston: Ticknor & Fields, 1866), 175–76.

136. *N.S.AppJPHA, 1851*, 93.

137. *Knight Report on N.S. Fisheries*, 6.

138. *Halifax Commission Proceedings*, 3022.

139. Howard I. Chapelle, *The National Watercraft Collection* (Washington: Government Printing Office, 1960), 165; Chapelle, *American Fishing Schooners*, 36.

140. *Mackerel Fishery Materials*, 84.

141. Chapelle, *American Fishing Schooners*, 75.

142. *Knight Report on N.S. Fisheries*, 6–7.

143. *Goode Report*, sec. 5, 1:248.

144. *RJ*, news item, 6 August 1852; Wasson and Colcord, 268–69.

145. Harold A. Innis, *The Cod Fisheries: The History of an International Economy* (2nd ed. rev.; Toronto: University of Toronto Press, 1954), 258.

146. Eugene D. Genovese, *The Political Economy of Slavery: Studies in the Economy and Society of the Slave South* (New York: Random House, 1961), 44; Kenneth M. Stampp, *The Peculiar Institution: Slavery in the Antebellum South* (New York: Alfred A. Knopf, 1967), 282; Ulrich B. Phillips, *Life and Labor in the Old South* (Boston: Little, Brown & Co., 1929), 197.

147. Robert W. Fogel and Stanley L. Engerman, *Time on the Cross: The Economics of American Negro Slavery*, 2 vols. (Boston: Little, Brown & Co., 1974), 1:110–11.

148. Mitchell, *History of the Greenbacks*, 455–64.

149. Genovese, 106–15.

150. *Historical Statistics, U.S.*, 9.

151. Maldwyn Allen Jones', *American Migration* (Chicago: University of Chicago Press, 1960), 93–94; Marcus L. Hansen, *The Atlantic Migration, 1607–1860* (Cambridge: Harvard University Press, 1940), 280.

152. Hansen, *Atlantic Migration*, 9.

153. Jones, 94; Hansen, *Atlantic Migration*, 280.

154. Oscar Handlin, *Boston's Immigrants: A Study in Acculturation* (2nd ed. rev.; Cambridge: Harvard University Press, 1959), 244; Robert Ernst, *Immigrant Life in New York City, 1825–1863* (New York: King's Crown Press, 1949), 61–62.

155. Earl F. Niehaus, *The Irish in New*

Orleans, 1800–1860 (Baton Rouge: Louisiana State Press, 1965), v, 25.

156. Jones, 139.

157. Handlin, 51; Jones, 108–9.

158. Handlin, 59.

159. Ernst, 62.

160. Handlin, 253; Niehaus, 43.

161. Handlin, 54–123.

162. Jones, 110–17.

163. Ibid., 117–18, 139.

164. *U.S.AppCG,* 34th Cong., 3rd Sess. (1857), 221.

165. Mitchell, *History of the Greenbacks,* 455–62.

Chapter 2

1. Thomas Jefferson, *The Papers of Thomas Jefferson,* ed. Julian P. Boyd, 20 vols. (Princeton, N.J.: Princeton University Press, 1950–82), 19:220.

2. Small, 184; Greene, 362.

3. McFarland, 143, 285.

4. Johnson et al., 2:161–63; McFarland, 134–37, 162.

5. *Halifax Commission Proceedings,* 3182–3207.

6. *ASP, CN,* vols. 1, 2: statements on fishing tonnage by customs district.

7. *ASP, CN,* 1:733, 1018, and 2:14, 164.

8. *U.S.AppAC,* 5th Cong., 1st Sess. (1797), cols. 3701–2; *U.S.AppAC,* 13th Cong., 1st Sess. (1813), cols. 2735–38.

9. *U.S.AppAC,* 15th Cong., 2nd Sess. (1819), cols. 2531–35.

10. *Davis Report,* 63; Sylvanus Smith, 53; *U.S.AppCG,* 35th Cong., 1st Sess. (1858), 436.

11. *U.S.CG,* 34th Cong., 3rd Sess. (1857), 379.

12. *ASP, CN,* vols. 1, 2: statements on fishing tonnage by customs district.

13. PMM, GC, MS 229.

14. *Goode Report,* sec. 2, 691; *U.S. RFCN, 1829,* 270–71.

15. *Goode Report,* sec. 2, 707; PMM, GC, MS 229.

16. Samuel Eliot Morison, *The Maritime History of Massachusetts, 1783–1860* (Boston: Houghton Mifflin Co., 1921), 145.

17. *Anderson Report,* 2.

18. Small, 184.

19. *Davis Report,* 64.

20. Ibid.

21. Elijah Kellogg, *The Fisher Boys of Pleasant Cove* (Boston: Lee & Shephard, 1874), 62.

22. *U.S.AppCG,* 34th Cong., 3rd Sess. (1857), col. 220.

23. *Halifax Commission Proceedings,* 2350.

24. Ibid.

25. *Anderson Report,* 1.

26. *U.S.CG,* 34th Cong., 3rd Sess. (1857), 379.

27. PMM, GC, MS 229.

28. Calculated from: PMM, GC, MSS 6, 125; PMM, WP, Miscellaneous Vessels, box 2, files 1, 21: schooner *Redwing,* settlement of coasting voyage to Boston, March 1854, and schooner *Martha Burgess,* settlement of Grand Banks voyage, 6 May 1856; BLH, WC, case 19: marine-insurance policies for various Castine fishing schooners, 1853; NA, RBC (RG 36), CDR, Penobscot District Fishing Articles of Agreement: articles for schooners *Amazon, Lagrange,* and *Minerva* of Castine, May–June 1854; Castine Tax Valuation Book for 1854; Wasson and Colcord, 317; *U.S. AppAC,* 15 Cong., 2nd Sess. (1819), cols. 2531–35; *EA,* Boston wholesale prices current, 6, 13, 20 March 1854.

29. *U.S.AppCG,* 32nd Cong., 1st Sess. (1852), col. 920.

30. PMM, GC, MS 229.

31. Ibid.

32. William H. Rowe, *The Maritime History of Maine: Three Centuries of Shipbuilding and Seafaring* (W. W. Norton & Co., 1948), 269.

33. *First Clay Report,* 6.

34. *Second Clay Report,* 7.

35. John L. Locke, *Sketches of the History of the Town of Camden, Maine* (Hallowell, Me.: Masters, Smith & Co., 1859), 254; William Williamson, 2:701.

36. *Andrews Report,* 655; *First Clay Report,* 6; *Second Clay Report,* 7.

37. *Andrews Report,* 655.

38. Coolidge and Mansfield, 104.

39. *U.S.AC, U.S.RDC,* and *U.S.CG:* 2nd Cong., 1st Sess. (1792) to 39th Cong., 1st Sess. (1866).

40. *Historical Statistics, U.S.,* 691–92.

41. *U.S.AppAC,* 5th Cong., 1st Sess. (1797), cols. 3701–2.

42. *U.S.CG,* 25th Cong., 3rd Sess. (1839), 143.

43. *U.S.CG,* 34th Cong., 3rd Sess. (1857), 378.

44. *U.S.AC,* 13th Cong., 1st Sess. (1813), cols. 458–62; *BDAC,* 1065.

45. *U.S.AC,* 2nd Cong., 1st Sess. (1792), col. 401; *BDAC,* passim; Joseph G. E. Hopkins, ed., *Concise Dictionary of American Biography* (New York: Charles Scribner's Sons, 1964), passim. For Madison's seminal role in the establishment of the fishing-bounty law, see Wayne M. O'Leary, "Fish and Politics in Jacksonian Maine," *The New England Quarterly* 67 (March 1994): 111–14.

46. *U.S.AC,* 2nd Cong., 1st Sess. (1792), col. 65; *BDAC,* passim; Hopkins, passim.

47. *U.S.AC,* 2nd Cong., 1st Sess. (1792), col. 401; *BDAC,* passim.

48. *U.S.AC,* 14th Cong., 1st Sess. (1816), col. 744; *BDAC,* passim.

49. *U.S.CG,* 25th Cong., 3rd Sess. (1839), 158–59; *BDAC,* passim; Hopkins, passim.

50. *U.S.CG,* 35th Cong., 1st Sess. (1858), 2239; *BDAC,* passim.

51. *Historical Statistics, U.S.,* 693.

52. *U.S.AC,* 2nd Cong., 1st Sess. (1792), cols. 363–400.

53. *U.S.AC,* 13th Cong., 1st Sess. (1813), cols. 449–62; *U.S.AC,* 14th Cong., 1st Sess. (1816), cols. 738–44.

54. *U.S.CG,* 25th Cong., 3rd Sess. (1838–39), 83, 149–59; *U.S.CG,* 26th Cong., 1st Sess. (1840), 186, 345–48; *U.S.CG,* 29th Cong., 1st Sess. (1846), 538–39, 1193.

55. *U.S.CG,* 35th Cong., 1st Sess. (1858), 1934–2238.

56. *U.S.AC,* 2nd Cong., 1st Sess. (1792), col. 364.

57. Ibid., cols. 379, 382.

58. Ibid., col. 393.

59. *U.S.CG,* 25th Cong., 3rd Sess. (1838), 83.

60. *U.S.CG,* 26th Cong., 1st Sess. (1840), 186.

61. Thomas Hart Benton, *Thirty Years'* *View,* 2 vols. (New York: D. Appleton & Co., 1856), 1:317.

62. *U.S.CG,* 34th Cong., 3rd Sess. (1857), 379.

63. *U.S.CG,* 35th Cong., 1st Sess. (1858), 2053.

64. Ibid., 2082.

65. *U.S.AppCG,* 34th Cong., 3rd Sess. (1857), 221.

66. *U.S.CG,* 35th Cong., 1st Sess. (1858), 1934.

67. *U.S.AC,* 2nd Cong., 1st Sess. (1792), col. 377.

68. *U.S.CG,* 29th Cong., 1st Sess. (1846), 539.

69. *U.S.AppCG,* 32nd Cong., 1st Sess. (1852), 921.

70. *U.S.AppCG,* 34th Cong., 3rd Sess. (1857), 221.

71. *EA,* editorial, 18 March 1840.

72. *WC,* editorial, 22 May 1858.

73. *U.S.AC,* 14th Cong., 1st Sess. (1816), col. 739.

74. Ibid., col. 743.

75. Ibid., cols. 739–40.

76. *U.S.CG,* 26th Cong., 1st Sess. (1840), 186; *Benton Report,* 26.

77. *U.S.AppCG,* 14th Cong., 2nd Sess. (1817), 1286.

78. *Andrews Report,* 634.

79. *Sabine Report,* 164–69.

80. *Andrews Report,* 632–33; *Brown Report,* 88.

81. *Browne Report,* 88.

82. *First Clay Report,* 9–10.

83. *U.S.CG,* 34th Cong., 3rd Sess. (1857), 379.

84. *U.S.CG,* 35th Cong., 1st Sess. (1858), 2025.

85. *U.S.AppCG,* 34th Cong., 3rd Sess. (1857), 219; *U.S.CG,* 35th Cong., 1st Sess. (1858), 2026.

86. *U.S.CG,* 35th Cong., 1st Sess. (1858), 2049.

87. Ranlett and Colcord, 12.

88. Sylvanus Smith, 53.

89. *Salt Documents,* 111–32; Letter from Henry McCobb, Collector of Customs, Bath, Maine, to Amos Nourse, Collector of Customs, Waldoboro, Maine, 18 December 1845 (in possession of George W. Bostwick, M.D., Bangor, Maine).

90. *Anderson Report,* 2.

91. *Sabine Report*, 165.

92. Richard K. Murdock, "Cod or Mackerel: Bounty Payment Disputes, 1829–32," *Essex Institute Historical Collections* 105 (October 1969): 309, 315.

93. Robert Sobel, ed., *Biographical Directory of the United States Executive Branch, 1774–1971* (Westport, Conn.: Greenwood Publishing Co., 1971), 60, 68, 141–42, 331.

94. *First Clay Report*, 8.

95. *RJ*, editorial, 21 April 1854; see also *Browne Report*, passim.

96. *First Clay Report*, 9.

97. Ibid., 10.

98. *U.S.AppCG*, 35th Cong., 1st Sess. (1858), 222.

99. Joseph Reynolds, *Peter Gott, the Cape Ann Fisherman* (Boston: John P. Jewett & Co., 1856), 262–63.

100. *Second Clay Report*, 8.

101. *U.S.CG*, 35th Cong., 1st Sess. (1858), 2029.

102. Adam Smith, *An Inquiry into the Nature and Causes of the Wealth of Nations*, ed. Edwin Cannan (New York: Modern Library, 1937), 484.

103. Charles W. Cole, *Colbert and a Century of French Mercantilism*, 2 vols. (New York: Columbia University Press, 1939), 1:97.

104. Charles Cole, 1:347, 472.

105. William Cunningham, *The Growth of English Industry and Commerce*, 3 vols. (5th ed.; Cambridge: Cambridge University Press, 1910–12), 2:483.

106. *U.S.AC*, 1st Cong., 1st Sess. (1789), col. 134.

107. Clinton Rossiter, ed., *The Federalist Papers* (New York: New American Library, Mentor Books, 1961), 88–89.

108. Jefferson, 19:218.

109. *U.S.AC*, 2nd Cong., 1st Sess. (1792), col. 370.

110. Ibid., col. 366.

111. *U.S.AC*, 5th Cong., 1st Sess. (1797), col. 446.

112. *U.S.AC*, 13th Cong., 1st Sess. (1813), col. 45l.

113. *U.S.AC*, 14th Cong., 1st Sess. (1816), col. 743.

114. John Fairfield, *The Letters of John Fairfield*, ed. Arthur G. Staples (Lewiston, Me.: Lewiston Journal Co., 1922), 393.

115. *U.S.CG*, 29th Cong., 1st Sess. (1846), 539.

116. *U.S.AppCG*, 32nd Cong., 1st Sess. (1852), 902–3.

117. Ibid., 903.

118. *Andrews Report*, 661–66.

119. *U.S.CG*, 34th Cong., 3rd Sess. (1857), 379.

120. *U.S.AppCG*, 34th Cong., 3rd Sess. (1857), 221.

121. *U.S.CG*, 35th Cong., 1st Sess. (1858), 329.

122. Ibid., 2071.

123. Ibid., 2022.

124. *WC*, news item, 25 May 1858.

125. *U.S.CG*, 35th Cong., 1st Sess. (1858), 1991–92.

126. Ibid., 1993–94.

127. Ibid., 1995.

128. Ibid., 1996–97.

129. *U.S.AppCG*, 35th Cong., 1st Sess. (1858), 436.

130. *Historical Statistics, U.S.*, 711; *Andrews Report*, 635; *Second Clay Report*, 7.

131. *U.S.AppCG*, 35th Cong., 1st Sess. (1858), 436.

132. *Me.LR, 1840*, chap. 77; *Me.LR, 1858*, chap. 135.

133. *RJ*, editorial, 21 April 1854.

134. *WC*, editorial, 22 May 1858.

135. *Sabine Report*, 199–204.

136. Kellogg, 55.

137. *U.S.CR*, 50th Cong., 1st Sess. (1888), 807.

138. *U.S.AC*, 2nd Cong., 1st Sess. (1792), col. 364.

139. *Benton Report*, 58.

140. *U.S.CG*, 35th Cong., 1st Sess. (1858), 2238.

141. Harold and Margaret Sprout, *The Rise of American Naval Power, 1776–1918* (2nd ed. rev.; Princeton, N.J.: Princeton University Press, 1966), 110.

142. Ibid., 157–62, 164.

143. *PA*, news item, 2 August 1866.

144. *U.S.AC*, 13th Cong., 1st Sess. (1813), col. 452; see also Jefferson, 19:210.

145. *U.S.AppCG*, 34th Cong., 3rd Sess. (1857), 220.

146. *U.S.CG*, 35th Cong., 1st Sess. (1858), 1993.

147. *Me.LR, 1840*, chap. 77.

148. *U.S.AC,* 2nd Cong., 1st Sess. (1792), cols. 368–69.

149. Ibid., col. 366.

150. Ibid., cols. 383–84, 389–90.

151. Ibid., cols. 363–64.

152. Adam Smith, 488.

153. Cunningham, 2:484.

154. Adam Smith, 483–89.

155. Ibid., 486.

156. Cunningham, 2:593; George Rogers Taylor, *The Transportation Revolution, 1815–1860* (New York: Rinehart & Co., 1951), 353; Arthur M. Schlesinger, Jr., *The Age of Jackson* (Boston: Little, Brown & Co., 1945), 314–17.

157. *U.S.CG,* 35th Cong., 1st Sess. (1858), 379.

158. *RJ,* editorial, 21 April 1854.

159. *U.S.AppCG,* 34th Cong., 3rd Sess. (1857), 221.

160. *U.S.CG,* 34th Cong., 3rd Sess. (1857), 379.

161. *U.S.CG,* 35th Cong., 1st Sess. (1858), 2055.

162. Schlesinger, 307–8, 314–17.

163. *U.S.CG,* 35th Cong., 1st Sess. (1858), 1992; *U.S.AppCG,* 35th Cong., 1st Sess. (1858), 436.

164. *Browne Report,* 98–99.

165. *U.S.CG,* 35th Cong., 1st Sess. (1858), 1935.

166. Leonard D. White, *The Federalists: A Study in Administrative History* (New York: Macmillan Co., 1948), 442–43; see also *U.S.AppAC,* 2nd Cong., 1st Sess. (1792), cols. 1329–32.

167. *Sabine Report,* 165–69.

168. Reynolds, 235–36.

169. Sylvanus Smith, 53.

170. *Me.LR, 1861,* chap. 60.

Chapter 3

1. *Halifax Commission Proceedings,* 2362.

2. Compiled from: *Goode Report,* secs. 2, 5; *Halifax Commission Proceedings,* vols. 1–3; *Hague Arbitration Proceedings,* vol. 2; *Mackerel Fishery Materials;* Johnson et al., vol. 2; Pierce; Procter, *Fishermen's Own Book; EA, RJ, EH, EAm,* and *ES,* marine lists, 1840–90.

3. *Goode Report,* sec. 5, 1:188, 234, 324–25.

4. Compiled from: *Goode Report,* secs. 2, 5; *Halifax Commission Proceedings,* vols. 1–3; *Hague Arbitration Proceedings,* vol. 2; *Mackerel Fishery Materials;* Johnson et al., vol. 2; Pierce; Procter, *Fishermen's Own Book; N.S.AppJPHA, 1853; Can.AppRFB, 1870;* PMM, GC, MSS 6, 125, 354; *EA, RJ, EH, EAm,* and *ES,* marine lists, 1840–90.

5. Ibid.

6. Ibid.

7. Ibid.

8. *U.S.RFCN,* 1830–65, statements on fishing tonnage by customs district.

9. *Sabine Report,* 170; Procter, *Fishermen's Own Book,* 6, 36; Jefferson, 19:226.

10. *Goode Report,* sec. 2, 32–33, 39,

43–44, 60, 63, 83; *EA,* marine lists, 8 November and 1 December 1841.

11. *Halifax Commission Proceedings,* 2528.

12. *Goode Report,* sec. 3, opp. 62, opp. 65; Kellogg, 51; *Halifax Commission Proceedings,* 2432.

13. *Goode Report,* sec. 1, 1:220.

14. *RJ,* Boston wholesale prices current, 6 September 1850.

15. *Goode Report,* sec. 2, 155–56, 691.

16. Adams, 256.

17. *EA, RJ, EAm,* marine lists, 1 July to 30 November 1850–60; see also PMM, GC, MSS 6, 354, and *EA,* marine list, 7 July 1857.

18. *Goode Report,* sec. 2, 707; *Halifax Commission Proceedings,* 1995.

19. Sylvanus Smith, 69.

20. PMM, GC, MS 6.

21. *EA,* marine lists, 1 July to 15 November 1853; *RJ,* marine lists, 1 July to 15 November 1853.

22. *EAm,* marine list, 19 August 1859.

23. *EA,* marine list, 29 July 1863.

24. *Goode Report,* sec. 2, 32–33, 42, 45, 68.

25. *U.S.FCB, 1887,* 454.

26. *Sabine Report,* 170; *Goode Report,* sec. 2, 135.

27. McFarland, 153.

28. Morison, *Maritime History of Massachusetts,* 136, 143.

29. *Goode Report,* sec. 2, 16, 41, and sec. 5, 1:147; Greenleaf, *Survey,* 251.

30. *Goode Report,* sec. 5, 1:147.

31. Wasson and Colcord, 217-465 passim; *EA, RJ, EH,* and *EAm,* marine lists, 1850-59.

32. Kellogg, 52; *Goode Report,* sec. 5, 1:137-39, 143; *Knight Report on N.S. Fisheries,* 26.

33. *Sabine Report,* 170; *Goode Report,* sec. 5, 1:140-41, 146; *Knight Report on Shore and Deep-Sea Fisheries,* 26.

34. *Sabine Report,* 170.

35. *Goode Report,* sec. 2, 78, and sec. 5, 1:146-47.

36. Ibid., sec. 2, 33, and sec. 5, 1:146.

37. *Halifax Commission Proceedings,* 474.

38. *Goode Report,* sec. 5, 1:145-47.

39. Ibid., sec. 2, 20, 32, and sec. 5, 1:50, 146; *N.S.AppJPHA, 1853,* 120; *RJ,* marine lists, 15 November 1850 and 3 October 1851; *EA,* marine lists, 25 September 1858 and 9 June 1860.

40. *Halifax Commission Proceedings,* 820; Innis, 327.

41. *Goode Report,* sec. 3, opp. 16, and sec. 5, 1:137.

42. *EA,* marine lists, 1 July to November 1856-65.

43. Kellogg, 52; Greene, 367; *Goode Report,* sec. 5, 1:138.

44. *N.S.AppJPHA, 1853,* 120-21.

45. Ibid.

46. *Goode Report,* sec. 2, 25, 41, 60, 63; Greene, 367; PMM, WP, Miscellaneous Vessels, box 2, file 23: schooner *William and John,* account book, April 1825.

47. *Sabine Report,* 173.

48. *Goode Report,* sec. 2, 56, 65,

49. *Sabine Report,* 173; *Hague Arbitration Proceedings,* 2:336-37; 340-47, 358, 360-63; *Goode Report,* sec. 2, 16, 30, 32, 39.

50. *Hague Arbitration Proceedings,* 2: 419-21, 427, 430-31.

51. *Sabine Report,* 173.

52. Ibid.

53. Ibid.

54. Kellogg, 52.

55. *EAm,* marine lists, 1 July to 15 November 1858-64.

56. *Halifax Commission Proceedings,* 2514.

57. Pierce, 82.

58. *Goode Report,* sec. 5, 1:124.

59. Ibid., sec. 2, 50, 68, 70-71; *Hague Arbitration Proceedings,* 2:326; *EA,* marine list, 10 June 1846.

60. *Goode Report,* sec. 3, opp. 67.

61. Ibid., sec. 2, 8, 70.

62. *Hague Arbitration Proceedings,* 2:422; *EA,* marine list, 20 May 1844; *RJ,* marine list, 20 August 1847.

63. *Goode Report,* sec. 2, 32, 60.

64. *RJ,* marine lists, 25 April and 27 June 1851; *EA,* marine lists, 27 May 1854, 1, 6, 20, 28 June 1855, 8 May and 11 June 1857, 28 June 1858, and 15 July and 23 August 1859.

65. *RJ,* marine lists, 25 April and 27 June 1851; *N.S.AppJPHA, 1853,* 120; *EH,* marine list, 8 July 1853; *EA,* marine lists, 26 September 1854, 28 June 1855, 12 September 1856, and 23 July 1858; *EAm,* marine list, 9 July 1858.

66. *EA,* marine list, 13 August 1886; *U.S.FCB, 1886,* 241; see also *EA,* marine lists, 1886-90.

67. For the *Woodruff*'s dimensions and tonnage, see *RAFS, 1891,* 544.

68. *Halifax Commission Proceedings,* 2432.

69. *EA,* marine lists, 15 July and 23 August 1859; see also *EA, RJ, EAm,* marine lists, 1 July to 15 November 1850-59.

70. PMM, GC, MSS 6, 354.

71. *RJ,* marine lists, 26 May and 2, 9 June 1854; *EA,* marine lists, 14, 26 September and 2 November 1854.

72. *RJ,* marine lists, 28 April, 7 July and 10 November 1854; *EA,* marine list, 22 September 1854.

73. *RJ,* marine lists, 4, 25 April and 11 July 1851, and 11 March and 8 April 1853.

74. *EA,* marine lists, 7 April and 8 May 1865.

75. *RJ,* marine lists, 17 June, 11 August, 16 September and 4 November 1853.

76. Greene, 369.

77. *Halifax Commission Proceedings,* 2162.

78. *Goode Report,* sec. 2, 68.

79. *EA,* marine lists, 3 April 1858 and 25 September 1865.

80. *Goode Report,* sec. 2, 70.

81. *EA,* marine lists, 8 May and 11 June 1857.

82. Ibid., 1 July to 15 November 1880–89.

83. *U.S.FCB, 1887,* 70.

84. Ibid., 454.

85. Reynolds, 166.

86. *Anderson Report,* 2.

87. Pierce, 83.

88. *Mackerel Fishery Materials,* 420–29.

89. *Goode Report,* sec. 1, 1:295.

90. Ibid., sec. 3, 20, and sec. 5, 1: 276–77; *N.S.AppJPHA, 1851,* 169.

91. *Halifax Commission Proceedings,* 253–54, 697, 791, 968, 2403, 2412, 2470; *EA,* marine lists, 1 July to 15 November 1857–65.

92. Procter, *Fishermen's Memorial and Record Book,* 63; *Halifax Commission Proceedings,* 2305.

93. *Goode Report,* sec. 2, 40, 48, 83, and sec. 5, 1:276; *EA,* marine list, 10 November 1835.

94. *Halifax Commission Proceedings,* 2757, 3301.

95. *Sabine Report,* 185.

96. *Halifax Commission Proceedings,* 254, 791, 943, 967, 1018–19, 1110, 1418, 2499.

97. *N.S.AppJPHA, 1853,* 120–29.

98. *U.S.RFCN, 1852,* 323–25.

99. *Halifax Commission Proceedings,* 598, 2470.

100. Ibid., 791, 968, 1019.

101. *Goode Report,* sec. 2, 40; *Halifax Commission Proceedings,* 2162.

102. *Halifax Commission Proceedings,* 253.

103. *Mackerel Fishery Materials,* 246.

104. Pierce, 28.

105. *Halifax Commission Proceedings,* 697.

106. *Mackerel Fishery Materials,* 102.

107. *Halifax Commission Proceedings,* 288, 2790.

108. Ibid., 1435.

109. Ibid.

110. *Halifax Commission Proceedings,* 1430.

111. *Goode Report,* sec. 5, 1:291.

112. *Halifax Commission Proceedings,* 228.

113. Donald C. Masters, *The Reciprocity Treaty of 1854* (2nd ed.; Toronto: McClelland and Stewart, 1963), 140–44.

114. *Halifax Commission Proceedings,* 1–6, 8, 81, 96.

115. Ibid., 253.

116. Ibid., 2414.

117. Brebner, *Canada,* 204.

118. *Halifax Commission Proceedings,* 678.

119. *EA,* marine list, 9 August 1878.

120. *Halifax Commission Proceedings,* 197–212.

121. *Mackerel Fishery Materials,* 430.

122. *Can.AppRFB, 1870,* 324.

123. *Mackerel Fishery Materials,* 337.

124. *Halifax Commission Proceedings,* 226–29.

125. *Mackerel Fishery Materials,* 126.

126. Ibid., 420–29.

127. *Goode Report,* sec. 2, 152.

128. *Mackerel Fishery Materials,* 328.

129. *Halifax Commission Proceedings,* 2499.

130. *Goode Report,* sec. 3, 42.

131. Ibid., sec. 5, 1:247, 276–77; *Halifax Commission Proceedings,* 2472; Pierce, 84.

132. *Mackerel Fishery Materials,* 243.

133. *EA,* marine list, 19 September 1853.

134. *Mackerel Fishery Materials,* 244; see also Chapelle, *National Watercraft Collection,* 4–6.

135. *Mackerel Fishery Materials,* 219; Procter, *Fishermen's Memorial and Record Book,* 62.

136. *U.S.RFCN, 1831,* 277.

137. *Halifax Commission Proceedings,* 2412.

138. *RJ,* marine list, 4 November 1859.

139. *Goode Report,* sec. 3, 24.

140. *Halifax Commission Proceedings,* 614–15.

141. Ibid., 246.

142. Ibid., 124.

143. *Goode Report,* sec. 5, 1:247, 277; *U.S.FCB, 1898,* 196.

144. *Goode Report,* sec. 3, 75–76.

145. *Mackerel Fishery Materials*, 220; Procter, *Fishermen's Own Book*, 40.

146. *Mackerel Fishery Materials*, 232.

147. *Goode Report*, sec. 5, 1:275.

148. *EA*, marine list, 19 May 1857; *Goode Report*, sec, 2, 51.

149. *Goode Report*, sec. 5, 1:275.

150. Ibid., 274, 277; *U.S.FCB, 1898*, 194-95.

151. Pierce, 83.

152. *Mackerel Fishery Materials*, 125, 420-29.

153. Ibid., 420-29.

154. *U.S.FCB, 1898*, 195-96; Pierce, 81.

155. Pierce, 78.

156. *U.S.FCB, 1898*, 195; McFarland, 271.

157. *Goode Report*, sec. 5, 1:422.

158. Joseph Smith, 90; *Goode Report*, sec. 5, 1:425.

159. *Goode Report*, sec. 1, 1:563, and sec. 5, 1:421.

160. *Halifax Commission Proceedings*, 706.

161. *Goode Report*, sec. 5, 1:421-22; 476.

162. Ibid., sec. 1, 1:562; sec. 3, 21; and sec. 5, 1:420, 460.

163. *Sabine Report*, 195; *Goode Report*, sec. 5, 1:462-63.

164. *Goode Report*, sec. 5, 1:462.

165. *Sabine Report*, 195.

166. *EA*, marine lists, 18 April, 28 May, and 2 June 1859.

167. *Halifax Commission Proceedings*, 614-15.

168. *EA*, marine list, 25 April 1859; *RJ*, marine lists, 1 July and 11 November 1859.

169. *Goode Report*, sec. 5, 1:147.

170. Ibid., 462.

171. *Goode Report*, sec. 3, 21, and sec. 5, 1:422, 474, 479.

172. Ibid., sec. 5, 1:479.

173. Ibid., 474.

174. *Goode Report*, sec. 2, 16, 19.

175. Ibid., sec. 5, 1:459.

176. Ibid., sec. 2, 41, 69, 71.

177. Ibid., sec. 5, 1:467.

178. Ibid., sec. 2, 19, 23, 32, 50, 71.

179. Ibid., sec. 5, 1:467.

180. Adams, 256; *Goode Report*, sec. 2, 12.

181. *Goode Report*, sec. 5, 1:475.

182. Ibid., 474.

183. *U.S.FCB, 1898*, 478-79.

184. *Goode Report*, sec. 5, 1:468, 475; *Wasson Report*, 80.

185. *Halifax Commission Proceedings*, 2513.

186. *EA*, marine lists, 21 April and 5 June 1883.

Chapter 4

1. *U.S.RDC*, 20th Cong., 1st Sess. (1828), cols. 2069-70.

2. *Sabine Report*, 175-78, 316.

3. *U.S.RFCN*, 1821-90, statements on domestic exports; *Sabine Report*, 176-77.

4. *U.S.RFCN, 1869*, 165; *U.S.RFCN, 1870*, 183; *U.S.Cen., 1870*, 3:793.

5. *U.S.FCB, 1898*, 406.

6. *U.S.RFCN, 1860*, 18-19.

7. *Sabine Report*, 178, 316.

8. *U.S.RFCN, 1870*, 183; *Mackerel Fishery Materials*, 209.

9. Greene, 362.

10. *Goode Report*, sec. 5, 1:146-47.

11. Ibid., sec. 2, 41.

12. Morison, *Maritime History of Massachusetts*, 309; see also Johnson et al., 2:165.

13. *U.S.RFCN, 1821*, 66-67; *U.S.RFCN, 1830*, 198-99.

14. *U.S.RFCN*, 1840-65, statements on domestic exports by country.

15. *U.S.RFCN, 1845*, 4-5.

16. Ibid.

17. *U.S.RFCN*, 1830-60, statements on domestic exports by country.

18. José R. Alvarez Diaz et al., *A Study on Cuba: The Cuban Economic Research Project*, trans. Raul M. Shelton and Rafael M. Zayos (Coral Gables, Fla.: University of Miami Press, 1965), 82, 128-29.

19. Robert G. Albion, *The Rise of New York Port, 1815-1860* (New York: Charles Scribner's Sons, 1939), 180-81; Innis, 227-58.

20. Shannon Ryan, *Fish Out of Water: The Newfoundland Saltfish Trade, 1814-1914* (St. John's, Nfld.: Breakwater Books, 1986), 230; see also Innis, 343-44.

21. Frank Tannenbaum, *Slave and Citi-*

zen: The Negro in the Americas (New York: Alfred A. Knopf, 1947), 34; Noel Deerr, The History of Sugar, 2 vols. (London: Chapman & Hall, 1949-50), 2:307; Fogel and Engerman, 1:34.

22. Arthur F. Corwin, Spain and the Abolition of Slavery in Cuba, 1817-1886 (Austin: University of Texas Press, 1967), 311; Philip S. Foner, A History of Cuba and Its Relations with the United States, 2 vols. (New York: International Publishers Co., 1962-63), 2:292-93; Ramiro Guerra y Sánchez, Sugar and Society in the Caribbean: An Economic History of Cuban Agriculture, trans. Marjory M. Urquidi (New Haven, Conn.: Yale University Press, 1964), xxv; Magnus Morner, Race Mixture in the History of Latin America (Boston: Little, Brown & Co., 1967), 152; Fogel and Engerman, 1:33-34; Deerr, 2:307.

23. Philip Sherlock, West Indian Nations: A New History (New York: St. Martin's Press, 1973), 129, 221.

24. Diaz et al., 9.

25. Halifax Commission Proceedings, 863.

26. Reynolds, 98, 122, 254-55.

27. Hugh Thomas, Cuba: The Pursuit of Freedom (New York: Harper & Row, 1971), 178.

28. Diaz et al., 105.

29. Gilberto Freyre, The Masters and the Slaves: A Study in the Development of Brazilian Civilization, trans. Samuel Putnam (New York: Alfred A. Knopf, 1946), xxiv, 43-47, 51-59, 468-69.

30. U.S.RFCN, 1825, 124-25.

31. Thomas, 126.

32. Sánchez, 62; Thomas, 123.

33. Thomas, 184.

34. Diaz et al., 71, 112.

35. Thomas, 145, 179.

36. Sherlock, 129-30.

37. PMM, WP, Schooner Commerce Collection, file 5: price-current newsletters, J. C. Burnham & Company, Havana, 13, 27 March and 28 July 1852.

38. Diaz et al., 105, 113.

39. Goode Report, sec. 2, 65.

40. George W. Rice, The Shipping Days of Old Boothbay (Portland, Me.: Southworth-Anthoensen Press, 1938), 268, 326.

41. Goode Report, sec. 2, 32.

42. Richard W. Hale, Jr., The Story of Bar Harbor (New York: Ives Washburn, 1949), 121.

43. EA, marine list, 28 September 1848.

44. Coolidge and Mansfield, 236; EA, marine list, 18 April 1862.

45. PMM, WP, Bark Sarah L. Bryant Collection, files 3, 4, 5: captain's letter of instructions and cargo invoice, Castine to Havana, 12 November 1847; sales receipt for freight, Havana, 18 January 1848; and freight account, Havana to London, 27 April 1848.

46. Goode Report, sec. 2, 83.

47. EA, marine lists, 17 December 1830, 7 April 1846, 21 March and 3 April 1848, 2 November 1857, and 24 November 1858.

48. U.S.RFCN, 1856, 560-62.

49. Greenleaf, Survey, 244-46.

50. Sabine Report, 176, 178.

51. U.S.RFCN, 1856, 298-99.

52. U.S.RFCN, 1861, pt. 2, 16-17.

53. U.S.RFCN, 1860, 318-19.

54. Greenleaf, Statistical View, 55-56.

55. U.S.RFCN, 1856, 298-99; U.S.RFCN, 1865, 71; U.S.RFCN, 1875, 380-81.

56. U.S.RFCN, 1870, 246-49; U.S.RFCN, 1880, 244-45.

57. U.S.RFCN, 1856-65, statements on domestic exports by customs district.

58. U.S.RFCN, 1861, pt. 2, pp. 16-17.

59. U.S.RFCN, 1856, 229, 235, 280, 476, 477.

60. U.S.RDC, 20th Cong., 1st Sess. (1828), col. 2069; U.S.RFCN, 1860, 474-75.

61. EA, marine lists, 19 May 1855, and 2 August and 18, 19 November 1856.

62. U.S.RFCN, 1840-60, statements on fishing tonnage by customs district and on domestic exports.

63. Greenleaf, Survey, 250-51.

64. Albion, New York Port, 129.

65. Taylor, 170.

66. Maine Reference Book for 1845, 56; EA, marine lists, 4 February 1856 and 1 January 1857.

67. Anderson Report, 1.

68. EA, marine lists, 10 January 1840, 12 February 1849, 19 February 1855, and 9 June and 5 November 1858.

69. Ibid., 4 May 1854 and 19 February 1855.

70. Ibid., 9 March 1840 and 26 July 1851.

71. Ibid., 18 January 1856 and 3, 6 December 1860; see also Small, 200.

72. *EA*, marine lists, 17 December 1841, 3 February 1844, 15 February and 9 April 1845, 14 February 1846, 5 March 1847, 30 April 1849, 7 May 1850, 21 January 1856, 3 February and 23, 25 April 1857, and 18 November 1859; *ES*, advertisement, 9 April 1856.

73. *EA*, wholesale prices current and Boston market quotations, 5 September 1854; PMM, WP, Witherle & Company's Early Business, box 2, file 47: price-current newsletter, Baltimore Merchants' Exchange, 2 September 1854.

74. *U.S.Cen.*, *1860*, 4:536.

75. *Halifax Commission Proceedings*, 2887.

76. Ibid.

77. *EA*, wholesale price current and Boston market quotations, 6 November 1854; *N.O.PC*, 8 November 1854.

78. *EA*, advertisement, 10 February 1860.

79. PMM, WP, Ship *Canova* Collection, box 1, file 4: cargo invoice, Castine to New Orleans, and captain's letter of instructions, 17 November 1823.

80. See, for example, PMM, WP, Miscellaneous Vessels, box 1, file 8: schooner *Eothen*, settlement of banks voyage, 17 April 1861.

81. PMM, WP, Ship *Antioch* Collection, box 1, file 21; box 2, file 26; and box 3, file 52: cargo invoices and freight lists, Castine to New Orleans, 1 October 1833, January 1835, and 23, 27 November 1840.

82. NA, RBC (RG 36), CDR, Penobscot District Coastwise Manifests, boxes 3, 4: outward manifests of various Castine vessels, 1849–58.

83. Ibid., box 4: outward manifest of ship *Adams*, Castine for New Orleans, 18 December 1857; Castine Tax Valuation Book for 1854.

84. NA, RBC (RG 36), CDR, Penobscot District Coastwise Manifests, box 4: outward manifest of ship *Picayune*, Castine for New Orleans, 17 November 1857.

85. Ibid., boxes 3, 4: outward manifests of ships *William Jarvis* and *William With-erle*, Castine for New Orleans, 24 October 1850 and 17 December 1851; *New Orleans Registers and Enrollments*, 5:40, 74, 141–42, 209; Wasson and Colcord, 317–18.

86. NA, RBC (RG 36), CDR, Penobscot District Coastwise Manifests, box 4: outward manifests of ships *William With-erle* and *Ostervald*, Castine for New Orleans, 17 December 1851 and 9 November 1852.

87. Albion, *New York Port*, 95–96.

88. *Salt Documents*, 168–69; *WC*, 18 February 1846.

89. PMM, WP, Ship *Canova* Collection, box 1, file 4: cargo invoice, Castine to New Orleans, and captain's letter of instructions, 17 November 1823; and freight bill, New Orleans to Havre, 13 February 1824.

90. PMM, WP, Ship *Antioch* Collection, box 2, files, 26, 28: cargo invoice, Castine to New Orleans, and captain's letter of instructions, January 1835; freight list, New Orleans to Liverpool, 12 May 1835; and cargo invoice, Liverpool to Castine, 28 July 1835.

91. For a detailed examination of the British-Canadian aspects of Maine's salt trade, see Wayne M. O'Leary, "The Maine Transatlantic Salt Trade in the Nineteenth Century," *The American Neptune* 47 (Spring 1987): 92–102.

92. John G. B. Hutchins, *The American Maritime Industries and Public Policy, 1789–1914: An Economic History* (Cambridge: Harvard University Press, 1941), 262.

93. Castine Tax Valuation Book for 1854.

94. *New Orleans Registers and Enrollments*, 5:137, 277.

95. NA, RBC (RG 36), CDR, Penobscot District Coastwise Manifests, box 3: outward manifest of ship *William Jarvis*, Castine for New Orleans, 24 October 1850; *EA*, marine lists, 27 November 1850, and 14 January, 29 March, and 23, 25 April 1851.

96. Albion, *New York Port*, 96.

97. NA, RBC (RG 36), CDR, Penobscot District Coastwise Manifests, box 3: outward manifest of ship *Adams*, Castine for New Orleans, 12 November 1849; *EA*,

marine lists, 8 December 1849 and 5 February 1850; *RJ*, marine lists, 14 December 1849 and 8, 27 March 1850.

98. PMM, WP, Miscellaneous Vessels, box 3, file 3: ship *St. Leon*, freight list, Mobile to Boston, February 1849, and cargo invoice, Liverpool to Castine, 12 July 1849; see also *EA*, marine list, 12 November 1849.

99. *Sabine Report*, 173.

100. *Goode Report*, sec. 5, 1:435.

101. Ibid., sec. 1, 1:566, and sec. 5, 1:482.

102. *Halifax Commission Proceedings*, 2551; *Goode Report*, sec. 5, 1:435.

103. *EA*, marine list, 16 March 1885.

104. *Mackerel Fishery Materials*, 233.

105. Thomas S. Berry, *Western Prices Before 1861: A Study of the Cincinnati Market* (Cambridge: Harvard University Press, 1943), 320.

106. *U.S.RFCN, 1837*, 225; *U.S.RFCN, 1838*, 215; *U.S.RFCN, 1839*, 217.

107. *EA*, marine list, 31 July 1858.

108. Greenleaf, *Survey*, 251.

109. Eliot, 34.

110. *EA*, marine lists, 14 October and 2 December 1846, and 23 August 1856; *Goode Report*, sec. 2, 48, 68.

111. *Goode Report*, sec. 2, 50–51, 56, 71.

112. Ibid., 45.

113. *EA*, marine lists, 25 December 1841, 1 December 1848, 26 September 1854, and 15 October 1857.

114. *EA*, marine lists, 1, 11, 14 February 1854.

115. PMM, WP, Miscellaneous Vessels, box 1, files 8, 11, 26, 40, and box 2, files, 1, 21: schooners *Julia Ann, Glendower, Eothen, Redwing, Rubicon*, and *Martha Burgess*, memos of fish sales and settlements of fishing and coasting voyages, 1852–61; see also *The New England Business Directory, 1860* (Boston: Adams, Sampson & Company, 1860), 580.

116. NA, RBC (RG 36), CDR, Penobscot District Coastwise Manifests, boxes 3, 4: inward manifests of schooners *Lucullus, James Henry, Glendower*, and *Redwing*, Castine from Boston, 24 April 1850, 4 February and 3 November 1851, and 7 April 1854.

117. Eliot, 19; *Goode Report*, sec. 2, 32–33; *EA*, marine lists, 1, 7 December 1840.

118. *Goode Report*, sec. 5, 1:160; *Anderson Report*, 1.

119. *EA*, marine lists, 23 January 1850 and 26 January 1861; PMM, WP, Miscellaneous Vessels, box 1, file 40: schooner *Julia Ann*, memo of fish sales, December 1853.

120. *EA*, marine lists, 1840–60.

121. Ibid.

122. *U.S.RFCN, 1856*, 298–99; *U.S.RFCN, 1857*, 286–87; *U.S.RFCN, 1858*, 318–19; *U.S.RFCN, 1859*, 314–15; *U.S.RFCN, 1860*, 318–19; *U.S.RFCN, 1861*, pt. 2, 16–17.

123. *EA*, marine lists, 1840–60.

124. Ibid., 21 January 1843 and 6 September 1848.

125. *EA*, marine list, 17 September 1860.

126. *EA*, marine lists, 13 February 1844, 18 October 1847, 14 March 1855, and 23 November 1858; *ES*, advertisements, 25 February 1857, 18 August 1858, and 2 May and 31 October 1860.

127. *EA*, advertisements, 14 April and 18 August 1858, and 2 May and 31 October 1860.

128. *Goode Report*, sec. 5, 1:482–83.

129. *U.S.FCB, 1898*, 195.

130. *Goode Report*, sec. 2, 90–91.

131. Luther Maddocks, "Looking Backward: Memories from the Life of Luther Maddocks" (unpublished typescript, Maine State Library, Augusta), 7.

132. *RJ*, advertisement, 6 April 1860.

133. *EA*, advertisements, 29 November 1847 and 17 January 1850.

Chapter 5

1. *EA*, supplement, 28 July 1888.

2. *Goode Report*, sec. 2, 31, 51, 708.

3. Ibid., sec. 4, 82.

4. McFarland, 160.

5. George W. Dalzell, *The Flight from the Flag: The Continuing Effect of the Civil War Upon the American Carrying Trade* (Chapel Hill: University of North Carolina Press, 1940), 112–13.

6. *EAm*, news item, 22 August 1862.

7. *Halifax Commission Proceedings,* 2787.

8. Greene, 427–33.

9. The average for nine fishing towns was 24 percent. See: Greene, 427–35; George A. Wheeler, *History of Castine, Penobscot and Brooksville, Maine* (2nd ed. rev.: Cornwall, N.Y.: The Cornwall Press, 1923), 312–15; George A. Wheeler and Henry W. Wheeler, *History of Brunswick, Topsham and Harpswell, Maine* (Boston: Alfred Mudge & Son, 1878), 913–15; John Johnston, *A History of the Towns of Bristol and Bremen in the State of Maine* (Albany, N.Y.: Joel Munsell, 1873), 453–59; Reuel Robinson, *History of Camden and Rockport, Maine* (Rockland, Me.: Huston's Book Store, 1907), 334; William A. Kilby, ed., *Eastport and Passamaquoddy: A Collection of Historical and Biographical Sketches* (Eastport, Me.: Edward E. Shed & Co., 1888), 433; Clayton W. Woodford, *History of York County, Maine* (Philadelphia: Everts & Peck, 1880), 135–36.

10. Greene, 434–35; U.S. MS Census Pop. 1860: Lincoln County, Maine, town of Southport; see also Pierce, 64.

11. *U.S.RFCN, 1861,* pt. 2, 496–97; *U.S.RFCN, 1862,* 322–23; *U.S.RFCN, 1863,* 330–31; *U.S.RFCN, 1864,* 382–83; *U.S. RFCN, 1865,* 720–21.

12. Morison, *Oxford History,* 666.

13. George Wheeler, 1st ed., 370–71.

14. Morison, *Oxford History,* 621; Bell Irwin Wiley, *The Life of Billy Yank: The Common Soldier of the Union* (New York: Bobbs-Merrill Co., 1951), 299, 303; James M. McPherson, *Ordeal by Fire: The Civil War and Reconstruction* (New York: Alfred A. Knopf, 1982), 357.

15. Based on data for 1,738 fishermen derived from U.S. MS Census Pop., 1860: Cumberland County, Maine, city of Portland; Lincoln County, Maine, towns of Boothbay and Southport; Knox County, Maine, towns of Vinalhaven and North Haven; Hancock County, Maine, town of Deer Isle; and Washington County, Maine, city of Eastport. See also John J. Pullen, *The Twentieth Maine: A Volunteer Regiment in the Civil War* (Philadelphia: J. B. Lippincott Co., 1957), 14.

16. Greene, 427–33; U.S. MS Census Pop., 1860: Lincoln County, Maine, town of Boothbay.

17. See, for example, war casualties for Southport, Castine, Harpswell, Bristol, Bremen, Camden, Eastport, Kittery, Deer Isle, and Belfast in Greene, 434–35; George Wheeler, 2nd ed., 312–15; Wheeler and Wheeler, 913–15; Johnston, 453–59, 503–6; Robinson, 334; Kilby, 433; Woodford, 135–36; George L. Hosmer, *An Historical Sketch of the Town of Deer Isle, Maine* (Boston: Stanley & Usher, 1886), 215–16; *Wasson Report,* 16; and Joseph Williamson, *History of the City of Belfast in the State of Maine* (2 vols.; Portland, Me.: Loring, Short & Harmon, 1877), 1:499.

18. Hosmer, 264; U.S. MS Census Pop., 1860: Hancock County, Maine, town of Deer Isle. See also U.S. Census Pop., 1850, 1860: Maine counties of York, Cumberland, Lincoln, Knox, Waldo, Hancock, and Washington, coastal residents by occupation.

19. Greene, 427–33; Hosmer, 264; U.S. MS Census Pop., 1860, 1870, 1880: Lincoln County, Maine, town of Boothbay, and Hancock County, Maine, town of Deer Isle, numbers of resident fishermen by year; *Halifax Commission Proceedings,* 3104–6, 3180–81, 3197–3207.

20. *Mackerel Fishery Materials,* 283.

21. *U.S.RFCN, 1863,* 331; *U.S. RFCN, 1864,* 383.

22. *U.S.RFCN,* 1830–90, statements on fishing tonnage by customs district.

23. *U.S.RFCN, 1861,* pt. 2, 496–97; *U.S.RFCN, 1862,* 322–23; *U.S.RFCN, 1863,* 330–31; *U.S.RFCN, 1864,* 382–83.

24. *U.S.RFCN, 1860,* 18–19; *U.S. RFCN, 1861,* pt. 1, 18–19; *U.S.RFCN, 1862,* 6–7; *U.S.RFCN, 1863,* 7.

25. Dalzell, 4.

26. Wiley, 239.

27. *Halifax Commission Proceedings,* 2283.

28. Ibid., 2611.

29. Ibid.; see also *U.S.RFCN, 1864,* 42.

30. *Halifax Commission Proceedings,* 2296.

31. *Mackerel Fishery Materials,* 284.

32. *Halifax Commission Proceedings,* 3205.

33. *EA,* marine list, 14 December 1864; see also PMM, WP, Miscellaneous Vessels, box 1, files 8, 26, and box 2, file 21: schooners *Glendower, Martha Burgess,* and *Eothen,* settlements of banks voyages, 18 April 1854, 6 May 1856, and 17 April 1861.

34. Small, 185.

35. Joseph Smith, 33.

36. McFarland, 183.

37. *EA,* wholesale prices current on or near 1 September 1830–90; see also wholesale prices at Gloucester, 1830–81, in Procter, *Fishermen's Own Book,* 19.

38. *EA,* wholesale prices current, 16 May 1860, 15 May 1861, and 5 May 1862.

39. *Mackerel Fishery Materials,* 283–84.

40. *EA,* wholesale prices current, 16 May 1860 and 17 May 1864.

41. Mitchell, *History of the Greenbacks,* 450; see also PMM, GC, MS 125.

42. *EA,* wholesale prices current, 16 May 1860 and 17 May 1864.

43. Ibid., 16 May and 3 September 1860, and 17 May and 22 August 1864.

44. Ibid., July 1864–April 1865, passim.

45. Ibid., 16 May 1860, 15 May 1861, 5 May 1862, 13 May 1863, 17 May 1864, and 1 May 1865.

46. *Halifax Commission Proceedings,* 2137, 2220, 2610, 2663, 2767.

47. Robert P. Sharkey, *Money, Class and Party: An Economic Study of Civil War and Reconstruction* (2nd ed., Baltimore: Johns Hopkins University Press, 1967), 53; Irwin Unger, *The Greenback Era: A Social and Political History of American Finance, 1865–1879* (Princeton, N.J.: Princeton University Press, 1964), 15–16.

48. Harold U. Faulkner, *American Economic History* (6th ed. rev.; New York: Harper & Brothers, 1949), 358, 536.

49. F. W. Taussig, *The Tariff History of the United States* (2nd ed. rev.; New York: G. P. Putnam's Sons, 1894), 160.

50. Taussig, 156–57, 167; Sidney Ratner, *The Tariff in American History* (New York: D. Van Nostrand Co., 1972), 24, 26, 29–30.

51. Jefferson, 19:210.

52. *Me.LR, 1840,* chap. 77.

53. *EA,* advertisements, 28 October 1846 and 9 July 1852; *ES,* advertisements, 8 March 1854 and 6 May 1857; Procter, *Fishermen's Own Book,* 248.

54. *Goode Report,* sec. 2, 76; *EA,* marine list, 21 November 1853; see also *U.S.RFCN, 1857,* 394, and *U.S.RFCN, 1861,* pt. 2, 182.

55. *U.S.RFCN, 1860,* 355, 432, 454, 456, 458, 460, 474, 488.

56. U.S. MS Census Ind., 1850: Hancock County, Maine, town of Bucksport, returns for fishing firms; PMM, GC, MS 125.

57. *Halifax Commission Proceedings,* 2622; *U.S.FCB, 1898,* 393, 397; U.S. MS Census Ind., 1870: Cumberland County, Maine, city of Portland, return for firm of Henry Trefethen & Company.

58. Jefferson, 19:277.

59. Morison, *Maritime History of Massachusetts,* 145, 301.

60. *First Jackson Report,* 114.

61. *Goode Report,* sec. 2, 36; *WC,* news item, 18 February 1846.

62. *Salt Documents,* 168–69.

63. PMM, GC, MS 125.

64. Garnett Eskew, *Salt, the Fifth Element: The Story of a Basic American Industry* (Chicago: J. G. Ferguson & Associates, 1948), 93.

65. *Davis Report,* 69.

66. Eskew, 94.

67. Arthur H. Cole, *Wholesale Commodity Prices in the United States, 1700–1861: Statistical Supplement* (Cambridge: Harvard University Press, 1938), 315.

68. Robert P. Multhauf, *Neptune's Gift: A History of Common Salt* (Baltimore: Johns Hopkins University Press, 1978), 251; *U.S.RFCN,* 1830–60, statements on foreign imports.

69. *U.S.RFCN, 1856,* 51, 520; *U.S.RFCN, 1857,* 514, 520; *U.S.RFCN, 1858,* 486, 526; *U.S.RFCN, 1859,* 484, 518. For a full discussion of the salt trade, see O'Leary, "Maine Transatlantic Salt Trade," 83–107.

70. Morison, *Maritime History of Massachusetts,* 301.

71. *Wells Report,* 28, 40; Johnson et al., 2:162–63; see also Taussig, 113–15, and Ratner, 21–25. For the political ramifications of antebellum tariff policy in the Maine

fishing districts, see O'Leary, "Fish and Politics," 106–9.

72. Taussig, 159.

73. *Wells Report*, 40; see also *U.S.CG*, 35th Cong., 1st Sess. (1858), 1933.

74. *Wells Report*, 43–45; *Lynch Report*, 100; Ida M. Tarbell, *The Tariff in Our Times* (New York: Macmillan Co., 1911), 59–60.

75. *EA*, advertisements, 14, 24 April 1868, and marine lists, 14, 21 April 1868.

76. Taussig, 162–63.

77. *U.S.AppCG*, 37th Cong., 2nd Sess. (1862), 374; *U.S.AppCG*, 38th Cong., 1st Sess. (1864), 205, 222; *Wells Report*, 28, 40.

78. Taussig, 162–63, 185; Tarbell, 59.

79. *U.S.RFCN*, *1861*, pt. 1, 482; *U.S. RFCN*, *1862*, 347–49, 355, 357, 363, 365; *U.S.RFCN*, *1870*, 368; *U.S.AppCG*, 37th Cong., 2nd Sess. (1862), 398–99, 401; *U.S.AppCG*, 38th Cong., 1st Sess. (1864), 201–2, 204–5; Taussig, 123–24, 131.

80. Taussig, 167–69, 230, 249–50; Ratner, 31, 34.

81. Taussig, 179, 184.

82. *EA*, wholesale prices current, 16 May 1860 and 5 May 1870; see also BLH, WC, MSS 172, 181: Journals of Fishing Outfits, Witherle & Company, 1860 and 1870.

83. U.S. MS Census Ind., 1860, 1870: Hancock County, Maine, town of Castine, returns for firms of John W. Dresser and John M. Dennett.

84. PMM, WP, Miscellaneous Vessels, box 1, file 7: schooner *Eothen*, bills and receipts, April–October 1860; BLH, WC, case 19: schooner *Eothen*, marine-insurance policies, 14, 15 May 1860; *EA*, marine lists, 27 April and 20 July 1860, and 14 May 1870; Wasson and Colcord, 319; *ALR*, *1863*, 427; *ALR*, *1874*, schrs., 67, 92; U.S. MS Census Ind., 1870: Hancock County, Maine, town of Lamoine, return for firm of Coolidge Brothers; Chapelle, *National Watercraft Collection*, 205–6; *RAFS*, *1879*, 476.

85. PMM, WP, Miscellaneous Vessels, box 1, file 7: schooner *Eothen*, bills and receipts, April–October 1860; U.S. MS Census Ind., 1870: Hancock County, Maine, town of Lamoine, return for firm of Coolidge Brothers.

86. U.S. MS Census Ind., 1870: Hancock County, Maine, town of Castine, return for firm of John W. Dresser; *U.S. RFCN*, *1870*, 638.

87. *EA*, wholesale prices current, 16 May 1860 and 5 May 1870; *U.S.RFCN*, *1870*, 627, 653.

88. *U.S.AppCG*, 39th Cong., 1st Sess. (1866), 419.

89. *EA*, wholesale prices current, 16 May 1860 and 22 May 1868; *U.S.RFCN*, *1870*, 650; see also *Goode Report*, sec. 2, 169.

90. *Goode Report*, sec. 2, 169, 210; see also *U.S.FCB*, *1898*, 392–93, 395–96, 433–34.

91. *U.S.AppCG*, 42nd Cong., 2nd Sess. (1872) 762; Taussig, 185.

92. BLH, WC, case 19: marine-insurance policies, various Castine fishing schooners, 1853–63.

93. PMM, WP, Miscellaneous Vessels, box 2, file 1: schooner *Redwing*, settlements of banks voyages, 24 January 1861 and 3 January 1864.

94. Dalzell, 112; Morison, *Oxford History*, 664.

95. Procter, *Fishermen's Memorial and Record Book*, 24–33.

96. Dalzell, 112.

97. Rice, 275.

98. BLH, WC, case 19: marine-insurance policies, schooners *Eothen*, 22 April 1861; and *Mentora*, 16 May 1861.

99. Ibid., schooners *Eothen*, 16 May 1860 and 15 April 1861; and *Mentora*, *Redwing*, and *Ella Rose*, 19 May 1862.

100. Robert G. Albion and Jennie B. Pope, *Sea Lanes in Wartime: The American Experience, 1775–1942* (New York: W. W. Norton & Company, 1942), 170.

101. *Halifax Commission Proceedings*, 2622.

102. BLH, WC, case 19: marine-insurance policies, schooner *Mentora*, 19 May 1862 and 29 May 1865.

103. *Halifax Commission Proceedings*, 2220, 2550, 2610.

104. PMM, WP, Miscellaneous Vessels, box 1, file 8, and box 2, file 1: schooners *Eothen* and *Redwing*, settlements of banks voyages, 24 January and 18 April 1861, and 7 March 1863; BLH, WC, case 19: marine-insurance policies, schooners *Eothen* and

Redwing, 14 May 1860 and 19 May 1862.

105. BLH, WC, case 19: marine-insurance policies, schooners *Mentora,* 7 May 1860 and 29 May 1865; and *Ella Rose,* 14 May 1860 and 29 May 1865.

106. Albion and Pope, 169.

107. Ibid., 169-70.

108. PMM, WP, Miscellaneous Vessels, box 2, file 1: schooner *Redwing,* settlements of banks voyages, 24 January 1861 and 3 January 1864; see also *EA,* wholesale prices current, 15 May 1861 and 13 May 1863.

109. BLH, WC, case 19: marine-insurance policies, schooners *D. T. Patchin,* 24 May 1867 and 20 May 1869; *Mentora,* 20 May 1869; and *Ella Rose,* 11 June 1870.

110. Ibid., schooner *Ella Rose,* 14 May 1860 and 11 June 1870.

111. Albion and Pope, 170-72.

112. *EA,* marine list, 10 February 1864; *ALR, 1863,* 64; Wasson and Colcord, 315.

113. *EA,* marine lists, 9 July and 16 August 1861; see also *New Orleans Registers and Enrollments,* 5:137.

114. Wheeler, 2nd ed., 153.

115. Hutchins, 321; Johnson et al., 2: 57-59; Faulkner, 243, 531.

116. *U.S.RFCN, 1860,* 650-51; *U.S. RFCN, 1861,* pt. 2, 496-97; *U.S.RFCN, 1862,* 322-23; *U.S.RFCN, 1863,* 330-31;

117. *U.S.RFCN, 1864,* 382-83; *U.S.RFCN, 1865,* 720-21, 728-29.

117. Rowe, 282; Greene, 370; Maddocks, "Looking Backward," 8; *Wasson Report,* 20, 75; Louis C. Hatch, ed., *Maine: A History,* 3 vols. (New York: American Historical Society, 1919), 3:674.

118. *U.S.RFCN,* 1865-92, and *U.S. RCN,* 1893-1900: statements on fishing vessels and tonnage by customs district.

119. *U.S.AppCG,* 39th Cong., 1st Sess. (1866), 419.

120. *U.S.RFCN, 1864,* 382-83; *U.S. RFCN, 1865,* 720-21; *U.S.RFCN, 1866,* 438, 446-47; *U.S.RFCN, 1867,* pt. 1, 314-15.

121. *EA,* wholesale prices current, 1 May 1865, 14 May 1866, 6 May 1867, 22 May 1868, and 5 May 1869.

122. *U.S.RFCN, 1866,* 438, 446-47; *U.S.RFCN, 1867,* pt. 1, 314-15.

123. Greene, 370.

124. *Halifax Commission Proceedings,* 2350.

125. *Goode Report,* sec. 2, 40; see also U.S. MS Census Ind., 1860, 1870: Hancock County, Maine, town of Deer Isle, returns for fishing firms.

126. *U.S.RFCN,* 1865-85: statements on fishing tonnage by customs district.

127. *U.S.RFCN, 1866,* 438, 446-47; *U.S.RFCN, 1867,* pt. 1, 314-15.

Chapter 6

1. Rudyard Kipling, *Captains Courageous: A Story of the Grand Banks* (New York: Century Co., 1896), 97.

2. *Goode Report,* sec. 5, 1:123, 138, 148, 247, 271.

3. PMM, GC, MS 6.

4. PMM, GC, MS 21: Log of the Schooner *Black Hawk,* 1846-47.

5. *RJ,* marine list, 11 July 1851.

6. *Goode Report,* sec. 5, 1:129.

7. Pierce, 43.

8. *EA,* marine lists, 1 July-15 November 1853-59, 1880-89; *RJ,* marine lists, 1 July-15 November 1850-54, 1859.

9. *Goode Report,* sec. 5, 1:159-160; Pierce, 66-69; *Halifax Commission Proceedings,* 791.

10. *ME.RBILS, 1887,* 116; PMM, GC, MS 354.

11. *EA,* marine lists, 1 July-15 November 1853, 1883; *RJ,* marine lists, 1 July-15 November 1853; Wasson and Colcord, 293-94, 315-17, 410; *RAFS, 1882, 1891,* passim.

12. *Goode Report,* sec. 5, 1:123.

13. *U.S.FCB, 1887,* 427.

14. *Halifax Commission Proceedings,* 1262.

15. *Goode Report,* sec. 1, 1:220, and sec. 5, 1:138, 160.

16. *RJ,* article, 30 November 1882.

17. Joseph Smith, 34.

18. *Halifax Commission Proceedings,* 253-54, 260, 318; *Mackerel Fishery Materials,* 334; Small, 187; *RJ,* marine list, 4 August 1848; *EA,* marine list, 25 September 1856.

19. *Goode Report,* sec. 5, 1:269.

20. Pierce, 28.

21. Ibid., 76–77; *Goode Report*, sec. 5, 1:265–66.

22. *EA*, marine lists, 5 April 1875 and 23 September 1876; *Mackerel Fishery Materials*, 327; *Halifax Commission Proceedings*, 3315; *Goode Report*, sec. 5, 1:268–69.

23. Goode, 12.

24. *Halifax Commission Proceedings*, 3315; *Goode Report*, sec. 5, 1:265; Pierce. 74.

25. *Goode Report*, sec. 5, 1:123; Pierce, 33; *EA*, advertisement, 14 April 1868.

26. *Goode Report*, sec. 2, 60, 72, and sec. 5, 1:124.

27. PMM, WP, Miscellaneous Vessels, box 1, file 7: schooner *Eothen*, bill for dory blocks, 14 April 1860; BLH, WC, MS 172: outfitting account of schooner *Redwing*, 11 May 1860; *EA*, marine lists, 24 May and 20 July 1860.

28. *Goode Report*, sec. 5, 1:123.

29. *EA*, marine lists, 22 February and 24 March 1870, and 5 September 1873; *Halifax Commission Proceedings*, 3003, 3011.

30. *Goode Report*, sec. 5, 1:123.

31. Ibid., 158–59; *Halifax Commission Proceedings*, 1997, 2007.

32. *Goode Report*, sec. 5, 1:138, 159.

33. *EA*, news item, 18 April 1857.

34. Joseph Smith, 67.

35. *Goode Report*, sec. 5, 1:159–60.

36. Pierce, 66.

37. Celia Thaxter, *Among the Isles of Shoals* (Boston: James R. Osgood & Co., 1873), 84; *Goode Report*, sec. 2, 57; Procter, *Fishermen's Own Book*, 150.

38. Pierce, 69–70.

39. *Goode Report*, sec. 5, 1:270–71.

40. Ibid., sec. 2, 63, 65, 70, and sec. 5, 1:270–71.

41. Ibid., sec. 5, 1:271–72; *Mackerel Fishery Materials*, 286.

42. *Goode Report*, sec. 5, 1:463.

43. Ibid., sec. 2, 40; Small, 185.

44. *Goode Report*, sec. 5, 1:247, 272.

45. Ibid., 308.

46. *U.S.FCB, 1887*, 455.

47. Small, 184.

48. *Goode Report*, sec. 5, 1:282–83.

49. Chapelle, *American Fishing Schooners*, 65–75; Greene, 292, 368; *EA*, marine lists, 26 April, 13 June and 20 December 1851; *RJ*, marine list, 4 June 1852.

50. *Halifax Commission Proceedings*, 3377; Sylvanus Smith, 66–67.

51. *U.S.Cen., 1870*, 3:792.

52. *Halifax Commission Proceedings*, 3196–3200.

53. Pierce, 33, 70; *Goode Report*, sec. 2, 84.

54. *U.S.FCB, 1887*, 455.

55. *Halifax Commission Proceedings*, 2979, 2982, 2995, 3011, 3026, 3086; PMM, GC, MS 125; PMM, WP, box 1, file 26, and box 2, file 1: schooners *Glendower* and *Redwing*, settlements of banks voyages, 1854–59; U.S. MS Census Ind., 1850: Hancock County, Maine, town of Bucksport, returns for fishing firms. See also Kellogg, 58.

56. *Halifax Commission Proceedings*, 3003, 3011; *U.S.FCB, 1887*, 426.

57. *Halifax Commission Proceedings*, 2979, 2992, 2995, 3011, 3018, 3026.

58. *Goode Report*, sec. 5, 1:292; *Halifax Commission Proceedings*, 2606, 3022.

59. *Halifax Commission Proceedings*, 2607, 2618; *Hall Report*, 20; *U.S. FCB, 1887*, 426.

60. *Goode Report*, sec. 5, 2:126, 149, 151; Pierce, 34, 45.

61. *Halifax Commission Proceedings*, 736; Greene, 367; *Goode Report*, sec. 5, 1: 127, 130–31; PMM, GC, MS 354.

62. PMM, GC, MS 125; *U.S.FCB, 1887*, 426.

63. *Halifax Commission Proceedings*, 2607, 2618; *Goode Report*, sec. 5, 1:151; PMM, GC, MS 125.

64. *Goode Report*, sec. 5, 1:251–52, 255–58; *Hall Report*, 21; *Halifax Commission Proceedings*, 668, 2606.

65. *Goode Report*, sec. 4, 96.

66. Greene, 370.

67. *Halifax Commission Proceedings*, 261, 2992, 3022; *Me.RBILS, 1887*, 115; *Me.RBILS, 1892*, 47; *EA*, marine list, 18 April 1883.

68. *Halifax Commission Proceedings*, 3336.

69. Procter, *Fishermen's Own Book*, 213.

70. *Goode Report*, sec. 5, 1:160; *Halifax Commission Proceedings*, 473, 1262.

71. *Me.RBILS, 1892*, 47.

72. *Goode Report*, sec. 5, 1:52–54; *Hall Report*, 21.

73. *Goode Report*, sec. 5, 1:252.

74. Ibid., 253–54; *Me.RBILS, 1892*, 47.

75. *Mackerel Fishery Materials*, 56–58, 78.

76. Greene, 370.

77. *Mackerel Fishery Materials*, 58.

78. Ibid., 78; *Me.RBILS, 1892*, 47.

79. *Me.RBILS, 1892*, 47.

80. *Goode Report*, sec. 3, 42.

81. *Halifax Commission Proceedings*, 338, 646; *Goode Report*, sec. 5, 1:254.

82. *EA*, marine list, 11 September 1883; see also *EA*, marine lists, 5 September 1873, 23 March 1882, and 19 April 1887, and news item, 1 January 1877.

83. *Hall Report*, 19.

84. Pierce, 81; *Mackerel Fishery Materials*, 55.

85. *EA*, marine list, 15 April 1884.

86. *Goode Report*, sec. 5, 1:164, 179.

87. *Me.RBILS, 1887*, 115; *EA*, 7 August 1877 and 14 August 1884.

88. *EA*, marine list, 18 April 1883.

89. *Halifax Commission Proceedings*, 3449; see also BLH, WC, case 19: marine-insurance policies, various Castine fishing schooners, 1870–77.

90. Pierce, 70.

91. *Halifax Commission Proceedings*, 2271, 2273; *Goode Report*, sec. 5, 1:152.

92. *U.S.FCB, 1887*, 426–27; *Goode Report*, sec. 5, 1:127; Greene, 367–68; *Halifax Commission Proceedings*, 3003; Pierce, 44; PMM, GC, MSS 6, 125, 354.

93. *Halifax Commission Proceedings*, 631, 2269–70, 2280, 2588.

94. *Goode Report*, sec. 5, 1:151–52, 161–63, 182–87, 436–37; *Halifax Commission Proceedings*, 85, 96, 1344, 2271–73, 2280.

95. *Halifax Commission Proceedings*, 2272, 2275, 3249, 3252; *Goode Report*, sec. 5, 2:151, 183–85, 437.

96. *Goode Report*, sec. 5, 1:151–52, 437; *Halifax Commission Proceedings*, 2271–72.

97. *Halifax Commission Proceedings*, 2803.

98. Ibid., 3249.

99. Ibid., 2272, 2607, 3251–52.

100. Ibid., 2272.

101. Ibid., 2271–72; *Goode Report*, sec. 5, 1:127.

102. *Goode Report*, sec. 5, 1:291–92.

103. Ibid., 160.

104. *Goode Report*, sec. 2, 84.

105. *Halifax Commission Proceedings*, 2801.

106. Ibid., 2017.

107. *Me.RBILS, 1887*, 111–16.

108. *Halifax Commission Proceedings*, 1255, 1387, 1416, 1997, 3233.

109. Ibid., 2801; Sylvanus Smith, 84–85, 90; *Can.RFB, 1890*, pt. 3, 15–16; *Can. AppRFB, 1890*, 142.

110. Joseph Smith, 36.

111. *Can.AppRFB, 1890*, 140.

112. *Goode Report*, sec. 5, 1:303.

113. *Me.RBILS, 1887*, 115–16; see also 111–14.

114. Goode, 66.

115. *Can.RFB, 1890*, lxx.

116. *Knight Report on N.S. Fisheries*, 9–10.

117. *Halifax Commission Proceedings*, 2801.

118. *Can.AppRFB, 1890*, 147.

119. *Mass.Cen., 1885*, 2:1389; *Mass.Cen., 1895*, 6:111.

Chapter 7

1. *Goode Report*, sec. 4, 18.

2. *Mackerel Fishery Materials*, 194–201; see also *U.S.RFCN*, 1830–65, statements on fishing tonnage by customs district.

3. *U.S.RFCN*, 1840–92, and *U.S.RCN*, 1893–1900: statements on fishing vessels and tonnage by customs district.

4. *Goode Report*, sec. 2, 83, 134, 173, 189, 227, 234.

5. *Mackerel Fishery Materials*, 207–8; see

also *MIJ*, news item, 28 November 1884.

6. *U.S.RFCN*, 1879–92, and *U.S.RCN*, 1893–96: statements on fishing vessels and tonnage by customs district.

7. *U.S.RFCN, 1883*, 875–76; *MIJ*, news item, 14 December 1883.

8. *MIJ*, news item, 26 December 1884.

9. *U.S.RFCN, 1870*, 767; *U.S.RFCN, 1880*, 860; *U.S.RFCN, 1885*, 910; *Mackerel Fishery Materials*, 207–8.

10. *U.S.RFCN, 1865*, 485; *U.S.RFCN, 1870*, 124–25; *U.S.RFCN, 1880*, 119–20.

11. *MBD, 1871*, 130, 132; *MBD, 1885*, 166–67, 169–70.

12. *U.S.RFCN*, 1845–60 and 1870–85, statements on fishing vessels and tonnage by customs district.

13. *Goode Report*, sec. 2, 83.

14. *EA*, marine lists, 1866–90; *U.S.MV, 1884*, passim; *RAFS, 1879, 1882, 1891*, passim; *ALR, 1874;* William A. Baker, *A Maritime History of Bath, Maine and the Kennebec River Region*, 2 vols. (Bath, Me.: Marine Research Society of Bath, 1973), 2:840–70 passim. See also *U.S. RFCN, 1868*, pt. 3, 70, and *U.S.RFCN, 1883*, 875.

15. *Goode Report*, sec. 2, 35.

16. *EA*, marine list, 14 July 1868; *Goode Report*, sec. 2, 40.

17. *U.S.RFCN*, 1830–80, statements on fishing tonnage by customs district.

18. *Goode Report*, sec. 5, 76.

19. *EA*, marine lists, 9, 14 June 1866, 7, 25 June 1867, and 10 June 1868; *Halifax Commission Proceedings*, 3191–92.

20. *Goode Report*, sec. 2, 68; Rice, 326.

21. *Mackerel Fishery Materials*, 423–29; *U.S.MV, 1884*, passim; *RAFS, 1879*, passim; *RAFS, 1882*, passim.

22. *Goode Report*, sec. 2, 38.

23. *EA*, marine list, 21 August 1888; *PDRB, 1885*, 589.

24. Arthur C. Bining and Thomas C. Cochran, *The Rise of American Economic Life* (4th ed. rev.: New York: Charles Scribner's Sons, 1964), 410–12; August C. Bolino, *The Development of the American Economy* (Columbus, Ohio: Charles E. Merrill Books, 1961), 438–39; see also Faulkner, 548–49, and Unger, 213, 220, 226, 265, 324.

25. *EA*, wholesale prices current on or near 1 September 1873–79; Procter, *Fisherman's Own Book*, 19.

26. *Halifax Commission Proceedings*, 254.

27. *EA*, wholesale prices current on or near 1 September 1873–79; *Goode Report*, sec. 2, 169.

28. *Halifax Commission Proceedings*, 2767.

29. *EA*, wholesale prices current, 5 May 1870 and 18 April 1877.

30. BLH, WC, MSS 181, 183: Journals of Fishing Outfits, Witherle & Company, 1870, 1874; BLH, WC, case 19: marine insurance policies, schooners *D. T. Patchin*, 11 June 1870 and 6 June 1877, and *Ella Rose*, 29 May 1865 and 6 June 1877.

31. *Halifax Commission Proceedings*, 2655, 2768; *EA*, marine list, 28 May 1866.

32. *Halifax Commission Proceedings*, 2607, 2655.

33. *EA*, marine list, 1 November 1860; Hutchins, 387–88.

34. U.S. MS Census Ind., 1860: Hancock County, Maine, town of Trenton, return for firm of Hodgkins Brothers; U.S. MS Census Ind., 1870: Hancock County, Maine, town of Lamoine, returns for firms of Coolidge Brothers and King Brothers.

35. *Lynch Report*, 42, 130, 142, 145, 195–96; *Hall Report*, 97–98.

36. *EA*, wholesale prices current on or near 1 May 1870–79.

37. *Hall Report*, 101.

38. *Goode Report*, sec. 5, 1:169; *EA*, wholesale prices current on or near 1 May 1873–79.

39. *EA*, marine list, 5 April 1875.

40. *U.S.RFCN, 1870*, 767; *U.S.RFCN, 1880*, 860.

41. *Halifax Commission Proceedings*, 3104–7, 3179–3211.

42. U.S. MS Census Ind., 1850: Lincoln County, Maine, towns of Boothbay, Southport, and Westport, returns for fishing firms; *Halifax Commission Proceedings*, 3194–3208.

43. U.S. MS Census Ind., 1870: Lincoln County, Maine, town of Southport, returns for fishing firms; *Halifax Commission Proceedings*, 3194–96.

44. U.S. MS Census Ind., 1860, 1870: Hancock County, Maine, town of Deer Isle, returns for fishing firms; *Halifax Commission Proceedings*, 3104–6, 3180–81.

45. U.S. MS Census Ind., 1860: Knox County, Maine, town of North Haven, returns for fishing firms; *Halifax Commission Proceedings*, 3179–80.

46. PMM, GC, MS 78: Castine District

Customs Collector's Abstract of Licenses Issued to Fishing Vessels, 1870–89.

47. PMM, GC, MS 229; NA, RDT (RG 56), GR, Abstracts of Fishing Bounty Allowances, vol. 417: Penobscot District allowances, 1st quarter 1849.

48. U.S. MS Census Ind., 1850: Hancock County, Maine, towns of Castine and Bucksport, returns for fishing firms. See also Castine Tax Valuation Book for 1854: valuations for schooners *Mary Brewer, Amanda Powers,* and *Silver Cloud; EH,* marine lists, 28 January, 11 February, 20 May, and 26 August 1853; *RJ,* marine list, 9 June 1854; and NA, RBMIN (RG 41), VDR, Penobscot District Enrollments, vol. 40: certificates of enrollment, schooners *Amanda Powers* and *Mary Brewer,* 4 November 1851 and 21 May 1852.

49. *Goode Report,* sec. 2, 76, and sec. 4, 95.

50. NA, RDT (RG 56), GR, Abstracts of Fishing Bounty Allowances, vol. 417: Penobscot District allowances, 1st quarter 1849; see also PMM, GC, MS 229.

51. U.S. MS Census Ind., 1850: Hancock County, Maine, towns of Castine and Deer Isle, returns for fishing firms.

52. Ibid., town of Deer Isle, return for firm of S. & H. Grove.

53. U.S. MS Census Ind., 1860 and 1870: Hancock County, Maine, town of Deer Isle, returns for fishing firms.

54. Goode, 22.

55. NA, RBMIN (RG 41), VDR, Portland-Falmouth District Registers and Enrollments, 1876–80: certificates of registry and enrollment for various schooners; *Mackerel Fishery Materials,* 420–29 passim; *PDRB, 1877, 1881,* passim; *MBD, 1880,* passim; *MIJ,* news item, 26 December 1884.

56. NA, RBMIN (RG 41), VDR, Belfast District Enrollments, 1850–52, and Portland-Falmouth District Registers and Enrollments, 1876–80: certificates for various schooners; *RJ,* news item, 6 August 1852; *Mackerel Fishery Materials,* 420–29 passim.

57. NA, RBMIN (RG 41), VDR, Portland-Falmouth District Registers and Enrollments, 1876–80: certificates for vari-

ous schooners; *Mackerel Fishery Materials,* 420–29 passim; *PDRB, 1877, 1881,* passim; *MBD, 1880,* passim; *MIJ,* news item, 26 December 1884; see also U.S. MS Census Ind., 1850: Hancock County, Maine, towns of Bucksport and Castine, returns for fishing firms.

58. NA, RBMIN (RG 41), VDR, Belfast District Enrollments, 1850–52, and Portland-Falmouth District Registers and Enrollments, 1876–80: certificates for various schooners; *RJ,* news item, 6 August 1852; *Mackerel Fishery Materials,* 420–29 passim.

59. *Hall Report,* 13.

60. Procter, *Fishermen's Own Book,* 273.

61. NA, RBMIN (RG 41), VDR, Portland-Falmouth District Registers and Enrollments, 1877–83: certificates for various schooners; *Mackerel Fishery Materials,* 420–29 passim; *PDRB, 1877, 1881,* passim; *MBD, 1880,* passim; *MIJ,* news item, 26 December 1884.

62. Sylvanus Smith, 69–70.

63. Joseph Smith, 234.

64. *Halifax Commission Proceedings,* 2379.

65. Ibid., 2285, 2291, 2296.

66. *Halifax Commission Proceedings,* 2428; Procter, *Fishermen's Own Book,* 19.

67. *Halifax Commission Proceedings,* 2238–40, 2428, 2636.

68. Ibid., 2636.

69. Ibid., 2238, 2240.

70. *Goode Report,* sec. 4, 96.

71. *Halifax Commission Proceedings,* 2428.

72. *U.S.FCB, 1898,* 196.

73. Joseph Smith, 37.

74. *Me.RBILS, 1887,* 112.

75. *EA,* news item, 4 November 1882.

76. Ibid., 22 November 1882; *MIJ,* news item, 24 November 1882.

77. *RJ,* news item, 30 November 1882.

78. *EA,* supplement, 28 July 1888.

79. *MIJ,* news item, 4 April 1884.

80. *EA,* news item, 2 November 1882.

81. *Me.PL, 1821,* chap. 150; *Mackerel Fishery Materials,* 372–78.

82. *MBD, 1880,* 134–36, 178; *MIJ,* news item, 14 December 1883 and 26 December 1884.

83. *U.S.FCB, 1898*, 498; *Mackerel Fishery Materials*, 153.

84. *Halifax Commission Proceedings*, 2418.

85. *Mackerel Fishery Materials*, 152–53.

86. *Me.PL, 1875*, chap. 2, sec. 5.

87. *EA*, wholesale prices current, 2 September 1878.

88. *Me.PL, 1832*, chap. 36; *Me.PL, 1836*, chap. 199.

89. *Mackerel Fishery Materials*, 100–2.

90. Henry Demarest Lloyd, *Wealth Against Commonwealth* (New York: Harper & Brothers, 1894), 494.

91. *U.S.AppAC*, 2nd Cong., 1st Sess. (1792), col. 1331.

92. *Sabine Report*, 166; see also *Perley Reports*, 172.

93. *Goode Report*, sec. 2, 179, 184, 707, 724, and sec. 5, 1:130, 132.

94. Morison, *Maritime History of Massachusetts*, 310; *Goode Report*, sec. 4, 165.

95. NA, RBC (RG 36), CDR, Penobscot District Fishing Articles of Agreement: articles for schooners *Dolphin* of Vinalhaven, 22 April 1830; and *Pamelia* of Islesboro, 5 July 1830. See also Kellogg, 59–60, 194, 271–72.

96. Reynolds, 109; Morison, *Maritime History of Massachusetts*, 309; *Halifax Commission Proceedings*, 2173–74; *Wright Report*, 16.

97. *Anderson Report*, 1; *Goode Report*, sec. 2, 71, and sec. 5, 1:146. See also NA, RBC (RG 36), CDR, Penobscot District Fishing Articles of Agreement: articles for Castine schooners *Charles*, 7 April 1838; *Olive*, 3 May 1845; *Amazon*, 4 May 1854; *Lagrange*, 6 June 1854; and *Minerva*, 22 June 1854.

98. PMM, WP, Miscellaneous Vessels, box 2, file 19: schooner *George Henry*, fishing articles of agreement, 18 June 1858; Small, 180. See also NA, RBC (RG 36), CDR, Penobscot District Fishing Articles of Agreement: articles for schooners *Andover* of Deer Isle, 22 April 1846; *Superb* of Sedgwick, 21 May 1847; and *Ames* of Deer Isle, 22 April 1848.

99. Procter, *Fishermen's Memorial and Record Book*, 82–87; Procter, *Fishermen's Own Book*, 28–35; *Goode Report*, sec. 4, 95.

100. *Goode Report*, sec. 2, 84, 145, 235, and sec. 5, 1:23; *Halifax Commission Proceedings*, 295, 2223, 2550, 2603, 2979; Small, 186; *Me.RBILS, 1887*, 115.

101. *U.S.FCB, 1881*, 234–35; *Goode Report*, sec. 2, 145–46, 194.

102. *Goode Report*, sec. 2, 145, and sec. 5, 1:157–58; *Halifax Commission Proceedings*, 2597, 3321.

103. PMM, WP, Miscellaneous Vessels, box 1, file 26: schooner *D. T. Patchin*, settlement of banks voyage, 24 December 1870; Pierce, 62; *Halifax Commission Proceedings*, 2979; *Goode Report*, sec. 5, 1:83.

104. Kellogg, 58; *Goode Report*, sec. 4, 97–98.

105. Nicolas P. Gilman, *Profit Sharing Between Employer and Employee: A Study in the Evolution of the Wages System* (3rd ed.; Boston: Houghton, Mifflin & Co., 1896), 26.

106. *Halifax Commission Proceedings*, 267, 269, 295.

107. *Goode Report*, sec. 2, 146, and sec. 4, 95.

108. Ibid., sec. 2, 32, 45, and sec. 4, 95; *Halifax Commission Proceedings*, 2175; see also *MIJ*, news items, 16 January, 24 April, and 25 December 1885.

109. *Halifax Commission Proceedings*, 2388.

110. Morison, *Maritime History of Massachusetts*, 137, 310; NA, RBC (RG 36), CDR, Penobscot District Fishing Articles of Agreement: articles for Castine schooners *Amazon*, *Lagrange*, and *Minerva*, 4 May and 6, 22 June 1854.

111. BLH, WC, MS 172; *Goode Report*, sec. 2, 83–84, 194.

112. *Goode Report*, sec. 2, 14; *Halifax Commission Proceedings*, 2173–74.

113. *Goode Report*, sec. 2, 708.

114. *Halifax Commission Proceedings*, 2801.

115. *EA*, marine lists, 8 October 1855, 2 October 1858, 19 September 1859, 25 September 1884, and 13 August and 11 September 1886; *Goode Report*, sec. 2, 32, and sec. 5, 1:129.

116. *Goode Report*, sec. 4, 159; *Halifax Commission Proceedings*, 614–15.

117. *Halifax Commission Proceedings*, 167.

118. *Perley Reports,* 173.

119. *Goode Report,* sec. 4, 160–61.

120. Ibid., sec. 5, 1:149.

121. *Halifax Commission Proceedings,* 1338.

122. Ibid., 270.

123. *Goode Report,* sec. 2, 45, and sec. 5, 1:146; *EA,* supplement, 28 July 1888.

124. Procter, *Fishermen's Memorial and Record Book,* 85.

125. *Goode Report,* sec. 2, 83–84, 89, 145, 156–59, and sec. 5, 1:234; Procter, *Fishermen's Own Book,* 213–14.

126. *Goode Report,* sec. 4, 96.

127. *EA,* supplement, 28 July 1888.

128. Robert C. Brown, *Canada's National Policy, 1883–1900: A Study in Canadian-American Relations* (Princeton, N.J.: Princeton University Press, 1964), 5–6; John B. Brebner, *North Atlantic Triangle: The Interplay of Canada, the United States and Great Britain* (Toronto: Ryerson Press, 1945), 185; Innis, 224; Masters, 20–21, 140–41.

129. *U.S.AppAC,* 14th Cong., 2nd Sess. (1817), col. 1286.

130. *Halifax Commission Proceedings,* 1, 8, 85, 94, 96; Johnson et al., 2:229; *EA,* supplement, 28 July 1888.

131. *Halifax Commission Proceedings,* 265.

132. Ibid., 3250.

133. Ibid., 612.

134. Ibid., 3101; *EA,* supplement, 28 July 1888.

135. *Halifax Commission Proceedings,* 3272, 3298.

136. Ibid., 3214, 3232–33, 3245, 3250, 3272.

137. Henry Steele Commager, ed., *Documents of American History,* 2 vols. (4th ed.; New York: Appleton-Century-Crofts, 1948), 1:436.

138. *EA,* supplement, 28 July 1888.

139. *MIJ,* news item, 3 April 1885.

140. *U.S.FCB, 1890,* 103, 133.

141. *Goode Report,* sec. 5, 1:247–48, 277.

142. Ibid., sec. 4, 7.

143. Ibid., 95.

144. *Mackerel Fishery Materials,* 305.

145. *MIJ,* news item, 5 November 1886.

146. *Halifax Commission Proceedings,* 2459.

147. Ibid., 2302, 2379, 2459.

148. *Goode Report,* sec. 5, 1:96.

149. *Halifax Commission Proceedings,* 3181–94; Wesley C. Mitchell, *Gold, Prices, and Wages under the Greenback Standard* (Berkeley: University of California Press, 1908), 601–2.

150. *Halifax Commission Proceedings,* 2379.

151. Ibid., 2388.

152. Ibid., 2515.

153. *Me.RBILS, 1887,* 112.

154. *Halifax Commission Proceedings,* 2290.

155. Calculated from U.S. MS Census Pop. 1850: Cumberland County, Maine, towns of Harpswell and Freeport; Lincoln County, Maine, towns of Georgetown, Phippsburg, Wiscasset, Westport, Boothbay, Southport, and Damariscotta; Waldo County, Maine, towns of Searsport, Vinalhaven, and North Haven; Hancock County, Maine, towns of Castine, Blue Hill, Eden, Trenton, and Hancock; and Washington County, Maine, towns of Steuben, Harrington, Milbridge, Machias, Machiasport, Jonesboro, and Jonesport.

156. Ibid., 1860, 1870: York County, Maine, town of Kennebunkport; Cumberland County, Maine, city of Portland; Sagadahoc County, Maine, town of Georgetown; Lincoln County, Maine, towns of Westport, Southport, and Boothbay; Knox County, Maine, towns of Vinalhaven and North Haven; Hancock County, Maine, towns of Deer Isle and Swan's Island; and Washington County, Maine, town of Lubec and city of Eastport.

157. *Goode Report,* sec. 4, 13.

158. Ibid., 11; see also U.S. MS Census Pop., 1880: Cumberland County, Maine, city of Portland.

159. *Goode Report,* sec. 2, 89.

160. *Historical Statistics,* U.S., 90; Faulkner, 477.

161. *Sabine Report,* 314, 316; Sylvanus Smith, 117; Morison, *Maritime History of Massachusetts,* 311; *U.S.AppCG,* 34th

Cong., 3rd Sess. (1857), 221; *U.S.CG,* 35th Cong., 1st Sess. (1858), 2023.

162. *U.S.AppCG,* 34th Cong., 3rd Sess. (1857), 221; Kellogg, 197.

163. Calculated from: PMM, GC, MSS 6, 125; PMM, WP, Miscellaneous Vessels, box 2, files, 1, 21; schooner *Redwing,* settlement of coasting voyage to Boston, March 1854, and schooner *Martha Burgess,* settlement of Grand Banks voyage, 6 May 1856; BLH, WC, case 19: marine-insurance policies for various Castine fishing schooners, 1853; NA, RBC (RG 36), CDR, Penobscot District Fishing Articles of Agreement: articles for various Castine schooners, 1854; Wasson and Colcord, 317; *U.S.AppAC,* 15th Cong., 2nd Sess. (1819), cols. 2531-35; *EA,* Boston wholesale prices current, 6, 13, 20 March 1854.

164. Innis, 334; *Goode Report,* sec. 4, 96; *MIJ,* news item, 6 October 1882; Leone Levi, "The Economic Condition of Fishermen," *The International Fisheries Exhibition Literature,* vol. 4: *Conferences Held in Connection with the Great International Fisheries Exhibition of 1883,* pt. 1 (London: William Clowes & Sons, 1884), 18-19, 40.

165. *U.S.AppCG,* 34th Cong., 3rd Sess. (1857), 220.

166. *Halifax Commission Proceedings,* 2351.

167. Kellogg, 197, 275.

168. Ibid., 70.

169. *Halifax Commission Proceedings,* 2589.

170. Ibid., 2428; see also Frederick William Wallace, *Blue Water: A Tale of the Deep Sea Fishermen* (Toronto: Musson Book Co., 1914), 61.

171. Wallace, 59-61.

172. *EA,* marine list, 28 August 1858; PMM, WP, Miscellaneous Vessels, box 1, file 26: schooner *Glendower,* settlement of banks voyage, 15 March 1859.

173. *Goode Report,* sec. 4, 95.

174. PMM, GC, MS 125: outfitting accounts of schooners *Redwing* and *Martha Burgess,* 6, 9 May 1853.

175. *U.S.CG,* 35th Cong., 1st Sess. (1858), 2024; Reynolds, 246; Sylvanus Smith, 53.

176. *Goode Report,* sec. 2, 146, and sec. 4, 95.

177. *Halifax Commission Proceedings,* 2379; *Goode Report,* sec. 2, 146, and sec. 4, 95; Sylvanus Smith, 118.

178. PMM, WP, Miscellaneous Vessels, box 1, file 26: schooner *D. T. Patchin,* settlement of banks voyage, 24 December 1870; Sylvanus Smith, 118.

179. Sylvanus Smith, 53; Daniel Remich, *History of Kennebunk From its Earliest Settlement to 1890* (Kennebunk, Me.: private printing, 1911), 389.

180. *Goode Report,* sec. 2, 40.

181. Ibid., 40-41.

182. Ibid., 84.

183. *Goode Report,* sec. 4, 94.

Chapter 8

1. Willis Barnstone, ed. and trans., *Greek Lyric Poetry* (Bloomington: Indiana University Press, 1962), 199.

2. *U.S.FCB, 1886,* 49.

3. *MIJ,* news item, 16 January 1885.

4. *EA,* marine list, 18 October 1841.

5. Compiled from: *RJ,* marine lists and news items, 1840-60; *EA,* marine lists and news items, 1840-90; *Andrews Report,* 657; *Halifax Commission Proceedings,* 222-25; George Wheeler, 1st ed., 99; Joseph Williamson, 1:815-22 passim; Small, 199; Hosmer, 215-16.

6. Greene, 325, 383-84; Rice, 257-58; 292, 304; *Halifax Commission Proceedings,* 223; *EA,* marine lists, 16 August, 27 October, and 20 December 1851, 23 October 1867, 19 September 1868, 9 July 1869, and 5 September 1873; *RJ,* marine list, 22 August 1851.

7. *Halifax Commission Proceedings,* 3182-94 passim.

8. *EA,* marine list, 11 November 1858; see also Hosea Wardwell, "Diary of Events in Penobscot, Maine, 1873-1913, with Notes on Earlier Years" (typed transcript in possession of Mr. Reed Sinclair, Penobscot, Maine).

9. *EA*, marine list, 26 October 1846.

10. Greene, 383.

11. Calculated from U.S. MS Census Pop., 1860, 1870, 1880: Cumberland County, Maine, city of Portland; Lincoln County, Maine, towns of Boothbay and Southport; Knox County, Maine, towns of Vinalhaven and North Haven; Hancock County, Maine, town of Deer Isle; and Washington County, Maine, city of Eastport.

12. Calculated from: *RJ*, marine lists and news items, 1840-60; *EA*, marine lists and news items, 1840-90; *Andrews Report*, 657; *Halifax Commission Proceedings*, 222-25; George Wheeler, 1st ed., 99; Joseph Williamson, 1:815-22 passim; Small, 199; Hosmer, 215-16.

13. *Halifax Commission Proceedings*, 262; see also *Goode Report*, sec. 3, 21.

14. *N.S.AppJPHA, 1853*, 118.

15. *Goode Report*, sec. 3, opp. 16, and sec. 4, 107; *Halifax Commission Proceedings*, 2078.

16. *EA*, marine list, 19 October 1858.

17. *Mackerel Fishery Materials*, 253.

18. *Goode Report*, sec. 5, 1:468.

19. *MN*, news item, 13 October 1851; *EA*, news item, 25 October 1851; *Mackerel Fishery Materials*, 249. See also *Halifax Commission Proceedings*, 599.

20. *EA*, news item, 14 October 1851.

21. Ibid., 18 October 1851; *MN*, news item, 15 October 1851.

22. Compiled from: *Andrews Report*, 657-59; Greene, 383-84; Hosmer, 216; Small, 199; *EA*, news items, 13-27 October 1851 and 26 January 1852; *RJ*, news items, 3, 17, 22, 31 October 1851; *WC*, news items, 14-17 October 1851; *EH*, news item, 6 November 1851.

23. *EA*, news item, 18 October 1851.

24. *EH*, news item, 6 November 1851.

25. *EA*, marine lists, 10 January 1849, 25, 28 October 1853, 6, 19 October 1858, 18, 23 October 1867, 5, 11 September 1873, and 24 September 1886; Rice, 257; Greene, 380; George Wheeler, 1st ed., 99; Joseph Williamson, 1:819; Hosmer, 215-16; *Mackerel Fishery Materials*, 253; *Goode Report*, sec. 4, 107-8, and sec. 5, 1:468; *Halifax Commission Proceedings*, 222-25; *U.S.FCB,*

1886, 273; see also George W. Blunt, ed., *The American Coast Pilot* (16th ed.; E. & G. W. Blunt, 1850), 64-66.

26. *Sabine Report,* 170; *Goode Report* sec. 3, 65; and sec. 5, 1:148; *Hague Arbitration Proceedings,* 1: map insert no. 1.

27. *EA*, marine lists, 15 September 1853, 2 October 1854, 3 September 1856, 13 August and 5 October 1857, 22 August and 12 October 1859, 15 August and 8 October 1860, and 26 August and 5 October 1861; PMM, GC, MSS 6, 354; see also *Hague Arbitration Proceedings,* 1: map insert no. 1.

28. Blunt, 119-20.

29. Ibid., 12; *Sabine Report,* 170; Samuel Eliot Morison, *The European Discovery of America: The Northern Voyages,* A.D. 500-1600 (New York: Oxford University Press, 1971), 476.

30. Blunt, 12; see also *Andrews Report,* 593.

31. *Goode Report,* sec. 4, 105-6.

32. *EA*, marine lists, 23 September 1873, 9 September 1881, and 23 March 1882.

33. Ibid., 5 September 1873 and 12 August 1889; PMM, GC, MS 249: Castine District Customs Collector's Record of Wreck Reports, 1884-1900, 40, 91.

34. *RJ*, marine list, 1 October 1850; *EA*, marine lists, 11 September 1852, 7 October 1854, 22 September 1855, and 31 August 1857.

35. *EA*, marine lists, 20 September 1844 and 11 September 1852; *RJ*, marine list, 1 October 1850; PMM, GC, MS 249, 29.

36. *RJ*, marine list, 10 November 1854.

37. Ibid., 1 October 1850; *EA*, marine lists, 20 September 1844, 7 October 1854, 22 September 1855, 31 August 1857, 29, 30 July 1885, and 12 August 1889.

38. *EA*, marine list, 30 July 1885.

39. *RJ*, marine list, 6 August 1852; *EA*, marine lists, 11 September 1861 and 19 September 1868.

40. Robert G. Albion, *Square Riggers on Schedule: The New York Sailing Packets to England, France, and the Cotton Ports* (Princeton, N.J.: Princeton University Press, 1938), 6-8; Albion and Pope, 27; see also Herman Melville, *Redburn: His First Voyage* (New York: Harper & Brothers, 1863), 127.

41. *EA,* marine lists, 12 July 1848, 30 July 1849, and 20 September 1859.

42. Ibid., 19 May 1846, 30 July 1849, 11 August 1851, 20 September 1859, and 26 September 1874; see also Melville, 127.

43. *EA,* marine list, 30 June 1848.

44. Ibid., marine lists, 16, 19, 26 September 1874.

45. Procter, *Fishermen's Memorial and Record Book,* 4.

46. *Goode Report,* sec. 5, 1:149, 155, 228; *Robertson Report,* 7-8.

47. Procter, *Fishermen's Own Book,* 21.

48. *EA,* marine lists, 11 April 1872 and 3 June 1873.

49. Ibid., marine list, 8 June 1876.

50. Procter, *Fishermen's Own Book,* 150.

51. *EA,* marine list, 29 August 1888.

52. Procter, *Fishermen's Own Book,* 66-85 passim.

53. Ibid., 179; Procter, *Fishermen's Memorial and Record Book,* 4; *Robertson Report,* 5.

54. *Robertson Report,* 6-9.

55. *MIJ,* news item, 9 January 1885.

56. *Robertson Report,* 6.

57. *U.S.CR,* 50th Cong., 1st Sess. (1888), 1514.

58. Matthew F. Maury, *The Physical Geography of the Sea* (2nd ed.; New York: Harper & Brothers, 1856), 291-92; Blunt, 16*.

59. PMM, GC, MS 6: 1 October 1853; Blunt, 18*, 25*.

60. PMM, GC, MS 6: 13 October 1853.

61. *EA,* marine lists, 4 December 1857, 9 July 1869, and 12 September 1883.

62. *RJ* marine list, 30 April 1852; *EA,* obituaries, 8 November and 1 December 1841, and marine lists, 7 October 1846, 29 October 1853, and 19 April 1887.

63. *EA,* marine lists, 27 October and 21 December 1852, 27 September 1855, and 6 June 1859; *ES,* marine list, 21 July 1858.

64. PMM, GC, MSS 6, 125, 354; *Goode Report,* sec. 4, 102.

65. *Goode Report,* sec. 4, 102-3; *Halifax Commission Proceedings,* 985.

66. *Goode Report,* sec. 2, 41; *Halifax Commission Proceedings,* 2478.

67. Eliot, 36.

68. Calculated from: Procter, *Fishermen's Memorial and Record Book,* 38-53, 168-72; Procter, *Fishermen's Own Book,* 66-85; *U.S.RFCN,* 1868-81, statements on fishing vessels and tonnage by customs district.

69. Wallace, 50.

70. *Goode Report,* sec. 5, 1:147.

71. Ibid., 128, 131, 193-94; see also Norman J. Ware, *Labor in Modern Industrial Society* (Boston: C. D. Heath & Co., 1935), 94-95, 163, 450-51.

72. Reynolds, 50.

73. PMM, GC, MS 6: 10 September 1853; see also entries for 13, 20, 31 July 1853.

74. Goode, 25; Reynolds 106; *Goode Report,* sec. 4, 9, 94.

75. *U.S.RDC,* 20th Cong., 1st Sess. (1828), col. 2077.

76. *Goode Report,* sec. 4, 55.

77. Ibid., 9; Goode, 25.

78. PMM, GC, MS 125; *Goode Report,* sec. 4, 90, and sec. 5, 1:132; Procter, *Fishermen's Own Book,* 43, 231; Reynolds, 52-54; Greene, 368-69; Pierce, 30-31; Kellogg, 108-9.

79. PMM, GC, MS 6: 11, 18, 31 August and 23 September 1853.

80. *Good Report,* sec. 2, 170, and sec. 4, 89, 91; *Halifax Commission Proceedings,* 2617; Pierce, 31.

81. Pierce, 43-45.

82. PMM, GC, MS 125.

83. *EA,* marine lists, 28 June 1850, 16 September 1853, 4 June 1875, and 13 May 1886.

84. Ibid., 28 June 1850, 24 May 1884, and 19 October 1888.

85. Ibid., marine list, 17 July 1844.

86. Ibid., 30 April 1855.

87. Ibid., marine lists, 28 June 1850, 30 April 1855, 1 July 1869, and 23 July 1888.

88. *Goode Report,* sec. 4, 9.

89. Ole E. Rölvaag, "The Romance of a Life," in *Ole Edvart Rölvaag: A Biography,* by Theodore Jorgenson and Nora O. Solum (New York: Harper & Brothers, 1939), 5.

90. PMM, GC, MS 6: 12 October 1853.

91. Ibid., MS 354; *Goode Report,* sec. 5, 1:128.

92. Melville, 127.

93. Reynolds, 56-57.

94. *EA,* marine list, 26 July 1841.

95. PMM, GC, MS 6.

96. Sylvanus Smith, 117; Procter, *Fishermen's Own Book*, 43; Procter, *Fishermen's Memorial and Record Book*, 73; *Goode Report*, sec. 4, 91, 94.

97. *Hague Arbitration Proceedings*, 2:342, 385; Greene, 368–69.

98. Ranlett and Colcord, 11; *RJ* article, 30 November 1882.

99. *Me.PL, 1851*, chap. 211.

100. Pierce, 55; *Goode Report*, sec. 5, 1:152; *Halifax Commission Proceedings*, 2449; PMM, GC, MSS 6, 354; Procter, *Fishermen's Own Book*, 43.

101. *Goode Report*, sec. 5 1:152.

102. Ibid., 152–56.

103. *Halifax Commission Proceedings* 2386.

104. *Goode Report*, sec. 4, 50, and sec. 5, 1:277; Sylvanus Smith, 71–72, 84.

105. *Mackerel Fishery Materials*, 61–64.

106. *EA*, marine list, 7 October 1846; *RJ*, marine list, 3 October 1851.

107. *RJ*, marine lists, 17, 21 October 1851; *EA*, marine lists, 29 October 1853, 25 July 1864, 13 June 1866, 14 September 1869, 20 April 1872, and 15 September 1873.

108. PMM, GC, MS 249, 105, 141.

109. *Hall Report*, 14–17; *Halifax Commission Proceedings*, 2607–8.

110. Pierce, 70.

111. Ibid., 80, 151, 156; Procter, *Fishermen's Own Book*, 20; *Mackerel Fishery Materials*, 75.

112. *Halifax Commission Proceedings*, 2889.

113. *RJ*, marine lists, 25 April 1851 and 7 October 1853; *EA*, marine lists, 18 May and 10 September 1855, 25 September and 8 October 1857, and 23 June 1858; see also PMM, GC, MS 6: 14, 29 July and 3 August 1853.

114. *Goode Report*, sec. 5, 1:6, 125, 127, 148–49.

115. Ibid., 125, 190; *Halifax Commission Proceedings*, 2608, 2663–64, 2890; PMM, WP, Miscellaneous Vessels, box 1, files 7, 27, and box 2, file 21: schooners *Glendower*, *Martha Burgess*, and *Eothen*, bills for anchors and cables, 23 January 1853, 22 May 1855, and 18, 28 May 1860.

116. BLH, WC, case 19: marine-insurance policies, various Castine fishing schooners, 1853–77; *Halifax Commission Proceedings*, 3449–50.

117. *Halifax Commission Proceedings*, 2608, 3450.

118. *Goode Report*, sec. 4, 95.

119. Calculated from: Procter, *Fishermen's Memorial and Record Book*, 9–51, 168–71; Procter, *Fishermen's Own Book*, 66–81.

120. BLH, WC, case 19: marine insurance policies, various Castine fishing schooners, 1853–70; PMM, GC, MSS 195, 249: Castine District Customs Collector's Record of Wreck Reports, 1874–84, 1884–1900; *Halifax Commission Proceedings*, 3181–3208.

121. PMM, GC, MS 195, 70.

122. *Halifax Commission Proceedings*, 271; see also *Goode Report*, sec. 5, 1:247.

123. *EA*, marine lists, 26 April and 20 December 1851.

124. Ibid., marine list, 16 October 1865.

125. Ibid., 26 October 1846.

126. U.S. MS Census Ind., 1850: Lincoln County, Maine, town of Westport, firm of Ezekiel Tarbox; *EA*, marine list, 19 October 1858.

127. *EA*, marine lists, 31 July 1869, 3 June 1880, and 6 August 1885.

128. Calculated from Procter, *Fishermen's Memorial and Record Book*, 14–41.

129. BLH, WC, case 19: marine insurance policies, schooners *Mentora*, 1853, 1859–62, 1865, 1869; *Glendower*, 1858–60; *Redwing*, 1860, 1862; *Rubicon*, 1853; *Eothen*, 1860–61; *Ella Rose*, 1858–62, 1865, 1870; and *D. T. Patchin*, 1867, 1870.

130. Procter, *Fishermen's Memorial and Record Book*, 17; *EA*, marine list, 4 April 1854.

131. BLH, WC, case 19: marine insurance policy, schooner *D. T. Patchin*, 24 May 1867; Wasson and Colcord, 319.

132. *EA*, marine list, 24 October 1877.

133. *U.S.AppCG*, 34th Cong., 3rd Sess. (1857), 220.

134. Goode, 25.

135. *Me.PSL, 1833*, chap. 371; *Me.PSL, 1837*, chap. 259.

136. Sylvanus Smith, 38–39.

137. *Halifax Commission Proceedings*, 2619.

138. Ibid., 1682.

139. Sylvanus Smith, 109.

140. Ibid., 24; see also *Halifax Commission Proceedings*, 3139–40.

141. *New England Business Directory, 1860,* 831; *Halifax Commission Proceedings,* 3117–18, 3121–22, 3451.

142. *Halifax Commission Proceedings,* 3453.

143. *U.S.RFCN, 1860,* 650–51.

144. *Me.PSL, 1858,* chap. 159; *New England Business Directory, 1860,* 827–28.

145. BLH, WC, case 19: marine-insurance policies, various Castine fishing schooners, 1853–70; *New England Business Directory, 1860,* 830.

146. *Halifax Commission Proceedings,* 2079, 3449–51.

147. *Me.PSL, 1868,* chap. 442.

148. *Me.PSL, 1874,* chap. 620; *EA,* advertisement, 13 March 1884; see also *Halifax Commission Proceedings,* 3182–86, 3193–94, 3449.

149. *EA,* marine lists, 19 September 1876, 24 October 1877, and 15 October 1878.

150. *Goode Report,* sec. 2, 235; *Me.PSL, 1858,* chap. 159; *Me.PSL, 1868,* chap. 442; *Me.PSL, 1874,* chap. 620; *Halifax Commission Proceedings,* 3449.

151. *Halifax Commission Proceedings,* 2190, 2222, 2548, 2556, 2606–8, 2655, 2768, 2891, 2935, 2992, 3003, 3011, 3018; *EA,* marine list, 28 May 1866; U.S. MS Census Ind., 1870: Hancock County, Maine, town of Lamoine, return for firm of Coolidge Brothers, and town of Trenton, return for firm of King Brothers.

152. Procter, *Fishermen's Memorial and Record Book,* 70; *EA,* marine lists, 15 January and 5 April 1875, 16 March 1880, 28 June 1882, and 31 March and 20 May 1884; PMM, GC, MSS 195, 249.

153. *Halifax Commission Proceedings,* 3105, 3107–42, 3181, 3198, 3202–3.

154. *Goode Report,* sec. 4, 12.

155. Ibid., sec. 2, 70, 83–84, and sec. 5, 1:188; Pierce, 150; *EA,* news item, 1 January 1877.

156. *Goode Report,* sec. 2, 145.

157. *Halifax Commission Proceedings,* 2284, 3108–41 passim.

158. *EA,* advertisement, 13 March 1884.

159. *Halifax Commission Proceedings,* 2161–63, 2170–72, 3114–15.

160. U.S. MS Census Pop., 1880: Essex County, Massachusetts, city of Gloucester.

161. See, for example, data in U.S. MS Census Pop., 1860, 1870, 1880: Cumberland County, Maine, city of Portland; Lincoln County, Maine, towns of Boothbay and Southport; Knox County, Maine, towns of Vinalhaven and North Haven; Hancock County, Maine, town of Deer Isle; and Washington County, Maine, city of Eastport.

162. *EA,* news item, 1 January 1877.

163. *Goode Report,* sec. 2, 707.

164. Procter, *Fishermen's Memorial and Record Book,* 52.

165. Reynolds, 79–84, 87–92.

166. *Goode Report,* sec. 4, 127.

167. Ibid., 128.

168. *Halifax Commission Proceedings,* 2596–2603.

169. Commager, 2:512.

170. *Goode Report,* sec. 4, 128.

171. Ibid., 129.

172. Ibid., 127.

173. W. W. Clayton, *History of Cumberland County, Maine* (Philadelphia: Everts & Peck, 1880), 198.

174. *Goode Report,* sec. 4, 126–27.

175. *EA,* marine lists, 4 April and 3 May 1854, and 16 May 1859; Procter, *Fishermen's Memorial and Record Book,* 10, 21.

176. *Goode Report,* sec. 4, 12.

177. U.S. MS Census Pop., 1880: Essex County, Massachusetts, city of Gloucester; Procter, *Fishermen's Own Book,* 244; *Goode Report,* sec. 2, 137–38.

178. *Goode Report,* sec. 2, 41; Wheeler, 1st ed., 242.

179. *MIJ,* news item, 3 April 1885.

180. *Goode Report,* sec. 4, 12.

181. U.S. MS Census Pop., 1880: Essex County, Massachusetts, city of Gloucester; *Goode Report,* sec. 5, 1:6.

182. *Halifax Commission Proceedings,* 3144, 3295, 3330, 3338–39.

183. U.S. MS Census Pop., 1860: Knox County, Maine, town of Vinalhaven.

184. *Halifax Commission Proceedings,* 2667.

185. *U.S.CG,* 35th Cong., 1st Sess. (1858), 1996.

186. Harold F. Wilson, *The Hill Country of Northern New England: Its Social*

and Economic History, 1790–1930 (New York: Columbia University Press, 1936), 54, 103. See also *U.S.Cen., 1860,* 1:200–206; *U.S.Cen., 1870,* 1:158–62; and *U.S. Cen., 1880,* 1:199–203.

187. Wilson, 56.

188. *Halifax Commission Proceedings,* 256.

189. Wilson, 7–8.

190. *Lynch Report,* 150.

191. Ibid., 213.

192. Wilson, 139–41.

193. Pierce, 33–34.

194. *Goode Report,* sec. 4, 14.

195. Ibid., 14–16; see also Marcus Lee Hansen, *The Mingling of the Canadian and American Peoples* (Toronto: Ryerson Press, 1940), 161.

196. *Halifax Commission Proceedings,* 3062, 3067, 3071, 3075; *Goode Report,* sec. 4, 89.

197. PANS, ZC, MS 189: Ships' Account Book, Zwicker & Company, 1876–83; PMM, GC, MS 125.

198. *Halifax Commission Proceedings,* 3250.

199. *Goode Report,* sec. 4, 6, 14.

200. Ibid., 14; Hansen, *Canadian and American Peoples,* 120. See also data in U.S. MS Census Pop., 1860: York County, Maine, town of Kennebunkport; Cumberland County, Maine, city of Portland; Sagadahoc County, Maine, town of Georgetown; Lincoln County, Maine, towns of Boothbay and Southport; Knox County, Maine, towns of Vinalhaven and North Haven; Hancock County, Maine, town of Deer Isle; and Washington County, Maine, town of Lubec and city of Eastport.

201. *U.S.AppAC,* 14th Cong., 2nd Sess. (1817), col. 1286.

202. *N.S.AppJPHA, 1853,* 117; *Halifax Commission Proceedings,* 430, 598, 614–16, 697, 791, 942, 967–68, 1019, 1021, 1418, 2170.

203. *Halifax Commission Proceedings,* 430.

204. Pierce, 33, 46.

205. U.S. MS Census Pop., 1860, 1870: Cumberland County, Maine, city of Portland.

206. Ibid.: Washington County, Maine, city of Eastport; *Halifax Commission Proceedings,* 752.

207. *Goode Report,* sec. 4, 7.

208. Ibid., sec. 2, 10, and sec. 4, 6.

209. Sylvanus Smith, 84.

210. *Me.RBILS, 1887,* 115.

211. *U.S.FCB, 1890,* 103.

212. *Halifax Commission Proceedings,* 2305.

213. *Goode Report,* sec. 4, 17.

214. *Halifax Commission Proceedings,* 3214, 3232–33, 3245, 3272.

215. Ibid., 482.

216. *Mass.Cen., 1885,* 2:1432.

217. Ibid., 1429–30.

218. U.S. MS Census Pop., 1880: Cumberland County, Maine, city of Portland.

219. *U.S.FCB, 1890,* 96, 127.

Chapter 9

1. *Halifax Commission Proceedings,* 676.

2. *U.S.RFCN,* 1865–92, and *U.S.RCN,* 1893–1900: statements on fishing vessels and tonnage by customs district.

3. Johnson et al., 2:183.

4. *Halifax Commission Proceedings,* 2824–25.

5. *MIJ,* news item, 29 January 1886.

6. *U.S.RCN, 1900,* 412.

7. *Halifax Commission Proceedings,* 2813.

8. Ibid., 2812, 2915.

9. Ibid., 2812–13.

10. Johnson et al., 2:202.

11. *Statistics of Commerce,* 155.

12. *Halifax Commission Proceedings,* 2826–27.

13. Johnson et al., 2:202.

14. *Halifax Commission Proceedings,* 2551, 2827; see also *EA,* marine list, 16 March 1885.

15. *Halifax Commission Proceedings,* 2914.

16. Ibid., 2552, 2746, 2887.

17. Johnson et al., 2:211–12; see also *Cutts Report,* 6–7.

18. *Goode Report,* sec. 2, 168.

19. Goode, 34; Johnson et al., 2:213.

20. Homer E. Gregory and Kathleen Barnes, *North Pacific Fisheries* (San Francisco: American Council of Pacific Relations, 1939), 310–11.

21. *Halifax Commission Proceedings*, 2765.

22. *MIJ*, news item, 19 September 1884.

23. *U.S.FCB, 1898*, 368, 383.

24. *U.S.FCB, 1893*, 413–14.

25. Ibid., 417.

26. *U.S.FCB, 1890*, 95.

27. *Fisheries of the U.S., 1908*, 139.

28. *Halifax Commission Proceedings*, 2450.

29. Ibid., 129–30.

30. Luther Maddocks, *The Menhaden Fishery of Maine* (Portland, Me.: B. Thurston & Co., 1878), 14, 17; Greene, 371–73; *Goode Report*, sec. 2, 28.

31. Maddocks, *Menhaden Fishery*, 21, 25.

32. Greene, 371, 373.

33. Small, 193–94.

34. Bishop, 347.

35. Maddocks, *Menhaden Fishery*, 18.

36. U.S. MS Census Pop., 1870: Lincoln County, Maine, town of Boothbay.

37. Maddocks, *Menhaden Fishery*, 18–19.

38. *U.S.FCB, 1890*, 107.

39. Small, 192; *U.S.FCB, 1899*, 244.

40. *Goode Report*, sec. 2, 10–11.

41. *U.S.FCB, 1899*, 250, 257, 264.

42. *U.S.FCB, 1890*, 78.

43. *U.S.FCB, 1899*, 250.

44. Hale, 126, 131.

45. Farrow, 308.

46. Green, 376.

47. *U.S.FCB, 1899*, 257.

48. Goode, 49–50.

49. *U.S.FCB, 1899*, 252, 255.

50. Charles A. E. Long, *Matinicus Isle: Its Story and Its People* (Lewiston, Me.: Lewiston Journal, 1926), 54; Bishop, 347; George A. and Henry W. Wheeler, *History of Brunswick, Topsham and Harpswell, Maine* (Boston: Alfred Mudge & Son, 1878), 618; *Goode Report*, sec. 2, 51.

51. *Me.RBILS, 1887*, 112.

52. *U.S.FCB, 1887*, 165–69, 174–76; see also Howard I. Chapelle, *American Small Sailing Craft: Their Design, Development and Construction* (New York: W. W. Norton & Co., 1951), 262, and Chapelle, *National Watercraft Collection*, 250–52.

53. *Goode Report*, sec. 5, 1:422, 425.

54. *U.S.FCB, 1887*, 165, 169, 174.

55. Ibid., 167.

56. Ibid., 168, 174–75, 181–82; *EA*, supplement, 28 July 1888; *Goode Report*, sec. 2, 45.

57. *U.S.FCB, 1887*, 188.

58. Ibid., 163; *Goode Report*, sec. 2, 10, 12; Goode, 44.

59. *U.S.FCB, 1887*, 188.

60. *U.S.FCB, 1890*, 78; *Goode Report*, sec. 2, 11.

61. *U.S.FCB, 1887*, 182.

62. Richard O. Cummings, *The American and His Food: A History of Food Habits in the United States* (Chicago: University of Chicago Press, 1940), 11; Frederick Marryat, *A Diary in America with Remarks on its Institutions,* ed. Sydney Jackman (New York: Alfred A. Knopf, 1962), 379; see also Thoreau, 197.

63. *Sabine Report*, 173.

64. John S. Springer, *Forest Life and Forest Trees* (New York: Harper & Brothers, 1851), 72; Harold A. Davis, *An International Community on the St. Croix, 1604–1930* (Orono: University of Maine Press, 1950), 135.

65. *Goode Report*, sec. 5, 1:241.

66. *Sabine Report*, 173.

67. Frances Trollope, *Domestic Manners of the Americans,* ed. Donald Smalley (New York: Alfred A. Knopf, 1949), 243, 281, 297, 390.

68. Oscar E. Anderson, Jr., *Refrigeration in America: A History of a New Technology and its Impact* (Princeton, N.J.: Princeton University Press, 1953), 8–9, 14.

69. Cummings, 83.

70. *Halifax Commission Proceedings*, 2283.

71. Ibid., 2552.

72. Cummings, 28; see also Sylvanus Smith, 118.

73. Wiley, 239.

74. J. Ogden Armour, *The Packers, the Private Car Lines and the People* (Philadelphia: Henry Altemus Co., 1906), 306.

75. Cummings, 77, 88.

76. Armour, 346.

77. *Cutts Report,* 80.

78. *Halifax Commission Proceedings,* 2748.

79. Ruth F. Grant, *The Canadian Atlantic Fishery* (Toronto: Ryerson Press, 1934), 35, 89–90.

80. *Goode Report,* sec. 4, 90, and sec. 5, 1:132.

81. Pierce, 368.

82. Greene, 435–36.

83. Reynolds, 52.

84. *Goode Report,* sec. 4, 75, 91; Procter, *Fishermen's Own Book,* 22.

85. Pierce, 45.

86. *Halifax Commission Proceedings,* 313.

87. Charles L. Cutting, *Fish Saving: A History of Fish Processing from Ancient to Modern Times* (London: Leonard Hill Books, 1955), 155.

88. *Halifax Commission Proceedings,* 737–38.

89. Bishop, 351.

90. *Goode Report,* sec. 1, 228; Pierce, 149.

91. Innis, 419.

92. Cutting, 173.

93. *EA,* news item, 3 February 1859.

94. *U.S.CG,* 34th Cong., 3rd Sess. (1857), 379.

95. *RJ,* news item, 3 March 1854.

96. *Goode Report,* sec. 5, 1:435.

97. Cummings, 37–39; see also Russel B. Nye, *The Cultural Life of the New Nation, 1776–1830* (New York: Harper & Brothers, 1960), 132.

98. Anderson, 26–27.

99. Ibid., 22–24, 27.

100. Ibid., 44, 53–54.

101. Willard F. Williams and Thomas T. Stout, *Economics of the Livestock-Meat Industry* (New York: Macmillan Co., 1964), 12–16; Armour, 17–19.

102. Williams and Stout, 13, 19; Armour, 124.

103. Williams and Stout, 20; Armour, 292–95.

104. Anderson, 31.

105. Cummings, 62; *U.S.FCB, 1898,* 367; Williams and Stout, 21; Armour, 19–20.

106. Williams and Stout, 21–22; Anderson, 57.

107. *Meat Products Hearings,* 428, 430.

108. Armour, 53.

109. Williams and Stout, 22.

110. Armour, 115, 306, 321.

111. Ibid., 178.

112. Williams and Stout, 22.

113. Anderson, 57–58; Armour, 295, 319–20.

114. Ray Ginger, *Age of Excess: The United States from 1877–1914* (New York: Macmillan Co., 1965), 25; Alfred D. Chandler, Jr., *Strategy and Structure: Chapters in the History of American Industrial Enterprise* (Cambridge: M.I.T. Press, 1962), 26.

115. *U.S.AppCG,* 34th Cong., 3rd Sess. (1857), 221.

116. Armour, 24–25; Anderson, 58.

117. Sylvanus Smith, 25, 36; *U.S.FCB, 1898,* 405.

118. *Meat Products Hearings,* 423.

119. *Goode Report,* sec. 5, 1:31; *U.S.FCB, 1898,* 359.

120. *Goode Report,* sec. 2, 168, and sec. 5, 1:31–37; *U.S.FCB, 1898,* 341–42.

121. Procter, *Fishermen's Memorial and Record Book,* 67; Chapelle, *American Fishing Schooners,* 64–65.

122. Morison, *Maritime History of Massachusetts,* 308; Cummings, 60.

123. *MIJ,* news item, 14 December 1883.

124. *Goode Report,* sec. 5, 1:31–32, 38–39.

125. *New England Business Directory, 1860,* 94–95, 580.

126. *Goode Report,* sec. 2, 89, 193.

127. Ibid., sec. 2, 9–11, 118–21, and sec. 5, 1:308.

128. Ibid., sec. 2, 133, 138–39, 178–79, 183, 187–88, 215–16, 225–26, 254–55, 259, 263; *U.S.FCB, 1890,* 130–31.

129. *Goode Report,* sec. 2, 13–14, 22, 29–30, 37, 46–47, 53–54, 66–67, 73, 77–78, 93–95; *U.S.FCB, 1890,* 100–101.

130. *U.S.FCB, 1890,* 75, 85, 103, 133.

131. *U.S.FCB, 1898,* 194–95, 431.

132. Ibid., 193, 199–201.

133. Ibid., 431.

134. *Goode Report,* sec. 2, 10, 108, 117, 120, 138, 188, 193, 284, 314.

135. *MIJ,* article, 10 October 1884; *Goode Report,* sec. 2, 193; *U.S.FCB, 1890,* 149.

136. *MIJ*, articles, 19 September and 10 October 1884; *U.S.FCB, 1890,* 147.

137. *Goode Report*, sec. 2, 10, 77, 89.

138. William L. Lucey, *The Catholic Church in Maine* (Francetown, N.H.: Marshall Jones Co. 1957), 156, 227-28.

139. Ibid., 160-61.

140. U.S. MS Census Pop., 1880: Cumberland County, Maine, city of Portland.

141. Leon E. Truesdell, *The Canadian Born in the United States: An Analysis of the Statistics of the Canadian Element in the Population of the United States, 1850-1930* (Toronto: Ryerson Press, 1943), 77; Lucey, 228.

142. *Me.RRC, 1872,* 23; see also Edward C. Kirkland, *Men, Cities and Transportation: A Study in New England History, 1820-1900,* 2 vols. (Cambridge: Harvard University Press, 1948), 1:198.

143. Kirkland, 1:212-13; George P. Geer, ed., *Geer's Express Directory and Railway Forwarder's Guide: The New England States* (Springfield, Mass.: C. R. Chaffee & Co., 1858), 270-71.

144. Kirkland, 1:479-83.

145. *U.S.AppCG,* 32nd Cong., 1st Sess. (1852), 923.

146. *MIJ*, news item, 14 December 1883.

147. Ibid., article, 19 September 1884.

148. *Halifax Commission Proceedings,* 2552, 2746, 2764, 2887, 2914.

149. Morison, *Maritime History of Massachusetts,* 308; Kirkland, 1:123, 135; see also Anderson, 31.

150. Cummings, 60; Kirkland, 1:320.

151. Geer, 270-71.

152. *Halifax Commission Proceedings,* 677, 683, 2765; *U.S.FCB, 1898,* 362; Goode, 9.

153. *MIJ*, article, 10 October 1884; Joseph Smith, 234.

154. *Goode Report*, sec. 2, 190; *U.S.FCB, 1890,* 149.

155. Wasson and Colcord, 192.

156. Kirkland, 1:199-200.

157. Ibid., 2:125-28.

158. Clayton, 79.

159. Kirkland, 1:284, 2:350.

160. Coolidge and Mansfield, 18.

161. *U.S.RFCN, 1860,* 650-51.

162. William A. Wheeler, *The Maine Central Railroad, 1847-1947* (n.p.: Maine Central R.R., 1947), 6; Hatch, 3:170.

163. William Wheeler, 2-8; Hatch, 3: 709-12; see also Henry V. Poor, *History of the Railroads and Canals of the United States of America* (New York: John N. Schultz & Co., 1860), 25.

164. *Me.RRC, 1890,* map insert; Edmund S. Hoyt, ed., *Maine State Year-Book and Legislative Manual for the Year 1879-80* (Portland, Me.: Hoyt, Fogg & Donham, 1880), map insert.

165. William Wheeler, 7, 9.

166. *Me.RRC, 1890,* map insert; Hoyt, map insert.

167. Kirkland, 1:220, 2:119.

168. Clayton, 19.

169. *Me.RRC, 1872,* 25; *Me.RRC, 1873,* 23.

170. *Goode Report*, sec. 2, 13-14, 22, 29-30, 37, 46-47, 53-54, 66-67, 73, 77-78, 93-95.

171. *U.S.FCB, 1890,* 97-99.

172. *U.S.RFCN,* 1870-92, and *U.S. RCN,* 1893-1900: statements on fishing vessels and tonnage by customs district.

173. *Goode Report*, sec. 2, 90.

174. *EA*, marine lists, 23 June, 2, 13, 15, 21, 30, 31 July, 5, 9, 10, 14 August, and 24 September 1880.

175. Ibid., 2, 17, 18, 23 March, 6 May, and 1, 24 June 1882; 15, 17 March, 11, 28 April, 2, 7 May, and 4, 6 June 1883; 10 February, 9, 21 March, and 20 May 1885; 3 April 1886; and 4 March 1889.

176. *Goode Report*, sec. 2, 87, 89-92, 147-49, 168, 190-93, 204-7.

177. *U.S.FCB, 1890,* 147.

178. Kirkland, 1:197, 467, 495.

179. *Goode Report*, sec. 2, 89.

180. Kirkland, 1:479-84.

181. *Goode Report*, sec. 2, 89, 138; *U.S. FCB, 1890,* 101, 107, 130, 137.

182. Sylvanus Smith, 61; *Hall Report,* 13; *Goode Report*, sec. 4, 51; Maddocks, "Looking Backward," 8, 48.

183. *MIJ*, news items, 19 December 1884 and 9 January 1885.

184. *U.S.RFCN,* 1865-90, statements on fishing vessels and tonnage by customs district.

185. Harold A. Innis and Arthur R. M. Lower, eds., *Select Documents in Cana-*

dian Economic History, 1783–1885 (Toronto: University of Toronto Press, 1933), 667.

186. Kirkland, 2:119; Grant, 30, 83; Stanley A. Saunders, *Studies in the Economy of the Maritime Provinces* (Toronto: Macmillan Co. of Canada, 1939), 261.

187. *U.S.FCB, 1893,* 343.

188. *U.S.FCB, 1884,* 460–62.

189. *Knight Report on N.S. Fisheries,* 5; *Can.RFB, 1885,* xviii.

190. Joncas, commentary, 46.

191. M. C. Urquhart, ed., *Historical Statistics of Canada* (Toronto: Macmillan Co. of Canada, 1965), 394–95, 399.

192. *Can.AppRFB, 1885,* 141; Grant, 16.

193. *Halifax Commission Proceedings,* 2894.

194. NA, RDT (RG 56), GR, Abstracts of Fishing Bounty Allowances, vol. 417: Penobscot District allowances, 1st quarter 1849; *Can.Cen., 1871,* 4:238; *U.S.RFCN, 1851,* 2*.

195. *Second Clay Report,* 16; *Can.Cen., 1871,* 4:356; see also *U.S.RFCN, 1859,* 636–37.

196. *Can.Cen., 1881,* 3:272, 278; *Goode Report,* sec. 2, 11; *U.S.RFCN, 1880,* 860.

197. DesBrisay, 468; PANS, ZC, MS 129: Export and Clearance of Fish Record Book, Zwicker & Company, 1882–86, news clippings of returns for the Lunenburg banks fleet, 1884–85; *EA,* marine list, 11 September 1886.

198. *Mass.Cen., 1895,* 6:116.

199. *U.S.AppCG,* 32nd Cong., 1st Sess. (1852), 924; see also *Davis Report,* 64.

200. *Cutts Report,* 44; *U.S.RFCN, 1866,* 32; *U.S.RFCN, 1867,* pt. 1, 36.

201. PANS, ZC, MS 128: Export and Clearance of Fish Record Book, Zwicker & Company, 1878–82, news clippings of fish exports from Halifax to the West Indies, 1877–80; PANS, ZC, MS 129: news clippings of fish exports from Halifax to the West Indies, 1882–83; *U.S.RFCN,* 1877–83, statements on domestic exports by country; see also Berton A. Balcom, "Production and Marketing in Nova Scotia's Fish Trade, 1850–1914" (M.A. thesis, Memorial University of Newfoundland, 1980), 90.

202. *U.S.FCB, 1898,* 406; *Halifax Commission Proceedings,* 863, 839, 1294.

203. PMM, WP, Schooner *Commerce* Collection, file 5: price-current newsletters, J. C. Burnham & Company, Havana, 17 December 1850 to 7 April 1853; *Cutts Report,* 44; *U.S.RFCN,* 1865–80, statements on domestic exports by country; Balcom, 203.

204. *U.S.FCB, 1898,* 406.

205. *Andrews Report,* 562.

206. Ryan, 81; *Andrews Report,* 562; *U.S.RFCN, 1851,* 7.

207. Diaz, 105; *U.S.RFCN, 1846,* 5; *U.S.RFCN, 1856,* 11; see also PMM, WP, Schooner *Commerce* Collection, file 5: price-current newsletters, J. C. Burnham & Company, Havana, 1850–53.

208. *Cutts Report,* 44; Balcom, 90, 203; Ryan, 82; *U.S.RFCN, 1866,* 33; *U.S.RFCN, 1867,* pt. 1, 36; *U.S.RFCN, 1868,* 49.

209. PANS, ZC, MS 128: news clippings of fish exports from Halifax to the West Indies, 1877–80.

210. Innis, 372.

211. Ibid., 331.

212. *Historical Statistics, U.S.,* 12–13; Urquhart, 14.

213. *Halifax Commission Proceedings,* 3302.

214. Ibid., 3003; see also *Cutts Report,* 31.

215. *Halifax Commission Proceedings,* 2995.

216. PANS, ZC, MS 189: accounts for schooner *Sibyl.*

217. *Knight Report on N.S. Fisheries,* 5; *Knight Report on Shore and Deep-Sea Fisheries,* 10.

218. Grant, 11.

219. H. W. Hewitt, "History of the Town of Lunenburg" (unpublished typescript, Public Archives of Nova Scotia, Halifax), 75; PANS, ZC, MS 129: news clippings of returns for the Lunenburg banks fleet, 1884.

220. *Halifax Commission Proceedings,* 2982; see also 2989, 2992, 2995, and 3011.

221. Ibid., 3062, 3067, 3071, 3075.

222. Ibid., 3049; *Lynch Report,* 19.

223. *Hall Report,* 20; *LP,* news item, 31 May 1881.

224. *Halifax Commission Proceedings,* 611, 2979, 2982, 2985, 2992, 3003–4, 3007, 3011, 3022.

225. Ibid., 2989, 2999, 3049, 3222.

226. Ibid., 3022, 3030, 3057, 3083.

227. Ibid., 3022.

228. Ibid., 3030; *Lynch Report,* 100; *Cutts Report,* 31.

229. *Halifax Commission Proceedings,* 2985, 3057.

230. Grant, 17.

231. *Halifax Commission Proceedings,* 8, 120–21, 127, 197, 205; *Goode Report,* sec. 2, 153.

232. *Can.AP,* 45 Vict. (1882), chap. 18.

233. *Can.RFB, 1883,* lxxiii–lxxiv.

234. *Can.RFB, 1890,* ix; see also *Can. RFB, 1884,* iii.

235. *U.S.FCB, 1893,* 342.

236. Joncas, 56; *Can.ODHC,* 4th Parl., 4th Sess. (1882), 1512, 1514.

237. *N.S.App.JPHA, 1851,* 170.

238. *N.S.App.JPHA, 1853,* 118.

239. *Halifax Commission Proceedings,* 3018, 3022.

240. *EA,* marine list, 22 April 1884.

241. *Can.AppRFB, 1884,* xxx; Joncas, 46.

242. *U.S.FCB, 1884,* 458.

243. *U.S.FCB, 1893,* 344.

244. *Can.App.RFB, 1870,* 319.

245. *Can.ODHC,* 4th Parl., 4th Sess. (1882), 1512.

246. *Can.RFB, 1890,* xix.

247. *Goode Report,* sec. 4, 6, 14; *U.S. FCB, 1887,* 452; *U.S.FCB, 1890,* 79.

248. *Can.AppRFB, 1884,* 82; *Can.App RFB, 1885,* 56–57.

249. *Can.AppRFB, 1885,* 58–59, 141; *Can.RFB, 1883,* lxxix.

Selected Bibliography

While published and unpublished treatises on the deep-sea fisheries of Maine are regrettably few, the existing historical literature on the Atlantic sea fisheries of North America in general is considerable and of excellent quality. Fortunately, the international nature of the industry and its operational uniformity from one geopolitical jurisdiction to another during the age of sail encourage a wide use of sources in pursuing fisheries history. The primary and secondary materials found most applicable to the foregoing study on Maine are cited fully in the text endnotes or in the accompanying list of abbreviations, but several, including some consulted but not cited, deserve special mention.

Essential to any consideration of the North Atlantic fisheries in the nineteenth century is Harold A. Innis, *The Cod Fisheries: The History of an International Economy* (2nd ed. rev.; Toronto: University of Toronto Press, 1954), a classic of research and synthesis originally published in 1940. Also important is Raymond McFarland, *A History of the New England Fisheries* (New York: D. Appleton & Co., 1911), dated but still the best overall treatment of the leading sea-fishing region in the United States. Robert G. Albion, William A. Baker, and Benjamin W. Labaree, *New England and the Sea* (Middletown, Conn.: Wesleyan University Press, 1972), contains a more recent survey of the same subject, in several brief but readable sections. A basic source on nineteenth-century fisheries history, technology, geography, biology, and economics, as well as a pioneering examination of the social aspects of the industry, is the monumental U.S., Commission of Fish and Fisheries, *The Fisheries and Fishery Industries of the United States,* ed. George Brown Goode (5 secs., 7 vols.; Washington: Government Printing Office, 1884–87). A smaller companion work to that comprehensive federal study, U.S., Commission of Fish and Fisheries, *Materials for a History of the Mackerel Fishery,* by George Brown Goode et al. (Washington: Government Printing Office, 1883), provides a detailed supplement on a particular fishery. U.S., Department of the Treasury, *Report on the Principal Fisheries of the American Seas,* by Lorenzo Sabine, 3rd Cong., 2nd Sess., 1853, Sen. Exec. Doc. 22, is the first published history of the American North Atlantic sea fisheries, and, though stylistically archaic, it remains pertinent for the period prior to 1850. Also useful are several addresses and research papers on a variety of contemporary and historical topics contained in *The International Fisheries Exhibition Literature: Conferences Held in Connection with the Great International Fisheries Exhibition of 1883* (13 vols.; London: William Clowes & Sons, 1884), the outgrowth of a worldwide gathering of industry experts including representatives from North America.

Emory R. Johnson et al., *History of Domestic and Foreign Commerce of the United States* (2 vols.; Carnegie Institution, 1915), has several chapters by T. W. Van Metre that provide a broad overview of the various American fisheries from 1789 to 1910, with an emphasis on political, economic, and diplomatic developments. Emphasizing fisheries-related diplomacy exclusively is Charles E. Cayley, "The North Atlantic Fisheries in United States–Canadian Relations" (Ph.D. diss., University of Chicago, 1931), a general history of the treaties and agreements covering the cooperative use of the fisheries resource. Ronald D. Tallman, "Warships and Mackerel: The North Atlantic Fisheries in Canadian-American Relations, 1867–77" (Ph.D. diss., University of Maine, 1971), is a detailed examination of one aspect of the international problem, the conflicts and negotiations over fishing rights leading to the Treaty of Washington and subsequent arbitrations.

Of more narrowly regional interest are several state and provincial studies. Foremost among these is Samuel Eliot Morison, *The Maritime History of Massachusetts, 1783–1860* (Boston: Houghton Mifflin Co., 1921), which devotes two unsurpassed chapters to the antebellum fisheries of the Bay State. A less successful effort in this vein is the generally superficial William H. Rowe, *The Maritime History of Maine: Three Centuries of Shipbuilding and Seafaring* (New York: W. W. Norton & Co., 1948), which contains two chapters on Maine's fisheries, one of them dealing with the nineteenth century. The political attitudes of Maine's fishermen and the state's reaction to nineteenth-century federal fisheries policy are summarized in Wayne M. O'Leary, "Fish and Politics in Jacksonian Maine," *The New England Quarterly* 67 (March 1994). Shannon Ryan, *Fish Out of Water: The Newfoundland Saltfish Trade, 1814–1914* (St. John's, Nfld.: Breakwater Books, 1986), offers an in-depth look at that province's export trade in dried cod, with an emphasis on statistics. Nova Scotia's dried-cod industry is similarly examined in Ruth F. Grant, *The Canadian Atlantic Fishery* (Toronto: Ryerson Press, 1930), an economic study less comprehensive than the title suggests, in that it focuses primarily on the historical development of one province's offshore fishery.

A number of useful local studies compensate to some degree for the dearth of regional monographs on the nineteenth-century Atlantic sea fisheries. Several of these specifically concern the Maine scene. Charles W. Eliot,

John Gilley: Maine Farmer and Fisherman (Boston: American Unitarian Assoc., 1904), provides a unique biographical account of the life of a Maine fisherman from the Mount Desert Island region. George L. Wasson and Lincoln Colcord, *Sailing Days on the Penobscot . . . with a Record of Vessels Built There* (Salem, Mass.: Marine Research Society, 1932), contains a chapter on the Isle au Haut fisheries of Penobscot Bay and an indispensable list of ships, including fishing schooners. Francis B. Greene, *History of Boothbay, Southport and Boothbay Harbor, Maine* (Portland, Me.: Loring, Short and Harmon, 1906), is the best of the multitude of Maine coastal town histories from the standpoint of the fishing industry. Also worth mentioning is H. W. Small, *A History of Swan's Island, Maine* (Ellsworth, Me.: Hancock County Publishing Co., 1898), which presents a detailed look at a leading mackerel-fishing community.

Several works on fishing localities outside of Maine also contribute to an understanding of the North American fisheries. George H. Procter, comp., *The Fishermen's Memorial and Record Book* (Gloucester, Mass.: Procter Brothers, 1873), and Procter, comp., *The Fishermen's Own Book* (Gloucester, Mass.: Procter Brothers, 1882), both compiled by an active fish merchant, are irreplaceable collections of historical facts and statistics, stories, poems, and contemporary descriptions pertaining to the important port of Gloucester, Massachusetts. Two formal histories, John J. Babson, *History of the Town of Gloucester, Cape Ann, including the Town of Rockport* (Gloucester, Mass.: Procter Brothers, 1860), and James B. Connolly, *The Port of Gloucester* (New York: Doubleday, Doran & Co., 1940), provide overviews of Gloucester's early and later periods, respectively. Berton A. Balcom, *History of the Lunenburg Fishing Industry* (Lunenburg, N.S.: Lunenburg Marine Museum Society, 1977), is an excellent modern study of Gloucester's latter-day Nova Scotia rival, while Mather B. DesBrisay, *History of the County of Lunenburg* (3rd ed.; Bridgewater, N.S.: Bridgewater Bulletin, 1967), is an early work useful for fisheries developments in that locale prior to 1895.

Several secondary works on specialized technical aspects of fisheries history are worth consulting. Setting the standard on the subject of naval architecture as applied to fishing vessels in the sailing era are Howard I. Chapelle's *The American Fishing Schooners, 1825–1935* (New York: W. W. Norton & Co., 1973) and sections of his *American Sailing Craft* (New York: Kennedy Brothers, 1936) and *The National Watercraft Collection* (Washington: Government Printing Office, 1960). Informative as well is W. M. P. Dunne's *Thomas F. McManus and the American Fishing Schooners: An Irish-American Success Story* (Mystic, Conn.: Mystic Seaport Museum, 1994), a ground-breaking study of North America's premier fishing-schooner designer. Also instructive are Joseph W. Collins, "Evolution of the American Fishing Schooner," *New England Magazine* 18 (May 1898); Wayne M. O'Leary, "The Antebellum Maine Fishing Schooner and the Factors Influencing Its Design and Construction," *The American Neptune* 44 (Spring 1984); and the first chapter of U.S., Superintendent of the Census, *Report on the Ship-Building Industry of the United States,* by Henry Hall (Washington: Government Printing Office, 1882). For the historical development of dories and other small craft used in the sailing fisheries, the best sources are Howard I. Chapelle, *American Small Sailing Craft: Their Design, Development and Construction* (New York: W. W. Norton & Co., 1951), and John Gardner, *The Dory Book* (Camden, Me.: International Marine Publishing Co., 1978).

Of particular value for its description of nineteenth-century fishing methods and technology, as well as insights into the fishing way of life, is Wesley G. Pierce, *Goin' Fishin': The Story of the Deep-Sea Fisheries of New England* (Salem, Mass.: Marine Research Society, 1932). L. B. Jensen, *Fishermen of Nova Scotia* (Halifax: Petheric Press, 1984), is an illustrative work useful for its accurate drawings of vessels, gear, and techniques, both historical and modern. Informative on the drying, smoking, pickling, and refrigeration of fish is Charles L. Cutting, *Fish Saving: A History of Fish Processing from Ancient to Modern Times* (London: Leonard Hill Books, 1955). The most complete American treatise on the same subject is Charles H. Stevenson, "The Preservation of Fishery Products for Food," *Bulletin of the United States Fish Commission, 1898* (Washington: Government Printing Office, 1899).

Only a few good fisheries memoirs exist. One relating to the state of Maine is Harold B. Clifford, *Charlie York: Maine Coast Fisherman* (Camden, Me.: International Marine Publishing Co., 1974), the collaborative semi-autobiography of a Casco Bay fisherman who witnessed the last days of sail on the offshore banks and along the down-east coast. Especially helpful for the earlier period is Sylvanus Smith, *Fisheries of Cape Ann* (Gloucester, Mass.: Gloucester Times Co., 1915), the recollections of a former Gloucester schooner captain and fish merchant. Superior to these as literature, and perhaps the finest work of its kind, is Frederick William Wallace, *Roving Fisherman: An Autobiography Recounting Experiences in the Commercial Fishing Fleets and Fish Industry of Canada and the United States, 1911–24* (Gardenvale, Que.: Canadian Fisherman, 1955). Also highly worthwhile is Raymond McFarland, *The Masts of Gloucester: Recollections of a Fisherman* (New York: W. W. Norton & Co., 1937), which describes a future historian's youthful experiences aboard a mackerel seiner of the 1890s.

More in the form of reportage than memoir are a handful of narratives of fishing voyages or anecdotal descriptions of life among the fishing population. The best of these firsthand reports for nineteenth-century Maine are: William H. Bishop, "Fish and Men in the Maine Islands," *Harper's New Monthly Magazine* 61 (August–September 1880); Joseph W. Smith, *Gleanings from the Sea* (Andover, Mass.: private printing, 1887); and Celia Thaxter, *Among the Isles of Shoals* (Boston: James R. Osgood, 1873). Henry David Thoreau, *Cape Cod* (Boston: Ticknor and Fields, 1866), provides a similar service for the fishing districts of Massachusetts. Two twentieth-century accounts succeed in capturing the flavor of the early banks fisheries. Frederick William Wallace, "Life on the Grand Banks," *National Geographic Magazine* 40 (July 1921), is particularly useful for its depictions of dory fishing and daily shipboard life. From a much later period, but still concerned with fishing under sail in the traditional fashion, is Alan Villiers's fine *The Quest of the Schooner* Argus: *A Voyage to the Banks and Greenland* (New York: Charles Scribner's Sons, 1951), which chronicles the last of the deep-water schoonermen.

In the absence of extensive personal accounts or autobiographies relating to the Atlantic fisheries in the nineteenth century, the best source of firsthand commentary on the nature of the North American fishing industry and the way of life it created is to be found in the prolific fiction it inspired, much of it highly accurate and realistic. The earliest of the genre is Joseph Reynolds, *Peter Gott, the Cape Ann Fisherman* (Boston: John P. Jewett & Co., 1856). Descriptive of Maine's pre–Civil War fisheries is Elijah Kellogg, *The Fisher Boys of Pleasant Cove* (Boston: Lee and Shephard, 1874). Most famous of all is Rudyard Kipling, *Captains Courageous: A Story of the Grand Banks* (New York: Century Co., 1896), a highly evocative novel all the more remarkable for its author's lack of sea experience.

Based more fully on intimate personal knowledge are the works of American James B. Connolly and his Canadian contemporary Frederick William Wallace. Connolly's *Out of Gloucester* (New York: Charles Scribner's Sons, 1905) is the author's first and best-known book of short stories, the finest of which were later collected under the title *Gloucestermen: Stories of the Fishing Fleet* (New York: Charles Scribner's Sons, 1930). Wallace's work on Nova Scotia is best represented by *Blue Water: A Tale of the Deep Sea Fishermen* (Toronto: Musson Book Co., 1914) and *The Shack Locker: Yarns of the Deep Sea Fishing Fleets* (Toronto: Hodder and Stoughton, 1916). In a slightly different category are two books bridging the gap between fiction and memoir. James B. Connolly, *The Book of the Gloucester Fishermen* (New York: John Day Co., 1927), is a collection of true tales presented in a short-story format. Joseph Berger [Jeremiah Digges], *In Great Waters: The Story of the Portuguese Fishermen* (New York: Macmillan Co., 1941), a semi-fictional account combining history and folklore, grew out of W.P.A.–sponsored research and interviews among the immigrant fishermen of Provincetown, Massachusetts.

United States government documents form the research backbone for any serious study of the North American sea fisheries. In addition to those already mentioned, several federal primary sources are of special relevance. U.S., Department of State, *Documents and Proceedings of the Halifax Commission, 1877, under the Treaty of Washington of May 8, 1871,* 3 vols., 45th Cong., 2nd Sess., 1878, House Exec. Doc. 89, provides invaluable testimony from fishermen and fish merchants on all phases of the Canadian and American industries in the mid-to-late nineteenth century. U.S., Department of State, *Proceedings of the North Atlantic Coast Fisheries Arbitration before the Permanent Court of Arbitration at the Hague,* 12 vols., 61st Cong., 3rd Sess., 1911, Sen. Exec. Doc. 870, contributes useful compilations of official correspondence and other documents relating to the diplomatic aspects of fisheries history. U.S., Department of the Treasury, *Report on the Trade and Commerce of the British North American Colonies and of the Great Lakes and Rivers,* by Israel D. Andrews, 32nd Cong., 1st Sess., 1852, Sen. Exec. Doc. 112, includes an extensive review of the status of the New England fishing industry at midcentury. Beginning in 1871 and 1881, respectively, the *Annual Report* and *Annual Bulletin* of the United States Commission on Fish and Fisheries, popularly known as the U.S. Fish Commission, contain innumerable authored monographs and reports of historical interest, including several on Maine. For nineteenth-century government statistics on American fishing tonnage, fish exports, and the like, the chief sources are: U.S., Congress, *American State Papers, Commerce and Navigation* (2 vols.; Washington: Gales and Seaton, 1832–34); U.S., Department of the Treasury, *Annual Report on the Foreign Commerce and Navigation of the United States,* 1821–92; and U.S., Department of the Treasury, *Annual Report of the Commissioner of Navigation,* 1893–1900. Also useful for statistical data on fishermen and fishing firms on a state-by-state basis are the federal manuscript census schedules for population and industry, 1850–1880, which are unpublished but available in microfilm form at various libraries and archives.

Selected Canadian government documents also shed light on the history of the Atlantic fisheries. Canada, Ministry of Marine and Fisheries, *Annual Report of the Department of Marine and Fisheries, Fisheries Branch,* 1868–on (published periodically as *Report of the Department of Fisheries* and *Report of the Commissioner of Fisheries*), is the leading source for statistics, reports, and miscellaneous commentary on that nation's sea fisheries, beginning with Confederation. The best source of official documentation for the earlier period is Nova Scotia, *Appendix to the Journal and Proceedings of the House of Assembly,* various years, which includes periodic reports and data on American as well as Canadian activities. Two individual government studies, Nova Scotia, Office of the Provincial Secretary, *Shore and Deep Sea Fisheries of Nova Scotia,* by Thomas F. Knight (Halifax: A. Grant, 1867), and New Brunswick, Office of Lieutenant Governor, *Reports on the Sea and River Fisheries of New Brunswick,* by M. H. Perley (Fredericton, N.B.: J. Simpson, 1852), offer the best pre-Confederation surveys of the fishing industries of those two provinces.

Another important primary source of fisheries history in the nineteenth century is the contemporary press, especially the daily or weekly newspaper columns containing shipping news. These variously titled "marine lists" record entrances and clearances, vessel losses and damage reports, ship launchings, fish-catch returns, and other miscellany. On the Maine fishing industry in particular, Portland's *Eastern Argus* is indispensable for its statewide coverage. Also useful for selected periods and localities are the *Republican Journal* of Belfast, the *Ellsworth Herald* and *Ellsworth American,* the *Machias Union,* and the *Eastport Sentinel,* as well as the *Mining and Industrial Journal,* a commercial weekly published in Bangor. Nova Scotia's *Lunenburg Progress* offers extensive commentary on that major port's activities after 1875 and provides a ready reference for cross-border comparative study.

In addition to published government documents and printed newspapers, significant primary materials for fisheries history may be found in a limited number of widely scattered manuscript collections. For Maine's deep-sea industry, the most valuable papers are those pertaining to the Witherle family of Castine, prominent fish merchants for most of the nineteenth century. Two collections of Witherle papers exist, one at the Penobscot Marine Museum, Searsport, Maine, and one at the Baker Library, Harvard University Graduate School of Business Administration, Cambridge, Massachusetts. Of comparable value for Nova Scotia's Atlantic fisheries are the business papers of Zwicker & Company of Lunenburg, housed at the Public Archives of Nova Scotia, Halifax. Three collections at the United States National Archives, Washington, D.C., contain important public documentation pertinent to the history of the New England fishing industry as a whole. The records of the Bureau of Customs (RG 36) yield such items as fishing articles of agreement, fishing journals, and cargo manifests for entrances and clearances at American ports. The records of the Bureau of Marine Inspection and Navigation (RG 41) include the certificates of enrollment issued to vessels engaged in the fisheries, providing essential information on builders, construction characteristics, and ownership. The records of the Department of the Treasury (RG 56) contain the federal government's abstracts of fishing-bounty payments made in the various collection districts, a unique source of socioeconomic data on the antebellum fisheries of Maine and Massachusetts.

Finally, reference should be made to the many published pictorial works bearing on the history of the North American sea fisheries. Fishing schooners and their crews became objects of attention for many noted marine photographers of the late nineteenth and early twentieth centuries. Those interested in the physical appearance of the world in which the sailing fishermen of the North Atlantic worked are referred to the following volumes of photographs and commentary: Albert Cook Church and James B. Connolly, *American Fishermen* (New York: W. W. Norton & Co., 1940); Joseph C. O'Hearn, *New England Fishing Schooners* (Milwaukee: Kalmbach Publishing Co., 1947); Andrew Merkel and W. R. MacAskill, *Schooner Bluenose* (Toronto: Ryerson Press, 1948); Gordon W. Thomas, *Fast and Able: Life Stories of Great Gloucester Fishing Schooners* (Gloucester, Mass.: Gloucester 350th Anniversary Celebration, Inc., 1973); Andrew W. German, *Down on T Wharf: The Boston Fisheries as Seen Through the Photographs of Henry D. Fisher* (Mystic, Conn.: Mystic Seaport Museum, 1982); and Joseph E. Garland, *Down to the Sea: Fishing Schooners of Gloucester* (Boston: David R. Godine, 1983).

APPENDIXES

Appendix 1   Maine's Share of American Cod- and Mackerel-Fishing
Tonnage, 1800–1900

	Vessels and Boats			*Vessels Only*		
	Maine Tonnage	*U.S. Tonnage*	*ME's Share of National Total*	*Maine Tonnage*	*U.S. Tonnage*	*ME's Share of National Total*
1800	5,354	29,427	18.2 %	2,522	22,932	11.0 %
1805	9,466	57,465	16.5	5,829	48,088	12.1
1810	5,454	34,828	15.7	1,661	26,251	6.3
1815	7,371	36,937	20.0	2,588	26,510	9.8
1820	16,322	72,040	22.7	11,325	60,843	18.6
1825	20,315	81,462	24.9	14,118	70,626	20.0
1830	28,822	97,530	29.6	26,930	94,015	28.6
1834	25,032	117,756	21.3	23,074	113,825	20.3
1840	21,742	104,305	20.8	17,784	96,196	18.5
1845	34,934	98,404	35.5	31,076	91,239	34.1
1850	53,937	151,918	35.5	49,264	143,758	34.3
1855	52,987	133,539	39.7	48,535	124,553	39.0
1860	75,252	162,764	46.2	69,913	153,619	45.5
1865	54,896	139,287	39.4	46,043	124,067	37.1
1870	22,433	91,460	24.5	18,221	82,612	22.1
1875	20,366	80,207	25.4	14,934	68,703	21.7
1880	18,785	77,538	24.2	14,694	64,935	22.6
1885	20,981	82,565	25.4	17,529	73,975	23.7
1890	11,842	68,367	17.3	9,615	61,507	15.6
1895	10,709	69,059	15.5	7,396	60,837	12.2
1900	7,701	51,629	14.9	4,570	43,694	10.5

Sources: ASP, CN, vols. 1, 2, *U.S.RFCN,* 1825–90, and *U.S.RCN,* 1895, 1900: statements
on fishing tonnage by customs district.

Note 1: Figures for 1800–1865 represent "old-measurement" tonnage; figures for
1870–1900 represent "new-measurement" tonnage. For explanation, see Appendix 2.

Note 2: The term "vessels" applies to craft of twenty or more tons engaged primarily in the
offshore deep-sea fisheries; the term "boats" applies to craft of less than twenty tons engaged
in the inshore or coastal fisheries.

Appendix 2 Maine Tonnage (o.m.) in the Cod and Mackerel Fisheries: 1830–1895

	Vessels & Boats	Vessels Only		Vessels & Boats	Vessels Only
1830	28,822	26,930	1863	74,880	68,676
1831	24,291	22,515	1864	74,532	68,256
1832	19,673	17,852	1865	54,896	46,367
1833	26,147	24,229	1866	51,362	43,043
1834	25,032	23,074	1867	31,082	24,128
1835	—	—	1868	33,150	25,557
1836	25,340	22,556	1869	33,203	26,808
1837	34,186	31,433	1870	33,650	27,332
1838	33,829	30,615	1871	33,957	26,919
1839	19,775	16,333	1872	28,185	21,590
1840	21,742	17,784	1873	69,294	63,323
1841	30,446	26,422	1874	25,173	18,821
1842	28,360	25,387	1875	30,549	22,401
1843	18,321	15,191	1876	33,323	26,568
1844	30,571	27,036	1877	54,820	47,426
1845	34,934	31,076	1878	31,406	25,014
1846	41,346	37,206	1879	29,039	22,920
1847	37,289	33,275	1880	28,178	22,041
1848	43,936	39,978	1881	29,495	23,711
1849	45,207	41,418	1882	28,097	22,691
1850	53,937	49,264	1883	51,261	45,056
1851	55,384	51,092	1884	31,722	25,820
1852	62,902	59,150	1885	31,472	26,294
1853	73,578	68,635	1886	31,179	26,222
1854	62,488	57,401	1887	31,073	27,038
1855	52,987	48,535	1888	24,452	20,715
1856	60,408	56,395	1889	22,089	18,830
1857	63,432	58,550	1890	17,763	14,423
1858	72,687	67,896	1891	17,534	13,883
1859	73,290	68,239	1892	16,340	11,771
1860	75,252	69,913	1893	16,218	11,211
1861	98,694	92,727	1894	17,337	12,339
1862	91,568	85,280	1895	16,064	11,094

Source: U.S.RFCN, 1830–90, statements on fishing tonnage by customs district.

Note 1: Figures for period 1830–1865 based on calculations from official government returns in "old-measurement" (o.m.) tons. Post-1865 figures based on official returns in "new-measurement" (n.m.) tons converted to "old measurement" for purposes of comparison. Conversion made according to the rule-of-thumb formula that old tonnage exceeded new tonnage by approximately one-third. (See Halifax Commission Proceedings, 2298, and EA, marine list, 26 April 1865.)

Note 2: Unusually high tonnages for 1873, 1877, and 1883 denote inflated vessel figures for Waldoboro, Bath, and Passamaquoddy districts, respectively, resulting from apparent errors in government statistics.

Appendix 3   Maine and Massachusetts Tonnage (o.m.) in the United
States Cod Fishery: 1830–1867 (Vessels and Boats)

	Maine	*Massachusetts*	*Other States*	*Total U.S.*
1830	18,733	34,864	7,959	61,556
1831	14,710	38,624	7,644	60,978
1832	11,619	36,813	6,596	55,028
1833	14,702	41,359	6,660	62,721
1834	13,586	34,068	9,020	56,674
1835	—	—	—	—
1836	14,859	37,020	11,428	63,307
1837	22,101	49,500	8,952	80,553
1838	22,529	38,328	9,207	70,064
1839	16,589	45,146	10,524	72,259
1840	17,355	48,415	10,266	76,036
1841	29,157	29,580	7,815	66,552
1842	23,272	25,605	5,928	54,805
1843	18,089	36,585	6,550	61,224
1844	29,372	47,139	8,714	85,225
1845	31,728	41,055	4,208	76,991
1846	33,208	38,546	7,564	79,318
1847	31,524	37,824	8,333	77,681
1848	36,053	44,795	8,999	89,847
1849	36,670	34,294	10,792	81,756
1850	41,891	41,553	10,362	93,806
1851	45,527	39,981	10,109	95,617
1852	47,823	51,125	11,625	110,573
1853	56,368	39,725	13,135	109,228
1854	48,694	54,022	9,211	111,927
1855	46,155	54,847	10,912	111,914
1856	51,334	41,892	9,226	102,452
1857	52,871	49,722	9,275	111,868
1858	61,631	49,336	8,285	119,252
1859	63,475	56,918	9,244	129,637
1860	66,590	59,982	10,081	136,653
1861	74,647	52,259	10,939	137,845
1862	68,133	54,356	11,112	133,601
1863	54,050	54,720	8,520	117,290
1864	52,054	48,744	2,944	103,742
1865	37,140	44,614	8,057	89,811
1866	32,120	41,358	3,883	77,361
1867	19,770	41,853	5,228	66,851

Source: U.S.RFCN, 1830–67, statements on fishing tonnage by customs district. Figures
for 1866–1867 converted from new-measurement tons (see note 1, Appendix 2).

Note: Separate tonnage statistics for individual sea fisheries were not kept after 1867.

Appendix 4   Maine and Massachusetts Tonnage (o.m.) in the United
States Vessel Cod Fishery: 1830–1867 (Vessels of 20 or More Tons)

	Maine	Massachusetts	Other States	Total U.S.
1830	18,733	34,864	7,959	61,556
1830	16,841	34,151	7,049	58,041
1831	12,935	37,633	6,671	57,239
1832	9,798	36,290	5,637	51,725
1833	12,473	40,174	5,922	58,569
1834	11,628	33,304	7,811	52,743
1835	—	—	—	—
1836	12,075	36,216	10,123	58,414
1837	19,348	48,409	7,299	75,056
1838	19,315	37,044	7,615	63,974
1839	13,147	43,260	8,761	65,168
1840	13,397	46,099	8,431	67,927
1841	25,133	27,782	7,641	60,556
1842	20,299	24,086	5,557	49,942
1843	14,959	34,953	4,989	54,901
1844	25,837	45,445	6,897	78,179
1845	27,870	39,595	2,361	69,826
1846	29,068	36,913	6,535	72,516
1847	27,510	36,230	6,438	70,178
1848	32,095	43,157	7,400	82,652
1849	32,881	32,022	8,979	73,882
1850	37,218	40,024	8,404	85,646
1851	41,233	38,110	8,133	87,476
1852	44,071	48,938	9,650	102,659
1853	51,425	37,632	10,933	99,990
1854	43,607	51,462	7,125	102,194
1855	41,703	52,463	8,762	102,928
1856	47,321	40,627	7,868	95,816
1857	47,989	48,548	8,036	104,573
1858	56,840	47,232	6,824	110,896
1859	58,424	54,558	7,595	120,577
1860	61,251	57,949	8,308	127,508
1861	68,680	49,633	8,997	127,310
1862	61,845	51,880	9,138	122,863
1863	47,846	52,162	6,552	106,560
1864	45,778	46,047	920	92,745
1865	28,611	40,756	5,224	74,591
1866	23,801	39,146	1,394	64,341
1867	12,816	38,633	3,615	55,064

Source: U.S.R.F.C.N, 1830–67, statements on fishing tonnage by customs district. Figures
for 1866–1867 converted from new measurement tons (see note 1, Appendix 2).

Appendix 5 Maine and Massachusetts Tonnage (o.m.) in the United
States Vessel Mackerel Fishery: 1830–1867 (Vessels of 20 or More Tons)

	Maine	Massachusetts	Other States	Total U.S.
1830	10,089	25,665	220	35,974
1831	9,580	34,943	1,688	46,211
1832	8,054	38,701	673	47,428
1833	11,756	35,196	1,773	48,725
1834	11,446	47,368	2,268	61,082
1835	—	—	—	—
1836	10,481	31,238	3,705	45,424
1837	12,085	33,438	1,288	46,811
1838	11,300	44,915	434	56,649
1839	3,186	31,920	878	35,984
1840	4,387	23,827	55	28,269
1841	1,289	10,032	0	11,321
1842	2,115	13,709	273	16,097
1843	232	11,544	0	11,776
1844	1,199	14,972	0	16,171
1845	3,206	17,712	495	21,413
1846	8,138	27,736	589	36,463
1847	5,765	25,017	669	31,451
1848	7,883	35,206	470	43,559
1849	8,537	34,057	348	42,942
1850	12,046	42,895	3,171	58,112
1851	9,857	39,416	1,266	50,539
1852	15,079	54,694	2,773	72,546
1853	17,210	41,281	1,360	59,851
1854	13,794	19,816	1,431	35,041
1855	6,832	13,709	1,084	21,625
1856	9,074	20,425	388	29,887
1857	10,561	17,530	237	28,328
1858	11,056	18,437	101	29,594
1859	9,815	17,038	217	27,070
1860	8,662	17,017	432	26,111
1861	24,047	29,945	804	54,796
1862	23,435	56,576	586	80,597
1863	20,830	29,692	497	51,019
1864	22,478	32,445	575	55,498
1865	17,756	31,371	349	49,476
1866	19,242	47,940	2,703	69,885
1867	11,312	34,637	1,298	47,247

Source: U.S.RFCN, 1830–67, statements on fishing tonnage by customs district. Figures
for 1866–1867 converted from new-measurement tons (see note 1, Appendix 2).

Appendix 6 Percentage of Maine and Massachusetts Vessel
Tonnage Engaged in Cod and Mackerel Fishing, 1830–1867
(Vessels of 20 or More Tons)

	Maine		Massachusetts	
	Cod	Mackerel	Cod	Mackerel
1830	62.5%	37.5%	57.1%	42.9%
1831	57.5	42.5	51.9	48.1
1832	54.9	45.1	48.4	51.6
1833	51.5	48.5	53.3	46.7
1834	50.4	49.6	41.3	58.7
1835	—	—	—	—
1836	53.5	46.5	53.7	46.3
1837	61.6	38.4	59.1	40.9
1838	63.1	36.9	45.2	54.8
1839	80.5	19.5	57.5	42.5
1840	75.3	24.7	65.6	34.4
1841	95.1	4.9	73.5	26.5
1842	91.7	8.3	65.1	34.9
1843	98.7	1.3	75.3	24.7
1844	95.6	4.4	75.2	24.8
1845	89.7	10.3	70.2	29.8
1846	78.4	21.6	56.9	43.1
1847	82.5	17.5	59.0	41.0
1848	80.2	19.8	55.1	44.9
1849	79.5	20.5	48.5	51.5
1850	75.5	24.5	48.2	51.8
1851	80.7	19.3	49.2	50.8
1852	74.6	25.4	47.1	52.9
1853	75.4	24.6	48.1	51.9
1854	75.8	24.2	72.3	27.7
1855	86.0	14.0	78.8	21.2
1856	83.9	16.1	67.2	32.8
1857	81.9	18.1	73.5	26.5
1858	83.8	16.2	72.0	28.0
1859	86.6	13.4	76.4	23.6
1860	87.1	12.9	77.3	22.7
1861	74.2	25.8	62.5	37.5
1862	72.9	27.1	47.2	52.3
1863	69.6	30.4	63.4	36.6
1864	67.6	32.4	59.0	41.0
1865	61.7	38.3	56.5	43.5
1866	55.3	44.7	45.0	55.0
1867	53.4	46.6	52.7	47.3
Avg.	74.3	25.7	59.6	40.4

Source: U.S.R.F.C.N, 1830–67, statements on fishing tonnage by customs district.

Appendix 7A Percentage of Maine Sea-Fisheries Tonnage Owned in the Various Customs Districts: 1800–1845 (Based on Vessels of 20 or More Tons)

District	1800	1805	1810	1815	1820	1825	1830	1835	1840	1845
Passamaquoddy	5.3	8.1	0.0	0.0	1.6	4.7	3.1	7.3	6.6	4.8
Machias	4.3	3.8	8.2	5.3	5.5	2.0	2.6	2.3	2.1	1.1
Frenchman's Bay	14.1	17.8	7.3	7.8	7.3	5.3	4.4	3.2	10.2	8.6
Penobscot (Castine)	5.2	14.4	17.0	11.3	16.6	20.2	22.9	34.6	36.6	31.0
Belfast	—	—	—	—	10.0	4.8	6.0	8.0	5.8	4.5
Waldoboro	—	13.1	8.1	11.5	8.9	9.6	7.0	6.0	0.6	12.8
Wiscasset	1.0	3.9	14.0	18.0	11.7	14.3	18.5	0.0	20.4	13.0
Bath	2.9	6.7	7.6	4.8	13.9	9.8	6.1	6.0	7.8	6.3
Portland-Falmouth	19.9	19.4	26.5	22.4	17.7	24.3	25.9	27.9	8.1	15.0
Biddeford (Saco)	6.1	3.8	6.7	0.0	1.1	1.5	0.6	0.6	1.3	0.8
Kennebunk	—	5.7	0.0	8.1	2.0	1.4	1.6	3.3	0.3	1.4
York	41.2	3.2	4.6	10.8	3.7	2.1	1.3	0.8	0.1	0.7
Eastern Maine (total)	28.9	44.1	32.5	24.4	41.0	37.0	39.0	55.4	61.3	50.0
Western Maine (total)	71.1	55.9	67.5	75.6	59.0	63.0	61.0	44.6	38.7	50.0

Appendix 7B Percentage of Maine Sea-Fisheries Tonnage Owned in the Various Customs Districts: 1850–1895 (Based on Vessels of 20 or More Tons)

District	1850	1855	1860	1865	1870	1875	1880	1885	1890	1895
Passamaquoddy	3.7	1.2	4.3	9.3	3.9	6.4	4.1	2.2	5.5	0.0
Machias	0.3	0.6	2.6	0.0	0.2	1.4	1.3	0.8	0.7	0.3
Frenchman's Bay	11.2	12.4	16.2	9.3	8.5	8.6	8.0	8.2	13.8	14.6
Penobscot (Castine)	31.4	33.9	29.3	23.9	32.6	16.3	16.4	13.8	11.0	12.1
Bangor	1.1	0.5	2.2	1.5	2.2	0.0	0.0	0.0	0.0	0.0
Belfast	10.8	15.0	12.3	11.6	8.7	6.9	7.2	9.6	10.2	2.5
Waldoboro	8.7	12.3	9.1	7.7	10.1	17.8	18.9	14.8	9.8	9.2
Wiscasset	12.4	4.2	9.9	24.5	23.9	21.8	16.6	11.8	11.4	12.5
Bath	5.5	5.0	3.9	3.6	1.4	1.0	0.8	0.8	0.5	0.0
Portland-Falmouth	12.7	10.1	7.8	7.0	7.8	18.7	25.8	36.5	35.2	46.8
Biddeford (Saco)	1.1	1.1	0.6	0.1	0.0	0.2	0.2	0.3	0.0	0.0
Kennebunk	1.1	2.6	1.5	1.0	0.6	0.9	0.4	1.2	1.9	2.0
York	0.2	1.1	0.4	0.6	0.0	0.0	0.2	0.0	0.0	0.0
Eastern Maine (total)	58.4	63.6	67.0	55.5	56.2	39.6	37.0	34.6	41.2	29.5
Western Maine (total)	41.6	36.4	33.0	44.5	43.8	60.4	63.0	65.4	58.8	70.5

Sources: ASP; CN, vols. 1, 2, and U.S.RFCN, 1825–95: statements on fishing tonnage by customs district.

Note 1: "Western Maine" refers to that portion of the state's coastline located west of the port of Rockland, including the customs districts of York, Kennebunk, Biddeford (later Saco), Portland-Falmouth, Bath, Wiscasset, and Waldoboro. "Eastern Maine" denotes that portion of the coastline situated east of Rockland and includes the districts of Belfast, Bangor, Penobscot (later Castine), Frenchman's Bay, Machias, and Passamaquoddy.

Note 2: Biddeford District was renamed Saco District in 1807, and Penobscot District became Castine District in 1866. Belfast and Bangor districts were created in 1818 and 1847, respectively. (See *Hough Report*, 104–5, and Wasson and Colcord, 253.)

Note 3: Tonnage data for Kennebunk and Waldoboro districts unavailable prior to 1804.

Appendix 8 Relative Dominance of Portland in the Maine Sea Fisheries: 1868–1898 (Based on Numbers of Vessels of 20 or More Tons, n.m.)

	Port.-Falm. District Vessels	Vessels of Other Maine Districts	Total Maine Vessels	Percentage of Vessels Owned in Port.-Falm. District
1868	31	326	357	8.7%
1869	36	336	372	9.7
1870	37	343	380	9.7
1871	44	335	379	11.6
1872	50	254	304	16.4
1873	52	478	530	9.8
1874	52	218	270	19.3
1875	59	265	324	18.2
1876	70	304	374	18.7
1877	75	421	496	15.1
1878	76	283	359	21.2
1879	70	261	331	21.1
1880	79	244	323	24.5
1881	81	248	329	24.6
1882	98	237	335	29.3
1883	113	328	441	25.6
1884	104	225	329	31.6
1885	104	220	324	32.1
1886	98	213	311	31.5
1887	95	182	277	34.3
1888	81	152	233	34.8
1889	76	142	218	34.9
1890	57	119	176	32.4
1891	60	113	173	34.7
1892	54	91	145	37.2
1893	52	82	134	38.8
1894	55	83	138	39.9
1895	52	81	133	39.1
1896	48	83	131	36.6
1897	47	78	125	37.6
1898	31	57	88	35.2

Source: U.S.RFCN, 1868–92, and U.S.RCN, 1893–98: statements on fishing vessels by customs district.

Note: Reduced Portland share of total vessels in 1873, 1877, and 1883 caused by government statistical errors in compiling data for Waldoboro, Bath, and Passamaquoddy districts, respectively.

Appendix 9 Leading Customs Districts in the Maine Sea Fisheries, 1830–1895 (Based on Tonnage in Cod and Mackerel Vessels of 20 or More Tons)

	District	Tonnage	% of Total		District	Tonnage	% of Total
1830	Port.-Falm.	6,989	26.0	1863	Wiscasset	15,191	22.1
1831	Penobscot	8,053	35.8	1864	Wiscasset	15,557	22.8
1832	Port.-Falm.	6,147	34.4	1865	Penobscot	11,070	23.9
1833	Penobscot	8,288	34.2	1866	Penobscot	8,936	31.1
1834	Penobscot	7,975	34.6	1867	Belfast	3,683	22.9
1835	—	—	—	1868	Castine	5,204	30.5
1836	Penobscot	8,429	37.4	1869	Castine	5,874	32.9
1837	Penobscot	10,911	34.7	1870	Castine	5,946	32.6
1838	Penobscot	10,752	35.1	1871	Castine	5,524	30.8
1839	Port.-Falm.	4,234	25.9	1872	Castine	4,482	31.1
1840	Penobscot	6,514	36.6	1873	Waldoboro	31,452	74.5
1841	Wiscasset	6,664	25.2	1874	Wiscasset	3,126	24.9
1842	Penobscot	5,271	20.8	1875	Wiscasset	3,251	21.8
1843	Penobscot	3,301	21.7	1876	Wiscasset	3,495	19.7
1844	Penobscot	7,187	26.6	1877	Bath	13,328	42.2
1845	Penobscot	9,648	28.5	1878	Port.-Falm.	3,665	22.0
1846	Penobscot	12,408	33.3	1879	Port.-Falm.	3,301	21.6
1847	Penobscot	8,631	25.9	1880	Port.-Falm.	3,797	25.8
1848	Penobscot	12,871	32.2	1881	Port.-Falm.	4,172	26.4
1849	Penobscot	13,682	33.0	1882	Port.-Falm.	5,327	35.2
1850	Penobscot	15,472	31.4	1883	Port.-Falm.	6,522	21.7
1851	Penobscot	16,025	31.4	1884	Port.-Falm.	6,130	35.6
1852	Penobscot	15,935	26.9	1885	Port.-Falm.	6,400	36.5
1853	Penobscot	17,666	25.7	1886	Port.-Falm.	6,346	36.3
1854	Penobscot	16,467	28.7	1887	Port.-Falm.	6,232	34.6
1855	Penobscot	16,457	33.9	1888	Port.-Falm.	5,168	37.4
1856	Penobscot	16,093	28.5	1889	Port.-Falm.	4,804	38.3
1857	Penobscot	17,850	30.5	1890	Port.-Falm.	3,380	35.2
1858	Penobscot	19,182	28.3	1891	Port.-Falm.	3,467	37.5
1859	Penobscot	19,685	28.8	1892	Port.-Falm.	3,223	41.1
1860	Penobscot	20,512	29.3	1893	Port.-Falm.	3,461	46.3
1861	Penobscot	21,618	23.3	1894	Port.-Falm.	3,650	44.4
1862	Waldoboro	20,959	24.6	1895	Port.-Falm.	3,459	46.8

Sources: U.S.RFCN, 1830–92, and U.S.RCN, 1893–95: statements on fishing tonnage by customs district.

Note 1: Tonnage totals are in new measurement (n.m.) tons beginning in 1866 and in old-measurement tons (o.m.) prior to that year. High tonnage figures and percentages for 1873 and 1877 reflect inaccuracies in official data for Waldoboro and Bath districts, respectively. Low Portland-Falmouth percentage for 1883 reflects an overcounting of statewide tonnage due to an inflated figure for Passamaquoddy District.

Note 2: Penobscot District was renamed Castine District in 1866.

Appendix 10 Portland Wholesale Fish Prices on or Near
the First of September: 1830–1890 (Highest Price)

	Cod (per qtl.)	#1 Mackerel (per bbl.)		Cod (per qtl.)	#1 Mackerel (per bbl.)
1830	$ 2.50	$ 4.75	1861	$ 3.00	$ 7.00
1831	3.00	5.25	1862	4.00	8.00
1832	3.00	5.00	1863	5.50	8.00
1833	3.00	5.62	1864	8.00	20.00
1834	2.50	6.00	1865	8.00	16.50
1835	3.00	—	1866	7.75	20.50
1836	3.50	9.50	1867	7.00	20.00
1837	4.50	8.00	1868	7.00	23.50
1838	4.50	—	1869	7.25	24.00
1839	3.75	—	1870	6.25	25.00
1840	2.50	—	1871	5.25	20.00
1841	2.25	—	1872	5.50	16.00
1842	—	—	1873	5.75	24.50
1843	2.75	9.50	1874	5.00	14.50
1844	2.50	10.25	1875	5.25	18.50
1845	2.25	—	1876	5.25	15.50
1846	3.00	12.50	1877	5.25	18.00
1847	3.25	12.00	1878	4.25	16.50
1848	3.00	9.00	1879	4.00	18.00
1849	2.50	9.50	1880	6.75	—
1850	3.00	10.25	1881	4.50	16.00
1851	3.25	10.00	1882	6.50	11.00
1852	3.75	12.00	1883	5.75	19.00
1853	3.50	12.00	1884	4.50	18.50
1854	3.50	16.00	1885	4.00	13.50
1855	3.75	16.00	1886	3.00	30.00
1856	3.25	14.00	1887	4.00	18.00
1857	4.00	18.00	1888	4.75	24.00
1858	3.25	14.00	1889	4.75	29.00
1859	4.00	16.00	1890	5.75	24.00
1860	3.75	16.00			

Source: EA, wholesale prices current, 1830–90.

Note: A quintal of dried salt cod weighed 112 pounds, and a barrel of pickled mackerel weighed two hundred pounds. (See *U.S.FCB, 1898,* 424, 426.)

Appendix 11 Average Yearly Cod Landings by Vessels of the Hancock County Grand Banks Fleet in the Deck- and Dory-Fishing Eras

	Catch per Vessel (thousands of fish)	Catch per Vessel (quintals of fish)	Number of Returns
		Deck Fishing	
1850	26,000	867	3
1851	22,000	733	2
1852	31,000	1,033	3
1853	22,000	733	31
1854	25,000	833	18
1855	27,000	900	21
1856	28,000	933	6
1857	28,000	933	21
1858	30,000	1,000	20
1859	25,000	833	24
Avg. (1850–59)	26,000	864	15
		Dory Fishing	
1880	41,000	1,375	4
1881	40,000	1,333	9
1882	39,000	1,308	6
1883	43,000	1,433	11
1884	52,000	1,718	14
1885	47,000	1,578	9
1886	52,000	1,747	7
1887	42,000	1,415	10
1888	44,000	1,646	11
1889	47,000	1,563	8
Avg. (1880–89)	45,000	1,512	9

Sources: EA, marine lists, 1853–59; 1880–89; *RJ,* marine lists, 1850–54, 1859.

Note: Catch averages based on returns recorded between July 1 and November 1 of each year. Averages for 1850–1859 computed from returns in thousands of fish. Averages for 1880–1889 computed from returns in quintals of fish. Conversions made according to the formula that thirty banks cod equalled one dried quintal. (See *U.S.FCB, 1893,* 344.)

Appendix 12   Comparative Performances of Deck-Fishing and Dory-Fishing Schooners in the Hancock County Grand Banks Fishery

Highliners in the Deck-Fishing Fleet of 1853

Name	Port	Dimensions (feet)	Landed Catch (fish)
John Perkins	Castine	75 × 21 × 8	37,000
Albion	Castine	75 × 22 × 8	35,000
Redwing	Castine	75 × 20 × 8	35,000
Martha Burgess	Castine	76 × 21 × 8	31,000
Howard	Bucksport	65 × 17 × 8	26,000
Patapsco	Castine	73 × 18 × 8	26,000

Average Vessel Dimensions (feet)   — 73 × 20 × 8
Average Calculated Tonnage (o.m.) — 103 tons
Average Landed Catch (no. fish)   — 32,000

Highliners in the Dory-Fishing Fleet of 1883

Name	Port	Dimensions (feet)	Landed Catch (fish)
Bertha D. Nickerson	Bucksport	90 × 25 × 10	90,000
Annie G. Quiner	Bucksport	86 × 22 × 8	78,000
Walter M. Young	Ellsworth	83 × 23 × 8	51,000
Carrie A. Pitman	Bucksport	72 × 20 × 8	45,000
Amy Knight	Bucksport	66 × 20 × 8	42,000
Princess	Bucksport	70 × 19 × 8	33,000

Average Vessel Dimensions (feet)   — 78 × 22 × 8
Average Calculated Tonnage (o.m.) — 120 tons
Average Landed Catch (no. fish)   — 57,000

Increase in Average Vessel Tonnage (1853–83) — 17%
Increase in Average Landed Catch (1853–83)   — 78%

Sources: EA, marine lists, 1 July–1 November 1853, 1883; *RJ,* marine lists, 1 July–1 November 1853; Wasson and Colcord, 293–94, 315–17, 410; *RAFS, 1882, 1891,* passim.

Note: Average old-measurement (o.m.) tonnage calculated from vessel dimensions as per the formula used by customs officials from 1789 to 1865. (See *U.S.AppAC,* 1st Cong., 1st Sess. [1789], 2162; see also Albion, *Square Riggers on Schedule,* 298.)

Appendix 13 Major Markets for United States Dried- and Smoked-Fish Exports: 1830–1860 (Quintals Shipped and Percentages of Total Exports)

	Cuba[a]	Haiti[b]	Other Spanish West Indies[c]	Entire Spanish Caribbean	Total (all markets)
1830	73,948 (32%)	35,499 (15%)	6,075 (3%)	80,023 (35%)	229,796
1831	67,514 (29)	42,011 (18)	8,267 (4)	75,781 (33)	230,577
1832	87,736 (38)	43,400 (19)	10,071 (4)	97,807 (42)	230,514
1833	79,433 (32)	50,034 (20)	15,679 (6)	95,112 (38)	249,689
1834	79,262 (31)	60,154 (24)	19,165 (8)	98,427 (39)	253,132
1835	77,757 (27)	75,847 (26)	21,763 (8)	97,610 (35)	287,722
1836	87,779 (36)	58,250 (24)	17,637 (7)	105,416 (44)	240,763
1837	75,004 (40)	39,419 (21)	13,151 (7)	88,155 (47)	188,943
1838	89,393 (43)	39,683 (19)	16,900 (8)	106,293 (52)	206,028
1839	78,278 (38)	44,635 (21)	24,770 (12)	103,048 (49)	208,720
1840	69,018 (33)	53,365 (25)	27,993 (13)	97,011 (46)	211,425
1841	77,289 (31)	67,991 (27)	34,939 (14)	112,228 (44)	252,199
1842	86,110 (34)	57,532 (23)	36,774 (14)	122,884 (48)	256,083
1843	46,007 (26)	43,089 (25)	26,242 (15)	72,249 (41)	174,220
1844	107,493 (40)	58,408 (22)	35,638 (13)	143,131 (53)	271,610
1845	123,000 (43)	59,427 (21)	37,905 (13)	160,905 (56)	288,380
1846	118,592 (43)	57,483 (21)	36,687 (13)	155,279 (56)	277,401
1847	128,950 (50)	55,672 (22)	25,833 (10)	154,783 (60)	258,870
1848	94,685 (46)	38,973 (19)	21,753 (11)	116,438 (56)	206,549
1849	197,457 (48)	30,526 (15)	20,880 (11)	218,337 (59)	197,457
1850	49,835 (30)	48,127 (29)	16,215 (10)	66,050 (40)	168,600
1851	37,509 (25)	56,263 (37)	15,208 (10)	52,717 (35)	151,088
1852	38,691 (29)	49,790 (37)	9,084 (7)	47,775 (35)	134,732
1853	30,726 (23)	45,718 (35)	11,226 (9)	41,952 (32)	131,665
1854	41,076 (31)	29,840 (23)	15,481 (12)	56,557 (43)	131,316
1855	37,653 (31)	25,653 (21)	12,712 (11)	50,365 (42)	119,926
1856	59,854 (35)	34,232 (20)	12,379 (7)	72,233 (43)	168,971
1857	44,796 (26)	46,882 (27)	12,461 (7)	57,257 (33)	174,765
1858	41,772 (26)	46,935 (29)	11,516 (7)	53,288 (33)	161,269
1859	73,226 (35)	49,399 (24)	18,029 (9)	91,255 (44)	209,350
1860	59,719 (27)	55,652 (25)	12,704 (6)	72,423 (33)	219,628
Average (1830–60)	76,115 (36%)	48,384 (23%)	19,521 (9%)	95,636 (46%)	209,400

Source: U.S.R.FCN, 1830–60, statements on domestic exports by country.

[a] Leading individual export market, 1830–50, 1854–56, and 1859–60; second leading market, 1851–53 and 1857–58.

[b] Leading individual export market, 1851–53 and 1857–58; second leading market, 1830–50, 1854–56, and 1859–60.

[c] Third leading combined export market, 1838–51 and 1854; fourth leading market, 1853 and 1855–60. "Other" Spanish West Indies refers principally to Puerto Rico and Santo Domingo.

Appendix 14 Representative Fish Shipments from the Passamaquoddy Region of Maine, 1840–1860 (Based on Reports of Vessels Damaged, Disabled, or Lost at Sea in Transit)

Vessel	Home Port	Port of Origin	Port of Destination	Approximate Date	Cargo
Schr. *Bride*	Eastport	Eastport	New York	December 1840	Pickled fish
Schr. *General Marshall*	Eastport	Eastport	Philadelphia	October 1841	Plaster and fish oil
Schr. *Lucy & Margaret*	New York	Eastport	New York	January 1843	Laths and smoked herring
Schr. *Martha*	—	Eastport	Portland	December 1844	Fish
Schr. *Oread*	Eastport	Eastport	Philadelphia	December 1845	Plaster, laths, herring
Brig *Otis Norcross*	Eastport	Eastport	Havana	August 1848	Timber and fish
Schr. *Matilda*	Lubec	Eastport	New York	September 1848	Fish and laths
Schr. *Emily*	Lubec	Lubec	Boston	November 1848	Dried fish
Schr. *Alpine*	—	Eastport	Richmond, Va.	January 1849	Plaster, laths, smoked herring
Schr. *Esther Eliza*	—	Lubec	New York	February 1850	Plaster, pickled fish, laths
Schr. *Chief Sachem*	Lubec	Lubec	New York	June 1850	Plaster and fish
Schr. *Oread*	Lubec	Lubec	New York	November 1851	Fish and plaster
Schr. *Umpire*	—	Lubec	Bangor	December 1852	Fish and ground plaster
Schr. *Rough & Ready*	Eastport	Eastport	Philadelphia	March 1853	Fish and laths
Schr. *Mozart*	Lubec	Lubec	New York	April 1853	Plaster, fish, laths
Brig *R. B. Clark*	Lubec	Lubec	New York	December 1853	Laths, pickets, fish
Brig *Albert Fearing*	—	Eastport	Philadelphia	December 1853	Fish and plaster
Schr. *Flora*	Eastport	Eastport	Philadelphia	March 1854	Plaster and fish
Schr. *Frederick Reed*	Eastport	Eastport	Boston	September 1854	Plaster and fish
Schr. *Mary Peavey*	—	Eastport	Baltimore	December 1854	Laths and fish
Schr. *Mozart*	Lubec	Lubec	New York	December 1854	Stone, plaster, herring, laths
Schr. *Mary H. Case*	Lubec	Eastport	New York	March 1855	Plaster, laths, fish
Schr. *Challenge*	—	Eastport	Baltimore	January 1856	Fish and palings
Schr. *Texan*	Eastport	Eastport	New York	November 1856	Fish and laths
Schr. *Matilda*	Lubec	Lubec	Boston	October 1857	Plaster and herring
Schr. *Olive*	Eastport	Eastport	New York	September 1858	Laths and smoked herring
Schr. *Ocean Herald*	—	Eastport	Alexandria, Va.	October 1858	Plaster and fish
Schr. *Turk*	—	Lubec	New York	February 1860	Ground plaster and herring
Schr. *Tilton*	Eastport	Eastport	New York	September 1860	Mackerel, herring, laths

Source: EA, marine lists, 1840–60.

Appendix 15 Social Characteristics of Resident Fishermen in Various Maine Communities: 1860–1870

	Average Age		Percentage Married		Percentage Born Out of State		Percentage Born Outside U.S.		Percentage Born in Atlantic Canada	
	1860	1870	1860	1870	1860	1870	1860	1870	1860	1870
Portland	34 yrs.	33 yrs.	66%	64%	18%	27%	12%	26%	10%	20%
Boothbay	29	33	50	60	11	13	8	10	6	8
Southport	34	33	57	49	10	14	9	10	4	6
Vinalhaven	29	33	55	51	5	4	2	2	1	1
North Haven	27	31	44	55	2	4	3	4	2	2
Deer Isle	31	30	58	53	5	4	4	2	3	2
Eastport	35	37	58	56	50	64	47	64	42	60
7 communities	31 yrs.	32 yrs.	55%	55%	12%	14%	10%	12%	8%	10%

Source: U.S. MS Census Pop., 1860, 1870: Cumberland County, Maine, city of Portland; Lincoln County, Maine, towns of Boothbay and Southport; Knox County, Maine, towns of Vinalhaven and North Haven; Hancock County, Maine, town of Deer Isle; and Washington County, Maine, city of Eastport.

Note: Based on total combined samples of 1,738 fishermen for 1860 and 1,320 fishermen for 1870. For numbers of fishermen in individual communities, see Appendix 16.

Appendix 16   Lack of Financial Assets Among Resident Fishermen
in Various Maine Communities: 1860–1870

	1860		*1870*	
	Total Fishermen	*Those Reporting No Assets*	*Total Fishermen*	*Those Reporting No Assets*
Kennebunkport	73	19 (26%)	93	37 (40%)
Portland	105	38 (36)	101	72 (71)
Georgetown	137	78 (57)	132	84 (64)
Westport	121	49 (40)	113	75 (66)
Southport	141	57 (40)	109	56 (51)
Boothbay	390	211 (54)	302	134 (44)
Vinalhaven	282	116 (41)	135	75 (56)
North Haven	153	81 (53)	121	65 (55)
Deer Isle	502	172 (34)	435	243 (58)
Swan's Island	90	24 (27)	115	69 (60)
Lubec	95	21 (22)	147	55 (37)
Eastport	165	68 (41)	117	58 (50)
12 communities	2,254	934 (41%)	1,920	1,023 (53%)

Source: U.S. MS Census Pop., 1860, 1870: York County, Maine, town of Kennebunkport;
Cumberland County, Maine, city of Portland; Sagadahoc County, Maine, town of Georgetown; Lincoln County, Maine, towns of Boothbay, Southport, and Westport; Knox County,
Maine, towns of Vinalhaven and North Haven; Hancock County, Maine, towns of Deer Isle
and Lubec; and Washington County, Maine, town of Lubec and city of Eastport.

Note: Financial assets refer to both realty and personalty holdings, as related to census enu-
merators.

Appendix 17 The Major Maine Sea Fisheries
and Participating Communities

Grand Banks Cod Fishery

Bangor	Camden	Hancock	Orland	Tremont
Belfast	Castine	Harpswell	Penobscot	Trenton
Boothbay	Cranberry Isles	Jonesport	Portland	Vinalhaven
Bristol	Deer Isle	Kennebunkport	Sedgwick	
Brooklin	Ellsworth	Lamoine	So. Thomaston	
Brooksville	Frankfort	Monhegan	Sullivan	
Bucksport	Gouldsboro	North Haven	Swan's Is.	

Gulf of St. Lawrence Cod Fishery

Addison	Bucksport	E. Machias	Mt. Desert	Waldoboro
Belfast	Camden	Harpswell	Portland	Westport
Boothbay	Castine	Isle au Haut	Southport	Wiscasset
Bremen	Cushing	Kennebunkport	Trenton	York
Bristol	Deer Isle	Monhegan	Vinalhaven	

Labrador Cod Fishery

Boothbay	Deer Isle	Lamoine	Tremont	Wiscasset
Camden	Eastport	Lubec	Trenton	
Castine	Harpswell	Portland	Vinalhaven	
Cranberry Isles	Jonesport	Southport	Westport	

Western (Sable Island) Bank Cod Fishery

Belfast	Camden	Georgetown	Lamoine	Swan's Is.
Boothbay	Castine	Gouldsboro	North Haven	Trenton
Bremen	Deer Isle	Hancock	Portland	Vinalhaven
Bristol	Eastport	Harpswell	St. George	Westport
Bucksport	Friendship	Kennebunkport	Southport	

Quereau Bank (Banquereau) Cod Fishery

Belfast	Bucksport	Kennebunk	Portland	Tremont
Boothbay	Camden	Kennebunkport	Searsport	Vinalhaven
Bremen	Castine	Lamoine	Sedgwick	Waldoboro
Bristol	Deer Isle	Orland	Southport	
Brooklin	Eastport	Penobscot	Thomaston	

Cape Sable & "Cape Shore" Cod Fishery

Belfast	Cranberry Isles	Machiasport	Vinalhaven	York
Boothbay	Deer Isle	Portland	Westport	
Bristol	Eastport	Rockland	Wiscasset	
Bucksport	Georgetown	Southport	Woolwich	

(*continued*)

Appendix 17 (*continued*)

Bay of Fundy Cod Fishery

Addison	Camden	Eden	Lamoine	Swan's Is.
Belfast	Castine	Friendship	Lubec	Trenton
Boothbay	Cranberry Isles	Gouldsboro	Machiasport	Vinalhaven
Brooklin	Cutler	Hancock	Matinicus	Waldoboro
Brooksville	Deer Isle	Harrington	Portland	Winterport
Bucksport	Dennysville	Islesboro	Sedgwick	
Calais	Eastport	Jonesboro	Sullivan	

Gulf of St. Lawrence Mackerel Fishery

Addison	Cape Elizabeth	Georgetown	Monhegan	So. Thomaston
Belfast	Castine	Gouldsboro	Mt. Desert	Southport
Boothbay	Damariscotta	Hampden	North Haven	Swan's Is.
Bremen	Deer Isle	Harpswell	Orland	Tremont
Bristol	E. Machias	Isle au Haut	Portland	Vinalhaven
Brooklin	Eastport	Kennebunk	St. George	Westport
Bucksport	Frankfort	Kennebunkport	Scarborough	Wiscasset
Camden	Freeport	Lubec	Sedgwick	Woolwich

Northern (New England Shore) Mackerel Fishery

Belfast	Castine	Islesboro	Portland	Tremont
Biddeford Pool	Cranberry Isles	Kittery	Rockland	Vinalhaven
Boothbay	Deer Isle	Matinicus	St. George	Westport
Bristol	Eastport	Monhegan	Sedgwick	Wiscasset
Brooklin	Friendship	North Haven	Southport	Woolwich
Camden	Isle au Haut	Northport	Swan's Is.	

Southern Spring Mackerel Fishery

Belfast	Brooklin	North Haven	St. George	Southport
Boothbay	Deer Isle	Portland	Sedgwick	Swan's Is.
Bremen	Georgetown			

Magdalen Islands Herring Fishery

Belfast	Cranberry Isles	Eastport	Lubec	Westport
Boothbay	Cutler	Gouldsboro	Milbridge	
Bucksport	Damariscotta	Hancock	Mt. Desert	
Camden	Deer Isle	Isle au Haut	Tremont	
Castine	E. Machias	Lamoine	Vinalhaven	

Sources: Goode Report, secs. 2, 5; *N.S.AppJPHA, 1853,* 120–29; *Can.AppRFB, 1870,* 350–60; PMM, GC, MSS 6, 125, 354; *EA,* marine lists, 1840–90; *RJ,* marine lists, 1840–60; *EH,* marine lists, 1851–54; *EAm,* marine lists, 1855–65; *ES,* marine lists, 1854–60; NA, RBC (RG 36), CDR, fishing logbooks for Maine customs districts; see also *Halifax Commission Proceedings, Hague Arbitration Proceedings* (vol. 2), *Mackerel Fishery Materials,* Pierce, Johnson et al. (vol. 2), and Procter, *Fishermen's Own Book, passim.*

Appendix 18   Financial Reconstruction of a Voyage to the Grand Banks of Newfoundland, May 17–October 17, 1853, by the Schooner *Martha Burgess* of Castine, Maine

Description of Vessel:	Type—Deck Hand-liner
	Tonnage—118 tons (o.m.)
	Dimensions—76′ × 21′ × 8′
	Builders—Mayo & Perkins, Castine, Me.
	Date of Launch—April 22, 1853
	Building Cost—$5,500
Owners of Vessel:	William Witherle, William H. Witherle, and
	Benjamin D. Gay (partners, William Witherle & Co.),
	George H. Witherle (clerk, William Witherle & Co.),
	and Joseph W. Sylvester (captain), all of Castine.
Size of Crew:	11 (9 sharesmen, cook, and boy)
Outfitting Firm:	William Witherle & Co., Castine
Time of Voyage:	5 months (4 months actual fishing)
Total Catch:	31,386 cod
Product after Processing:	942 quintals of dried cod and 14 barrels of codfish oil
Market Price of Fish (Boston wholesale market, March 1854):	$3.50 per quintal
Market Price of Oil (estimated):	$15.00 per barrel
Fishing Bounty Payment (maximum allowance based on tonnage):	$360.00

Gross Stock of Voyage (wholesale value of fish & oil)		$3,507.00
Vessel's Expenses:	"Great General" (salt, bait barrels, fuel, lighting, etc.)	882.89
	Insurance on Great General (3% of full valuation)	26.49
	Freight & Insurance to Wholesale Market	129.47
	Total Vessel Expenses	$1,038.85
Net Stock of Voyage (gross minus vessel's expenses)		$2,468.15
Owners' Share of Net Stock ($\frac{1}{2}$)		1,234.08
Owners' Expenses: Insurance on Vessel	(3% of full valuation)	165.00
	Total Owners' Expenses	$ 165.00
Owners' Share of Net Stock After Expenses		$1,069.08
Owners' Share of Bounty Allowance ($\frac{3}{8}$)		135.00
Owners' Share of Total Proceeds		$1,204.08

(*continued*)

Shoreman's Share of Net Stock for Curing & Drying ($\frac{1}{18}$)	$137.12
Crew's Share of Net Stock ($\frac{8}{18}$)	$1,096.96
Crew's Expenses: "Small General" (provisions, fishing apparatus)	310.17
Insurance on Small General (3% of full valuation)	9.31
Cook's Wages ($20.00 per month)	100.00
Cook's Compensation for Fish Caught ($12.00 per 1,000)	8.11
Boy's Wages ($10.00 per month)	50.00
Boy's Compensation for Fish Caught ($12.00 per 1,000)	0.47
Total Crew Expenses	$478.06
Crew's Share of Net Stock After Expenses	618.90
Crew's Share of Bounty Allowance ($\frac{5}{8}$)	225.00
Crew's Share of Total Proceeds.	$843.90

Individual Settlements (Owners)

	Share in Vessel	Share of Net Stock	Share of Bounty	Total Share	Bounty as a % of Total Share
William Witherle	$\frac{1}{4}$	$267.27	$33.75	$301.02	11.2%
William H. Witherle	$\frac{1}{4}$	267.27	33.75	301.02	11.2
Benjamin D. Gay	$\frac{1}{4}$	267.27	33.75	301.02	11.2
George H. Witherle	$\frac{1}{8}$	133.64	16.88	150.51	11.2
Joseph W. Sylvester (Capt.)	$\frac{1}{8}$	133.63	16.88	150.51	11.2
	100%	$1,069.08	$135.00	$1,204.08	11.2%

Individual Settlements (Sharesmen)

	Fish Catch	Catch Percentage	Share of Net Stock	Cook's/ Boy's Share of Net Stock	Share of Bounty	Cook's/ Boy's Share of Bounty	Total Share
Highliner	4,729	15.07%	$93.27	$1.57	$33.91	$0.57	$129.32
2nd Sharesman	4,583	14.60	90.36	1.57	32.85	0.57	125.35
3rd Sharesman	4,360	13.89	85.96	1.57	31.25	0.57	119.35
4th Sharesman[†]	3,464	11.04	68.33	1.57	24.84	0.57	95.31
5th Sharesman	3,370	10.74	66.47	1.57	24.16	0.57	92.77
6th Sharesman	2,643	8.42	52.11	1.57	18.94	0.57	73.19
7th Sharesman	2,620	8.35	51.68	1.57	18.79	0.57	72.61
8th Sharesman	2,594	8.26	51.12	1.56	18.59	0.57	71.84
9th Sharesman	2,308	7.35	45.49	1.56	16.54	0.57	64.16
Cook & Boy (non-sharesmen)	715	2.28%	$ 14.11	—	$ 5.13	—	—
Total	31,386	100.00%	$618.90	$14.11	$225.00	$5.13	$843.90

† Captain

(*continued*)

Appendix 18 *(continued)*

Earnings of Sharesmen after Deduction of Individual Debts Owed to Outfitter

	Share of Voyage	Outfitting Debt	Actual Income	Bounty Payment	Bounty as a % of Total Share	Bounty as a % of Actual Income
Highliner	$129.32	$7.30	$122.02	$34.48	26.7%	28.3%
2nd Sharesman	125.35	5.06	120.29	33.42	26.7	27.8
3rd Sharesman	119.35	60.93	58.42	31.82	26.7	54.5
4th Sharesman [†]	245.82	none	245.82	42.28	17.2	17.2
5th Sharesman	92.77	3.53	88.78	24.73	26.7	27.9
6th Sharesman	73.19	32.24	40.95	19.51	26.7	47.6
7th Sharesman	72.61	none	72.61	19.36	26.7	26.7
8th Sharesman	71.84	6.93	64.91	19.16	26.7	29.5
9th Sharesman	64.16	22.50	41.66	17.11	26.7	41.1
Average (total)	$110.49	$15.39	$ 95.05	$26.87	24.3%	28.3%
Avg. (minus Capt.)	$ 93.57	$17.31	$ 76.21	$24.95	26.7%	32.7%

[†] Captain

Individual Settlements (Captain):	Fishing Share	$ 95.31
	Owner Share	150.51
		$245.82

Sources: PMM, GC, MSS 6, 125; PMM, WP, Miscellaneous Vessels, box 2, files 1, 21: schooner *Redwing,* settlement of coasting voyage to Boston, March 1854, and schooner *Martha Burgess,* settlement of Grand Banks voyage, 6 May 1856; BLH, WC, case 19: marine-insurance policies for various Castine fishing schooners, 1853; NA, RBC (RG 36), CDR, Penobscot District Fishing Articles of Agreement: articles for various Castine schooners, 1854; Castine Tax Valuation Book for 1854; Wasson and Colcord, 317; *U.S.AppAC,* 15th Cong., 2nd Sess.(1819), cols. 2531–35; *EH,* marine list, 29 April 1853; *EA,* Boston whole-sale prices current, 6, 13, 20 March 1854.

Note 1: Since the cook and boy worked for wages paid by the crew, their portions of the catch and bounty were divided equally among the sharesmen.

Note 2: The captain, J. W. Sylvester, was a working member of the crew. He fished and received a commensurate share of the crew's portion of the catch and bounty, as well as a share as part owner of the vessel.

Appendix 19   Comparison of Maine Fishing Operations at a Major
Commercial Center and a Regional Outport, 1850

	Castine	*Deer Isle*
Total Capital Invested	$68,700	$60,900
Number of Firms/Owners	10	43
Average Capital Investment per Firm	$6,870	$1,416
Capital Investment of Largest Firm	$17,000	$10,000
Total Number of Vessels Owned	39	52
Number of Single-Vessel Owners	3 (30%)	36 (84%)
Number of Multiple-Vessel Owners	7 (70%)	7 (16%)
Average Number of Vessels per Owner	3.9	1.2
Number of Vessels Owned by Largest Firm	8	4
Total Number of Men Employed	320	382
Average Crew Size per Vessel	8.2	7.4
Total Monthly Wages Paid	$6,330	$7,500
Average Monthly Wages per Man	$19.78	$19.63
Cod Catch (quintals)	23,350	14,490
Value of Cod Catch	$59,000	$36,350
Average Catch Value per Unit	$2.53/qtl.	$2.51/qtl.
Cod Oil Production (barrels)	299	231
Value of Cod Oil	$4,621	$ 3,465
Mackerel Catch (barrels)	0	12,165
Value of Mackerel Catch	$0	$67,390
Average Catch Value per Unit	$0	$5.54/bbl.
Average Cod Catch per Vessel	599 qtls.	279 qtls.
Total Product Value	$63,621	$107,205
Annual Return per Firm (before expenses)	$6,362	$2,493
Annual Return per Firm (after deduction of wages)	$5,729	$2,318

Source: U.S. MS Census Ind., 1850: Hancock County, Maine, towns of Castine and Deer Isle.

Note 1: Production statistics reflect year 1849.

Note 2: Vessel ownership refers to primary or managing ownership.

Appendix 20   Economic Structure of the Penobscot District
Cod-Fishing Fleet: 1829–1848

	1829 Fleet	*1839 Fleet*	*1848 Fleet*
Total Vessels	108	200	267
Vessels 20 Tons or Over (vessel class)	82 (76%)	160 (80%)	235 (88%)
Vessels Under 20 Tons (boat class)	26 (24%)	40 (20%)	32 (12%)
Average Tonnage (entire fleet)	28.7	37.3	40.0
Average Tonnage (vessel class)	33.6	43.5	43.9
Average Tonnage (boat class)	13.3	12.5	11.6
Number of Vessels Under 50 Tons	93 (86%)	157 (79%)	199 (75%)
Number of Vessels 20–49 Tons	67 (62%)	117 (59%)	167 (63%)
Number of Vessels 20–30 Tons	54 (50%)	59 (30%)	74 (28%)
Number of Vessels 50 Tons or Over	15 (14%)	43 (21%)	68 (25%)
Number of Vessels 50–90 Tons	13 (12%)	30 (15%)	53 (20%)
Number of Vessels Over 90 Tons	2 (2%)	13 (7%)	15 (6%)
Vessels Owned by Single-Vessel Owners	78 (72%)	97 (48%)	111 (42%)
Vessels Owned by Multiple-Vessel Owners	30 (28%)	103 (52%)	156 (58%)
Vessels Owned by Masters (entire fleet)	61 (56%)	73 (37%)	—
Vessels 20 Tons or Over Owned by Masters	47 (57%)	51 (32%)	—
Vessels Under 20 Tons Owned by Masters	14 (54%)	22 (55%)	—
Total Owners (primary or managing ownership)	90	130	149
Single-Vessel Owners	80 (89%)	102 (78%)	111 (74%)
Owners of 2 or More Vessels	10 (11%)	28 (22%)	38 (26%)
Owners of 3 or More Vessels	2 (2%)	9 (5%)	23 (15%)
Owners of 6 or More Vessels	0 (0%)	2 (1%)	8 (5%)
Owners of 10 or More Vessels	0 (0%)	1 (−1%)	2 (1%)
Average Number of Vessels per Owner	1.2	1.5	1.8

Sources: PMM, GC MS 229; NA, RDT (RG 56), GR, Abstracts of Fishing Bounty
Allowances, vol. 417: Penobscot District allowances, 1st quarter, 1849.

Note: Vessel ownership refers to primary or managing ownership, not minority
shareholding.

Appendix 21   Pre– and Post–Civil War Vessel-Ownership Patterns in the
Maine Sea Fisheries: A Comparison of Two Ports

	Belfast *1852*	*Portland* *1880*
Total Vessels	33 (100%)	28 (100%)
Single-owner vessels	14 (42)	1 (4)
Multiple-owner vessels	19 (58)	27 (96)
Vessels solely owned by master	7 (21)	0 (0)
Vessels in which master was managing owner	12 (36)	5 (18)
Vessels in which master owned shares	17 (52)	12 (43)
Total shareholders	97 (100%)	184 (100%)
Resident shareholders	62 (64)	100 (54)
Nonresident shareholders	35 (36)	84 (46)
Out-of-state shareholders	10 (10)	7 (4)
Single-vessel shareholders	77 (79%)	155 (84%)
Shareholders in 2 or more vessels	20 (21)	29 (16)
Shareholders in 3 or more vessels	8 (8)	13 (7)
Shareholders in 4 or more vessels	3 (3)	6 (3)
Shareholders in 5 or more vessels	0 (0)	3 (2)
Average number of shareholders per vessel	3.9	8.6
Most common division of shares	16ths	32nds

Sources: NA, RBMIN (RG 41), VDR, Belfast District Enrollments, 1850–52, and Portland-
Falmouth District Registers and Enrollments, 1876–80: certificates for various schooners;
RJ, news item, 6 August 1852; *Mackerel Fishery Materials,* 420–29 passim.

Note: Vessel total for Portland represents only the city's mackerel fleet, while Belfast total
represents all fishing vessels.

Appendix 22 Comparative Construction Costs of Two Maine Grand Banks Cod-Fishing Schooners of the Prewar and Postwar Periods

Name	*Eothen*	*Harvest Home*
Tonnage	130 tons (o.m.); 101 tons (n.m.)	120 tons (o.m.); 78 tons (n.m.)
Register Dimensions	84′ × 22′ × 8′	78′ × 22′ × 8′
Materials	Mixed woods; iron and copper fastenings	Mixed woods; iron and copper fastenings
Builders	Mayo & Perkins, Castine	Coolidge Brothers, Lamoine
Date of Launch	April 1860	May 1870
Cost of hull and spars	$4,225 (materials and labor)	$ 2,890 (materials only)
Cost of iron work	338 (materials and labor)	640 (materials only)
Cost of sails and rigging	583 (materials and labor)	3,300 (materials only)
Miscellaneous costs (painting, etc.)	37 (materials and labor)	—
Cost of labor	—	2,340
Basic building cost	5,183	9,170
Estimated market value	$6,000	$10,000

Sources: PMM, WP, Miscellaneous Vessels, box 1, file 7: schooner *Eothen*, bills and receipts, April–October 1860; BLH, WC, case 19: schooner *Eothen*, marine-insurance policies, 14, 15 May 1860; U.S. MS Census Ind., 1870: Hancock County, Maine, town of Lamoine, return for firm of Coolidge Brothers; Wasson and Colcord, 319; Chapelle, *National Watercraft Collection,* 205–6; *EA,* marine lists, 27 April and 20 July 1860, and 14 May 1870; *ALR, 1863, 427; ALR, 1874,* schrs., 67, 92; *RAFS, 1870,* 476.

Appendix 23   Maine Vessels Wrecked or Sunk in the Gulf of
St. Lawrence during the "Yankee Gale" of October 3–5, 1851

Vessel	Port	Lives Lost
Lion	Castine	8
Mary Moulton	Castine	12
Martha Ann	Castine	0
George	Castine	0
Leo	Frankfort	0
Reward	Deer Isle	0
Rapid	Deer Isle	0
Norna	Deer Isle	0
Sarah	Deer Isle	7
Sophronia	North Haven	0
Ruby	North Haven	0
Commerce	North Haven	0
Liberator	Swan's Island	0
Fly	Swan's Island	0
Henry Clay	Tremont	—
America	Lubec	9
Eliza	Lubec	0
W. R. Burnham	Southport	—
Tamarlane	Southport	—
Larakey	Boothbay	13
C. G. Matthews	Boothbay	0
Caledonia	Portland	11
Fair Play	Portland	0
Hickory	Portland	0
William	Portland	0
Regulator	Portland	0
Triumph	Cape Elizabeth	0
Washington	Freeport	7
Golden Grove	Kennebunk	0
Stoic	Kennebunkport	10

Towns Suffering Losses	14
Total Vessels Lost	30
Total Lives Lost	77

Sources: Andrews Report, 657–59; Greene, 383–84; Hosmer, 216; Small, 199; *EA,* news items, 13–27, October 1851 and 26 January 1852; *RJ,* news items, 3, 17, 22, 31 October 1851; *WC,* news items, 14–17, October 1851, *EH,* news item, 6 November 1851.

Appendix 24 Partial List of Penobscot Region Vessels
Lost in the Fisheries, 1839–1889

Vessel	Port	Year	Lives Lost	Location
Georgiana	Castine	1839	7	Chaleur Bay
Two Sons	Belfast	1841	9	North Atlantic
Clay	Sedgwick	1841	—	Georges Bank
Replaced	Deer Isle	1841	—	Gulf of St. Lawrence
Madison	Orland	1844	0	Grand Banks
Active	Castine	1846	6	Coast of Maine
Albion	Orland	1849	0	Grand Banks
Delight	Castine	1849	0	Coast of Maine
Fame	Belfast	1849	6	Gulf of Maine
Mary Lou	Bucksport	1850	0	Grand Banks
Sarah & Mary	Belfast	1850	1	Coast of Maine
Cherokee	Vinalhaven	1850	0	Magdalen Islands
Lion	Castine	1851	8	Coast of Prince Edward Island
Mary Moulton	Castine	1851	12	Gulf of St. Lawrence
George	Castine	1851	0	Coast of Prince Edward Island
Martha Ann	Castine	1851	0	Coast of Prince Edward Island
Mary Farley	Castine	1851	0	North Atlantic
New England	Castine	1851	0	North Atlantic
Reward	Deer Isle	1851	0	Coast of Prince Edward Island
Rapid	Deer Isle	1851	0	Coast of Prince Edward Island
Norna	Deer Isle	1851	0	Coast of Prince Edward Island
Sarah	Deer Isle	1851	7	Chaleur Bay
Sophronia	North Haven	1851	0	Coast of Prince Edward Island
Ruby	North Haven	1851	0	Coast of Prince Edward Island
Commerce	North Haven	1851	0	Coast of Prince Edward Island
Liberator	Swan's Island	1851	0	Coast of Prince Edward Island
Fly	Swan's Island	1851	0	Coast of Prince Edward Island
Leo	Frankfort	1851	0	Coast of Prince Edward Island
Dolphin	Camden	1851	0	Coast of Labrador
Coral	Castine	1852	0	Grand Banks
Duroc	Castine	1852	—	Coast of Nova Scotia
Raven	Belfast	1853	—	Mirimichi Bay
Champion	Deer Isle	1853	—	Coast of Prince Edward Island
Vesta	Belfast	1854	—	North Atlantic
Trumpet	Camden	1854	0	Grand Banks
Equator	Bucksport	1855	0	Strait of Canso
Rich	Castine	1857	0	Grand Banks
Ocean Wave	Penobscot	1858	9	Grand Banks
Hannibal	Deer Isle	1858	0	Gulf of St. Lawrence
John Bell	Vinalhaven	1858	0	Coast of Prince Edward Island
Good Intent	Castine	1859	—	Coast of Nova Scotia
Coquette	Bucksport	1859	0	Quereau Bank

(continued)

Appendix 24 (*continued*)

Foaming Billow	Belfast	1860	14	Gulf of St. Lawrence
Louisa	Belfast	1860	0	Coast of Maine
Jenny Lind	Belfast	1865	0	Coast of Maine
J. M. Tilden	Castine	1867	18	Magdalen Islands
Island Queen	Deer Isle	1869	0	Coast of Rhode Island
William E.	Belfast	1869	—	Coast of Maine
Mary Elizabeth	Belfast	1869	—	Coast of Maine
Maine	Belfast	1869	—	Coast of Maine
Rebecca S. Warren	Deer Isle	1873	—	Gulf of St. Lawrence
Grace Darling	Camden	1873	—	Gulf of St. Lawrence
Ceylon	Camden	1873	—	Gulf of St. Lawrence
Lalla Rookh	Swan's Island	1876	0	Coast of Maine
Emma Campbell	Camden	1880	—	Coast of Maine
Astoria	Bucksport	1885	0	Grand Banks
M. E. Torrey	Sedgwick	1887	0	Coast of Cape Breton Island
Isaac Keene	Bucksport	1888	0	Grand Banks
William Tell	Bucksport	1889	0	Grand Banks

Sources: Andrews Report, 657; *Halifax Commission Proceedings,* 222–25; PMM, GC, MSS 195, 249; *RJ,* marine lists and news items, 1840–60; *EA* marine lists and news items, 1840–90; George Wheeler, 1st ed., 99; Joseph Williamson, 1:815–22; Small, 199; Hosmer, 215–16.

Appendix 25 Regional Tabulation of United States Senate Votes on the Fishing-Bounty Question, 1839 and 1858

	Vote to Table Bounty-Repeal Bill, January 29, 1839			*Vote to Pass Bounty-Repeal Bill, January 30, 1839*		
	Yes	*No*	*Not Voting*	*Yes*	*No*	*Not Voting*
Northeast	7	7	6	5	12	3
New England	(4)	(4)	(4)	(4)	(7)	(1)
Mid-Atlantic	(3)	(3)	(2)	(1)	(5)	(2)
South	4	11	7	8	7	7
Southeast	(2)	(3)	(5)	(1)	(4)	(5)
Southwest	(2)	(8)	(2)	(7)	(3)	(2)
Northwest	1	6	1	7	0	1
Total	12	24	14	20	19	11

	Vote to Extend Bounty Temporarily, May 12, 1858			*Vote to Repeal Bounty Immediately, May 19, 1858*		
	Yes	*No*	*Not Voting*	*Yes*	*No*	*Not Voting*
Northeast	15	3	3	4	14	1
New England	(12)	(0)	(0)	(0)	(12)	(0)
Mid-Atlantic	(3)	(3)	(3)	(4)	(2)	(1)
South	2	18	5	18	2	4
Southeast	(0)	(9)	(3)	(9)	(0)	(3)
Southwest	(2)	(9)	(2)	(9)	(2)	(1)
West	10	7	3	8	8	4
Northwest	(8)	(6)	(2)	(6)	(6)	(4)
Far West	(2)	(1)	(1)	(2)	(2)	(0)
Total	27	28	11	30	24	9

Sources: U.S.CG, 25th Cong., 3rd Sess. (1839), 157–59; U.S.CG, 35th Cong., 1st Sess. (1858), 2082, 2239.

Index

main
55.-

Book slight
with
odor
5/6/99
LmS